THE SOUTH REPORTS
THE CIVIL WAR

THE SOUTH REPORTS
THE CIVIL WAR

BY J. CUTLER ANDREWS

PRINCETON UNIVERSITY PRESS

PRINCETON, NEW JERSEY

1970

Library of Congress Number: 75-90942

I.S.B.N.: 0-691-04597-6

This book has been composed in Linotype Caledonia

Printed in the United States of America
by Princeton University Press

Second Printing, 1971

Contents

~~~~~~~~~~~~~~~

List of Illustrations

Preface

~~~~~~~~~~~~~

In January 1956, shortly after the University of Pittsburgh Press published my *The North Reports the Civil War*, I received a letter from R. Miriam Brokaw, then Managing Editor of the Princeton University Press. Her letter was prompted by a review of my book by the late dean of American journalism historians, Frank Luther Mott, who suggested that "Southern journalism badly needs a historian." Was I already at work on a companion book, *The South Reports the Civil War*? Miss Brokaw asked. If so, and if the manuscript were not already otherwise committed, would I be interested in submitting it to the Princeton University Press for consideration? I had visualized my study of Northern reporting as a terminal enterprise, doubting my qualifications for a similar investigation of Southern journalism. Also, I had no agreement with the University of Pittsburgh Press to do a Southern volume. But after considering the idea carefully, I found its symmetry attractive and decided to begin the investigation which resulted in this book.

It was almost inevitable that these twin books should deal with much the same kind of subject matter and employ a generally similar approach. When I write I prefer a combination of narrative and expository history to the topical, or problem-oriented, approach favored by many present-day American historians. In my view, history should tell a meaningful story as well as analyze the character and behavior of its principals—individuals and social groups. And so I have attempted to convey in this work an understanding of what antebellum Southern journalism was like, to reconstruct the historical matrix within which it operated, and to relate the reporting of the military and political events from 1861 to 1865 by the Southern press to the events themselves as they unfolded from Sumter to Appomattox.

The problems of research and writing were much the same as those I encountered in my book on Northern reporting. The scattered files of the Southern Civil War press, which constituted a major source of information for this book, proved less readily available than the Northern newspapers I had used earlier, however. The ravages of the Civil War wrought havoc with the contents of Southern newspaper offices, destroying many back files and dispersing others. For example, considerably less than half of the *Montgomery Advertiser*'s wartime issues have survived. (A pioneer effort of gathering up and preserving some of these scattered newspapers was performed by the historian Francis Parkman, whom the Boston Athenaeum commissioned to purchase any printed publications of the Confederacy he could find when he visited Richmond with a friend in June 1865. The wartime file of the *Richmond Examiner* that cost him $325 became the nucleus of the Athenaeum's valuable collection of almost 3,000 Confederate imprints, the largest in existence.) Moreover, the office records of Confederate newspaper establishments have almost entirely disappeared, and contemporary letters and diaries of Southern editors and war correspondents are extremely rare. One of the more important discoveries that my research netted, as the result of a search from Bangor, Maine to Santa Cruz, California, was the handwritten campaign notebook of Reporter Samuel Chester Reid, Jr., covering the last three years of the war.

A second problem, similar to that which I faced in my earlier project, was that of blending my account of the Southern reporting of the war with the story of the war itself. In so doing I have attempted to describe the military and political events of the period at sufficient length to make the reporting of an Alexander or a de Fontaine understandable, and to provide a factual backdrop to compare with the reporting. Yet I have sought to minimize the repetition of occurrences with which Civil War buffs may already be familiar and to emphasize the reporting of events rather than the events themselves.

A third, very real, problem was that of identifying anonymous or pseudonymous reporters. After considerable effort I have been able to expand to ninety-four the list of nine Southern war correspondents and army artists whose names appear on the arch on South Mountain dedicated to the war correspondents and newspaper artists of the American Civil War. Also, in a number of instances I have been able to discover the various pseudonyms used by a given reporter in several different newspapers. Thus I learned that the Dr. William G. Shepardson, who was the "Bohemian" of the *Richmond Dispatch*, was also the "Evelyn" of the *Mobile Register*, that the "Sallust" of the *Richmond Dispatch*, who had previously been unidentified by historians, was in reality the Peter Alexander who corresponded for the *Savannah Republican* under the byline of "P.W.A.," that the "Dixie" of the *Memphis Appeal* apparently was the poet John R. Thompson rather than the John Barton to whom this pseudonym was ascribed in a recent article in the *Journal of Southern History*,[1] and that "Hermes," "Gamma," "Malou," and "Pan" were all pen names of the same Richmond correspondent, George W. Bagby. In some other cases, one of which I discuss in Appendix I, I have thus far been unable to pierce the veil of anonymity that enshrouds particular newspaper pseudonyms.

Although this book emphasizes military reporting, I give some attention to political reporting at Montgomery, Richmond, and other Southern cities insofar as that reporting related to the conduct of the war. To the extent that slavery and the Negro may appear to be neglected themes of Confederate news coverage, it should be realized that Southern army correspondents seldom came into direct contact with Negroes other than the body servants of army officers, and that so long as the war was going well for the South, Negro slaves did not seem newsworthy to the newspaper correspondents of the South. Northern reporters allotted much more space to Southern Negroes and slavery in their newspaper correspondence than Southern war reporters did.

LIKE most historians I owe a heavy debt of gratitude for their invaluable assistance to a host of librarians, archivists, professional colleagues, scholarly organizations, and friends. I am especially indebted to the Library of Congress for the opportunity to examine its extensive manuscript and newspaper collections and to the Boston Athenaeum for the privilege of using its files of Confederate newspapers. For their many helpful suggestions about research opportunities I wish to thank Mr. Handy B. Fant, Mr. Neil Franklin, and Mr. Elmer O. Parker of the National Archives staff; Mr. William A. Runge of the Alderman Library of the University of Virginia; Dr. James W. Patton, Curator of the Southern Historical Collection of the University of North Carolina; Miss Mattie Russell, Curator of the Division of Manuscripts of the Duke University Library; Mr. E. L. Inabinett, Director of the South Caroliniana Library of the University of South Carolina; Miss Jessie E. Cobb, Librarian of the Alabama State Department of Archives and History; Miss Peggy J. Duckworth of the University of Alabama Library; Miss Ruth Walling, Reference Librarian of the Emory University Library; Miss Charlotte Capers, Director of the Mississippi Department of Archives and History; Miss Dorothy Whittemore and other members of the staff of the Tulane University Library; and Dr.

[1] T. H. Baker, "Refugee Newspaper: The Memphis *Daily Appeal*, 1862-1865," *Journal of Southern History*, xxix (August 1963), 334.

Preface

Ray A. Billington, Director of Research at the Huntington Library.

Historical societies have been generous along with archives and university libraries with both their resources and advice. While it is practically impossible to include everyone whom I should like to thank in this connection, I should like to mention especially Miss Virginia Rugheimer, Librarian of the Charleston Library Society, Mrs. Granville T. Prior of the South Carolina Historical Society, Mrs. Lilla M. Hawes, Director of the Georgia Historical Society, Mrs. D. B. Alexander, Archivist of the Atlanta Historical Society, Mr. Howson W. Cole, Curator of Manuscripts at the Virginia Historical Society, and Mrs. Alene Lowe White, Librarian of the Western Reserve Historical Society. For the opportunity to use manuscript material in private collections, I wish to express my appreciation to Mr. Harry M. Rhett of Huntsville, Alabama, and Mr. Samuel Chester Reid of Santa Cruz, California.

Some Civil War scholars from whom I have received useful suggestions and other assistance are Professor Bell I. Wiley of Emory University, Mr. Clifford Dowdey of Richmond, Virginia, Quintus C. Wilson, Dean of the School of Journalism of West Virginia University, Professor James P. Jones of Florida State University, and Mr. Richard Harwell, Librarian of Smith College.

Many people have provided me with family photographs and other memorabilia to illustrate this book: Mrs. Florence A. Blomquist, the picture of her great-uncle Peter W. Alexander; Mrs. Wallace S. Pitts, the picture of her husband's grandfather, William Wallace Screws; Mr. W. H. de Fontaine, the picture of his grandfather, Felix Gregory de Fontaine; Mrs. Harry Da Ponte, the picture of her husband's grandfather, Durant Da Ponte; and Mr. Samuel Chester Reid, the picture of his grandfather, Samuel Chester Reid, Jr., a prominent Southern war correspondent.

Various historical societies and other libraries also have supplied me with illustrations: the Virginia Historical Society, the pictures of John M. Daniel and George W. Bagby; the Virginia State Library, Richmond, Va., the picture of James McDonald; the Charleston Library Society, the pictures of Robert Barnwell Rhett, Jr. and Henry Timrod; the Carolina Art Association, the picture of Aaron Willington; the University of South Carolina Library, the picture of William A. Courtenay; the Library of Congress, the picture of the Brady photograph of Colonel John Forsyth; and the Wyoming State Archives and

Preface

Historical Department, the picture of James B. Sener. Mr. Franklin Garrett of Atlanta, Ga. made available the picture of the *Atlanta Intelligencer* office in 1860. The National Archives, the Western Reserve Historical Society, and the New York Historical Society have permitted me to reproduce letters written by Peter Alexander, Samuel C. Reid, Jr., and Secretary of War Judah P. Benjamin from manuscript collections in their libraries, for book illustrations.

The American Philosophical Society awarded me a summer grant which made possible newspaper research in Richmond, Charleston, and Savannah. I am likewise grateful to Chatham College for a year's leave of absence from teaching for research on this book, and for a series of grants from Chatham College's Central Research Fund, which underwrote travel costs incident to research in various libraries, the purchase of newspaper microfilm, and a part of my typing expense. Special mention also should be made of my indebtedness to Professor Robert L. Zetler of the University of South Florida, whose expert advice in matters of style and presentation proved invaluable, to Mr. Peter R. Knights, onetime Mellon Fellow at the University of Pittsburgh, for useful suggestions relating to a number of features of this book, and to my secretary, Mrs. Armand A. Kihm, who gave indispensable aid in manuscript preparation.

J. Cutler Andrews

Chatham College
Pittsburgh, Pennsylvania
September 6, 1969

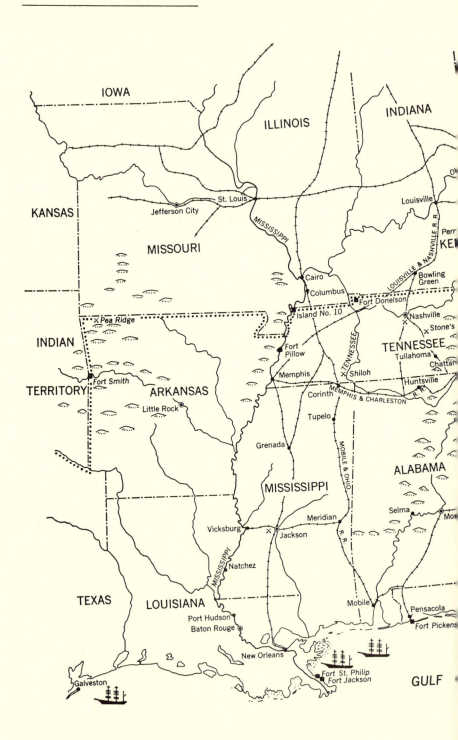

PENNSYLVANIA

Pittsburgh

Harrisburg

Philadelphia

NEW

Gettysburg

JERSEY

OHIO

MD.

Baltimore

Frederick

Harper's Ferry

POTOMAC

DELAWARE

Winchester

Washington D.C.

Cincinnati

(WEST VIRGINIA
ADMITTED 1863)

SHENANDOAH
VALLEY

Fredericksburg

RAPPAHANNOCK

CHESAPEAKE BAY

ankfort

VIRGINIA

Gordonsville

JAMES

Fortress Monroe

Lynchburg

Richmond
Petersburg

Norfolk

CKY

VIRGINIA & EAST TENNESSEE R.R.

ROANOKE
ISLAND

CUMBERLAND
GAP

Raleigh

Goldsboro

CAPE
HATTERAS.

NORTH   CAROLINA

Charlotte

Dalton

Wilmington

Columbia

Fort Fisher

SOUTH   CAROLINA

Atlanta

Augusta

Charleston

ATLANTIC

Milledgeville

Fort
Sumter

OCEAN

Macon

GEORGIA

Savannah

Fort
McAllister

N

nery

W   E

S

MEXICO

FLORIDA

◎ State Capital

■ Confederate Forts

✕ Battle

⚓ Blockaded Port

Drawn by Howard N. Ziegler

0   80   160
MILES

THE SOUTH REPORTS
THE CIVIL WAR

CHAPTER 1

Civil War in the Making

It was seven o'clock in the evening on Thursday, April 11, 1861. At the wharf in Charleston, South Carolina, a reporter for the *Charleston Mercury* was climbing aboard the steamer *Seabrook*, one of the two vessels comprising the navy of South Carolina, which was about to cruise off the Charleston Bar. Approaching a middle-aged, weather-beaten gentleman, the reporter inquired for Captain Hartstene.

"I am that gentleman," replied the mariner.

"I have a permit to visit Sullivan's Island to write an account of the battle for the *Mercury*," explained the reporter with a pleading note in his voice.

"We are not going to Sullivan's Island, sir," rejoined the captain. "We're going to sea, and the steamer will leave in a moment, and so you had better go ashore."

The reporter hesitated for a moment, then blurted out: "I must make my report, sir, and I'll go to sea with you, if I can obtain your permission."

"Well, you can go, sir," was the reply, "but we expect warm work, and you may be landed at Stono tomorrow morning, or find yourself shortly in New York with a halter round your neck."

"Aye, aye, sir. I'll take my chance," said the *Mercury* man gleefully as he waved a greeting to the crowd on shore, for the steamer was even then casting off and he could not have remained behind had he wished to.

As the *Seabrook* and the *General Clinch* sailed down the channel, their crews looked anxiously in the direction of Fort Sumter, which lay dead ahead on a shoal in the center of the harbor, about three miles from the city. The reporter and everyone else aboard knew that the commander of the fort, Maj. Robert Anderson of the First United States Artillery, had received a summons to surrender that afternoon by a deputation of officers from Confederate Brig.Gen. P.G.T. Beauregard. It was rumored in Charleston that Anderson had already rejected the surrender demand, and almost everyone there believed that the Confederate shore batteries which ringed the harbor would open

3

fire on the fort at eight o'clock that night. On board ship conjectures about the future course of events were cut short by the lookout reporting a rocket seaward. As all eyes focused in that direction, two red rockets burst in the air, followed by the burning of a blue light. The Confederate Fort Johnson on James Island, about 1¼ miles south of Fort Sumter, promptly recognized the signal that an enemy had made his appearance, and sent up the answering rocket almost the instant that the blue light displayed by the *General Clinch* disappeared.

Excitement mounted as howitzers were manned, decks stripped, and guns, revolvers, and ammunition distributed on both ships in preparation for whatever lay ahead. As they approached Fort Sumter's black shape in the distance, suddenly a hail was heard, and a hoarse voice shouted, "The pirates are off the bar!" "What steamer?" Captain Hartstene wanted to know. "The *Harriet Lane*, twelve miles out," announced the same gruff voice, adding that she alone of all the expected Yankee cruisers had been sighted. The authorities in Charleston fully expected that the *Harriet Lane* would attempt to land U.S. troops in boats to reinforce the Sumter garrison. It was the mission of Hartstene's South Carolina navy to prevent this.

A pilot boat, a little later, furnished confirmation of the arrival of the *Harriet Lane*, and at eight o'clock, when the Confederate batteries were expected to open fire, all eyes turned in the direction of Fort Sumter. Minutes passed, yet the stillness and blackness of the fort remained unbroken. The impression was now current on the *Seabrook* that Major Anderson must have surrendered.[1]

In Charleston hundreds of spectators thronged Battery Square and the wharves until after midnight, waiting for the bombardment to begin. Most of them had gone home to bed, however, before it was known, about 3:30 in the morning, that a second attempt by Beauregard's aides to persuade Anderson to capitulate had failed and that the bombardment would begin within an hour.

In THE stillness preceding the first gunshots, the aged editor of the *Charleston Courier*, Aaron S. Willington, remained sleepless at his home on New Street, contemplating the situation which seemed about to erupt into war. Dazed by the rapid course of events, vexed and distracted by his own increasing irritation, "astounded by the glaring

[1] *Charleston Mercury*, April 15, 1861.

treachery of our enemies, [and] lost in wonder at their egregious stupidity," Editor Willington had not found an opportunity until this moment to reflect seriously about the full extent of the crisis he and his fellow citizens in Charleston faced.[2] To be sure, an editorial published in his newspaper only two days before had told the world that, "with implicit reliance on the God of Battles, we go forth to meet the deadly foe. Let the strife begin—we have no fear of the issue."[3] But this was the kind of rhetoric Southern political leaders and the great majority of Southern newspapers had been mouthing for months. Now that the strife to which the *Courier* had so airily referred was about to begin, was it surprising that an elderly man who could not sleep should reflect and pray and seek to elevate his spirit with "glorious memories"?

Perhaps Willington recalled the time, almost fifty-nine years before, when as a young printer employed in a Boston newspaper office he had left Massachusetts to accept a position as a foreman in the plant of the newly established *Charleston Courier*. He might have remembered that it had been a fortunate move on his part, for within a few years Willington, the printing foreman from Boston, had become the editor of the *Courier*; under his management the paper had emerged as one of the leading commercial newspapers in the South and as an exponent of Southern Unionism. In Willington's office, the famous editor of the *New York Herald*, James Gordon Bennett, had been taught the essentials of the newspaper business, and during the last fifteen years Willington had been the president of the New England Society of Charleston, managing its affairs with wisdom and tact.[4]

Life in Charleston had been good to Willington. Although his education had largely been confined to the printing office or the compositor's frame, he had played a prominent part in the political and business activities of the city. He had at various times been an alderman, a member of the state legislature, and a director in a number of leading banks and insurance companies. Also, he had made four European tours, during which he had climbed Mont Blanc and the Great Pyramid of Cheops, stood on the Bridge of Sighs in Venice, and wandered, guidebook in hand, through various museums and art

[2] *Charleston Daily Courier*, April 13, 1861.

[3] *Ibid.*, April 10, 1861.

[4] *Ibid.*, February 3, 1862; undated newspaper clipping, South Carolina Historical Society.

galleries. His last trip abroad in 1855 had provided the material for a book describing his travel in Europe that summer.[5]

The Charleston for which Willington had come to hold a deep affection was in 1861 the largest American seaport south of Baltimore. The city had a population of 29,000 whites and 37,000 Negro slaves.[6] It was a town of impressive beauty and grace, essentially English in tone and manner, and reflecting the prestige and influence of a landed aristocracy who were the nearest thing to a peerage in America. Charleston was located on a peninsula bounded by the Ashley and Cooper Rivers with the Battery Square at their junction. Characteristic of the layout of the town were its paved streets with brick sidewalks, crossing each other at right angles and fringed with rows of Pride of India trees along their outer edges. The architecture of this old seaport was predominantly red brick and white marble; its quaint old houses, generally separate from each other, were usually built at an angle to the street so as better to catch the breeze from the ocean. A striking feature of the houses were their verandas, constructed in a light Oriental style from the ground to the very top, so that the rooms on each story enjoyed the advantage of a shady open walk. Distinctive likewise were the high-walled gardens which surrounded the houses, abounding with flowers and shrubs of all kinds, with double and triple rows of orange trees, and displays of large white roses. On her thirty-eighth birthday the wife of Senator James Chesnut received from her friends the Rutledges an exquisite bouquet from their rose garden, which prompted her to write rapturously in her diary, "Are there such roses anywhere else in the world?"[7]

Near the Battery at the lower end of the town were the fashionable churches, St. Michael's and St. Philip's, St. Andrew's Hall, where Louis Agassiz had lectured in the early eighteen-fifties when he was professor of science at the College of Charleston and where the Ordinance of Secession had been passed the previous December, and the Bond Street Theater where the world-famous diva Adelina Patti and an English troupe from the Royal Italian Opera House had performed the previous autumn. Near the Quay was the U.S. Customs House, whose

[5] *Charleston Daily Courier*, February 3, 1862.

[6] Roy Meredith, *Storm over Sumter; The Opening Engagement of the Civil War* (New York, 1957), p. 14.

[7] I. D. Martin and M. L. Avery, eds., *A Diary from Dixie* (New York, 1905), p. 27. This is Mary Chesnut's diary.

unfinished structure was symbolic in some measure of the hostile attitude of South Carolinians toward the tariff policy of the United States government.[8]

It had been the custom in Charleston for many years for the planter aristocracy from the up-country to come to town for the winter shopping and social season, the horse races in February, the St. Cecilia Ball in St. Andrew's Hall, and the theater. Hugers and Pinckneys set the tone for a cultivated and moneyed leisure class, whose social activities were mirrored in Mary Boykin Chesnut's famous diary. One of the elements of Charleston society that participated in these activities was the "codfish aristocracy" of transplanted Bostonians, to which Willington belonged. To Charleston over the years had come a number of foreign visitors—among them the Englishmen Capt. Basil Hall and novelist William Makepeace Thackeray, and the Swedish traveller Frederika Bremer—to view the local scene and record their impressions in books that might expect wide circulation. What interested them most were the multitude of Negroes, the revolting slave auctions, and the public market with its stalls of fruit and flowers presided over by portly colored women and with its flocks of unsavory turkey buzzards.[9]

To Charleston also had come a young college student from Massachusetts the spring before to enjoy a vacation and watch the proceedings of the first Democratic national convention ever held in South Carolina. The student, Edward G. Mason, had been impressed by and a little amused at the efforts of his hosts to convince him that slavery was the best possible condition for the black man. But he could not help but notice that at night the whole city was under martial law, that any Negro found on the streets after nine o'clock without a pass from his master was immediately arrested and thrown in jail. The mounted police, mainly of Irish birth, were drilled and armed as sol-

[8] W. H. Russell, *My Diary North and South* (London, 1863), p. 100. Otherwise descriptive of antebellum Charleston are Meredith, *Storm over Sumter*, pp. 14-17; W. A. Swanberg, *First Blood, The Story of Fort Sumter* (New York, 1957), pp. 187-88; H. K. Leiding, *Charleston, Historic and Romantic* (Philadelphia, 1931), pp. 193-94; W. S. Hoole, "The Literary and Cultural Background of Charleston, 1830-1860," unpub. Ph.D. diss. (Duke University, 1934), pp. 69-73.

[9] Eyre Crowe, *With Thackeray in America* (New York, 1893), pp. 145-50; A. E. Benson, ed., *America of the Fifties: Letters of Frederika Bremer* (New York, 1924), pp. 96-97. See also *The Family Tourist, A Visit to the Principal Cities of the Western Continent* (Philadelphia, 1848), pp. 396-98.

diers and officered by graduates of South Carolina military schools. Between them and the younger and more active Negroes was a long-standing feud that erupted whenever a venturesome young Negro applied the hated epithet "buzzard" to one of the mounted police.[10]

As a Southern Whig of Northern background, Willington had opposed both nullification and secession in South Carolina for more than thirty years. The *Courier* had been the leading Union organ in the state at the time of the nullification crisis in 1832; and in the midst of the threats of secession that the Compromise of 1850 only briefly checked, this venerable newspaper upheld the flag of the Union. In Willington's opinion, however, the election of a sectional president in 1860 had sounded the death knell of the Union, and he silently acquiesced when in December 1860 the State of South Carolina in Convention assembled took the lead in bringing about the secession of the Lower South. Other Charlestonians, including Robert Barnwell Rhett, Jr., of the *Mercury*, had expressed irritation at the continuing presence on South Carolina soil of a garrison of U.S. troops, which moved from Fort Moultrie on Sullivan's Island to Fort Sumter on the day after Christmas.[11]

Although Anderson, a West Point-trained officer of Southern birth and pro-slavery sympathies, had taken this step to ward off a possible attack from the mainland and thus avoid precipitating civil war, South Carolinians generally interpreted it as a warlike move. When President James Buchanan refused to disavow Anderson's action and order him back to Moultrie, commissioners representing the State of South Carolina and the newly-formed Confederate government, successively initiated negotiations in Washington for the peaceful withdrawal from Sumter of Anderson's garrison of artillerymen. Even so, war was narrowly averted in January when the *Star of the West*, a Northern supply vessel carrying reinforcements to Fort Sumter, was driven off by fire from a Charleston shore battery.

As time went on, the *Courier*'s jingoistic competitor, the *Charleston Mercury*, began to lambaste Governor Francis Pickens for permitting Anderson to receive mail through the Charleston post office and fresh provisions from the local market. Pickens, a stout man with oversized

[10] E. G. Mason, "A Visit to South Carolina in 1860," *Atlantic Monthly*, LIII (February 1884), 241-43; "An Englishman in South Carolina," *Continental Monthly*, III (January 1863), 113.

[11] *Charleston Daily Courier*, February 3, 1862; Bruce Catton, *The Coming Fury* (New York, 1961), pp. 154-56.

head, watery eyes, and flabby features, was looked upon as something of a renegade for having deserted South Carolina in her hour of crisis to accept a diplomatic assignment to Russia from 1858 to 1860. It was party talk in Charleston that Pickens had been pressured into going abroad by his beautiful third wife, Texan Lucy Holcombe; a speech he was supposed to have made, in which he boasted that he was "born insensible to fear," only made his critics laugh the more.[12] Yet it was Pickens and not the elder Robert Barnwell Rhett, who craved the honor for himself, whom the voters placed in the governor's chair when he returned from Europe. Willington must have smiled mischievously when he heard the story about *Mercury* editor Rhett rushing into Pickens' office on Meeting Street to demand that he stop shillyshallying and occupy Fort Sumter forthwith.

"Certainly, Mr. Rhett," Pickens was supposed to have replied blandly. "I have no objection! I will furnish you with some men and you can storm the work yourself."

"But, sir, I am not a military man!" Rhett shot back.

"Nor I, either," retorted the governor, "and therefore I take the advice of those who are."[13]

Willington's *Courier* had reported the arrival in Charleston on March 3 of the Confederate Commander-in-Chief whom Governor Pickens had been requesting of Jefferson Davis for weeks. The Montgomery government's choice, General Beauregard, had been Superintendent of West Point and custodian of the lake defenses in his native Louisiana before he took command at Charleston of the South Carolina troops who were already gathering there. Beauregard had agreed with his engineering officer, Maj. William Whiting, that there would be no difficulty in overpowering Sumter's tiny garrison, and had recommended changes in the location of batteries in preparation for active measures.[14]

Like many other Charlestonians, Willington must have pored over the columns of the Northern press for indications of the policy that President-elect Abraham Lincoln could be expected to pursue after March 4 toward the seven states that had already seceded, and toward

---

[12] *Dictionary of American Biography* (hereafter referred to as *D.A.B.*), xiv, 559-561; W. F. Guess, *South Carolina, Annals of Pride and Protest* (New York, 1960), p. 225; Martin and Avery, *Diary*, p. 3n; Russell, *My Diary*, p. 121.

[13] Swanberg, *First Blood*, p. 189.

[14] T. H. Williams, *P.G.T. Beauregard, Napoleon in Gray* (Baton Rouge, 1955), p. 51; Swanberg, *First Blood*, p. 217; Leiding, *Charleston*, pp. 213-14.

efforts, Northern and Southern, to bring about a peaceful evacuation of Sumter. Back in 1855, at the age of seventy-five, Willington had been made almost totally blind when an operation for cataracts in both eyes, performed by a New York doctor, was unsuccessful. Then, following a restful summer at Swampscot on the Massachusetts coast, the aged editor gradually regained the sight of one eye. At length he was able to walk about Charleston without assistance once more and to read the newspapers with unflagging persistence and interest, often detecting typographical errors that had escaped the notice of full-sighted copyreaders.[15]

At his "Woodlands Plantation" the eminent South Carolina author William Gilmore Simms had decided that Lincoln's inaugural address meant war and had written to a friend in New York in protest against the "lies" in the Northern press about widespread suffering and divided opinion in South Carolina.[16] Moderates like Willington, who still hoped to avoid war, must have felt reassured when Lincoln's friends, Col. Ward H. Lamon and Stephen Hurlbut, arrived in Charleston on a peace mission on March 24. Although Lamon told Pickens he had come there solely to arrange for the removal of Anderson's garrison, he did not reveal that the real purpose of their mission was to assess at first hand the amount of Unionist sentiment in South Carolina.[17]

Lamon determined that there were practically no Union sympathizers in Charleston, which was essentially the same conclusion to which the Massachusetts college student Edward Mason had come when he visited Charleston the year before. At that time Mason had gone out to the country home of an old Union man named Talbot, who had supported Andrew Jackson in Nullification times. In Mason's hearing, Talbot told several of his friends:

"You have all gone mad together. There is no end to this separation business. You want to separate the South from the North; and then you want to separate South Carolina from North Carolina; and then the district south of the Ashley River from the district north of the Ashley River; and then the district south of the Cooper River from the district

---

[15] *Charleston Daily Courier*, February 3, 1862.

[16] William Gilmore Simms to James Lawson, March 15, 17, 1861, in M.C.S. Oliphant, ed., *The Letters of William Gilmore Simms* (Columbia, S.C., 1952-56), IV, 347-48, 350. Simms specifically denounced the New York papers, including the *Times*.

[17] Swanberg, *First Blood*, p. 238.

10

north of the Cooper River; and then, sir, by Jove, sir! you will want to separate husband and wife!"[18]

Yet at the time of Lamon's visit to Charleston there were doubters, even in official circles, as to the wisdom of secession. According to Senator Louis Wigfall of Texas, both Governor Pickens and Assistant Secretary of State William H. Trescot had been openly against secession before they left Washington, and Trescot "does not pretend to like it now."[19] But the only out-and-out Unionist in Charleston in March 1861 was 72-year-old attorney James L. Petigru, who had distinguished himself by his fine work in codifying the laws of South Carolina.

Willington no doubt was personally acquainted with Petigru, who had consistently opposed disunionist doctrines since the days of Nullification. With his mantle of snowy hair and the odd falsetto voice and rolling gait that had attracted the attention of the poet Paul Hamilton Hayne when the old man strolled through Russell's Book Shop with his friend Alfred Huger, Petigru was an unforgettable figure. His predictions of disaster and ruin for the secessionist cause were probably regarded by most Charlestonians as the ravings of an amiable and half-senile old man whose great age and aristocratic birth entitled him to complete freedom of speech.[20]

Lamon's fears for his own personal safety in Charleston were the topic of common gossip there when Editor Joseph Clisby of the *Macon* (Ga.) *Daily Telegraph* arrived there from Macon on the evening of March 27. Clisby, who, like Willington, was of New England birth, had left his newspaper office to see for himself what was happening in Charleston Harbor. Clisby found Charleston swarming with business activity. He was kept awake in his hotel room there on the night of his arrival by the hammering of the packers in the jobbinghouses. Early the next morning the sidewalks along Meeting and Hayne Streets in the vicinity of the hotel were completely filled with boxes of goods marked for shipment to various destinations in South Carolina, Georgia, Alabama, and Florida.

The hotel clerks told Clisby that Lincoln's frightened law partner had entered his name on the register there as being from Virginia.

---

[18] Mason, "Visit," pp. 246-47.

[19] Martin and Avery, *Diary*, p. 29.

[20] P. H. Hayne, "Ante-Bellum Charleston," *Southern Bivouac*, n.s. i (November 1885), 328; *D.A.B.*, xiv, 514-15; Martin and Avery, *Diary*, p. 24n; Russell, *My Diary*, p. 117.

Also, some boys at the hotel had taken great delight in adding to the Northern man's fears by every imaginable expedient, "although not the slightest purpose of harming him existed."[21]

Although Clisby had concluded that public opinion in Charleston was becoming "wonderfully impatient" with the delay in the occupation by the Confederate authorities of Fort Sumter, the editor of the *Charleston Mercury* was hopeful that there would be no fighting at either Sumter or the only other remaining Federal fortification in the South, Fort Pickens in Florida. In a letter to one of his newspaper correspondents on April 2, Rhett predicted that Sumter would be given up; also Pickens: "when the Confederate States are ready to take it. But, as we have no naval force, the North will hold Key West and Tortugas for the time."[22]

These illusions about Lincoln's intentions, which Lamon's visit to Charleston may have helped to foster, were rudely dissipated within a few days after Rhett wrote his letter. On April 6 a prominent Washington newspaperman who had formerly lived in Charleston telegraphed his Charleston friend, Judge A. G. Magrath, some startling information that he had just obtained directly from Lincoln's Secretary of State, William H. Seward. "Positively determined not to withdraw Anderson," the telegram said. "Supplies go immediately supported by a naval force . . . if their landing be resisted."[23]

It was possible, of course, that newspaperman James E. Harvey had misunderstood Seward, but it was not possible for Pickens to disregard the unsigned message from the President of the United States that Capt. Theodore Talbot and State Department Chief Clerk Robert S. Chew delivered in Charleston two days later. Lincoln's message informed Pickens and Beauregard that an attempt was going to be made to supply Fort Sumter with provisions only and that if no resistance were offered, no effort to supply Sumter with men, arms, or ammunition would take place without further notice or unless in case of an attack on the fort. Advising Talbot and Chew to get out of town in

[21] *Macon Daily Telegraph*, March 30, 1861.

[22] R. B. Rhett, Jr. to G. W. Bagby, April 2, 1861, George W. Bagby Papers, Virginia Historical Society.

[23] *War of the Rebellion: A Compilation of the Official Records of the Union and Confederate Armies* (Washington, D.C.), Ser. I, vol. i, p. 287, hereafter referred to as *O.R.* (Army). Because of conflicting evidence as to the intentions of the Lincoln administration, however, Governor Pickens questioned the accuracy of Harvey's telegram. Swanberg, *First Blood*, p. 278.

a hurry, Pickens and Beauregard decided that a peaceful solution of the Sumter crisis was no longer possible unless Anderson capitulated before the arrival of the supply mission. Beauregard did not believe the Lincoln administration's "provisions only" story. He was convinced that the Federals had every intention of attacking his forces and that they were planning to land a large force on Morris Island to capture the batteries from the rear.[24]

Between April 8 and 12 preparations for war accelerated. The streets of Charleston were alive with soldiers as troops from the South Carolina up-country poured in. War correspondents from the North suddenly appeared, among them Samuel R. Glen and Felix Gregory de Fontaine of the *New York Herald*, to scramble for news items in competition with *New York Times* man George H. C. Salter, who had been in Charleston for almost three months.[25] At the Confederate capital in Montgomery, Alabama a telegraphic dispatch reporting that General Beauregard had opened fire on seven war steamers that had appeared off the Charleston Bar created tremendous excitement on April 9, until it was disclosed that the telegram had been a hoax.[26] Over the same telegraph line from Montgomery to Charleston there passed on the following day a message from the Confederate Secretary of War to Beauregard, directing him to demand Sumter's evacuation post haste and in the event of a refusal to "reduce it."[27]

Willington knew nothing about the struggle that had taken place in Anderson's mind when he received Beauregard's surrender ultimatum. Nor was he informed of the mishaps arising out of a tug-of-war between Lincoln's advisers that would deprive the relief expedition of the means to provide the Sumter garrison with the supplies it so badly needed. Yet civil war was obviously at hand; for a Charleston editor of New England birth the prospect must have been fully as disturbing as it was for anyone within earshot of the gunfire that was about to open in the early morning hours of April 12.

Perhaps Willington would have been more sanguine about the out-

[24] *Ibid.*, p. 286.

[25] *Charleston Daily Courier*, April 8, 1861; *New York Times*, April 2, 17, 1861. De Fontaine's name appeared among a list of passengers who sailed from New York on the steamer *Columbia* (bound for Charleston) on March 31, 1861. *Ibid.*, April 1, 1861.

[26] *Charleston Daily Courier*, April 13, 1861.

[27] S. W. Crawford, *The Genesis of the Civil War, The Story of Sumter, 1860-1861* (New York, 1887), p. 421; *O.R.* (Army) Ser. I, vol. i, p. 297.

come of the battle if he had realized the heavy odds Anderson's men faced. During the past three months the besiegers had erected batteries at every available point along Sullivan's, Morris, and James Islands, so that Sumter now stood alone within a semicircle of hostile guns. Altogether, Beauregard could bring to bear on the fort thirty guns, many of them of large caliber, and eighteen mortars. In the fort Anderson had forty-eight guns of various calibers and not a single mortar. Twenty-seven pieces of his heaviest ordnance were situated in the barbette on top of the fort, which provided a better view of enemy positions and a more advantageous angle of fire. Unfortunately, with hardly more than one-tenth of the fort's full complement of 650 men, Anderson, in view of his exposed position, did not dare use the barbette guns. Another disadvantage he faced was the fact that if the Confederates chose to storm his fort, the six thousand men they had under arms in the vicinity of Charleston provided them with odds of about one hundred to one.[28]

FROM aboard the *Seabrook* in Charleston Harbor the anonymous *Charleston Mercury* correspondent watched the signal shell for the opening of the bombardment arch skyward from a battery at Fort Johnson shortly after 4:30 A.M., on Friday, April 12. As the *Mercury* man later recalled the sequel: "Shell followed shell in quick succession; the harbor seemed to be surrounded with miniature volcanoes belching forth fire and smoke. Still Major Anderson gave no sign of resentment, save the defiance expressed at his flag-staff. But a shell from Cumming's Point[29] bursts on the parapet—the brave Cummings Pointers are getting the range! Another falls quite within, and now Fort Moultrie seems to have got the range and the Floating Battery, which the North believed a humbug, begins to indicate her position. She's not exactly at her wharf in Charleston, nor is it positive she will not take a position nearer still to Fort Sumter. It is getting to be warm work for Major Anderson."[30]

[28] Swanberg, *First Blood*, pp. 288, 293, 295.
[29] Located on Morris Island.
[30] *Charleston Mercury*, April 15, 1861. The floating battery alluded to in this quotation, which had been designed by John Randolph Hamilton, a grandson of Alexander Hamilton, had been towed out from the city and moored at the west end of Sullivan's Island to command the harbor entrance and participate in the bombardment of Fort Sumter. Mrs. H. H. Ravenel, *Charleston, the Place and the People* (New York, 1906), p. 491; Swanberg, *First Blood*, p. 289; *Richmond Daily Dispatch*, April 12, 1861.

From somewhere in the city a *Richmond Dispatch* correspondent who signed himself "Virginius" timed the opening shot at 4:27 A.M. and noted that it was followed in quick succession by another. There was, he reported, an interval of fifteen minutes; then two other shots were fired.

Off goes the fifth. Its deep, terrible report, the jarring of the windows and shaking of the house only tells its power and its destructiveness. It comes from Stevens' Iron Battery.

Off goes [*sic*] Nos. 6,7,8,9,10 in rapid succession. I hasten to the wharf. There goes a shell and bursts just over Sumter. Quick flashes of lurid light are seen, and in twenty seconds, the hoarse voice of the dog of war is heard. Moultrie plays into Sumter. There goes a shot from the Floating Battery—it strikes. There goes one of Anderson's shells—it falls near to his terrible adversary. There goes another shot from Anderson's Barbette. I see the white column of smoke rise at the Iron Battery; the very earth shakes—it is Stevens' 10-inch Columbiad. There is another flash and presently the report and the whistle of the ball, though three miles and more off—it is the Rifle cannon. There goes Moultrie again, and then the Floater. Anderson answers each manfully. Another shell bursts just over Sumter. All is enveloped in smoke, and I can see neither Sumter nor the Islands.

Six o'clock arrives. Our batteries continue, but Anderson does not answer! Shells and balls fly thick and fast around him but he answers not. His flag still waves. What can the matter be? Seven o'clock arrives. —He remains silent. They are pouring into him from Johnson, Stevens', the Howitzer Battery, Moultrie, the Floater and two Mortar Batteries. A heavy shower of rain comes up; but it stops not the heavy throats of the ordnance, nor drives away the thousands of spectators lining the wharves and housetops. Eight o'clock— Anderson opens his fire from his Columbiads in his Casemates, his Barbettes being deserted on account of the shower of shell that falls around him. All the batteries are now playing into him, and he playing upon Stevens, on the South, and Moultrie and the Floater on the northeast. "There goes Stevens," exclaims one—The earth trembles again. That is a terrible gun. All is now enveloped in smoke, and the glass aids me not. . . .[31]

There are some interesting inaccuracies in "Virginius's" report that suggest it was written in haste. Although he describes counterfire from the fort as taking place before six o'clock, the fact is that Anderson's

[31] *Richmond Daily Dispatch*, April 16, 1861. The Stevens Battery, located at Cummings Point on Morris Island, was the invention of Clement H. Stevens, Superintendent of the Citadel Academy in Charleston. Stevens was later killed in the Atlanta campaign after attaining the rank of brigadier general. The Stevens Battery, mounting ten guns, was ingeniously constructed from heavy timbers overlaid with railroad iron so as to present an inclined surface. Its three ten-inch columbiads were fired through embrasures (openings) fitted with thick iron shutters. Ravenel, *Charleston*, p. 491.

gunners did not open fire until some time around seven. It is possible, of course, that the reporter's watch was at least one hour slow,[32] but his nearly accurate timing of the opening of the bombardment would seem to invalidate this explanation. Also, his identification of one of the fort's casemate guns as a "Columbiad" was erroneous. Anderson probably wished that all of his Columbiads (his longest-range guns) had been on the casemate level, but unfortunately none was.[33]

The *New York Times* correspondent in Charleston, George Salter, was already at the warf when "Virginius" arrived there that morning. Since one hour after midnight Salter had been perched on a cotton bale on the long Adger Pier with opera glass in hand, awaiting the sound of the opening gun. His only companions were a young bride of three months, whose husband had left her to join the Palmetto Guards on Morris Island, and her little brother. Salter could hear the young woman sobbing bitter tears as streaks of light began to appear in the eastern sky.

When the bombardment began, another reporter for the New York press, de Fontaine of the *Herald,* was on the alert, to watch how the sleeping Charlestonians were startled from their slumbers by the sound of the guns. Years later he recalled how: "Lights flash on as if by magic from the windows of every house, and in the twinkling of an eye, as it were, an agitated mass of people are rushing impetuously toward the water front of the city. Grave citizens, whose dignity under ordinary circumstances is unimpeachable, are at the top of their speed dressing as they run, and sending up wild hurrahs as if they must have some such safety-valve for their enthusiasm or be suffocated. There are men *sans* coats, women *sans* crinoline, and children in their night-gowns."[34]

After watching the bombardment for six hours straight, *Times* man Salter climbed down and went to his rooming house on King Street to eat a late breakfast and take a nap. While he was there a party of armed men arrived to tell him he was under arrest by order of the

[32] According to an eyewitness of the bombardment, Confederate Capt. Stephen D. Lee, Fort Sumter did not respond with its guns until 7:30 a.m. R. U. Johnson and C. C. Buel, *Battles and Leaders of the Civil War* (New York, 1887), i, 77.

[33] Swanberg, *First Blood*, p. 293. The heaviest guns in Sumter's casemate tier were three forty-two-pounders; the other eighteen guns were relatively inoffensive thirty-pounders. The range of a columbiad was two to three miles, compared with the half-mile range of Anderson's eight-inch howitzers. *New York Times*, April 5, 1861.

[34] F. G. de Fontaine, "The First Day of Real War," *Southern Bivouac*, ii (July 1886), 77.

government of South Carolina on charges of being a spy. Expostulation was in vain. Salter spent the rest of the day and until noon of the next in the Charleston guard house, at which time he was warned to leave the city at once.[35]

About the time Salter left the Adger Pier, the South Carolina naval vessel on which the *Charleston Mercury* reporter was embarked sighted a steamer and a brig which Captain Hartstene believed to be a part of the Lincoln relief expedition. Both the *Seabrook* and the *General Clinch* weighed anchors and headed for Cummings Point on Morris Island, about 1,200 yards southeast of Sumter. As they passed battery after battery, the reporter could see the gunners on the beach waving their hands and could hear them cheering. The steamer, first tentatively identified as the Federal transport *Harriet Lane*, proved to be the merchant vessel *Nashville* bound from New York to Charleston. She hoisted the Palmetto flag as the *Seabrook* passed her and continued on her way into the harbor. Failing to make contact with the Yankee squadron, the South Carolina naval expedition cleared the harbor and followed the coast northward to Stono Inlet, thus depriving the *Mercury* representative of any further opportunity to witness the Sumter fight.[36]

Throughout Friday April 12 the bombardment of Sumter and its counterfire continued. At the Charleston home of Caroline Gilman, the wife of a Unitarian minister, friends drifted in and out all day; as they arrived they were put to work making cartridge bags for the gunners. The bags were made of a strong red woolen fabric called baize and were sewed with worsted cotton thread to make them ignite more easily. There was little conversation among the women thus busily employed except when rumors about the progress of the fighting were brought in by the few gentlemen who called, "and then we clustered around them, as if life and death hung on their words."[37]

The *Richmond Dispatch* reporter was convinced at different times during the forenoon that he could see a breach in Sumter's sixteen-foot brick walls.[38] At eleven o'clock a messenger from Morris Island brought word that the projectiles from Anderson's guns were glancing off the iron-covered Stevens battery at Cumming's Point like marbles

[35] *New York Times*, April 17, 1861.

[36] *Charleston Mercury*, April 15, 1861.

[37] C. H. Gilman, "Letters of a Confederate Mother, Charleston in the Sixties," *Atlantic Monthly*, cxxxvii (April 1926), 507.

[38] *Richmond Daily Dispatch*, April 16, 1861.

thrown by a child on the back of a turtle. At one-thirty it was reported that two of the guns in the Stevens Battery had been temporarily disabled, but that they were soon back in commission again. At three o'clock Anderson's guns bearing on the Iron Battery were silenced, but he continued to blaze away from his northeastern guns at Moultrie a little over a mile away and at the floating battery on Sullivan's Island. Beauregard's aide, W. Porcher Miles, arrived from Moultrie at five o'clock to report that all was well in that quarter. About 7:00 P.M. the bombardment slackened, and only desultory firing continued during the night. Sometime during the evening, one of the *Mercury's* special reporters at Fort Moultrie turned up at the newspaper office with a trophy in the form of a thirty-two-pound ball of Yankee origin which had lodged in one of the sandbags at the Fort.[39] Shortly after midnight General Beauregard left his headquarters in the Charleston Hotel to go to Morris Island.[40]

The telegraph had already flashed the news of the attack to distant points of the Confederacy and elsewhere. Authentic information about developments at Charleston did not get to Richmond until the middle of Friday afternoon. All morning Richmond had been deceived by a bulletin, supposedly concocted by the city's stockbrokers, that everything was still quiet in Charleston at 9:00 A.M. When the news of the firing finally came, it was in the form of a private dispatch from John Tyler, Jr. in Montgomery to his father, the former president. As evidence of the high tension that prevailed in Richmond that day, a Unionist member of the Richmond state convention named Marmaduke Johnson assaulted Editor John M. Daniel of the *Richmond Examiner* with a cane and was held over for court action.[41]

As soon as they learned fighting had broken out in Charleston, the editors of both of the Savannah daily newspapers, William Tappan Thompson of the *Morning News* and James R. Sneed of the *Republican* boarded the first train for Charleston at one o'clock in the afternoon. The train was crammed with citizens of Savannah, who having heard only a few minutes before the exciting news from Charleston, were determined to go there to see for themselves and take part in the fight if there was an opportunity. On meeting the down train from Charleston some thirty or forty miles out of Savannah, the two editors

[39] *Charleston Daily Courier*, April 13, 1861; *Charleston Mercury*, April 13, 1861.
[40] Meredith, *Storm*, p. 172.
[41] *Charleston Mercury*, April 16, 1861.

obtained confirmation of the earlier news and sundry exciting rumors of what was happening in Charleston at the time of their departure from the passengers. Among the rumors (quite inaccurate as it turned out) were reports that several Confederate gunners at Fort Moultrie had been killed and that Moultrie had suffered damage from the fire of Fort Sumter. Thompson and Sneed were told at a station farther up the line that the firing of heavy guns had been heard there until about one o'clock, when the sound of firing had ceased. Could Anderson have surrendered? Had Beauregard been defeated? Was the battle over? Then at the next station the sound of firing could be heard again as a number of South Carolina soldiers who had been on leave at their homes trooped on board the northbound train to rejoin their units. As the editors and their fellow passengers from Savannah left the train at the Ashley River to take the steam ferry across to Charleston, they not only could hear the sound of the firing more distinctly than ever, they could smell the sulphurous fumes of saltpeter in the air. After checking in at one of the Charleston hotels the editor of the *Savannah News* ate a hurried supper and hastened to the battery, where in spite of a light rain an immense crowd of men, women, and even children were watching the battle.

Editor Thompson remained at the battery until one the next morning staring at the pyrotechnic display. According to the *Richmond Dispatch* reporter, the firing reached maximum intensity about ten o'clock; notwithstanding the rainstorm the streets of the city were thronged with people throughout most of the night. The *Savannah News* editor left instructions at his hotel for him to be awakened at 4:00 A.M., and by 4:30 he was back on the battery. There in the darkness he watched the clouds of white smoke curl up from the Confederate forts and batteries and, although the wind was now unfavorable, listened to the rumbling of the guns.[42]

Although the Federal relief expedition made no obvious attempt to run supplies into the harbor under the cover of darkness, one ship did enter the harbor that night. It was a sloop with a cargo of wood belonging to one of the Charleston citizens, and its pilot was an old Negro. When warned of the danger he would encounter by running the gauntlet of gunfire, the pilot shrugged off the warning, saying, as quoted by a *Charleston Courier* reporter: " 'Caint hep that. Must go

[42] *Savannah Daily Morning News*, April 15, 1861.

to de town tonight: if anybody hurt dis boat, Massa see him about it, shuah.' "[43]

At sunrise on Saturday, April 13 the rain clouds had disappeared, and with fine weather in prospect, male and female, white and black, young and old Charlestonians selected observation points for the resumption of the bombardment. At first, random shots were exchanged by the combatants, but at about eight o'clock, after a hot shot from the Stevens battery had found its mark, the cry arose from the wharves and spread throughout the city, "Fort Sumter is on fire!" In the distance could be seen four Yankee war vessels ranged in line beyond the bar; the spectators watched in suspense to see whether they were going to enter the harbor to engage the batteries. At half past ten Maj. Anderson ceased fire to give undivided attention to the conflagration. Hardly had his men brought it under control when a shell from Sullivan's Island set the east side of the fort on fire. Toward noon flames burst out from every quarter and jetted from many of the port holes. To make matters worse, the wind was still from the west, driving the smoke of Sumter's guns back into the embrasures where the gunners were at work.[44]

At Richmond, Virginia, where business was generally suspended that morning, the citizenry were clustered around the newspaper and telegraph offices, awaiting the latest news from Charleston. At the office of the *Richmond Whig* a large crowd of curious people gaped at a coast survey chart of Charleston Harbor on display, with the positions of all the batteries designated. The place where the Floating Battery was supposedly anchored was also indicated, but there was considerable uncertainty among the watchers about its exact position.[45]

At a quarter of one, the *Charleston Courier* posted a bulletin on the board outside its office: "Fort Sumter's flag down. The iron battery has just now cut the flag staff down."[46] The general impression among the spectators was that Anderson had surrendered, but their murmurs of joy changed to expressions of regret when about twenty minutes later the Federal flag reappeared on a short staff above the part of the fort facing Moultrie. The firing went on until about two o'clock, when a

[43] *Charleston Daily Courier*, as reprinted in Meredith, *Storm*, p. 192.

[44] *Richmond Daily Dispatch*, April 16, 1861; *Charleston Mercury*, April 15, 1861.

[45] *Charleston Mercury*, April 16, 1861.

[46] Meredith, *Storm*, p. 183; *Charleston Daily Courier*, April 15, 1861.

white flag appeared on the same staff and the Stars and Stripes was hauled down. The *Richmond Dispatch* reporter said: "You may imagine, but you cannot realize the joy, as the shouts of joy went up from thousands on the decks, wharves, houses, and steeples."[47] With the cessation of firing, the appearance of the harbor changed dramatically. Beauregard dispatched steamers with fire-fighting equipment to the fort, and sailing vessels could be seen darting about everywhere, conveying gentlemen from the city to see their friends on the islands. As soon as the news of the surrender was made known, the bells of the city began to ring, and salutes were fired from the Cadet's Battery, the School Ship, and the cutter *Lady Davis*. The excitement continued unabated when several Confederate officers returned from Fort Sumter with the surrender agreement. At the head of the crowd as it surged in the direction of Beauregard's headquarters were Col. James Chesnut and handsome former Governor John Manning. As the procession passed the Charleston Hotel at the corner of Meeting and Hayne Streets, Governor Pickens appeared on the balcony and delivered a bombastic victory speech.

A reporter for the *Columbus* (Ga.) *Times* was present when General Beauregard received the announcement of the surrender before a jubilant and cheering throng. The swarthy little general rose to the occasion in fitting oratorical style, exclaiming: "Noble Carolinians! accept my warmest congratulations on your victory—not won by me, but by the gallant men who so promptly obeyed my orders. The war has been commenced; we must continue our exertions until the enemy is driven from our harbor." That evening there was a grand fete at Ashley Hall, the country home of Col. William I. Bull, which was attended by hundreds of city folk and country gentry. Among the guests were wealthy planter Wade Hampton, General Beauregard, and other celebrities. Many of the ladies added color to the scene under the moss-draped oaks with their jockey caps and velvet Renfrew hats, decorated with black and white plumes.[48]

In Richmond that night the newspaper offices of the *Enquirer, Examiner,* and *Dispatch* were handsomely lit, with bonfires blazing before each of them. Red, white, and blue lights and fireworks of all kinds enhanced the brilliancy of the spectacle. Perhaps only a few of

[47] *Richmond Daily Dispatch*, April 16, 1861.
[48] *Columbus Daily Times*, April 17, 1861; Leiding, *Charleston*, pp. 216-17.

the celebrants of the victory took notice of the fact that the office of the *Richmond Whig*, true to its Unionist tradition, was dark.[49]

The formal surrender of Fort Sumter did not take place until the next day. Although no newspaper reporters were permitted to visit the fort on Saturday or Sunday, the editor of the *Charleston Courier*, now relieved of his anxiety, managed to get inside Fort Sumter on Sunday morning and report what he saw. Willington said:

"When we went into Sumter through the port hole we found the Major busy distributing letters to the officers and men of his force. He appeared to be in perfect health. He was all smiles, and chatted in an easy vein. The men were hearty looking and cheerful. If they were not in transports they soon will be, and what matters a few hours? All of the poor fellows wanted whisky, and many were the silent gesticulations they made to ascertain if any could be had."[50]

In reporting the action, the Charleston newspapers emphasized the excellent morale of the South Carolina troops and their contempt for the "mighty men of war" off the bar who made no effort to come to the relief of their distressed comrades.[51] Of course, the newspapermen had no way of knowing that the failure of two of the most important units of the expedition to appear and its lack of landing craft were decisive factors in keeping the "men of war" from coming to Major Anderson's assistance.[52] The journalists who witnessed the bombardment also expressed surprise that the nearly four thousand shells expended by the shore batteries had failed to make a breach in Sumter's walls and that no casualties had taken place on either side during the two-day bombardment.[53]

Yet a correspondent of the *Macon Telegraph* who was in Charleston at the time of the surrender reported that the interior of Fort Sumter was "an unsightly mass of embers." He also admitted that although Confederate Fort Moultrie had performed wonders during the battle, "old Moultrie received pay in her own coin from Sumter, for the offi-

[49] *Memphis Daily Appeal*, April 18, 1861.
[50] *Charleston Daily Courier*, April 15, 1861.
[51] See e.g. *Charleston Mercury*, April 16, 1861.
[52] Meredith, *Storm*, p. 185. Swanberg, *First Blood*, p. 323 is more specific, crediting Beauregard's batteries with having fired 3,341 shot and shell and with having scored 600 direct hits.
[53] *Charleston Daily Courier*, April 15, 1861; *Savannah Republican*, April 15, 1861. The publication by a local printing firm of a compilation in book form of accounts of the bombardment in the Charleston newspapers was announced in the *Charleston Mercury*, April 18, 1861.

cers' quarters are badly damaged, and many of the houses on the Island bear testimony to the power of the balls which were shot from Sumter."[54]

An interesting feature of the reporting of the Sumter story by the Charleston newspapers was the absence of large type in the modest two-line head the *Courier* used. Also the editorial "we" was generously interspersed through the reports that the *Courier* and *Mercury* published; there was no attempt by either paper to separate news from editorial opinion.[55]

After the formal surrender of Fort Sumter on Sunday afternoon Major Anderson and his men were permitted to go on board the U.S.S. *Baltic* for transportation back to New York. Between the local newspapermen, who had not been allowed to witness the surrender ceremony, and Beauregard's officers apparently there was very little cordial feeling. When the famous British war correspondent William H. Russell arrived in Charleston from the North later that week, he was the witness of a scene on board a ship in the harbor in which Maj. Whiting "dressed down" one of the Charleston newspapermen. Russell told how Whiting pulled out of his pocket a "ragged little sheet" and brandished it in the face of its representative. Then Whiting proceeded to contradict in the most unqualified terms the statements contained in "the full and accurate particulars of the Bombardment of Fort Sumter" that had appeared in that issue of the paper. "If I knew who wrote it," rasped the major, "I'd make him eat it!"[56]

Naturally the Southern press was jubilant at the easy triumph Beauregard had won and confident that the border states would make common cause with the Confederacy if President Lincoln attempted any further coercion. Lincoln's proclamation of April 15, calling for 75,000 militia to suppress uprisings in the seven secessionist states too powerful to be suppressed by ordinary law courts and marshals, left little doubt in anyone's mind that force would be used. Civil war was now a reality, and the reporting of it would soon become a major function of Editor Willington's *Charleston Courier* and the other newspapers of the Southern Confederacy.

[54] *Macon Daily Telegraph*, April 16, 1861.

[55] In this connection see *Charleston Sunday News*, April 17, 1898, as reprinted in *Southern Historical Society Papers*, xxvi, 101-109.

[56] Russell, *My Diary*, p. 102.

CHAPTER 2

A Bird's Eye View of Wartime
Journalism in the South

WHEREAS IN the eighteen-fifties relatively few Southerners read books and magazines published below the Mason and Dixon Line, Dixieland's newspapers ranked with the best in the country. Experienced editors such as the *Louisville Journal's* pungent George D. Prentice, George W. Kendall of the *New Orleans Picayune,* and John Forsyth of the *Mobile Register* were sectional spokesmen whose gifted pens were quite as influential as the rhetoric of clergymen and political orators in shaping Southern opinion and giving direction to Southern action. Moreover, editors of the South invited contributions on topics of public interest from prominent political friends and reserved considerable space in their columns for the reprinting of good literature. Thus Southern newspapers in some measure provided the equivalent of literary magazines and magazines of opinion, and their editors tended to be a cross between the statesman-politician and the man of letters.

To an even greater extent than was true elsewhere in the country, the partisan political press dominated prewar Southern journalism. During the conflicts over nationalism and states' rights that had arisen in the Jacksonian period, the printer-editor who formerly had published a newspaper as a secondary interest and had interpreted the news with some degree of impartiality faced the choice in some instances of aligning himself with a party or discontinuing publication. Although the number of Southern newspapers greatly increased between 1830 and 1860, the publication of newspapers in that section was rarely profitable, and the privilege of publishing legislative journals and state laws was therefore a significant perquisite of party journalism. Also in an era when personal journalism was in its heyday, the editor as a man of consequence was admitted to the inner councils of his party and often became a powerful political force.

What the Southern editor wrote was more interesting to his readers than the meager supply of news that appeared in his paper. Antebellum

A Bird's Eye View of Wartime Journalism

Southern newspapers gave more space to national and foreign news than to local events and problems. The newspapers of Jackson, Mississippi, for example, frequently ignored the results of local elections and made no reference whatever to such events of local import as the completion of the Vicksburg and Jackson Railroad and the arrival of the first train in Jackson.[1]

The typical daily Southern newspaper of the period ran to four pages and varied from four to eight columns in width. Headlines were limited to a single column, but big stories such as a steamboat disaster or the fiasco of the Walker filibustering expedition in Nicaragua might be extended in multiple decks to almost a half-column. The first page usually consisted of news and a copious supply of advertising. Page two contained editorial articles, letters from prominent individuals, city items, and more advertising. Pages three and four included a slim budget of telegraphic news, marketing and other commercial reports, and serialized fiction, along with advertisements.

How a leading Southern newspaper of the day was put together probably conforms with the experience of A. B. Meek, who edited one of the Mobile papers in the eighteen-fifties. Meek would first select two important newspapers from each of the larger cities represented among his newspaper exchanges and clip a dozen or so small articles, which he would then hand to the waiting printer. Then he would clip articles for solid matter, leaving just enough space for the lead editorial. When the printer told him that enough material had been found for the day's edition, he would knock off the editorial rapidly but with care. Then he would read the editorial aloud to his editorial associate, Thaddeus Sanford. They would consult about its language, scope, and bearing on the prominent issues of the day, rigidly excluding any sentiment that did not harmonize with the editorial policy of the paper. The local editor never began to write his article before nine o'clock in the evening and rarely took more than half an hour to collect the necessary items.[2]

Hand presses were still in use in most Southern newspaper offices

[1] W. D. McCain, *The Story of Jackson* (Jackson, Miss., 1953), i, 218. For other comments on the Southern antebellum press see C. C. Sydnor, *Development of Southern Sectionalism, 1819-1848* (Baton Rouge, 1948), pp. 306-307; Avery Craven, *Growth of Southern Nationalism, 1848-1861* (Baton Rouge, 1953), p. 275; W. B. Hesseltine, *History of the South, 1607-1936* (New York, 1936), pp. 343-44; T. C. De Leon, *Four Years in Rebel Capitals* (Mobile, 1892), pp. 288-89.

[2] M. C. Boyd, *Alabama in the Fifties* (New York, 1931), pp. 206-207.

at the beginning of the Civil War. On April 24, 1862 the *Knoxville Daily Register* announced that to enable its press run to meet the increased demand of wartime circulation it had decided to discard the hand press on which the paper had been printed up to that time and replace it with a power press.

Somewhere around eight hundred newspapers were published, daily, weekly, and tri-weekly, in the eleven states of the Confederacy in April 1861. About ten percent were dailies, with Virginia having the largest number (fifteen), followed by Georgia and Louisiana with twelve and eleven respectively.[3] With a population of over 168,000 New Orleans was at the time the largest city in the South. Yet Richmond, with a population of less than one-fourth that of New Orleans in 1860, was the hub of Confederate news enterprise for almost the entirety of the war. Its four daily newspapers (the *Enquirer*, *Whig*, *Examiner*, and *Dispatch*), later joined by a fifth newspaper, the *Sentinel*, exerted considerable influence over the remainder of the Confederate press.[4] In the opinion of the capable Northern journalist Whitelaw Reid: "The newspapers of Richmond, throughout the war, were in many respects the ablest on the continent. Their writing was often turgid, but it was always effective; and it shaped the public sentiment of the whole Confederacy. . . . In the midst of their destitution they managed to keep up double the number of average dailies that we had in Washington, and the editorials of each were generally the productions of educated thinkers, as well as red-hot partisans."[5]

One of the oldest Southern newspapers was the *Richmond Enquirer*, established as a semi-weekly in 1804 by a youthful Virginian named

[3] E. M. Coulter, *The Confederate States of America, 1861-1865* (Baton Rouge, 1950), p. 493n; Sidney Kobre, *Foundations of American Journalism* (Tallahassee, 1958), p. 315.

[4] For a competent treatment of a significant aspect of the Richmond press during the Civil War see H. A. Trexler, "The Davis Administration and the Richmond Press," *Journal of Southern History*, XVI (May 1950), 177-95. See also *New Orleans Daily Picayune*, October 19, 1861; *Charleston Daily Courier*, February 12, 1862. The offices of the five Richmond newspapers were located in the same general area. Both the *Enquirer* and *Dispatch* were in the same block on Main Street, between 12th and 13th Streets. The *Whig* and *Sentinel* offices faced each other at the intersection of Governor and Franklin Streets. The *Examiner* establishment was on the west side of Governor, south of Franklin.

[5] Reid, *After the War* (Cincinnati and New York, 1866), p. 319. For a not entirely unprejudiced estimate of the worldwide attention the power and brilliancy of the Richmond press evoked, see E. A. Pollard, *Life of Jefferson Davis* (Philadelphia, Chicago, etc., 1869), p. 444.

Thomas Ritchie, who had studied law and medicine and taught school in Fredericksburg before going into newspaper work. With the assistance of the great statesmen of the old Virginia school, the tall, lean, quick-moving editor with brilliant eyes and impressive profile made the *Enquirer* a power in the land. It had become a daily newspaper by the time "Father Ritchie" left it in 1845 to edit the organ of the Polk administration in Washington. Ritchie's sons managed their father's paper for a few years, but by the time the war came the name "Ritchie" had disappeared from the *Enquirer's* masthead, and the firm of Tyler, Wise, and Allegre was in control. At the time of the purchase of the *Enquirer* by this firm in August 1860, the old newspaper landmark was valued by the partners at $36,000.

At the beginning of the war both Editors Nathaniel Tyler and O. Jennings Wise, the son of Governor Henry A. Wise, left Richmond to enter military service. The remaining partner, W. B. Allegre, a practical printer and the business manager of the paper, was not suited for editorial duties. So first the veteran Virginia journalist Bennett M. De Witt and then Richard M. Smith, a refugee editor from Alexandria, Virginia functioned as "working editor" of the *Enquirer*. When Tyler's regiment was disbanded in December 1862, he resumed his former position as senior editor, but permitted the Irish patriot John Mitchel to write a large proportion of the *Enquirer's* editorials until Mitchel left the paper after a quarrel with Tyler at the end of 1863.

During the first part of the war the *Enquirer* had the reputation of being the "organ" of the Davis administration. Indeed, the popular report was that Davis occasionally and Secretary Judah P. Benjamin frequently wrote its leading articles. If Benjamin was a frequent contributor to the *Enquirer*, this must have been true for only a limited period of time. The *Enquirer* admitted that it had recommended his dismissal from the War Department early in 1862 after a succession of military disasters and that it had opposed his conduct of the office of Secretary of State. Cautious and conservative, the *Enquirer* prided itself on the literary quality of its content and the care with which its editors distinguished between verified news and unauthenticated reports.[6]

[6] M. D. Evans, "The Richmond Press on the Eve of the Civil War," *John P. Branch Historical Papers of Randolph Macon College* (January 1951), 16-20; *Charleston Daily Courier*, February 12, 1862; *Daily Richmond Enquirer*, January 6, 1863; *Mobile Daily Advertiser and Register*, December 23, 1863; Nathaniel

As its name implies, the *Richmond Whig* was for many years the organ of the Whig party in Richmond and the long-time political opponent of the *Enquirer.* John Hampden Pleasants, its founder in 1824 and one of the ablest editors in the South, died of wounds sustained in a duel with one of Thomas Ritchie's sons in 1846. The *Whig* opposed secession with much vigor until Lincoln's call for 75,000 militia on April 15, 1861, whereupon Editor Robert Ridgway was forced out of his editorship, and the *Whig* overnight switched to the opposite side. Ridgway's successor, Alexander Mosely, was the titular editor of the *Whig* during the first two years of the war, but James McDonald, a product of the fecund Lynchburg newspaper world,[7] exercised most of the prerogatives of the editorship, becoming senior editor after Mosely retired to his farm in Nelson County in March 1863.

Although it displayed all the zeal of a new convert for the cause of Southern Independence, the *Whig* viewed with a jaundiced eye the domination of the Confederate government by its erstwhile political opponents. It was therefore periodically critical of Davis and prone to advocate restrictions on the Executive that if carried out would have rendered the government powerless. Apparently the office of the *Richmond Whig* was a favorite meeting place for Confederate congressmen, whose "angular and elongated frames, shabby overcoats, and deliberate strut" were the subject of humorous comment by a Richmond newspaperman who was no stranger there.[8]

In Whig-dominated Richmond, the *Whig* had proved more than a match for the *Enquirer* in the days before the war; so in 1847 the local Democratic politicians had sanctioned the establishment of a second

---

Tyler, estimate of value of the (Richmond) *Enquirer*, Brock Collection, Huntington Library. According to this last source, the receipts of the *Enquirer* firm between August 11, 1860 and October 19, 1862 were $159,889.77. Expenditures of $104,025.40 during the same period permitted the newspaper to make a profit of $55,864.37, amounting to an average figure of about twenty-five thousand dollars a year.

[7] During the early part of the nineteenth century Lynchburg had provided a training ground for fledgling journalists who moved on from there to positions on larger and more influential newspapers. In 1866 the Lynchburg correspondent of the *Richmond Whig* called attention to the fact that the *Whig* had been the preserve of Lynchburg editors, proprietors, and agents almost from its beginning. J. L. King, Jr., *Dr. William Bagby* (New York, 1927), p. 18. See also letter of John R. Thompson to the *London Index*, March 26, 1863, John R. Thompson Papers, University of Virginia.

[8] Evans, "Richmond Press," pp. 20-21; *Charleston Daily Courier*, February 12, 1862; *New Orleans Daily Crescent*, December 5, 1861.

Democratic organ there. Almost from its beginning the dynamic John M. Daniel had been the editor of the Democratic semi-weekly *Richmond Examiner*, which became a daily shortly before the war. In early 1862 the Richmond correspondent of the *Charleston Courier* described the *Examiner* as an "enterprising sheet, [which] always has the news, is fond of the sensational, pitches into everybody and everything, and is altogether one of the most readable and attractive newspapers in the South."[9] A somewhat less friendly critique of the *Examiner* characterized it as: "the Ishmael of the Southern press, so far as it is against everybody. All parties, all men, and, we may add, all measures, are in turn censured in the *Examiner*. In nine cases out of ten the censure is undeserved, but the articles are almost invariably written with wit and smartness. Clever young men who have to make their mark or clever men who have failed to make their mark naturally vent their spleen in the *Examiner*, and when there is some ground for censure no paper is more calculated to bring about a redress of the grievance or abuse."[10]

To a marked degree the journalistic character of the *Examiner* was the personality of Daniel writ large. The *Examiner* editor was a man of striking appearance with a small beautifully shaped head and a dark, refined "decidedly Jewish" face and thin-lipped mouth, partially concealed by a heavy black moustache. A slightly aquiline nose, a closely trimmed jet-black beard, and thick black eyebrows shading deepset hazel eyes were other features of his countenance which attracted the attention of even the casual observer.

Born the son of a country physician in Stafford County, Virginia, about halfway between Richmond and Washington, D.C., Daniel obtained practically all his schooling from the books in his father's library. He took up, but soon abandoned, the study of law and after working for a time as the superintendent of a small library in Richmond, entered journalism in the mid eighteen-forties. Daniel was first employed in an editorial capacity by an agricultural magazine called the *Southern Planter*. In May 1847 he switched over to the *Examiner* as joint editor along with B. M. De Witt, and a year later became sole owner of the paper. His quick sharp intelligence and slashing literary style were the credentials for his journalistic success. During Pierce's administration Daniel left the *Examiner* for several years to accept a

[9] *Charleston Daily Courier*, February 12, 1862.
[10] *London Index*, November 27, 1862; *Charleston Mercury*, January 28, 1863.

diplomatic appointment at the Sardinian Court. There his tactlessness involved him in difficulty when a private letter of his was published by mistake in an American newspaper. Daniel had told of being "sponged on" for seats at the opera by counts "who stink of garlick as does the whole country" and of receiving visits from diplomats "with titles as long as a flagstaff, and heads as empty as their hearts."

Although he rode out the storm occasioned by his indiscretion, Daniel returned to the United States in December 1860 and resumed the editorship of the *Examiner*, remaining at his desk during the war years except for two interludes of military service. On the first of these two occasions, in the fall of 1861, the duties of Editor-in-Chief were performed by L. Q. Washington, subsequently Confederate Assistant Secretary of State; on the other, during McClellan's campaign against Richmond, by the vivacious and prolific writer, Edward A. Pollard. Although at all other times Daniel was emphatically *the* editor of the paper, the *Examiner* had a large pool of contributing editors during the war period, all of whom wrote editorials which Daniel purchased with the understanding that he was to have the authority to accept or reject any or all parts of them.

Daniel aimed to make his paper not only a political power but a "school of literature." It was one of his chief endeavors to write simple, plain, Anglo-Saxon English, discarding all Americanisms. He was not interested in writing pretty sentences; yet by a careful selection of words he achieved unexcelled vigor. Few American editors of his day employed more severe invective or resorted more to sarcasm. According to Pollard, Daniel did not himself write more than a few of the articles published in his paper, although he always insisted on preparing a New Year's column reviewing the events of the previous year and expressing his own philosophy in connection with them. Daniel was even a better editor than he was a writer. He corrected and strengthened everything that went into his columns, including advertisements. And when he received a clever letter he used it with his own emendations as subject matter for an editorial. Abhorring slovenliness in dress or print, he was wont to say that a man who goes into print should remember that he is making his appearance before the best society and that he owes it both to himself and to that society not to appear in undress. It was Daniel's objective to have two or three really good editorials in each issue of his paper. He had little use for short pointed paragraphs, believing that a column or column and a half of newspaper space was essential for an effective editorial. His journalistic model was the *London Times,* and he promised himself in the event of Confederate success to make the *Examiner* equal in all respects to the famous *Thunderer.*

Daniel was a misanthrope, a cynic, and a somewhat unstable individual, who was easily provoked into controversy. He both despised men and used them, taking advantage of their meannesses and weak points and evaluating their intellectual caliber with marvelous exactness. From early youth he had shunned society, preferring instead a small circle of intimate friends. In later life he was a recluse who lived among his books and had a horror of visitors. To judge from his editorials, Daniel admired only two public men of his day, John C. Calhoun and Stonewall Jackson. He esteemed Calhoun for his depth and precision of thought, strength of character, and steady nerve; Jackson for the quickness of his perception, which the editor likened to that of Napoleon.[11]

The relationship of Virginian Pollard to Daniel's *Examiner* was never clearly defined. Apparently he joined the newspaper in 1861 after being educated at Hampden-Sydney College and the University of Virginia, travelling extensively as a journalist in various parts of North America, Europe, and the Far East, and working as a government clerk in Washington during the Buchanan administration. Pollard was variously identified as editor, co-editor, associate editor, editorial writer, and contributor to the *Examiner.* For the most part he seems to have functioned as associate editor, assisting Daniel in the preparation of the editorial columns of the paper while his brother Henry Rives Pollard served as news editor.

As a contemporary historian of the war, as well as in the capacity

[11] *D.A.B.,* v, 67-68; G. W. Bagby, *John M. Daniel's Latch-Key* (Lynchburg, Va., 1868); J. M. Daniel, *The Richmond Examiner during the War* (New York, 1868), pp. 218-32; A. N. Wilkinson, "John Moncure Daniel," *Richmond College Historical Papers,* i, no. 1, pp. 73-95; R. W. Hughes, *Editors of the Past* (Richmond, 1897), pp. 18-30. In her reminiscences of wartime Richmond, Constance Cary Harrison, the wife of Jefferson Davis's private secretary, describes the *Examiner* as "a clever, acrid sheet, keeping up to the last an invincible determination to sustain the flag of Walker's Dictionary against that of the Northern authority, Webster. Its bitter, brilliant philippics against the weakness of authorities on both sides of the war line . . . made a brave show of the final *k* in such words as eccentrick and dyspeptick, and of the neglected *u* in favour, flavour etc. Mr. Daniel was a very unpopular man, a sort of a social sphinx. . . ." William Dillon, *Life of John Mitchel* (London, 1888), ii, 197; Pollard, *Life of Davis,* p. 189.

of journalist, Pollard has been characterized as "the ablest and most prolific Southern writer of his day." Although he lacked the elegant diction and crushing force that marked the writing style of Daniel at his best, the unusual vigor of Pollard's language excited the admiration and praise of his newspaper colleagues.[12]

Financially, the *Examiner* was very successful during the Civil War. During the last two years of the war its net receipts were between $1,000 and $1,500 per week, providing a margin of almost $50,000 a year after all personal expenses had been deducted.[13] Daniel spared no expense in providing his newspaper with good equipment, both material and intellectual, and the experiment paid off ten-fold. The *Examiner* was well known from Texas to Virginia, and actually had more subscribers in some of the distant states of the Confederacy than in the immediate vicinity of its place of publication.

Yet from a news standpoint probably the most important of the Richmond dailies was the four-page, fourteen-by-twenty-inch news sheet which James Cowardin and William H. Davis established in Richmond on October 19, 1850. The *Dispatch* was the result of Cowardin's dream to produce a newspaper patterned after the *Baltimore Sun*, a newspaper "devoted to the interest of the city and free and independent in its political views." In thus establishing the first American penny paper south of Baltimore, Cowardin and his partner obviously ran counter to the prevailing trend of Southern journalism. They made their venture pay after a slow start, however. By March 1861 the 18,000 subscribers to the *Dispatch* exceeded in number the paid circulation of all the other Richmond newspapers combined.[14] At that time the *Dispatch* probably outpaced in circulation the entire Southern press, with the exception of one or two of the daily newspapers of New Orleans.

Cowardin, the wartime publisher of the *Dispatch*, like Aaron Willington, had entered journalism via the printing business. A native

[12] *D.A.B.*, xv, 47-48; *National Cyclopedia of American Biography*, vi, 339; J. S. Wilson, in E. A. Alderman et al., eds., *Library of Southern Literature* (New Orleans and Atlanta, 1909), ix, 4,147-50; Michael Houston, "Edward Alfred Pollard and the Richmond *Examiner*: A Study of Journalistic Opposition in Wartime," unpub. M.A. thesis (American University, 1963), p. 63; *Atlanta Daily Intelligencer*, October 25, 1863.

[13] Bagby, *Daniel's Latch-Key*, p. 22.

[14] Lester Cappon, *Virginia Newspapers, 1821-1935* (New York and London, 1936), pp. 8, 169; Evans, "Richmond Press," p. 26.

Virginian from Bath County, he had spent his apprenticeship in the composing rooms of the Danville and Lynchburg newspapers before coming to Richmond in the early eighteen-thirties. In Richmond Cowardin worked under Thomas Ritchie as chief clerk of the *Enquirer* and secured an interest in the *Richmond Times and Compiler* with the intention of converting it from a political into a commercial newspaper. In 1848, finding that the *Times and Compiler* was languishing under his management, Cowardin (as he thought) said farewell to journalism forever and embarked in the banking and brokerage business with his brother-in-law. But the disappointed journalist did not like being a cashier and returned to the newspaper business as joint founder of the *Dispatch*.[15]

The first editor of the *Dispatch* was Hugh R. Pleasants, a brother of the deceased editor of the *Whig*. At the beginning of the war Oliver P. Baldwin, a graceful paragraphist, succeeded Pleasants, but both men continued to write editorials for the *Dispatch*, as did Cowardin when he found time from his other duties. Baldwin's employment as a part-time clerk in the War Department early in 1862 gave the *Dispatch* an advantage in access to war news. In spite of the handicap of a wretched typography and the other difficulties it experienced along with the other members of the Confederate press, the *Dispatch* continued to increase its circulation, reaching a peak of 30,000 by the end of the war.[16]

Making its bow to the public for the first time on March 11, 1863, the *Richmond Sentinel* was soon reputed to have replaced the *Enquirer* as the organ of the Davis administration. Its editor-in-chief, Richard M. Smith, had once edited a newspaper of the same name in Alexandria, Virginia, and had done editorial work for the *Enquirer* after the Yankee occupation of Alexandria at the beginning of the war forced him to become a refugee.

Another Richmond publication of a somewhat different character was the weekly *Southern Illustrated News*. Patterned after a London pictorial with a similar name, it was established in Richmond in the late summer of 1862 to fill the void created by the unavailability of *Harper's*

---

[15] *National Cyclopedia of American Biography*, II, 51; *Richmond Daily Dispatch*, November 22, 1882.

[16] *Richmond Times-Dispatch*, October 22, 1950; *Memphis Daily Appeal*, March 21, 1863; *Charleston Mercury*, February 4, 1862. In September 1861 the *Dispatch* claimed a daily circulation of 26,000, "while the weekly is 10,000 and the semi-weekly, 6,000." *Richmond Daily Dispatch*, September 9, 1861.

Weekly and other Northern illustrated journals. With a distinguished roster of contributors that included the poet and novelist William Gilmore Simms, John R. Thompson, James R. Randall (who wrote "Maryland, My Maryland"), and Alabamian Henry Flash, it acquired a circulation of twenty thousand within a few weeks. Its principal war correspondent was the novelist John Esten Cooke, who was a staff officer at one time or another of both Jeb Stuart and Stonewall Jackson, and also contributed war correspondence to some of the Richmond dailies.[17]

During the first year of the war the press of New Orleans effectively competed with the Richmond newspapers in both news enterprise and editorial influence. Charleston, Augusta, Savannah, Atlanta, Mobile, and Memphis were other important centers of Confederate journalistic enterprise.

Six daily newspapers, the *Picayune, Delta, True Delta, Crescent, Bulletin,* and *Bee,* operated in New Orleans at the beginning of the war. Founded in 1837, the *Picayune* had acquired a national reputation for news enterprise at the time of the Mexican War, when it made use of a system of pony expresses and fast steamships to scoop the world in reporting military events from the Mexican battlefields. Strangely enough, there was a strong New England influence among the *Picayune* staff at the time of the Civil War. Both the publisher, Alva M. Holbrook, and the chief editor, Samuel F. Wilson, were from Massachusetts, and the literary editor, J. F. Otis, was a Bostonian. Perhaps this Northern influence in part explained the fact that, like the *Richmond Dispatch,* the *Picayune* followed the precepts of the "New Journalism" of Benjamin H. Day and Moses Beach by remaining aloof from political ties, giving prominence to local news, and avoiding personalities of an acrimonious character.[18]

[17] R. B. Harwell, *The Confederate Reader* (New York, 1957), p. 130; R. B. Harwell, "John Esten Cooke, Civil War Correspondent," *Journal of Southern History,* xix (November 1953), 501-16; J. O. Beaty, *John Esten Cooke, Virginian* (New York, 1922), p. 80; *Mobile Daily Advertiser and Register,* February 26, March 8, 1863; *New York Evening Post,* October 22, 1864.

[18] T. E. Dabney, *One Hundred Great Years; The Story of the Times-Picayune* (Baton Rouge, 1944), pp. 56, 106; *New York Times,* May 8, 1862; Frederic Hudson, *Journalism in America* (New York, 1873), pp. 493-95; Henry Rightor, *Standard History of New Orleans* (Chicago, 1900), pp. 272-75. For the high incidence of Southern journalists of New England origin in the antebellum South see G. F. Mellen, "New England Editors in the South," in E. H. Ford, *Selected Readings in the History of American Journalism* (Minneapolis, 1939), pp. 234-47.

Two prominent figures in the *Picayune* establishment during its early days—George W. Kendall and Judge Alexander C. Bullitt—were no longer actively engaged in newspaper work when the war came. Kendall, one of the joint founders of the *Picayune* and its most prominent war correspondent in the Mexican War, had retired to an extensive plantation in Texas where he lived as a landed proprietor on a princely scale.[19] Bullitt, a Kentuckian who first applied the nickname of "Old Rough and Ready" to General Zachary Taylor and edited the national organ of the Whigs in Washington during the Taylor administration, had gone home to Louisville before the outbreak of war. Bullitt continued, however, to contribute articles to the *Picayune* from Kentucky during the early months of the war, which led a Mobile editor to style him "the most elegant and eloquent newspaper writer in the Confederacy."[20]

From the time of its founding in 1845, the *Delta* was identified with the ultra-Secessionist school of Southern politics. Its weekly edition circulated throughout the Gulf States area from Texas to Georgia. Its most prominent editors at the time of the war were Judge Alexander Walker and Durant Da Ponte. Walker, a Virginian, had the reputation of being the most scholarly man in the New Orleans press.[21] Da Ponte, a grandson of the composer of the libretto for the opera "Don Giovanni," had come to New Orleans from southern Illinois when he was twelve years old, had broken in as a local reporter for the *Crescent* two years later, and was a member of the paper's editorial staff by the time he was sixteen. The gossips of New Orleans whispered it about that Da Ponte owed his advancement to the influence of his uncle, Thomas J. Durant, an eminent jurist and large slaveholder. It was conceded, however, that young Da Ponte wielded a bold and vigorous pen and that he was singularly well informed about Northern politics. Like Walker, he was also a man of scholarly interests, speaking and writing seven languages fluently, translating a number of Italian poems into English, and displaying talent in watercolor painting.[22]

The *Crescent*, which came into existence about the same time as the *Delta*, had been a Know-Nothing paper in the eighteen-fifties and had opposed secession up to the time of John Brown's raid in Virginia

---

[19] *D.A.B.*, x, 327-28; Hudson, *Journalism in America*, p. 495.

[20] *Mobile Daily Advertiser and Register*, October 6, 1861. See also *Biographical and Historical Memoirs of Louisiana* (Chicago, 1892), II, 159.

[21] *New York Times*, May 8, 1862.

[22] *New Orleans Daily Picayune*, August 8, 1894; *New York Times*, May 8, 1862.

(1859). Walt Whitman had been "scissors editor" of the *Crescent* for a few months during the early days of its history. His younger brother Jeff was with him at the time, but Jeff grew homesick and complained so much about the New Orleans climate that Whitman resigned and the two brothers went back north. The chief owner of the *Crescent* in 1861 was a native of New Jersey named J. O. Nixon whose success as a politician placed the *Crescent* in a favorable position for municipal patronage.[23]

Charleston, Augusta, and Savannah followed the pattern of those Southern cities in which two newspapers of opposite political persuasion divided the newspaper field. In Charleston the rival newspapers were the *Courier* and *Mercury*, in Augusta the *Constitutionalist* and the *Chronicle and Sentinel*, in Savannah the *Republican* and the *Morning News*.

Prominently associated with Willington in the management of the *Charleston Courier*, the oldest daily newspaper in the Carolinas, were Richard Yeadon and Thomas S. Simons. After Willington's death in February 1862 terminated his career of nearly sixty years as senior editor of the paper, Yeadon and Simons shaped the *Courier*'s policies for the remainder of the war.[24]

The wartime editor of the *Charleston Mercury*, Col. Robert Barnwell Rhett, Jr., was the scion of a famous Charleston family and the eldest son of Senator Robert Barnwell Rhett. The younger Rhett was also a Phi Beta Kappa from Harvard, graduating in the same class with President Charles W. Eliot, with whom he corresponded up to the last few years of his life. Within less than four years after young Barnwell came to the helm of the paper in March 1857, the *Mercury* quadrupled its circulation; the strident editorials Barnwell and his brother Edmund published in the *Mercury* during those years were generally regarded as instrumental in bringing about the secession of South Carolina.[25] In a reversal of policy after the war began the *Mercury*

---

[23] *New York Times*, May 8, 1862; *New Orleans Daily Picayune*, January 25, 1887; Frances Winwar, *American Giant, Walt Whitman and His Times* (New York and London, 1941), pp. 120, 133-35, 141; H. S. Canby, *Walt Whitman* (Boston, 1943), pp. 73-74. There are indications in the Winwar biography that Whitman's employers on the *Crescent*, McClure and Hayes, had become disenchanted with him before they quarreled with him over salary matters at the time of his departure from the newspaper.

[24] H. T. Malone, "The Charleston *Daily Courier*, Standard Bearer of the Confederacy," *Journalism Quarterly* (Summer 1952), p. 307.

[25] *Charleston News and Courier*, February 22, 1905; T. A. Deland and A. D.

came to be known as an anti-administration paper and remained critical of Davis's policies throughout the war.

The "working editor" of the *Mercury* was a youthful and devout Roman Catholic Virginian named Bartholomew R. Riordan who had attracted Rhett's attention when in the spring of 1860 he visited Charleston to report the Democratic national convention for the *New Orleans Delta*. One of the New York papers described Riordan as the factotum on the *Mercury* staff, "who is obliged to read so many exchanges that it is a wonder he is not made an idiot in the flower of his youth; that being who clips, who wafers, who writes out the 'markets,' who deciphers raving and incomprehensible telegrams, who looks after the editorials, and has an eye on the local column, who reads miles of proofs, who must know who dies and who gets married, who attends to that mysterious and awful duty the 'making up' of the paper, who 'sees the paper to press,' who, finally, works like a galley slave from 12 o'clock in the day to 3 o'clock in the morning of the next day, day in and day out, year in and year out, until the hot, unwholesome atmosphere of the editorial 'den,' drafts, a continual cramped position, want of physical exercise, and a perpetual mental strain, cause the scissors to drop from his stiffened fingers, and necessitate the writing, by a brother quill, of a dead head obituary." After the Confederate Associated Press was founded Riordan assumed in addition to this alarming combination of duties the responsibility of acting as the Associated Press reporter in Charleston at a time when the city was being subjected to almost daily bombardment.[26]

The internal affairs of the *Mercury* as a family enterprise were not always harmonious. In the Rhett Papers is an undated letter from Edmund Rhett to his father, probably written before the Civil War, complaining of interference with the composition of his editorials on the part of his elder brother. Noting that his brother Barnwell was "a religious man and not a man of the world," Edmund objected to Barnwell's practice of "taking up my articles, for which I alone am responsible and striking out this, as irreligious, that, blasphemous, a third as harsh, a fourth as improper &c &c. . . . If I am fit to edit the Paper,

---

Smith, *Northern Alabama, Historical and Biographical* (Birmingham, 1888), pp. 256-59; W. L. King, *The Newspaper Press of Charleston, S.C.* (Charleston, 1872), p. 155.

[26] *Daily Richmond Examiner*, October 21, 1861; *Savannah Republican*, September 23, 1863; *New York Daily Tribune*, March 22, 1897.

my own judgement must also be respected. If not, I am not fit for the position, and he had much better get a wiser and more efficient man. . . . No paper can in these times pay that is not sharp, aggressive, and pungent. It is not possible to publish the views of the *Charleston Mercury* without giving offense to somebody. Edit it, if you please, like the bleating of a lamb and some opponent may any morning find excuse for offensive remark. I desire to edit the Paper to make it pay. But it will never pay when subscribed to only by church members."[27]

The contrasting demeanor of the two rival Charleston newspapers during the Civil War, one strongly pro-administration and the other just as strongly opposed, was the theme of an interesting editorial in another South Carolina newspaper:

"The Courier is practical and the Mercury speculative. The Courier deals with the present and the past, and the Mercury more with the future. The Courier is content to meet events as they occur, and the Mercury anticipates them. There is more diffusion in the Courier, and more compactness in the Mercury. The Courier is pleased to hold on the even tenor of its way; and the Mercury is bold, dashing, presumptive, and prophetic . . . both are popular. . . . The Courier . . . however is, and must be, ever more popular . . . [being] highly domestic, and more a favorite with families."[28]

Although Atlanta was a smaller city in 1860 than Augusta or Savannah, it was a more active newspaper center than either during the wartime sixties. In July 1864 a leading Confederate war correspondent went on record as saying that "next to Richmond, Atlanta may boast of the ablest conducted Press in the country, the most unflagging enterprise, and some of the most accomplished of gentlemen among its editors."[29]

In 1861 the "Gate City," as it was then popularly known, possessed two morning newspapers, the *Intelligencer* and the *Southern Confederacy*, and a lively evening newspaper, J. S. Peterson's *Commonwealth*. After the *Commonwealth* failed in mid-1862 Peterson, a former New Englander, made a second attempt in the Atlanta journalistic field, but his *Atlanta Daily Gazette*, founded August 10, 1863, ran into diffi-

27 Edmund Rhett to Robert Barnwell Rhett, n.d., Robert Barnwell Rhett Papers, Huntsville, Alabama.

28 *Barnwell* (S.C.) *Sentinel*, as quoted in *Charleston Daily Courier*, May 6, 1862.

29 *Savannah Republican*, July 15, 1864.

culties and expired in December of that year. When the Union army overran Tennessee, Atlanta became the sanctuary of a number of refugee newspapers, among them the *Memphis Appeal*, the *Knoxville Register*, and the *Chattanooga Rebel*. Among the better known names associated with Atlanta journalism during the war were those of George W. Adair and J. Henly Smith, who were editorially connected with the *Southern Confederacy*, and John H. Steele, the editor of the *Intelligencer*.[30]

Mobile, a city of 40,000 inhabitants, had four daily morning newspapers in April 1861, the *Advertiser*, *Register*, *Tribune*, and *Mercury*, and two evening papers, the *News* and *Telegraph*, which were published as evening editions of the *Advertiser* and *Tribune* respectively. The *Mercury* suspended publication in the early summer of 1861, and in June, the *Advertiser* and the *Register* merged, to become under John Forsyth's editorship one of the best-known and most frequently quoted newspapers in the Confederacy.

Forsyth's connection with the *Register* dated back to 1837, two years after his arrival in Mobile from his native Georgia. Forsyth was the able son of a distinguished father of the same name who had been successively attorney general and governor of Georgia, a member of Congress for fifteen years, minister to Spain, and secretary of state for six and a half years under Presidents Jackson and Van Buren. The younger Forsyth was educated abroad and at Princeton, where he was the valedictorian of the class of 1832. After four years as one of the owners of the *Register*, Forsyth returned to Georgia for family reasons and there edited the *Columbus Times* for twelve years. In 1853 he returned to Mobile and resumed the editorship of the *Register*. Although his connection with the paper was further interrupted by a diplomatic assignment in Mexico between 1856 and 1858, he championed the

[30] Biographical information about Adair appears in *National Cyclopedia of American Biography*, II, 425; *Atlanta Journal*, September 27, 1899. Adair later recalled having sold the *Atlanta Confederacy* for $200,000 in August 1863. With the money he bought gold which his wife sewed into her skirt for safekeeping just far enough apart to keep the gold pieces from rattling. *Atlanta Daily Constitution*, August 1, 1897; *Confederate Veteran*, v (August 1897), pp. 402-405. For information about the journalistic careers of J. Henly Smith and John H. Steele see *Atlanta Daily Constitution*, February 26, 1907; *Atlanta Daily Intelligencer*, January 12, 1871. Interesting accounts of Atlanta journalism at the time of the war can be found in H. T. Malone, "Atlanta Journalism during the Confederacy," *Georgia Historical Quarterly*, XXXVII (September 1953), 210-19; *New York Evening Post*, October 14, 1864.

cause of "Douglas Democracy" in the columns of his newspaper with such fervor that in the election of 1860 Douglas carried the city and county of Mobile over both the Bell and Breckinridge tickets. It was at this time that Forsyth became Mayor of Mobile and in March 1861 a member of the famous but futile peace commission the Davis government dispatched to Washington.[31]

Of the four leading Memphis newspapers (*Appeal, Argus, Avalanche,* and *Bulletin*) by far the most interesting and important was the *Memphis Appeal,* which was already valued at $75,000 in 1860. Under the joint editorship of Col. John R. McClanahan and Benjamin F. Dill, the *Appeal* impressed everyone with its indomitable spirit and the extent of its news coverage. Keeping one step ahead of the Yankees while publishing at various times during the war in Grenada and Jackson, Mississippi, Atlanta and Columbus, Georgia, and Montgomery, Alabama, the *Appeal* was one of the finest examples of Confederate journalism.[32]

Illustrative of the spirit of the *Appeal's* owners was an incident in December 1862. A war correspondent of a Knoxville newspaper at the Bowman House in Jackson, Mississippi noticed the door of a room with the sign "Memphis Headquarters" in large letters inscribed on it. Through the open door the reporter from Knoxville saw a number of men around a table listening to McClanahan expound on the glowing prospects of his newspaper. The colonel, who was a Mexican War veteran, swore that he had not been compelled by the approach of the enemy to move the *Appeal* from Grenada to Jackson. His action had been merely a "change of base" that he had planned months beforehand. During the outburst of laughter at the colonel's witticism at the expense of General McClellan, one of his listeners laughingly observed that the *Appeal's* maneuver had truly provided a splendid example of military strategy.[33]

Another peripatetic Southern newspaper that established an envi-

---

[31] *National Cyclopedia of American Biography,* VIII, 471; *Mobile Daily Register,* May 3, 1877; Thomas Owen, *History of Alabama and Dictionary of Alabama Biography* (Chicago, 1921), III, 598. The early history of the *Register* is briefly summarized in *Mobile Register, 100th Anniversary, 1814-1914* (privately printed), pp. 9-13.

[32] T. H. Baker, "Refugee Newspaper: The Memphis Daily Appeal, 1862-1865," *Journal of Southern History,* XXIX (August 1963), 326-44; Robert Talley, *One Hundred Years of the Commercial Appeal, 1840-1940* (Memphis, 1940), p. 19.

[33] *Knoxville Daily Register,* December 17, 1862.

able reputation for news enterprise was the saucy little *Chattanooga Rebel*. First published in August 1862 at Bowling Green, Kentucky, it "changed base" several times before it arrived in Chattanooga, where it flourished for a time under the editorship of Henry Watterson. The *Rebel* was primarily an army newspaper and under Watterson's editorship the most widely read newspaper in the Western army of the Confederacy. Watterson parted company with his newspaper soon after the fall of Chattanooga in September 1863, and the *Rebel* continued the wanderings that took it from Tennessee to Georgia and finally to Alabama.[34]

The war brought about many of the same changes in Confederate newspaper practice that were characteristic of wartime journalism in the North—changes in newspaper makeup, including more prominent headlines; an increasing emphasis on news, especially telegraphic news; a spate of extra editions;[35] the employment of newsboys in the larger cities to replace much of the old subscription trade; the use of special correspondents to supplement the amount of news obtained from the publisher's exchanges; and the evolution of a cooperative news-gathering service. With these changes came problems which constricted the area in which change was possible, problems of considerably greater magnitude than those with which journalism in the North had to contend. Wartime scarcities and skyrocketing costs of paper and other printing materials, the increasing obsolescence of presses and typographical equipment, the problem of finding printers and other office help to replace the employees that were called away to the

[34] J. W. Livingood, "The Chattanooga *Rebel*," *Publications of East Tennessee Historical Association*, No. 39 (1967), pp. 42-55; J. F. Wall, *Henry Watterson, Reconstructed Rebel* (New York, 1956), pp. 37-43; *Daily Richmond Examiner*, September 17, 1863. Watterson was a Tennesseean who had done newspaper work in Washington, D.C. before the war. During the war he was at various times the editor of the *Nashville Banner*, the *Chattanooga Rebel*, the *Atlanta Southern Confederacy*, and the *Montgomery Mail* and one of the ablest journalists the war produced.

[35] On August 17, 1861 the *New Orleans Daily Delta* announced that it had published five editions of the *Delta* the day before and that each contained the announcement of a victory. The diarist J. B. Jones declared in the October 1, 1862 entry of his diary that the Richmond newspaper extras were mere slips of paper, rarely more than a column wide, which were reproduced in the next regular issue of the paper. J. B. Jones, *A Rebel War Clerk's Diary* (Philadelphia, 1866), I, 161. To fill the news vacuum in Richmond over the weekend, a new Sunday newspaper was established there during the summer of 1863. *Augusta Daily Constitutionalist*, July 21, 1863.

army, communication difficulties resulting from abnormal pressures on and deterioration of telegraph and postal facilities, and periodic encounters with military censorship limited the effectiveness of the Confederate press and caused subscription rates to soar to heights undreamed of at the beginning of the war. Also, there was a steady attrition in the number of Confederate dailies and weeklies.

Paper that had cost three to five dollars a ream before the war was retailing at fifty to sixty dollars in July 1864 and was frequently unavailable even at that price.[36] The cost of ink, glue, oil, molasses, wood, potash, and other essentials of newspaper manufacture mounted in similar proportion. With only five percent of the nation's paper mills in 1860, the South could not produce nearly enough paper to meet even the section's peacetime needs, and it was not possible to smuggle enough through the blockade or to accelerate domestic production sufficiently to meet the wartime demand for newsprint.[37]

To conserve their paper supply, publishers restricted the size of their sheets and made use of smaller type or diminished their frequency of issue. By July 1862 all the Richmond dailies were being published on half (single) sheets; soon thereafter, this became the practice of almost all the Confederate dailies and many of the weeklies. Beginning in September 1861 the *Charleston Courier* reduced its size on several occasions, until by February 13, 1865 its single sheet measured only ten by fifteen inches, with but four columns to the page. Also, newspapers offered high prices for clean cotton and linen rags and made use of inferior grades of paper, including writing paper, wrapping paper, and even the reverse side of wallpaper.[38] In Richmond it was common practice for newspapers to borrow paper from each other, returning the borrowed amount whenever possible to enable the lender to issue his edition promptly. The *Richmond Examiner* told how: "Brown paper, waste paper, backs of old letters, and rejected essays, and unpaid bills (made out to delinquent subscribers), bits of foolscap torn from the copy books of youth, and the ledgers of busi-

---

[36] *Mobile Daily Advertiser and Register*, July 10, 1864. For bitter complaint about the way in which rag speculators in Savannah forced up the price of paper after the destruction by fire of the Bath Paper Mills near Augusta, see *Savannah Republican* as quoted in *Wilmington Daily Journal*, April 30, 1863.

[37] F. L. Mott, *American Journalism* (New York, 1941), pp. 362-63.

[38] J. M. Lee, *History of American Journalism* (Garden City, 1917), pp. 305-306; *Savannah Republican*, June 3, 1864. The wallpaper editions of the *Vicksburg Citizen* are particularly well known.

ness men furnish the manuscript of the thunderous 'editorials' and horrible 'locals' of the press of the Confederacy. An editor in Alabama says he has been using a shingle for two months, wiping out one editorial as it is set up, and indicting [*sic*] another; and a brother editor replies that he is working out his editorial 'sums' on an old slate he used to con over when he went to school."[39]

The scarcity of ink also induced the use of homemade substitutes which did not enhance the typographical appearance of the hard-pressed news sheets. Some newspapers (the *Memphis Appeal* among them) were obliged to print their sheets with ordinary shoe-blacking. When during the last year of the Civil War the type of the *Richmond Daily Dispatch* was worn out, its business manager, J. D. Hammersley, undertook to run the blockade and go to England for a new outfit. He secured the outfit and got it through the blockade and into the *Dispatch* office, but before it could be used for the first time the building that housed it was consumed in the flames that destroyed every newspaper office in Richmond but one.[40]

Of the approximately eight hundred printers who made up the entire printing force of the Confederacy in 1863, at least seventy-five percent either had been or were in the army by June 1864.[41] Substantial numbers of pressmen, mailing clerks, reporters, and editors likewise shouldered the rifle, which placed a heavy burden on those who remained behind.[42] Of the small number of employees performing the tasks of the *Savannah Republican* office in September 1864, two were disabled war veterans, two others were soldiers detailed by the government for work in the office because of their skill as practical printers, and a third pair, occupying positions filled by able-bodied men before the war, were ladies![43]

Expanding labor costs and increased telegraph tolls were substantial factors in the price squeeze that constricted newspaper operation. A

[39] *Daily Richmond Examiner*, June 1, 1863.

[40] Talley, *One Hundred Years of Commercial Appeal*, p. 21; *Richmond Times-Dispatch*, October 22, 1950.

[41] *Daily Richmond Examiner*, October 31, 1863; *Augusta Daily Constitutionalist*, June 16, 1864.

[42] *Charleston Mercury*, November 12, 1861. In February 1862 the editorial, operative, and other employees of the *Charleston Courier* establishment numbered twenty-two. *Charleston Daily Courier*, February 5, 1862. A year later, the *Jackson Mississippian* employed twenty compositors, two editors, six clerks, and four "penmen." *Chicago Tribune* as reprinted in *New York Times*, May 29, 1863.

[43] *Savannah Republican*, September 17, 1864.

twenty-five-percent increase in the printing rates of Mobile in November 1863 involved an increase in the *Mobile Register's* expenditures of about $9,000 a year. During the first six months of 1864 the total operating costs of this same newspaper (Sundays excepted) ran to one thousand dollars a day.[44] After the Southern Telegraph Company twice doubled its wire service rates between January and June 1864, a Texas newspaper complained of telegraph bills ranging from $600 to $800 a week.[45]

Pressures of this kind forced upward the subscription price of most Southern dailies from an average of around five dollars a year to levels of $100 and even $125 in the spring of 1865. By 1864 many newspapers were taking subscriptions for only three months at a time, and by the end of the war, the quoting of monthly and even daily rates exclusively had become standard practice.[46]

Under the weight of the same pressures many other newspapers went out of business or were merged into more profitable enterprises. During the first year of the war forty newspapers suspended publication in Virginia alone, and in Texas fifty out of sixty. In Mississippi only nine out of the prewar total of seventy-five were still in operation at the end of 1863. Military occupation by the enemy and financial stringency continued to silence other presses until by January 1865 there were not as many newspapers in the entire Confederacy as there were in the state of Virginia before the war. Probably no more than twenty Southern dailies were still functioning at the time of Lee's surrender.[47]

The difficulties of a Southern wartime editor were well described in a front-page article by the senior editor of the *Atlanta Confederacy* describing a typical day in his newspaper office in 1863:

As we enter our office in the morning, the confidential clerk who opens our letters hands us a short communication, quietly remarking that "them" fellers at Marietta have *ris* again in the price of their paper. We hastily glance

[44] *Mobile Daily Advertiser and Register,* December 1, 1863.

[45] *Montgomery Mail* as reprinted in *Charleston Daily Courier,* June 14, 1864; *Savannah Republican,* July 1, 1864; *Augusta Daily Constitutionalist,* July 2, 1864.

[46] Coulter, *Confederate States,* p. 494. In March 1865 the subscription price of the *Macon Daily Telegraph* was $120 a year.

[47] *Lynchburg Daily Republican,* December 23, 1861; *Savannah Republican,* February 11, 1862; *Lynchburg Virginian* as reprinted in *Mobile Daily Advertiser and Register,* February 1, 1865. Among the more important Confederate dailies which fell into enemy hands between December 1864 and the end of March 1865 were the *Savannah Republican* and *Morning News,* the *Charleston Mercury* and

at the contents and find that the paper mills have made a heavy advance upon us. We indignantly pass on to the press-room and find a good portion of the floor flooded with water. We ask Billy what is the matter and he replies, "Nothing but a chip in one of the flues and the engine boiled over." We then ask Billy how there came to be so many waste papers . . . on the floor. . . . "Well," says he, "the last paper you got at Marietta ain't no account. About a fifth of it is split up, so it won't run through." We start back, and the mailing clerk accosts us saying, "Can't write without fire such a morning as this." We call the porter and ask why a good fire is not made, when he replies that he can't make it burn, as the last load of coal is nearly all rocks. Our confidential clerk again asks us what he shall do with a lot of indistinct, blotted, torn-up, badly patched shinplasters signed "S. Smith," all sent in a letter from a post office in Alabama, in which the writer asks us to "fling him in" one subscription for a year, for having made for us a club and sent the money, (the aforesaid batch of Alabama shinplasters).

We step to the front door a moment to catch the free air, while we try to arrive at a solution of the troubles just named, when a little negro comes dashing up and says, "Missus wants a paper; Wesley flinged hern over de fence in de yard and de puppy tored it up." Just then a red-faced man, with a dilapidated military coat on, steps up and inquires who is the man who wants to go as a substitute? We tell him to walk into the office and the clerk will give him the name. He has scarcely passed us, when another man asks if we can tell where he can hire a little nigger gal to sorter help his folks as they are most all sick. We answer that we cannot as none are advertised this morning. "We don't take a paper," the man replies, "'lowed you knowed". . . .

After an hour spent in this way, we hurry up to our sanctum to look over exchanges and correspondence; find but few papers, and none from Richmond, Charleston, or Mobile; find one or two letters from men we never knew or heard of before, asking us to change their paper to some post office, without stating where they are now taking it, as though we had plenty of time to look through all those "eight ponderous volumes" to find his name.

Soon there is a rap at the door of our sanctum. We invite the person to come in, when a soldier asks if we have any "payrolls" or "scriptive lists." Of course we have nothing of the kind in our sanctum, but we have to tell him where we can find them. We have not more than got ourselves well squared up to our desk to fix something for the paper, when our Foreman comes in hurriedly saying, "Copy, sir." We have none ready, and have to give him something that is only half ready or something that we would not put in the paper, if we had anything else prepared; but the printer can't wait, and must have *something* to work on.

We impatiently turn to our desk and have not more than got ourself composed and our mind in proper train of thought on (what we consider) an important editorial when we hear three quick, light, but distinct raps at

Courier, the *Columbia Guardian* and *Carolinian*, the *Wilmington Journal*, and the *Goldsboro Journal*. For a partial list of daily newspapers still in operation in the Confederacy at the end of the war see *Columbus Daily Sun*, April 13, 1865.

the door. We at once know that it is a woman. We say "come in" when the visitor introduces herself, gives the most satisfactory references of unsurpassed talents and accomplishments, and wants to furnish us with a six column article on love, or the education of women, and a piece of poetry twice a week, dedicated to all the distinguished and handsome Generals of the war, for handsome pay of course. We are compelled through politeness to a lady—a *literary* lady—of the genuine blue-stocking sisterhood, to sit for a half hour and talk, and hear her talk, the most consummate nonsense; and in less than one minute after she is gone, another printer comes dashing in for "more copy," when we have not a single paragraph to give him. We however rummage over a pile of selections and communications that have been laid aside for some time, make some clippings from our exchanges at random, write a few short paragraphs, and weave into them as much *spice* as possible, hoping they will please, if not instruct our readers; and so we fill the hands of our printers for the day with "copy."

We then start out upon the street to transact some very important business that should have been attended to several days ago. We meet three men at the door as we enter the street, each one of whom, in his turn, asks us a question in the following order:

"Got any dispatches since morning?" — "Any news from Vicksburg, and will the Yankees take Wilmington?" "Do you think Congress will repeal the *exemption* act? I believe I'll look-round for a *sub.*; we'll all have to go yet." Soon we meet a man on the street who asks, "when are you going to publish Sen. Hill's speech? You always publish such things in the *Confederacy*, and I've been looking for this speech for two weeks." We tell him we will publish it next week. . . .

Soon after dinner persons commence coming in and asking: "Evening paper out yet?" "No sir," we reply. "What time will it be out?" "Five o'clock," we again reply; and these questions are asked and the same answer given with but few variations, a hundred times a day. Occasionally one will give it a little variety by saying he can't wait, and then ask if we have "anything good in the paper to-day."

These are not the half of our daily troubles, and the most serious and important of them are not alluded to in this article. Now, under these circumstances if our wife should happen to die, and our head become a little frosted over, and we should happen to go out among the girls just for recreation, we hope the dear creatures will remember this recital of our woes and not think we are growing old.[48]

Near the end of 1864 Editor James Sneed of the *Savannah Republican* wrote to President Davis in Richmond to ask a favor. He explained that the supply of type and nearly every other kind of material in his

---

[48] *Atlanta Daily Southern Confederacy*, February 1, 1863. For a description, blending fact and fancy, of a Southern newspaper office during war days (that of the *Savannah Republican*) see the letter of "Personne" in *Charleston Daily Courier*, March 18, 1862.

office had been depleted by wartime usage, "until we are now reduced to the necessity of printing a paper which, half the time, nobody can read." Since there was no foundry left in the Confederacy to provide the necessary supplies to keep his paper in operation, Sneed wanted the President to grant him permission to ship ten bales of cotton from Wilmington to Nassau in a blockade runner in which the government had reserved space. Sneed solemnly promised to devote the proceeds of this transaction to the purchase of materials for his newspaper. There is no record of Davis's response to the editor's plea, but before it could have been favorably acted upon, Sherman's army had reached Savannah and Sneed's publishing career was at an end.[49]

Nearly all the more prominent Confederate daily newspapers at the beginning of the war used the first page for the display of advertisements and notices, and published editorials and war news on the later pages. As the war progressed, war news and even editorials took over the first page, while the amount of advertising diminished and was relegated to the back of the newspaper. Employing with obvious reluctance a term popularized by the *New York Herald*, which Bennett in turn had copied from the *London Times*, some Southern newspapers gave prominent place to "situation" articles to summarize the war news that they obtained from various sources.[50]

In spite of the difficulties the war created for Confederate editors and publishers, it stimulated greater public interest in news in the South than had ever been known before. The Confederate press continued to rely on its newspaper exchanges for information from other parts of the Confederacy and on Northern papers whenever they came to hand for their reports of news happenings in the North and other parts of the world. "Such is the scarcity of Northern intelligence that ten, fifteen and even twenty dollars are freely paid for a single New York paper," declared the Richmond correspondent of a Charleston newspaper in June 1861. In time, enterprising journalists reduced to a system the collection of Northern papers by flag-of-truce boats and various underground channels.[51] Also, whereas telegraphic news rarely

---

[49] James Roddy Sneed to Jefferson Davis, November 17, 1864, Jefferson Davis Papers, Duke University.

[50] For comment about the use of the term "situation" in the *London Times* and *New York Herald* in connection with military operations see *Petersburg Daily Express*, February 19, 1862; *Knoxville Daily Register*, December 3, 1862; *Atlanta Daily Register* as quoted in *Mobile Daily Advertiser and Register*, March 25, 1864.

[51] *Charleston Daily Courier*, June 21, 1861. On October 26, 1864 the Richmond

exceeded a column in the antebellum press,[52] Confederate newspapers expended large sums on and devoted proportionately large amounts of space to telegraphic reports of the latest news from Richmond, Louisville, Nashville, Memphis, Chattanooga, New Orleans, and other news-gathering centers.

In the early days of the war nearly every Southern newspaper of any size made extensive use of volunteer correspondents, both officers and enlisted men, to report news from the army. The larger newspapers also employed special correspondents of their own, and occasionally editors such as John Forsyth and George W. Adair visited the armies briefly to gather material.

The *Richmond Dispatch*, the *Mobile Advertiser and Register*, the *Memphis Appeal*, and the *New Orleans Delta* were among the more active Southern newspapers in publishing war correspondence during the first year of the war. From evidence provided by the newspapers themselves, it appears that although the number of Confederate war correspondents was considerably less than the number of "Bohemians" with the Northern armies, over one hundred army correspondents represented the Confederate press in the field at various times during the war.[53] Equipped with horse, spyglass, writing materials, and other essentials, the Confederate war correspondent, if he was not already a soldier, often found it expedient to obtain a staff appointment to facilitate access to army news. There was probably a wide variation in the amount of compensation reporters received. When Henry Timrod joined the Army of the West as a war correspondent for the *Charleston Mercury* soon after the Battle of Shiloh, the terms of his appointment were six dollars a day and travelling expenses paid. Samuel Chester Reid's weekly pay as a war correspondent for the *New Orleans Picayune* at the beginning of 1862 amounted to twenty-five dollars a week. By the end of 1863 he was receiving four times

---

correspondent of the *Augusta Chronicle* stated that the Richmond press received Yankee newspapers regularly each day from the army lines below the city, having made special arrangements with officers at the front to obtain copies of the Baltimore, Philadelphia, and New York papers, which were usually two days old. *Augusta Daily Chronicle and Sentinel*, November 2, 1864.

[52] "Before the civil war the Nashville press depended but to a limited extent on the telegraph for its news. Occasionally a paragraph of general news was injected into the market reports which the telegraph company furnished to the newspapers printed here, charging therefor a reasonable sum." J. Wooldridge, *History of Nashville* (Nashville, 1890), p. 362.

[53] This figure includes both special and volunteer correspondents.

that amount from the *Mobile Tribune* with a supplementary allowance for horse feed. Altogether Reid's monetary payments from his various newspaper employers over a period of about two and a half years appears to have amounted to about $12,000.[54]

The distinction between volunteer and special (paid) correspondents was not always clear-cut. Indeed, on some occasions Dixie newspapers employed as special correspondents soldiers or ex-soldiers who had already demonstrated their proficiency as volunteer journalists. Also, in some cases newspapers differentiated between telegraphic and letter correspondents, although in others both functions were combined in the same person.

It was the common practice of Confederate newspaper reporters to attach pseudonyms to their correspondence in place of their real names. If a reporter wrote for more than one newspaper, as was frequently the case, he was accustomed to use a different signature in each paper. Thus Reid, the "Sparta" of the *New Orleans Picayune* and *Memphis Appeal*, was the "Ora" of the *Mobile Advertiser and Register* and the "290" of the *Atlanta Intelligencer*. Similarly Dr. William G. Shepardson was the "Bohemian" of the *Richmond Dispatch* and the "Evelyn" of the *Mobile Register*. In a letter written to George W. Bagby before the war, when Bagby was still the Washington correspondent of the *Charleston Mercury*, Editor R. B. Rhett, Jr. signified some of the reasons for the anonymity of reporters:

"I consider your connection with the Washington Correspondence [of the *Mercury*], as strictly confidential. No one in South Carolina, out of the *Mercury* office, knows your name; and if you will be as discrete [*sic*] as I will, no one shall ever know. The wisdom and consequent usefulness of your letters will depend entirely upon this. If you are known, it is impossible to criticise and use names as you otherwise can do, to the great benefit of the southern cause.

"Crandall was my correspondent for some time, and was very useful in exposing the intrigues of sundry would be fireeaters at Washington until he, through imprudence, allowed them to ferret him out. After

[54] Virginia Clare, *Harp of the South* [biog. Timrod] (Ogelthorpe University, Ga., 1936), p. 65; Diary of Samuel Chester Reid, Jr., Samuel Chester Reid Papers, Santa Cruz, Calif. As a Washington correspondent of the *Richmond Whig* and *Charleston Mercury* before the war, George W. Bagby received a flat rate of compensation of three to five dollars a letter. R. B. Rhett, Jr. to G. W. Bagby, January 27, 1858, Bagby Papers, Virginia Historical Society; G. W. Bagby to R. Ridgway, March 31, 1858, Brock Collection, Huntington Library.

that, he was of no account. Jones of New York has just been exposed, either through his own indiscretion, or the treachery of some telegraph operator—All this by way of caution."[55]

Two reporters, Peter W. Alexander and Felix Gregory de Fontaine, stood head and shoulders above the others in the realm of news correspondence. Although primarily identified with the *Savannah Republican*, Alexander also reported at various times during the war for the *Atlanta Confederacy*, the *Columbus Sun*, the *Mobile Advertiser and Register*, the *Richmond Dispatch*, and the "Thunderer" of the English press, the *London Times*. De Fontaine was the "Personne" of the *Charleston Courier* until the end of 1863, when he became editor and part owner of the *Columbia Daily South Carolinian*. "Personne" returned to the field during 1864, however, for brief tours of reporting duty in the service of his own newspaper and the *Savannah Republican*. Although for the most part, Alexander and de Fontaine operated in different war theaters, their paths crossed occasionally. In October 1863 a special correspondent of the *Atlanta Register* stationed near Chattanooga noted one of the crossings: "Since I began writing, 'Personne' and 'P.W.A.,' correspondents of the Charleston Courier and Savannah Republican, have spent an hour at our quarters during a thunder shower; both of whom we found to be intelligent and interesting gentlemen—quite as entertaining in conversation as attractive in writing. The latter is still cruising in the craft of celibacy; the former has been twice married, and when speaking of his state of life, with him the interrogation point (?) had been twice answered, but with his friend, if she should be fortunate, there would be an exclamation point (!) in admiration of the occurrence."[56]

"The Prince of Correspondents," as the *Courier* flatteringly styled Alexander, was a native of Ruckersville, Georgia, and a graduate of the University of Georgia in the class of 1844. At the University Alexander carefully schooled himself in English composition. In contrast with the other students who generally followed the practice of preparing rough drafts of their literary exercises and then of rewriting them for presentation to their professors, Alexander would carefully write his essays in full and then revise them twice, with marked improvement each time. He surpassed almost all his fellow students as a writer

[55] R. B. Rhett, Jr. to G. W. Bagby, January 30, 1861, Bagby Papers, Virginia Historical Society.

[56] *Atlanta Register* as reprinted in *Charleston Daily Courier*, October 27, 1863.

and in other academic respects as well, finishing second in his class only to the famous orator (subsequently Confederate States senator) Benjamin H. Hill.

Alexander began the study of law after leaving the University and was admitted to practice in neighboring Thomaston. The contributions which as a loyal Whig he made to the Whig party press brought the opportunity for editorial work on the *Savannah Republican*, then the leading organ of the Whig party in Georgia. From 1853 to 1857 Alexander was editor-in-chief of the *Republican*. Then he returned to Thomaston to resume his law practice and remained firm to the end in his opposition to the disruption of the Union as a member of Georgia's secession convention.

Having resigned himself to the inevitability of separation Alexander accepted an appointment as a war correspondent of the *Republican* when hostilities began, and travelled north to the front in Virginia. Using the bylines "P.W.A." or simply "A." ("Sallust" when writing for the *Richmond Dispatch*), Alexander soon gained the confidence of the Confederate authorities and obtained facilities as a correspondent which few of his competitors could match. The graphic style of his letters and the abundance and reliability of the information they contained caused them to be copied and read in every portion of the South and even beyond the warring sections.[57]

De Fontaine was of foreign parentage. Two of his uncles, after whom he was named, were Italian professors attached to the Austrian and French courts. His father, Louis Antoine de Fontaine, was a French nobleman who accompanied the Bourbon monarch Charles X into exile. The elder de Fontaine came to the United States late in 1830 and married an American girl connected with the family of the Revolutionary War patriot, Ethan Allen. Two years later (1834) Felix was born in Boston.

After receiving his education from private tutors de Fontaine learned shorthand (or phonography as it was then called) at a time when the system was still uncommon. In time he became a congressional reporter in Washington and also was charged with preparing the official reports of the famous trial of the Harvard Professor John H. Webster for the murder of Dr. Parkman in Boston (1849) and that of Congressman

[57] *Atlanta Constitution*, September 24, 1886; L. L. Knight, *Georgia's Landmarks, Memorials, and Legends* (Atlanta, 1914), II, 569, 720; *New York Evening Post*, October 22, 1864.

Dan Sickles for the shooting of Barton Key in Washington (1859).[58] He was also connected with the New York press for a number of years until he moved to Charleston, S.C. on the eve of the war. In Charleston he gained the friendship and confidence of the Creole General Beauregard and received the general's permission to provide the *New York Herald* with a telegraphic report of the attack on Fort Sumter.

It was a peculiar turn of fortune that made it possible for one of the two leading war correspondents on the Confederate side to furnish a Northern newspaper with a news scoop of the first action of the Civil War. But de Fontaine's sympathies apparently were with the South, and in May 1861 "Little Felix," as he had been known in Boston, accompanied the First South Carolina Regiment to Virginia as a military correspondent with the rank of major. Within a few weeks he was providing the readership of the *Charleston Courier* with portrayals of the poetry and humor, the pageantry and occasional dullness of Confederate camp life.[59]

A step removed from Alexander and de Fontaine was a group of war correspondents who, although somewhat less notable, performed the duties of their craft with distinction. They included the versatile Samuel Chester Reid, Jr., James B. Sener, Dr. William G. Shepardson, Albert J. Street, John H. Linebaugh, and Israel Gibbons. Sener and Shepardson were primarily identified with the *Richmond Dispatch*, although both men reported for other papers. Street was the "N'Importe" of the *Mobile Register*; Linebaugh covered the operations of the Army of Tennessee for the *Memphis Appeal*; Gibbons was accredited to the *New Orleans Crescent* until New Orleans fell and was subsequently an occasional correspondent of the *Mobile Register*. As already noted, Reid reported for a number of papers, including the *New Orleans Picayune*, the *Memphis Appeal*, the *Mobile Register*, *Mobile Tribune*, *Montgomery Advertiser*, and *Atlanta Intelligencer*.

Three of the six reporters (Reid, Street, and Gibbons) were of North-

[58] Webster, a chemistry professor at Harvard, murdered Dr. Parkman following a quarrel over a sum of money Webster owed Parkman. Webster was convicted on circumstantial evidence, the focal point of which was some teeth found in Webster's furnace that were identified as Parkman's false teeth. This famous murder case is described in *D.A.B.*, xix, 592-93; S. H. Holbrook, "Murder at Harvard," *American Mercury*, lxvi (February 1948), 228-33.

[59] *D.A.B.*, v, 196; *Charleston News and Courier*, December 12, 1896; E. A. Perry, *The Boston Herald and Its History* (Boston, 1878), pp. 34-35; *New York Evening Post*, October 22, 1864.

ern birth, but at least two of the three had lived in the South for some time previous to the war. Aged 24 in 1861 Sener was the youngest of the lot and the only college graduate (University of Virginia) among them. In terms of experience the six men presented a variety of backgrounds. Reid and Gibbons had done newspaper work for the New Orleans press, Reid for the *Picayune* and Gibbons as a compositor and local reporter for the *New Orleans Crescent*. In addition to his newspapering, Reid, the son of a famous sea captain, had shipped on a merchantman at the age of 16 and, after studying law in the office of Gen. John A. Quitman of Mississippi, had served as U.S. deputy marshal and as a member of the Texas Rangers during the Mexican War. Street had been a Confederate soldier during the first part of the Civil War, Linebaugh an Episcopal clergyman. It seems likely that Dr. Shepardson, whose early history is almost completely unknown, had at one time been a physician and studied in Europe. Two of the six reporters died during the war, Street from an accidental gunshot wound and Linebaugh from drowning. Gibbons died soon after the war from tuberculosis contracted in the army.[60]

Other Confederate reporters who performed creditably as army correspondents, for periods of relatively short duration in most cases, were: Alexander St. Clair-Abrams of the *Atlanta Intelligencer*; Charles D. Kirk (the "Se De Kay" of the *Louisville Courier, Chattanooga Rebel*, and *Augusta Constitutionalist*); William Wallace Screws of the *Montgomery Advertiser*; Leonidas W. Spratt and Dr. John D. Bruns of the *Charleston Mercury*; and Henry Watterson of the *Mobile Register* and *Augusta Constitutionalist*.

Abrams was a Louisianan of Spanish descent who had been a soldier during the siege of Vicksburg before he entered wartime newspaper work in Atlanta. Kirk was a native Kentuckian who returned to Louisville after the war and was editor of one of the newspapers there at his death in 1870. Screws was a soldier correspondent of the *Advertiser* whose war correspondence so impressed the editor of that newspaper that Screws was invited to join its editorial staff after the war. As the editor of the *Montgomery Advertiser* for almost fifty years

[60] For newspaper obituaries of Reid, Sener, Street, Linebaugh, and Gibbons see *New York Daily Tribune*, August 16, 1877; *Washington Evening Star*, November 19, 1903; *Richmond Times-Dispatch*, November 20, 1903; *Mobile Daily Advertiser and Register*, May 17, 1864; *Montgomery Daily Mail*, November 16, 1864; *New Orleans Daily Crescent*, November 2, 1866.

Screws played a large role in shaping the policies of the Democratic party in Alabama during most of that time. The Leonidas W. Spratt who was a prominent lawyer in Charleston for more than twenty years before the war and a delegate to the South Carolina secession convention was the same Spratt who reported the First Battle of Manassas for the *Charleston Mercury*. His colleague Bruns, on the other hand, was a Charleston physician and teacher who was an intimate friend of Timrod and Simms.[61]

As the most important news center of the Confederacy after May 1861, Richmond was host for the representatives of most of the important Confederate dailies. Perhaps the ablest and most frequently quoted of the Richmond correspondents of the Southern press were Louis J. Dupré of the *Knoxville Register*, John R. Thompson, the "Dixie" of the *Memphis Appeal*, Salem Dutcher of the *Augusta Constitutionalist*, and George W. Bagby, who represented a number of different newspapers. Dupré, a Mississippian, had been connected with the Memphis press before the war, and had served in the army before the *Register* sent him to Richmond in January 1863.[62] Thompson, a leading literary light in Richmond, was the editor of the influential *Southern Literary Messenger* for thirteen years before the war. During the war, in addition to covering the Richmond newsfront for the *Appeal*, he edited the pictorial newspaper, the *Southern Illustrated News*, and contributed letters to Henry Hotze's weekly propaganda publication, the *London Index*.[63] Dutcher was a native of New York state who had been employed as a newspaper reporter in Washington before he joined the Confederate army in 1861. After his discharge from the army in May 1862 he was employed as a Treasury Department clerk in Richmond and contributed articles to the *Augusta Chronicle*, in addition to his work as Richmond correspondent of the *Constitutionalist*.[64]

Bagby, a Virginian and Thompson's successor as editor of the *South-*

[61] *Jacksonville* (Fla.) *Times Union*, October 5, 1903, June 6, 7, 1931; *Louisville Daily Sun*, February 18, 1870; *D.A.B.*, xvi, 514-15, xix, 552-55; Letter of Zack Spratt to this writer, June 3, 1960; *Charleston News and Courier*, May 21, 1883.

[62] *Knoxville Daily Register*, May 12, July 25, 1863.

[63] *D.A.B.*, xviii, 464.

[64] *Augusta Daily Constitutionalist*, August 6, 1864; *Augusta Chronicle*, December 24, 1917; information prepared and presented to the Augusta-Richmond County Public Library, Augusta, Ga., by Ralph W. Donnelly, Charlotte, N.C.

ern *Literary Messenger,* was simultaneously the "Hermes" of the *Charleston Mercury,* the "Gamma" of the *Mobile Register,* the "Pan" of the *Columbus* (Ga.) *Sun,* and an occasional correspondent of about twenty other Confederate newspapers. In addition, he contributed editorials to the *Richmond Examiner* and for a time was an associate editor of the *Richmond Whig.* In short, Bagby was the workhorse of the Richmond newspaper world, and in the opinion of a Florida editor, "literally the best newspaper writer in the Confederate States."[65] Well informed about both Confederate politics and Southern military operations, he adhered to the anti-Davis coterie of the Confederate press; as the war dragged on he nourished increasing doubts as to whether Davis's leadership could end otherwise than in disaster.[66]

At the outbreak of the Civil War the newspapers of the Confederacy received most of their news of events outside the South from the Southern headquarters of the New York Associated Press in Louisville, where a representative of the Southern press, M. W. Barr, worked alongside the Yankee agent George W. Tyler. The termination of telegraph service between Washington and Richmond on June 1, 1861 and the subsequent occupation of Louisville by Federal troops severed the news connection of the Southern press with the New York A.P. and obliged it to rely on a number of competing news agencies for telegraphic news reports.[67]

The principal news agency in the South in 1861 was operated by a South Carolinian named William H. Pritchard, who had been the agent of the New York A.P. in South Carolina, Georgia, and Alabama since 1856, with headquarters at Augusta.[68] When Pritchard contracted diphtheria and died very suddenly in Richmond in March 1862, his son William H. Pritchard, Jr., took over control of his father's Southern

[65] *Gainesville* (Fla.) *Cotton States* as reprinted in *Charleston Mercury,* July 10, 1863.

[66] E. A. Alderman et al., *Library of Southern Literature* (New Orleans and Atlanta, 1908-1913), I, 141-46; *Richmond Daily Dispatch,* November 30, 1883; Introduction by D. S. Freeman to G. W. Bagby, *The Old Virginia Gentleman* (Richmond, 1948), xvii-xxvii; King, *Press of Charleston, passim.*

[67] Oliver Gramling, *AP, The Story of News* (New York and Toronto, 1940), p. 38; *New Orleans Daily Picayune,* June 26, 1861; *New Orleans Daily True Delta,* July 2, 1861.

[68] *Richmond Daily Dispatch,* March 26, 1862; *Augusta Daily Constitutionalist,* March 26, 1862; *Savannah Republican,* March 26, 1862. William H. Pritchard to Secretary (L.P.) Walker, May 6, 1861. Office of Confederate Secretary of War 1861-1865, Letters Received, 1047-1861, National Archives.

Associated Press. Dissatisfaction with the high cost and poor quality of the service provided by Pritchard's agency[69] led to a series of meetings of Confederate newspaper publishers to discuss means of improving their news-gathering service and other problems common to their profession. Their first meeting, held in Atlanta in March 1862, was poorly attended; in the interval between their first and second meetings, the Richmond press improvised a "telegraphic news system" with John Graeme, Jr. of the *Richmond Whig* as general manager to compete with Pritchard's Augusta-based agency.[70] Dissatisfaction with the service provided by both agencies brought about renewed activity on the part of the publishers to find a more satisfactory solution. The culmination of these efforts was the establishment of the Press Association of the Confederate States of America in Augusta on March 1, 1863. The new association, comprising all Confederate dailies east of the Mississippi River and a few tri-weeklies, elected Dr. Robert W. Gibbes, editor of the *Columbia South Carolinian*, as its president, and selected John S. Thrasher of Galveston, Texas as general manager. Thrasher was an experienced newspaperman who at one time had been connected with the Cuban and New Orleans press and later had worked as a travelling correspondent of the *New York Herald* in Latin America.[71]

After establishing the headquarters of the new organization in Atlanta, Thrasher went on a tour of the Confederacy to recruit correspondents and effect satisfactory arrangements with the telegraph companies. He secured permission to transmit press dispatches over the lines of the military telegraph and both the Southern and Southwestern Telegraph Companies at half the usual rate. Also, Generals Beauregard, Bragg, Joseph E. Johnston, and Pemberton promised to cooperate with the association in providing access to news about military operations insofar as it was compatible with the Confederate public interest.[72]

[69] According to the *Daily Richmond Enquirer* of November 26, 1862, the joint contributions of the Southern press to Pritchard's news service amounted to between $8,000 and $9,000 a year, and Pritchard did not spend more than $5,000 during the same period for the employment of a maximum of five or six telegraphic reporters.

[70] *Daily Richmond Examiner*, November 5, 27, 1862; *Richmond Daily Dispatch*, November 5, 1862; *Mobile Daily Advertiser and Register*, December 6, 1862.

[71] *D.A.B.*, IX, 509-10; *Savannah Republican*, May 1, 1863.

[72] Q. C. Wilson, "Confederate Press Association, A Pioneer Press Agency,"

Thrasher instructed the reporters he posted with each of the principal armies in the field and at the larger news centers to keep their news stories objective, to discriminate carefully between fact and rumor, and never to be beaten by a special correspondent. The association paid its correspondents twenty-five to thirty dollars per week, plus a modest allowance for travel and maintenance, and permitted them to supplement their income by contributing special reports to individual newspapers. Persuading Graeme to become the Richmond agent of the P.A., Thrasher dispatched a second correspondent, J. Henly Smith, to Richmond during the winter of 1863-1864 to help Graeme obtain full coverage of Southern congressional news. Other members of Thrasher's reporting organization included two reporters with Lee's Army of Northern Virginia, Jonathan W. Albertson and a reporter named Smoot; A. J. Wagner, the controversial agent at Jackson, Mississippi; Will O. Woodson, who ran afoul of Bragg at the time of the Battle of Chickamauga; Riordan; and John E. Hatcher. In May 1863 the P.A. had about twenty news agents scattered throughout the area from the Potomac to the Mississippi whom the *Savannah Republican* rated as being "for the most part men of intelligence, judgment, and well acquainted with the wants of the press. . . ."[73]

Each member of the association received a weekly news report not to exceed 3,500 words, at a flat rate of twelve dollars. For any excess, newspapers had to pay at the rate of ten cents a word. During the first three months of its existence the P.A. spent between $17,000 and $18,000 for collecting news and transmitting it to different newspapers throughout the Confederacy. By the end of 1863 the sum total of news that it had sent by telegraph exceeded 150,000 words. To protect itself from the pilferage by the telegraph companies and the sale of P.A news at a fraction of its cost to the press to private groups of subscribers, the P.A. copyrighted its news dispatches.[74]

Journalism Quarterly, xxvi (June 1949), 162; *Atlanta Daily Southern Confederacy*, April 28, 1863; J. S. Thrasher to Robert McKee, August 29, 1863, Robert McKee Papers, Alabama State Department of Archives and History, Montgomery.

[73] L. T. Griffith and J. E. Talmadge, *Georgia Journalism, 1763-1950* (Athens, Ga., 1951), p. 74; Coulter, *Confederate States*, pp. 497-98; *Atlanta Daily Southern Confederacy*, March 14, 1863; *Savannah Republican*, May 6, 1863; *Memphis Daily Appeal*, July 16, 1863.

[74] Wilson, "Confederate Press Association," pp. 164-65; R. F. Tucker, "The Press Association of the Confederate States of America in Georgia," unpub. M.A. thesis (University of Georgia, 1950), pp. 36, 44, 47; *Mobile Daily Advertiser and Register*, August 11, 1863.

Probably its greatest accomplishment was the mutual system whereby member editors sent news from their own localities to newspapers in other cities. This practice provided a means of absorbing inflated costs and created a feeling of solidarity within a profession that was habituated to deadly competition with fellow editors. Although the P.A. met serious problems in its dealings with the army, the telegraph companies, a powerful Richmond press that generally refused to cooperate, and Northern armies which destroyed the plants of its member papers and disrupted communications, it kept on reporting news throughout the war and proved a valuable asset to Confederate journalism.[75]

These, then, were the principal components of the press organization that attempted to provide the Southern people with an adequate conception of the war as it unfolded during the years 1861-1865. The part played by the newspaper correspondents of the South and their editors in gathering and disseminating war news will be the theme of succeeding pages.

[75] Tucker, "Press Association," pp. 32-33.

CHAPTER 3

"A Great Battle Has Been
Fought . . . and Won"

~~~~~~~~~~~~~

As THE Confederate capital during the opening days of the war, Montgomery, Alabama acted as a magnet for newspapermen from far and near. Major Northern and European newspapers were represented there, along with Southern journals, between February and April. During the latter part of April and throughout May 1861, the Montgomery dateline was a familiar heading in the news columns of the Southern press.

Situated on high bluffs at a large bend in the Alabama River, 331 miles by river above Mobile, Montgomery in 1861 was an attractive town of about 9,000, whose frontier heritage was still visible. Originally founded by a New Englander named Andrew Dexter under the name of New Philadelphia, the town had been rechristened, according to one explanation, in honor of the Revolutionary War general, Richard Montgomery, who had been killed in an unsuccessful effort to storm Quebec. It had been just fifteen years since the capital of the state had been moved there from the less accessible Tuscaloosa. And now that Montgomery, which reputedly was the richest municipality of its size in the country, was the seat of the Confederate government in a time of war, the city's three hotels—the Exchange, Montgomery Hall, and Madison House—along with various private boardinghouses, were filled to overflowing with government officials, office seekers, soldiers, and newspapermen.[1]

Reporters for out-of-town newspapers wrote flatteringly of the beautiful site of the city, its tasteful private residences, the majority of which were constructed in the style of the Italian villa, and its expensive and carefully kept gardens with their luxuriant flowers and shrubbery. In Montgomery on May 6, 1861 a correspondent for the *New Orleans Delta* described the town as having "thrown off its dreamy appearance of a country village" and of its shining forth "with

[1] L. H. Powell, *Historic Towns of the Southern States* (New York and London, 1900), pp. 381-84, 405.

all the splendor of a fashionable metropolis. All that was attractive in the society of Washington has been transferred to the gay capital of this rising republic. The streets are filled with beautiful women and with patriotic men, and the avenues are rendered lively and attractive by numerous carriages."[2] But already in May, statesmen and their ladies were complaining about the debilitating heat, the miserable hotel facilities, and the predatory behavior of the swarms of carnivorous mosquitoes.

Among the reporters of the Southern press who forwarded copy to their newspapers from Montgomery at this time were William G. Shepardson of the *Mobile Register* and *Columbus* (Ga.) *Times*, David G. Duncan of New Orleans, a native Scotsman and the telegraphic correspondent of a number of Confederate newspapers, and N. E. Foard and Henry Sparnick of the *Charleston Courier*. Sparnick had attended the College of Charleston and had represented the *Courier* at the State Capital in Columbia before the newspaper dispatched him to Montgomery early in 1861.[3]

William H. Russell of the *London Times*, the most famous war correspondent of his day, came to Montgomery in the early days of May to get an impression of the future prospects of the new nation. Although Russell experienced the sensation of being isolated because of the interruption of communication with the outside world, he was impressed with the confidence the leadership of the Confederacy displayed in the invincible power of cotton and in the prospects for a short war. He met and talked in general terms with President Jefferson Davis in the large red brick building that housed the offices of the new government. The English correspondent's practiced eye observed the sinewy figure, erect soldier-like bearing, regular features, and thin, care-worn face of the Confederate president. He also recorded in his notebook a conversation with a former governor of Alabama who assured him that "sooner than submit to the North, we will all become subjects to Great Britain again."[4]

For the most part, the Confederate government exercised a tight control over news issuing from the government departments, and the

[2] *New Orleans Sunday Delta*, May 12, 1861.

[3] J. P. Jones and W. W. Rogers, "Montgomery as the Confederate Capital: View of a New Nation," *Alabama Historical Quarterly*, xxvi (Spring 1964), p. 5.

[4] *London Times*, May 30, 1861; W. H. Russell, *My Diary North and South* (Boston and New York, 1863), pp. 172-74.

practice of secret sessions by the Confederate Congress proved extremely irritating to special correspondents whose employers wanted to know why so little important news was coming out of Montgomery. When Beauregard arrived in Montgomery from Charleston on May 4, the "Jenkinses of the Capital" scrambled to surround him, therefore, and multiply descriptions of his erect military bearing, his dark olive complexion, and his quick, expressive eye.[5] The *Charleston Mercury* registered a scoop by publishing on May 8 the full text of the act of Congress declaring war against the United States, furnished by its enterprising Montgomery correspondent. When they were not grousing about the dearth of news, other members of the Montgomery press corps described the appearance of the various government departments, commented on the pressure of work devolving on President Davis and Secretary of War Leroy P. Walker, and speculated on the possibility of the Confederate capital being moved from Montgomery to some other place.

Virginia's decision to join the Confederacy, made public during the last week of April, had an important bearing on the location of the capital. The information that the Virginia convention had extended an invitation "to make this state the seat of government of the Confederacy" had been leaked to the press by May 1, and the news hawks were soon predicting the removal of the capital to Richmond within the next thirty days. Congress adjourned on May 21 to meet in Richmond two months later, and when Davis left Montgomery on May 26 on his way to Virginia, a correspondent of the *New Orleans Delta* tried in vain to wire the news of the President's departure to his newspaper in New Orleans. The only explanation given the reporter for suppressing his telegram was "to prevent the usual enthusiastic manifestations on the part of the people."[6] A Virginia newspaper[7] had already revealed the fact, however, that Davis was en route from Montgomery to Richmond. When Davis reached Richmond on May 29 the capital newspapers gave full publicity to the large crowds that greeted him,

[5] *New Orleans Sunday Delta*, May 12, 1861. The term "Jenkins" was commonly used by journalists in the eighteen-sixties to signify a snobbish or servile penny-a-liner. The London *Punch* is supposed to have first made use of the term with reference to a vulgar reporter of fashionable events for the *Morning Post* who was said to have been originally a footman. H. F. Reddall, *A New Handbook of Fact, Fancy, and Fable* (Chicago, 1892), p. 286.

[6] *New Orleans Daily Delta*, May 31, 1861.

[7] *Petersburg Daily Express*, May 25, 1861.

first at the railroad depot and then at the Spotswood Hotel, and to the speeches the President and other members of his party made in response.

A rival center of Confederate press interest was Pensacola, Florida, where Brig.Gen. Braxton Bragg commanded a force of several thousand volunteers which had gathered there to reduce Federally occupied Fort Pickens. The same day that Fort Sumter surrendered a correspondent of one of the Pensacola newspapers was arrested on Bragg's order and sent under guard to the War Department in Montgomery. The correspondent, a certain L. H. Mathews of the *Pensacola Observer*, was charged with publishing information which tipped off the enemy as to Bragg's intention of attacking Pickens on the evening of April 12. Mathews, who wrote for his newspaper under the pseudonym "Nemo," was honorably acquitted of being a spy and released from imprisonment within two or three days. In refutation of newspaper stories alleging that he was a "Northern man," Mathews addressed a letter to the editor of the *Montgomery Advertiser* explaining that he was an Irish immigrant who had lived in the South since 1848 and had been an employee of the *Pensacola Observer* for five years. Rather than having any affinity with Northern principles, he had "been repeatedly accused of being an ultraist on Southern rights." Mathews apparently had no further difficulty with Bragg, but the incident signified the general's intention to hold army newspapermen strictly accountable for breaches of military security.[8]

Among the first special correspondents at Pensacola were Alexander Walker of the *New Orleans Delta*, Capt. Francis F. De Gournay of the *New Orleans Picayune*, and a reporter named Wright who was

[8] *Montgomery Daily Advertiser* as quoted in *Columbus* (Ga.) *Daily Times*, April 24, 1861. See also *Charleston Mercury*, April 18, 20, 23, 1861; *Atlanta Daily Southern Confederacy*, April 19, 1861; *Richmond Daily Dispatch*, April 22, 1861; A. D. Richardson, *The Secret Service, the Field, the Dungeon, and the Escape* (Philadelphia, Cincinnati, Chicago, 1865), p. 104. In a letter to his newspaper from Pensacola on May 25, 1861, a correspondent of the *Memphis Appeal* reported that Mathews was a "quiet, gentlemanly man" who in 1848 was an associate of the Irish patriot John Mitchel and like Mitchel was forced to go into exile because of his political views. "Like the most of intelligent Irishmen, he is stout built and of medium height, with heavy whiskers, a frank, open countenance, and mild-blueish gray eyes. Like every true Irishman too, he is a stout partisan for the land of his adoption, the birthland of his Louisiana wife. . . . He is at this time the active editor of the *Observer*, and as careful of the rights and interests of our loved South as you or I can be." *Memphis Daily Appeal*, May 31, 1861.

accredited to the *New Orleans Bee*.[9] Walker and an unidentified correspondent of the *New Orleans Crescent* accompanied Col. A. H. Gladden's First Louisiana Regiment when it left New Orleans for Pensacola on April 17. When they reached Pensacola about three days later, the two reporters found that Bragg had a force of over 6,000 men; they were understandably impatient for signs of activity in the Confederate camp. Peering across the one-and-a-half mile stretch of water that separated the Warrington Navy Yard from the Federal position on Santa Rosa Island, the *Crescent* man caught glimpses of Fort Pickens' big guns and the heavy armament of the four large Federal ships of war anchored on the sea side of the island. His conclusion was that in the event of a bombardment, "our quarters would be rather uncomfortable."[10]

With Bragg imposing tight security restrictions on communications between the fort and the mainland and on reports of military movements as well, the local correspondents had to piece out their letters with feature material. Reporter Walker told how when one of Davis's presidential messages reached Pensacola, the publisher of the *Observer* was in a quandary because most of his compositors were away from the office performing military duty with the Florida regiment. In his perplexity the publisher turned to the commander of one of Bragg's rifle companies, who promptly ordered a muster of his men and called for volunteer printers to help set up the message of President Davis. Immediately a dozen or so former printers stepped forward, marched to the office of the *Observer*, and lining up behind the cases, enabled the editor to get out the earliest and largest edition of the paper that he had ever published.[11]

On another occasion Walker noticed with some amusement how Bragg fell victim to his own system of strict surveillance. This occurred when the commanding general was about to descend from a steamboat onto the Pensacola wharf. A sentinel of the Louisiana Guards promptly halted Bragg as he started to go ashore and required him to show his pass.

"I have none," replied the general.

"Then you can't pass," responded the youthful disciplinarian in blue roundabout and white gaiters.

[9] *Charleston Mercury*, April 19, 1861.
[10] *New Orleans Daily Crescent*, April 27, 1861.
[11] *New Orleans Daily Delta*, May 11, 1861.

"I have no one to grant me a pass," replied the general, rather enjoying the joke.

"Yes, sir, you can, if you are an officer, as I take you to be; you can get a pass from Col. Gladden or Gen. Bragg."

"But what if I am Gen. Bragg himself?"

"That must be proved," said the stout little guardsman.

The Corporal of the Guard No. 9 was accordingly called, and that officer immediately recognizing the General, he was allowed to pass.[12]

From time to time during the spring of 1861 reporters for various Southern newspapers visited Pensacola in spite of the "stringent regulations" enforced by Bragg against the entrance of news writers into his lines. A correspondent of the *Atlanta Confederacy* was struck by the novel sight of the cannon barrels of the War of 1812 vintage planted at every street corner in the town about halfway in the ground, with the mouth down, serving as the equivalent of the granite posts that adorned the street corners in Atlanta.[13] For those who chafed at the lack of any apparent effort on Bragg's part to destroy Fort Pickens and its defenses, a *Memphis Daily Avalanche* reporter offered the soothing advice: "as we are bound to have Pickens eventually, it does not make much difference whether that time is a little sooner or a little later."[14] One by one the abler reporters drifted away as it became clear that Bragg's continuing inactivity and his phobia against newspapermen militated against the possibility of interesting war correspondence. Among the defectors was *Delta* correspondent Walker who irritated Bragg because of his slapdash descriptions which never contained anything flattering about camp life unless it pertained to a good dinner![15]

Even before the Confederate capital was moved from Montgomery to Richmond, other Confederate newspapermen were on their way north to cover the troop movements in northern Virginia. One of the first journalists to arrive in Richmond was Riordan, who had taken a leave of absence from his post as managing editor of the *Charleston Mercury* to act as a war correspondent for that newspaper.[16] In report-

[12] *Ibid.*, May 14, 1861.

[13] *Atlanta Daily Southern Confederacy*, May 26, 1861.

[14] *Memphis Daily Avalanche*, June 1, 1861.

[15] *New York Times*, May 8, 1862. The *Mobile Register* correspondent at Pensacola in the early part of July 1861 was apparently a man named Oliver Jeter. *Mobile Daily Advertiser and Register*, July 18, 1861.

[16] *Charleston Mercury*, April 30, 1861. Riordan was a Virginian who had

ing Riordan's arrival in Richmond the regular Richmond correspondent of the *Mercury* told of his letter being written in an office which had been hurriedly vacated because it had been selected as the headquarters of Brig.Gen. Milledge L. Bonham. "Your correspondent is put to his wits' end by the necessity of writing at railroad speed in the midst of a confusion surpassing anything he ever witnessed; for, through the open windows (the day is very warm) comes a din of a thousand commingled noises, not the least of which is the steady tramp of soldiers marching out to the great encampment at the Fair grounds."[17]

Apparently Riordan did not remain in Richmond very long, for on May 4 the *Mercury* contained a letter from him postmarked Alexandria on April 30, describing a hasty visit to Washington. Chartering an omnibus, the adventurous Riordan succeeded in passing the Yankee guards at the Washington end of the Long Bridge and in remaining in Washington long enough to report the "Reign of Terror" he claimed to have witnessed there. Meanwhile, in the corridors of the Spotswood and the other Richmond hotels, Riordan's *Mercury* colleague, Leonidas W. Spratt, as well as de Fontaine and J. W. Kennedy of the *Charleston Courier*, Donelson C. Jenkins of the *New Orleans Delta*, George W. Stoddard of the *New Orleans Crescent*, and Andrew A. H. Dawson of the *Mobile Register*, sauntered up and down, pumping their acquaintances for news items.

In the first of his long series of letters to the *Courier* postmarked Weldon, North Carolina on May 8, de Fontaine described the enthusiasm for the war evident in the Tarheel State, with Confederate flags flying everywhere and young men rallying to the colors. On the same northbound train with "Personne" were two companies of Georgians, one of which contained at least 45 soldiers who were not less than six feet tall. At every depot where the train stopped, de Fontaine saw crowds of men with ribbons and rosettes attached to their coats and secession flags in their hats, who extended ovations while floral offerings from fair feminine hands were brought into the cars.[18]

---

received his journalistic training in the office of the Washington *Union*. He made a flattering impression on the editor of the *Charleston Mercury* when he visited Charleston in 1860 to cover the Democratic national convention for the *New Orleans Delta*. Rhett persuaded Riordan to join the *Mercury* staff, with which the latter remained connected throughout the war. W. L. King, *The Newspaper Press of Charleston* (Charleston, S.C., 1872), p. 180; *Charleston News and Courier*, 150th Anniversary Edition, January 11, 1953.

[17] *Charleston Mercury*, April 30, 1861.

[18] *Charleston Daily Courier*, May 11, 1861.

Already at the end of April the Richmond to which de Fontaine and his fellow war correspondents were hastening was one vast bustling army camp, where business appeared to have been suspended except for the sale of arms and military clothes and equipment. Richmond citizens swarmed out to the encampments located on the Agricultural Fair Grounds outside the city. Every few minutes on the afternoon of a dress parade, trains crowded with passengers left the depot of the Richmond, Fredericksburg, and Potomac Railroad bound for one of the drill grounds. Frequently as many as three or four thousand spectators were on hand to watch beardless cadets from the Virginia Military Institute drilling men twice their age.[19]

Situated at the foot of the Great Falls of the James River at the head of tidewater navigation, Richmond in 1861 was a rather provincial city of about 40,000, connected by canal with Lynchburg, the leading tobacco market of the state, and with some pretensions to being a railroad center. It had been all hills, valleys, and ravines belonging to the celebrated Col. William Byrd of Westover before it became the state capital of Virginia in 1779. At the time of the Civil War some of the precipices and deep gullies were still in evidence north of the town, presenting a forbidding aspect.

Covering about three and a half square miles, the geographical setting of Richmond was beautiful, even romantic. To the simple countryman from a remote distance who visited the chief city of his state perhaps once a year to market his tobacco crop, it was a magnificent metropolis. After having dined at Zetelle's and beheld what he regarded as the pinnacle of comfort and luxury at Ballard's Exchange Hotel, the country visitor returned home to describe the sights of Richmond and the adventures he had experienced to his admiring friends.

A tributary of the James River named Shockoe Creek bisected the town. On the high ground on either side of the creek in the areas known as Shockoe and Richmond Hills were the upper class residences and the public buildings. About two fifths of the population of Richmond was Negro, a large proportion of whom were free Negroes. The Negro dwellings, located for the most part in the suburbs, were in drab contrast to the handsome mansions of the dominant whites.

On Shockoe Hill in the western part of Richmond stood the Capitol, a showy edifice with Doric columns that had been designed by Thomas Jefferson. In the basement were the council-room of the Confederate

---

[19] *Columbia Daily Southern Guardian,* May 6, 1861.

government and the meeting place of the Confederate Congress. The state library and governor's offices graced the upper story. The War Department, housed in what had formerly been the Mechanic's Institute, and most of the other government offices were along Broad and Franklin Streets. The clerks who worked in these offices at meager salaries were for the most part exiles from Maryland, and the detective force of the city was composed to a man of former members of the Baltimore police. Surrounding the Capitol was a beautiful square of about eight acres where throngs of citizens and their wives gathered in the evening to exchange gossip and hear renditions of "Dixie" and other lively airs. Main Street, running generally southeast and northwest, was the principal thoroughfare of the town, and the Spotswood Hotel at the corner of Tenth and Main was the focal point of the business section.

In addition to being a great slave market where Negroes from the border states were sold to purchasers from the Lower South, Richmond had before the war exported flour to tropical markets and imported coffee in exchange, for re-export to the South and Southwest. The leading industry of the town was flour milling. In 1861 the Richmond Flour Mills, which formed a huge cluster of brick buildings towering up to what was then considered an amazing height, were reputed to be the largest in the world. The city also boasted several large iron foundries, of which the Tredegar works, covering thirty-two acres, were the most notable, and manufactured cotton and woolen goods, paper, and tobacco as well. Yet Richmond's city fathers had refrained from encouraging the investment of surplus capital in industrial expansion lest the influx of a manufacturing class give to that element of society a numerical preponderance in the community.[20]

By the end of May, as the governmental and military center of the Confederacy, Richmond had been taken over by strangers. Relegated to the past was the repose and respectability of Richmond's exclusive residential district on Shockoe Hill. Soldiers were everywhere in the city, crowding the daguerreotype galleries from morning till night to

[20] *Memphis Daily Appeal*, June 13, 1861; *New Orleans Daily Crescent*, January 22, 1862; S. P. Day, *Down South* (London, 1862), i, 56, 63-68, 78-90; "Richmond and Washington during the War," *Cornhill Magazine*, vii (January 1863), 98; E. A. Pollard, *Life of Jefferson Davis* (Philadelphia, 1869), pp. 129-30; Mrs. R. A. Pryor, *Reminiscences of Peace and War* (New York and London, 1904), p. 171.

obtain likenesses of youthful faces for parents and sweethearts.[21] As a special correspondent of the *Columbus* (Ga.) *Times* entered a Richmond barber shop one morning in July, he noticed in the next chair a young soldier with a beardless but downy cheek who had come there to be shaved. The French barber, not seeing any beard and knowing of but one other purpose for which his services could be required, asked solicitously, "Sair, shall I coute ze hair?" An English barber interpreted, "He wishes to know if you want your hair cut." "The devil, no," was the reply. "It has been so short that I have not been able to get hold of it in a week. I want to be shaved"—and shaved he was, although barber Johnny Crapeau looked as mystified as no doubt he really was.[22]

By the time most of the leading war correspondents had reached Richmond, the situation in Virginia had assumed a warlike aspect. Davis had already made up his mind to pursue a generally defensive policy and await intervention from cotton-starved Europe. Now that Virginia had turned over the control of its armed forces to the Confederate government, Davis had between 35,000 and 40,000 soldiers available to repel attack. There were about 7,000 men in and around the great Confederate naval base at Norfolk, 5,000 more on the lower peninsula between the James and York Rivers guarding the approaches to Richmond from the southeast, some 2,700 in the vicinity of Fredericksburg, and between 7,000 and 8,000 at Manassas, about 80 miles north of Richmond in a direct line. There were between 5,000 and 6,000 soldiers in Richmond itself and nearly 8,000 at Harper's Ferry and in the lower Shenandoah Valley.[23]

Harper's Ferry, with its important Federal arsenal, had fallen into Confederate hands without resistance during the early days of the war. To that point came the grim-faced Col. Thomas J. Jackson a short time afterward to assume command of the garrison and organize the defense of the post. On May 23 another of the Confederacy's leading generals arrived to replace Jackson. The new arrival was a courtly Virginian named Joseph E. Johnston, who had come all the way by rail from Montgomery after receiving his commission as brigadier general in the Regular Army of the Confederate States.[24]

[21] *Charleston Mercury*, April 26, 1861.

[22] *Columbus Daily Times*, July 15, 1861.

[23] Allan Nevins, *The Improvised War, 1861-1862* (New York, 1959), p. 207; Bruce Catton, *The Coming Fury* (Garden City, 1961), p. 401.

[24] Nevins, *Improvised War*, pp. 156-57; G. E. Govan and J. W. Livingood, A

To cover the operations of these separated commands the Confederate press augmented its representation in Virginia. Up from Pensacola came Henry Perry to represent the *New Orleans Picayune* in Richmond. From New Orleans came Durant Da Ponte to join the *Delta's* D. C. Jenkins and a soldier correspondent of that newspaper named Louis M. Montgomery. Other new arrivals on the scene included a Mr. Emmett of the *New Orleans True Delta,* a reporter named Stone for the *Memphis Appeal,* and M. W. Cluskey, junior editor of the *Memphis Avalanche,* who was an officer in the Fourth Tennessee Regiment.[25]

With the Mobile Cadets, an elite outfit made up of members of Mobile's leading families, which left there for Virginia soon after the war began, was the Swiss immigrant Henry Hotze, who had worked under John Forsyth on the *Mobile Register* before he went off to war. During the march and later in camp near Norfolk, Hotze contributed war correspondence to the *Register,* using the pseudonym "Cadet." A typographical error in the printed version of one of his letters involved the reporter from Mobile in difficulties with his comrades. He had written that only one other company excelled his own in drill, but a blundering compositor had substituted the word "equalled" for "excelled," and forthwith every other company regarded itself as having been insulted in the most sensitive area of its self-respect.[26]

One of the first correspondents to enter the field in northern Virginia was de Fontaine, who in early May embarked on an adventurous itinerary which took him deep into the enemy's country. After stopping at Manassas Junction, to which he devoted a none too flattering description, he continued to Winchester in the Shenandoah Valley. Writing from there on May 13 he improvised a piquant paragraph about the ladies of the town whom he characterized as being "as full of war talk as a tea cup is full of scandal." Apparently the ladies gave him a difficult time, subjecting him as a stranger without a letter of introduction to an inquisitorial fire of cross-questions. "They are perfect conversational battering rams," he added, "bustling with moral excellence

---

Different Valor, the Story of General Joseph E. Johnston (Indianapolis and New York, 1956), pp. 34-35.

[25] *New Orleans Daily Picayune,* June 4, 1861; *New Orleans Daily Delta,* June 8, 1861; *Richmond Whig* as reprinted in *Mobile Daily Advertiser and Register,* June 11, 1861; *Memphis Daily Avalanche,* June 6, 1861.

[26] Henry Hotze, *Three Months in the Confederate Army* (University, Ala., 1952), pp. 31, 35.

which they could never discover in anybody else." He admitted, however, that these "crinoline tongue batteries" were an imported crop, although he did not make clear from what area they had been imported.[27] From Winchester he apparently travelled incognito to Baltimore and from there to Annapolis where he visited some camps of Federal troops which he later described. Back in Confederate territory once more at Harper's Ferry, de Fontaine portrayed for his newspaper in vivacious fashion the garrison, which included a considerable number of Indians from North Carolina and a goodly share of lower class Baltimoreans whom he referred to as Baltimore "plugs."

"Their distinguishing feature is generally an abbreviated crop of hair, which, to use their favorite expression, has been filed 'down'; a nose which bears the marks of contact with that indefinite substance yclept a 'brick bat,' before which the graceful proportions of that organ have ignominiously retreated, and a style of conversation so miscellaneous and emphatic that it would require a thorough revision of Webster's unabridged to embrace its numerous improvements upon the Anglo-Saxon."

In the Confederate camp at Harper's Ferry was also a fair sampling of the citizenry of a number of Southern states. De Fontaine was impressed by the fact that the command included some of the wealthiest and most influential citizens of Alabama and Mississippi—lawyers, doctors, professors, editors, printers, merchants, and planters, along with a strong infusion of the sturdy yeoman element. The Kentuckians, he decided, were in a class by themselves. "They are generally a large, well formed, robust set of men, splendid marksmen, independent as the air; and, in their careless, yet not ungraceful movements, one may almost carry his thoughts back into the past and imagine our forefathers of the forest borders around him. When they first arrived, being without arms, it was proposed to give them muskets, but they were refused under any circumstances. The boys said they didn't know how to shoot 'soger' tools, and if they couldn't have rifles they 'would rather throw rocks.' Considering the length of time they have now been here, their regiment is probably the worst drilled at Harper's Ferry. But the fault is entirely their own. . . . A military gentleman who visited their encampment in the mountains remarked to a little group that he regretted they were not better drilled. 'What's the good of that?' said one of the men. 'We come here to wade in any whar, and when we see a good shot,

[27] *Charleston Daily Courier,* May 20, 1861.

you may bet your life, stranger, we're goin to shoot.' 'See here,' continued the beef eater, 'here's our drill,' and taking his bowie knife from his belt he fixed it in a tree with the edge of the blade outwards. Then marching off a distance of sixty or seventy yards, aimed his rifle and split a bullet upon the blade. 'You see stranger, if we ain't much on sogerin, we are powerful good at drawin' a bead.' "[28]

By June 7 de Fontaine was back in Richmond, too late to report the arrival there, three days earlier, of the crack battalion of Washington Artillery from New Orleans, who prided themselves on being descended from the best families of Louisiana. The *Picayune* reporter, Perry, was on hand to greet them, however, and to report how in spite of their long and tedious journey, every member of the command looked "fifty per cent better than when I saw them at home two weeks ago."[29] Later the same reporter told how in camp near Richmond it took a full week to break in their horses to the gun carriages and half of another to accustom these same horses to cannon fire. And when at the end of three weeks there was a grand parade of horses, guns, officers, and men, on a June evening, all Richmond, including President Davis, turned out to see the svelte performance of this beautifully uniformed detachment.[30]

A favorite topic of Richmond reporters during these June days was the health and appearance of President Davis. A correspondent of the *New Orleans True Delta* who was present at the review of the Washington Artillery on June 26 commented that the President appeared to enjoy good health, "and his usual thinness of figure does not, I think, justify the remarks of some writers, who have recently described him as looking haggard and emaciated." In reporting a reception Davis gave at the Spotswood Hotel a week earlier, de Fontaine observed that "the President always looks well" and proceeded to give a flattering description of his "irresistible smile," his "brilliant scintillations of thought," and his "fine conversational abilities."[31]

Soon the Washington Artillery would be on their way to Manassas

[28] *Ibid.*, June 3, 1861.

[29] *New Orleans Daily Picayune*, June 12, 1861; F. G. de Fontaine, "Shoulder to Shoulder, Reminiscences of Confederate Camps and Fields," *XIX Century*, I, (September 1869), 299.

[30] *New Orleans Daily Picayune*, June 27, 1861; *Richmond Daily Dispatch*, November 5, 1861.

[31] *New Orleans Daily True Delta*, June 27, 1861; *Charleston Daily Courier*, June 21, 1861.

to report to General Beauregard, who had been summoned from Charleston on May 28 to report to Davis in Richmond. At a conference with Davis and Gen. Robert E. Lee, acting commander of all Confederate forces in Virginia, Beauregard learned of his assignment to Manassas, which was already threatened by Federal attack.[32]

It was at Manassas that Reporter Jenkins of the *New Orleans Delta* found Beauregard when he went there in the company of Da Ponte and telegraphic correspondent Duncan on Friday, June 21. About six o'clock that evening the three reporters called on the general at his headquarters, which was in a small frame house near the northeast angle of the camp. No doubt Beauregard, a native of New Orleans, recognized the advantage of good press relations with this group of influential journalists from his own city. Jenkins likewise understood the advantages of winning the general's favor, so for the delectation of the *Delta's* readers he prepared a pen portrait of the Creole general that could hardly fail to enhance Beauregard's image. Jenkins reported:

"The General received us with that kind of quiet, easy cordiality which finds its way to the heart more readily than profuse and pointed demonstrations can. There was nothing pronounced in his appearance or manner. He is not a man, though full of power, to waste energy, like a steam engine with leaks in the flues and boiler. He was standing in the yard, with an unconscious grace and dignity as we approached. There were no 'tigers,' no 'toadies' around him. His dress was as simple as a uniform could well be—a blue frock coat, blue pants, a fatigue cap. He held his spurs in his hand, thus unconsciously displaying an emblem of a man of action—a General of the field, and not of the closet. As you know, he is somewhat below the middle height; but his appearance betokens health and vigor, and you can not feel that you are in the presence of a small man in any respect, when in his. His face was composed, his eye serene. He had never studied the military stare affected by some officers of small calibre. He conversed freely and without the faintest tone of professional dogmatism. In a word, he impresses one as an accomplished gentleman."[33]

As the party of correspondents was preparing to leave, one of them

[32] T. H. Williams, *P.G.T. Beauregard, Napoleon in Gray* (Baton Rouge, 1954), p. 67.

[33] *New Orleans Daily Delta,* June 27, 1861. For an interesting description of Beauregard's headquarters at Manassas written by another New Orleans reporter, see *New Orleans Daily Picayune,* July 14, 1861.

was curious to know when the great fight would take place. Parrying the inquiry with a smile, the general remarked that his questioner had better telegraph General Scott, the Federal Commander-in-Chief, for that information.

It was about this time that Peter Alexander came up from Savannah to Richmond to represent the *Savannah Republican* and the *Atlanta Southern Confederacy* at the Confederate capital. With some degree of elation, the *Confederacy* editor J. Henly Smith had told Vice President Alexander H. Stephens in mid-June that "Pete Alexander will correspond for us regularly from the Army in Va. . . . over his initial 'A.' "[34] When Alexander arrived in the capital in the latter part of June, he got the impression from reporters and others that a great battle near Washington was imminent. In the wake of several other newspapermen Alexander left Richmond on the morning of June 27 and arrived at Beauregard's headquarters in Manassas Junction at two o'clock that afternoon. Finding no signs of military activity there, he continued north another fourteen miles to Fairfax Court House. From there, the next day, he addressed a letter to the *Savannah Republican* reporting that "the advanced posts of the Hessians are not exceeding six miles from where I now sit, and their drums can be distinctly heard from my window as they beat their evening and morning calls. This letter is written, therefore, as it were, at the mouth of the enemy's guns."[35] To the disappointment of the reporters it soon became evident, however, that the prognostications of an impending battle were premature.

Most of them had already missed the first military action of the war on June 10 at Big Bethel on the York peninsula, thirteen miles from Yorktown. In an attempt to capture a Confederate battery posted there, Maj.Gen. Benjamin F. Butler, commanding Federal troops in and around Fort Monroe, had sent out 4,000 troops in two columns on a night march. In the darkness they became confused, fired on each other, and were finally driven back by Col. John B. Magruder's artillery. In a fight lasting about four hours the Federals suffered seventy-six killed and wounded, compared with Confederate casualties of only eight.[36] Detailed accounts of the "glorious victory" appeared in extra

[34] J. Henly Smith to Alexander H. Stephens, June 16, 1861, Alexander H. Stephens Papers, Library of Congress.
[35] *Savannah Republican*, July 8, 1861. See also *Memphis Daily Appeal*, June 29, 1861; *New Orleans Daily Picayune*, June 30, 1861.
[36] Catton, *Coming Fury*, p. 437; Shelby Foote, *The Civil War, A Narrative*,

editions of the *Richmond Dispatch*, the *Petersburg Express*, and the *Norfolk Day Book*. Three *Richmond Dispatch* reporters, H. C. Tinsley, Hugh Pleasants, and a former bookkeeper of the newspaper named Rady, were on the spot at Big Bethel to report the action in abundant detail for their newspaper.[37] A *New Orleans Crescent* correspondent, W. P. Reyburn, emerged from the affair with something less than glory. Being a portly gentleman and perhaps not overly courageous, Reyburn inspired raucous merriment among the staff of "Prince John" Magruder by his unsuccessful efforts to find a tree sufficiently large to conceal himself in.[38]

Durant Da Ponte of the *New Orleans Delta* was at Pig Point on the opposite side of Hampton Roads that day, within earshot of the fighting, but was unable to discover what had happened until the next day. In a letter commenting on the skirmish, Da Ponte praised the "glorious result," but warned his readers not to attach too much importance to the action from a military point of view. In his opinion it did not by any means demonstrate that Confederates were sure to whip the enemy when the latter possessed a numerical superiority of four to one, three to one, or even two to one. He was also impressed by the fact that despite the mismanagement of Butler, enemy troops had, by advancing three times to the assault, displayed their fighting spirit.[39]

From the viewpoint of the Confederate high command the reporting of the Big Bethel affair told too much. Apparently one of the Southern newspapers rejoiced prematurely because the Yankee raw recruits had aimed entirely too high in their excitement. Unfortunately this information fell into enemy hands, and according to the *Richmond Enquirer*, "a thousand limping soldiers have cursed the indiscretion."[40]

The Big Bethel engagement was the only action of any consequence that Confederate correspondents in the Norfolk area had the opportunity to report during 1861. The editor of the *Fredericksburg* (Va.)

Fort Sumter to Perryville (New York, 1958), pp. 56-57; Hal Bridges, *Lee's Maverick General* (New York, Toronto, London, 1961), pp. 28-29.

[37] *Richmond Daily Dispatch*, June 13, 1861.

[38] *New York Times*, May 8, 1862.

[39] *New Orleans Daily Delta*, June 20, 1861. In contrast to Da Ponte's opinion as to the ability of Federal troops is the statement of another New Orleans correspondent, Henry Perry: "I do not believe . . . that on a fair field our men can be whipped by double their number. They cannot be whipped at all. They certainly have not been yet." *New Orleans Daily Picayune*, June 25, 1861.

[40] *Daily Richmond Enquirer*, May 21, 1863.

News on one occasion came under the fire of Federal warships when he ventured too near the shore in the vicinity of Aquia Creek.[41] At another time, Stoddard of the *New Orleans Crescent* in the company of an army captain gave chase in a sailboat to a deserter swimming away from one of the Confederate shore batteries near Norfolk. But the deserter, the son of a professor at Hampton College, had too long a start and made good his escape to Newport News in a small boat which picked him up in midstream.[42]

Soon after the Big Bethel episode, the Confederate press was considerably disturbed when a Federal major general named Robert Patterson moved south from Chambersburg, Pennsylvania with 15,000 Yankee soldiers and compelled Johnston to evacuate Harper's Ferry. Both Davis and Lee were unhappy about the withdrawal, fearing an adverse effect on public opinion, but Johnston realized that his position could be easily turned and believed that the possible capture of his garrison was the greater danger.[43] Although Confederate editors and reporters were mystified by Johnston's retreat and some were honest enough to admit it, their general response was to interpret it as a brilliant stroke of strategy on Johnston's part, designed to entrap an exposed portion of the enemy force.[44]

Lack of confidence in Johnston's generalship was voiced in a letter written for publication by an occasional correspondent of the *Memphis Appeal* and *Avalanche* named J. P. Pryor, who was at Winchester during the first week of July. Pryor was particularly concerned by the lack of security precautions in the Army of the Shenandoah. He charged in a letter published by the *Avalanche* that on the very night before the retreat from Martinsburg it had been possible as late as ten or eleven o'clock for a strange officer to pass through Johnston's lines and reach the door of his headquarters without being challenged by a sentry. In a letter that he mailed to the same newspaper the following day, Pryor evidently had second thoughts about the prudence of criticizing the commanding general. Although he still doubted that Johnston inspired as much confidence among his troops as a commanding general should, Pryor declared that the general had the confidence

[41] *New Orleans Daily Delta*, June 29, 1861.

[42] *Ibid.*, July 17, 1861.

[43] Govan and Livingood, *A Different Valor*, pp. 37-39.

[44] *Daily Richmond Enquirer*, June 21, 1861; *Mobile Daily Advertiser and Register*, June 23, 1861; *Atlanta Daily Southern Confederacy*, June 26, 1861.

of President Davis, and expressed regret about the disparaging comments that had appeared in his previous letter.[45]

To prevent the publication by Confederate war correspondents of information adverse to security, the Confederate War Department began to impose tighter security measures. On July 1 through the columns of the *Richmond Enquirer*, Secretary of War Leroy P. Walker addressed an open letter to Confederate newspaper correspondents which many newspapers reprinted in its entirety. In his letter Walker, an Alabamian, while professing his belief in an unshackled press and his continued willingness to permit any of the representatives of the press to visit the camps in Virginia, appealed to the army newspapermen to refrain from the transmission and publication of such information as might be injurious to the Confederate cause. He added:

"It must be obvious that statements of strength, or of weakness, at any of the points in the vicinity of the enemy, when reproduced in the North, as they would be in spite of all the vigilance in our power, would warn them of danger to themselves, or invite an attack upon us; and, in like manner, any statements of the magnitude of batteries, of the quantity and quality of arms, or of ammunition, of movements in progress or in supposed contemplation, of the condition of troops, of the Commissariat, &c., might be fraught with essential injury to the service."[46]

It might be conjectured that some serious breaches of security by the Confederate press had preceded Walker's action—and this was evidently the case. In a letter to his newspaper from Richmond, written on the day before Walker's protest, Dawson of the *Mobile Register* accused the press of the South of having been its curse and listed a number of disclosures by loose-tongued journalists which had adversely affected Southern interests.[47]

---

[45] *Memphis Daily Avalanche*, July 13, 18, 1861.

[46] *Daily Richmond Enquirer*, July 1, 1861; *Charleston Daily Courier*, July 4, 1861; *New Orleans Daily True Delta*, July 10, 1861. Almost four weeks earlier a former editor of a Petersburg newspaper, A. D. Banks, had written to Secretary Walker at the request of the Richmond press, asking the secretary to permit the press to employ war correspondents at various points subject to telegraphic censorship by the War Department. A. D. Banks to Hon. L. P. Walker, Richmond, June 4, 1861, Office of Confederate Secretary of War, 1861-1865, Letters Received 1265-1861, National Archives.

[47] *Mobile Daily Advertiser and Register*, July 7, 1861. Dawson accused the New Orleans press in particular of leaking the information of the purchase of 7,000 Enfield rifles in Europe and alleged that another press indiscretion alerted

For the most part, Southern editors reacted favorably to Walker's admonition and showed penitence. A notable dissenter was the *Charleston Mercury,* which Peter Alexander accused of having published the offending specimen of army correspondence that had prompted Walker's appeal.[48] In an editorial which it published on July 6 the *Mercury* scoffed at the notion that the military authorities at Washington looked to the Southern press for information about the Army of the Confederate States. Also, it defended the right of the press to inform its readers about everything relating to the operations of the government or the conduct of the war. If the press had been derelict, the *Mercury* added, its deficiency lay not in having injured the cause of the Confederacy by indiscreet disclosures but rather in concealing from the people facts of which they had a right to be informed.

In private as well as in public, the *Mercury* argued strenuously for its own conception of the freedom of the press. In reply to a dispatch from General Beauregard censuring the newspaper for the publication of information about his army, Editor Rhett further explained his position. Rhett asserted that he would never publish in the *Mercury* anything which in his judgment would be injurious to Confederate interests and that it would be the subject of sincere regret to him if Beauregard should deem anything injurious that appeared in Rhett's paper. "But I must in all frankness say to you that it does not seem to me, any army intelligence published in Charleston can be harmful. Scott has his own agents throughout Virginia. *The Mercury is not sent to any place or portion of the North.* Letters sent from Manassas take several days to reach Charleston. From here, after publication the intelligence takes several days more to reach Virginia or Kentucky. So that, if news contained in the Mercury *was* sent North and was not *already known,* in

---

the Federal authorities to the removal of cannon from the Gosport Navy Yard. He added: "No regiment has ever passed Lynchburg that Lincoln has not had the fullest notice of. There is not a battery in the country that has not been as fully described by correspondents as Frank Leslie's or Harper's artist could have done. They keep old Scott as well posted about the strength of our forces at every point . . . as if he were present at every dress parade and heard the morning orders read." For an example of this kind of disclosure see *New Orleans Sunday Delta,* June 2, 1861.

[48] *Savannah Republican,* August 27, 1861. According to Alexander, the *Mercury* had been guilty of two separate infractions, the second of which apparently occurred after the publication of Walker's letter. See also *Charleston Mercury* editorial, July 6, 1861.

Washington through other channels, it would at least be stale and *behind the times.*

"As to the facts themselves, you may be assured that I shall publish only such as I shall be satisfied are true."[49]

Whatever Rhett might say in defense of his conduct the Confederate authorities had no intention of permitting the press to discuss army movements freely. As a result there was a perceptible tightening of security arrangements in Virginia during early July, and the Richmond correspondents complained bitterly of the rumors that masqueraded as news on the streets of the capital. Reliable information from Johnston's army near Martinsburg was particularly difficult to obtain. On July 5 the Richmond correspondent of the *Memphis Appeal* informed his newspaper that Johnston had been attacked by Patterson's division three times the day before, that each time the Federals had been repulsed with heavy loss, that when they finally drew off, Johnston had intercepted their retreat, had hemmed them in at Martinsburg, and was preparing to bombard the town after directing the citizens to withdraw their women and children. Within twenty-four hours this ingenious story was demonstrated to be simply the latest specimen of a long series of such fabrications. Perhaps the fact that at this time none of the Richmond newspapers had a single reliable correspondent in the vicinity of Johnston's army partly explained the vogue of the stories.[50]

Writing from Beauregard's army near Fairfax Court House at about the same time, Alexander complained of communication difficulties which beset his attempts both to forward and receive information at that place. He explained that he had resorted to the Express Company, to private individuals bound for Richmond, and to the mail bags for these purposes. "Indeed, I have made every effort, except by employing couriers, to communicate with you [the *Savannah Republican*]

[49] Robert Barnwell Rhett, Jr. to Pierre Gustave Toutant Beauregard, July 13, 1861, Robert Barnwell Rhett Papers, Duke University.

[50] *Memphis Daily Appeal,* July 11, 1861; *New Orleans Sunday Delta,* July 14, 1861. An interesting description of the rumors current in Richmond about army operations during the first week of July appears in Dawson's letter in the *Mobile Daily Advertiser and Register,* July 11, 1861. For the request of a volunteer correspondent that the *Richmond Dispatch* provide a corrected version of a skirmish in which the Mecklenburg cavalry took part near Cockletown, Va., see William H. Jones to the *Richmond Dispatch,* July 21, 1861, Brock Collection, Huntington Library.

regularly and punctually, and if I have failed, you must attribute the failure to the circumstances under which I write."[51]

Indicative of the widening scope of press censorship was an order published at Yorktown in mid-July over the signature of Col. D. H. Hill of the First Regiment of North Carolina Volunteers. Hill alluded to a general order from army headquarters forbidding "newspaper scribblers" from giving information to the enemy of the movements of troops, the results of battles and skirmishes, the number of forces at particular points, etc. Hill went on to say that since this order had been violated to the "manifest prejudice of the service" he was directing the commanders of regiments and detachments within his command to use every means to frustrate "this foolish and pernicious itching for newspaper notoriety."[52]

Hill's assault on the prerogatives of the press met with a sharp response from the army newspapermen. Both de Fontaine and the Richmond correspondent of the *Memphis Appeal* countered with charges that in his "itching for notoriety" the same Colonel Hill had immediately after the fracas at Big Bethel rushed into print with an account stressing the gallant conduct of himself and his own men, the first official report of the affair to receive newspaper publication. Furthermore, Hill had given no credit in his report to the governor of North Carolina to Colonel Magruder, the department commander, who was also present at the battle. In his travels around Richmond the *Appeal* correspondent "Virginius" picked up another news squib. Its purport was that Hill himself was a member of the corps of correspondents whom he referred to as "newspaper scribblers" and that as such he contributed letters to one of the Richmond newspapers under the pseudonym "Yorktown."[53]

In such an atmosphere of tightened security regulations and press unhappiness with the regulations came the foreshadowing of important news developments. About six weeks had elapsed since Federal troops had crossed the Potomac at Alexandria and Arlington Heights to establish bridgeheads in Virginia. On July 10 Beauregard learned that the Federal field commander, Maj.Gen. Irvin McDowell, was preparing to march south toward Richmond. Six days later a Confederate woman

[51] *Savannah Republican*, July 11, 1861.
[52] *Memphis Daily Appeal*, July 19, 1861.
[53] *Charleston Daily Courier*, July 22, 1861; *Memphis Daily Appeal*, July 19, 1861.

spy courier brought definite information from Washington that the movement would begin the very next day.[54]

To meet the threatened advance of McDowell's army of 35,000 Beauregard had a force of 23,000 posted north of the important rail junction of Manassas. Some 55 miles northwest of Manassas near the Potomac end of the Shenandoah Valley, Joe Johnston with 11,000 men faced Patterson's force of 14,000 based at Harper's Ferry. In preparation for McDowell's advance Beauregard drew up his battle line along the south bank of Bull Run, a Potomac tributary flowing southeast about three miles below Centreville and to the north of Manassas Junction. He also asked Davis for reinforcements; in response the government on July 17 ordered Johnston to move down from Winchester along the Manassas Gap Railroad to form a junction with Beauregard.[55]

According to the *Mobile Register* there were at this time some twenty or thirty representatives of the press in Richmond who had passes from the War Department entitling them to visit the army.[56] Few of them were at Manassas on the 18th, however, when a Federal brigade under Brig.Gen. Dan Tyler probing the Confederate line met a sharp check at Blackburn's Ford in the Confederate center. The losses in this brief skirmish were comparatively modest—sixty-three Confederate soldiers killed and wounded and perhaps double the number of casualties on the Union side. But Confederate newspaper accounts of the action magnified the skirmish into a battle and considerably exaggerated the extent of the Federal defeat. Alexander's special dispatch to the Georgia press sent from Richmond on the afternoon of the 18th claimed that the Federals had been repulsed with great slaughter and were retreating to Alexandria.[57] The *New Orleans Picayune* correspondent was even further from the mark, reporting a Federal loss in killed and wounded of four to five thousand![58]

[54] Williams, *Beauregard*, p. 75; Ishbel Ross, *Rebel Rose, Life of Rose O'Neal Greenhow, Confederate Spy* (New York, 1954), pp. 113-15.

[55] Williams, *Beauregard*, p. 76.

[56] *Mobile Daily Advertiser and Register*, July 24, 1861. According to this same source, passes issued by the War Department to newspaper correspondents authorizing them to visit the army at this time required the holder to certify "upon his honor as a man that he will not communicate in writing or verbally for publication *any fact ascertained by him.*"

[57] *Savannah Republican*, July 19, 1861; *Atlanta Daily Southern Confederacy*, July 19, 1861.

[58] *New Orleans Daily Picayune* July 28, 1861; T. E. Dabney, *One Hundred*

"A Great Battle Has Been Fought"

The telegraph lines north of Richmond were already under the exclusive control of the government. On the 18th Beauregard issued a general order requiring all civilians with the exception of residents to leave the camp before military operations commenced and retire beyond a distance of four miles.[59] Some few army correspondents found ways and means of getting to Manassas, however, among them Alexander and de Fontaine. Alexander left Richmond on Saturday morning, July 20 and spent the greater part of the day reaching Manassas by the circuitous train route through Gordonsville. De Fontaine, who was representing the *Richmond Enquirer* as well as the *Charleston Courier*, did not get away from the capital until the evening of the 20th, barely in time to make connections with the battle of the next morning.[60]

Perry of the *New Orleans Picayune*, who had just gone up from Manassas to visit Johnston's Army of the Shenandoah, preceded the army as it marched from Winchester to Piedmont, boarding the limited rolling stock of the Manassas Gap Railroad there to complete its journey by rail. Writing to his newspaper on the same day that de Fontaine left Richmond, Perry described the high spirits of Johnston's men as they fell in on the left side of Beauregard's battle line, and reported (inaccurately) that Johnston's troop movement had already been completed. Predicting that the combined armies would move forward "tomorrow morning," Perry permitted himself some sentimental reflections on the eve of what he correctly forecast would be a great battle:

"To-night, the two armies, each 60,000 strong at least, sleep within five miles of each other. Their pickets are hourly having affrays along the whole line, which is now upward of eight miles in length. Except

---

Great Years; The Story of the Times-Picayune from Its Founding to 1940 (Baton Rouge, 1944), p. 129. Probably the best account of the Blackburn Ford skirmish appeared in the *Richmond Examiner*.

[59] *New Orleans Daily Picayune*, July 28, 1861. On July 19 the Richmond correspondent of the *Memphis Appeal* advised his newspaper that "the government has the exclusive control of the telegraph east of this place, and no private messages are allowed to pass over the wires. Today an embargo has also been laid on the railroad, so far as the passage of citizens is concerned, the entire services of the road being necessary for the transportation of men and munitions of war." *Memphis Daily Appeal*, July 25, 1861.

[60] *Savannah Republican*, July 25, 1861; *Charleston Daily Courier*, July 24, 1861; Tyler, Wise & Allegre to the Hon. Sec. of War, July 19, 1861, Office of Confederate Secretary of War 1861-1865, Letters Received 2508-1861, National Archives. The usual travelling time from Richmond to Manassas by rail in 1861 was about six hours. Richard Taylor, *Destruction and Reconstruction* (New York, 1879) p. 13.

81

these occasional shots, however, all is quiet. It is now midnight. It is the stillness of death. To-morrow will break upon a bloody battle-field."[61]

While Perry was penciling these lines, Beauregard with the approval of the senior commander, Johnston, was preparing a battle order calling for a wide envelopment of the Union left. Unknown to Beauregard was the fact that McDowell, the Union commander, had simultaneously planned to flank the Confederate left, making use of a diversionary movement against the Confederate position at the Stone Bridge to conceal his real objective. By two o'clock in the morning of July 21 the Union attack force of 14,000 was forming up to make a wide sweep to the right to cross Bull Run at a ford near Sudley Springs and come in behind the Confederate left flank. At 3:30 A.M. the sound of reveille in the Confederate camp roused Perry from his bed. Excitedly he penned a postscript to the letter he had composed a few hours before. "The whole army is up and ready for the advance. . . . We shall probably move about six."[62]

But the Confederate operation was not proceeding according to plan. Ambiguities in the phrasing of Beauregard's combat order made it difficult for his subordinates to know when the advance was to begin, the precise character of the movements intended, and which of the two generals associated in the command was the field commander. Because of poor staff work, moreover, the combat order did not reach most of the brigade commanders who were expected to lead off the attack. At an early morning hour headquarters received a message from General Bonham who commanded a Confederate brigade near Mitchell's Ford that the Federals had appeared on his left and that another enemy force was moving along the Warrenton Pike toward the Stone Bridge on the extreme left of the Confederate line. At 5:30 the Union feint at the Stone Bridge began. But it was conducted in such lackluster fashion that Col. "Shanks" Evans, who faced the Stone Bridge with a brigade of two small regiments, correctly divining that it was a feint, swung the greater part of his force around clockwise to the left and moved north across the turnpike to check the flanking movement. When the head of the Federal column appeared over the hills a little after nine o'clock, Evans' men opened fire and the battle was on. As the pressure mounted against him, Evans called for rein-

[61] *New Orleans Daily Picayune,* July 28, 1861.
[62] *Ibid.*

forcements, and from the reserve force Bee's brigade of Johnston's Army of the Shenandoah moved to Evans' support without specific orders from Johnston or Beauregard. As the Confederates fell back across the turnpike to a hill on the Henry farm, Beauregard realized that his offensive movement would have to be abandoned, and began moving troops from his right to his left to prevent the Federals from sweeping through to his rear.[63] By this time it was clear that the battle was going to be fought at right angles to the line of battle selected by the two opposing commanders.

At seven o'clock that morning a party of war correspondents consisting of de Fontaine, Alexander, Spratt of the *Charleston Mercury*, Shepardson of the *Montgomery Advertiser* and the *Columbus* (Ga.) *Times*, and Duncan of the *Richmond Dispatch* had left Manassas Junction for the battlefield. So great was their excitement that they were entirely unprepared either in the way of food or of field glasses for viewing maneuvers at a distance. Had it not been for the foresight of an officer they picked up along the way who had powerful field glasses and his making them available, they would have been handicapped that day.

At about eight o'clock they reached a hill above Mitchell's Ford that was almost bare of trees and sufficiently high to afford them an unobstructed view of the heights on the opposite side of Bull Run. Noting the heavy clouds of dust which pinpointed the direction in which the enemy was moving, the correspondents sought the shade of a tree, where they began recording their observations. At that moment the reporters had an interesting meeting with the venerable planter Edmund Ruffin, who had been present at the attack on Fort Sumter and had fired one of the opening shots of the war. With his eighty-odd years and flowing white hair, Ruffin had come to Manassas to take part in the fight and encourage the young soldiers by his presence and example.

Presently Generals Beauregard, Johnston, and Bonham came galloping up the hill to the summit where they engaged in earnest conversation. In a little while their position became the target of some Federal rifle batteries, whereupon one of Beauregard's staff officers suggested that the reporters look for a safer spot. As they moved off, a shell burst not twenty feet away. It was now about eleven o'clock, and the heavy booming of cannon, followed immediately by the sharp

---

[63] Catton, *Coming Fury*, pp. 448-54.

crack of musketry off to the left, served notice that the engagement had begun in earnest. As the generals rode off in the direction of the heaviest firing, the correspondents followed at a respectful distance, pausing at one of the field hospitals to which the wounded were already being brought. About half past twelve de Fontaine managed to get a ride in a passing ambulance to Stone Bridge. As he rode along, he noticed a regiment of Virginians who were just going into the fight at that point, having run the whole distance from the railroad station at Manassas Junction, panting and cheering.[64]

By two o'clock the battle was at its height, with 18,000 Union troops making attack after attack on the Confederate position on the Henry House Plateau. General Bee was mortally wounded, but before he died he had helped to create a legend. When his brigade had dwindled to a mere handful, he rode up to General Jackson and said, "General, they are beating us back." Jackson's reply was: "Sir, we'll give them the bayonet." Bee returned to his brigade and pointing with his sword toward Jackson's command shouted, "There is Jackson standing like a stone wall. Let us determine to die here, and we will conquer. Follow me." General Bee's principal aide told the story to a correspondent of the *Charleston Mercury*, and through the medium of that paper the name of Stonewall Jackson came into history.[65]

The turning point of the action came with the capture of two Federal batteries which mistook an advancing regiment of Confederate infantry for friends, followed by the arrival on the battlefield of Early's brigade from the extreme right of the Confederate line and Kirby Smith's brigade, which had just come in from Winchester. Immediately before this happened, the *Dispatch* reporter, Duncan, had heard General Johnston exclaim to Brig.Gen. Philip St. George Cocke, "Oh, for four regiments!" and the appearance of these reinforcements seemed

---

[64] *Richmond Daily Dispatch*, July 25, 1861.

[65] *Richmond Daily Whig*, July 29, 1861; *Charleston Mercury*, July 25, 1861; undated clipping, M. J. Solomon Scrapbook, Misc. MSS, Duke University. Some other comments on the origin of Stonewall Jackson's sobriquet may be found in F. E. Vandiver, *Mighty Stonewall* (New York, Toronto, London, 1957), p. 65; D. S. Freeman, *Lee's Lieutenants* (New York, 1945), I, Appendix v. The most recent biographer of Jefferson Davis, Hudson Strode, takes issue with the implication of the *Charleston Mercury* correspondent that General Bee was expressing admiration for Jackson in his use of the appelation "Stonewall." Strode contends that Bee was bitter because Jackson had remained in a good tactical position on the Henry House Plateau instead of coming to the rescue of Bee's hard-pressed South Carolinians. Hudson Strode, *Jefferson Davis, Confederate President* (New York, 1959), p. 119n.

almost as if in answer to his wish.[66] About 3:30 Beauregard ordered an advance along his entire front; the wearied Federals, convinced the day was lost, broke and fled across Bull Run in the direction of Centreville. A correspondent of the *New Orleans True Delta*, who had unluckily stationed himself earlier that day at the extreme right of the Confederate line, finally reached Mitchell's Ford just in time to see the beginning of the Union retreat. According to the *True Delta* man:

"Our men were perfectly frantic. Regiment after regiment ran up the hill in the wild excitement of pursuit. They were only stopped about two miles this side of Centreville by Gen. Bonham, who saw, I presume, that in the confusion they might be led into a trap. The men shouted, 'to Washington,' 'to Baltimore,' &c &c, and I believe, if left to themselves they would have neared the first point, for the enemy were in a perfect rout. In the rush up the hill I found another detachment of the Washington Artillery, under Lieut. Garnett, who did not get a chance to fire at the enemy at all. I came back with them to Bull Run; rain came on in the night, and I crawled under one of their wagons and took a snooze. It was the best accommodation they had for themselves and of course the best they could offer me."[67]

Perhaps the unluckiest of all the Confederate war correspondents at the First Battle of Manassas was Reporter J. P. Pryor. Venturing too near the enemy lines, he was "gobbled up" and made a Federal prisoner.[68]

Another late arrival on the battlefield was President Davis, who had left Richmond at six o'clock that morning and reached the scene just in time to witness the Federal retreat. According ·to Alexander, his appearance was greeted with shout after shout and was the equivalent of a reinforcement of five thousand men.[69]

[66] *Richmond Daily Dispatch*, July 25, 1861.

[67] *New Orleans Daily True Delta*, July 31, 1861. Even Spratt, who was nearer the scene of action than the *True Delta* man, admitted that not until 1:15 in the afternoon did he realize that the enemy attack at Mitchell's Ford was nothing more than a feint. Another prominent Confederate war correspondent who missed being present at the battle was the "Se De Kay" of the Louisville *Courier*, Charles D. Kirk. Kirk's Kentucky battalion of General Johnston's army was detained at Piedmont by a railroad accident and did not reach the battlefield until the fighting was over. Kirk, however, wrote an account of the battle for the *Courier*, which was reprinted in Frank Moore, *Rebellion Record* (New York, 1862), II, 375-76.

[68] *Memphis Daily Appeal*, July 28, 1861.

[69] *Savannah Republican*, July 29, 1861.

The appearance of the battlefield that night was the theme of a letter Junior Editor Cluskey of the *Memphis Avalanche* contributed to the *Avalanche*. Cluskey described realistically the groans of the wounded as they were hauled from the field to the hospital, the ghastly appearance of the dead, the tramp of the courier horses, the clattering sound and speedy movements of heavy ambulances and baggage wagons, and the red breeches of the stricken Ellsworth Zouaves serving under a full moon "as beacons to the spot where the conflict had been the bloodiest."[70] Meanwhile the weary *Savannah Republican* reporter walked seven miles from the battlefield to Manassas Junction. Arriving there about one o'clock in the morning he dispatched an exuberant telegram to his newspaper that began: "Glory to God in the highest!" and announced that "A great battle has been fought and a victory won!!"[71]

Sunday July 21 was a quiet day in Richmond, with the streets practically deserted and no sign of the newspaper bulletin boards that had attracted great crowds during the last three days of the preceding week. About four o'clock on Sunday afternoon, as he was on his way to the Express office, the Richmond correspondent of the *Columbus* (Ga.) *Times* heard from a Confederate congressman that a great battle had taken place at Manassas that morning, but that no details had yet been received.[72] Later that evening crowds besieged the newspaper and telegraph offices clamoring for news about the great battle the congressman had heard about. At length under a full moon a dispatch from President Davis was read to the crowd in front of the Spotswood House, announcing that the Confederates had gained a "glorious though a dearly bought victory" and that the enemy was in full flight, closely pursued by Beauregard's forces.[73]

There was still a vast crowd around the hotel the next morning. Their enthusiasm was mingled with grief, however; a correspondent of the *Petersburg Express* saw an affianced young lady whose betrothed had been at the front lose control of herself and, breaking away from her escort, race to the Richmond telegraph office. There, according to the reporter, her frantic appeals to the telegraph operator for information about the names of the killed and wounded brought tears

[70] *Memphis Daily Avalanche*, August 1, 1861.
[71] *Savannah Republican*, July 23, 1861.
[72] *Columbus Daily Times*, July 27, 1861.
[73] *Memphis Daily Appeal*, July 28, 1861.

to the eyes of spectators.[74] Unfortunately it was raining heavily in Richmond that morning, and weather interference with the functioning of the telegraph caused reports from the battlefield to come in very slowly. About noon it was learned that President Davis had officially communicated the news of the victory to the War Department; his dispatch, addressed to Adjutant General Samuel Cooper, was posted on the newspaper bulletin boards.[75]

The front page of the *Richmond Dispatch* that morning did not contain a word about the battle, but on an inside page was an editorial captioned "The Great Victory," purporting to give details of the battle, including grossly exaggerated estimates of the number of troops engaged on both sides. The same issue of the *Dispatch* included a special dispatch from its telegraphic correspondent at Manassas Junction reporting tremendous slaughter of both Union and Confederates, the shooting of General Beauregard's horse from under him, and a mortal wound (completely imaginary) inflicted on the Federal commander, McDowell.

In succeeding issues of the *Dispatch* and other newspapers, the Confederate press made use of official statements, special correspondence, and bombastic editorials to extract the full measure of satisfaction from the details of the inglorious Yankee rout. Especially popular with their readers were the battle reports of Alexander and de Fontaine, the *Charleston Mercury*'s Spratt, and Montgomery of the *New Orleans Delta*.[76]

There were numerous inaccuracies in the reporting of the battle,

[74] *Petersburg Daily Express*, July 23, 1861. The townspeople of Richmond indulged in no uproarious expressions of joy at the result of the First Battle of Manassas if the statements of a Richmond correspondent of the *New Orleans Crescent*, published several weeks after the battle, can be taken at their face value. According to the *Crescent* reporter, although the citizenry exchanged hearty congratulations with their neighbors and friends whom they met on the streets, "there was no shouting, no cannon firing, no noisy intoxication—everything was staid, sober and quiet." *New Orleans Daily Crescent*, September 11, 1861.

[75] *Richmond Daily Dispatch*, July 23, 1861.

[76] *Savannah Republican*, July 29, 1861; *Atlanta Daily Southern Confederacy*, July 27, 1861; *Columbus* (Ga.) *Daily Sun*, July 29, 1861; *Charleston Daily Courier*, July 30, 1861; *Charleston Mercury*, July 26, 29, 1861; *New Orleans Daily Delta*, August 22, 23, 1861. The editor of the *Savannah Republican* claimed on August 20, 1861 that he had received "hundreds of applications" for back numbers of the paper containing Alexander's "able and graphic letters on the late battle of Manassas Plains." Probably the best account that appeared in the Richmond press was D. G. Duncan's battle report in the *Richmond Dispatch* of July 25, 1861.

especially in the first reports based on hearsay information from train passengers and others who were not actually present during the fighting. The first telegraphic reports transmitted by Pritchard's Southern Associated Press made it appear that President Davis had arrived on the battlefield in time to take a prominent part in the battle. Indeed, the *Richmond Dispatch* credited Davis with commanding the center of the Confederate line in person and with deciding the fortune of the day by a charge that he ordered at four o'clock that afternoon. Subsequently Spratt and other Confederate reporters rectified the errors, making clear that Davis had taken no part in military operations while the battle was in progress.[77] The journalist E. A. Pollard, who was no friend of Davis's, explained the mistake by alleging that it was the President's intention when he left Richmond that (Sunday) morning to take command of the army in person. According to Pollard, Davis had revealed his intention to a few close friends in Richmond who passed the information on to some of the Richmond newspapermen, and the president never forgave Beauregard for fighting and winning the battle before he (Davis) got to Manassas.

Confederate press reports of casualty figures on both sides were considerably wide of the mark. Citing as authority official information from the Confederate government, the press presented a picture of 15,000 Confederates defeating 35,000 Yankees and inflicting losses of 10,000 to 15,000, as compared with Confederate casualties of 1,500 to 3,000. In reality, the aggregate Union loss amounted to 2,896, compared with Confederate casualties of 387 killed, 1,582 wounded, and 13 missing.[78]

The tendency of particular special correspondents to enlarge on the achievements of the commands from their own states produced controversy between the Richmond and Charleston press and evoked angry letters from military personnel who objected to what they regarded as discrimination against their units.[79] In an attempt to minimize dis-

[77] *Richmond Daily Dispatch*, July 22, 1861. See also J. B. Jones, *A Rebel War Clerk's Diary* (Philadelphia, 1866), I, 65.

[78] Dabney, *One Hundred Great Years*, p. 130.

[79] Diary of Benjamin F. Perry, August 18, 1861, Southern Historical Collection, University of North Carolina. The Richmond press was particularly irritated by the publication in Charleston of a pamphlet made up from the special correspondence of the *Charleston Mercury* which gave the impression that the victory had been won mainly by South Carolina troops. For Rhett's response to the complaints

satisfaction with the injection of regional bias into the reporting of the battle, the editor of the *Richmond Whig* stated that he was not surprised that some of the reporters had confined their praise to the troops with whom they were most closely associated. He added: "This seeming discrimination is natural enough; and moreover it was impossible for any individual participating in a battle like that at the Stone Bridge, unless acting in a high official capacity, to observe the movements of troops at a distance with sufficient accuracy to form a just estimate of their relative bravery or skill. . . . Every correspondent, however, should endeavor to render the meed of praise wherever it is due, without offensive partiality, and should by all means abstain from ungenerous depreciation [*sic*] of others."[80]

In their desire to magnify the extent of the victory and the odds against which it was achieved, Confederate reporters made it appear that Patterson's Harper's Ferry command had joined McDowell in time to participate in the Battle of Manassas.[81] Moreover, they considerably exaggerated the number of Federal cannon captured by the Confederates when they claimed the capture of sixty-five pieces of artillery. Confessing that he wished the report were true, a soldier correspondent of the *Columbus Times* asserted that the true number was twenty-eight as ascertained by his actual count and the official report of captured property. "The only way in which the number could have been made to approximate sixty-five was by counting the caissons as pieces of artillery, and most probably this was done."[82] Commenting on the tendency of the press to reiterate endlessly the circumstances of the triumph, a South Carolina officer confessed several weeks later in a letter to his mother that he was tired of hearing about the battle. ". . . everybody has talked and still talks so much, and as to the newspapers they are perfectly absurd; I hope you don't believe one-tenth of what you read. All about the [Hampton] Legion I know, and it is amusing

---

of the *Richmond Examiner* and other Richmond newspapers see *Charleston Mercury*, August 19, 1861. See also Officers of Stephens Light Guard to Alexander H. Stephens, August 2, 1861, Stephens Papers, Library of Congress.

[80] *Richmond Daily Whig*, August 5, 1861.

[81] See e.g. *New Orleans Daily Picayune*, July 30, 1861.

[82] *Columbus Daily Times*, August 16, 1861. Captured Federal equipment consisted of twenty-eight field guns, thirty-seven caissons, a half-million rounds of field ammunition, and other valuable military property. *O.R.* (Army), Ser. i, vol. ii, pp. 502-503.

to read the accounts of what the papers give of where we were, what we did and who came to our relief."[83]

Writing from Richmond to the *Savannah Republican* fully a month after the battle, Reporter Alexander admitted that no "full, fair and satisfactory account" of the First Battle of Manassas had been published. Yet he expressed the opinion that under the rules adopted by the military authorities to prevent full coverage by the army correspondents it was a wonder that the correspondents' accounts were as full as they were.[84] In similar language the *Richmond Dispatch* defended the press against the faultfinders who sneered at the large number of errors in its news columns. In response to such criticisms, the *Dispatch* maintained that "no newspaper does or can be expected to vouch for the entire accuracy of every item that appears in its columns. Its conductors have no power to summon their informants before them, and put them on oath, subject to the pains and penalties of perjury. The most they are bound to do is to sift as fairly and accurately as they can the mass of matter before them and conscientiously suppress what they honestly believe to be untrue in itself or unjust to any individual. This duty they perform, as far as we know, about as honestly as the world at large discharges any of its obligations. . . . The real wonder is that so many of the multitudinous items of information in a daily journal should be as correct as they are."[85]

Perhaps the most controversial issue in the Southern reporting of First Manassas related to the performance of Brig.Gen. Richard S. Ewell. In his full-length account of the battle, Alexander referred to the order addressed by Beauregard to Ewell on the morning of the battle, directing him to attack the left flank of the enemy line. Alexander stated further that for some unexplained reason the order was not executed and that if it had been, the complete destruction of General McDowell's army would have followed.[86]

Another reporter, the correspondent of the *Columbus* (Ga.) *Sun*, insinuated that Ewell had been guilty of treason, but retracted his statement and apologized when he was called on to furnish authority for

---

[83] James Conner, *Letters of General James Conner, C.S.A.* (Columbia, S.C., 1933), p. 54.

[84] *Savannah Republican*, August 27, 1861.

[85] *Richmond Daily Dispatch*, July 29, 1861.

[86] *Savannah Republican*, July 29, 1861.

his statements.[87] A correspondent of the *Columbus* (Ga.) *Enquirer* sought to clear Ewell of the implication of having disobeyed Beauregard's order.[88] Apparently none of the army correspondents was aware that this order was never in Ewell's hands and that in the situation of changed orders, recalled orders, and confused orders that followed, Ewell's Second Brigade ended the day with a frustrating record of more than twenty miles marching and countermarching with hardly a glimpse of a Yankee.[89]

Army correspondents basked in some of the glory Beauregard and other Confederate officers reaped in full measure from their stunning victory. In months to come enterprising book publishers would rush into print some of the leading newspaper narratives of the battle. Also, Leonidas W. Spratt of the *Charleston Mercury* embarked on a lecture tour to relate to admiring audiences in Richmond, Charleston, Lynchburg, and other cities the exploits of the men on the Manassas battlefield of July 21.[90] But the more farsighted editors were aware that Confederate independence was not yet an accomplished fact, that there would be more fighting to test the Southern people, along with the efficiency of the South's news-gathering organization.

[87] Photocopy of Civil War Reminiscences of Major Campbell Brown, I, 9, Richard S. Ewell Papers, Southern Historical Collection, University of North Carolina.

[88] *Columbus Daily Enquirer* as quoted in *Savannah Republican*, August 14, 1861. See also *Columbus Daily Sun*, September 12, 1861. For Alexander's rejoinder to the *Enquirer* man's defense of Ewell see *Savannah Republican*, August 23, 1861.

[89] P. G. Hamlin, *"Old Bald Head"*: *The Portrait of a Soldier* (Strasburg, Va., 1940), pp. 65-66.

[90] See e.g. *Lynchburg Daily Republican*, September 4, 1861; *Savannah Republican*, September 17, 1861; *Memphis Daily Appeal*, September 18, 1861; *Columbus Daily Times*, September 5, October 5, 1861; *Charleston Mercury*, September 18, 30, 1861.

CHAPTER 4

Great Expectations and Minor Accomplishments

IN THE AFTERMATH of the unexpected victory at Manassas the columns of the Confederate press reflected a widespread belief that the battle had ended the war. On the third morning after the rout of the Union forces the *Mobile Register* likened the result to the English defeat of the Spanish Armada in 1588; on July 25 the same newspaper predicted that "on the centre of his line in Virginia the vanguard of [the enemy's] army will never again advance beyond cannon shot of Washington." Similar statements appeared in newspapers like the *Richmond Examiner* and *Dispatch* and the *Louisville Courier*.[1]

Editors like Rhett and Daniel had confidently expected that in the afterglow of Manassas Johnston and Beauregard would vigorously pursue the retreating enemy. Indeed, reports were current in Richmond on the twenty-fifth that Beauregard's troops had already entered Alexandria, just below Washington, without firing a gun. In relaying this information to its readers the *Petersburg Express* hopefully added: "We presume the next movement will be against Arlington Heights, and then 'on to Washington!' "[2]

When it became clear that the main Confederate army had not advanced beyond Centreville the impatience of the newspaper generals with what they regarded as Davis's defensive strategy found expression in curiosity as to why there had not been an effective pursuit. They did not then know that on the evening following the battle President Davis had recommended such a course and the capture of Washington to his generals. In reply Beauregard and Johnston pointed out that the army lacked sufficient food, equipment, and transportation, and warned the President of the possibility of a counterattack by a fresh Union army nearby; Davis yielded to the objections. The heavy rainstorm the following day, which converted the Virginia countryside

[1] *Mobile Daily Advertiser and Register*, July 24, 1861; T. H. Williams, *P.G.T. Beauregard, Napoleon in Gray* (Baton Rouge, 1954), p. 91; D. S. Freeman, *Lee's Lieutenants* (New York, 1942), i, p. 80.

[2] *Petersburg Daily Express*, July 26, 1861.

92

into a quagmire, interposed further obstacles to a Confederate advance. Nonetheless, Confederate editors expressed strong dissatisfaction with Johnston's failure to exploit the fruits of his victory; both editors and their reporters predicted and continued to watch for signs of an advance on Washington.[3]

Their hopes rose early in August when at Beauregard's prompting Johnston ordered an advance. From Centreville the main body of the army marched to Fairfax Court House, and advanced elements of Beauregard's command went all the way to the heights overlooking Washington on the south side of the Potomac.[4]

For a period of almost two weeks after the battle, Reporter Peter Alexander was prostrated in Richmond by an attack of illness induced by exposure and fatigue. With only a scant breakfast and a solitary cracker to quiet his hunger pangs on the day of the Battle of Manassas, he had walked twenty miles through hot sun and heavy dew after the fighting had ended. Added to the effects of his great mental and physical excitement during the fight was the undermining experience of revisiting the battlefield the following Wednesday amid the heavy stench arising from scores of unburied horses. By the end of the first week of August, however, he was back on his feet, ready to resume the tasks of an army correspondent.[5]

His competitors for news of Confederate operations in northern Virginia included his former associates, de Fontaine, the *Picayune* reporter Perry, Montgomery of the *New Orleans Delta,* and Charles D. Kirk of the *Louisville Courier.* The *Charleston Mercury* sent a for-

---

[3] G. E. Govan and J. W. Livingood, *A Different Valor, The Story of General Joseph E. Johnston, C.S.A* (Indianapolis, 1956), pp. 59-60; J. E. Johnston, *Narrative of Military Operations* (New York, 1874), pp. 59-60; R. W. Winston, *High Stakes and Hair Trigger* (New York, 1930), p. 198; W. C. Harris, *Leroy Pope Walker* (Tuscaloosa, Ala., 1961), p. 88; R. D. Meade, *Judah P. Benjamin* (New York and London, 1943), p. 189; *Richmond Daily Dispatch,* July 30, 1861; *New Orleans Sunday Delta,* August 4, 1861; *Savannah Republican,* August 27, 1861. According to the war memoir of Gen. Richard Taylor, the amount of confusion in the Confederate camp for several days after the battle was "extreme." "Regiments seemed to have lost their colonels, colonels their regiments. Men of all arms and all commands were mixed in the wildest way. A constant fusillade of small arms and singing of bullets were kept up, indicative of a superfluity of disorder, if not of ammunition." Richard Taylor, *Destruction and Reconstruction* (New York, 1879), pp. 13-14.

[4] Williams, *Beauregard,* p. 99.

[5] *Savannah Republican,* August 9, 15, 1861; *Atlanta Daily Southern Confederacy,* August 15, 16, 1861.

mer physician named John D. Bruns to Virginia to replace Spratt early in August. In a letter to South Carolina Congressman W. Porcher Miles, Bruns confided that "Mr. S." (evidently Spratt) had not made himself "convenable" to the Confederate authorities and that the editorial policy of the *Mercury* had been of such a character as not to entitle the paper to very favorable consideration at either Richmond or Manassas. Bruns exuded confidence, however, in his own ability to foster harmony between the "powers that be" and his prospective newspaper employers in Charleston; he promised Miles he would not reveal any important strategic movements or make himself obnoxious in army circles by gratuitous comment or criticism. Perhaps Rhett was less optimistic than Bruns about the latter's ability, for a little later he dispatched another correspondent, William A. Courtenay, northward to reinforce Bruns.[6]

Another of Peter Alexander's journalistic competitors was the *Delta* correspondent Durant Da Ponte. Da Ponte, who had evidently gone back to New Orleans after the Battle of Manassas, reappeared in Johnston's army in September in the dual capacity of a reporter and a staff officer with the rank of captain on Maj.Gen. Earl Van Dorn's staff.[7]

The *Charleston Courier* stole a march on the other newspapers by employing a lady correspondent. In a letter to the editor signed "Spartan Mother," she had proffered her services as a Virginia correspondent of the *Courier* to be near her twenty-year-old son who was attached to Johnston's army.[8] In stating her qualifications, the would-be feminine newspaper reporter said:

"You may, perhaps, think a woman is not competent to grasp the issues now presented to our people. I admit it; at the same time I think a woman proves many times a more attractive correspondent than a man. Her perceptions are keener—she picks up items of interest al-

---

[6] J. Dickson [John D.] Bruns to W. P. Miles, August 4, 1861, William Porcher Miles Papers, Southern Historical Collection, University of North Carolina. Since Miles was at this time the chairman of the Military Affairs Committee of the Confederate House of Representatives, Bruns was no doubt seeking to enlist his influence in smoothing the acceptance of a new *Charleston Mercury* correspondent in the army.

[7] *Vicksburg Sun* as reprinted in *Mobile Daily Advertiser and Register*, September 13, 1861. See also Mrs. Burton Harrison, *Recollections Grave and Gay* (New York, 1911), pp. 61-63. For a reference to Montgomery as the color-sergeant of the Washington Artillery see S. P. Day, *Down South* (London, 1862), i, 317.

[8] *Charleston Daily Courier*, August 7, 1861.

most intuitively, and can often times glean many from a mass where a man would detect nothing. Should I go to Virginia, I shall remain in as close proximity to the camp as is consistent with my dignity as a woman, seeking shelter in farm house or village, as the case may be. Should there be wounded to nurse, my mission will be among *them.*"[9]

The first of her letters, appearing over the signature of "Joan," was dated at Richmond on the Monday following the Battle of Manassas. Over the period of the next four months she wrote two or three letters a week to the *Courier* from Virginia, in which she portrayed the war from the woman's point of view with remarkable perspicacity. She described visits to the Yankee prisoners confined in the tobacco factory at the foot of Main Street, an interview with Vice President Stephens, with whom she was obviously fascinated, the war work of the Richmond ladies busily employed as seamstresses for the soldiers in almost every church of the city, and the general appearance of the Confederate capital. After spending almost eight weeks in Richmond she finally managed to secure permission to go to the front and be re-united with her son.[10]

Dr. Shepardson, who had represented the *Montgomery Advertiser* and the *Columbus Times* at Manassas, transferred his allegiance to the *Richmond Dispatch* in September. For the next six months his war correspondence for the *Dispatch* over the signature of "Bohemian" received wide distribution through the columns of the Confederate press. It was during this period that two of the leading Richmond correspondents of out-of-town newspapers also began their reporting from the capital. The poet John R. Thompson became the Richmond correspondent of the *Memphis Appeal* in August 1861, and the piquant letters of "Hermes," otherwise known as George W. Bagby, first began to appear in the *Charleston Mercury* about two months later.

Throughout August and September the Dixie press continued to agitate for another forward movement, and Beauregard finally con-

---

[9] *Charleston Daily Courier* as reprinted in *Daily Richmond Enquirer*, July 19, 1861.

[10] *Charleston Daily Courier*, July 25, August 3, 5, 9, 31, September 10, 24, 1861. The *Courier* was not the only Southern newspaper to employ a woman war correspondent, however. In the *Mobile Daily Advertiser and Register* of August 24, 1861 is the first of a series of letters to that newspaper from a lady correspondent in Norfolk who signed herself "Virginia." The *Knoxville Register* also had a lady correspondent with Johnston's army at Fairfax Station whose signature was "E. L. McE." *Knoxville Daily Register*, September 15, 1861.

vinced Johnston that it was essential to launch a decisive blow to interfere with the Federal concentration for a spring campaign against Richmond. Late in September in response to an invitation from Johnston, President Davis went up to Fairfax Court House to discuss the proposed offensive.[11] Perry of the *Picayune*, who happened to be at army headquarters at the time, described the President's arrival in camp. He told how Davis came up from Richmond by special train as far as Fairfax Station and travelled on horseback the remaining four miles, being met en route by General Beauregard and Beauregard's aide, Lt.Col. John S. Preston. Perry noted the fact that the President rode quite erect on a white horse a little in advance of the party as they entered the town and then dropped back to engage in earnest conversation with Beauregard. "He was dressed, as usual, in plain citizen's dress of Confederate colors, and appeared quite well, though thin from the loss of flesh during his recent illness. After a hearty supper he received the calls of all the principal officers of the army and later in the evening was honored with a serenade by the handsome band of the First Virginia Regiment. The first piece was of course 'Hail to the Chief,' the last the inevitable 'Dixie,' after which the President withdrew to more private counsel with the generals commanding."[12]

According to the *Richmond Dispatch* reporter, Shepardson, Davis's visit was unheralded and therefore unexpected. Yet he was by no means unwelcome, since both the local citizenry and the soldiers were chafing at the army's inaction and were wanting to know what was to be done to meet Yankee encroachment. Shepardson described the festivities of that evening and told how on the following morning President Davis made a personal reconnaissance of the outposts, accompanied by a large retinue of officers.[13]

This and the grand review of several brigades and the Washington Artillery that took place just before Davis's departure on October 4 provided the grist for reporters' letters, along with conjectures as to the purpose of the visit. Apparently newspapermen were barred from the conference of October 1 at which Beauregard's plan for an invasion of Maryland was discussed. Davis wanted to know how many men would be needed. When he learned that 60,000 (20,000 more than

[11] Williams, *Beauregard*, p. 100; Meade, *Benjamin*, p. 184.
[12] *New Orleans Daily Picayune*, October 10, 1861.
[13] *Richmond Daily Dispatch*, October 4, 1861.

were already under the command of Johnston and Beauregard) was the minimum figure, he said that he could not reinforce the army to that extent and even if he could, there were not enough arms to equip the reinforcements. Both generals rejected as impractical and dangerous his counterproposal to send a small raiding party across the Potomac. It was apparent to them, if not to the press, that there would be no further offensive operations in northern Virginia for the remainder of the year.[14]

Da Ponte of the *New Orleans Delta* arrived from Richmond too late to see the President before his departure. From someone who had been more fortunate he received the rather misleading impression that "we should not remain long in expectation of another encounter with the enemy." Da Ponte heard from the same informant that when Brig.Gen. James Longstreet told President Davis that if he had come a few days earlier he would have had an opportunity to see Washington, Davis replied, "Well, well, you will all have a chance to see it again, but you will have to fight your way to it."[15]

Another newspaperman who was at Fairfax at the time of Davis's visit was de Fontaine, who, like Alexander, had earlier been incapacitated by an illness of several weeks' duration. "Personne" had left Richmond at the end of the first week of August to make a flying trip to General Magruder's "Army of the Peninsula." To document the discomforts of his experience he described his journey from Richmond to Yorktown in shorthand fashion:

"Cars crowded, sun hot, atmosphere dusty, occupy six inches of a metaphorical seat, the remainder of which is divided between a very fat Irish woman and a very large basket. Old lady in a decided state of distillation. At once discovered an odor of strong water as if she had freely indulged in burning fluid and sugar, seasoned with onions.— Her face is broad, red, moist, and oleaginous, suggestive of a scarcity of soap and water, and is a sort of base from which protrudes a gigantic twenty-four pounder of a nose—a patriarchal ornament out of which a beard has grown . . . for the last half hour . . . the stout dame has subjected me to an inquisitorial bombardment, compared with which that of Sumter was mild and trivial. I let off my artillery in minute

---

[14] Williams, *Beauregard*, p. 101; Govan and Livingood, *A Different Valor*, pp. 75-77.

[15] *New Orleans Daily Delta*, October 15, 1861.

monosyllables. She finally leaves at a way station. . . ."[16] The remainder of his letter conveyed a picture of the boat trip from West Point to Yorktown in a crowded fore and aft schooner, the going ashore in a "ricketty boat," trudging along the beach for a quarter of a mile through sand ankle deep, the party of four or five planters who had come a long way to visit their sons in camp, and the consternation of the pious old father who found a bottle of whisky and a pack of cards in his boy's tent!

"Personne" had contracted the illness alluded to previously following his return to Richmond, and after his recovery had gone to Culpeper to convalesce. At the beginning of September Pritchard of the Southern Associated Press had arranged for "Personne" to go to Manassas to report by telegraph and letter facts relating to the results of "skirmishes and engagements," together with lists of killed and wounded.[17] Thus employed by Pritchard and the *Charleston Courier,* de Fontaine was at Fairfax Court House to report the abortive Davis visit to the army.

Throughout August and September there was chronic excitement in Richmond over stories of offensive movements and clashes with the enemy that for the most part were false. Writing from Richmond on August 27 a *Picayune* correspondent informed his newspaper that "they get up rumors here about battles and results as readily as Yankees get up patents for machinery, and both are about equally valuable and reliable. This is the most difficult city I have been in to discriminate between truth and falsehood, and you must not be surprised at the groundless reports you sometimes receive by telegraph."[18] Similarly "Personne" told about Rumor being the ruling god in Richmond, and Da Ponte admitted that the public had become weary of reading about severe engagements in which "heavy firing, valiant charges, and disorderly retreats terminate in an infinitessimal list of casualties."[19] Apparently the *Charleston Mercury* had come to recognize the need of exercising greater caution in discussing army movements in its news columns. In a letter to Edmund Rhett in Charleston, another member of

[16] *Charleston Daily Courier,* August 15, 1861.

[17] W. H. Pritchard to Hon. L. P. Walker, Secretary of War, September 2, 1861, Office of Confederate Secretary of War 1861-1865, Letters Received, 3966-1861, National Archives.

[18] *New Orleans Daily Picayune,* September 3, 1861.

[19] *Charleston Daily Courier,* September 7, 1861; *New Orleans Daily Delta,* September 25, 1861.

the Rhett family, who was with the army near Fairfax Court House, cautioned him to be "exceedingly careful how you write in the *Mercury*, or publish anything to give to the enemy a knowledge of our numbers, or position, or equipments."[20]

On October 18 the Richmond newspapers published reports that Johnston's army had pulled back from the Potomac and taken up a new triangular position with its apex at Centreville. Perry of the *Picayune* was at Fairfax when the movement took place, to furnish his newspaper with an eyewitness account. In his newspaper story he underlined the excitement of the townspeople who had not expected the order and were unprepared to remove their families, servants, and household effects within a matter of hours, and he depicted the picturesque aspects of the midnight march of October 15-16.[21] Not being apprised as to the reasons for the retreat, the army correspondents did their best to put a good face on it. De Fontaine, for example, assured his readers that the army's new position was more defensible than the old and more likely to provoke the Union commander, Maj.Gen. George B. McClellan, into making an attack.[22] De Fontaine did not know, although he may have surmised, that the decision to withdraw had originated with Johnston, who regarded the position of his army as being exposed and dangerous.[23]

The attack "Personne" had expected Johnston's retreat to provoke materialized within less than a week when a Union brigade crossed the upper Potomac near Leesburg at the left end of the Confederate line and sustained a bloody repulse. To the mortification of the press no special correspondent of any leading Southern newspaper was present to record the Confederate success at Ball's Bluff. When the news of the victory in the form of a dispatch from General Johnston to the War Department was first posted on the *Enquirer* bulletin board about ten o'clock in the morning of October 22, almost the whole population of Richmond rushed into the streets to ascertain the truth of the report.[24] Mindful of the fact that the officer in command of the Confederates, Colonel "Shanks" Evans, was a South Carolinian, the Rich-

---

[20] A. Barnwell Rhett to Edmund Rhett, October 14, 1861, Robert Barnwell Rhett Papers, Southern Historical Collection, University of North Carolina.

[21] *New Orleans Daily Picayune*, October 23, 1861.

[22] *Charleston Daily Courier*, October 24, 1861.

[23] Williams, *Beauregard*, p. 101; Govan and Livingood, *A Different Valor*, p. 79.

[24] *New Orleans Daily Picayune*, November 1, 1861; *Charleston Daily Courier*, October 29, 1861; *Savannah Republican*, October 28, 1861.

mond correspondent of the *Charleston Mercury* expressed exuberant sentiments:

"Three times three and a tiger for the heroic South Carolinian, General Evans! I knew the man was game to the backbone the first time I laid eyes on him. . . . And now with three Regiments and *no artillery*, he has given Stone a terrible lambasting, killed Baker of Oregon (an excellent thing,), taken 6 pieces, 800 prisoners, and killed, wounded, and drowned 1200 more."[25]

There was a general scramble of army correspondents (Alexander, de Fontaine, Shepardson, and Perry among others) to interview the participants in the action and collect trophies from the battlefield. A series of battle accounts that "Personne" pieced together from such sources came nearest to presenting a comprehensive account of the engagement. In the opinion of the editor of the *Richmond Dispatch*, "Personne's" October 29 letter from Leesburg far surpassed "in vivid description and intense soul-thrilling language" all his other letters that had yet been published. Writing about the battlefield of Ball's Bluff, "Personne" described with sickening realism and a sense of disgust a drove of pigs feasting on Yankee corpses that had been buried in shallow graves and a party of men in a boat along the river rifling the pockets of dead Yankees who were floating on top of the water.[26]

From the widely-differing accounts he obtained from the Mississippi regiments that took part in the fighting, a special correspondent of the *New Orleans Crescent* concluded that Ball's Bluff had been purely a "helter skelter, up and down hill, bush fight" won by the energy and superior marksmanship of the men in the ranks.[27] Indeed, he thought, generalship had had very little to do with the outcome. Before long both Da Ponte and de Fontaine felt obliged to defend Evans against press criticism to the effect, first that he had fought the Battle of Ball's Bluff contrary to orders, and second that he had made a grave error in not attacking the Federal force at Edward's Ferry on the opposite side of the river on the day after the battle.[28]

The arrival at Manassas and later in Richmond of the prisoners captured at Ball's Bluff was the theme of several letters from special cor-

[25] *Charleston Mercury*, October 28, 1861.

[26] *Richmond Daily Dispatch*, November 12, 1861; *Charleston Daily Courier*, November 8, 1861.

[27] *New Orleans Daily Crescent*, November 11, 1861.

[28] *Charleston Daily Courier*, November 8, 1861; *New Orleans Daily Delta*, November 20, 1861.

respondents. There were about five hundred prisoners in the first echelon, belonging to the 15th and 20th Massachusetts, the 42d New York "Tammany" Regiment, and Colonel Baker's California Regiment. John R. Thompson of the *Memphis Appeal* reported that the prisoners were generally well clothed, although a dozen or more were barefooted, having taken off their shoes in the course of their retreat preparatory to recrossing the Potomac. Although Thompson was of the opinion that as a body they displayed a hang-dog look, Da Ponte thought that many of them seemed to take their misfortune quite good humoredly. "A few wore a defiant and even a ferocious expression, which excited the merriment of the spectators." Perry reported that as the prisoners entered Manassas they were received with cheers from the assembled crowd "such as only they can give who have the invaders of their homes in their hands." Da Ponte stated, however, that the citizens of Richmond as a rule displayed no tendency to exult over their captive enemies or otherwise to mistreat them, although humorous expressions such as "Glad to see you; how do you like Richmond?" and "Where did you leave Scott?" were abundant.[29]

It was about this time that rumors of difficulties between Beauregard and the Davis administration began to appear in the press. Within two weeks after the Battle of Manassas the *Charleston Mercury* published unconfirmed reports from its Richmond correspondent to the effect that the President had been responsible for stopping the pursuit of the fleeing enemy.[30] To counter such gossip Davis followed the unusual course of asking his generals to deny the rumor officially. Beauregard complied at once, but in his official report of the battle he implied that the rejection of his original plan to combine the two armies had prevented the Southern armed forces from getting to Washington. Unfortunately the Confederate War Department failed to forward Beauregard's report to the President, and the first Davis knew about it was when a summary of it appeared, first in the *Richmond Dispatch* and later in the *New Orleans Delta*. Davis promptly obtained the complete report from the War Department, read it, and on October 30 addressed a letter of protest to Beauregard, saying that the newspaper synopsis had been verified by the text of the report.[31] As the news of

[29] *Memphis Daily Appeal*, October 29, 1861; *New Orleans Daily Picayune*, October 31, 1861; *New Orleans Daily Delta*, November 1, 1861.

[30] *Charleston Mercury*, August 7, 1861.

[31] *Richmond Daily Dispatch*, November 1, 1861; *New Orleans Daily Delta*,

the quarrel became public through the press, the friends of Beauregard entered the fray, and Beauregard himself ventilated the controversy in the newspapers in a remarkable letter which he authorized the *Richmond Whig* to publish on November 7.

Heading his letter "Centreville, Va., Within hearing of the Enemy's Guns, November 3, 1861," Beauregard declared that the excerpts from his report in the newspapers had been published without his knowledge or authority. He went on to say (apparently with Davis in mind), "if certain minds cannot understand the difference between *patriotism*, the highest civic virtue, and *office-seeking*, the lowest civic occupation, I pity them from the bottom of my heart." Also he disclaimed any interest in becoming a candidate for any civil office in the gift of the people. Taking notice of the distinctive heading of Beauregard's letter, a rival newspaper posed the query, "Are we expected to give special credit to the General's lucubrations because of a fact certainly not very unusual in military operations?" In general the press reaction to Beauregard's theatrical stance was adversely critical, although the New Orleans press continued to plead the general's cause.[32]

With the approach of winter there were increasing indications that Johnston's army was about to go into winter quarters. Yet the press continued to exploit the possibilities of an attack by McClellan. On December 9 Da Ponte reported that during the last two days everybody in Richmond had become firmly convinced that McClellan was advancing in force, and "Fighting at Centreville," "Fighting at Evansport," and "Fighting at Dumfries" were exclamations that could be heard at every street corner. On the strength of such reports Da Ponte hustled to the War Department, only to be informed by the imperturbable Assistant Secretary of War Albert T. Bledsoe that no information to confirm the scare stories had been received from army headquarters. ". . . I flew to the hotels, and found the ladies calmly discussing feminine affairs in the parlors; I hastened to the telegraph office, and sent a dispatch to the army, inquiring if there was any evidence of an advance of the army, and received for answer the emphatic monosyllable, 'none.' "[33]

October 26, 1861, February 4, 1862; Shelby Foote, *The Civil War, A Narrative, Fort Sumter to Perryville* (New York, 1958), p. 124.

[32] P.G.T. Beauregard to the Editors of the *Richmond Whig*, November 3, 1861, Letterbook, 1861-1863, Beauregard Papers, Library of Congress; *Richmond Whig*, November 12, 1861.

[33] *New Orleans Daily Delta*, December 15, 1861.

On the following day Da Ponte learned at last that the army was preparing to go into winter quarters.

In view of this, "Personne," "P.W.A.," and most of the other army correspondents left Centreville to return home. By Christmas Eve Alexander was back in Savannah, where he received the congratulations of his newspaper friends at the *Republican* office.[34]

Throughout the fall campaign in northern Virginia the right to report had been restricted by the military authorities and affected by the sensitiveness of interested parties to overly frank judgments by reporters. In a letter from Richmond on August 16 Alexander Walker of the *New Orleans Delta* advised his newspaper that so rigid was the requirement of secrecy with regard to military operations that he felt "considerably embarrassed" as to what he might and might not say. Three weeks later another Richmond correspondent complained that "everything here is kept secret" and that General Johnston had stopped the mails from Manassas to Richmond. In succeeding weeks it proved almost impossible for civilians in Richmond to obtain passes to visit the army.[35]

In performing their reportorial duties army correspondents frequently ran the risk of being treated as spies. In September 1861 Shepardson told about Spratt being arrested at the instigation of a "female custodian of the public welfare." According to Shepardson, Spratt escaped imprisonment with some difficulty, although he demonstrated a clear record and proved that he had made secession speeches ever since he was first elected to the South Carolina legislature years before.[36] Likewise a special correspondent of the *Petersburg Express* named Frank Smyth, who aroused the suspicion of the local militia, was thrown in jail in Winchester, Virginia and languished there until the Secretary of War brought about his release.[37] In announcing his decision to ter-

[34] *Richmond Daily Dispatch,* December 6, 1861; *Charleston Daily Courier,* December 11, 1861; *Savannah Republican,* December 18, 24, 1861.

[35] *New Orleans Sunday Delta,* August 25, 1861; *New Orleans Daily Crescent,* September 16, 1861. On October 27, 1861, the *Mobile Advertiser and Register* stated: "The Richmond papers announce that all civilians are now rigidly excluded from our lines at Manassas."

[36] *Richmond Daily Dispatch,* September 23, 1861.

[37] Frank Smyth to Hon. L. Pope Walker, Secretary of War, August 18, 1861, Office of Confederate Secretary of War, 1861-1865, Letters Received, 3423-1861, National Archives. In his letter to Walker, Smyth claimed to have been born in Ireland, but reared and educated in Richmond, of which he had been a loyal citizen for the past fifteen years.

minate his special correspondence, Spratt said frankly that he had every reason to believe that the military authorities were displeased because he had continued reporting so long and that since the position of an outsider in a military camp was not pleasant, he saw no reason for remaining there any longer.[38]

Both de Fontaine and Courtenay ran into difficulties of a somewhat different nature because of controversial statements which appeared in their special correspondence. "Personne" aroused the ire of a Leesburg paper for imputing disloyalty to the citizens of Loudon County (the county in which Leesburg was located). The editor of the *Leesburg Democratic Mirror* retorted:

"That there are disloyal citizens in the county of Loudon . . . we shall not deny . . . but to denounce the county for the disloyalty of a few unworthy people who chance to have an abiding place within her limits is like denouncing the works of deity because at times dark spots appear on the disc of the sun. . . ."

"Loudon is a border county, and there is of course more diversity of sentiment than in an interior county of South Carolina, but whatever of disloyalty exists in the county is almost confined to one section, Waterford and the German settlement. . . ."

"The *Courier*'s correspondent may have been ignorant of these facts, if so he should not have written—if he knew them and still wrote— he is to be pitied."[39]

Courtenay's difficulty was the result of a letter addressed to the editor of the *Charleston Mercury*. In the letter, not intended for publication, he alleged that the South Carolina troops were "fast getting disgusted" and predicted that nearly all the twelve-months volunteers would go home at the expiration of their enlistments because they felt they had been "sold." The *Mercury*, probably inadvertently, published Courtenay's letter, whereupon a South Carolina company in Johnston's army, the Palmetto Guards, took umbrage and wrote to the editor of the *Mercury* to denounce the letter as "false . . . slanderous, and totally unworthy of a true Carolinian." Courtenay interpreted the blast from the Palmetto Guards as a reflection on his honor, and the result was a duel between Courtenay and Capt. G. B. Cuthbert of the Guards near Manassas on November 21. Neither party was hurt, and after an

[38] *Charleston Mercury*, August 3, 1861.
[39] J. D. Patch, *The Battle of Ball's Bluff* (Leesburg, Va., 1958), pp. 107-11; *Charleston Daily Courier*, November 8, 1861.

exchange of shots, the difference of opinion was amicably settled. Subsequently there was a series of letters between Cuthbert and Editor Robert Barnwell Rhett, Jr. over a statement about Cuthbert that had appeared in the *Mercury*. Eventually Rhett succeeded in mollifying the resentment of his military adversary and avoiding a second duel.[40]

The most common themes of Confederate army reporting in Northern Virginia during the autumn of 1861 were picket firing, army diet and recreation, profiles of leading generals, descriptions of the terrain in which the army was operating, the routine of camp life, sickness in the army, and the need for blankets and clothing.

Writing on September 17 from Munson's Hill, a small bare elevation within sight of Washington, "Personne" referred to the constant succession of shots that continued daily between the two opposing lines of pickets from daylight until dusk. The interval between the lines was less than nine hundred yards; from where "Personne" was situated he could every now and then see the enemy pickets pushing aside the corn that concealed them or peeping from behind some temporary barricade. Although he confessed that the very proximity of danger coupled with the beauty of the surrounding countryside created such a magnetic attraction that "you forget the risk in yielding to the charm," he admitted that the firing was desultory and that no more than four casualties had occurred on the Confederate side thus far.[41]

Viewing picket actions from the same vantage point, *Picayune* reporter Perry alluded to the large amount of space given in the newspapers to the "murderous practice" of soldiers on the picket line, but asserted that the justice of such strictures did not seem evident from on-the-spot observation. He went on to say that "the officers in command have given strict orders never to fire unless it may be in self defense, or necessary to maintain a post, and so far as I have seen, the men are inclined of themselves to obey these instructions."[42] Even

[40] *Charleston Mercury*, November 6, 1861; *Richmond Daily Dispatch*, November 23, 1861; *Memphis Daily Appeal*, November 29, 1861; G. B. Cuthbert to R. B. Rhett, Jr., March 7, 10, 14, 1862; R. B. Rhett, Jr., to G. B. Cuthbert, March 10, 13, 1862, Robert Barnwell Rhett Papers, Huntsville Alabama.

[41] *Charleston Daily Courier*, September 21, 1861. For an uncomplimentary allusion to the "black-hearted traitor" Munson, after whom the hill was named and who had fled to Washington with his family when the Confederate troops approached his home, see *New Orleans Daily Delta*, September 11, 1861.

[42] *New Orleans Daily Picayune*, September 18, 1861. General Johnston had written to "Jeb" Stuart on September 2, 1861: "Can you not do something to prevent this critical [continual?] picket fighting? It is useless between equal troops—

at this early stage of the war fraternizing between the pickets was not unheard of. At one juncture, however, according to *New Orleans Delta* reporter Montgomery, the Confederate military authorities discovered a plot by the enemy to use gifts of whisky to soften up the Confederate pickets, and issued orders to suspend any further communication between the picket lines.[43]

The culinary arrangements for breakfast in the army were the subject of a letter *Charleston Mercury* correspondent Courtenay addressed to his paper from Centreville in October 1861. Courtenay was rather less than impressed by the process of army bread-making do-it-yourself style. He described how the raw flour was mixed with water and greased with bacon fat to make a loaf that when baked in the oven, was "brown outside, raw inside, and only palatable on account of the grease—otherwise it would choke you." Courtenay wanted to know why well-baked bread was not supplied to all the soldiers in the army, but encountered only a blank look from the officers when he told them about the portable sheet iron ovens used for this purpose by the French in the Crimea. The various primitive methods of grinding coffee in the army interested and slightly appalled him, and he could not forbear mentioning by way of comparison that even the "detested Yankee" issued ground coffee to the men in paper packages of one ration each.[44]

One of the best products of Courtenay's reporting from Virginia during the fall and early winter of 1861 was a feature story about military road-building. Courtenay stated that the amount of daily transportation about the camp to provide the soldiers with the necessary rations was almost incredible. Moreover, he was impressed with the cheery teamwork manifested by former merchants, professional men, and spare-built townsfolk in keeping open the roads in country where, after a light shower of rain, a team and wagon could easily become mired six to ten inches deep.[45]

I mean such as are equal in quality—but disadvantageous to the better troops, when the parties are not equal in quality. . . . So don't let our men teach our adversaries to fight—or make them less afraid of whizzing bullets." J.E.B. Stuart Papers, Huntington Library.

[43] *New Orleans Sunday Delta*, September 29, 1861.

[44] *Charleston Mercury*, November 4, 5, 1861.

[45] *Ibid.*, November 20, 1861. After his return to Charleston toward the end of the year, Courtenay, who had been the business manager of the newspaper before he became its war correspondent, provided the *Mercury* with a ten- to twelve-column story of the disastrous fire that destroyed a large portion of the city on

In commenting on camp recreation the army reporters told about the various kinds of army sports, dances, convivial dinners among the officer corps, concerts, and serenades. "Personne," in describing the range of sporting activity, discoursed on the popularity of racing between men, mules, crack horses, and even greased pigs; told anecdotes about the horseplay between the soldiers and the good humor of the victims; and made mention of blindfold attempts to stick a hot poker into a target. With feminine dance partners almost nonexistent, officers and enlisted men would sometimes dance together in what the men jestingly referred to as "grasshopper soirees."[46]

Having ridden up to Dumfries on the Potomac River to observe movements on the Confederate right, *Dispatch* correspondent Shepardson was an interested spectator at a dance in a private home. The refreshments consisted of a shoulder of mutton, a few boxes of sardines, some fresh fish, and a few other meager tidbits; the orchestra was a good-natured volunteer who played the fiddle. Although the evening passed pleasantly enough, at one point the organizer of the dance wanted to know of Shepardson:

"Does this not remind you of Brussels before the battle of Waterloo?"

"We are indeed dancing in the face of the enemy," agreed Shepardson. "What would you do should we hear the sound of his guns?"

Shepardson's hostess did not appear intimidated, nor did she err on the side of politeness. "I would stay to see our victory; for I have too much confidence in the brave men between me and the enemy to believe they can be driven back."[47]

Humor sometimes flavored the reporter's recital of the leisure time pursuits of camp life. On one occasion Shepardson was at Fairfax when the band of the First Virginia Regiment serenaded one of the

December 11-12, 1861, the most complete account that appeared in any Southern newspaper. During the postwar years Courtenay came to public attention again as the "earthquake mayor" of the city from 1879 to 1887. *Charleston Mercury*, December 12-16, 1861; *Charleston News and Courier*, March 18, 1908; *Year Book*, City of Charleston, 1908, p. 365.

[46] *Charleston Daily Courier*, October 18, 1861. For other reportorial comments on army recreation see *Richmond Daily Dispatch*, November 13, 1861; *Savannah Republican*, November 9, 1861; *New Orleans Daily Delta*, November 12, 1861; *Atlanta Daily Southern Confederacy*, September 8, 1861. Diet and recreation in Johnston's army in 1861 are discussed in B. I. Wiley, *The Life of Johnny Reb* (Indianapolis and New York, 1943), pp. 90, 151ff.

[47] *Richmond Daily Dispatch*, November 28, 1861.

generals. According to Shepardson, the whole town turned out to listen to the sweet music on a night so quiet one could almost hear the beating of his own heart. "After the band had ceased, a fine tenor voice commenced singing a low ditty under the window of a fair-faced girl. . . . The sash was thrown up and the fair face testified her pleasure by her appearance on the stage. A crowd began to collect around, and the young man went on from song to song, gaining in confidence and enthusiasm every moment, and finally struck up that beautiful air from the Bohemian Girl, "Then you'll remember me." . . . But there were those among the listeners who did not appreciate the music as much as we did, for a soldier interrupted the song by shouting at the top of his voice: "He's a married man! he's a married man!" This sudden descent from the sublime to the ridiculous changed the scene completely. In popped the fair face; down crashed the window; the wicked soldier laughed all the way from his boots, and the mortified minstrel ended his tenor solo in basso curses."[48]

Gustavus Smith, Earl Van Dorn, and the cavalry leader Jeb Stuart were among the generals to whom the army correspondents applied their descriptive talents. Both de Fontaine and Shepardson provided their newspapers with pen portraits of Stuart, with "Personne" expressing the conviction, "there is not a more interesting individual occupying a share of the public attention at this moment than Col. Stuart. . . ." De Fontaine was struck with Stuart's handsome physique (which reminded him of Garibaldi), his well-developed head, clear blue eyes, and alertness. The reporter expressed the opinion that "no man in the South is more hated and more feared by the Yankees" than Stuart. "Personne" more or less accurately prophesied that the dashing soldier would yet fill a niche in two categories, "first with his trusty sabre upon some flying Yankee's caput, and second, with his proud untarnished name in the temple of Southern freedom."[49] Shepardson described Stuart in similar language, commenting on the excellent horsemanship, "that I have never seen excelled except by Captain Nolan, who was killed at the battle of Balaklava during Lord Cardigan's famous charge." Shepardson went on to say that during Stuart's period of active service he had never been caught napping nor had he failed in any plan that he had attempted. "If I do not have some-

[48] *Ibid.*, October 9, 1861.
[49] *Charleston Daily Courier*, September 21, 1861.

thing further to record of him before many weeks, it will greatly surprise me."[50]

To keep themselves otherwise occupied the Confederate reporters
composed vignettes of the points of military interest in the war zone:
Manassas Junction, Centreville, Falls Church, Munson's Hill, and Dumfries. In the language of an *Atlanta Confederacy* correspondent, Manassas Junction was neither a city nor a village but simply a railroad
junction with three or four houses, a shoe shop, a post office, and a
telegraph office situated in the boxcar of a passenger train. Another reporter described the telegraph office as consisting of two cars placed at
right angles to each other. In one car was the battery and in the other
a sending and receiving room which served as a dining room by day
and a dormitory by night for the busy operators. "From early morning
until far into the night the steady click of the instrument is heard, and
the busy operators are seen intently engaged upon their work unmind-
ful of the noise and din without. . . . The chief operator here is Mr.
Barnes, who has two assistants, and as can be easily supposed, the three
are kept as busy as bees."[51]

On a visit to Centreville in October 1861, Thompson of the *Memphis
Appeal* observed the contrast between the appearance of the town by
night, with its campfires and tent lanterns causing it to look like a vast
crowded city, and the scene the next morning when it had lost its
metropolitan aspect in spite of the numerous white tents with which it
was surrounded. Thompson pictured Centreville as "a long straggling
street, with dilapidated houses at considerable intervals, the roadway
very much obstructed by rocks . . . camps all around, horses hitched to
every rail of the tumble-down fences . . . small specimens of 'peculiar institution,' other 'contraband of war' peddling chickens and chestnuts. . . ."[52]

To a *Dispatch* correspondent Falls Church resembled nothing so
much as Goldsmith's deserted village, with a majority of its houses
having been closed up by their Northern owners after the defeat of
McDowell's army at Bull Run, and in some cases reopened for Confederate soldiers.[53]

[50] *Richmond Daily Dispatch*, October 8, 1861.
[51] *Atlanta Daily Southern Confederacy*, September 7, 1861; *Richmond Daily
Dispatch*, September 16, 1861.
[52] *Memphis Daily Appeal*, November 8, 1861.
[53] *Richmond Daily Dispatch*, September 11, 1861.

How "Personne" and Shepardson obtained their first view of Dumfries was explained in a letter which Shepardson mailed to the *Dispatch* shortly after the middle of October. While on their way from Centreville to Manassas in search of something better than camp fare, the two reporters heard a dull, booming sound coming from the direction of the Confederate batteries on the lower Potomac.

"There's a gun," said "Personne," as he quietly smoked his Havana, "and another, and another, and another."

"They are rolling ten-pins down on the river," quipped Shepardson.

"And there's a ten-stroke," ejaculated the *Courier* man as a Columbiad emptied its contents and caused the hills to vibrate with its tremendous report."

"Shall we go down?"

"Agreed!"

Ten minutes later the two reporters were in the saddle on their way to Occoquan. The morning was wet and disagreeable. Galloping between sunshine and shower, beneath giant elms, through oak forests, and past dark perennial pines, the pair reached Dumfries that evening, covered with the dirtiest kind of mud, their horses jaded and bespattered. From every man, woman, and child in the town they inquired about the newsworthy happenings in the vicinity, but the success of their undertaking was in inverse proportion to the distance they had travelled. Finally they caught up with a strange-looking person wearing an immense ante-revolutionary white hat and bestride a mule that would have passed in a menagerie for a wild beast. "Personne" hailed him:

"My friend, what was the firing about this morning?"

"Wall, I dun 'no, reckon they're firing at the Yanks. I heard they landed down by Occoquan."

"But do you know anything about it?"—with a peculiar emphasis on the word *know*.

"Nary time," was the facetious reply.

The correspondents discovered later that the occasion for the cannonading had been the capture of a couple of Federal schooners bound upstream for Washington with provisions and stores.[54]

In one of his subsequent letters, Shepardson described the town of Dumfries, where only about twenty residences remained to mark the

[54] *Ibid.*, October 24, 28, 1861.

site of a flourishing city of 10,000 inhabitants two generations before.[55] The faded glories of Dumfries were also the theme of a letter from Da Ponte which the *New Orleans Delta* published in mid-December. Three and a half miles below the town were the Evansport batteries, used by the Confederates to block the navigation of the Potomac River; it was rumored that General McClellan was about to launch an attack on them. In the parlor of the old tavern in Dumfries, Da Ponte encountered Senator Wigfall of Texas, who was now a general with headquarters (which was in the tavern). After a late dinner Da Ponte received a military briefing from the senator-turned-general. Wigfall explained the nature of the terrain, the preparations that had been made to throw back the enemy, the forces apportioned to this part of the Confederate line, and other particulars. As a result Da Ponte came to the conclusion, which the general no doubt wanted him to derive, that the enemy would have a difficult time dispersing the Confederate forces stationed in the area.[56]

During the autumn of 1861 the incidence of infectious diseases—measles, mumps, and typhoid fever in particular—was high among the Confederate troops in Virginia, many of them recruited from rural areas where resistance to such diseases was low. The Confederate press made no attempt to suppress this information. Indeed, the alarming extent of camp sickness, the lack of camp sanitation (which no doubt was a factor), and the delinquencies of the medical department figured prominently in the army correspondence of that period. Writing from Richmond on August 14, *Charleston Courier* correspondent "Joan" estimated that at Charlottesville and Culpeper there were over three thousand soldiers under the care of physicians. About two weeks later a Richmond correspondent of the *Mobile Register* placed the number of Confederate wounded and sick at fifteen thousand. In letters describing these conditions, reporters stressed the need for improved army diet, called on governors and mayors of cities to raise funds for army hospitals, and sounded the call for a reorganization of the army's medical department.[57]

[55] *Ibid.*, November 26, 1861.
[56] *New Orleans Daily Delta*, December 12, 1861.
[57] *Charleston Daily Courier*, August 17, 1861; *Mobile Daily Advertiser and Register*, September 4, 1861. Alluding to the apparent surprise of the Northern press at the publicity given to army sickness in the Confederate newspapers, the editor of the *Richmond Examiner* boasted that "the Southern papers, and letter writers, and Southern officials, tell the whole truth about the condition of their

In some instances reporters found that illness was caused by a soldier's carelessness. Courtenay of the *Charleston Mercury* was present when a soldier burst into a regimental surgeon's tent about midnight with the plea, "Doctor, Oh Doctor! —— is dying and wants you to come and see him." While the surgeon unrolled his woolens and began to dress, questioning as to the case proceeded.

"What does he complain of?"

"He's very bad off, Doctor!"

"What has he been eating?"

"Don't know, Doctor."

"Went down to Manassas yesterday?"

"Yes, Sir."

"Eat raw corn on the way back?"

"Believe so, sir."

The doctor started out with a shawl about him and was back in about twenty minutes. His patient had gone down from Centreville to the Junction, eaten and drunk a variety of things, had returned to camp and eaten half a dozen "dodgers" and as many half-roasted ears of corn, and as a natural consequence was about to "die" during the night. He did not die, however, and was very penitent the next day.[58]

As it became apparent that the war was going to last through the winter, the army reporters began to point up the need for blankets and warm clothing for the army. Alexander was the first of the army newspapermen to present the problem, and in October, Courtenay addressed an angry letter to the *Mercury*, accusing the Confederate States of America of being the only nation in the civilized world that failed to do justice to its soldiers by furnishing them clothing. Da Ponte made similar allegations with regard to the attire of the Louisiana troops.[59]

Such complaints were part of a general press campaign against abuses in army administration. The brunt of the criticism fell on the Commissary and Quartermaster's Departments. Alexander wrote bitterly of army baggage literally rotting at Manassas from insufficient

---

army, whether good or bad, favourable or unfavourable, and thus the people of the South are at all times informed of the real condition of affairs." *Daily Richmond Examiner*, September 25, 1861. See also H. H. Cunningham, *Doctors in Gray* (Baton Rouge, 1958), pp. 45-46, 188.

[58] *Charleston Mercury*, November 5, 1861.

[59] *Savannah Republican*, September 24, 1861; *Charleston Mercury*, October 26, 1861; *New Orleans Daily Delta*, November 22, 1861.

protection against the weather. After he had left the army to return home for the winter, he unleashed a full-scale attack on such abuses. In particular, he accused the Quartermaster's Department of having impressed all the transportation and forage in the counties adjacent to Manassas, thereby creating hardship among the local farmers, who were left without equipment to grow another crop. As for the Commissary Department, he pointed out: "the hides taken from the cattle slaughtered for the use of the army will shoe the army; the tallow will light the army, while the oil from the feet is sufficient to keep all the harness, wagons and artillery in good order. As it is, not half of the hides are saved in proper condition while four-fifths of the tallow and all the oil is wasted. In the meantime, the Government is paying large sums for shoes, harness and candles."

Alexander reserved some of his plainest language for the shortcomings of the Medical Department. Its administration, he contended, was "not only stupid but brutal. In former letters I have spoken of the ignorance and criminal negligence of regimental surgeons, many of whom have had no practical experience in surgery, and who in a whole year never had as many cases as they are frequently called upon to visit every day in the army." He went on to deplore the meager supply of certain important medicines which the Medical Department insisted on trying to obtain from Richmond, where the prices were highest and the supply smallest, although, he claimed, such medicines were readily available elsewhere in the Confederacy. "Meanwhile the best and bravest men who ever drew a sword are dying for want of these medicines."[60]

THE Confederate press depended almost exclusively on volunteer correspondents and the telegraph for coverage of military operations in western Virginia. In May 1861 a Federal force under General McClellan had gotten the jump on the Confederates by occupying Grafton, an important railroad junction 175 miles west of Harper's Ferry by rail. Early in June the Confederates were defeated at Philippi, fifteen miles south of Grafton. To meet the serious threat to Confederate rail connections with western Virginia, Lee's adjutant general, Col. Robert

---

[60] *Savannah Republican*, December 5, 20, 1861. Deficiencies in the Confederate Commissary Department were vigorously attacked by the *Richmond Examiner* in October 1861. The shortages of drugs and medicine in the South during the war are discussed in M. E. Massey, *Ersatz in the Confederacy* (Columbia, S.C., 1952), pp. 115-23.

S. Garnett, was commissioned a brigadier general and dispatched to the Allegheny Mountains area. Early in July, with an ample force General McClellan attacked Garnett at Rich Mountain, outflanked him, and defeated him at Carrick's Ford on July 13 in a battle in which Garnett was killed.[61]

Three days later the first news of the defeat reached Richmond by telegraph through Louisville and by the more direct, but less expeditious, route via Staunton.[62] The first detailed stories were reprints from the Cincinnati papers. Not until July 27 was the *Richmond Dispatch* able to publish an account from its own special correspondent "Ned," dated at McDowell, Virginia, four days earlier.

Having placed Brig.Gen. W. W. Loring in temporary command in northwestern Virginia to replace Garnett, Lee left Richmond for western Virginia on the morning of July 28. His mission, the subject of speculation on the part of the Richmond correspondents, was to reorganize an offensive in the Cheat Mountain area and diminish the rivalry between Brig.Generals John B. Floyd and Henry A. Wise in the Kanawha region. "Personne" had written a flattering piece on Lee for the *Courier's* readers early in May.[63] And now as Lee was departing from Richmond to perform his first field duty for the Confederacy, Thompson of the *Memphis Appeal* recorded his impressions of the general, whom he noted the Southern people had heard very little about during the past three months.

"His life, since he assumed the chief command of the Virginia forces, has been a model of soldierly patience and energy and watchfulness. Six o'clock in the morning has seen him regularly enter his office, which, with rare exceptions, he has not left, save at meal times, till eleven at night. A man of few words, of unvarying courtesy, but of a singularly cold and distant manner, he has kept his own counsels with more than the impenetrable secrecy of Louis Napoleon, and no one has dared to trifle with his time upon unimportant or frivolous mis-

---

[61] D. S. Freeman, *R. E. Lee, A Biography* (New York and London, 1934), I, 503-504, 519-20, 532-34; Frank Klement, "General John B. Floyd and the West Virginia Campaign of 1861," *West Virginia History*, VIII (April 1947), 319-21.

[62] *Memphis Daily Appeal*, July 21, 1861.

[63] *Charleston Daily Courier*, May 14, 1861. "Personne" singled out as Lee's most prominent features his "broad, expansive forehead . . . fine profile . . . keen expressive dark brown eye . . . nose, slightly on the Roman style of architecture . . . and a mouth full of spirit and determination." He described Lee's manners as "affable, courteous, and refined" and his dress as consisting of plain black clothes with an old felt hat, which "nine times out of ten, is knocked in on one side."

sions. If the visitor had business, he was requested to state it in the briefest or most direct way; if he came through sheer curiosity to see the man, or converse with him idly about public affairs, Gen. Lee excused himself so promptly and coolly that he never ventured to call again."[64]

The retreat of the First Georgia Regiment from Rich Mountain to Monterey after the Battle of Carrick's Ford was the subject of an interesting letter by a special correspondent of the *Atlanta Southern Confederacy*, which the *Confederacy* did not publish until August 17. The correspondent, J. N. Bass, told of the regiment marching a hundred miles through the most difficult country in five days and four nights with nothing to eat during all that time. He also described the large amount of sickness in camp and the unauthorized action of the colonel in furloughing the members of his sick regiment for a period of thirty days, an act of humanity which exposed him to the hazards of a court-martial.

Lee's efforts to recapture the Cheat Mountain stronghold failed; then the news spotlight shifted south to the Kanawha area, where Floyd and Wise, both of them former politicians, held quasi-independent commands with the sanction of Jefferson Davis. Floyd, who had arrived in western Virginia in mid-July with a brigade of riflemen, was assured favorable publicity by the presence of several newspaper editors on his staff. One of these was John M. Daniel of the *Richmond Examiner*, who left his newspaper in the charge of the former Collector of the Port of San Francisco, L. Q. Washington, while he went off to the wars.[65]

The second of Floyd's editors, Maj. Robert Henry Glass of the *Lynchburg Republican*, arrived in camp just in time to report the Battle of Cross Lanes for his newspaper. After considerable quarreling between Floyd and Wise over the issue of uniting their commands, Floyd on August 26 surprised the Seventh Ohio at Cross Lanes and defeated it roundly without any assistance from his rival. In trenchant prose Glass described the opening of the action:

"At 4 o'clock A.M., the Brigade was in motion, and the clear ring of the General's stentorian voice was heard along the lines in the fresh morning air like the blast of a trumpet. We were all instantly to our

---

[64] *Memphis Daily Appeal*, August 6, 1861.

[65] *Ibid.*, September 24, 1861. Subsequently Washington left the *Examiner* to become Confederate Assistant Secretary of State.

arms and to our saddles, and advanced rapidly, at double quick. A heavy fog hung over the hills and along the valleys, and we approached almost upon the enemy's pickets before they saw us. They fired and ran, distinctly in our view, and not a hundred yards in our advance. Our men gave a shout at that sort of music, and dashed on with accelerated speed. In a few minutes we discovered the blue coats of the enemy, as they stood drawn up near a church by the road side, while to our right and behind a fence stood another column of the enemy."[66]

Glass went on to depict the charge of the two Confederate regiments across a cornfield and to a still higher eminence where the sharpest part of the conflict ensued. As artillery was hurried to the front, the enemy broke into full retreat, and the pursuit was continued for some eight or ten miles. Glass was astonished at how few were killed and wounded in proportion to the number of shots fired in battle. "As we rode through the field this morning, the enemy's bullets could be heard cutting through the corn and whistling by your ears as thick as hail, and yet but few of our men were touched. The calculation recently made by some one, that it requires seven hundred balls to kill one man is really true, though the calculation is not of much consolation to the poor fellow who gets the fatal shot."[67]

Glass was also present at Carnifex Ferry two weeks later when one of Rosecrans' Federal brigade commanders prematurely attacked Floyd and was repulsed by the Confederates. Glass's account of the fighting was considerably briefer than his report of Cross Lanes, though it was not inaccurate. Moreover, he was highly complimentary in telling about Floyd's withdrawal to the south side of the Gauley River, which he termed "as brilliant a success as our defense. We lost in this movement not a man, a gun or a wagon, and would not have lost a single article, had not the removal of our large number of sick required the use of an unusual portion of our means of transportation. The road was terrible, and wide enough only for the passage of a single wagon, while the rapid and rugged Gauley had to be crossed on two flat-boats and a temporary foot bridge, just completed on the

---

[66] *Lynchburg Daily Republican,* September 5, 1861. Glass, whose son Carter was destined for a distinguished public career as Secretary of the Treasury and United States Senator from Virginia, was of Scotch-Irish stock, "a rather spare man of medium height, perhaps five feet, ten inches, with reddish brown hair, bright, penetrating brown eyes, [and] prominent nose." Rixey Smith and Norman Beasley, *Carter Glass, a Biography* (New York and Toronto, 1939), pp. 4-12.

[67] *Lynchburg Daily Republican,* September 5, 1861.

morning of the fight. The feat was accomplished in less than five hours, and in the darkness of the night."

At the close of his letter Glass described the adverse conditions under which it had been written. The rough sheets on which it was scrawled had been given to him, he said, by a lady along the road, and a bad pencil had traced the lines with nothing but a fence rail for a desk. "Besides, they are written upon an empty stomach, with the prospect of it becoming much emptier before our tents are pitched and our supper prepared."[68]

Following the battle, Floyd continued his retreat from the Gauley, preceded by Wise, to Big Sewell Mountain, a distance of at least twenty miles. From there Glass wrote a long letter to the *Republican* describing the mountain scenery.[69] Then, after a conference with Wise, Floyd withdrew twelve miles farther to Meadow Bluff, where he could not easily be flanked by Rosecrans' superior numbers. Glass reported the retreat, which took place by night, graphically enlarging on the rain which fell in torrents, thoroughly drenching the marchers. The experience induced him to philosophize on camp life with its numerous tests of human patience and endurance.

"Clean linen here once a week is a great luxury, and a shirt which has never felt starch or the polish of an iron makes a man feel proud and 'better than other people.' For silver spoons we have pewter; for china cups and plate, tin; saucers, none; table-cloth, none; cream, none; vegetables, none. Good beef and tolerable bread, with a cup of creamless coffee constitute our principal fare, at breakfast, dinner and supper. Those who are so fortunate as to pick up an occasional chicken by the wayside, kill it before getting to camp, for fear its squall may attract the attention of the nearest mess, and make them guests for the next meal."[70]

At the end of September news reached the public in Richmond of the acrimonious disharmony between Generals Floyd and Wise, and on the twenty-seventh Glass reported the recall of Wise to Richmond, leaving the "Wise Legion" to be turned over to General Floyd.[71] That same morning a storm hit Floyd's camp, dashing tents to the earth, washing away bridges, and obliterating roads. Glass and his tent mate,

[68] *Ibid.*, September 21, 1861.
[69] *Ibid.*, September 24, 1861.
[70] *Ibid.*, September 26, 1861.
[71] *Ibid.*, October 5, 1861. See also *New Orleans Daily Picayune*, October 13, 1861.

a certain Captain W., kept themselves tolerably dry by propping their tent poles during the height of the storm, but when they looked for an alcoholic stimulant they found that there was not a drop in the camp. In the midst of the storm their young messmate bravely volunteered to get some from a point a mile away. Donning his oil cloth trappings and mounting his horse, he dashed off on his errand. After heroically fording several artificial streams created by the torrent, he returned with the disheartening tidings of "nary a drop." As a result the tent mates had to retire to bed and make the most of the warmth of their blankets for the night.[72]

At the end of October Glass left the army and returned to Lynchburg. His excellent war reporting, widely reprinted in newspapers throughout the Confederacy, had added color to a drab campaign which ended with disappointing results for the Confederates. There was no indication of this, however, in the "thank you" letter Glass addressed to Floyd after his return home. Glass assured Floyd that having conversed with great numbers of people at Richmond and in other parts of the state, he had heard no other opinion expressed than that "you are the best General in the mountains—that your campaign has been the most energetic & brilliant of any & that had you been left to yourself & been properly supported by the govt. in men the enemy would have been expelled the Valley before you."[73]

On the other hand, the military reputation of Lee was under a cloud because of his failure to bag Rosecrans. Bagby, the Richmond correspondent of the *Charleston Mercury*, set the tone for newspaper criticism in a letter whose opening sentence was, "Poor Lee! Rosecrans has fooled him again." "Are the roads any worse for Lee than Rosecrans?" asked Bagby, who went on to say: "The people are getting mighty sick of this dilly-dally, dirt digging, scientific warfare; so much so that they will demand that the Great Entrencher be brought back and permitted to pay court to the ladies."[74]

Lee responded in rather mild fashion to such newspaper jibes. "I am sorry, as you say," he confided to Mrs. Lee, "that the movements of our armies cannot keep pace with the expectations of the editors of the papers. I know they can arrange things satisfactory to themselves

[72] *Lynchburg Daily Republican*, October 5, 1861.

[73] R. H. Glass to Brig.Gen. John B. Floyd, November 13, 1861, John B. Floyd Papers, Duke University.

[74] *Charleston Mercury*, October 14, 1861.

118

on paper. I wish they could do so in the field. No one wishes them more success than I do, and would be happy to see them have full swing."[75]

By the middle of November John M. Daniel was back in Richmond, and the western Virginia campaign, essentially barren of result, was over.

CAMPAIGN reporting in the West during 1861 was mainly in Kentucky and Tennessee.[76] From the beginning of the war until September, Kentucky preserved an uneasy neutrality while both opponents bid for the state's support. At Cairo, Illinois, a point of concentration for Federal troops, the *Memphis Argus* in August had a special correspondent making note of his observations of the enemy "at the risk of his neck."[77] About the same time the *New Orleans Picayune* sent north a member of its staff, Samuel C. Reid, to take soundings of public opinion in Kentucky. After spending some time in Louisville and other parts of the state, Reid came to the conclusion that a majority of Kentuckians favored the Confederate cause, but a majority of the citizens of Louisville were for the North "some from principle, and many from policy."[78]

On September 3, 1861 Kentucky's breathing spell came to an end when Maj.Gen. Leonidas Polk occupied Columbus, an important strategic point on the Mississippi River. The Federal commander, Brig.Gen. U. S. Grant, reacted by moving up the Ohio from Cairo to take possession of Paducah at the mouth of the Cumberland River, and Brig.Gen. Robert Anderson, who had been recruiting Kentucky volunteers for the Union army, transferred his headquarters from Cincinnati to Louisville on September 7. Before the month was out the Louisville agent for Pritchard's Associated Press was arrested by the Federal authorities and incarcerated at Fort Warren in Boston Harbor, and his office was closed.[79]

[75] Robert E. Lee to his wife, October 7, 1861 as reprinted in Freeman, *Lee*, I, 598.

[76] Apparently Price's Missouri campaign received very scant coverage in the Confederate press. Reporters at Columbus, Kentucky, gave incidental attention to the activities of the bushwhacker "Jeff" Thompson in southeastern Missouri. See e.g. *Charleston Mercury*, September 12, 1861; *Memphis Daily Appeal*, November 1, 1861.

[77] *Mobile Daily Advertiser and Register*, August 9, 1861.

[78] *New Orleans Daily Picayune*, August 15, September 4, 5, 1861.

[79] *Wilmington* (N.C.) *Daily Journal*, September 26, 1861. On June 11, 1861 the

About the middle of September Gen. Albert Sidney Johnston, then commonly regarded as the South's best general, arrived in Nashville from Richmond to take command in the West. Indicating his approval of Polk's occupation of Columbus, he dispatched Brig.Gen. Simon P. Buckner with a force of 4,000 to occupy Bowling Green, Kentucky, on the main line of the Louisville and Nashville Railroad. To Cumberland Gap at the other end of the Kentucky-Tennessee line, Johnston sent Brig.Gen. Felix K. Zollicoffer with a force of 3,000 to 4,000 men.[80]

Israel Gibbons of the *New Orleans Crescent* was at Columbus on September 19 when Johnston arrived there to confer with Polk and inspect his fortifications. "His arrival was a source of universal joy," reported Gibbons. "Last night he was splendidly serenaded, and in response made a stirring speech—so I am told—for I could not be present though I could distinctly hear the music and excitement at our camp on the hill."[81] After remaining a few days at Columbus, Johnston moved on to Bowling Green, where he established his headquarters. It was at this latter point that a correspondent of one of the Tennessee papers saw Johnston about a month later and improvised a flattering description. According to the reporter Johnston was "a prompt, decisive man, possessing an indomitable will and the greatest tenacity of purpose. . . . In age, he is perhaps a little the turn of fifty. He is the very picture of good health. He is considerably above the medium size. He is heavy set, but not the least corpulent. His hair is dark, and not being cut closely, exhibits a tendency to curl a little. He has a deep-set, dark and piercing eye. In general appearance, he is self-reliant, bold, and dauntless, exhibiting the hero of leonine courage and unquailing energy."[82]

From Columbus *Crescent* reporter Gibbons wrote a series of letters to his newspaper during the fall and winter of 1861, portraying in folksy style the everyday life of the Confederate soldier in the West during military inactivity. Gibbons' conception of his function as a reporter was well expressed in a letter he wrote to the *Crescent* during the first week of December. In it he indicated awareness of the curiosity of his readers about the likelihood of an enemy attack on Columbus.

Memphis Daily Appeal had identified Barr as "the special and recognized agent of the New Orleans Associated Press" at Louisville.

[80] S. F. Horn, *The Army of Tennessee* (Norman, Okla., 1941), pp. 55-56; J. H. Parks, *General Leonidas Polk, C.S.A.* (Baton Rouge, 1962), pp. 185-86.

[81] *New Orleans Daily Crescent*, September 25, 1861.

[82] *Nashville Republican Banner*, November 3, 1861.

Yet he disclaimed any intention of investing his opinions with an authority which they did not really possess by intimating that he had breakfasted with Colonel This and dined with General That and had derived his information from the most highly reliable and severely respectable sources. Nor did he seek to display his erudition by launching forth in a labyrinth of possibilities and probabilities as to what the enemy might or might not do in words of "learned length and thundering Sound." "If you wish my opinion as to the probability of an early battle, I answer that I have none, and do not pretend to calculate events one day ahead of the present time. I will just give you such items as float around camp, and from them, if you can, you may form your own opinion."[83]

Gibbons was as good as his word. In one of his most delightful letters he pictured life aboard the steamboat *Charm*, in which he was then ensconced and which Johnston had considered making his temporary headquarters. Aboard the *Charm* on the evening that Gibbons was writing his letter were some attractive Kentucky ladies who had come up from Hickman on a pleasure excursion to see the sights of Columbus. To Gibbons, famished like many a soldier for the sight of a feminine face, the girls appeared "as sweet as preserved peaches." Would the correspondent like to be introduced to them? Fresh from the trenches, Gibbons in his own words looked "as rusty and ugly as an old chestnut burr." And so, recalling the kid gloves, patent leather shoes, white shirts, and other peacetime luxuries he had left behind in New Orleans, he sighed—and declined the invitation.

He stayed for supper, nevertheless, and was amused at the alacrity with which officers from all parts of the camp scrambled aboard to meet the *Charm's* charmers. To prevent the craft from being capsized by the inundation of cocked hat, sword, and spur, the captain stationed the mate and several of his men at the foot of the gangway. It proved impossible to stem the tide, however, so the captain retired to bed in disgust. When Gibbons and the ship's doctor returned to the *Charm* later that evening they found that the military gentlemen were well acquainted with the ladies, and to the tunes of "Rackensack," "Leather Breeches," "Gal on the Log," etc., were shaking themselves in a regular old-fashioned country hoe-down.[84]

On another occasion Gibbons enlivened his reporting with a descrip-

[83] *New Orleans Daily Crescent*, December 11, 1861.
[84] *Ibid.*, October 1, 1861.

tion of a Northern war correspondent who came down the river from Cairo on a gunboat under a flag of truce for an exchange of prisoners. After telling about some of the "official deadheads" on board, Gibbons came to the point of his story, representing that "the gassiest deadhead of all was a chap named Chapman representing himself as reporter and correspondent extraordinary for the *New York Herald.* He was successively social and impudently inquisitive, relating, unasked, his many wonderful experiences, and endeavoring to obtain, in return, some idea of our army around Columbus. But the man who reported the whole of the Charleston Convention, took a ride on the Great Eastern, and saw Douglas die, left Columbus about as wise as he came. I would like to have been aboard to see the animal; they say he is one of the real live Jenkinses of the New York press."[85]

The same flag-of-truce boat provided another Confederate reporter, J. J. Lane of the *New Orleans Delta,* with an anecdote about a newsboy who was offered a half-dollar by a Federal officer for a recent issue of the *Memphis Appeal.* According to the reporter, the boy picked up the coin which the officer had tossed in his direction and remarking that he could afford to *give* the Federal a paper and didn't want any of his damned Yankee money, pitched the coin into the river. This defiant act on the part of one so young evoked a number of hurrahs from the crowd and even smiles from the Federals themselves.[86]

Both Gibbons and Lane were away from Columbus when the only important military action of the year in the Kentucky-Tennessee theater took place. Although it was not much of a battle in comparison with the great struggles of 1862, the Battle of Belmont created a stir quite out of proportion to the numbers engaged and its effect on the military situation.[87]

To prevent the transmission of any reinforcements from Kentucky to the Confederate forces in Missouri, Grant started south from Cairo with five regiments of volunteers on November 6 to make a demonstration near Columbus. On the following morning Polk learned of a Federal landing on the Missouri side of the river north of Belmont, a shabby settlement of three houses and a steamboat landing just across the river from Columbus. As soon as he heard of Grant's movement, Polk sent

[85] *Ibid.,* October 30, 1861. For another view of Frank Chapman several months later see F. B. Wilkie, *Pen and Powder* (Boston, 1888), pp. 111-12.

[86] *New Orleans Daily Delta,* October 29, 1861.

[87] Horn, *Army of Tennessee,* p. 63; Parks, *Polk,* p. 192.

Brig.Gen. Gideon Pillow across the river with four regiments to reinforce the regiment that was already encamped at Belmont. The battle began about 10:30 A.M. when Grant attacked Pillow's pickets.[88]

According to the *Memphis Appeal* reporter the Confederates were in a disadvantageous position, being drawn up in an open field, while the enemy line was partially screened by a wood. Although the raw and inexperienced troops on both sides fought bravely, the Federals gradually pressed the Confederates back to the river bank and took possession of their camp. At this point three more regiments of reinforcements came over from Columbus under Brig.Gen. B. F. Cheatham with Polk accompanying them, and the big Whitworth rifled gun at Columbus began to rake the Federal position. As Grant fell back, Cheatham effected a flanking movement which threw the retreaters into disorder and transformed a withdrawal into a rout.[89]

According to the account of the battle which the *Memphis Avalanche* published:

". . . it was when [the Federals] reached their boats and embarked on L. M. Kennett, supported by their gunboats, that the butchery was most terrific. Packed together on the boat lying at the shore, in dense masses, Smith's [Confederate] regiment poured on them for half an hour, from a distance of only eighty yards, an incessant fire. An immense number were killed and wounded, the gutters around the boat filled with torrents of blood, which crimsoned the river around for a considerable distance, and the decks so slippery the men could scarcely stand. Those who approached the wheel were shot down as fast as they appeared so that they were compelled to move the boat into the stream without guidance."[90]

In Memphis, the hometown of about three thousand of Polk's soldiers, the news of the battle created intense excitement. From an early hour on November 8 the Memphis telegraph office was crowded with an eager multitude wanting to know, "What's the news?" As they waited private dispatches came through with laconic messages such as "I am safe" or so-and-so "is badly wounded," but nothing about the battle. Between ten and eleven o'clock that morning, the *Appeal* issued an extra containing an interesting letter from the scene of the

[88] Horn, *Army of Tennessee*, p. 64.

[89] *Memphis Daily Appeal* as reprinted in Frank Moore, *The Rebellion Record* (New York, 1862), III, 295-96.

[90] *Memphis Daily Avalanche* as reprinted in Moore, *Rebellion Record*, III, 297-98.

battle and a few particulars gleaned from passengers on the down train from Columbus, which partly allayed the excitement.[91]

A correspondent of the *New Orleans Picayune* censured the accounts of the battle that appeared in the Memphis papers because they overlooked the part played in the fighting by the Eleventh Louisiana Regiment. Also, the *Memphis Argus* exposed itself to criticism from one of the Nashville papers for an editorial blasting General Polk for having been surprised by the enemy at Belmont.[92] Not surprisingly, the Confederate newspaper accounts of the battle generally minimized their own losses and magnified that of the enemy.

A few days after the battle, Lane of the *New Orleans Delta* accompanied a flag-of-truce expedition to Cairo to effect another exchange of prisoners. He wryly commented that the expedition was "a rather dry one," the Federals withholding the champagne refreshments that had been distributed to them when they visited Columbus. Lane also concluded that the result of the battle had made their hosts all rather taciturn and morose. Before he returned to Columbus, he managed to secure copies of Northern newspapers that gave the Northern version of the battle. Apparently Lane did not get to see Grant on this occasion, but later he reported a meeting of Generals Polk and Grant halfway between Cairo and Columbus which enabled him to limn a cursory pen picture of the enemy commander. Lane described Grant as "a good looking, apparently even-tempered man with dark chesnut hair and blue eyes. He is about five feet nine or ten inches high and weighs about 160 pounds. His full name is Ulysses S. Grant."[93]

Apart from some reporting of Zollicoffer's movements in eastern Tennessee[94] in semi-humorous vein by Albert Roberts, the "John Hap-

[91] *Memphis Daily Appeal*, November 9, 1861; Robert Talley, *One Hundred Years of the Commercial Appeal, 1840-1940* (Memphis, 1940), pp. 17-18. The refusal of the Confederate authorities to permit news about the battle to be sent over the telegraph lines between Columbus and Memphis for a period of forty-eight hours after the battle was the subject of an indignant editorial in the *Appeal* of November 10, 1861.

[92] *Nashville Republican Banner*, November 15, 1861.

[93] *New Orleans Daily Delta*, November 17, 19, 1861.

[94] See e.g. *Nashville Republican Banner*, July 30, 31, August 13, 20, 22, October 22, 30, 1861. Another war correspondent who reported from the East Tennessee area at this time was T. D. Wright of the *Atlanta Southern Confederacy*. Writing from Greenville, Tenn. on November 30, 1861, Wright reported an amusing conversation with an elderly Tennessee woman illustrative of the ignorance of the mountain folk about military matters. *Atlanta Daily Southern Confederacy*, December 8, 1861.

py" of the *Nashville Banner,* Confederate reporting in the West for 1861 was now virtually completed. Much of the reporting had been not much more than a training exercise for the campaigns that were yet to come. Yet the reporters with the western army had received a foretaste of the suffering and privation that were to be their lot as the war entered a deadlier phase in 1862.

CHAPTER 5

Alexander Exposes a "Lost Opportunity"

RELATIVELY FEW Confederate war correspondents were on the scene to report the opening of the 1862 campaign in the West. No reporter of any consequence was in the vicinity of Bowling Green, Kentucky, the headquarters of the Western Department, nor at Forts Henry and Donelson in Tennessee, which were soon to become the center of some important fighting. Apparently the New Orleans editors regarded Columbus, Kentucky, where Johnston still had a force of 17,000 troops under the command of General Polk, as a more important center of war news. At any rate, three New Orleans war correspondents, J. J. Lane of the *Delta*, Israel Gibbons of the *Crescent*, and a *Picayune* reporter who gave no other clue to his identity than the initials "A.M.," were in Columbus during January, sharing quarters at the home of the Jollee family and engaging in friendly competition for news.[1]

They do not seem to have been as apprehensive about a Federal attack from the direction of Cairo as General Pillow had been before he left town in a huff after a quarrel with General Polk. But life in Columbus for soldier or newspaperman was far from being luxurious or comfortable, as Gibbons made clear in a letter that he mailed to his newspaper on January 17. Scarcities of every kind were the theme of his semi-humorous complaint—bacon, coffee, and edible beef, blankets, boots, and stationery of any kind. Forage for horses and mules was in short supply, and as for the straw for man and beast specified in army regulations, "not a wisp" was in sight. Gibbons reported that as a result of the shortage of hay ". . . the horses and mules suffer much from colics and lampers, and gnaw and chew everything they can get their noses at. Many of the wagon-bodies are almost entirely eaten up. . . . The mules can't be held by rope halters; they chew themselves loose, and eat up the poles and stumps they are hitched to; pen them up, and they will eat through the fence. . . . There is an epicurean mule in our battalion, who, whenever he gets loose, goes around chewing the horses' tails. . . . I call him the old fool mule, for he has the face of a prize-fighter, from kicks administered by horses who don't wish their tails

[1] *New Orleans Daily Crescent*, February 15, 1862.

126

barberized."[2] Apparently Gibbons' plaintive description of the privations of men and mules at Columbus touched a chord of pity among his newspaper readers. About three weeks later there arrived in camp a lambswool scarf knitted by Miss Bettie N. of Claiborne Parish, Louisiana, and addressed to the Western Military Correspondent of the *New Orleans Daily Crescent.*[3]

When fighting erupted in mid-January it took place not at Columbus but at the opposite end of Albert Sidney Johnston's long line from Indian Territory west of the Mississippi to the barrens of eastern Kentucky. The setting was the bend of the Cumberland River, about seventy miles northwest of Cumberland Gap. There, near a place called Mill Springs, a force of about 4,000 Confederates under the joint command of a West Pointer named George Crittenden and former Congressman Zollicoffer faced a Union division of about 5,000. A dawn surprise attack on January 19 by Zollicoffer miscarried. The Confederate commander rode too close to a Union regiment which he confused with one of his own and was shot down. A Federal counterattack routed the Confederates and drove them pell-mell back across the Cumberland River minus their artillery, wagon train, and the body of their lamented commander.[4]

The only Confederate reporter of any note at what Southern newspapers referred to as the Battle of Fishing Creek was the *Nashville Banner's* Albert Roberts.[5] The first reports of the reverse to reach Richmond came from Northern sources; to the mortification of Southern

[2] *Ibid.*, January 23, 1862.

[3] *Ibid.*, February 14, 1862. For an amusing description of "Flunkyism in Office" pertaining to the press relations of General Polk's staff see *ibid.*, February 20, 1862.

[4] Shelby Foote, *The Civil War, A Narrative, Fort Sumter to Perryville* (New York, 1958), pp. 177-80; R. G. McMurtry, "Zollicoffer and the Battle of Mill Springs," *Filson Club Quarterly*, xxix (October 1955), 303-19.

Albert Sidney Johnston's Western Department carried the notation of Department No. 2 in the Confederate military organization. Coastal defense was the prerogative of Department No. 1, which included most of the state of Mississippi. Bragg's separate department of Alabama and West Florida was informally joined to Department No. 2 after Bragg evacuated Pensacola in March 1862. Archer Jones, "Some Aspects of George W. Randolph's Service as Confederate Secretary of War," *Journal of Southern History*, xxvi (August 1960), 306-307.

[5] Roberts' account of the fight was reprinted in *Memphis Daily Avalanche*, January 31, 1862; *Atlanta Daily Southern Confederacy*, February 6, 1862. The *Mobile Register*, however, rated the account of the battle written by the correspondent of the *Bowling Green Courier* as "the most intelligent narrative we have yet seen of the circumstances of the position of Crittenden's army prior to the battle and of the battle itself." *Mobile Daily Advertiser and Register*, February 6, 1862.

127

readers information received by the Confederate War Department disclosed that the facts were even more disastrous than enemy sources had indicated. Although the Confederate casualty list was not excessive,[6] the enemy apparently had opened an invasion route into the strong Unionist area of east Tennessee, and the editor of the *Atlanta Confederacy* was actually fearful for the safety of Atlanta.[7]

A Savannah newspaper tried to counteract the damaging effects of the Fishing Creek disaster on public opinion with "a bear story" about the capture of St. Louis by Brig.Gen. Sterling Price.[8] Several Tennessee newspapers, on the other hand, made General Crittenden the scapegoat for the first damaging Southern defeat since Rich Mountain. Unluckily for him, Crittenden labored under the incubus of the reputation for habitual intemperance that he had acquired during his years of service in the United States army. The Southern press accused him of drunkenness, recklessness, and even disloyalty to the Confederate cause. Although the *Memphis Appeal* and a few other newspapers defended him, the adverse findings of a court of inquiry eventually brought about his retirement from the Confederate army.[9]

While Confederate editors were still wrangling with each other about the setback to their cause in southeastern Kentucky, a threat to the critical center of Johnston's line claimed their attention. To prevent two northward flowing streams, the Tennessee and Cumberland Rivers, from providing highways of invasion to the South, Johnston's predecessors in command in the West had planned the construction of a fort to guard each river. The two strong points, Fort Henry on the right bank of the Tennessee River and Fort Donelson on the left bank of the Cumberland, were located, twelve miles apart, in Tennessee, just south of the Kentucky line. On February 6 a Union gunboat flotilla

---

[6] Probably somewhat over five hundred men, killed, wounded, and missing. The Federal loss was about half this.

[7] *Atlanta Daily Southern Confederacy*, January 25, 1862.

[8] *Daily Richmond Examiner*, February 1, 1862.

[9] *Louisville Daily Courier* as reprinted in *Knoxville Daily Register*, January 29, 1862; *New Orleans Daily Delta*, January 30, 1862; *Memphis Daily Appeal*, January 28, February 5, 1862; *New Orleans Daily Crescent*, February 5, 1862; *Memphis Daily Avalanche*, February 7, 1862; *Raleigh Standard* as reprinted in *Memphis Daily Appeal*, February 12, 1862. Attorney General Thomas Bragg noted in his diary on January 24, 1862 that it was current gossip in Richmond that Crittenden was very intemperate and that that fact was known when he was appointed to military command. "The Enquirer alludes to his habits this morning in no very delicate terms." Diary of Thomas Bragg, Southern Historical Collection, University of North Carolina.

under Commodore Andrew H. Foote came storming up the Tennessee River. Fort Henry was poorly constructed, and after a token resistance the Confederate brigadier in command, named Lloyd Tilghman, surrendered, having already sent most of his men cross-country to Fort Donelson. The *Memphis Appeal* carried headlines the next morning: "From The Tennessee River! — The Fight Commenced! — Fort Henry Fallen! . . . — Two Federal Gunboats Disabled! — Fate of Gen. Tilghman's Command Unknown!"

The break in his line caused Johnston to evacuate Bowling Green and Columbus, which were now outflanked, and concentrate part of his forces at Fort Donelson. To give up Donelson would mean the loss of the capital of Tennessee, a supply depot and industrial center of great importance. Unfortunately Johnston remained in Nashville, about 50 miles southeast of Donelson, and permitted three officers of approximately equal rank to exercise a divided command at the point of attack.

The breezy manner in which the *Nashville Banner* editorialized about the news of the evacuation of Bowling Green amused and amazed the Northern war correspondent Whitelaw Reid when a copy of the newspaper in which it appeared fell into his hands several weeks later. Reid quoted the *Banner* as saying:

"We do not regard the latest news of last evening from Bowling Green as of such consequence as to excite fear or foreboding. The seizure of a certain number of cars and engines, with the debris of our provisions and munitions amounting in all to a very inconsiderable quantity . . . should be considered as simply the natural result either of negligence or breach of trust on the part of some one or other. The Yankees undoubtedly had full knowledge of our movements; they were advised of our intended evacuation; they had full information of the very hour of our departure, and so they marched in as we marched out, firing a few shells for appearance sake. . . . There is no use to be downhearted. Up with the heart and up with the flag! We have a work of defense to perform, and by the help of God we'll do it."[10]

After having beaten off an attack by Foote's gunboat flotilla the defenders of Donelson decided to attempt to break out of the encirclement effected by Grant's force. Beginning at 5:30 A.M. Saturday morning, February 15, Pillow's Tennesseans on the Confederate left attacked the right side of Grant's line, forcing McClernand's division back, and by noon had opened the Nashville escape route. Then for

---

[10] *Cincinnati Daily Gazette*, March 10, 1862.

reasons that were not clear at the time and were the subject of controversy afterward, Pillow called off further pursuit and talked his colleagues, Floyd and Simon Buckner, into retiring to their original position. That night, with victory having thus inexplicably turned into defeat, the three generals decided that the fort would have to be surrendered. Floyd and Pillow, who outranked Buckner, succeeded in making their escape, leaving Buckner with the onus of surrendering a Confederate army of more than 12,000.[11]

The first telegraphic reports of the battle that came out of Nashville were understandably jubilant. Pritchard's Press Association reporter rejoiced on February 14 that the enemy had been "whipped by land and water," and on the sixteenth the *Memphis Appeal* printed a special dispatch from Nashville signed W. B. Galbreath, signifying that the battle on the fifteenth had resulted in a "complete rout" of the Federals and the capture of 1,000 enemy soldiers. On the same day the *New Orleans Picayune* published a dispatch from a Nashville source of "undoubted reliability" claiming that the Yankees had suffered a greater defeat than Manassas at Fort Donelson.

On Sunday, February 16 the telegraph failed to confirm the optimistic reports that had come over it the day before. In Memphis that evening as rumors of defeat and victory alternated, a large crowd milled about in front of the telegraph office until a late hour, hoping to obtain reliable news. The following morning the editor of the *Memphis Avalanche* undoubtedly reflected the mood of his readers when he said, "We are standing on tiptoe of fear and hope." By the time the editorial containing these words was in print, everybody in Memphis knew the worst: Fort Donelson had surrendered to a large force of the enemy with at least part of its garrison. From Nashville and Memphis private dispatches reporting the surrender streamed over the wires to Chattanooga, Atlanta, Savannah, New Orleans, and more distant parts of the Confederacy. Yet fully a week after the surrender, Richmond still refused to confirm the accuracy of these reports, contenting itself with the observation that they were considered "extravagant."[12]

Once the initial effects of the shock had passed, the public wanted to know the particulars of the events preceding the surrender. But again, as at Fishing Creek, the Confederate press had been caught

[11] S. F. Horn, *The Army of Tennessee* (Norman, Okla., 1953), pp. 88-95; R. S. Henry, *First with the Most Forrest* (Indianapolis and New York, 1944), pp. 57-59.
[12] *Memphis Daily Avalanche*, February 17, 1862; *Savannah Republican*, February 19, 1862.

napping. The *Nashville Union and American* and the *Memphis Appeal* were the only Southern newspapers in a position to publish eyewitness accounts. The author of the *Union's* relatively brief battle account was Col. John C. Burch, one of the editors of that newspaper and a member of General Pillow's staff.[13]

Defects of the kind usually present in the reporting of a military defeat were evident in the Confederate battle reports of Donelson, both mail and telegraphic. The press exaggerated the size of the enemy's forces, presented a wide range of estimates of the number of Confederate prisoners, and minimized the scope of the disaster to preserve public morale. Buckner at first received undeserved blame because he remained behind to conduct the surrender. Then the suspension of Floyd and Pillow from their commands by the Davis administration caused the press to revise its opinion of Buckner. And when Pillow and Floyd violated army regulations by releasing their official reports to the press before sending them to the War Department in Richmond, the irregularity of this procedure inspired widespread press criticism.[14]

When Johnston learned early Sunday morning that Fort Donelson was being surrendered, he decided it was more important to save the remnants of his army than to try to hold Nashville. According to a Mobile reporter, at breakfast that morning Johnston explained to the lady with whom he and his staff took their meals that his soldiers had fought as bravely as ever soldiers did, but they were not made of steel and could not hold out day after day against impossible odds. Johnston told her to "stay at home. Tell all your friends from me to stay at home. I cannot make a fight before Nashville, and for the good of the city shall retire. I know Gen. Buell well. He is a gentleman, and will not suffer any violence to peaceable citizens or disturb private property."[15] Later in the day Johnston decided to march Hardee's 17,000 men southeast from Nashville to Murfreesboro, dispatch reinforcements to Chat-

---

[13] *Nashville Union and American,* as reprinted in *Atlanta Daily Southern Confederacy,* February 25, 1862; *Wilmington Daily Journal,* March 1, 1862; *Memphis Daily Appeal* as reprinted in *Atlanta Daily Southern Confederacy,* March 5, 1862; *Knoxville Daily Register,* May 2, 1862.

[14] See e.g. *Memphis Daily Avalanche,* February 27, 1862; *New Orleans Daily Delta,* March 1, 19, 1862; *Atlanta Daily Southern Confederacy,* March 7, 1862. The *Confederacy* tartly commented: "Gen. Pillow is a wire working politician and has been all his life; and the publication of his report before sending it to the War Department is entirely characteristic of such a man."

[15] *Mobile Daily Tribune* as reprinted in *Memphis Daily Appeal,* March 2, 1862.

tanooga, and await a junction with Polk's troops, which had been recalled from Columbus.

At least two reporters from out-of-town newspapers and an editorial
correspondent were eyewitnesses of the panic that seized the inhabitants of Nashville in spite of Johnston's reassuring words. About nine
o'clock Sunday morning, February 16, a correspondent of the *Mobile
Tribune* rode out into the country from Nashville to dine at the farmhouse of a friend. Returning that afternoon, he came on to the turnpike
south of town about four o'clock and asked the first man he met about
the latest news from Fort Donelson, expecting to hear tidings of a
great triumph.

"News! What's the last you've heard?"

"Last night's dispatches."

"None since? The last out and plenty of it. Fort Donelson has fallen
and Nashville is surrendered. They say the white flag is waving now
on the Capitol and the gunboats will be up before sundown."

The newspaperman thought his informant was hoaxing him, but
involuntarily quickened his pace, only to hear the same tale repeated
endlessly with interesting variations by a stream of refugees hurrying
south along the turnpike toward Franklin. On reaching the tollgate
at the top of a hill which overlooked Nashville, the *Mobile Tribune*
reporter strained his eyes in an effort to distinguish the white flag on
the state capital. There was no flag of any kind; the flagstaff was bare.

Along Broad Street by the Nashville and Decatur road he caught
sight of Governor Isham Harris, scrambling aboard a special train
for Memphis with the fugitive members of the state legislature and
the archives of the state. A seemingly endless line of Confederate soldiers and wagons was passing across the wire bridge that spanned the
Cumberland River and moving in the direction of the Murfreesboro
turnpike. Crossing the bridge to the north bank of the river, the *Tribune*
man rushed to his home in Edgefield to remove his family to a safe
place in Decatur.[16]

Another reporter who recorded his impressions of Nashville at the
height of the panic was the *New Orleans Crescent* correspondent, Gibbons, who had come there after the evacuation of Columbus. Gibbons
was disagreeably affected by the destruction of several million dollars
worth of government property during the outburst of hysteria that accompanied the evacuation. Nevertheless, he remained in Nashville

[16] *Ibid.*

132

throughout the week that followed the surrender of Donelson, expecting Buell's Army of the Ohio to arrive at any moment and looking for some means of getting out of town before it did. Finally at three o'clock on Saturday afternoon, February 22, a solitary car and engine bound for Murfreesboro left the railroad station with the *Crescent's* correspondent jammed in among the other passengers. One of them was Governor Harris, who had returned from Memphis and was now making his escape a second time.

When the train reached Mill Creek several miles out of town, it was discovered that the stream was flooded from the morning's rain, and the bridges looked precarious. The train crossed the first bridge cautiously but safely. The second bridge with its wooden supports looked so dangerous, however, that the engineer decided not to cross until he had tested it with the locomotive alone. Some of the passengers walked across in advance. Then the locomotive crossed and returned slowly, but just as it reached the abutment on the Nashville side of the creek, the bridge collapsed and was swept off in the torrent. Gibbons and the other passengers who had not walked to the other side on the bridge now had to walk back to Nashville and look for other means of escaping from the city.

Carriages, horses, or other means of conveyance were unavailable for any amount of money, so Gibbons started out for Murfreesboro on foot the next morning, leaving his carpetsack with the railroad agent at the depot to be forwarded to Decatur by train. On the way he found a travelling companion in the person of a Texas soldier who had escaped capture at Fort Donelson. By managing to get a twelve-mile ride on an ammunition wagon, they were able to reach Murfreesboro, 31 miles from Nashville, by nine o'clock that night. At Murfreesboro Gibbons felt more secure, and relished the privilege of sleeping on the bare floor in the house of a Mrs. Hagan for the sum of four "bits," with the sleeper furnishing his own blankets.[17]

The editorial correspondent who was in Nashville at the height of the excitement was Glass of the *Lynchburg Republican*, who had come west with some of the Virginia troops. Glass described the consternation that the news of the fall of Fort Donelson inspired as being unequalled since the First Battle of Manassas. He admitted that the spectacle of women in tears aroused his sympathy and that many other things that happened in Nashville on that Sunday occasioned his

[17] *New Orleans Daily Crescent*, March 3, 1862.

laughter, "but the cowardly conduct of hundreds of men was the subject of unmitigated loathing."[18]

The telegraph operators, as well as the newspapermen, had fled by the time Buell's army finally occupied Nashville on February 25. Already Johnston was receiving hot criticism in the Confederate press for the loss of both Kentucky and middle Tennessee.[19] These momentous developments, in contrast to the relative quiet that prevailed east of the mountains, caused Confederate news managers to hustle their best reporters to Tennessee. On February 22, one week after Fort Donelson fell, Peter Alexander was on his way west from Richmond, travelling by way of Atlanta and Chattanooga, to cover the campaign for the *Savannah Republican* and *Mobile Register*. The *Atlanta Confederacy*, for which he had reported from Virginia during the previous year, had intended to reemploy him in 1862, but the provisions of his contract with the *Republican* prevented this. So the *Confederacy* was obliged to reprint his letters from the *Republican*, one day later than if they had been written for the Atlanta paper. Alexander visited the *Confederacy* office when he stopped in Atlanta and picked up information about the military situation in Tennessee from Walter N. Haldeman, the refugee editor of the *Louisville Courier*.[20]

Alexander reached Chattanooga on the afternoon of February 28; after a couple of days there he started for Murfreesboro by rail. The train was crowded, and there were frequent stops to make way for troop trains and southbound trains laden with refugees. From Tullahoma, where he was unable to proceed any farther, he had to retrace his journey to Stevenson, Alabama. There, while waiting for a westbound train, he had an interesting conversation with a stranger named Kellogg, who claimed to be a brother-in-law of President Lincoln.

[18] *Lynchburg Daily Republican*, February 26, 1862.

[19] *New Orleans Daily Crescent*, February 19, 1862; *Knoxville Daily Register*, February 21, 1862; *Atlanta Daily Southern Confederacy*, February 23, March 20, 1862. Jefferson Davis's concern with the "reckless . . . statements" critical of Johnston in the Mississippi Valley press was voiced in a letter to Johnston dated March 12, 1862. Albert Sidney Johnston Papers, Tulane University Library. Following Johnston's death in battle, a Southern editor improvised the romantic explanation that Johnston had needlessly exposed himself to danger because of the "foul injustice" accorded him by the Southern press. *Knoxville Daily Register*, April 8, 1862.

[20] *Savannah Republican*, February 26, March 3, 1862; *Atlanta Daily Southern Confederacy*, January 26, February 27, 1862. Alexander's first letter for the *Mobile Register* appeared in the March 27, 1862 issue of that newspaper. Alexander ceased reporting for the *Register* on May 19, 1862 according to his own statement in the *Savannah Republican*.

Alexander had planned to go from Stevenson to Huntsville, where it was expected that General Johnston would establish his new headquarters. Learning, however, that a battle was imminent at New Madrid on the upper Mississippi, he continued west to Memphis, arriving there on March 4.[21]

In the letters he subsequently wrote from Memphis, Alexander had relatively little to say about the town's appearance. When Gibbons had been there about a month earlier for his first visit in ten years, he had been greatly surprised at its expansion and the great amount of military and private business. The quantity of sugar and molasses was "positively tremendous," and the draymen of Memphis were "getting rich under the sweet pressure" of hauling sugar from the landing to the Charleston depot for as much as five or even ten dollars a load. For evening entertainment there was "an excellent band of Ethiopian minstrels" and parties "where were assembled some of the prettiest of the Memphian belles."[22]

Early in March another prominent reporter came west to join Alexander at Memphis. The new arrival was Perry of the *New Orleans Picayune*, who had been at Manassas and Norfolk before he started west in search of "the real seat of war." The *Charleston Courier's* ace correspondent, de Fontaine, was destined to arrive in Mississippi before the next great battle, but at this time he was in Georgia, contributing letters to the *Courier* from Augusta, Savannah, and Atlanta.[23]

In the meantime Johnston had discarded his defensive policy and was laboring mightily to gather enough troops from outlying points to strike a blow. Up from the Florida coast marched Braxton Bragg, leaving Pensacola to the mercy of the Yankees. The War Department stripped New Orleans of its infantry defenses to provide 5,000 more troops. To Arkansas went orders to Van Dorn to march the army recently defeated at the Battle of Pea Ridge to Corinth, Mississippi, where Johnston planned to concentrate his army. These reinforce-

[21] *Savannah Republican*, March 6, 10, 13, 1862; *Atlanta Daily Southern Confederacy*, March 15, 1862.

[22] *New Orleans Daily Crescent*, February 14, 1862.

[23] The *Memphis Appeal* reported Perry's arrival in Memphis on March 16. *Memphis Daily Appeal*, March 18, 1862. See also *New Orleans Daily Picayune*, March 22, 1862. De Fontaine's Georgia correspondence is reprinted in James M. Merrill, ed., "Personne Goes to Georgia: Five Civil War Letters," *Georgia Historical Quarterly*, XLIII (June 1959), 202-11. These letters first appeared in the *Charleston Daily Courier* of March 4, 10, 17, 18, 20, 1862.

ments, combined with the troops salvaged from the disaster at Donelson, would provide an army of about 40,000 to challenge a deeper penetration of the South.[24] Since even an army of this size would be outnumbered by the two Federal armies under Grant and Buell in Tennessee, Johnston planned to attack Grant in his camp on the left bank of the Tennessee River before Buell's 30,000 bluecoats could march from Nashville to join him.

Alexander had been misinformed about the location of general headquarters. Johnston's army was gathering at the junction point of the Mobile and Ohio and the Memphis and Charleston Railroads at Corinth, 93 miles east of Memphis. Not being certain where the great battle was going to be fought, several of the more prominent reporters remained at Memphis, attempting to keep track simultaneously of developments on the upper Mississippi River and in northeastern Mississippi.

After the evacuation of Columbus, Kentucky on March 2, Polk had transported less than half of his army about thirty miles down the river to New Madrid, Missouri, near the Kentucky-Tennessee line. He established batteries there and at Island No. 10 on the opposite side of the river to impede the invaders. Within a week's time a joint U.S. army-navy expedition under Commodore Foote and a Yankee brigadier named John Pope were blasting away at the batteries. Not all the Confederate correspondents who were reporting this fight were doing so from the safe distance of Memphis. Fresh from his Nashville adventure, Gibbons had gone North to report the resistance of the garrison at Island No. 10 for the *New Orleans Crescent*. A reporter named J. W. Youngblood was there to represent the *Memphis Appeal*, and the *New Orleans Delta* had a special correspondent in the vicinity who used the pen name "Mimosa."[25]

Expressing disappointment at the "stern necessity" that had dictated the evacuation of Columbus, Gibbons was not impressed by the reassurances of the Confederate high command, that "this is a better place to defend the river than Columbus was." The fall of New Madrid on March 13 in some measure justified his skepticism, but Island No. 10 held out against the mortar fire of the Union attack force, which con-

[24] Foote, *Civil War*, p. 319; Horn, *Army of Tennessee*, pp. 114-15; D. H. Maury, *Recollections of a Virginian* (New York, 1897), p. 158.

[25] *Memphis Daily Appeal*, April 11, 1862. Youngblood's letters were written over the signature "Juvenis." See also *New Orleans Daily Delta*, March 25, 1862.

tinued day after day. An animated description of the bombardment which Gibbons wrote for the *Crescent* inspired favorable comment in Richmond when it was reprinted in the *Examiner*. On April 7 Reporter Youngblood estimated that up to that time the enemy had hurled over ten thousand shells of the heaviest caliber at the Confederate position. "Even while I write, the shells from their thirteen inch mortars are bursting around me but, so far, have done little or no damage."[26]

Alexander was still in Memphis on April 2, but other reporters were flocking to Corinth to be in readiness for the great battle which the *New Orleans Delta* had predicted editorially on March 21. One of the first arrivals on the scene was the *Delta* editor Walker who came up with the New Orleans troops to Corinth early in the last week of March. Walker was impressed by the strict discipline Bragg maintained in his corps, and noted in particular the taboo on "that great bane of our country—whisky." Walker was correspondingly critical of the system prevalent in the Western army, of soldiers electing their own officers and of the lax discipline to which it frequently gave rise.[27]

Disparaging comments about army discipline likewise appeared in the correspondence of the *New Orleans Picayune* reporter, Reid, who turned up in Corinth on the second day after Walker's arrival. Reid did not like the "political jugglery and wire working" which ambitious soldiers employed to obtain rank and which he felt had an utterly demoralizing effect on their men. He was pleased, however, to meet in camp many old friends from distant points. One of his friends was Col. Calhoun Benham from California, a member of General Johnston's staff. "There are also many old habitués of Washington City to be met here, who once were considered 'elegant dogs,' and flourished extensively among the women kind, who are now roughshod, and so disguised in long beards and dirty shirts that it is hard to recognize the kidgloved, champagne-dining fraternity."[28]

On the day after Reid dated his letter, General Beauregard and his

[26] *New Orleans Daily Crescent*, April 14, 1862; *Memphis Daily Appeal*, April 11, 1862. Excerpts from Gibbons' account of the bombardment, together with favorable editorial comment, appeared in the *Atlanta Daily Southern Confederacy*, April 2, 1862.

[27] *New Orleans Daily Delta*, March 28, 1862. Walker's first letter of his Shiloh campaign correspondence appeared in the *New Orleans Daily Delta* of March 27, 1862.

[28] *New Orleans Daily Picayune*, March 30, 1862. Reid's first letter in the *Picayune*, signed "Sparta," appeared in that newspaper on March 28, 1862.

staff arrived in camp from Jackson, Mississippi, with considerable fanfare. Newspaperman Walker was in the Louisiana encampment on a ridge just outside Corinth when the general appeared there on March 29, inspiring warm greetings and loud hurrahs. Beauregard acknowledged his reception with a little speech to the commanders of the Louisiana regiments, in which he expressed unbounded confidence in the splendid army assembled there and promised that the Louisianians would soon have the opportunity of meeting the invader on an equal field. While the general was speaking Walker saw a mettlesome horse come galloping down the avenue at full speed, carrying an officer who seemed completely unable to control him and who cried out lustily, "Clear the track!" The horse plunged through the crowd around General Beauregard, scattering the general's staff and catapulting the rider to the ground within a few feet of Beauregard. Several bystanders helped the unhorsed officer to his feet and found that he was not seriously injured. Walker learned from them that the victim of this exciting interlude was a regimental quartermaster named Maj. J. F. Caldwell, who had the reputation of being one of the most useful and active officers in his regiment.[29]

Johnston's arrival on March 25 and his reorganization of the army into four corps had already provided the subject matter of another interesting Walker letter.[30] On April 2 Beauregard and Bragg recommended a forward movement on the basis of intelligence information indicating that Grant's Federals were preparing to make a full-scale attack on Memphis. Johnston preferred to wait for the arrival of Van Dorn's reinforcements from the Trans-Mississippi, but finally agreed to march north to attack Grant's army in its camp at Pittsburg Landing on the Tennessee River.[31]

An unsigned correspondent of the *Picayune* reported that the order to advance, issued later that night, had been preceded by great activity in the army. "Ambulances have been distributed to the various brigades, the medicos have been busy in preparing their splints and bandages, the rattling of shell and shot in heavy wagons for distribution among the artillery and mortar batteries, the hurrying to and fro of aids and orderlies with messages, groups of scouts in their brown linsey dresses, slouched hats and top boots . . . standing around the different

[29] *New Orleans Sunday Delta*, April 6, 1862.
[30] *New Orleans Daily Delta*, March 29, 1862.
[31] Williams, *Beauregard*, p. 126; Foote, *Civil War*, p. 325.

quarters of our generals, or holding their horses by their bridles . . . looking like paintings of Italian brigands, or reminding you of pictures of scenes in the old revolution, the sharp ringing click of the hammer and anvil of the different forges, all give dread note of preparation for the coming battle."[32] To guard against premature disclosures of his attack plan, Johnston arrested a correspondent of the *Mobile Tribune*, W. B. Fowler, whose letter containing full information about the size and position of Johnston's army had already been published in the *Tribune*.[33]

Neither Fowler nor any of the other Confederate army correspondents could have anticipated how badly the plans for the march would miscarry. Lack of training and previous battle experience on the part of a majority of the troops produced delays and confusion. As a result, the projected one-day march over a distance of twenty-three miles required three days.

Reid was one of the war correspondents who accompanied the army on its march to Pittsburg Landing. Unable to obtain the horse that had been promised him, the reporter had to ride on the first day of the march over a rough road in a jolting ambulance belonging to the 4th Louisiana Volunteers, drawn by a miserable wind-broken horse that had been palmed off on the government for $250. In Monterey, Tennessee, ten miles from Corinth, Reid sent off a letter to his newspaper by courier, explaining that Monterey was not on a telegraph line and that "the news will have to be sent by couriers to Corinth."[34]

Not until Sunday morning, April 6, was Johnston's army in attack position along a front three miles long, confronting the Union camp. Hardee's corps augmented by one of Bragg's brigades was in front, with the remainder of Bragg's corps constituting a second line about five hundred yards in the rear. To the right and left, a half-mile behind Bragg, were the corps of Polk and John C. Breckinridge to provide support and act as a reserve force. Beauregard was convinced that the army's tardy advance had deprived it of all the advantages of surprise and was in favor of calling off the attack and returning to Corinth.[35]

There were probably no less than eleven Confederate army correspondents in the vicinity of the battlefield when Hardee's guns

---

[32] *New Orleans Daily Picayune,* April 6, 1862.

[33] *Ibid.*, April 8, 1862.

[34] *Ibid.*, April 10, 1862.

[35] Bruce Catton, *Terrible Swift Sword* (New York, 1963), p. 226; Williams, *Beauregard*, p. 131.

opened up on Sunday morning. The newspaper brigade included Alexander, who had come over from Memphis just in time for the battle, de Fontaine of the *Charleston Courier*, Perry of the *New Orleans Picayune*, Walker of the *Delta* and Stoddard of the rival *Crescent*, Robert Ette of the *Memphis Appeal*, two other Memphis newspapermen representing the *Memphis Avalanche* and *Argus*, and an unnamed correspondent of the *Montgomery Advertiser*. From far off Richmond there was a correspondent of the *Richmond Dispatch*, possibly de Fontaine, who provided no other clue to his identity than the pseudonym "Quel Qu'un."[36]

Alexander had reached Corinth the day before the battle, but finding it impossible to procure a horse to enable him to catch up with the army, had encamped for the night on one of the roads to Pittsburg Landing, 14 miles east of Corinth. At about ten o'clock the next morning he bought a mule and a hard Mexican saddle with no padding in the seat and got to the battlefield a little after noon.[37]

By that time the battle had been in progress for about six hours. Sweeping forward at daybreak with their screeching Rebel yell, Hardee's Graybacks had struck the enemy's front line and forced it back as Bragg came up to support Hardee. As the surprised Federals retreated, some of the Confederate soldiers fell out of line to sample their enemy's Sunday morning breakfasts; as brigades, regiments, and even companies became hopelessly intermingled, the Confederate plan of attack dissolved.[38]

The biggest problem of Johnston's corps commanders was a hard core of resistance on the Union left where Prentiss's Illinois division, with the help of some reinforcements from another division, made a stand in an old country lane along the crest of a gentle rise, that came to be known as the "Hornet's Nest." Past noon and into the afternoon they beat off repeated Confederate assaults. Attempting a flanking movement in that direction, Johnston rode to the far right, exposing himself unwisely. Apparently no newspaper reporter was near him at the time. Yet in his battle account of Shiloh, de Fontaine told how Johnston fell about half past two o'clock "while heading a charge upon the camp of the enemy, one ball piercing his body and another striking

---

[36] The style of this letter is very similar to that of de Fontaine in his letter correspondence. Also, de Fontaine used the pseudonym "Quel Qu'un" while writing for another newspaper during a later stage of the war.

[37] *Savannah Republican*, April 14, 1862.

[38] Catton, *Terrible Swift Sword*, pp. 232-33; Foote, *Civil War*, p. 338.

him below the knee, severing the poplitieal [*sic*] artery, from which he bled to death in about twenty minutes," after imparting to Governor Harris the information that "my wound is mortal."[39] Beauregard, who up to that time had been commanding the rear area from Shiloh chapel, took over the command of the army without informing the soldiers of Johnston's death.

Stoddard of the *New Orleans Crescent* had gotten a glimpse of the new army commander in the early part of the afternoon when the Crescent Regiment, to which Stoddard was attached, received orders to move forward. At that time Beauregard was standing by the roadside among his aides. To the newspaperman he appeared "somewhat older and much more gray than when I last saw him before the war." Yet he was still vigorous and bore himself as proudly as ever. Stoddard watched him wave his hat and point in the direction of a thick copse of trees where all pandemonium seemed to have broken loose and heard him exclaim, "On, on, my brave boys, and the day is ours."[40]

Now that he was in full command of the army, Beauregard decreed that there should be no let-up in the attack, using sixty-two guns to rake the "Hornet's Nest" with canister. Finally the Confederates worked around both flanks of Prentiss, surrounded his command, and obliged the survivors to surrender at about 5:30. There was still time, Beauregard thought, to launch another attack to drive the remnants of Grant's army into the river. But the Confederates had been fighting for more than twelve hours, they were nearly exhausted, and from the river the Yankee gunboats were lobbing huge shells over the heads of their comrades into the Confederate ranks. It was now sundown, and through the gathering twilight, Beauregard dispatched couriers with orders to call off the attacks and pull back to rest for a resumption of the fighting the next morning.[41]

Reporters Alexander and Perry were at Beauregard's headquarters that evening when the captured Union division commander, Brig.Gen. Benjamin M. Prentiss, was brought before Beauregard by one of Polk's staff officers. Both Alexander and Perry gave substantially similar accounts of the conversation between Beauregard and Prentiss.[42] Accord-

[39] *Charleston Daily Courier*, April 15, 22, 1862.

[40] *New Orleans Daily Crescent*, April 15, 1862.

[41] Foote, *Civil War*, pp. 340-42.

[42] Perry's account of Shiloh was published in the *New Orleans Daily Picayune* of April 11, 1862. The minor respects in which Perry's account of the conversation between Beauregard and Prentiss differs from that of Alexander include a

ing to Alexander, Prentiss opened the conversation by saying, "Well, sir, we have felt your power to-day, and have had to yield." To this, Beauregard replied somewhat theatrically, "That is natural, sir. You could not expect it to be otherwise. We are fighting for our homes, for our wives and children, for generations to come after us, and for liberty itself. Why does your government thus war upon us, and seek us upon our own soil?" When Prentiss answered that his fellow citizens could not bring themselves to consent to see the Union broken up, Beauregard retorted that the Union was already broken and that the last man, woman, and child in the South would willingly perish before the Union should be restored.

Then he asked Prentiss about the size of the Union force that had been engaged that day. With surprising candor, Prentiss, according to Alexander, replied: "Six divisions, numbering a little over 7,000 each—the whole not amounting to more than 40,000." He then attributed his misfortune to mismanagement and lack of support and informed Beauregard that if he (Prentiss) had been properly supported, "we should have broken your centre at the time we stopped your advance." Beauregard took issue with him on this point and then probed again, wanting to know if General Buell had arrived and the size of his force. This time, Prentiss was rather more wary, saying after some hesitation, "I do not know where Gen. Buell is, or the number of his forces. I have heard he was at Nashville, and then at Columbia, and also that he was on the road. We do not look for him under forty-eight hours." From that point on the conversation reflected the feelings of confidence that each officer had in the eventual triumph of his cause and included an exchange of compliments. Eyeing the distinguished prisoner closely, Alexander was surprised to find him "not at all depressed," and concluded that although he was apparently quite candid, "I thought I detected a disposition to evade, if not to deceive, in his reply as to the whereabouts of Buell."

That night Alexander slept in the tent of the quartermaster of the 53d Ohio Regiment, which Beauregard had assigned him and two of his friends to. Before he retired for the night he made use of the abundant supply of writing paper the Federal quartermaster had left

---

reference to Prentiss telling Beauregard that a large number of his men were sick before the battle, which Alexander fails to mention. Also, the question about Buell's whereabouts, which Alexander attributed to Beauregard, Perry indicates was addressed to Prentiss by an unnamed bystander, and Perry gives a somewhat different version of Prentiss's reply to the question.

behind to write up his impressions of the day's fighting. Up until sunset the weather had been mild and pleasant, but it was now raining very hard, the result, Alexander surmised, of the heavy cannonading that had gone on since early morning(!).[43]

His premonition that Buell was near at hand proved correct. During the night, 20,000 of Buell's troops crossed the river, and Grant's army was further reinforced by another division which had failed to come up in time to take part in Sunday's fight. Soon after sunrise the fighting resumed, with the combined forces of Grant and Buell attacking and the Confederates doggedly resisting as they fell back. Finally at two o'clock in the afternoon, Beauregard ordered a retreat, but the badly damaged Federal army made no more than a token pursuit as the Confederates withdrew toward Corinth.

The first official information about the battle to reach Richmond was a dispatch from Beauregard to Adjutant General Cooper that was received at the War Department on Monday morning. In his dispatch Beauregard claimed that he had gained a "complete victory" after a severe battle of ten hours, although the loss on both sides had been heavy, including the Confederate field commander.[44] The first dispatches sent by telegraphic reporters from the battle area likewise gave the impression that the Confederates had won a glorious victory, capturing numerous batteries and many prisoners. Subsequent newspaper dispatches admitted that the Confederates had retreated after the second day's fight "to a stronger position." The *Courier's* de Fontaine added the reassuring information that "our troops are in admirable spirits and ready for another fight."[45]

In New Orleans the office of the Southwestern Telegraph Company stayed open all Sunday night to provide information. According to the *New Orleans Delta* thousands of Louisianians were on the street the next morning to learn the content of the news dispatches. "The excitement was evidently a pleasant one to judge from the expression of faces, but there was no noise, no huzzaing or throwing up of hats. . . . When the bunting was thrown to the breeze, however, from our office and in other localities, the news boys gave vent to their feelings by a continued round of cheering. . . ."[46]

[43] *Savannah Republican*, April 14, 1862.

[44] *Richmond Daily Dispatch*, April 8, 1862.

[45] *Ibid.*, April 11, 1862. Apparently de Fontaine was acting as telegraphic correspondent for the *Richmond Dispatch*, as well as for the *Charleston Courier*.

[46] *New Orleans Daily Delta*, April 8, 10, 1862.

Neither was there occasion for cheering in the vicinity of the Shiloh battlefield, where the heavy toll of the fighting was only too apparent. "Personne" wrote his full-length account of the bloodbath at Shiloh from a sitting position on the floor of a hotel corridor in Corinth, with the bodies of the living and dead lying prone on either side of him as far as the eye could reach. As he labored over his copy he could not shut out of his consciousness the disturbing fact that "groans fill the air, surgeons are busy at work by candle-light, . . . the atmosphere is fetid with the stench of wounds, and the rain is pouring down upon thousands who yet lie out upon the bloody ground of Shiloh."[47]

Of major importance among the newspaper accounts of the battle were the battle reports of "Personne," Perry of the *Picayune*, the *Delta* correspondent Walker, and Alexander. Alexander's account of the action of the first day ran to more than two columns in the *Savannah Republican*, and his battle report of the second day was of equivalent length.[48] Alexander's reporting of Shiloh was much superior to his work at the First Battle of Manassas. No longer confining his attention to the military performance of the Georgia troops, he provided a much better general view of the action than in his Manassas narrative. At first Alexander refused to express an opinion as to the number of killed and wounded on either side. He hoped, he said, that the Confederate loss was not as large as many believed it to be, and he asserted his belief that the number killed was not in the usual proportion to the wounded because of the protection afforded by the trees. On the third day after the battle, Alexander ventured an estimate of battle casualties which proved ridiculously low. He placed the number of Confederate dead at 400-600 and the wounded at 2,000; the number of enemy killed and wounded he lumped together at 4,000. One week later he cautiously scaled upward his estimate of total loss on the Confederate side to 4,000, but contended that Northern estimates placing the Union loss at 18,000-20,000 were ridiculously high. By the beginning of May he had to concede that his revised estimate of Confederate loss had been too conservative, and that it was now believed to have been fully 10,000, one-fifth of whom were fatalities.[49]

[47] *Charleston Daily Courier*, April 15, 1862.

[48] Alexander's battle account of Shiloh was published in the *Savannah Republican* of April 14, 19, 1862. See also *Mobile Daily Advertiser and Register*, April 11, 1862.

[49] *Savannah Republican*, April 22, 23, 29, May 12, 1862. For reprints of Alex-

Walker's battle report of Shiloh was comprehensive, reasonably objective, and sufficiently popular with newspaper readers that it was later reprinted in book form. Walker was impressed by the fact that the enemy had fought "with unexampled vigor and obstinacy" throughout the battle; he admitted that the generals who led the Federal troops had been both able and gallant. He also refrained from making any claim that the Confederates had won a complete victory on the first day, and conceded that the loss of general officers on the Confederate side had been "terribly severe." As the correspondent of a Louisiana newspaper, he could be expected to express the viewpoint of and laud the performance of his state's leading general.[50]

Yet there were certain shortcomings in his report, as there were in the other Confederate battle narratives. For reasons that can be easily comprehended he gave greater space to the fighting of the first day than that of the second. Moreover, he appeared to be overly harsh in his strictures on the behavior of the exhausted Confederate soldiery toward the end of the first day's fighting. He was in error, too, in reporting the participation and death of Union General Buell in Sunday's fighting and in claiming the capture or destruction of all but one of the Union batteries that day. There were also interesting discrepancies between his opinion of the effect of the Union gunboat fire and that of the *Crescent* reporter Stoddard.[51]

Most of the errors that marred the Southern reporting of the battle were in the special dispatches that were telegraphed from the battlefield before their authors had had the time and opportunity to separate fact from rumor. These press telegrams exaggerated the extent of the Confederate success, implying that Beauregard had triumphed on the second day as well as the first, incorrectly estimated the size of the enemy force at 100,000 to 125,000, credited Buell with having been in

---

ander's Shiloh battle account see *Montgomery Daily Advertiser*, April 16, 1862; *Atlanta Daily Southern Confederacy*, April 17, 1862; *Richmond Daily Dispatch*, April 17, 1862; *Knoxville Daily Register*, April 20, 1862; *Richmond Semiweekly Enquirer*, April 22, 1862.

[50] *New Orleans Daily Delta*, April 12, 16, 17, 19, 23, 1862; Alexander Walker, "Narrative of the Battle of Shiloh," in H. C. Clarke, *Diary of the War for Separation* (Augusta, Ga., 1862), pp. 114-60.

[51] Stoddard was impressed by the "tremendous fire" of the Union gunboats which "swept every contiguous portion of the battlefield" and credited the enemy with knowing every foot of the country they were shelling. Walker, on the other hand, although he admitted that the constant shelling of the gunboats produced no little alarm among the Confederate troops, thought it caused little damage.

command of Grant's army on the first day of the battle and as having been either killed or captured, described the Confederate battle line as extending fourteen miles, and confused the names of the Confederate generals who were in command of the various sectors of the line. Five days after the battle, in a special dispatch to the *Memphis Appeal* from Corinth, Alexander inaccurately reported that Beauregard's army was still in possession of the Shiloh battlefield.[52]

There were press errors of omission, too. In a letter to the *Mobile Register* from near Corinth on May 17, 1862, a Confederate cavalry officer charged that "the newspapers have chronicled the heroic deeds of daring and skill performed by the infantry and artillery arms of our service on the bloody field of Shiloh, but scarcely a word has been said about the cavalry, possibly because we may not have a letter-writer among us."[53] The Tennessee newspapers made similar complaints about discrimination against Tennessee troops on the part of newspaper correspondents attached to the press of the Lower South. Alleging that the most efficient and successful fighting at Shiloh had been performed by Kentucky and Tennessee soldiers, the editor of the *Memphis Avalanche* expressed pained surprise that the correspondents of the New Orleans, Mobile, and Charleston newspapers had sought to create the impression that troops from the Gulf States had done the principal fighting on April 6-7.[54] Perhaps the most extraordinary of all the questionable statements about the Battle of Shiloh in the Confederate press was the assertion by the editor of the *Montgomery Advertiser* that the Confederate "victory" at Shiloh had broken the strength of the enemy's western army, and that "it will never be able to make another advance upon our lines in the same spirit of confidence as before."[55]

When several days after the battle the *New Orleans Picayune* correspondent Reid paid a call on General Bragg, with whom he had previously had good relations, he discovered that the general was displeased with the press coverage of his performance on the field. Reid asked

[52] *Memphis Daily Appeal*, April 13, 1862. In the same dispatch Alexander alleged that poisoned balls and poisoned quinine, presumably the work of the Federals, had been found on the battlefield. For criticism of exaggerations in the Southern press of the Confederate "great victory at Corinth" see the comments of Confederate Attorney General Thomas Bragg in his unpublished diary under date of April 19, 1862. Misc. MSS., Southern Historical Collection, University of North Carolina.

[53] *Mobile Daily Advertiser and Register*, May 22, 1862.

[54] *Memphis Daily Avalanche*, May 7, 28, 1862.

[55] *Montgomery Daily Advertiser*, April 16, 1862.

Bragg if he had seen the dispatches and letters Reid had forwarded to the *Picayune*. Bragg said that he had not, "and that it would seem, so far as the newspapers were concerned, that he was not in the battle at all!" Bragg then expressed in a brusque manner his "entire indifference to the press" and said that "he supposed when the official report should be published, it would appear where he was." Reid made known his surprise at the general's irritation and declared that he thought he had done full justice to Bragg in his reporting. When, however, he went on to request further particulars about the battle, Bragg complained about being unwell and referred him to the adjutant general. Several days later, when Reid visited a member of Bragg's staff who had promised to communicate some incidents of the battle, he was informed that the staff member had already forwarded them to the *Mobile Register* in the form of a communication highly laudatory of General Bragg, stating that he was the last officer to leave the battlefield. From then on, Bragg avoided Reid and endeavored unsuccessfully to bring about the ostracism of the other press correspondents.[56]

The controversies to which the Confederate reporting of the Battle of Shiloh gave rise continued to disturb the relations of the Confederate high command with the press for months. When in July 1862 the *Savannah Republican* published a letter from Alexander containing critical comment about Beauregard's performance at Shiloh, Beauregard induced his former adjutant general, Thomas Jordan, to make a formal reply. Alexander's letter, printed under the caption "A Lost Opportunity at Shiloh," had submitted evidence from an interview with General Prentiss on an Alabama River steamboat to substantiate the charge that General Beauregard had prematurely called off the pursuit of Grant's army on the evening of the first day at Shiloh because of false information communicated to him by his prisoner, General Prentiss. Suspecting that Alexander had been duped by certain officers working in the interest of General Bragg, Jordan argued with some degree of plausibility that Beauregard was already well informed about Buell's movements when he talked to Prentiss and that his decision to call back his troops was based on a sound estimate of the situation.[57]

[56] *Charleston Mercury*, September 26, 1862.

[57] P.G.T. Beauregard to Brig.Gen. Thos. Jordan, August 8, 1862, P.G.T. Beauregard Papers, Library of Congress. In his letter of August 14, 1862 to Beauregard, published in the *Official Records*, Colonel Jordan referred to Alexander as the "dupe" of an unnamed officer of high rank in the army and in his July 7, 1862

Two DAYS after the Battle of Shiloh the Memphis newspapers reported the fall of the Confederate strong point on the upper Mississippi, Island No. 10. Foote's gunboats had run past the Confederate batteries during the first week of April, and on April 7, the Union besiegers gobbled up the Confederate defense force of 7,000, along with more than a hundred pieces of artillery. Among the prisoners was the Confederate war correspondent Youngblood of the *Memphis Appeal,* who managed to escape after several days of captivity.[58]

So intent was the Confederate press on the danger presented by the southward advance of the Union gunboats along the upper Mississippi that Confederate editors paid relatively little attention, publicly at least, to the attack on New Orleans from below that now threatened. On a visit to New Orleans in the early part of September 1861, Editor Forsyth of the *Mobile Register* had reported that Maj.Gen. David E. Twiggs and Commo. George N. Hollins were hard at work constructing defenses, "doing all they can with the limited means at their disposal." Forsyth refrained from saying that the seventy-one-year-old Twiggs was inefficient, but *New Orleans Delta* editor Alexander Walker was more candid about the state of affairs in New Orleans in a private letter to Secretary of War Benjamin written about this time. Walker told Benjamin that New Orleans was not prepared to defend itself against an attack by the large expedition that Walker had learned was being fitted out in New York, and begged for a change of commanders.

The mouth of the Mississippi had been subject to Federal blockade since the end of May 1861. Forsyth had noticed when he was in New Orleans that although the city was full of people business was at a standstill and the levees were devoid of produce. But not until a fleet of Union mortars and gunboats undertook to force an entrance to the Head of the Passes at the upper end of the Mississippi Delta in mid-April 1862 did the New Orleans press abandon its indifference. In January the *Delta* had deprecated the needless alarm which the presence of 2,000 enemy troops at Ship Island inspired; in mid-February

---

letter to the same general implied that Alexander's criticisms of Beauregard had been motivated by Beauregard's expulsion of Alexander as a "letter writer" from the army. *O.R.* (Army) Ser. I, vol. xvii, pt. 2, pp. 640-642, 679-680; Gen. G. T. Beauregard, "Notes on E. A. Pollard's Lost Cause," *Southern Magazine,* x (January 1872), 61-64. The text of Colonel Jordan's letter of August 8, 1862 to the editor of the *Savannah Republican* was reprinted from the *Republican* in *Atlanta Daily Southern Confederacy,* August 26, 1862.

[58] *Memphis Daily Appeal,* April 18, 1862.

the *Crescent* had declared that "the only real danger we apprehend comes from the Upper Mississippi."[59] The changed aspect of New Orleans security was reflected in a long editorial that appeared in the *Delta* on April 2, 1862, speculating on the thirty or forty enemy vessels which had just emerged from the Mississippi Passes. Were the two star-shaped forts seventy-five miles downriver from New Orleans, that constituted the city's principal defense against an attack from below, proof against the gunfire of such a naval expedition?

As if to answer the question, Capt. David D. Porter of the U.S. Navy opened fire on Forts Jackson and St. Philip with his mortars on Good Friday, April 18, an attack which caused the *Delta* to report that New Orleans was in serious peril. Day by day during the following week the New Orleans press reported the progress of the bombardment on the basis of official dispatches from the commandant of Fort Jackson and other dispatches that he had cleared for publication. Apparently the only reporter for any out-of-town newspaper who was stationed at New Orleans at this time was a certain "D." who was affiliated with the *Memphis Appeal*. "D." must have been reporting under difficulties, for on April 20 he notified his newspaper that the press in New Orleans had been "expressly enjoined from publishing or telegraphing any of the movements or occurrences hereabouts, especially those of the [Confederate] navy. . . ."[60] Because of the censorship that was obviously at work, the tone of the dispatches that appeared in the New Orleans newspapers was reassuring. The carefully doctored news reports made it appear that the garrison at the forts were in good spirits and that the forts were likely to hold out indefinitely against the Yankee barrage. The *Delta* admitted, however, that shells from the mortars fell in and around Fort Jackson with uncomfortable frequency and that the fury of the bombardment was "unprecedented in the annals of warfare."[61] Moreover, its editor had accurately concluded on April 2 that more was to be feared from a sudden dash of the Federal steamers past the forts than from a slow and continuous assault upon them by mortars and long-range guns.

Still confident that the enemy's assault on the forts would be repelled, the citizens of New Orleans awoke on Thursday morning, April 24

[59] *New Orleans Daily Delta*, January 16, 1862; *New Orleans Daily Crescent*, February 14, 1862.

[60] *Memphis Daily Appeal*, April 26, 1862.

[61] *New Orleans Daily Delta*, April 19, 1862; *Richmond Daily Dispatch*, April 23, 1862.

to hear the stunning news that the enemy fleet under Capt. David G. Farragut had slipped past the forts the night before. The information came in the form of a dispatch from A. E. Tulda, the telegraph operator at the Quarantine Station, which Governor Thomas Moore at once made public.[62] The shock of this unexpected announcement created boundless excitement in the South's largest city. The alarm bells rang out, and all business was completely suspended in conjunction with the proclamation of martial law by Maj.Gen. Mansfield Lovell, who had replaced Twiggs as the army commander. The Confederate government tried to suppress the news of New Orleans' defenseless condition, but on Friday Mobile learned what was happening when telegrams from the New Orleans operators of competing telegraph lines were published in the *Register*. Later that afternoon Pritchard's Associated Press sent a dispatch confirming the *Register's* story and adding that the telegraph operators were expecting to leave New Orleans soon. The censors stopped delivery of the Press dispatch, and by the following morning the New Orleans telegraph office had closed. From Mobile the news of Farragut's success was telegraphed to Richmond in time to appear in Saturday morning's newspapers.[63]

Meanwhile the Union warships had continued upstream after passing the forts, had silenced the Chalmette batteries near the city with little effort, and appeared off New Orleans on Friday morning. With less than 3,000 soldiers to defend New Orleans, General Lovell declared it an open city and marched out. By the following Wednesday it had been occupied by Federal troops. Although the Confederate War Department had official information by April 27 of the evacuation of New Orleans,[64] the Confederate government never acknowledged the city's fall to the press. Nevertheless, the Richmond press referred to the disaster on April 28 with undisguised bitterness and surprise, although the *Dispatch* tried to pretend that the event had been anticipated and that public opinion was already prepared for it. In a letter to his newspaper from Richmond, the *Memphis Appeal* correspondent John R. Thompson hooted at the *Dispatch's* version of the situation. Thompson

[62] *New Orleans Daily Delta*, April 25, 1862.

[63] *Wilmington Daily Journal*, April 26, 1862; *Mobile Daily Advertiser and Register*, April 29, 1862; *Charleston Mercury*, April 29, 1862; Bragg Diary, April 26, 1862, Southern Historical Collection. For indications of the application of censorship to press dispatches north of Augusta that reported the surrender of New Orleans see *Wilmington Daily Journal*, May 1, 1862.

[64] *Memphis Daily Appeal*, May 8, 1862.

snorted that "the public mind had already been prepared for no such thing. On the contrary, no event was considered more unlikely during the whole progress of this war than that New Orleans would fall into the hands of the enemy."[65] But although in New Orleans the *Delta* lamented that Louisiana had been left alone to defend its great city with little or no aid from the government in Richmond, other newspapers followed the lead of the *Richmond Dispatch* in minimizing the significance of the capture of New Orleans. For the *Memphis Avalanche* the city's fall was simply an "inconvenience" and not a "disaster"; on the day Butler's Yankee troops entered it the editor of the *Montgomery Advertiser* professed that he saw nothing "in any or all of our reverses to discourage any man who appreciates the trials through which a people are required to pass to make them worthy of Independence."[66]

To alleviate the perplexity of its readers as to how a great city of 200,000, supposedly defended by 30,000 disciplined troops, immense fortifications along the river, and an ironclad monster (the *Louisiana*), more formidable than the *Merrimack*, had surrendered without firing a shot, the *Richmond Enquirer* published on May 14 and 15, 1862 a detailed account of the events that preceded the surrender. It seems likely that the account, addressed to the editor of the *Enquirer* and signed by John T. Monroe, Mayor of New Orleans, was written at least in part by Durant da Ponte, editor of the *New Orleans Delta*.

ONE REASON that there had been so few newspapermen in New Orleans to report its capture was that the eyes of the press were focused on northeastern Mississippi. There Beauregard's army was holding in check the advance of an army fully twice as large, commanded by Union General Henry W. Halleck.

A reporter for one of the Richmond newspapers was filled with admiration for the hardy physiques of the South's Western soldiers, whom he compared favorably with the Virginians and Carolinians he had already seen in the East. He reported that "the troops from Louisiana are small, wiry, quick as squirrels in their motions and thoroughly Gallic in their habits and associations. The men of Alabama and Mis-

[65] *Ibid.*

[66] *New Orleans Daily Delta*, April 30, 1862; *Memphis Daily Avalanche*, May 9, 1862; *Montgomery Daily Advertiser*, April 30, 1862. The responsibility of the Confederate Navy Department for the fall of New Orleans is the theme of H. A. Trexler's "The Confederate Navy Department and the Fall of New Orleans," *Southwest Review*, XIX (Autumn 1933), 88-102.

sissippi are taller, as a general thing less cosmopolized, yet full of Southern fire." The soldiers of the region that he characterized as the West—Texas, Missouri, Arkansas, Tennessee, and Kentucky—impressed the Richmond journalist with their independent, swaggering air, their "Sort of don't-care-a-damativeness," which he ascribed to their "wild and ragged ancestry." Whereas the soldiers from the Gulf States wore an approximation to a uniform, the western men seemed remarkable to this reporter because of the variety of their gear. "Here you see the well dressed gentleman with nothing to mark the soldier but the cartridge box, body belt and shot gun. There is a group of Mississippi boatmen in their slouched hats, red shirts, heavy pants, and cowhide boots, coming up to the knee. Again you encounter the bushwhackers of Arkansas, Texas and Missouri, large bearded, hard handed, tough, muscular fellows, who eat victuals with their bowie-knives and sleep on the butts of their guns. Some have rifles which have come down to them as heirlooms from an untainted ancestry and are historic with the bloody records of bar fights and wild cat adventures; thousands have nothing but the ordinary shotgun, but all, more or less, go armed with the inevitable knife and revolver. Many ride poor Rosinantes of beasts, sometimes a horse, but as frequently a mule; and thus equipped, go forth looking like dilapidated Don Quixotes, but acting like very devils when they smell blood."[67] An Eastern newspaperman could not fail to notice their lack of discipline, along with their qualities of hardiness and courage, and the fact that their officers, who were in the main big enough to whip any man in the command, were inclined to let them have their own way and not subject them to the rigid constraints of military life.

Alexander, de Fontaine, and Reid were with Beauregard's army during the major part of the Corinth campaign. After New Orleans fell and the *Picayune* came under Federal control, *Picayune* reporters Reid and Perry accepted employment as special correspondents of the *Memphis Appeal*.[68]

On April 24 poet Henry Timrod arrived in Corinth to represent the

[67] *Richmond Daily Dispatch*, April 29, 1862. This report, to judge from its treatment of its theme and the pseudonym "Quel Qu'un" used by its author, was probably written by de Fontaine.

[68] Reid apparently became the special correspondent of the *Mobile Register* at Corinth after Alexander voluntarily resigned his connection with that paper on May 19, 1862. *Savannah Republican*, June 9, 1862.

Charleston Mercury as its special correspondent with the Army of the West. Timrod had come west from Charleston by a roundabout route on a South Carolina troop train. He was surprised, he admitted, to find that Corinth was "quite a place." He had expected it to be an insignificant railway station with a hut or two and perhaps a shop and post office in one. Instead, it was a large village with hotel, churches, several streets lined with shops, and many attractive dwellings.[69] After he had been with the army for a few days Timrod described Corinth in greater detail, with its crowds of anxious faces clustered in front of the post office window awaiting the distribution of the dilatory mails. His pen picture went on to portray how: "Under an oak, at no great distance from the postoffice . . . is the 'Southern News Depot' where the latest papers are purchased at the price of ten cents apiece . . . .

"The scene at the Railway Depot, where the Mobile and Ohio and the Memphis and Charleston Roads intersect each other beggars description. The depot is . . . shaped like the letter L, but it is usually so thronged that my crowd hating habits have not allowed me to observe it with any accuracy. Near it is the Tishomingo Hotel, a long three-storied brick building with a triple piazza running around three sides of it. . . . On the railway platform is a complete chaos of barrels, boxes and bustle of noise and nastiness; of goods, groceries and guards! A space of about a hundred yards in breadth, where mules, horses, wagons and people are tangled together in inextricable confusion, divides the railway from a range of stores, once filled with everything salable from calico to cheese . . . but now converted into depots where quartermasters look important or commissaries reign supreme."[70] A few nights later, while on a visit to General Beauregard's headquarters, Timrod caught sight of the French Prince de Polignac playing the piano

---

[69] *Charleston Mercury*, May 7, 1862. Timrod gives the date of his departure from Charleston as April 15, 1862 in a letter of that date to a friend in Columbia, S.C., Miss Rachel Lyons. William Fidler, ed., "Unpublished Letters of Henry Timrod," *Southern Literary Messenger*, II (December 1940), 650. Timrod told his feminine friend: "You must not look for very brilliant letters, as I intend to do nothing but tell plain facts in the plainest of styles. Even of these, I distrust my power to gather much. My want of *savoir-faire*, and my comparative inability to make my way among strangers will put many difficulties in my way. However I bear strong and flattering testimonials to all the great men of the army from Beauregard down, and I have some hopes also of being appointed temporarily on the staff of Gen. Crittenden . . . and I shall thus possess greater facilities than newspaper correspondents usually have."

[70] *Charleston Mercury*, May 14, 1862.

for a waltz program which was none the less spirited because not a single crinoline was present![71]

The poet-correspondent was not destined to find camp life very healthful or congenial, however. In a letter addressed to the *Charleston Courier*, de Fontaine described the unappetizing fare—hard bread, water, molasses, and tough bacon, and told how a reporter in camp was obliged to scrape the dust off his person with a shingle and wash his face with water brought from a mud puddle. "About three times a week we have the chills, with which my friend 'Kappa' [Timrod] and myself were wont to shake 'like the dry bones in the valley of Jehosophat.' Of late, however, we have grown too lazy to shake and look charitable on each other under the inspiring emotions of ye ague yclept 'dumb!' "[72]

The chills to which de Fontaine referred were common among the rank and file of the Confederacy's western army. The hotels and private residences of Corinth were already jammed with the sick and injured. By the middle of May Beauregard had 18,000 soldiers on the sick list. Alexander was too discreet to communicate such statistics to his newspaper for publication, but he admitted that there was considerable sickness in the army, the principal diseases being dysentery, pneumonia, and measles.[73]

Still another obviously unsafe subject for army correspondents was the low morale of the Army of the Mississippi, which reached dangerous proportions in early May 1862. To some extent it was the result of the news of the fall of New Orleans and the penetration of the enemy's fleet into the lower Mississippi, which many of Beauregard's soldiers regarded as the death knell of the Confederacy. To some extent it resulted from the increasing unpopularity of General Bragg, whose brutal treatment of the Tennessee volunteers within his command

[71] *Ibid.,* May 20, 1862.

[72] *Charleston Daily Courier,* May 29, 1862. For Timrod's description of the difficulties of reporting resulting from his illness see *Charleston Mercury,* May 20, 1862.

[73] *Savannah Republican,* May 12, 1862. The heavy mortality in the army from disease is ascribed quite as much to impure water as to inadequate diet in H. H. Cunningham, *Doctors in Gray* (Baton Rouge, 1958), pp. 180-81. A *Richmond Dispatch* reporter made clear that bad water was one of the more serious problems in the army. "With every pint of fluid one has to drink half an ounce of dirt. . . . If every man in the army has not a thoroughly macadamized wind-pipe by the time this war is closed it will not be the fault of the gravel he takes into it." *Richmond Daily Dispatch,* May 30, 1862.

had given rise to newspaper protest. According to one observer whole-sale desertion and even breakup of the army were only averted by the feeling of indignation against the Yankees that was excited by the publication of General Butler's famous "woman" order in New Orleans on May 15.[74]

In his advance on Corinth Union General Halleck was maddeningly deliberate, taking more than a month to reach an objective that should not have required more than three days. Beauregard did all he could to slow or halt the Federal advance by sending out cavalry parties to raid Halleck's line of communications, but he did not have enough cavalry to provide serious interference. Beauregard also kept on the alert to entrap any part of Halleck's army that became separated from the main body.[75]

During the first week of May Alexander reported an incident at Farmington, Mississippi about four miles east of Corinth, where one of Halleck's corps commanders, John Pope, exposed himself. Alexander told how Pope's 20,000 Federals broke and ran like the Union troops at Bull Run to avoid the capture of the greater part of their command.[76] Later in the month Pope returned to his old position, and once again Beauregard tried to spring the trap. But the results were the same as before except that this time the Federals did not fall back. In a letter dated at Corinth on May 22 which was published in the *Savannah Republican*, Alexander attributed the failure of the movement to faulty reconnaissance.

[74] Butler's notorious Order No. 28, May 15, 1862, in which he, as military governor of New Orleans, decreed, "when any female shall by word, gesture, or movement insult or show contempt for any officer or soldier of the United States she shall be regarded and held liable to be treated as a woman of the town plying her vocation." To angry Southerners sensitive about the honor of their women, the author of the order became "Beast" Butler; at least one newspaper, the *Jackson Mississippian*, offered a $10,000 reward for his head! William Watson, *Life in the Confederate Army* (New York, 1888), pp. 368-71. A somewhat misleading report of the existence of high morale among Beauregard's soldiers appears in a letter from Special Correspondent Henry Perry published in the *Memphis Daily Appeal*, May 14, 1862. Quite as significant as what Perry had to say about army morale was his mention of the arrival in the army at this time of the Rev. Dr. Benjamin M. Palmer, a noted clergyman from New Orleans, whose morale-building sermons were of unusual effectiveness. For a comparison of Palmer's influence to that of the eighteenth-century pamphleteer Thomas Paine see J. W. Silver, *Confederate Morale and Church Propaganda* (Tuscaloosa, 1957), p. 17.

[75] Williams, *Beauregard*, p. 151.

[76] *Savannah Republican*, May 17, 1862.

Beauregard's second failure to drive back the Federals convinced him that he would never be able to hold Corinth if it came under a siege. So on May 25 he called a council of his generals, in which it was agreed to withdraw down the line of the Mobile and Ohio Railroad.[77] The Confederate commander took elaborate precautions to preserve the secrecy of the evacuation. Taking a leaf from Halleck's three days earlier, Beauregard had already on May 24 ordered the press correspondents to leave the army on the first train and not to remain within twenty-five miles of Corinth.[78]

The reporters at Corinth were understandably indignant. It was whispered about the camp that the misbehavior of a single correspondent, Sam Reid of the *Memphis Appeal*, had provoked Beauregard's wrath. Reid's alleged offense had been a dispatch to the *Appeal* which stated that "a general engagement is expected tomorrow. Our whole army marched out this evening."[79] In a letter which he wrote to the editor of the *Charleston Courier* to vindicate his record, Reid denied that his dispatch had constituted a breach of security and submitted as evidence the fact that it had been cleared for publication by military authority of no less degree than Beauregard's acting Adjutant General, Captain Jordan. Reid went on to infer that Bragg rather than Beauregard had been responsible for the order. He ascribed Bragg's animosity toward the reporters to pique resulting from the small attention given by the press to the part he had played in the Battle of Shiloh.[80]

Nonetheless, Beauregard's order effectively eliminated on-the-spot

[77] Williams, *Beauregard*, p. 153.

[78] *O.R.* (Army) Ser. i, vol. x, pt. 2, p. 543; *Richmond Daily Dispatch*, June 7, 1862; *Mobile Daily Advertiser and Register*, May 29, 1862; *Savannah Republican*, May 28, 1862.

[79] Both Alexander and de Fontaine attributed the expulsion order to Reid's alleged indiscretion, although Alexander was inclined to think that Reid was being made the scapegoat for the failure of Beauregard's flanking movement. *Savannah Republican*, June 2, 1862; Charleston *Tri-Weekly Courier*, June 10, 1862. Reid's difficulties with the army authorities are also noticed in a letter by the army correspondent of the *Memphis Daily Argus* as reprinted in *Savannah Republican*, May 31, 1862. Reid's controversial dispatch was published in the *Memphis Daily Appeal* of May 22, 1862. It alluded to Beauregard's abortive advance of that day which failed to pick off Pope's corps at Farmington.

[80] *Charleston Daily Courier*, June 21, 1862; *Charleston Mercury*, September 26, 1862. For another indication that Bragg was instrumental in the expulsion of the reporters from Beauregard's army see the *Memphis Argus* letter cited above and signed "H.L.P." See also entries for May 22, 24, 1862 in S. C. Reid Diary, Reid Papers, Santa Cruz, California.

press coverage of the evacuation of Corinth. In conformance with army regulations de Fontaine and Perry headed for Memphis while Alexander and Timrod, accompanied by Reid, started homeward. Timrod's reporting experience in the West had netted him little more than discomfort and frustration. Many years later the journalist James Ryder Randall recalled meeting Timrod in Mobile at this time and befriending the ailing war correspondent who was already in an early stage of tuberculosis. According to Randall, "he [Timrod] could hardly travel any distance without losing his valise; and he had that singular disease which makes one blind or nearly so at night. I had to carry him around, at dusk, as if he were sightless."[81]

In Mobile Alexander learned that Beauregard had evacuated Corinth on May 29, presenting Halleck with a bloodless victory and the uncomfortable feeling that he had been hoaxed. But the censorship Beauregard had imposed at Corinth was still in evidence even at that distance from the army. When Alexander tried on June 2 to send a telegraphic synopsis of the evacuation of Corinth from Mobile to Savannah, the military superintendent of the telegraph refused to sanction it, and referred him to the military commander at Mobile, Brig.Gen. John H. Forney. When Alexander finally got through to Forney the commander likewise refused to approve the telegram, even though the information it contained had already appeared in part in the Memphis and Jackson papers.[82] After remaining in Mobile for a few days Alexander returned to Georgia.

While in Mobile Alexander had encountered his former employer, Editor Adair of the *Atlanta Confederacy*, who was on his way to Corinth to see for himself what Beauregard and Halleck were doing and to establish a system of army correspondence for his newspaper. Having learned from Alexander that newspapermen were taboo in the army and that Corinth was already in enemy hands, Adair decided to go to Memphis by way of Jackson instead, corresponding for the *Confederacy*

---

[81] J. B. Hubbell, *The Last Years of Henry Timrod* (Durham, N.C., 1941), pp. 12-13.

[82] *Charleston Daily Courier*, June 9, 1862; *Savannah Republican*, June 6, 1862. For the editorial protest of the *Mobile Register* prompted by the announcement of the order excluding the newspaper correspondents from Beauregard's western army see *Mobile Daily Advertiser and Register*, May 29, 1862. The *Register* defended its own conduct by stating that the dispatches of *its* correspondents had been under the surveillance of army headquarters, "and we have offered to submit every letter to the censorship of the General in command here [Mobile], before venturing to put them in type."

en route. On May 31 he was at the Gayoso House in Memphis, which he found largely deserted in anticipation of a sudden visit by the Yankees. Adair concluded that it would be best not to tarry there and run the risk of a Federal occupation. So he headed back for Mobile, missing the train to Jackson as the result of a prolonged conversation with a fellow editor in Canton, Mississippi, and arriving in Mobile on the day before Memphis fell.[83]

BOTH "Personne" and Perry were still in Memphis when Adair reached there on May 31. Five days later they learned that Fort Pillow, seventy-five miles upstream from Memphis and thirty-five miles distant by land, had capitulated. Now the only protection Memphis had against the Federal gunboats was the eight-steamer Confederate flotilla under the command of Commodore J. E. Montgomery. Martial law was already in effect at Memphis, and the *Richmond Dispatch* correspondent who was stationed there told how "billiards and bar-rooms have been tabooed, and houses of ill-fame can only *be visited by means of a pass from the Provost Marshal* or his assistants—a document which frequently finds its way into the hands of eager applicants."[84]

The Memphis newspapers attempted to put the best face on a bad situation that resourceful editorializing could supply. The *Avalanche* informed its readers that the evacuation of Fort Pillow was generally regarded in military circles as a "great triumph," and that the Confederates had held it "as long as we wanted to hold it, and when we got ready we left it in our own way and in our own good time." Such comments could only be evaluated as "whistling in the dark." When word of the evacuation of Fort Pillow reached Memphis around noon on June 5, so excited was everyone that the common mode of salutation along Main Street was, "When do you think the Federals will be here?"[85]

The naval battle that was to determine the fate of Memphis was fought on the river just above the city on the morning of June 6 in full view of tens of thousands of Memphis citizens. Among the spectators who lined the bluffs even before dawn was the *Charleston Courier*

[83] *Atlanta Daily Southern Confederacy,* May 27, 30, June 3, 8, 10, 1862; *Mobile Daily Advertiser and Register,* June 6, 1862.
[84] *Richmond Daily Dispatch,* June 17, 1862.
[85] *Memphis Daily Avalanche,* June 6, 1862.

special, de Fontaine, who had been carried from a sickbed to an observation point. His account of the fighting, probably the best that was published from the Southern point of view, he wrote from between a pair of bed sheets.[86]

De Fontaine's description of the gallant but hopeless resistance by the diminutive Confederate gunboat fleet, mounting twenty-eight light cannon, in comparison with the sixty-eight mostly heavy guns of their Federal adversaries, could hardly fail to fire the Southern heart. In just over an hour the battle was over. One Confederate vessel had been sunk, two burned, four captured; the only survivor, the *Van Dorn*, escaped downstream. Subsequently Commodore Montgomery was criticized for not avoiding such a hopeless fight and for not saving his fleet by flight. "Personne" refuted the argument with the explanation that Montgomery's gunboat flotilla did not have enough coal to go down to Vicksburg and that while they were still endeavoring to augment their coal supply, they came under attack.[87]

The various Memphis newspapers, *Appeal, Avalanche*, and *Argus*, likewise covered the naval battle, and enlarged on the hostile behavior of the citizenry during the first hours of the Federal occupation.[88] "Personne" remained in the city for several days after the arrival of the Yankees, but finally resolved to leave when a friend warned him that his presence was known to the Federals and that they were looking for him. Disguising himself as a farmer, the reporter left the city by night in a horse-drawn buggy provided by the same friend and escaped

[86] *Charleston Daily Courier,* June 17, 1862.

[87] *Ibid.*

[88] See e.g. *Memphis Daily Avalanche,* June 7, 1862; *Memphis Daily Appeal,* June 9, 1862. For a statement indicating that Memphis had exhibited much pro-Union sentiment three months earlier see the letter of war correspondent Israel Gibbons in *New Orleans Daily Crescent,* March 10, 1862. In an editorial published June 13, 1862, the *Appeal* denied the Northern newspaper accounts which gave the Federals credit for the humane act of putting tugs to work picking up the crews of the disabled Confederate gunboats. The editor went on to say: "In company with hundreds of others and in the vicinity of the disaster, we witnessed the sinking of the Gen. Lovell, as she was heading for the Tennessee shore. Her crew was instantly struggling with the watery element, and some three or four small boats put out from the shore manned by civilians to rescue as many as possible. While engaged in picking them up, four shots were fired at them from two of the Federal vessels. After the drowning men were rendered non-combatants by the casualties of war, their further destruction, as well as that of those who attempted the rescue, was sought. This is the truth—let history assert it!"

south to Hernando, Mississippi.[89] From Hernando "Personne" returned to South Carolina by easy stages to recover his health and prepare to go to whatever battlefield in East or West the *Courier* chose to send him.

[89] *Charleston Daily Courier*, June 21, 1862.

CHAPTER 6

Editor Daniel Sows Dissension
Among Lee's Lieutenants

～～～～～～～～～

ON JANUARY 3, 1862 Reporter William G. Shepardson of the *Richmond Dispatch* addressed a cryptic letter to his newspaper. Written in sentimental style under a Richmond dateline, it informed the readers of the *Dispatch* that this was to be the last in Shepardson's long series of army correspondence from the Confederate "Army of the Potomac." Although it could be inferred that the removal of the army to winter quarters was the cause of his departure, "Bohemian" offered no explanation of why he had "looked my last upon the broad flats of Manassas plains."[1]

The real reason for Shepardson's separation from the army was conceivably embarrassing to him. Four days after the publication of his concluding letter in the *Dispatch*, the *Richmond Examiner* revealed the startling information that General Johnston had issued General Order No. 98 calling for the expulsion of all newspaper correspondents and reporters from his army. The *Examiner* attributed Johnston's drastic action to "alleged imprudent statements made by some of the newspaper correspondents in relation to movements of the army and military affairs on the Potomac."[2] Nosing his way about the government departments in Richmond, *Charleston Courier* correspondent de Fontaine had already ferreted out the fact that a certain publication in a Richmond newspaper had triggered the general's wrath.[3] Soon Alexander of the *Savannah Republican* discovered that Johnston had issued his order as the result of a letter written from Manassas and published in the *Dispatch*, in which the author located the various brigades nearby and specified the particular places where they had taken up their quarters for the winter. That most of the information in the *Dispatch* article was unsuitable for publication, "P.W.A." did not attempt to deny, but why, he asked, should the correspondents of all the other newspapers

---

[1] *Richmond Daily Dispatch*, January 6, 1862.

[2] *Daily Richmond Examiner*, January 10, 1862. The number of the order was referred to in *Richmond Daily Dispatch*, January 24, 1862.

[3] *Charleston Daily Courier*, January 16, 1862.

and all the readers of these papers be punished for the folly of a *Richmond Dispatch* reporter, whom he failed to identify? Yet Alexander must have known that the culprit was none other than the nostalgic Mr. Shepardson.[4]

Before Johnston issued his expulsion order he had asked Secretary of War Benjamin to punish Shepardson for his breach of military security. Benjamin had replied that the law provided no recourse for this "outrageous breach of duty of both the writer and publisher," and that he had appealed to the Military Committee of Congress for legislation that would apply to such an offense. Benjamin also advised Johnston: "I think some of the mischief . . . arises from your own too lenient tolerance of the presence of newspaper reporters within your lines. . . . I feel persuaded that this man Shepardson is a spy, and would be found guilty as such by a court-martial, and if he is caught again within your camp, I trust you will bring him to prompt trial as a spy."[5]

The Confederate press objected strenuously to Johnston's restrictions on the right to report. Alexander could find few among his friends in Richmond who justified the order, "and these few are generally persons who have had some quarrel with the press, or who feel that their performances in politics or in the field have not been duly appreciated and magnified by the chroniclers of the press." The *Atlanta Confederacy* sounded an editorial blast, warning that behind Johnston's news blockade a great deal of "criminal folly, official incompetence, shameful shortcomings, and no little rascality" was being concealed and that the public welfare would suffer a thousand times more from this policy of silence than from the fault of publishing too much. The *Confederacy* also voiced the dubious opinion that few Southern papers had published anything that would be harmful for the enemy to know and that few newspaper correspondents had "trespassed upon the bounds of propriety or sound discretion."[6] Other Southern dailies invoked the freedom of the press in similar language. When a conven-

[4] *Savannah Republican*, January 29, 1862. "Bohemian's" responsibility for the banishment of the reporters is stated in *Petersburg Daily Express*, April 5, 1862.

[5] Judah P. Benjamin to Gen. Jos. E. Johnston, Centreville, January 5, 1862, Misc. MSS, New York Historical Society. For a reply to an inquiry from Beauregard about Shepardson's whereabouts see Major J. B. Walton to Gen. Beauregard, December 31, 1861. Beauregard Papers, Duke University. The Shepardson letter which incurred the wrath of Benjamin and Johnston was published in the *Richmond Dispatch* on December 30, 1861.

[6] *Atlanta Daily Confederacy*, March 1, 1862.

tion of newspaper editors met in Atlanta on March 11-12 to discuss the problems of wartime newsgathering, it appointed a committee to draft a series of widely publicized resolutions critical of Johnston's order.[7] To Southern newspapermen in general it seemed inevitable that unless Johnston or the War Department could be induced to rescind the order the public would have to depend on private letters from the army and the austere language of official communiqués for information about the operations of the Confederacy's eastern army.

With its reporters shut out of Johnston's command, the Confederate press had to rely almost altogether on its various Richmond news sources during the spring of 1862. But Richmond in January of that year was far from being a satisfactory residence for reporters and other civilians. A floating element of some 15,000 government employees, political adventurers, and get-rich-quick gentry had been added to the permanent population, and a correspondent of the *Petersburg Express* was unfavorably impressed by the high price of all kinds of food, the housing shortage, and the scarcity of gas illumination and candles. "I will not say," he asserted, "that it is as hard for a poor man to live here, as it is for a camel to go through the eye of a needle, but I can say, without endangering my veracity, that the poor man who can live in Richmond need have no fear of starving upon any other portion of God's foot-stool."[8] The lawlessness that had become rampant there was also the theme of considerable head-shaking by the *Examiner* and the other Richmond newspapers.

There was surface optimism in Richmond about the eventual success of the Confederate cause, but the series of military defeats that began with the disaster at Fishing Creek in late January seriously affected the morale of the Confederate capital. Particularly damaging to public confidence and to the sangfroid of the Richmond press was the outcome of the battle at Roanoke Island on February 7-8.

Early in January it had become known in Richmond that a huge Union naval expedition commanded by Brig.Gen. Ambrose E. Burnside was on its way south from Hampton Roads to strike at some point along the south Atlantic coast. Writing on January 20 from Norfolk, where the *Dispatch* had sent him after his hasty departure from

[7] *Daily Richmond Examiner*, January 21, 1862; *Savannah Republican*, January 14, March 18, 1862. The committee of protesting newspapermen consisted of F. G. de Fontaine, J. R. Sneed, and J. Henly Smith.

[8] *Petersburg Daily Express*, January 28, 1862.

Johnston's army, Shepardson guessed from the light draught of its vessels and from tips gleaned from the Northern press that the Burnside expedition was destined for the coast of North Carolina.[9] During the previous autumn another Union naval expedition had penetrated the lower (Pamlico) sound and established a foothold on the North Carolina coast. The capture of Roanoke Island off Albemarle Sound would expose Norfolk and its valuable navy yard to an attack from the rear. Yet the only defenders of Roanoke Island were a small garrison of 2,500 troops commanded by General Wise.

Shaped like an hourglass nine miles long and in places as much as three miles wide, Roanoke Island provided adequate maneuvering room for defense purposes. But Wise was troubled by the small size of his command, by his shortage of ammunition, and by the ineffectual character of the Confederate navy's auxiliary "mosquito fleet." Appeals to the department commander at Norfolk, Maj.Gen. Benjamin Huger, and to Secretary Benjamin netted Wise exactly nothing; and just as the Burnside expedition, with its 13,000 soldiers and twenty Union gunboats, hove into view off the lower end of the island, Wise was stricken with pleurisy.[10]

Shepardson left Norfolk on February 2 on a steamer bound for Albemarle Sound.[11] Five days later he was on Roanoke Island to report its defense against amphibious assault for the *Dispatch*. Brushing aside the seven tiny Confederate war vessels with their one gun each, the Union gunboats with their armament of sixty-four guns smashed the Confederate shore defenses and covered the landing of Burnside's troops on the evening of February 7. After attending some of the wounded of the Seventeenth North Carolina Regiment, who had been under fire at Fort Bartow, Shepardson went down to the water battery along the shore that night to estimate the results of the bombardment. Although the night was intensely dark and misty he could see the red glare of the burning huts reflected on the ramparts of the damaged fort.[12]

On the morning of February 8 the defenders of the island held off the attack for four and a half hours until Union flanking columns penetrated some "impassable" marshes and captured the Confederate de-

[9] *Richmond Daily Dispatch*, January 11, 21, 1862.

[10] R. D. Meade, *Judah P. Benjamin, Confederate Statesman* (New York, 1943), pp. 220-24; J. S. Wise, *The End of an Era* (Boston and New York, 1899), p. 181.

[11] *Richmond Daily Dispatch*, February 5, 1862.

[12] *Ibid.*, February 27, 1862.

fenders' three-gun battery. Cut off from escape, Wise's Confederates had to surrender; along with them the *Dispatch* correspondent Shepardson was made prisoner.[13]

The news of the fall of Roanoke Island and the capture of Wise's men plunged Richmond into gloom. Some of the heaviest losses in the fighting had been among the company of "Richmond Blues" made up of the sons of the city's most prominent families. One of the victims was Capt. O. Jennings Wise, a former editor of the *Richmond Enquirer* and the son of General Wise.[14] The *Charleston Mercury* correspondent Bagby reported the arrival in Richmond of the body of young Wise, and described in sorrowful fashion the tearless grief of the young man's father. Bagby also joined the throng of spectators that filed past Wise's bier as he lay in state at the Capitol, and heard an aged Irishman murmur, "Farewell, noble and gallant young man; may your spirit soon be in Paradise."[15]

Before the Richmond press obtained full details of the defeat, the *Richmond Dispatch* published, probably for purposes of morale, a statement from its Norfolk correspondent that Great Britain had just recognized the independence of the Confederate States. The reporting of the action by the Richmond press inspired criticism elsewhere because of its not giving suitable attention to the part taken by troops from states other than Virginia. The Richmond newspapers, on the other hand, excoriated the blunder of leaving 2,000 troops on the island to be trapped by superior numbers and wanted to know why the island had not been properly fortified and why the Confederate generals had failed to provide the means of escape. Within a matter of weeks the criticism led to a congressional investigation which placed the blame on General Huger and Secretary Benjamin.[16] Subsequently

---

[13] *Ibid.*, February 11, 1862.

[14] Strode, *Davis*, p. 196.

[15] *Charleston Mercury*, February 18, 20, 1862.

[16] *Memphis Daily Appeal*, February 18, 1862; *Richmond Daily Whig*, February 15, 1862; Meade, *Benjamin*, p. 22. In a letter to his newspaper from Richmond, Alexander charged that "the correspondents of the Richmond papers are singularly remiss in their accounts of the parts taken by troops from other States. One would hardly know, if he confined himself to the Richmond journals, that any other forces participated in the fight except those of their own State." *Savannah Republican*, February 20, 1862. See also *Charleston Daily Courier*, February 17, 1862; Diary of Thomas Bragg, Southern Historical Collection, University of North Carolina, February 25, 1862. For a reference to a letter which appeared in the *Raleigh Standard* criticizing "Bohemian's" remarks about the performance

Shepardson was paroled and permitted to return to Richmond, along with the other Confederate parolees.

Just before the Battle of Roanoke Island the local editor of the *Richmond Enquirer*, Clifton W. Tayleure, had returned to the city after an adventurous journey to Baltimore via what the *Enquirer* referred to as the "Underground Railroad." Tayleure's wife, to whom apparently he was very much attached, was living in Baltimore at this time; learning that she had been ill, he determined to pay her a visit. He had been in Baltimore only a few days before he was arrested and haled before the Union military commander of the department, Maj.Gen. John A. Dix. On learning of Tayleure's Southern sentiments, the general placed him under parole and ordered him not to leave Maryland for the South without written permission. Apparently the *Enquirer* local concluded that a promise made under duress was not a bona fide promise. At any rate, he absconded from Baltimore with four friends in a small boat and sailed down Chesapeake Bay to Virginia. Back in Richmond, Tayleure published in the *Enquirer* a lively and interesting account of the journey, in which he maintained that the citizens of Baltimore were overwhelmingly in favor of the Confederate cause and were waiting as patiently as they could for their day of deliverance.[17]

In the midst of increasing criticism of the Davis administration from the press and Congress because of the recent military reverses, Alexander reported for the *Savannah Republican* on February 22 the inauguration of the Confederate President and Vice President for the six-year term to which they had been elected the previous autumn. The members of the press in Richmond accepted an invitation to participate in the inaugural procession. In spite of a downpour of rain that lasted almost all day, Alexander commented on the large crowd in Capitol Square of ladies in carriages and some on foot, of soldiers, citizens, and visitors. He went on to tell how the crowd received both the President and Vice President with "hearty and prolonged cheers," and the Right Reverend Bishop Johns offered a touching prayer. According to Alexander, the inaugural address that followed "was delivered with

---

of the thirty-first North Carolina Regiment see *Richmond Daily Dispatch*, March 14, 1862. The text of the report of the Gaither Committee is given in *Petersburg Daily Express*, April 18, 1862.

[17] *Petersburg Daily Express*, February 4, 1862; *Charleston Daily Courier*, February 10, 1862; *Daily Richmond Enquirer*, May 26, 1862.

great dignity, and yet with much feeling and grace, especially the closing sentence. Throwing up his eyes and hands to heaven, he [Davis] said: 'with humble gratitude and adoration, acknowledging the Providence which has so visibly protected the Confederacy during its brief but eventful career, to thee, Oh God! I trustingly commit my-self, and prayerfully invoke, Thy blessing on my country and its cause.' "

"It was a scene never to be forgotten. The lowering clouds above the gigantic statues of our revolutionary fathers, stern and motionless . . . the vast crowd spellbound and silent, and the chosen Chief of a new born Republic, standing with uplifted eyes and hands, committing him-self to the tender mercy of the Ruler of Nations and of men, and hum-bly invoking his blessing upon his country and his cause! There was not a heart in that great assembly which did not involuntarily respond to the invocation, amen!"[18]

But even so solemn an occasion was not without its anticlimax. After the oath of office had been administered to the President and Vice President, Alexander noticed that an effort was being made to induce Vice President Stephens to say something. Whether because he was un-prepared to speak or did not think it proper, the Vice President, who was clad in a suit of domestic jeans woven by two young ladies from his home county in Georgia, simply made a deep bow to the audience and returned to his seat. Then the band, which had played "Dixie" after the swearing in of President Davis, concluded the ceremonies with a rendition of the Marseilles Hymn.

Almost exactly a fortnight later the best piece of war news in months made the front page of the Confederate newspapers. Its subject was the exploits of the Confederate ironclad *Virginia*, which had emerged from the Gosport Navy Yard near Norfolk to wreak havoc on the un-armored Union blockading squadron in Hampton Roads. She had left her berth in the navy yard simply to make a trial run, and the encounter with the blockade squadron that followed was the result of a spur-of-the-moment decision of the *Virginia's* commanding officer, Commodore Franklin Buchanan. For this reason none of the Confederacy's better-known reporters was on the spot to write up the story.

The nearest city of any size to the scene of the battle was Norfolk, whose press, together with the Norfolk reporters of various out-of-town

[18] *Savannah Republican*, February 26, 1862. The *Petersburg Express* printed the full text of the address, obtained from its Richmond correspondent, in place of the telegraphic synopsis provided by the Southern Associated Press.

newspapers, were best situated to report the details of the fighting. A lady correspondent of the *Mobile Register*, who signed herself "Virginia," was in Norfolk on Saturday, March 8, when the redoubtable Confederate ironclad cut loose from her moorings and in the company of three wooden gunboats (the *Yorktown*, *Jamestown*, and *Teaser*) glided quietly down the Elizabeth River into Hampton Roads. According to the *Register*'s reporter, "throngs of animated and enthusiastic citizens" on the wharves of Norfolk cheered enthusiastically as the *Virginia* steamed by, but there was no response from Buchanan and his polyglot crew.[19]

The two best Southern newspaper accounts of the fight were those published in the *Norfolk Day Book* and the *Petersburg Express*. The *Day Book*'s battle report, which was probably written by its editor, John R. Hathaway, was the more factual. Rather more quotable was the lively narrative that a special correspondent who was identified simply as "Rifleman" furnished to the *Express*. Here is how the *Express* reporter, who evidently was a soldier, reported the battle for his Petersburg newspaper:

Dear Express: When I tell you that within the last few hours I have seen the conclusion of the grand naval fight of the campaign; that I have seen the flame and heard the explosion of the *Congress*; have seen the slanting spars—all that is now visible—of the formidable *Cumberland*, the whilom terror of all these parts, . . . and the partner for many a day of the *Pawnee* in the consternation of hundreds of doughty dwellers by the sea in these capes; that I have seen the splendid *Minnesota* with a breach amidships on her port side as wide as the famous parliamentary gap through which an Irish counselor swore a coach and six might be driven; that I have seen the *Jamestown* and *Yorktown*, erst peaceful common carriers of travellers and "truck," now grim with cannon, making their first visit to Norfolk for well nigh a twelve month; that I have seen the gallant *Virginia*, rough with honorable scars, shooting along like some huge "Saurian," with a jaunty little Confederate flag at her peak gaily flaunting over a superb "star-spangled;" that these hands have helped to fold up the said "star-spangled," and that thousands of freemen saw her trail astern of our iron boat without a sigh— when I tell you all this have I not sketched you a chapter of events that will make the 8th and 9th of March "white stone" days in the calendar of the young republic?

Let me detail these events at some greater length, avoiding as much as possible the statistical department, whereof the *Day Book* will furnish you information enough for all the Gradgrinds. . . .

The blockade of the James has for many months past been maintained by

19 *Mobile Daily Advertiser and Register*, March 29, 1862.

the *Congress* and the *Cumberland*, two first class sailing frigates of 63 guns, and the *Cumberland* being the nearest of them, was the first object of the *Merrimac*'s attentions. As she approached the C. on the starboard side, her deck was seen lined with sharpshooters to pick off our gunners through the port holes. We struck her on her quarter, tearing away a large section of her works, and at the same time discharged the bow gun, dealing death down the entire line of her gun deck. Then backing out and leaving her beak fast in the timbers of the doomed vessel, the *Merrimac* rounded her stern, delivering another fire and catching a broadside herself as she made the circuit. Coming up on her port side, she delivered her fire again, and the *Cumberland* with a stagger and lurch settled down with all on board, in the waters, going down by the head on the spot of her six months' anchorage, in full view of thousands of Yankee soldiers drawn up in battle array on the beach.

Within 25 minutes from the first shot, the flood of the James closed over the hull of the *Cumberland*, and it savors of poetic justice that her destruction should be the work of a vessel which would never have been built but for the crew of the *Cumberland*—the main instruments in the burning of the old *Merrimac*.

The latter now turned her attention to the *Congress*, and with the utmost coolness, regularity and precision, battered her sides with shot after shot, assisted by the *Yorktown* . . . and *Jamestown*, . . . the *Teazer* [sic], the *Raleigh* and one or two other boats. In a short time she ran up her white flag, hauled down her colors and surrendered. A crew was sent to take off her wounded and prisoners, when to the undying infamy of Lincolndom, be it said, that both from the vessel and the shore, the boat's crew were fired upon and forced to return.

Commodore Buchanan gave the order to recommence the engagement, and a shell was sent through her from stern to bow, dealing indiscriminate death in its passage. Her guns were now silenced, and again a boat put out to her, to find her decks one vast charnel house, her scuppers running blood, and her works a shapeless wreck. As she had been run near shore, most of her crew who were not wounded made their escape—the rest were taken and brought aboard the *Raleigh* and again the savages ashore fired at the crew on their errand of mercy, killing one of their *own men*.

The *Congress* was then fired, and she illumined the horizon till midnight, when the magazine exploded, and all that remained of the blockade of James River was the bare spars of the sunken *Cumberland*, and floating and charred fragments of her consort.

During this fight, the *Minnesota*, a magnificent steam frigate of 42 guns, with the *St. Lawrence*, and it is supposed the *Roanoke*, advanced from Old Point to the assistance of their beleaguered comrades. The *Merrimac* engaged them all, and for several hours a rain of shot and shell battered her unyielding sides. All retired, eventually, except the *Minnesota*, which ran aground about a mile and a half below Newport News.[20]

[20] *Petersburg Daily Express*, March 11, 1862.

Neither of the accounts published in the *Express* and the *Day Book* devoted as much space to the battle between the *Virginia* and the *Monitor* on the following day as they did to the more successful achievements of the *Virginia* in Saturday's engagement. The *Express* reporter claimed that twice the *Virginia* ran the *Monitor* down, but could not sink her because of having lost her long beak in the first attack on the *Cumberland*. The reporter for the *Day Book* described the "sharp encounter" that took place between the *Monitor* and the *Virginia* "during which time they were frequently not more than thirty or forty yards apart. Unfortunately the *Virginia* ran aground, and the *Ericsson* used her advantage, poured shot after shot into her, but without doing any serious damage. In a short while, however, the *Virginia* succeeded in getting off, and putting on a full head of steam, ran her bow into the *Ericsson* doing, as it is thought, great damage."[21] The first reports of the battle also made it appear that the *Minnesota* had been destroyed along with the *Congress* and *Cumberland*, inaccurately classed the *Cumberland* as a sloop of war rather than as a frigate, and referred incorrectly to the *Monitor* as a ram.[22] One of the *Day Book* staff made the accurate prediction that "this successful and terrible work . . . will create a revolution in naval warfare, and henceforth iron will be the king of the seas."[23]

Before Alexander left Richmond at the end of February to cover military operations in Tennessee he expressed concern about the Yankee onslaught he obviously expected. It was common knowledge that a large Federal army had been concentrated near Washington to attack Richmond as soon as weather conditions permitted. Yet the Confederate press had no way of knowing through direct observation from what direction the invasion was likely to come. Nor did any of the Richmond correspondents of out-of-town newspapers have the kind of confidential relations with President Davis that would enable them to communicate informed guesses about the enemy's intentions. Still Thompson of the *Memphis Appeal* expressed contempt for the "craven souls" who ran from one end of the town to the other, sounding the alarm that the Yankees would be in Richmond in ten days, that the

[21] *Norfolk Day Book*, March 11, 1862; Frank Moore, *Rebellion Record* (New York, 1862), IV, 276-79. Other accounts of the naval battle appeared in the *Richmond Daily Dispatch*, March 13, 1862; *Daily Richmond Examiner*, March 15, 1862.
[22] See e.g. *Mobile Daily Advertiser and Register*, March 11, 1862.
[23] *Norfolk Day Book*, March 11, 1862.

government was planning to abandon Virginia as a line of defense and make a stand in North Carolina, and that Richmond was filled with Union men who were prepared to betray the city at the first opportunity![24]

During the first week of March Richmond was put under martial law, and the subject of public morale at the capital preempted the attention of the Richmond reporters. Da Ponte of the *New Orleans Delta* conceded that the recent reverses in North Carolina and Tennessee had caused much "depression" in Richmond, but Bagby insisted in a letter to the *New Orleans Crescent* that in spite of the dangers presented by Union light-draught gunboats, the population of Richmond was bearing up very well. As an illustration of its resolute spirit he told of passing General Wigfall on the street and of asking the general if there was any news. "No," boomed Wigfall, "I don't believe we have been whipped since dinner; I expect, though, to hear of another defeat in the next five minutes!"[25]

By the latter part of March Thompson seemed convinced that public sentiment in Richmond was much more hopeful and determined. He described the situation as one in which "our people have made up their minds to a long and wasting war. . . . Volunteers are pouring in from all quarters. . . . The new feeling seems to have infused something of energy even into the departments."[26] Bagby disagreed, maintaining that it was idle to deny that the "good people of Richmond" were "scared."

"But the country people, and more particularly the men in the army, are in high spirits. For example, there was in my room today a talented young fellow belonging to [Stonewall] Jackson's command who discoursed me for an hour on the uprising of the people of the [Shenandoah] valley and the immense advantages we have derived from our

[24] *Memphis Daily Appeal,* March 5, 1862. On another occasion Thompson made reference to the comparatively small number of people who had the chance to see the President frequently and intimated that his knowledge of Davis was "from hearsay only." *Ibid.,* March 28, 1862.

[25] *New Orleans Daily Delta,* February 19, 1862; *New Orleans Daily Crescent,* February 20, 1862. In a letter to General Bragg mailed from Richmond on March 16, 1862, a Confederate congressman named G. L. Pugh conceded that "public confidence has been very much shaken in the Government, and while I do not participate in the general distrust . . . I cannot close my eyes to the fact that dissatisfaction prevails everywhere." Braxton Bragg Papers, Western Reserve Historical Society.

[26] *Memphis Daily Appeal,* March 28, 1862.

defeat at Donelson. . . . On Sunday, a friend from Lynchburg came to me . . . enthusiastic. 'By jings!' said he, 'you ought to see the way the soldiers and the militia are pouring into Lynchburg. Great strapping fellows from the mountains—men in the prime and vigor of life—none of your boys that get sick and break down, but real able-bodied busters.' Again to-day, a Captain, who is getting up a company here in the city, said to me as we met on the street, 'I've just got seven of the finest recruits you ever saw. What do you think of four brothers, the smallest weighting 195 pounds and the shortest reaching six feet two inches, and all from Louisa county?' . . . These are encouraging signs."[27]

Richmond citizens had reason for being "scared," for on April 2 McClellan arrived at Fort Monroe across from Norfolk with an army of 121,500 men that was obviously intent on the capture of Richmond. The day before McClellan's first contingents arrived the *Richmond Dispatch* had alerted its readers to the movement of the huge army from the neighborhood of Washington to the Virginia Peninsula, and had credited the Federals with acting on the premise that this would be a shorter and easier road to Richmond than *via* Manassas. Early in March Johnston had evacuated the Manassas-Centreville area, pulling back his troops first to the Rappahannock and then to the Rapidan. Yet at the beginning of April the Confederacy had only 12,000 men at Yorktown under Brig.Gen. John B. Magruder and 13,000 troops at Norfolk under Huger to confront McClellan's mighty host until Johnston could send reinforcements. When by April 4 it had become abundantly clear that the Federal army was about to advance on Richmond by way of the peninsula formed by the York and James Rivers, Johnston began withdrawing his army from north of Richmond to the southeast and established his new command post at Yorktown.[28]

An appreciative observer of these troop movements was Reporter Bagby. In a letter to the *Charleston Mercury* which he mailed on April 14, Bagby told of seeing eight or ten thousand soldiers march out of Richmond the day before toward the expected attack. "Most of them were Georgians, and a sturdier, more cheerful set has never passed through this city. . . . Thousands of people crowded the hills that overlooked the place of their departure. The lower part of Main street for

[27] *New Orleans Daily Crescent*, April 9, 1862.
[28] G. E. Govan and J. W. Livingood, *A Different Valor, The Story of General Joseph E. Johnston, C.S.A.* (Indianapolis, 1956), pp. 105, 107-108, 114.

many squares was perfectly lined with soldiers, sitting on the curb-
stones as contentedly as if they were in rocking chairs, smoking, talking, laughing and hurrahing at every stray dog that came along just
as though they were not going to, perhaps, the deadliest of all the
battles of the war. It was amusing to see some of them eating fat
bacon as if it were cheese. . . . Gen. Toombs was acting as commander
of the division. He rode a grey horse, and wore a big high crown
black slouch hat and a long red worsted comfort around his neck."[29]

Since civilian war correspondents were still persona non grata in
Johnston's army, the Confederate press had to depend on Richmond
news releases or the letters of soldier correspondents for the details of
the siege of Yorktown which lasted through April. On April 15 Secretary of War George W. Randolph informed Graeme, the Richmond
agent of the Southern Associated Press, that, "if the commanding general in the Peninsula has no objection," he could send an Associated
Press reporter to that area, "but all communications for the press must
be submitted for the approbation of the general in command."[30] In
the light of Johnston's hostility toward the press, Graeme must have
regarded such a promise as meaningless.

On May 6 the Richmond press published from Northern news sources
a report of the evacuation of Yorktown on May 4, which Johnston had
successfully carried out a matter of hours before McClellan was ready
to blast it with his big guns. During the next twenty-four hours the
Federal Army of the Potomac pursued the retreating Confederates up
the Peninsula, overtaking their rear guard at Williamsburg on May 5.
On May 7 the *Petersburg Express* published an extra, based on information received from one of General Magruder's dispatch bearers,
reporting the repulse of the enemy and a "glorious victory."[31] From
Petersburg the good news was telegraphed to Richmond and other
points.

Both sides in fact claimed the victory, the Federals because they
retained possession of the field after a conflict that had been confusion
from start to finish, and the Confederates because they had checked

[29] *Charleston Mercury*, April 17, 1862.

[30] *O.R.* (Army), Ser. i, vol. li, pt. 2, p. 540. On April 22, 1862 Attorney General
Thomas Bragg noted in his diary, "From Yorktown nothing transpires. The telegraph line is in the hands of the Gov't—the newspapers are wroth that they cannot
publish every thing, as they have been doing."

[31] *Petersburg Daily Express*, May 8, 1862.

the enemy's pursuit. Union casualties of 2,239 exceeded the South's losses of 1,703.[32]

The elation the Confederate version of the battle inspired was diminished by the almost simultaneous reports of the abandonment of Norfolk and the destruction of the ironclad, *Virginia*. With the collapse of the Yorktown line the Confederate high command had felt obliged to give up Norfolk and the Gosport Navy Yard. In an effort to escape up the James the crew of the *Virginia* removed everything from the ship but her supply of shot and powder, to enable her to draw no more than the requisite eighteen feet. But when the pilots still refused to move the ship, pointing out that the unarmored portions of the hull were now exposed, she had to be blown up to prevent her from falling into enemy hands. Again, as in the case of the evacuation of Yorktown, the Richmond newspapers obtained their first word of this discouraging news from Northern sources, and it was more than a week after the event before the Mobile press received official confirmation of the news by telegraph.[33]

Once more the morale of the people in Richmond sagged. In such an atmosphere of confusion and doubt almost any kind of rumor was likely to gain credence. On May 8 several Richmond newspapers reported that another bloody engagement between McClellan's and Johnston's forces had taken place at Barhamsville on the south bank of the York River, about twenty miles above Williamsburg. A courier who was supposed to have reached Richmond early that morning from the scene of the engagement was quoted as saying that the fight had been the most costly of any that had yet occurred during the war and that "when night closed upon the bloody scene, we had two thousand men killed and wounded, while the Yankee loss was estimated at 6,100." Unbounded anxiety prevailed in Richmond until three o'clock that afternoon when a dispatch dated at Barhamsville just before noon was received from General Johnston stating that all was quiet in the army and that the enemy appeared perfectly contented with his

[32] Shelby Foote, *The Civil War, A Narrative, Fort Sumter to Perryville* (New York, 1958), p. 411. On May 13, 1862 Attorney General Bragg confided to his diary that, "the fight at Williamsburg seems to have been severe. As usual *Virginia* papers speak only of *Va.* troops. But No. Ca. had at least two Regiments, McRae's and Scales' and the Ellis Art'y—Cap. Manly, in the action—and all suffered severely."

[33] J. T. Scharf, *History of the Confederate States Navy* (New York, 1887), pp. 221-23; *Mobile Daily Advertiser and Register*, May 14, 1862; *Petersburg Daily Express*, May 11, 13, 1862.

achievements at the Battle of Williamsburg. Neither statement was strictly accurate. An attack by Whiting's brigade on the skirmish line of General Franklin's Union division that morning had resulted in sharp fighting for several hours and a loss of a little over 200 men on both sides.[34]

McClellan's continued advance up the Peninsula caused panic to grip Richmond during the second week of May. It was bruited about the city that the Confederate Congress had adjourned and left town, that the president had sent his family to Raleigh, North Carolina for safety, and that the archives of the government were being boxed up for removal to Columbia, South Carolina. On May 16 Dr. Shepardson, who was now covering the Richmond news beat for the *Mobile Register*, informed his newspaper that hundreds of people were leaving the capital every day for distant points in Virginia and the North Carolina mountains and that the Danville railroad depot was piled high with the baggage of the refugees. Shepardson learned at the telegraph office that morning that the government had taken over control of the telegraph lines south and west of Richmond and that his news dispatch would have to be endorsed by some commanding officer. At the office of the provost marshal, General Winder's adjutant refused to authorize the transmission of Shepardson's dispatch in the general's absence, and referred him to Adjutant General Cooper. The adjutant general advised him to consult the secretary of war, who in turn curtly referred him to the president's chief military adviser, General Lee. Fortunately Shepardson met with courteous treatment from Lee; his dispatch was properly endorsed and sped over the wires to Mobile.[35]

Some indication of the appearance of Richmond at this juncture was communicated in a letter Thompson wrote to the *Memphis Appeal*. He told about "groups of excited men at every corner; dense crowds before the bulletin boards of the newspaper offices; long lines of army wagons rattling over the clamorous pavements; here and there, an officer in a smart, fresh uniform, in strange juxtaposition and contrast with a knot of pallid, ragged soldiers whom the bright sun had tempted to stroll out of the hated hospital; couriers, covered with the dust of

[34] *Petersburg Daily Express*, May 9, 1862; R. U. Johnson and C. C. Buel, *Battles and Leaders of the Civil War* (New York, 1956), II, 221.

[35] *Mobile Daily Advertiser and Register*, May 22, 1862; S. A. Putnam, *Richmond during the War* (New York, 1867), pp. 129-30.

the road, on broken down horses in feeble gallop towards the War Department."[36]

On May 15 anxious citizens at the capital could hear the sound of McClellan's gunboats pounding away at the Confederate shore batteries along the James at Drewry's Bluff. In some measure public confidence was restored when the press announced the next day that the Federal gunboats had been repulsed and that it had been determined in a cabinet meeting that the Davis government would remain in Richmond and defend the city to the last. Another factor in mitigating the panic was the resolute behavior of the Richmond press.[37]

On the 19th Shepardson informed the *Mobile Register* by letter that Johnston's army had crossed the Chickahominy River in its retreat up the Peninsula and was now only a few miles from the city. He added that Johnston's soldiers were desperate. "McClellan threatens to push them to the wall, and against it they will put their backs, and, like the fiery Fitz James, dare one and all to mortal combat."[38] The real state of affairs on the Peninsula was quite as little known to the Richmond press as to its readers. The editor of the *Richmond Dispatch* complained on May 29 that "seeking needles in bundles of hay" would be comparatively more easy than obtaining positive information about the army situation and that the military authorities had erected such an "impassible barrier" to newsgathering that it was physically impossible to evade its effectiveness or overcome the many impediments to free passage through the lines.

The press, therefore, was as unprepared as anyone else for the news of the Confederate counterstroke in what came to be known as the Battle of Seven Pines. Johnston was aware that two of McClellan's army corps (Keyes' and Heintzelman's) had crossed to the south bank of the Chickahominy and advanced to within seven miles of Richmond. He noted also that repeated rains had raised the level of the river to flood stage, making it difficult for McClellan to send reinforcements in the events of a sudden attack on these two corps. With an army of 63,000 divided into six divisions, Johnston decided to attack the exposed portion of his adversary's command.[39]

[36] *Memphis Daily Appeal*, May 22, 1862.

[37] *Mobile Daily Advertiser and Register*, May 22, 1862; *Richmond Daily Dispatch*, May 16, 1862; *Philadelphia Weekly Times*, November 16, 1878.

[38] *Mobile Daily Advertiser and Register*, May 27, 1862.

[39] Govan and Livingood, *A Different Valor*, pp. 146-47.

Johnston's plan was well thought out, but its bungled execution by his division commanders was a nightmare of confusion and delays. Longstreet and Huger became embroiled in a controversy over precedence, and an attack that was supposed to be launched on Saturday morning, May 31, did not get under way until two o'clock in the afternoon. The attack was finally delivered by the division of D. H. Hill who became tired of waiting for a signal that never came. Although Hill's attack was unsupported on either flank, it swept over the first line of Casey's Union division, and Longstreet's advance was similarly successful. But when Gustavus Smith's division, reinforced by four brigades from Magruder and A. P. Hill, marched down the Nine Mile Road to strike the Union General Keyes' exposed right flank, it collided instead with "Bull" Sumner's muddy Federal corps who had just crossed the river to relieve their hard-pressed comrades. Smith could make no headway against Sumner. To the south Hill's attack had stalled when it reached Keyes' third line. As night came on Johnston was struck down, first by a bullet and then by a shell fragment. Davis and Lee, who were nearby, went looking for Smith, who was second in command. Finding that Smith was mentally unstrung, Davis decided the next morning that Lee should assume command of what was henceforth to be known as the Army of Northern Virginia. There was only indecisive fighting on Sunday, June 1, as the army that had launched the attack disengaged itself for a future offensive stroke under its new commander.[40]

Editor Richard Yeadon had come up from Charleston on the eve of the battle for a reunion with his soldier nephew and adopted son, Corporal Richard Yeadon, Jr., and for the purpose of writing, at his son's request, an account of what promised to be "the greatest battle of the war." Yeadon had arrived in Richmond on Wednesday, May 28, and had gone out in search of his son's camp the next day in a horse and buggy which cost him ten dollars to hire. He located his son with some difficulty in the camp of the Hampton Legion and noticed with some surprise the privations and discomforts of camp life. The Legion, he was told, had been without tents since a retreat in which they were involved the previous March; their only bed was the ground.

On the morning the battle opened, Yeadon had gone to pay his respects to President Davis and several members of the President's cabinet, seeking to arrange for some military transfers for officer friends.

[40] Foote, *Civil War*, pp. 445-49.

Knowing that a battle was scheduled for that morning, Davis must have been little disposed to engage in casual conversation with a somewhat garrulous Charleston newspaper editor. Nevertheless, he received Yeadon "courteously and kindly." After taking leave of the President, Yeadon went in company with Secretary of the Treasury Memminger to see Benjamin, now secretary of state, with whom he enjoyed "a half hour of lively conversation." Yeadon returned to the army that afternoon, watched the Federal artillery in action, and had one more brief meeting with his son. Not until the next day did he learn of his son's death that afternoon while taking part in a charge. Yeadon's personal tragedy distracted him from the larger aspects of the battle.[41]

Editor Glass of the *Lynchburg Republican,* another prominent Confederate newspaperman who happened to be in Richmond at this time, contributed one of the more significant accounts of the battle. In a letter to his newspaper written on June 1, Glass told how "Judge Daniel, John Goode, and myself were on the field all day yesterday and to-day, and were favored with such positions as gave us a full sight and hearing of everything which transpired."[42] There was no indication in Glass's account of the battle of anything less than a complete success on the part of the Confederates. He told how Hill's division carried two strong lines of enemy entrenchments and declared, "when night closed the scene of carnage," Johnston's soldiers were "victors of the entire field." He credited Longstreet's and Hill's divisions with having done most of the fighting, and confessed his inability to make even an approximate guess as to the number of casualties. Later he estimated that the Confederate loss would not fall short of 2,000 and that the enemy's was fully as much, if not a thousand more, besides five hundred prisoners.[43]

The reporting of the Battle of Seven Pines by the Southern press was rather disappointing as a whole. Since reporters in civilian garb (as distinguished from editors) were not permitted within army lines, the Richmond newspapers had to depend on the statements of participants whose knowledge usually did not extend beyond the limits of a single regiment or even company. James R. Sneed, the editor of the *Savannah Republican,* was considerably disgruntled with the poor performance

[41] *Charleston Daily Courier,* June 13, 14, 16, 1862.
[42] *Lynchburg Daily Republican,* June 4, 1862.
[43] *Ibid.,* June 5, 1862.

of the Southern Associated Press. With scarcely concealed sarcasm, he snapped: "Whilst private individuals are telegraphing important information from Richmond concerning the late battles, we would be glad to know what that individual is doing who has set himself up at the capital as the agent of the Press and regularly comes forward with a bill for his services. . . . What are you at, Mr. Graeme, that everybody else can get important information, and you alone remain in the dark. . . ? For three whole days you have been burying the dead, without finding who they are, and watching with wonder and admiration the 'quiet' that reigns 'along the line'—is there nothing else you can do that would better interest the public for whom you set yourself up as a caterer of news?"[44]

Probably Sneed had not anticipated the rancor that his editorial would inspire in the breast of the Southern Associated Press manager, William H. Pritchard, Jr. Pritchard promptly dashed off an angry letter to the owner of the *Republican*, F. W. Sims, defending his Richmond agent and announcing his intention to strike the name of the *Savannah Republican* from his list of subscribers. Not simply did Pritchard carry out his threat; he also threatened to administer similar treatment to all newspaper proprietors who made their press dispatches available to the *Republican*.[45]

Yet Sneed was not alone in his dissatisfaction with the reporting of the battle. A subscriber to several Southern newspapers complained thirteen days after the battle that in none of them had he seen any attempt at a full account of the recent battle along the Chickahominy and that even the Richmond papers contented themselves with trivial items, lists of those killed, and lavish praise of their favorite military detachments. He added that the only connected narrative of the battle he had seen in the *Charleston Mercury* was reprinted from a Northern newspaper.[46] Omission of essential information was not the only charge that was directed against the battle reporting of the Richmond papers.

[44] *Savannah Republican*, June 5, 1862. For a statement by the editor of the *Richmond Dispatch* enlarging on the difficulties of giving an accurate and comprehensive picture of a battle like Seven Pines immediately afterward see *Richmond Daily Dispatch*, June 3, 1862.

[45] *Savannah Republican*, June 10, July 4, 1862.

[46] *Savannah Republican*, June 21, 1862. The *Mobile Register* on June 10 had quoted the *Richmond Whig* as placing the Confederate loss in the battle at 2,500 to 3,000, and had expressed the opinion that the Federal loss including prisoners was not less than 10,000. The actual losses were: 6,134 Confederates and 5,031 Federals. *O.R.* (Army) Ser. I, vol. xi, pt. 1, pp. 754, 762; pt. 2, p. 506.

In Fayetteville, North Carolina the *Observer* of that city published a letter from the colonel of the Fifth North Carolina Regiment alleging that "the Richmond papers (except the *Whig*) are so erroneous about the battle of Saturday that I propose to give you the facts. . . ."[47]

The failure of the Confederate government to supply official information about the battle excited the suspicion of the editor of the *Savannah Republican*. Taking into account other evidence that the Confederates had suffered heavy losses, Sneed expressed apprehension lest his side had gotten the worst of the fight. "Too many of our dead were left in the hands of the enemy for us to bragg [*sic*] too vociferously over the battle as a victory to our arms."[48]

As usual there were complaints of discrimination by the press against military units whose meritorious battle performance had been ignored. The anger of North Carolinians was aroused by a statement in the *Richmond Dispatch* that erroneously credited Longstreet's division with arriving on the field before the division commanded by the Carolinian Gen. D. H. Hill. Taking into account the bad feeling to which such discrimination gave rise, the *Richmond Enquirer* attributed these instances of injustice to the readiness with which some soldiers supplied the press with information while others were "tardy or neglectful." The *Enquirer* suggested that any soldiers who felt aggrieved by the lack of newspaper publicity for their commands should "quietly correct the omission as far as requisite" and remain patient. "The sad lists of casualties which we are publishing will tell the story better than the flowing sentences of the novelist, and the people will not fail to understand it."[49]

An unusually vivid description of the battlefield of Seven Pines, written on the third day after the battle, was contributed to the *Memphis Appeal* by its special correspondent, "T.E.C." The *Appeal* reporter pictured virtually impassable roads crowded with pedestrians and vehicles of every description moving toward or coming away from the field, ambulances laboring to and fro filled with the wounded and the dying, citizens on horseback or on foot along the roadside inquiring for relatives or friends, and orderlies, aides, and dispatch bearers splashing through mud and mire. He told of stretcher-bearers slowly creeping through the bushes searching for the wounded, guided by lantern

[47] *Richmond Whig*, June 9, 1862; *Fayetteville Observer*, June 5, 1862.
[48] *Savannah Republican*, June 7, 1862.
[49] *Daily Richmond Enquirer*, June 5, 1862.

carriers, of surgeons with coats peeled off and sleeves tucked up, plying "the horrid knife" in every cabin, of soldiers in camp hugging their blankets, and here and there a wounded man describing his "hair-breadth 'scapes'" and hungrily devouring scraps of bread and bacon.[50]

The Battle of Seven Pines had checked McClellan's advance, but did not remove the threat to Richmond. Meanwhile Confederate newspaper editors and their readers were beginning to hear exciting reports about a new military celebrity who had been giving a good account of himself in the Shenandoah Valley. Charged with the mission of tying down Federal forces considerably more numerous than his own and preventing the reinforcement of McClellan's army by McDowell's troops at Fredericksburg, Stonewall Jackson had on May 25 inflicted a serious defeat on Banks' division at Winchester and was about to play an interesting game of hide-and-seek with no less than three widely separated Federal commands.

Well in advance of other newspapermen Reporter George Bagby had taken note of Jackson. In a letter to the *New Orleans Crescent* written when Jackson was still comparatively unknown to the public, Bagby told his readers: "Jackson is described as a spare man, above the medium stature with dark hair and eyes, a sallow complexion, and a habit of holding his head back so that he never looks at the ground. He is as brave and cool as a human being can be; a Presbyterian who carries the doctrine of predestination to the borders of positive fatalism—the very man to storm the infernal regions in case of necessity. Silent and uncommunicative, exceedingly polite, yet short and prompt in his speech, he has but little to do with the commanders under him, but is devoted in his attentions to the men, especially to those who are sick."[51]

Unfortunately from the standpoint of news, special correspondence from the Shenandoah Valley during May and the early part of June

[50] *Memphis Daily Appeal,* June 17, 1862. Bagby's observations of the fringes of the battle area on the morning of June 1 conformed to the picture sketched by the *Memphis Appeal* reporter. According to Bagby, "the scene on the road beggars description. Omnibuses, wagons, caissons, and other vehicles were stalled and wrecked along the road for miles. Horsemen found it difficult to traverse the continuous mud puddles through which our brave fellows had marched. . . . I told my friend that our army must fall back, it being harder to provision it over those seven miles of mud than over the hundred miles of rail between this and Manassas." *Charleston Mercury,* June 6, 1862.

[51] *New Orleans Daily Crescent,* February 15, 1862.

was exceedingly sparse. Jackson was not on intimate terms with Confederate newspapermen; both the rapidity of his movements and the remoteness of his sphere of operation from centers of population made for spotty news coverage. The principal newspapers of tidewater Virginia had to depend for news of Jackson in large part on dispatches from telegraph operators at Lynchburg and other towns in the Valley and on accounts published in local Virginia newspapers. Yet by the end of May, on the strength of a series of brilliant successes from Winchester to Port Republic, the *Richmond Dispatch* was prepared to rate Jackson as "the hero of the war." Even the *Richmond Whig*, which had earlier been critical of him, published in mid-June a laudatory review of his campaign which maintained that "with a handfull of citizen soldiers, but partially drilled and poorly armed and equipped, he has, in little more than sixty days, marched over five hundred miles, fought about twelve battles—five of which were pitched battles—defeated four Generals—routed four armies—captured millions of dollars worth of stores &c and killed, wounded, and seized as prisoners almost as many of the enemy as he had soldiers under his command."[52]

Although Jackson appeared to be indifferent to what the press said about him, he read the Richmond papers at least occasionally. In E. A. Pollard's *Life of Jefferson Davis*, the former editor of the *Richmond Examiner* recalled having written for his paper on one occasion a paragraph eulogizing Jackson and remarking at the time that Jackson probably would never read it and undoubtedly cared nothing for public opinion. "You are utterly mistaken," retorted Editor-in-Chief John M. Daniel. "He is to-day the most ambitious man within the limits of the Southern Confederacy."[53]

[52] *Richmond Daily Dispatch*, May 29, 1862; *Richmond Daily Whig*, June 16, 1862. The regular correspondent of the *Richmond Dispatch* with Jackson was a soldier who signed himself "Massanutten" and who apparently had been a volunteer correspondent earlier in the campaign. *Richmond Daily Dispatch*, June 11, 1862. The account of the evacuation of Winchester by Jackson which the *Dispatch* published on March 17, 1862 had been obtained from Henry D. Beall, "lately of the *Winchester Republican* office." It seems likely that C. W. Hardwicke, a former member of the *Lynchburg Republican* staff who had left the newspaper to go into the army, reported Banks' defeat at the Battle of Winchester for the *Republican*. *Atlanta Daily Southern Confederacy*, June 5, 1862.

[53] Pollard, *Life of Jefferson Davis* (Philadelphia, 1869), p. 282. In a letter to Gen. Joseph E. Johnston dated March 6, 1862, Jackson mentioned a particular news story that he had seen in the (Richmond) *Whig* of "yesterday." Joseph E. Johnston Papers, Huntington Library. For a reference to one of the most widely-read newspaper descriptions of Jackson, contributed to the *Southern Illustrated*

Convinced that McClellan would, if left undisturbed, make use of his heavy guns to shell the Confederates out of Richmond, Lee concluded that he would have to strike McClellan's army before his opponent could get within artillery range of the capital. So he prepared to strip the Richmond defenses of every available man to launch a heavy blow at McClellan's right wing north of the Chickahominy. During the first part of June the tone of the Richmond press was buoyant, hopeful, and defiant of the enemy. Its predominant editorial theme was that McClellan was doomed to defeat before Richmond. Yet the advent of summer heat produced an atmosphere of listlessness and quiet such as was generally characteristic of Southern town life at that season of the year. In a letter to the *Memphis Appeal*, Richmond Reporter Thompson observed that "except for wagons and the occasional movements of troops our streets are as dull as the broad dusty road that leads through a county court house, and the bustling, active capital of three weeks ago seems, by some spell, to have been provincialized."[54]

On June 16 Richmond awoke from its stupor when Confederate cavalry leader Jeb Stuart rode into town to report a brilliant cavalry exploit. He had left Richmond, he said, on the previous Thursday morning with 1,200 men on a scouting movement in the enemy's rear. In performance of his mission he had ridden north out of Richmond and struck McClellan's main supply base at White House on the Pamunkey River, where he had captured three large transports and about a hundred wagons, whose contents he burned. Continuing southward he had pushed on to the Chicahominy River, arriving there a little before dawn on Saturday. There was no bridge across the river, and the ford was fifteen feet deep. Working against time and the possibility that their pursuers would be on them before they could finish, his cavalrymen found and repaired the bridge and safely crossed, carrying with them their artillery, prisoners, and spoils. Once more safely within Confederate lines, they rode back into Richmond, having made a complete circuit of McClellan's army and having covered about 150 miles in a little over forty-eight hours.

"What, then, was the general result?" asked a *Richmond Dispatch*

News by the war correspondent John Esten Cooke, see R. B. Harwell, "John Esten Cooke, Civil War Correspondent," *Journal of Southern History*, XIX (November, 1953) p. 507.

[54] Foote, *Civil War*, p. 469; *Mobile Daily Advertiser and Register*, June 11, 1862; *Memphis Daily Appeal*, June 21, 1862.

reporter of a wearied, dusty trooper who was watering his steed at a roadside spring. "The result?" repeated the trooper, proudly but with evidence of fatigue.

"We have been in the saddle from Thursday morning until Saturday noon, never breaking rein nor breaking fast; we have whipped the enemy wherever he dared to appear, never opposing more than equal forces; we have burned 200 wagons laden with valuable stores, sunk or fired three large transports, captured 300 horses and mules, lots of side-arms, &c, brought in 170 prisoners, four officers, and many negroes, killed and wounded scores of the enemy—pleased Stuart and had one man killed—poor Capt. Latane! This is the result, and $3,000,000 cannot cover the Federal loss in goods alone.

"As to myself," said he as he mounted and rode off, "I wouldn't have missed the trip for $1,000—history cannot show such another exploit as this of Stuart's!"[55]

"The more we think of Stuart's late feat," rhapsodized Bagby, "the more wonderful it seems. It is a question whether the annals of warfare furnish so daring a deed. . . . The Examiner calls Stuart a 'Circuit Rider,' and an extraordinary one he is."[56]

Two or three days after the triumphant conclusion of Stuart's raid, Richmond Reporter Thompson obtained permission from the authorities to drive out to the Confederate lines on the Nine Mile Road. Nothing could exceed the desolation of the countryside, with its depressing ensemble of fences torn down, wheat fields trodden underfoot, and abandoned farm houses and comfortable dwellings preempted for use as hospitals or officers' quarters. At the general's headquarters Thompson found everything as quiet "as if McClellan had carried off his troops to the moon." The general, whom he refrained from identifying, was reclining in slippers on the elm-shaded portico of a little wooden house, reading the latest issue of the *New York Herald*. Now and then a courier would come riding in from some command, or an aide-de-camp, pipe in mouth, would hand an order to the general for his signature. No one seemed to pay any attention to the occasional sharp crack of a field piece, which gave evidence that the Yankees

[55] Burke Davis, *Jeb Stuart, the Last Cavalier* (New York and Toronto, 1957) pp. 110ff; *Richmond Daily Dispatch*, June 16, 1862. For an account of Stuart's appearance in Richmond to report the results of his raid see "Dixie's" letter in *Memphis Daily Appeal*, June 24, 1862.

[56] *Charleston Mercury*, June 20, 1862.

on the other side of the Chickahominy were shelling one of the Confederate regiments.

After a while news was received by a courier (and immediately sent off to the next division headquarters by another) that the enemy was moving in a heavy column up the road on the opposite side of the river in the direction of Mechanicsville. At once horses were saddled and a reconnaissance carried out, which showed that about 20,000 Yankees had moved up the Chickahominy. Having thus obtained the feel of the army situation and some copy for an interesting letter to the *Memphis Appeal*, Thompson went back to Richmond.[57]

In a letter to his newspaper on June 21, a soldier correspondent of the *Savannah Republican*, V.A.S. Parks, expressed confidence that even with the best-appointed army in the world and with all his artillery and gunboats, McClellan would never attack the Confederates. Parks was convinced that if an attack was to be made in the neighborhood of Richmond it would have to be made by the Confederates, that in such case McClellan's army would be "beaten, driven back, routed, and totally demoralized."[58] At least the first part of his prediction proved remarkably accurate.

Meanwhile Lee, in an attempt to smash McClellan, had decided to concentrate every available soldier in front of Richmond. For this purpose he brought a division up from North Carolina and summoned Jackson to lead his veterans from the Shenandoah Valley cross-country to Richmond. In all, this would provide Lee with a force of 86,000 to meet McClellan's army of slightly more than 100,000. By a skillful arrangement of his troops, Lee intended to compensate for the disparity. He planned for Longstreet, the two Hills, and Jackson, with 55,000 men, to strike Porter's isolated Federal corps on the north bank of the Chickahominy, whose flank, Stuart's raid had disclosed, was unguarded. The remaining troops under Magruder, Huger, and Holmes would attempt to hold in check the bulk of McClellan's army.

It was essential for the success of Lee's plan that Jackson's movement be kept secret. Stories were planted in the Richmond press to make it appear that Jackson had been reinforced, ostensibly to mount another offensive in the Shenandoah Valley and threaten Washington.[59]

[57] *Memphis Daily Appeal*, June 27, 1862.
[58] *Savannah Republican*, June 26, 1862.
[59] Johnson and Buel, *Battles and Leaders*, II, 347. On June 24, 1862 the Rebel war clerk, J. B. Jones, jotted down the observation that "there are some vague

Unfortunately for Lee's plan Jackson arrived late. He had been expected to give the signal for the Confederate attack on Thursday morning, June 26, 1862. When nothing had been heard from him by three o'clock in the afternoon, the hot-blooded A. P. Hill ordered his oversized division on the left of Lee's line into action. Crossing the Chickahominy, he marched his men eastward to attack the corps of Fitz John Porter entrenched behind Beaver Dam Creek. As Hill's men moved into action, Longstreet and D. H. Hill followed his line of march to support the attack on Porter's strong position. As a result of A. P. Hill's impetuosity, Lee found himself making the frontal attack that he had wanted to avoid, without the advantage of Jackson being on the enemy's flank.

Porter was able to fling back the attackers that afternoon, but June 27 was a different story, for at last Jackson was in position. In the Battle of Gaines's Mill, fought eight miles from Richmond, Porter's line finally collapsed; by evening his broken divisions were in flight across the Chickahominy. At a council of his corps commanders held at headquarters that night, McClellan decided to cut loose from his base on the Pamunkey and retreat southward to the James.[60]

The reporters of the Richmond press were still excluded from the army, as two representatives of the *Richmond Examiner* found on the day of A. P. Hill's attack when they tramped out the York River Railroad to the point where the first picket was stationed. "So far, and no farther shalt thou go," was the message that the picket had for them. From the corporal of the guard they learned that by order of the commanding general no civilian, citizen, or any person other than a soldier could approach any nearer to the battlefield, with or without a pass.[61]

The *Examiner* was not entirely without eyes and ears in the army, however, for accompanying A. P. Hill's division in the capacity of aide to the division commander was the editor of the *Examiner*, John M. Daniel. An orderly of Stonewall Jackson caught sight of Daniel on the day of the Battle of Gaines's Mill as the editor rode up in the train of General Hill. The contrast between Hill's appearance and that of his subordinate was the most interesting feature of the occasion to

---

rumors about the approach of Stonewall Jackson's army but no one knows anything about it, and but few believe it." E. S. Miers, ed., *A Rebel War Clerk's Diary* (New York, 1958), p. 83.

[60] Johnson and Buel, *Battles and Leaders*, II, 353ff.

[61] *Daily Richmond Examiner*, June 27, 1862.

the orderly. Whereas Hill was "spare and short, dressed in a fatigue-jacket of gray flannel, with no plume, only a queer little felt hat, and the least possible insignia which could designate his rank," Daniel was the very model of a cavalier with every element of his equipment as near perfect as possible. In the orderly's judgment, Daniel's ensemble approached military foppery as near as good taste would permit. Within a few hours the exquisite uniform of the glamorous newspaper-man was destined to be dabbled with his own blood from the wound that ultimately would contribute to his death.[62]

Whatever restrictions on eyewitness reporting might exist, the Richmond telegraph office was open; from that office on June 26 the first press dispatches describing the fighting went out to remote parts of the Confederacy. The first telegram giving a detailed account of the fighting that day, which appeared in the Mobile papers, was written by Durant Da Ponte, who had come to Richmond after his *New Orleans Delta* had fallen into Federal hands.[63] All day Thursday the sound of cannonading could be heard distinctly in Richmond. Thompson of the *Appeal* was in the crowd that lined the hills to the north of the city during the long June twilight, listening to the guns and watching the flashes of prematurely bursting shells. Thompson could not help marvelling at the spectacle of "delicate women, hearing with composure the loud, incessant roar of artillery from the batteries of an enemy whose energies were . . . bent . . . upon the reduction of their city" and "children gambolling upon the grass and crying out with delight as the sudden, fitful explosion of the shells strewed the horizon with meteors. . . ."[64]

The calm of the civilian population was still undisturbed the next day, according to the *Richmond Whig*. During the afternoon people collected at some of the corners on Main Street to hear the latest reports from the battlefield, and there were similar gatherings at the hospitals when the wounded were brought in. On Saturday morning the *Whig* complained that the continued exclusion of reporters from the army had deprived it of the information about the military operations of the day before, which it had expected to provide its readers

[62] Anon., "What I Saw of the Battle of the Chickahominy," *Southern Magazine*, x (January 1872), 4. Jackson's orderly was the author.

[63] P.G.T. Beauregard to Gen. Thomas Jordan, July 12, 1862, Letterbook, 1861-1863, P.G.T. Beauregard Papers, Library of Congress.

[64] *Memphis Daily Appeal*, July 5, 1862; *Savannah Republican*, June 27, 1862.

with that morning. The War Department, it further indicated, had closed at an early hour the evening before, even though a battle had been raging nearly all day within earshot of the capital.[65]

Six thousand unoccupied beds had been set aside in various buildings for the reception of the wounded before the battles. On Saturday, June 28, the first wounded began coming in from the field, along with thousands of prisoners of war. Reporter Thompson was in the crowd along Main Street, scrutinizing the faces of the prisoners and observing the demeanor of his fellow Virginians. A captured Union flag bearing the legend "We never surrender" caught his eye, but he could see little evidence that it added much to the feeling of humiliation on the part of the captives, who "bore themselves with no little insolence, and despite their be-draggled and soiled condition made no mean appearance." Thompson was pleased to see that the spectators refrained from cheering and offered no insults to the prisoners. Elsewhere in the press, however, there were indications of ill-feeling in Richmond at the preferential treatment given high-ranking Union captives. Particularly irritating to some was the report of a Union major general (McCall) being housed and entertained at Richmond's best hotel, the Spotswood.[66]

As McClellan's army retreated south, fighting rearguard actions at Savage Station, Frayser's Farm, and Malvern Hill on June 29-July 1, the Richmond press was confident that Lee would capture McClellan's entire army, although newspaper accounts of the fighting admitted that the retreat was being conducted with great skill and that the Army of the Potomac was fighting with unusual courage and determination. In its report of the Battle of Frayser's Farm (Glendale), the *Richmond Dispatch* conceded that the Federals had resisted with more desperate determination and greater bravery than at any time since the recent fighting had begun and that the fire of their artillery and small arms had been deadly. The Richmond press as a whole, however, consistently underestimated the losses sustained by Lee's army throughout the Battles of the Seven Days.[67]

Especially culpable from the standpoint of good reporting were

[65] *Richmond Daily Whig*, June 28, 1862.
[66] *Richmond Daily Dispatch*, June 30, 1862.
[67] *Ibid.*, July 2, 1862, in which the writer stated that the Confederate loss at Frayser's Farm "will not amount to more than one-tenth that of the enemy." See also *Wilmington Daily Journal*, July 5, 1862; *Mobile Daily Advertiser and Register*, July 9, 1862.

the accounts in the Confederate press of the concluding battle of the Seven Days at Malvern Hill. There on an elevation of a hundred and fifty feet, Porter had concentrated an overpowering array of cannon; prudence would have dictated the avoidance of a frontal attack on such a position. There was a possibility, nevertheless, that Union army morale had reached the breaking point after its long retreat, so Lee attacked. The result was mass suicide, with 5,590 Confederate soldiers being killed and wounded on the slopes of Malvern Hill, compared with less than one-third that number of Federals. The withdrawal of McClellan's troops to Harrison's Landing on the James during the night was the only basis for the claim of victory that was voiced in the Confederate press. On both sides during an almost continuous week of fighting the losses had been appalling, although the Confederates, as the attacking force, had suffered a greater proportion of the casualties.[68]

Unfair and inaccurate reporting by the Richmond press of the Battles of the Seven Days caused angry protest by military and civilian critics. The presence of John M. Daniel on A. P. Hill's staff throughout the Peninsular campaign had prompted the *Examiner* to devote a disproportionate amount of attention to the performance of Hill's Light Division. The resentment Daniel's articles had aroused among the other commands finally came to a head when the *Examiner* published its account of the Battle of Frayser's Farm on July 2. The *Examiner* story, printed as its lead article on page 1, stated explicitly that at about four o'clock on the afternoon of June 30, when Longstreet was called away, Hill assumed command of Longstreet's division, as well as his own, and enabled both divisions to pluck a glorious victory from "desperate and threatening circumstances." To emphasize further the valor displayed by the Light Division, the *Examiner* told that out of a force of 14,000 with which it went into action on June 26, a week later it could not muster more than 6,000 able-bodied men.

The *Examiner*, with its extravagant praise of Hill and implied disparagement of the other divisions, was read in all the camps. Regarding the *Examiner's* statements as casting untrue aspersions on his adherence to duty, Longstreet thought Hill should have prevented such "fanciful distortions." It was true that Daniel's wound had ended his connection with the army before the Battle of Frayser's Farm and that

---

[68] Johnson and Buel, *Battles and Leaders*, II, 394; Foote, *Civil War*, p. 513; Bruce Catton, *Terrible Swift Sword* (New York, 1963), p. 337.

he was therefore beyond Hill's reach. Also, Hill did make the *amende honorable* in the official report of the battle that he submitted to the War Department. But Longstreet thought the record should be set straight in a more public manner. When he had completed a rough draft of a reply to the *Examiner* article, he showed it to his assistant adjutant general, G. Moxley Sorrel, asking Sorrel whether he would be willing to send such a letter over his own name to the rival *Richmond Whig*. Sorrel willingly complied with Longstreet's wishes, and on July 11, 1862 the *Whig* published a card signed by Sorrel making clear that Longstreet's absence from his command had been both brief and necessary and that the *Examiner's* figures for the casualties suffered by Hill's division were exaggerated.

Hill reacted impetuously to the publication of Sorrel's card, requesting that he be transferred from Longstreet's command. With deliberate unconcern, Longstreet forwarded Hill's letter to Lee with an endorsement recommending that Hill's request be granted. Lee tabled the correspondence, hoping that the tempers of both men might cool. Instead they became more explosive. Hill instituted an investigation of his own which convinced him that Longstreet had erred when he said that he had absented himself from the battlefield to send one of Hill's brigades into action. When Hill refused to have any further communication with Sorrel, Longstreet wrote sharply to his sulking lieutenant and finally directed Sorrel to place Hill under house arrest and confine him to the limits of his camp. For a time it looked as if there might even be a "hostile meeting" between the two generals. Finally Lee intervened, restored Hill to the command of his division, then transferred the Light Division to Stonewall Jackson's command in the Shenandoah.[69]

There was another protest against the Richmond press coverage of the Battles of the Seven Days when a wounded soldier friend of the editor of the *Wilmington* (N.C.) *Journal*, who had fought in the Peninsular campaign, wrote to the *Journal* to express his dissatisfaction with that press coverage. According to the *Journal's* correspondent, Richmond press reports of the battles had completely overlooked the performance of Branch's North Carolina brigade, the advance brigade

---

[69] W. W. Hassler, *A. P. Hill: Lee's Forgotten General* (Richmond, 1957), pp. 66-70; D. S. Freeman, *Lee's Lieutenants, A Study in Command* (New York, 1950), I, 644ff.; G. M. Sorrel, *Recollections of a Confederate Staff Officer* (New York, 1905), pp. 85-88. The card published in the *Richmond Whig* on July 11, 1862 appeared simultaneously in the *Richmond Dispatch*.

of A. P. Hill's division; although North Carolina and Georgia had furnished fully one-half of the forces engaged in those battles, "North Carolina and Georgia have found no place in the Richmond papers." Editor James Fulton of the *Wilmington Journal* agreed with the idea that the Richmond papers "are Virginia all over" and declared that when the Richmond press acknowledged the gallantry and services of troops from other states they did not do them the same justice that they would have done if the troops had been Virginians.

The *Richmond Enquirer* undertook to defend the fairness of the capital press against such accusations. Pointing out that it was military policy to exclude reporters from the lines of the army, the *Enquirer* contended that the Richmond newspapers had no way of knowing the events and casualties of the battles other than from information supplied voluntarily by acquaintances and interested parties. Moreover, the *Enquirer* and its sister papers had earnestly and repeatedly requested the adjutants of all the regiments in the army, from whatever state, to send them as speedily as possible the lists of casualties for publication. In some cases, apparently, the adjutants of regiments from distant states preferred to make their reports to their home papers instead of to those in Richmond. Likewise, as the *Milledgeville Union* pointed out, volunteer correspondents of regiments from states other than Virginia preferred to send their battle accounts to the papers at home, where they might be seen and read by those most interested, rather than to forward them to the newspapers in Richmond.[70]

In at least one instance involving the *Atlanta Confederacy*, a newspaper received criticism for an alleged pro-Yankee bias in its reporting. The *Atlanta Commonwealth* charged that the *Confederacy* had presented an "apology for McClellan's defeat" and by so charging precipitated an angry correspondence between Editor J. Henly Smith of the *Confederacy* and Editor J. S. Peterson of the *Commonwealth* which terminated in a challenge to a duel.[71]

Four days after McClellan's army reached the James River, de Fontaine of the *Charleston Courier* arrived in Richmond from South Carolina to prepare a comprehensive account of the Battles of the Seven Days. De Fontaine found Richmond in a state of confusion, with al-

[70] *Daily Richmond Enquirer*, July 14, 26, 1862; *Wilmington Daily Journal*, July 8, 1862.

[71] *Atlanta Daily Southern Confederacy*, July 16, 1862. The editorial to which the *Atlanta Commonwealth* took exception appeared in the *Confederacy* on July 8, 1862.

most countless wounded stretched out along the sidewalks, waiting for transportation homeward or to local hospitals. Strangers of both sexes thronged the streets looking for their relatives, and hearses and wagons filled with coffins were prominent. Later "Personne" visited the battlefield, seeking to reconstruct by personal interviews with officers and the comparison of conflicting accounts the military events that had taken place over an area of thirty or forty miles. He found it no easy task spending ten hours a day bouncing up and down on a hard trotting horse under a sun which produced temperatures of ninety-eight degrees in the shade and through country so desolate that it was almost impossible to find anything to eat. Moreover, when "Personne" sought information about the movements of one of the South Carolina brigades, he was informed that Gen. Maxcy Gregg, the brigade commander, would arrest any officer or private who imparted any information to him until after the publication of the brigade commander's official report.[72]

Thus official silence remained largely unbroken even after the conclusion of the campaign. It was patent to nearly everybody that Lee had flung back McClellan's army from the very gates of Richmond to a distance 30 miles by land and 60 miles by river from the capital. It was also clear that McClellan's army was safe at Harrison's Landing under the protection of the Federal gunboats. But in spite of angry editorial protests by the *Examiner* and the other Richmond newspapers,[73] Lee had no intention of giving the press carte blanche to report the movements of his army. Almost a week after the Battles of the Seven Days, he wrote to the Secretary of War to protest a paragraph that had appeared in the *Richmond Dispatch* that morning giving the precise location of three of his divisions. Calling attention to the fact that the entire Federal army was in his immediate front and that copies of the Richmond newspapers were available to the enemy, Lee urged the secretary of war to take the necessary steps to prevent the press from giving publicity to the strength and position of his army.[74]

[72] *Charleston Daily Courier*, July 11, 15, 18, 22, 23, 24, 28, 31, 1862.

[73] Writing to Andrew Dawson in Mobile on July 15, 1862, General Beauregard asked his correspondent, "Have you seen the able criticism of the Richmond Battles in the Examiner of the 8th inst? I wonder who wrote it. He overlooked, however, two or three points which would have made his remarks still stronger. . . ." Beauregard Papers, Library of Congress.

[74] *O.R.* (Army) Ser. I, vol. vi, pt. 3, pp. 635-36. Lee's letter carried the endorsement of Secretary of War Randolph, "Send copies of this letter to all the papers

A letter that has been preserved in the National Archives in Washington gives evidence of Secretary Randolph's compliance with Lee's request. The letter, written by Edward A. Pollard to the secretary of war, acknowledged receipt of the secretary's request that the newspapers should exercise care about revealing the strength, position, or movements of the Confederate armies. Pollard told Randolph that the *Examiner* understood the importance of this caution, "and we beg to assure you that in the future as in the past, the *Examiner* will be studious to observe that rule of reticence, which we agree with you is required by the interests of the public safety."[75] Probably Randolph did not overlook Pollard's sly disclaimer of past negligence.

Thus in the great series of battles that saved Richmond in the summer of 1862, the right to report had been severely circumscribed by considerations of public security which the Confederate military authorities impressed upon the Davis government. Neither Seven Pines nor Seven Days had provided the opportunity for battle reporting comparable to the best efforts of the Confederate army correspondents at Shiloh. It remained to be seen whether the South's press would have any better success reporting future campaigns in the East that were farther removed from the watchful eyes of the authorities in Richmond.

---

in the city, and express the hope that no steps may be necessary to stop such publications."

[75] Edwd. A. Pollard, Editor of *Examiner* to Hon. George D. Randolph, Secretary of War, July 11, 1862, Office of Confederate Secretary of War, 1861-1865, Letters Received, 398-P-1862, National Archives.

CHAPTER 7

"There Is a Smell of
Death in the Air"

〰〰〰〰〰〰〰

IN THE AFTERGLOW of McClellan's defeat before Richmond, the Confederate press discovered a new hero in Robert E. Lee. The *Richmond Dispatch* contended that "no Captain that ever lived could have planned or executed a better plan" than that of the Battles of the Seven Days, and the *Richmond Whig* asserted that Lee had "amazed and confounded his detractors by the brilliancy of his genius, the fertility of his resource, his energy and daring. He has established his reputation forever." Even the *Richmond Examiner*, which had saddled him with the epithet of "Evacuating Lee" when he assumed control of the army after Seven Pines, and had mocked his reliance on the ditch and spade, now refrained from further criticism.[1]

In succeeding months profiles of Lee and his lieutenants would appear with increasing frequency in the war correspondence of the leading Confederate newspapers. Both Peter Alexander and the army correspondent of the *Columbus* (Ga.) *Times* regarded Lee as comparable to George Washington in terms of his dignified manner and qualities of leadership. Alexander did not rate Lee as possessing "the first order of intellect." Yet insofar as he was able to plan and execute a military campaign on a large scale and direct the movements of a large army, Lee, in Alexander's opinion, surpassed all the other officers in the service and was "the peer of any living chieftain in the New World or the Old."[2]

---

[1] *Richmond Daily Whig*, July 18, 1862; *Richmond Daily Dispatch*, July 9, 1862; *Daily Richmond Enquirer*, September 3, 1862; Burke Davis, *Gray Fox, Robert E. Lee and the Civil War* (New York, 1956) p. 77. For further comment on the attacks on Lee that had appeared in the *Examiner* see E. P. Alexander, *Military Memoirs of a Confederate* (New York, 1907), p. 110.

[2] *Columbus Daily Times* as reprinted in *Knoxville Daily Register*, October 31, 1862; *Mobile Daily Advertiser and Register*, December 5, 1862. Alexander described Lee as being "in the prime and vigor of physical and intellectual manhood. . . . He is six feet in height, weighs about one hundred and ninety pounds; is erect, well formed, and of imposing appearance; has clear, bright, benignant black eyes, dark gray hair, and a heavy gray beard. . . . He wears an unassuming black felt hat, with a narrow strip of gold lace around it, and a plain Brigadier's

Neither Lee nor Stonewall Jackson was particularly interested in newspaper publicity, nevertheless.[3] Moreover, in mid-July Lee was troubled by the fact that McClellan's army was still within twenty-five miles of Richmond and that a new menace to Richmond's security was looming up in the form of Maj.Gen. Pope's newly created Army of Virginia, which was reported to be somewhere near Manassas. On July 12 Lee received the startling information that Pope had occupied Culpeper that morning and was in a position to threaten Gordonsville, a key point on the railroad line connecting Richmond with its supply centers in the Shenandoah Valley. Keeping an eye on McClellan's army southeast of Richmond, Lee dispatched Jackson with 12,000 men to Gordonsville and prepared to send A. P. Hill's Light Division after him. Fearful of newspaper publicity that might betray the gamble he was taking by thus dividing his army, Lee directed Hill to cover his movement by saying that he was moving against Suffolk and Norfolk. In a letter to the Secretary of War written on July 28, Lee raised the question whether an enigmatic paragraph to that effect in the *Dispatch* or entire silence would better deceive the enemy.[4]

In a letter from Richmond to the *Charleston Courier* mailed the following day, de Fontaine ventured the opinion that the South was about to shift from a defensive to an offensive strategy, although he declined to predict where the blow would be struck.[5] The implication in his letter that McClellan's army was about to evacuate the peninsula left it to be inferred, nevertheless, that Lee was about to march north.

The first step in the offensive movement that "Personne" had uncovered took place near Culpeper on August 9, when Stonewall Jackson seized the opportunity to pick off two understrength divisions under

---

coat, with three stars on the collar, but without the usual braiding on the sleeves. He travels and sleeps in an ambulance, when the army is in motion, and occupies a tent when it is stationary, and not the largest and best house in the neighborhood, as is the custom of some officers. In a few words he cares but little for appearances, though one of the handsomest men in the Confederacy, and is content to take the same fare his soldiers get."

[3] Jackson's aloofness toward the press is commented on in H. K. Douglas, *I Rode with Stonewall* (Chapel Hill, 1940), pp. 35-36. Yet his cordiality to two visiting newspapermen, Francis Lawley of the *London Times* and Frank Vizetelly of the *London Illustrated News*, at the time of their visit to Lee's army in October 1862 is described in *ibid.*, pp. 190-91.

[4] Clifford Dowdey and L. H. Manarin, eds., *The Wartime Papers of R. E. Lee* (Boston, 1961), pp. 240-42.

[5] *Charleston Daily Courier*, August 7, 1862.

Maj.Gen. Nathaniel P. Banks which Pope had left unsupported at Cedar Mountain. Although the Federals were outnumbered more than two to one, they fought well, routing the famous "Stonewall Brigade" before they were driven from the field. The Southern Associated Press claimed a "complete victory," however, and along with it the capture of three hundred prisoners. A break in the telegraph line between Richmond and Gordonsville prevented further details of the action from reaching the Confederate press for several days.[6]

A *Richmond Dispatch* correspondent who used the byline "Massanutten" was an eyewitness of the fight. During the flag of truce which the enemy made use of to bury their dead, the *Dispatch* reporter fraternized with the Yankee burial party and took the opportunity to get a look at the Federal general, Robert H. Milroy. "Massanutten's" appraisal of Milroy was, "he has red hair and whiskers and looks like a fighting General." While the burial party performed its task with obvious distaste, the less industrious members of the party gathered around the reporter from Richmond to hear what he described as some "wholesome truths."

One Ohioan, who formerly lived in Virginia, came to me to inquire for his relatives. I reproached him for fighting against his mother State. He professed to be doing it on pure principle, said he was a Democrat, and hated the Abolitionists worse than I did, who were keeping out of the war. I told the story about the monkey using the cat's paw to get out the hot chestnuts, and said "It will be a bitter thing when you Democrats of the Northwest wake up to find out that the New England Abolitionists made the war, and then made you fight it, while they kept out themselves." This produced a laugh, most of the crowd seeming to enjoy a good thing against their side, but the Ohioan looked grave, and the officers again tried to pull off from what might prove dangerous for them to hear. It was, however, literally "no go." Said one of the officers, "Its no use arguing. Each will think his own side right. It must be settled by other arguments." "Yes," said I, "such as those," pointing to their heaps of unburied dead. "I think we argued well last Saturday; but there is a disinterested party—the world—and the world is against you. They declare you have undertaken a hopeless task, and scorn the brutalities of your Butlers and your Popes." This only produced the maddened reply, "Yes, we want more such. We should have begun that sooner." But the crowd looked quiet and sober. I urged also on some that whereas all our men who fell in battle were missed and mourned

[6] Bruce Catton, *Terrible Swift Sword* (New York, 1963), p. 391; John B. Morris to General Earl Van Dorn, August 10, 1862, Van Dorn Papers, Alabama State Department of Archives and History; *Atlanta Daily Southern Confederacy*, August 14, 1862.

by the community, their death would be considered rather a blessing at the North. This, of course, was contradicted by some, but nevertheless did not seem without its effect on those to whom it was addressed. . . . I don't know, of course, whether I did any good by my preaching, but I do know some of that crowd came over to us that night, and I should be glad often to have the same chance to demoralize the Yankee troops.[7]

Although Jackson had beaten Banks at Cedar Mountain, inflicting a larger number of casualties than he sustained, he had not fought well. With almost 20,000 men under his command, he had failed to coordinate his attack or to reconnoiter the ground beforehand. After the battle he had to retreat across the Rapidan to escape from Pope, who was now heavily reinforced.[8] During Jeb Stuart's visit to Richmond the following week, Thompson of the *Memphis Appeal* heard about a conversation between Stuart and several Yankee officers, exchanged prisoners of war, with whom he had been associated in the United States army before the war. When the officers admitted that Pope had been decisively defeated at Cedar Mountain, Stuart predicted that Pope's official report would be considerably less candid and that in all probability the Yankee commander would claim a victory. Both sides accepted the wager of a basket of champagne on the outcome of Stuart's prediction. When later Pope claimed in his official report that he had badly whipped Jackson and received congratulations from the U.S. Chief of Staff on his brilliant success, Thompson voiced the opinion that Stuart had won the champagne and said he hoped it would not be paid in Newark cider![9]

Jackson's failure to suppress Pope caused Lee to send ten more brigades under Longstreet to Gordonsville. And when the Confederate army commander received reliable information on August 14 that McClellan's army was evacuating the peninsula, he decided to march north with the remainder of his army to crush Pope before McClellan could come to his rescue.[10] *Charleston Courier* reporter Felix de Fontaine had arrived at Orange Court House from Richmond the day before, just in time to accompany Lee's advance. Alexander was still in Richmond, hoping to leave there on the first train on which there

[7] *Richmond Daily Dispatch*, August 18, 25, 1862.

[8] F. E. Vandiver, *Mighty Stonewall* (New York, 1957), p. 344.

[9] *Memphis Daily Appeal*, August 28, 1862. Stuart's biographers make no mention of his being in Richmond after the Battle of Cedar Mountain, however, so this story may be apocryphal.

[10] Shelby Foote, *The Civil War, A Narrative, Fort Sumter to Perryville* (New York, 1958), pp. 604-608.

was standing room to take him to Gordonsville and catch up with Lee's men. "No passenger trains run on the road now," Alexander informed his newspaper, "and there is not transportation enough for the troops. Some entire divisions have had to march the entire distance." Alexander also confessed doubts that he would be able to communicate with the press by telegraph from Gordonsville. There was basis for his skepticism in the new regulations imposed by the War Department, limiting the transmission by telegraph of almost everything pertaining to army operations unless copied from Yankee newspapers.[11] Alexander added: "My letters must be few and brief also, except in the event of a battle. The regulations are such as to leave only a very narrow margin to correspondents from the field."[12] During the next two days train travel from Richmond to Gordonsville was suspended; when finally on August 26 the first Gordonsville dateline appeared in Alexander's war correspondence, he wrote gloomily that the nearer one got to the army, the less news there was to communicate.[13]

"Personne," on the other hand, was with Lee's army when it crossed the Rapidan on August 20. When he found that the rate of fifteen miles a day at which the army was marching would prevent him from communicating with his newspaper, he wrote up his notes of army operations in the form of a diary which he saved for a future publication. He noted on August 21 that "we live on what we can get—now and then an ear of corn, fried green apples, or a bit of ham fried on a stick, but quite as frequently do without either from morning until night." The following day he witnessed the hanging of a spy from Perrysville, Pennsylvania. When on August 23 the part of the army to which he was attached reached the Rappahannock, "Personne" gleefully predicted that "tomorrow will probably witness an advance of our army across the Rubicon. Then ho' for Washington and Baltimore."[14]

The star reporter of the *Charleston Courier* was in less exuberant spirits two days later when he composed a letter to his newspaper from "In the Field, near Brandy Station." He said frankly:

Writing on a march is not the most convenient or agreeable task in the world, however tantalizing may be the *cacaothes scribendi* of the scribbler. Though he may have any amount of mental pabulum on hand ready to be

[11] *Richmond Daily Whig*, August 27, 1862.
[12] *Charleston Daily Courier*, August 30, 1862; *Mobile Daily Advertiser and Register*, August 26, 1862.
[13] *Mobile Daily Advertiser and Register*, August 26, 1862.
[14] *Charleston Daily Courier*, August 30, 1862.

moulded into shape, there are few times or places when he can set himself consistently down to the work and do full justice to his material. The shelter of a house is not to be thought of; a tent is a palace; pen and ink are tabooed, and a man is forced to seek his epistolary comfort either at the crumbling end of a lead pencil, with a shady tree or its equivalent for a sanctum, and fence rail for his writing desk, or dispense with the same altogether. He must labor spasmodically in sunshine and storm, jerking out his thoughts whenever he can get a chance, and though he may have to lay himself out at full length beneath a baggage wagon, as I am at this moment doing, be content with accommodations which, if not princely, he must teach himself to believe are at least ample and independent. It is an ignominious rostrum from which to talk to twenty thousand people, but it is nevertheless a fitting illustration of the straits to which all connected with the army are more or less reduced.

I look around me and see men barefooted and ragged, bearing only their muskets and a single blanket each, yet all inspired by the hope of another battle. I have seen some, too, who were hungry—stragglers who would come up to the camp fire, tell a pitiful story of sickness or fatigues, and then ask for a bit of bread and meat. . . . Speaking of the bare feet, I suppose that at least forty thousand pairs of shoes are required to-day to supply the wants of the army. Every battle contributes to human comfort in this respect, but it is not every man who is fortunate enough to "foot" himself upon the field. It has become a trite remark among the troops, that "all a Yankee is now worth is his shoes;" and it is said, but I do not know how truly, that some of our regiments have become so expert in securing these coveted articles, that they can make a charge and strip every dead Yankee's feet they pass without coming to a halt.

While on this subject, I may add that it is the universal complaint of farmers throughout the region we are now passing, that our men are as unconscientious in stripping the country of every thing that can be eaten, as the the enemy themselves. Now and then there may be one who, if he takes a dozen ears of corn, will pin a two bit bill to a fence post as a token of his honesty; but as a general thing ducks, chickens, pigs, and meat are remorselessly "gobbled up" without the remotest conception of right or wrong. There are a few among our Brigadier-Generals who endeavor to restrain this utter looseness, and there are one or two who in a measure succeed. Generals Hood and Pryor belong to the latter class. I have seen their brigades on a march of fifty miles, and where others were followed by stragglers who might be counted by hundreds, I suppose that twenty-five would fully cover all who lagged behind the "old Texan" Brigade and the Floridians.[15]

In a letter of August 27 to the *Mobile Register* from Gordonsville, Alexander lamented that all of eastern Virginia north of the Rappahannock had virtually been converted into a desert by the military opera-

[15] *Ibid.*, September 3, 1862.

tions of both sides. He surmised that it would be difficult, therefore, to obtain subsistence for the army in the event of an advance to the Potomac. In the light of this state of affairs, he decided to remain in Gordonsville until he could ascertain the whereabouts of some friends in the advance elements of the army and join them.[16]

Probably neither Alexander nor de Fontaine knew (at least they gave no information about it in their correspondence) what strategy Lee was using to crush Pope before McClellan could come to his aid. Nor would any reader of the Confederate press have been likely to know during the last week of August that Stonewall Jackson had left Lee's army on a sweep to the northwest through Thoroughfare Gap to attack Pope's rear. Pope quickly learned of Jackson's movement, but erroneously interpreted it as a retreat. He was still on the defensive north of the Rappahannock when Jackson reemerged twenty miles in his rear along the Orange and Alexandria Railroad, near the huge Federal supply base at Manassas Junction. Neglecting to detach a strong force to hold Thoroughfare Gap, Pope started in pursuit of Jackson, and after much marching and countermarching made contact with him at Groveton, near Manassas, on the afternoon of August 28. Following a costly, indecisive action there, Pope remained on the old Bull Run battlefield to meet the combined forces of Jackson and Longstreet.[17]

"Personne" had been with Longstreet's corps as it marched up the south bank of the Rappahannock to Rock Ford and then followed Jackson's line of march through Salem to reach Thoroughfare Gap by midday of the 28th. "Personne" described the Gap as "a rude opening through the Bull Run Mountains, varying in width from one hundred to two hundred yards. . . . It is a place where a thousand determined troops could hold at bay for weeks ten times their number."[18] A single division of Union troops occupied the pass, but some of the men in Hood's division found a cleft in the ridge and opened a flanking fire which unplugged the gap. Longstreet's five divisions, totaling 32,000 men, marched southeast the next day to take up a position on Jackson's flank to the right of the Warrenton turnpike.

Both "Personne" and to a lesser degree Alexander were eyewitnesses of the Second Battle of Manassas on Saturday, August 30. Alexander

[16] *Mobile Daily Advertiser and Register*, September 4, 1862.

[17] Catton, *Terrible Swift Sword*, pp. 418-27.

[18] *Charleston Daily Courier*, September 10, 1862; J. B. Hood, *Advance and Retreat* (Bloomington, 1959) p. 32.

climbed aboard a freight train at Gordonsville at 9:00 A.M. on Friday, August 29, and reached Rapidan Station, the northern terminus of the Orange and Alexandria Railroad, at noon that day. There he got a horse, forded the Rapidan and the Rappahannock, and rode into Warrenton at one o'clock on the thirtieth. He rested his horse and started toward the battlefield, covering fourteen miles in one hour and fifteen minutes. He arrived just in time to witness the triumph of the Confederates.[19]

"Personne" saw at least part of the fighting from the heights occupied by Capt. Stephen D. Lee's battery. From the first account that he put together, composed at midnight on Saturday, it is obvious that he was unable to comprehend the general proportions of the battle.[20] But the six-column battle report he sent off three days later, after he had questioned various officers, was probably the best account of Second Manassas that appeared in the Confederate press.

The battle began about noon on August 30, when Pope, under the illusion that Jackson was retreating, ordered a vigorous pursuit. Pope's attack subjected Jackson to such pressure that he had to call on Lee for reinforcements. Lee ordered Longstreet to attack; after the artillery had checked Pope's advance, Longstreet's men stormed eastward along the south side of the turnpike, sweeping aside the skeleton force that opposed them and threatening to cut off Pope's escape route across the stone bridge over Bull Run. In his battle report, de Fontaine told how Hood's division moved obliquely to the right and forward to spearhead Longstreet's advance:

The whole army was now in motion. The woods were full of troops. . . . The din was almost deafening, the heavy notes of the artillery, at first deliberate, but gradually increasing in their rapidity, mingled with the sharp treble of the small arms, gave one an idea of some diabolical concert in which all the furies of hell were at work.—Through the woods, over gently rolling hills, now and then through an open field we travel on toward the front. . . . Hood and Kemper are now hard at it, and as they press forward . . . sometimes at a double quick, you hear those unmistakable yells, which tell of a Southern charge or a Southern success. . . .

We do nothing but charge—charge—charge! If the enemy make a bold effort to retrieve the fortunes of the day, (and they made many) and we are repulsed, it is but for the moment, and the regiments rallying upon their supports plunge back again into the tempest of fire that before swept them down. The minnie balls which fly in showers seem to bear a death warrant

[19] *Mobile Daily Advertiser and Register*, September 10, 1862.
[20] *Charleston Daily Courier*, September 6, 1862.

in every devilish screech; grape shot and cannister rake the men by scores; friends fall killed and wounded on every hand; shells with their shrill demoralizing shrieks course through the air like fiery monsters, striking where they are least expected, and scattering their fragments in all directions. . . .

It was a task of almost superhuman labor to drive the enemy from these strong points defended as they were by the best artillery and infantry in the Federal army, but in less than four hours our indomitable energy had accomplished every thing. . . .

The battle raged in the manner described until after dark, and when it was impossible to use fire arms the heavens were lit up by the still continued flashes of the artillery, and the meteor flight of shells scattering their iron spray. By this time the enemy had been forced across Bull Run, and their dead covered every acre from the starting point of the fight to the Stone Bridge. Had we been favored with another hour of daylight, their rout would have been as great as that which followed the original battle of Manassas. As it was, they retreated in haste and disorder to the heights of Centreville. We had driven them up hill and down a distance of two and a half miles, captured between twenty and thirty pieces of artillery, several hundred prisoners (though few soldiers cared to be troubled by the latter) and some six or eight thousand stand of arms.[21]

The lateness of Alexander's arrival on the battlefield made it more difficult for him to report the battle; after he had completed his battle account the next day, the problem of communicating with his newspaper handicapped him further. It was sixty-five miles from Bull Run to the nearest post office at Rapidan Station. Although Alexander was willing to pay as much as fifty dollars for courier service, no courier was immediately available. It was equally impossible for him to telegraph his account of the fighting, since all the telegraph wires and railroad bridges between the Rapidan and Manassas had been destroyed by the enemy. Yet he could not help thinking about the suffering of the private soldier in an army that might have been supposed to be jubilant over the smashing victory that it had just won. In a letter dated midnight, Monday, September 1, Alexander informed his readers that "the army has not had a mouthful of bread for four days, and no food of any kind except a little green corn picked up in the roadside, for thirty-six hours. The provision trains are coming up, but many of the troops will have to go another day without anything to eat. Many of them are also barefooted. I have seen scores of them to-day marching over the flinty turnpike with torn and blistered feet. They bear all

[21] *Ibid.*, September 11, 1862.

these hardships without murmuring; . . . As for tents, they have not known what it was to sleep under one since last spring."[22]

Richmond was in the dark about what had happened for several days after the battle.[23] On September 1 the *Dispatch* published reports about a battle that had occurred on Saturday, "and perhaps yesterday," in the vicinity of the old Manassas battlefield. But the first authentic information it published was a dispatch from General Lee to President Davis that reached Richmond late that afternoon. The dispatch stated that on Saturday "Gen Lee attacked the combined forces of McClellan and Pope, utterly routing them with immense loss."[24] On the third of September Reporter George Bagby informed the *Charleston Mercury* that Second Manassas was "a battle of far greater magnitude than we supposed." He reported incorrectly that McClellan, Pope, Burnside, and Hunter were all there, and confessed he did not know how they had managed to get together.[25] Army news sources were disappointingly uncommunicative for a period of several days after this. In an editorial entitled "Any Late News from the Army," which it published on September 6, the *Richmond Enquirer* commented on the fact that an entire week had elapsed since the end of the fighting and the public was still without any information about the details. Complaining that "no one knows who was killed—no one knows who was wounded," the *Enquirer* implored Secretary of War Randolph to take immediate steps to ascertain who had fallen and make their identity public.[26]

The paucity of information from the Army of Northern Virginia was in part attributable to Lee's decision to invade Maryland. Cavalry reconnaissance had disclosed that Pope's dispirited Federals were withdrawing to the fortified lines around Washington, where they could easily be reinforced by those units of McClellan's army that had not

[22] *Mobile Daily Advertiser and Register,* September 10, 1862.

[23] On the day of the Battle of Second Manassas, Attorney General Bragg inscribed in his diary: "we have no news today from any quarter. The telegraph at Gordonsville is under the control of the government and not used by individuals. The trains come through daily, but bring nothing but rumors—It is all right— We must wait—." Thomas Bragg Diary, Southern Historical Collection, University of North Carolina.

[24] *Richmond Daily Dispatch,* September 2, 1862.

[25] *Charleston Mercury,* September 6, 1862.

[26] Letter of "Hermes" in *Charleston Mercury,* September 10, 1862. For a similar complaint see the letter of the *Columbus Sun's* Richmond correspondent, R. J. Yarington, in *Columbus Daily Sun,* September 9, 1862.

yet joined them. The Washington fortifications were too strong for Lee to attack. Although he knew that his army was not equipped for extensive maneuvers, lack of supplies made it impossible for him to remain where he was. In Maryland, where the population was believed to be strongly sympathetic toward the Confederate cause, Lee estimated that the army could much better provision itself, get new recruits, and perhaps win the foreign recognition that was essential for Confederate success. So on September 5-6 the adventurous Confederates crossed the Potomac near Leesburg and marched north to Frederick.[27]

De Fontaine was at Leesburg the day before to witness the arrival of Lee's army and its cordial treatment by the citizens. In the excitement of the hour the streets were thronged with ladies, and "Personne" rejoiced:

"The doorways and curb stones are like living bouquets of beauty. Everything that wears crinoline or a pretty face is out, and such shouts and wavings of handkerchiefs and hurrahs by the overjoyed gender never emanated from human lips. . . .

" 'What regiment is that?' 'Sixth Georgia, Ewell's division.' 'Hurrah for you! Hurrah! Kill all the Yankees!' screamed a bevy of girls. 'Hurrah for the gals! Coming back to marry the whole town.' shout the Confederates. 'Got any tobacco?' says another. 'Got any shoes? Give us a slice of bacon and bread. Hoop, hi, hi!' and then the whole crowd break out into a series of yells and screeches that only require the addition of an Indian war dance to complete the scene. I never heard such tumult or saw such enthusiasm in my life."[28]

A couple of days later "Personne" watched the crossing of Longstreet's corps from a hill on the Maryland side of the river opposite White's Ford. The river below was dotted with thousands of men wading thigh deep over the rocky bed of the Potomac. An old gentleman of Maryland origin whose hospitality the reporter had already enjoyed exclaimed as he beheld the scene:

"Goodness gracious, look at the Seceshes!"

"Yes," rejoined "Personne" with an air of complacency, "but that is only a handfull."

"Wall, I declare," responded his companion. "I've been to shows and

[27] D. S. Freeman, *R. E. Lee, A Biography* (New York and London, 1935), II, 350-54.
[28] *Charleston Daily Courier*, September 11, 1862.

circusses and theaters and all them things but I never seen such a sight'n all my life. Why, you've got soldiers enough to whip all creation; but look yere, won't these fellers hurt us Marylanders? I'm a little afeard that when they get to ranging around the country, they'll interfere with my family and do something wrong. To tell the truth, I don't care to leave my farm house."

"Personne" reassured him about his and his family's safety and later saw the reassurance verified by the good behavior of the Confederate soldiery at the home of his erstwhile host.[29]

The Confederate army correspondents were much interested in the attitude of the Marylanders toward their would-be deliverers in the light of earlier expectations. Alexander told of the army being received with shouts and cheers; on September 7 "Personne" was of the opinion that the reception of the Confederate army had been "all that we could desire." He noticed, however, that although a few Marylanders had been highly demonstrative, "the majority content themselves with quiet manifestations of the warm sympathy they feel."[30] Still another (*Richmond Dispatch*) reporter expressed concern about the fact that on its march of some fifteen miles into Maryland the part of the army to which he was attached had "seen no enthusiasm for Southern Rights, not a white handkerchief from a window, though from the stateliness of some of the mansions there must be white handkerchiefs in them."[31]

For about four days Lee's army remained encamped a mile or two southeast of Frederick, watching for indications of an uprising against Federal authority and enlisting Confederate recruits.[32] Lee was also waiting for the arrival of former Governor Enoch L. Lowe of Maryland, a prominent Southern Rights man who was believed to have great influence with the people in that part of the state and who apparently was being groomed to head a provisional government in Maryland. About this time *Richmond Dispatch* correspondent "Massanutten" met President Davis in Gordonsville following Davis's return from a mission in the direction of Lee's army. According to one of the Richmond correspondents Lowe had been with Davis on the Sep-

[29] *Ibid.*, September 23, 1862.
[30] *Ibid.*
[31] *Richmond Daily Dispatch*, September 17, 1862.
[32] According to *ibid.*, September 15, 1862, about 1,500 Marylanders from Frederick and Montgomery Counties had enlisted in the Confederate army by September 10.

tember 7 that Davis left Richmond.[33] When Lowe failed to turn up at Frederick, Lee, at Davis's prompting, issued a proclamation to the people of Maryland explaining the peaceful purpose of his invasion and his desire to extend protection to the oppressed Marylanders. Lee planned to move west to Hagerstown and march north into Pennsylvania, but he was disappointed to find that continuing Federal occupation of Martinsburg and Harper's Ferry posed a threat to his communications. To safeguard his rear Lee decided to detach Jackson from the main army and send him down to Harper's Ferry to pick off the Federal garrison there.

While the army was still in Frederick, Alexander rode into town with a Confederate general to see an old friend of his. As they were passing along the street a young lady beckoned to Alexander and asked if the officer with whom he was riding was not General Jackson. When the reporter told her that she was mistaken, she wrung her hands and exclaimed:

"Oh! I shall go crazy if I don't see him."

"He is not much for good looks," Alexander replied, "but he fights like a lion."

"I know it," said she, "and that is the reason I am dying to see him. When will the army leave?"

"At daylight to-morrow morning."

"Oh! lordy," she cried, "what shall I do? Won't you come in and take some wine and cake with cousin and myself?"

Alexander excused himself, but regaled her with an anecdote about Old Stonewall during his march from Staunton to Richmond. At that time his officers were very curious to know where they were going, and finally an inquisitive colonel rode up to him and said: "General, we are all desirous to know what our destination is—can't you tell us?" Jackson approached him and inquired in a confidential manner, "Can you keep a secret?" "Oh, yes," answered the colonel. "Well, so can I," replied Jackson and rode on. The young lady laughed at the anecdote, and Alexander bade her good evening.[34]

On September 10 the Confederates marched out of Frederick, playing and singing "The Girl I Left Behind Me." The three divisions of McLaws, Walker, and Anderson were to converge on Harper's Ferry;

[33] *Memphis Daily Appeal,* September 15, 1862; *Richmond Daily Dispatch,* September 20, 1862.
[34] *Mobile Daily Advertiser and Register,* September 25, 1862.

Longstreet's command was to march across South Mountain to Hagerstown, followed by D. H. Hill's division. After the capture of Harper's Ferry, which was expected to take place on September 12 or 13 at the latest, Jackson's divisions were to rejoin Lee at Boonsboro to continue the campaign.[35]

Meanwhile General McClellan's reorganized Army of the Potomac marching north from Washington occupied Frederick on September 12, less than twenty-four hours after the last Confederates had departed. At Frederick, by a stroke of luck, McClellan came into possession of the Confederate plan of operations and learned of Lee's bold gamble of dividing his army in the presence of the enemy. With unusual celerity, McClellan started west from Frederick toward the gaps in South Mountain with the intention of destroying Lee's army.

While McClellan was still below Frederick newspaper correspondent Alexander was with General Toombs' brigade of Longstreet's corps, pushing westward along the mountain road to Hagerstown. In a letter to his newspaper dated September 11, "P.W.A." described the march of the last two days across the valleys of the Monocacy and the Catoctin and over the Blue Ridge. He declared he had never seen a more fruitful and lovely region or more picturesque and bewitching scenery: "the deep blue mountains running in parallel lines, the quiet valleys, the clear rocky streams, the white farm houses and immense barns, wheat stacks and hayricks, the great cattle grazing on the hillsides, the long dusty column of the Confederate army threading their way across the valleys and through the gaps in the mountains, and the clusters of simple country people who have gathered along the road side or in front of their houses to witness the passing spectacle."[36]

There were some delays in the Harper's Ferry operation, and on Sunday, September 14, Longstreet's corps was still encamped near Hagerstown. The *Richmond Dispatch* correspondent shared the opinion of most of the troops around him that the army was about to cross the Mason and Dixon line into Pennsylvania. He was greatly surprised,

[35] Foote, *Civil War*, p. 667; James Longstreet, *From Manassas to Appomattox* (Bloomington, 1960), p. 205.

[36] *Mobile Daily Advertiser and Register*, September 25, 1862. Although Alexander made no mention of this in his correspondence, the editor of the *Sandersville Central Georgian*, Ivy W. Duggar, on October 1, 1862 alluded to the fact that "P.W.A." had been with General Toombs "nearly ever since we left Richmond." Typed copy of Duggar's war correspondence for his Sandersville newspaper, Georgia State Archives.

therefore, when an order was received that afternoon to countermarch toward Frederick; he noted the many sad faces and anxious inquiries among the troops about the reason for the new order. At the end of an eight-hour march the *Dispatch* man heard reports about an artillery duel at Turner's Gap on South Mountain, which was of greater scope than he imagined.[37]

In a letter written at Boonsboro that evening, "Personne" told how D. H. Hill's five brigades, containing no more than 5,000 men, had fought a delaying action against two Federal army corps while the general waited for Longstreet to come to his rescue. "Personne" was considerably impressed with the "wonderful elasticity" with which the enemy had reorganized their broken army after the Second Battle of Manassas and started in pursuit of the Confederates. He explained that because of the uneven ground on South Mountain the Confederates were unable to make effective use of their artillery to check the masses of blue-uniformed infantry to whose numbers there seemed to be no end and who fought boldly and perhaps better than ever before. Also, Longstreet's troops were worn out by their long march under a broiling sun, and fully one-third of their number had dropped out of line, unable to keep up with the rapid pace of the others. As a result according to "Personne," "we barely held our own. Advance we could not. The enemy in numbers were like a solid wall. . . . Retreat, we would not, and thus we fought, doggedly giving and taking the fearful blows of battle until long after nightfall."[38]

Realizing that the Gap could not be held past daylight and that he was outnumbered four to one, Lee decided to recross the Potomac into Virginia. Then on the following day, he heard that Jackson had captured Harper's Ferry. The receipt of this gratifying news caused Lee to rescind his plan of retreating into Virginia and order his army to concentrate in the neighborhood of Sharpsburg, overlooking a tributary of the Potomac called Antietam Creek.

[37] *Richmond Daily Dispatch*, September 30, 1862.

[38] *Charleston Daily Courier*, September 29, 1862; Hal Bridges, *Lee's Maverick General, Daniel Harvey Hill* (New York, 1961), p. 93. According to the diarist Thomas Bragg, the *Richmond Enquirer* issued an extra on the evening of September 20 to give the first news of the Battle of South Mountain, fought six days earlier. Diary of Thomas Bragg, September 21, 1862. The first information about the action at South Mountain that the *Richmond Dispatch* received was in the form of a letter to that newspaper from N. B. Meade, editor of the *Winchester* (Va.) *Republican. Richmond Daily Dispatch*, September 20, 1862.

With the Confederate troops at Sharpsburg on the eve of the Battle of Antietam was a correspondent of the *Richmond Dispatch* who was attached to Stephen D. Lee's battery of Confederate artillery. The reporter observed that Sharpsburg was situated in a deep valley and that all around the town were very high, bald hills. "The country about Sharpsburg is exceedingly beautiful," he remarked appreciatively, "the farm houses and farms in the best condition." On Monday afternoon, September 15, and all day Tuesday, he watched the enemy taking his positions on the opposite side of Antietam Creek and listened to the crescendo of picket fire that both sides kept up all Tuesday night. As the *Dispatch* reporter remembered it, "it was a beautiful night, and no man who lay upon that field, and realized the deep tragedy which was to be enacted on the morrow could but be sad and thoughtful."[39]

Both "Personne" and "P.W.A." were on hand to provide eyewitness accounts of the battle, in which Lee's army faced odds of more than two to one. The greater part of Jackson's corps had returned from Harper's Ferry by the morning of September 17, but even so there were at most 35,000 Confederate troops along the Sharpsburg ridge to confront McClellan's army of about 87,000. Alexander was with Toombs' brigade on the Confederate right, near what came to be known as the Burnside bridge. "Personne" was situated in the center of the Confederate line.

The Battle of Antietam, or Sharpsburg, as the Confederates generally called it, was in fact three battles that occurred in succession from left to right. "Old Stonewall" was in command on the Confederate left when the fighting began. During the morning he managed to beat off a succession of attacks launched in division strength by Union Generals Hooker, Mansfield, and Sumner, with reinforcements obtained from the center and left.

Then it was the turn of D. H. Hill, commanding the Confederate center, to dig in along the sunken road which, in token of the piles of dead men clustered along it, was named "Bloody Lane." *Charleston Courier* reporter de Fontaine thus described the carnage that took

[39] *Richmond Daily Dispatch*, September 30, 1862. The *Dispatch* reporter's memory must have been playing tricks on him when he wrote this letter. In his *From Manassas to Appomattox*, p. 237, General Longstreet recalled that "a light rain began to fall at nine o'clock" on the evening of September 16, and there are other indications that the weather could hardly have been as mild as the *Dispatch* man indicated.

place in front of his observation point in the Confederate center shortly after twelve noon:

> From twenty different standpoints great volumes of smoke were every
> instant leaping from the muzzles of angry guns. The air was filled with the
> white fantastic shapes that floated away from bursted shells. Men were
> leaping to and fro, loading, firing and handling the artillery, and now and
> then a hearty yell would reach the ear, amid the tumult, that spoke of death
> or disaster from some well aimed ball. Before us were the enemy. A regiment
> or two had crossed the river, and, running in squads from the woods along
> its banks, were trying to form a line. Suddenly a shell falls among them,
> and another and another, until thousands scatter like a swarm of flies, and
> disappear in the woods. A second time the effort is made, and there is a
> second failure. Then there is a diversion. The batteries of the Federals open
> afresh; their infantry try another point, and finally they succeed in effecting
> a lodgement on this side. Our troops, under D. H. Hill, meet them, and a
> fierce battle ensues in the centre. Backwards, forwards, surging and swaying
> like a ship in a storm, the various columns are seen in motion. It is a hot
> place for us, but is hotter still for the enemy. They are directly under our
> guns, and we mow them down like grass. The raw levies, sustained by the
> veterans, come up to the work well, and fight for a short time with an ex-
> citement incident to their novel experiences of a battle; but soon a portion
> of their line gives way in confusion. Their reserves come up, and endeavor
> to retrieve the fortunes of the day. Our centre, however, stands firm as ada-
> mant, and they fall back.[40]

This is a vivid word picture of the outward appearance of what happened, but it conveys a somewhat misleading impression of its significance. By two o'clock in the afternoon Hill had only a skeleton force
left with which to hold off a Federal breakthrough, for which ample
U.S. reserves were available. Yet, not knowing how near they were to
complete victory, McClellan and Sumner withheld the knockout punch
that Franklin pleaded with them to let him deliver.

On the right, in the meantime, Longstreet had been able to prevent
Burnside from sweeping across Antietam Creek to drive the Confederates into the Potomac. Finally, about one o'clock, Burnside's men
got across; as he was regrouping his command the arrival of A. P.
Hill's division from Harper's Ferry blunted the force of his offensive
and forced his men back from the heights that they had spent all
morning trying to seize. On the following day the two armies remained within artillery range, neither venturing to attack the other.
Then on the night of the eighteenth, the remnants of Lee's army re-

[40] *Charleston Daily Courier*, September 29, 1862.

crossed the Potomac into Virginia, bringing the Maryland campaign to an end.[41]

"Personne" and "P.W.A." rated Sharpsburg as the severest and most hotly contested battle of the war. Most of the Confederate newspapermen who were present were impressed by the fine equipment and excellent performance of the Federal artillery. Alexander added that the Union soldiers fought well, too, "better in fact than the Federals have ever done before, except at Shiloh; and the new volunteers did about as well as the older troops." Yet Alexander gave the edge in artillery performance to the Confederate side. He pointed out that whereas the Federals directed their fire at the Confederate batteries, the Confederate artillerymen, by special order of General Lee, selected the infantry columns of the Federals for their targets. As a result, he wrote, "the enemy's assaulting columns were repeatedly repulsed by the well-directed fire of our artillerists."[42] The *Richmond Dispatch* correspondent viewed the efficiency of the Confederate artillery during the battle in a somewhat different light from Alexander. He asserted that "our artillery ammunition is almost worthless. The shells and spherical case generally don't explode at all."[43]

During a lull in the battle "Personne" rode back to the town of Sharpsburg and found that many of the houses had been damaged by gunfire and a few destroyed. Most of the citizens had remained in their homes, not supposing that a battle so near at hand could be very harmful, but when Sharpsburg came under artillery fire, they took refuge in their cellars or crouched behind a convenient stone wall.

Passing through the town where army hospitals were overflowing with the wounded, "Personne" went a mile beyond, watching the surgeons at work in farmhouses, barns, and sheds along the road.[44] He observed also the immense body of stragglers ("their number was legion") in the rear of the army and told how Lee's cavalry was used to round some of them up and push them back into the fight. The Richmond correspondent of the *Charleston Mercury* repeated several

[41] Longstreet, *Manassas to Appomattox*, p. 266; Catton, *Terrible Swift Sword*, pp. 451-58.

[42] *Mobile Daily Advertiser and Register*, October 2, 1862.

[43] *Richmond Daily Dispatch*, September 30, 1862. "Personne" likewise attested to the superiority of the Federal artillery, with its superior rifled cannon and ammunition, "which, unlike ours, exploded where it was sent. . . ." *Charleston Daily Courier*, October 14, 1862.

[44] *Charleston Daily Courier*, September 29, 1862.

months afterward a story that had come to his ears about General Lee's encounter at Sharpsburg with one of these stragglers.

"Where are you going, sir?" Lee had asked.

"Goin' to the rear."

"What are you going to the rear for?"

"Well, I've been stung by a bung, and I'm what they call demoralized." Divining that the innocent who had been "stung by a bung" had probably been "stunned by a bomb," Lee made no further attempt to interfere with his progress toward the rear.[45]

"Personne" did not mention in his battle report seeing Alexander, who wrote his battle account the following morning in the midst of the wounded and dying at an army hospital. Describing "amputated arms and legs, feet, fingers and hands cut off, puddles of human gore, and ghastly gaping wounds," Alexander went on to say: "There is a smell of death in the air, and the laboring surgeons are literally covered from head to foot with the blood of the sufferers."[46]

In Richmond, where the news of the capture of Harper's Ferry had prompted the *Enquirer* to bring out an extra,[47] the first reports of the battle, from Northern sources, occasioned considerable anxiety. Warrenton was the northern terminus of the telegraph line that extended from Richmond in the direction of Lee's army, and Harrisonburg was the nearest telegraph station to Winchester on the line from Richmond to the Shenandoah Valley.[48] Although the Southern Associated Press tallied the enemy loss in killed and wounded at 20,000, compared with 5,000 on the Confederate side, the refusal of the Confederate government to permit the publication of casualty lists in the newspapers seemed ominous.[49] Probably few well-informed persons in Richmond believed the statement of the editor of the *Richmond Enquirer* that

[45] *Charleston Mercury*, December 23, 1862.

[46] *Mobile Daily Advertiser and Register*, October 2, 1862.

[47] The extra, which was only of quarter-sheet size, was dated Friday afternoon, September 19, 1862.

[48] *Richmond Daily Whig*, September 22, 1862.

[49] *Memphis Daily Appeal*, September 25, 1862. The *Daily Richmond Enquirer* of September 30, 1862 stated: "As it has been deemed advisable for the present not to publish the list [of casualties] persons can obtain information in regard to their relatives in the army by calling at the Army Intelligence office in the Farmer's Bank, opposite the Post Office." The official reports of the losses sustained by both armies in the battle indicated that the total loss on both sides was about 23,000 (Union, 12,410, and Confederate, 10,700) *O.R.* (Army) Ser. I, vol. xix, pt. 1, pp. 204, 843, 861-62, 925, 974, 1,009, 1,015; Freeman, *Lee*, ii, 402n.

the battle at Sharpsburg had "resulted in one of the most complete victories that has yet immortalized the Confederate arms." To reassure its readers the *Enquirer* felt it necessary to contradict stories that the Confederate government was withholding important news from the public. Instead, maintained the *Enquirer*: "The government has been free and ready to furnish all legitimate information. The trouble lies here: Rumor, even when true, always flies faster than fact. . . . Government deals in facts and official reports; and for the sending of these, time is required to ensure accuracy. The passenger by the cars or other private information is generally ahead of even Jackson's brief telegrams."[50]

De Fontaine's story of Antietam was probably his outstanding battle report of the war and the best account that was published in the Southern press. It climaxed a seven-column newspaper narrative amounting to no less than 8,000-9,000 words, that began with the Battle of South Mountain and included the details of the capture of Harper's Ferry. De Fontaine's opening sentence was dramatic and direct: "Yesterday was fought, at this place [Sharpsburg], the severest battle that has yet marked the annals of the war." He went on to stress the heavy odds that faced Lee's men, odds that he reckoned at 3-1. Then he reconstructed the setting of the battle: the town of Sharpsburg situated in a bend of the Potomac River, the valley of the Antietam that separated the two armies, the succession of green hills occupied by the Confederates, and the lowlands thickly covered with fields of grain and corn. Antietam Creek, he explained, was fordable by infantry at any point, but not passable by artillery except on the bridges. Then briefly he sketched the order of battle on both sides, erroneously crediting McClellan with being in command on the Union right and admitting that it was impossible for him to describe so soon after the battle the position of brigades.

With these preliminary details out of the way he reported in suc-

[50] *Daily Richmond Enquirer*, September 22, 24, 1862. In a letter to the *Memphis Appeal* written from Richmond on September 22, journalist John R. Thompson reported that "since Friday [Sept. 18] the city has been painfully excited on this subject. The Philadelphia Inquirer of Thursday, received here by flag of truce boat from Varina on James River, contained such portentous paragraphs of Yankee success that we knew not what of disaster to expect. . . . Longstreet killed, Jackson wounded and in the hands of McClellan, forty thousand Confederate soldiers taken prisoner—such flaming headlines as these in large capitals seemed full of sorrow to the cause." *Memphis Daily Appeal*, October 1, 1862.

cession the preliminary skirmishing on Tuesday afternoon, the early morning action of Wednesday, September 17 on the Confederate left, and the noonday struggle between the centers of both armies. "Personne" was not so situated that he would see what was going on during the two and a half hours that the fighting on the Confederate left was at its height, but he could hear the din of the heavy guns, the whistling and the bursting of the shells, and the almost deafening roar of musketry. If the *Charleston Courier* correspondent indeed had no fears of the ability of the Confederate left to hold its ground, the reason could have been the "strange strength and confidence we all felt in the presence of that man, 'Stonewall Jackson.'"

In describing the struggle on the Confederate right that began about the middle of the afternoon, "Personne" acknowledged that he knew less about this portion of the field than any other. But he was an eyewitness of the arrival on the battlefield of A. P. Hill's dust-stained veterans from Harper's Ferry who stemmed the threatened Federal breakthrough at the end of the bruising 15-hour fight.

So far as "Personne" was concerned, the result of the Battle of Antietam was "a victory to our arms. If we failed to rout the enemy it was only because the nature of the ground prevented him from runing. . . . Last night we were inclined to believe that it was a drawn battle, and the impression generally obtained among the men that because they had not in their usual style got the enemy to running, they had gained no advantage, but to-day the real facts are coming to light, and we feel that we have indeed achieved another victory."[51]

Following the battle there was some confusion in Richmond about the exact whereabouts of Lee's army. The news of the recrossing of the Potomac by that army reached Davis in Richmond within thirty-six hours after it occurred, but Davis withheld it from the press for another day.[52] On September 23 the *Richmond Examiner* reported that Lee had crossed only a part of his army to the south side of the Potomac, leaving it to be inferred that he was planning another offensive movement. The *Dispatch* of the same date contained contradictory information about the recrossing of the Potomac, but on the following day its editor indicated that he was completely satisfied that Lee's entire army was on the south bank of the river. "The reports heretofore

[51] *Charleston Daily Courier*, September 29, 1862.
[52] *Charleston Mercury*, September 25, 1862.

received and which we were inclined to credit that only a portion of the army had re-crossed proved to have been not well founded."

Army correspondents were as mystified as their editors about the results of the Maryland campaign. In a letter from Shepherdstown on September 19, "Personne" had interpreted Lee's backward movement as "purely strategic, and totally different from the 'change of base' that recently took place upon the Chickahominy."[53] Alexander admitted that he was unable to determine whether the return of the Confederate army to Virginia had been the product of military necessity, the result of the attainment of the supposed object of the invasion, the capture of Harper's Ferry, or some hidden strategic purpose. Alexander had been with Lee's army on the night march of September 18; in his letter describing the movement he portrayed the contrast between the circumstances of its crossing into Maryland by the light of an early morning sun and its return to Virginia in silence and under the cover of night. "The columns wound their way over the hills and along the valleys, like some huge, indistinct monster. The trees and overhanging cliffs and the majestic Blue Ridge loomed up in dim but enlarged and fantastic proportions, and made one feel as if he were in some strange and weird land of grotesque forms, visited only in the hour of dreams."

Looking back on the Maryland campaign as a whole, Alexander admitted that he had been in favor of the movement into Maryland, but that under existing circumstances, "I now think it was a mistake. This conviction gradually forced itself upon my mind after I came with the army and saw the miserable condition in which it was. A fifth of the troops are barefooted; half of them are in rags; and the whole of them insufficiently supplied with food. . . . Since we crossed into Maryland, and even before they frequently had to march all day and far into the night, for three and four days together, without food of any kind, except such apples and green corn as they could obtain along the way. . . ."

"The political effect upon Maryland of our retrograde movement must be highly injurious. We shall doubtless lose ground among the people, and it may be we shall have to make up our minds to lose the State itself. It should be the direst necessity, however, that should compel us to abandon Maryland. The waters of the Chesapeake are in-

[53] *Charleston Daily Courier*, September 29, 1862.

dispensable to the Confederate States as a naval power, as well as for our security and defence."[54]

The bitter feeling that the apathetic response of Marylanders inspired in Lee's army was reflected in a letter an army correspondent of the *Memphis Appeal* addressed to his newspaper from Martinsburg on September 24. The *Appeal* reporter told how, "we found all stores closed, and an almost complete refusal to take any money but specie. And the women—God bless their pretty faces—didn't seem to appreciate the self-sacrificing devotion of the boys, and with a few exceptions took particular care, by a contemptuous elevation of their tiny proboscis, to show their contempt of 'you dirty rebels.' Maryland has a few noble patriots in her limits, but as a State, she resembles Ephraim—she is tied to her idol, the g-l-o-u-r-i-o-u-s Union, and ought to be let alone."[55]

LEE HAD hoped to resume the offensive within a few weeks after his return to Virginia, but first he had to strengthen his army by gathering up the stragglers. The letters of the army correspondents made clear that this was a larger task than he had anticipated. A war correspondent of the *Richmond Dispatch* reported on September 22 that there were not less than five thousand stragglers in the vicinity of Winchester, and a Winchester correspondent of the *Lynchburg Republican* estimated the total number in early October at 30,000![56] But if Lee could not advance, McClellan, it appeared, was in no mood to undertake a vigorous pursuit of Lee. On September 22 Sumner's corps occupied Harper's Ferry; but not until late in October did the Army of the

[54] *Mobile Daily Advertiser and Register*, October 2, 1862.

[55] *Memphis Daily Appeal*, October 13, 1862. "Personne" confirmed the disheartening effect on the army of the cool treatment accorded them by the civilian population, saying: "We were carried through the three worst Union counties in the State." *Charleston Daily Courier*, October 9, 1862. For a defense of the Maryland population against these charges of basic unfriendliness by an army correspondent of the *Richmond Dispatch* see *ibid.*, September 23, 1862.

[56] *Richmond Daily Dispatch*, September 26, 1862; *Memphis Daily Appeal*, October 9, 1862. The high incidence of straggling during the Antietam campaign was the subject of a letter addressed by General Lee to Jefferson Davis at the time of Lee's arrival in Frederick. He observed that "with some, the sick and feeble, it results from necessity, but with the greater number, from design. These latter do not wish to be with their regiments nor to share in their hardships and glories. They are the cowards of the army, desert their comrades in time of danger, and fill the houses of the charitable and hospitable in the march." R. E. Lee to Jefferson Davis, September 7, 1862, Robert E. Lee Papers, Duke University.

Potomac cross the river in force and begin to march southward east of the Blue Ridge. Remaining in the Shenandoah Valley near Winchester, Lee put his men to work destroying the track of the Baltimore and Ohio Railroad west of Harper's Ferry.[57]

During early October mishaps of a somewhat different character interrupted the army reporting of both de Fontaine and Alexander. Sometime around the first of October "Personne" suffered an accident when his horse was frightened suddenly. When the bridle fastened about his spur the animal dragged the correspondent for a distance of fifty to seventy-five yards, severely lacerating him but fortunately breaking no bones. An internal inflammation which complicated "Personne's" injuries caused him to return to South Carolina during the third week of October and separated him from Lee's army for the remainder of 1862.[58] "P.W.A.," on the other hand, fell ill in Winchester as a result of the scant food and other hardships of the Maryland campaign and went back to Richmond about the middle of October.[59] Before he left the army Alexander addressed to the two newspapers (the *Savannah Republican* and the *Mobile Register*) for which he was then correspondent a moving appeal in behalf of the enlisted man in Lee's army. Other newspapermen quickly echoed his remarks and widely circulated them throughout the Confederacy. In his letter Alexander enlarged on the hardships of Lee's men during the Maryland campaign, and then asked his readers:

Do you wonder, then, that there should have been stragglers from the army? that brave and true men should have fallen out of line from sheer exhaustion, or in their efforts to obtain a mouthful to eat along the roadside? or that many seasoned veterans should have succumbed to disease and been forced back to the hospital? I look to hear a great outcry raised against the stragglers. Already lazy cavalry men and dainty staff officers, who are mounted and can forage the country for something to eat, are condemning the weary private, who, notwithstanding his body may be covered with dust and perspiration and his feet with stonebruises, is expected to trudge along under his knapsack and cartridge box on an empty stomach and never to turn aside for a morsel of food to sustain his sinking limbs. Out upon such monstrous injustice! . . . . .

The men must have clothing and shoes this winter. They must have

[57] *Richmond Daily Dispatch*, October 30, 1862.

[58] *Charleston Daily Courier*, October 21, 1862; *Columbia South Carolinian* as reprinted in *Charleston Daily Courier*, October 23, 1862; *Savannah Republican*, October 23, 1862.

[59] *Mobile Daily Advertiser and Register*, October 2, 4, 25, 1862.

something to cover themselves while sleeping, and to protect themselves from the driving sleet and from storms when on duty. This must be done, though our friends at home should have to wear cotton and sit by the fire. The army in Virginia stands guard this day, and will stand guard this winter over every hearthstone in the South. The ragged sentinel who may pace his weary rounds this winter on the bleak spurs of the Blue Ridge, or along the frozen valley of the Shenandoah and the Rappahannock, will also be your sentinel, my friend at home. . . . He suffers and toils and fights for you, too, brave, true-hearted women of the South. Will you not clothe his nakedness then? Will you not put shoes and stockings on his feet? Is it not enough that he has written down his patriotism in crimson characters along the battle-road from the Rappahannock to the Potomac, and must his bleeding feet also impress their mark of fidelity upon the snows of the coming winter? I know what your answer will be. God has spoken through the women of the South, and they are his holy oracles in this day of trial and tribulation.[60]

Alexander's championing of the common soldier registered an understandable impact on the Confederate press and its readers. The editor of the *Richmond Dispatch* described it as "true eloquence, coming from the heart of a man who not only sees what he describes, but is himself a participant," and the *Charleston Courier* seconded the appeal, stressing the obligations of its readers "to work! to work!"[61] By the middle of November Alexander was in a position to testify to the gratifying success of the movement in Richmond in behalf of the destitute soldiers. "Jew and Gentile have responded with like generosity and promptitude, and it is believed that eight or ten thousand pairs of good shoes, and as many socks, have been raised, and some twenty-five or thirty thousand dollars."[62] One of the subscribers to the *Savannah Republican* who signed himself "Old Soldier" proposed to repay the debt that the Confederate public owed "P.W.A." for the courage and accuracy of his reporting by contributing to a purse of $1,000 to be invested in a suitable memorial to him. Alexander wrote a private note to the editor of the *Republican* when he heard about the proposed memorial, expressing his warmest thanks to the kind friends who had

[60] *Ibid.*, October 4, 1862. In *ibid.*, October 8, 1862, Alexander told of seeing Rodes' Alabama brigade pass through Richmond on August 19, 1862: ". . . it was there that I saw for the first time a barefooted Confederate soldier."

[61] *Richmond Daily Dispatch*, October 9, 1862; *Charleston Daily Courier*, October 6, 1862. According to the *Savannah Republican*, Alexander's letter depicting the sufferings of the army "has been copied, without exception by every exchange that comes to this office, and probably by every newspaper in the Confederate States. . . ." For appeals on behalf of the enlisted man by other reporters see *Memphis Daily Appeal*, October 17, 28, 1862.

[62] *Mobile Daily Advertiser and Register*, November 20, 1862.

placed such a flattering estimate on his work as a war correspondent. He said he hoped the one thousand dollars would be raised as soon as practicable, but in lieu of the proceeds being given to him, he urged that they be invested in shoes and clothing for the needy soldiers in Virginia.[63]

The *Richmond Enquirer* sounded the only sour note in the paean of journalistic praise of Alexander. Expressing the opinion that there had been a good deal of exaggeration and misapprehension about the deficiencies of army supply, the *Enquirer* made a sneering reference to "an army correspondent of papers near the Gulf, who usually writes very interesting letters [and who] tells of the recent arrival of clothing to our army, and claims the credit of having caused it by his letters." The *Enquirer* went on to say that it thought the correspondent was probably mistaken. "We suppose that, in the same way, a man might make the sun rise by dwelling beforehand upon its necessity."[64]

APPARENTLY no newspaper reporter was with Stuart's cavalry when it crossed the Potomac on October 9 on a raid into Pennsylvania. The main object of the raid was to cut the Cumberland Valley Railroad between Harrisburg and Chambersburg. Although this objective was not achieved, Stuart and his men covered eighty miles in twenty-seven hours with a loss of only three casualties and brought back 1,200 horses and thirty prisoners. A *Richmond Dispatch* reporter who was in the neighborhood of Winchester when Stuart returned from his Chambersburg raid claimed that "*horses* were what he [Stuart] went for and horses he obtained—horses of all sizes, shapes and colors. . . . Many of the horses were large and utterly worthless, except to pull a plow or a baggage-wagon; but some of them make elegant cavalry horses, and have already been initiated."[65]

[63] *Macon Journal and Messenger* as reprinted in *Knoxville Daily Register,* December 7, 1862; *Savannah Republican* as reprinted in *Charleston Daily Courier,* December 12, 1862.

[64] *Daily Richmond Enquirer,* November 3, 1862. Subsequently, during the month of November, the *Enquirer* and the *Richmond Whig* engaged in editorial controversy about attacks on the Davis administration by the *Whig* relating to alleged neglect of the army's needs by the Quartermaster's Department. In the *Memphis Appeal* of November 21, 1862, its Richmond correspondent contended that the sight of Confederate soldiers marching barefooted through the slush of the city during a snowstorm on November 7 had had more effect than Alexander's letters in bringing home to the citizens of Richmond the shoeless and blanketless condition of the army.

[65] *Richmond Daily Dispatch,* October 24, 1862; Freeman, *Lee,* II, 422.

A by-product of Stuart's raid, which created anguish among Confederate newspaper editors, was the announcement of a new policy by the War Department censors. When the Associated Press reporter prepared a dispatch summarizing the events of the movement as reported in the Northern press, the War Department refused to permit the dispatch to be sent over the wires until it had been cleared for transmission by the adjutant general. Since dispatches based on statements published in Northern newspapers had previously been authorized, the *Richmond Whig* protested the arbitrary character of the new rule and requested that it be withdrawn.[66]

Letters of Richmond correspondents reflected an escalation of wartime scarcities and lawlessness during the fall of 1862. Thompson of the *Memphis Appeal* told how "the scanty supply of coal has already deprived us of gaslight in the streets and thoroughfares, and the dearth of provisions is attested in the almost fabulous prices of all articles of daily consumption."[67] Similarly the *Mobile Register* correspondent Sam Reid, writing about a visit to the capital in the latter part of November 1862, pictured extortion as reigning supreme in Richmond. "Five dollars a day for board, and half rations at the hotels at that, whisky fifty cents per wine glass, rifled, and more deadly than solid shot, killing at a greater distance than a parrot gun. There is no such thing as public 'liquidizing' in Richmond, but if you want to indulge, you have to become initiated and work your way through, as if in a Mason's Lodge, when the alcoholic is measured out . . . at a price which in Porkopolis would buy two gallons of comparatively a vastly superior quality!"[68]

At the time of Reid's visit Richmond was still agog over the resignation of Secretary of War Randolph on November 15 and his replacement by James A. Seddon. Peter Alexander concluded from these events that Davis was in fact his own secretary of war. He went on to say that in his opinion the President exerted greater power at that time than General Jackson or George III ever aspired to in their prime. "He has exercised the veto power more frequently, perhaps, than all the Presidents of the United States ever did, and always with success. In no instance that has come to my knowledge, either in the Provisional or pres-

[66] *Richmond Daily Whig*, October 15, 1862; *Memphis Daily Appeal*, October 23, 1862.
[67] *Memphis Daily Appeal*, October 29, 1862.
[68] *Mobile Daily Advertiser and Register*, November 30, 1862.

ent Congress, did he ever fail to carry his point as against the Congress. . . . Nor is it known that he has ever been prevailed upon to yield to the public desire, when different from his own, except in the appointment of General Price and the transfer of Mr. Benjamin from the Department of War to that of Foreign Relations. No public man in our history ever stood closer to his friends, or conceded less to those who had crossed his path or arrayed themselves amongst his personal or political enemies. A man of great nerve and imperturbable coolness, combined with remarkable courtesy, or the most freezing politeness as the occasion may require, he yet manages as the Chief Magistrate of a Confederacy of sovereign States, under the limitations of a written constitution . . . to wield a power almost unlimited, and to exercise supreme control in every department of the government."[69]

The Southern press had already learned of the removal of General McClellan from the command of the Army of the Potomac on November 7. When his successor, General Burnside, quickly shifted the Federal army east to the vicinity of Fredericksburg in mid-November, the "old burg," as many Virginians called it, became the center of newspaper attention. Burnside had stolen a march on Lee and arrived at Falmouth on the opposite side of the Rappahannock from Fredericksburg on November 17. There he was disappointed to find that the pontoons for his river-crossing had not yet arrived. The same day Lee started his first contingents from Culpeper to Fredericksburg; by November 20 about half of his army had reached the historic old town to contest the advance of Burnside's army on Richmond.[70]

The Richmond newspapers carried news stories on November 22 about the demand for the surrender of the city that the Federals had served on Mayor Montgomery Slaughter the previous day. The excuse for the demand was the charge that Federal troops had been fired on

[69] *Ibid.*, November 26, 1862; *Memphis Daily Appeal*, November 28, 1862. Interviews with President Davis by Reporter Reid and Editor Richard Yeadon during November 1862 are mentioned and briefly described in *Mobile Daily Advertiser and Register*, November 30, 1862 and *Charleston Daily Courier*, November 13, 1862. According to Reid, Davis looked "remarkably well" at the time of the interview, and "notwithstanding his cares and laborious duties, evinces all the fire and energy with which he led his troops to battle in Mexico. . . ." Richard Yarington, the Richmond correspondent of the *Columbus Sun*, reported on December 8, 1862, however, that Davis was "very much absorbed in his Executive duties and never appears in public, except at St. Paul's Episcopal Church where he is a member and regular attendant at worship." *Columbus Daily Sun*, December 15, 1862.

[70] Freeman, *Lee*, ii, 433, 436.

from the streets of the town and that its manufactures were being used in behalf of the Confederate cause. General Burnside let it be known that if the city did not capitulate by 5:00 P.M. of that day, Federal artillery would open fire on the town at nine o'clock the next morning. To avert serious loss of life among the townspeople, General Lee advised them to leave the town as soon as possible.

When the Southern Associated Press tried to wire the story of the surrender demand from Richmond, it encountered difficulties. The Richmond telegraph office referred the agent of the Associated Press to the adjutant general, who in turn deferred to the judgment of Assistant Secretary of War Albert T. Bledsoe. Unwilling to take responsibility for the decision, Bledsoe advised the Associated Press man to see Secretary Seddon. Only then was the news service permitted to inform the public that Burnside had demanded the surrender of Fredericksburg. This series of incidents evoked the derisive comment from Bagby: "Have we a circumlocution office any where in the Confederacy?"[71]

A reporter for the rival Richmond Associated Press had boarded the midnight train for Fredericksburg the night before the Southern Associated Press man experienced these difficulties. When he arrived at his destination at dawn the next morning, the reporter from Richmond was amazed to see an exodus of refugees. Women and children were leaving in every direction, and aged and infirm men were bearing their household goods and other possessions on their backs. By November 25 Alexander learned in Richmond that nearly all the women and children, sick, and infirm had been removed from the threatened point. "Some were brought to this city; others were taken to Charlottesville, Petersburg, and other points in the State; but in the absence of further hostile demonstrations on the Rappahannock, they will probably return to their homes in the course of a week or two."[72]

Richmond newspapermen were puzzled by Burnside's movement. The Richmond correspondent of the *Memphis Appeal* could not understand why the new "generalissimo" of the Yankee army would choose "the very worst and most difficult route" for an advance upon Rich-

---

[71] *Charleston Mercury*, November 28, 1862.

[72] *Richmond Daily Dispatch*, November 25, 1862; *Mobile Daily Advertiser and Register*, December 2, 1862. The arrival in Richmond of the first refugee trains from Fredericksburg was described in *Daily Richmond Enquirer*, November 24, 1862.

mond.[73] The *Richmond Examiner* and the other Richmond newspapers suspected that Burnside's movement was only a feint, that the greatest danger of attack was from the south side of Richmond. When Alexander learned from the Northern press that it was the failure of the pontoon boats to arrive that had immobilized Burnside, he too was mystified. According to Alexander the Rappahannock was fordable almost everywhere above Fredericksburg; it was only below the city that bridges were required.[74]

A *Richmond Dispatch* reporter who was assigned to one of the artillery regiments in Lee's army carefully observed the advance units of the enemy host on the opposite side of the river. He reported that the enemy came down every day to the river bank and that when "one of our men asked one of the Yankees, the other day who was in command? he replied 'that d———d curly head Burnside.'" The *Dispatch* man added: "I understand the Federals are deserting daily."[75]

The strange inactivity of Burnside's army that had mystified the Richmond journalists finally came to an end on Thursday, December 11, when the Federal army engineers began to lay pontoon bridges across the river opposite Fredericksburg. When a brigade of Mississippi infantry that had been left in the town drove the pontooniers from their task, Burnside ordered his artillery to open fire on the town from across the river. An assault party crossed the river in boats when the artillery bombardment failed to rout the defenders, and in house-to-house fighting forced Barksdale's Mississippians out of the town and back onto the ridge behind Fredericksburg.[76]

Information of the attack reached Richmond that morning in the form of a dispatch from General Lee to the War Department reporting the repulse of the enemy. Later that day Alexander applied to the passport office in the War Department for authorization to rejoin the

[73] *Memphis Daily Appeal*, November 29, 1862.

[74] *Daily Richmond Examiner*, November 21, 22, 1862; *Mobile Daily Advertiser and Register*, December 14, 1862. If John R. Thompson's letter to the *Memphis Appeal*, published on December 19, 1862, is reliable evidence, the fact that Burnside's strange inactivity was attributable to the failure of his pontoons to arrive became known in Richmond on December 5 or shortly before.

[75] *Richmond Daily Dispatch*, December 3, 1862.

[76] An unsigned special correspondent of the *Richmond Enquirer* provided his paper with a vivid description of the performance of Barksdale's Mississippians, who were armed with Springfield rifles, and of the narrow escapes of the inhabitants of Fredericksburg who remained in their homes during the bombardment. *Daily Richmond Enquirer*, December 15, 1862.

army and report the results of the impending battle. The officer in charge provided the discouraging information that no one except persons engaged in government or army business was being granted a passport. When Alexander pointed out that reporters for three of the Richmond newspapers were proceeding without hindrance to the scene of action, he was advised that such clearance had been improperly extended by an officer who had no authority to do so.[77] Thus apparently by accident the Richmond press for almost the first time during the war was accorded the privilege of sending special correspondents to the army in Virginia at the time of a major battle.[78]

On Friday the 12th, the main body of Burnside's army crossed the river, occupied the town, and prepared to attack Lee's army, which was entrenched on the heights to the rear of the town. With an army of approximately 78,000 men Lee had the advantage of position over the roughly 120,000 men Burnside could bring to bear. That evening a reporter for the *Richmond Enquirer* described the Confederate lines as "enshrouded in a thick atmosphere of smoke, proceeding partly from the cannonading today, and, in part, from the camp fires of the armies. . . . The camp fires now gleam on every hill and hillside, and along the horizon flare up in broad sheets of pale light that indicate the presence of the 'ample forces.' Our men joke and laugh around their camp fires as they prepare rations for the morrow in careless confidence, for they know we have the men and the generals equal to the coming trial. Everybody expects the great battle will take place within the next twenty-four hours. Long trains of wagons are wending rearward, laden with baggage, hospital tents are being pitched, and ambulances ranged in convenient position, and the 'decks' generally cleared for action."[79]

[77] *Memphis Daily Appeal*, December 22, 1862; *O.R.* (Army) Ser. i, vol. xxi, p. 546; P. W. Alexander to Hon. Jas. A. Seddon, Secty of War, December 12, 1862, Office of Confederate Secretary of War, 1861-1865, Letters Received, 496-A-1862; *Mobile Daily Advertiser and Register*, December 18, 1862. In a letter written to the *Mobile Register* from Richmond on December 3, Alexander explained that his failure to join the army at Fredericksburg before then resulted from the fact that "our troops are still without their tents." *Mobile Daily Advertiser and Register*, December 9, 1862.

[78] Reporter Yarington stated in a letter from Richmond dated December 16, 1862: "for the first time, I think, since the war raged along the Potomac and in Northern Virginia, the Richmond press have enjoyed the privilege of sending special correspondents to the army and of which they have each availed themselves." *Columbus Daily Sun*, December 23, 1862.

[79] *Daily Richmond Enquirer*, December 15, 1862; Longstreet, *Manassas to Appomattox*, p. 317.

The Confederate line, which generally faced the northeast, was about four miles long and was divided into two main sectors. Longstreet commanded the Confederate left on Marye's Hill with four of his five divisions in line. On the right Jackson had Gen. A. P. Hill's division along his entire front, supported by three other divisions. Stuart's cavalry guarded and extend'd the Confederate right flank.[80]

In Richmond Correspondent George Bagby was fuming at the lack of information from Lee's army at Fredericksburg. About seven o'clock that (Friday) evening the War Department received a dispatch stating, "General Lee holds the enemy in check; the army is moving." But Bagby was unable to determine whether such a movement was to the front or rear. Why, he wondered, were the three Richmond reporters at Fredericksburg so silent about what was happening there?[81]

The correspondent of the *Richmond Enquirer* who was stationed on the Confederate right on Saturday morning, December 13, was impressed by the greyish dim cloud of fog and smoke that enveloped the landscape and gradually rose. About eight o'clock the sound of the enemy's artillery shattered the stillness of the scene and signalled the advent of another battle. In front of the Confederate position was a plain about six miles long and two and a half miles wide on which the enemy had established its battle formation. A few long narrow groves of leafless oaks broke the monotony of the plain, and here and there were clumps of cedar. Fences and ditches separated fields of about one hundred acres each, and in the center of the enemy line on rising ground near the river was posted a battery of twenty-one heavy enemy guns. The *Enquirer* man then observed that the fog had lifted, "revealing the dark and heavy columns of the enemy moving down the opposite bank of the river. Far down near the lower part of the valley, they are seen debouching. Whole fields are gleaming with bayonets. They continue to pour out upon the plain in a stream which seems to come from an inexhaustible fountain. The meadows are black with them, tens of thousands in solid columns. We can only vaguely conjecture at this distance the number. Old soldiers think there are sixty thousand. Where are our men?"

"The enemy, now formed in three heavy columns, advances to attack our right; on they go at double quick toward the woods, making the earth shake under their tread with colors flying and arms glistening

[80] Shelby Foote, *The Civil War, A Narrative, Fredericksburg to Meridian* (New York, 1963), p. 30.
[81] *Charleston Mercury*, December 16, 1862.

in the sunlight. Where are our men? A long sheet of flame from the skirt of the woods at the foot of the hills, a cloud of smoke, a roar and rattle of musketry tell their whereabouts. The advanced column halts, delivers a hasty fire. A continuous stream of fugitives from the front scour across the fields rearward; some are halted and formed in squads, but can never be forced again to go to the front except at the point of the bayonet. The smoke now mostly shuts the [combatants] from the view of the distant spectator. There is breaking of ranks among the enemy, rallying and rerallying, but to no avail. They cannot stand the murderous fire. They give it up as a bad job."[82]

Unfortunately neither "P.W.A." nor "Personne" were on the battle-field that day to give accounts of the most disastrous Yankee defeat since the First Battle of Manassas. Alexander did not reach Fredericks-burg until the battle was over. Yet his description of the battle, based on information obtained second-hand from participants, had the mas-ter's touch. His account of the fighting on the Confederate left, where the loss of life was particularly heavy, is especially vivid:

As the fog rolled away and the sun came out, the enemy were seen ad-vancing from the town in great force. Coble's and Kershaw's brigades, posted at the base of the hill, about a fourth of a mile from the edge of the town, were the first to receive the shock. Their position was behind a stone fence, while the heights in their rear were occupied by the New Orleans Washing-ton Artillery under command of the veteran Col. Walton and Cook's North Carolina brigade. These batteries poured a devouring fire into the ranks of the multitudinous foe as they advanced across the open plain between the town and our front line. The enemy made a desperate attempt to gain these heights. Assault upon assault was made, each time with fresh columns and increased numbers. They never succeeded, however, in getting nearer than seventy or eighty yards to the stone wall, from which the brave Georgi-ans and Carolinians saluted them with a fire that no mere human force could face and yet live. Our men did not pull a trigger until they got within easy range, and then taking deliberate aim, they poured volley after volley right into their faces.

In this way it is said the enemy brought up first and last 40,000 men against this position; and yet these two heroic brigades, or rather portions of them, (for all the regiments belonging to them were not engaged,) not only maintained their ground, with the assistance of the batteries on the hills above them, but repulsed the foe with a slaughter that is without a parallel in this war. I went over the ground this morning, and the remaining dead, after two-thirds of them had been removed, lay twice as thick as upon any other battlefield I have ever seen. . . .

[82] *Daily Richmond Enquirer*, December 17, 1862.

Just in front of our line is a thin plank fence, behind which the enemy sought shelter as they advanced to the attack. Some of the planks in this fence were literally shot away from the posts to which they were nailed, and one can hardly place his hand upon any part of them without covering a dozen bullet holes. Just at the foot of the stone wall behind which our men were posted, thousands of flattened musket balls may be picked up, whilst the hills behind it have been almost converted into a lead mine. . . .[83]

But if "Personne" and Alexander were not present at the Battle of Fredericksburg there was an observer whose account of the battle and of the events that led up to it was a stellar piece of reporting. Capt. John Esten Cooke, then serving as a staff officer of General Stuart, signed his battle report "J.E.C.," which was published in the *Richmond Whig.* Cooke's one-and-a-half-column newspaper story was written three days after the battle in a tent down whose log chimney a northwest wind accompanied by rain was driving the smoke.

Cooke described the enemy crossing of the Rappahannock on Thursday, the heroic resistance offered by Barksdale's Mississippi brigade, and the Federal bombardment of the town, which he watched from a hill just to the right of Telegraph Road as it descended to Fredericksburg. He declared he had never seen anything to compare with the repeated firing of those one hundred enemy guns that went on all day Thursday. ". . . it was that 'fire of hell' which Gortschakoff spoke of at Sebastopol. The quick puffs of smoke, touched in the centre with tongues of flame, ran incessantly along the lines of the enemy's batteries on the slopes, and as the smoke slowly drifted away, the bellowing roar came up in one continuous roll." With Cooke were Generals Lee, Longstreet, and Stuart, who were watching the artillery fire that swept the streets of the town with round shot, shell, and spherical case, and sent chimneys crashing down on the townspeople. Lee was dressed in an old gray coat, riding cape, and dark felt hat, and although he said but little, Cooke recalled his utterance in a grave tone tinged with sarcasm: "It is delightful to them to destroy innocent people, without being hurt themselves. *It just suits them.*"

Then Cooke told of riding down the next morning to the stone wall where Cobb's brigade had relieved Barksdale's exhausted Mississippians and of watching the sharpshooters at work on both sides. A gay young soldier with an attractive face was lying down reading, quite oblivious of the bullets that were plunking around him. In response

[83] *Mobile Daily Advertiser and Register,* December 25, 1862.

to Cooke's question as to what book he was reading, he answered politely, "History of Ireland, second volume."

"Are you from the old country?"

"No sir; I picked this up in camp."

Cooke did not undertake a comprehensive account of the bloody repulse of the Federals on Saturday. In part this was because the regular correspondents of the Richmond press had forestalled him, especially the correspondent of the *Richmond Examiner*, "who, though inaccurate in some particulars, has embodied most of the details in an interesting narrative." Instead, he concentrated his battle report for the *Richmond Whig* on the action that took place on the Confederate right which he himself saw.

Making note of the fact that soon after daybreak Lee, together with Jackson and Stuart, rode down to the right to reconnoiter the enemy position, Cooke was impressed with the confidence all three generals exhibited; he was surprised at the brand new uniform, so unlike his usual garb, that Stonewall Jackson was wearing. But he was correspondingly unimpressed with the tactics of the Federal generals, who seemed to be operating without any visible plan. "There was no generalship displayed, no power of combination or maneuvering. Their lines were pushed forward, and when mowed down by our artillery or musketry, new ones took their places—and the wavering, uncertain character of these movements continued. It has been stated in print that this was a Malvern Hill affair, with the position of the combatants reversed. But I think the writer is mistaken, at least as regards our right. The fight was on much more equal terms than is supposed—with this important difference, that the enemy very far outnumbered us, opposing two or three to one at every point of attack." Cooke asserted that the battle was chiefly an artillery engagement, with important exceptions at particular points of the line. He conceded that the enemy's artillery was well handled and that it inflicted much damage, but it was his opinion that the enemy were no match for the Confederate troops. "The truth is, that we fought them fair and open, one to their three and whipped them. . . ."[84]

All day Saturday while the battle was going on suspense in Richmond was building up. Not until nine that night did reliable news reach the

[84] *Richmond Daily Whig*, December 22, 1862. See also *Charleston Mercury*, December 29, 1862 and *Memphis Daily Appeal*, January 1, 1863, which identify Cooke as the author of the *Whig*'s Fredericksburg report.

Confederate capital, in the form of a dispatch from General Lee to the War Department. Lee's message was terse but fervent: "At 9 o'clock this morning, the enemy attacked our right wing, and as the fog lifted the battle ran along the whole line from right to left until 6 P.M. the enemy being repulsed at all points. Thanks be to God!"

"As usual, we have to mourn the loss of many of our own men."

"I expect the battle will be renewed at daylight to-morrow morning."[85]

Events did not fulfill Lee's prediction. For two days the two armies confronted each other in skirmish line contact. Then under cover of night Burnside recrossed the Rappahannock and abandoned his advance on Richmond over the Fredericksburg route.

Bagby pictured Stonewall Jackson's disappointment at the enemy's escape in a manner that suggests an attempt to embroider the Jackson legend. Without indicating the source of his story Bagby told how on the Sunday night after the battle "Old Stonewall" entered his tent about one o'clock in the morning and climbed into bed, without troubling to disrobe, with a friend whom he had invited to share his tent. The night was very cold, and the friend had slept as it seemed only a few minutes when Jackson sprang up, took off all his clothes, opened the door of his tent, and stalked outside in his unclad state. Calling his Negro servant, Jackson bade him dash over him two large buckets of water which had been standing in the freezing air. Then Jackson returned to the tent, rubbed himself down with a coarse towel, put on his new uniform, and went out to check the position of his forces, fully expecting to attack at daybreak. About seven o'clock he came back and woke up his friend, telling him to come to breakfast; the Yankees were "clean gone."[86]

Indignant accounts of the damage the Union army had inflicted on Fredericksburg were the theme of letters by the press correspondents attached to Lee's army. A special correspondent of the *Richmond Enquirer* stated that the "wanton destruction of property in town" could neither be imagined nor described. Estimating the property damage at $250,000, he told of furniture recklessly destroyed or thrown into the streets by Yankee soldiers, of beds ripped open, pictures disfigured

[85] *O.R.* (Army) Ser. i, vol. xxi, p. 546; *Richmond Daily Dispatch*, December 15, 1862. The newspaper version of Lee's dispatch quoted above varies somewhat from that printed in the *Official Records*.

[86] *Charleston Mercury*, December 29, 1862.

and destroyed, and pianos stripped of their keys.[87] Another *Enquirer*
correspondent calculated the damage to the town at $750,000, and
communicated an even more shocking picture of Yankee vandalism.[88]
What the correspondents failed to mention was that some of the destruction of property in Fredericksburg had been committed by Confederate soldiers who had occupied the city before the battle.[89]

The first telegraphic accounts of the Battle of Fredericksburg were
fairly conservative. As the extent of the disaster suffered by Burnside's
army became more apparent, however, Confederate newspaper editors
and reporters played the numbers game with both casualty figures and
estimates of the numbers of troops engaged. Perhaps the acme of such
foolishness was in a letter to the *Knoxville Register* from Richmond,
which credited Burnside with having had 200,000 soldiers participating in the battle while the Confederates had only 20,000 troops engaged. In the same letter the statistics of killed and wounded were
placed at 1,800 Confederates and 19,000 Yankees![90] The Richmond
correspondent of the *Memphis Appeal* likened the Yankee defeat to
Napoleon's defeat at Waterloo. And the editor of the *Richmond Dispatch* interpreted the result as "a complete victory to the Confederate
forces. We say complete, because, although the enemy's force was not
annihilated . . . the failure was entirely owing to the near neighborhood
of their strongholds. Had the battle been fought twenty miles this side
of the Rappahannock River there would have been such a rout as the
world did not witness in the forty-six years between the battle of
Waterloo and the first battle of Manassas."[91]

There were other deficiencies in the Confederate reporting of Fredericksburg besides the careless use of statistics. No correspondent's
letter gave any indication of the sizable gap in A. P. Hill's front line

[87] *Daily Richmond Enquirer*, December 18, 1862.

[88] *Ibid.*, December 20, 1862.

[89] According to a special correspondent of the *Richmond Enquirer* signed
"Flint," who was in Fredericksburg during the first week of December 1862, a
Confederate regiment stationed in the city after most of its population had left,
broke open houses, stole everything they could readily dispose of, and in one
instance seized all the clothing of two young ladies except what they had on their
persons. *Daily Richmond Enquirer*, December 6, 1862.

[90] *Knoxville Daily Register*, December 24, 1862. A Southern Associated Press
dispatch published in the *Memphis Daily Appeal* on December 18, 1862 considerably underestimated the loss on both sides. In his biography of Lee, II, 471, Freeman estimates the loss in Burnside's army at 12,653, compared with 5,309 on the
Confederate side.

[91] *Memphis Daily Appeal*, December 29, 1862.

on the Confederate right which enabled an enemy division commanded by Maj.Gen. George G. Meade to break the Confederate line before Meade's division was driven back by Jackson's counterattack.[92] Moreover, a *Richmond Enquirer* correspondent frankly admitted the inadequacies of his own reporting. He went on to say: "It was your correspondent's intention to have gone over the field with a capable and intelligent officer, who could have informed him as to the disposition of our forces and the parts which were borne respectively by regiments, companies, brigades, and divisions. Nothing would have afforded him greater pleasure, and the regret is sincere that pressing duties and the necessities of the hour should have . . . prevented this."[93]

In the more remote parts of the Confederacy the impairment of telegraph service caused considerable delay in reporting the battle and much grumbling on the part of newspaper editors.[94] Yet Lee's victory had given the Confederate press the text for many triumphant editorials. And if the performance of only one or two army reporters was particularly distinguished,[95] the reports of these same correspondents could hardly fail to stiffen the morale of soldier and civilian alike to meet the tests of death and suffering that lay ahead.

[92] In this connection see W. W. Hassler, *A. P. Hill: Lee's Forgotten General* (Richmond, 1957), pp. 118, 120-21, 123; Bruce Catton, *Never Call Retreat* (New York, 1965), p. 22. Catton expresses the opinion that if Meade's breakthrough had been properly exploited by the commander of Burnside's Left Grand Division, Maj.Gen. William B. Franklin, Burnside could have won the battle in spite of the bloody repulse of his men on the opposite end of the line.

[93] *Daily Richmond Enquirer*, December 18, 1862.

[94] See e.g. *Memphis Daily Appeal*, December 16, 1862; *Atlanta Daily Southern Confederacy*, December 17, 1862, in which the editor of the *Confederacy* lamented that "the persons employed by the press and well paid to send us news, have proven themselves incompetent to the task."

[95] Southern journalists excused the shortcomings of their battle reporting at Fredericksburg by pointing out that the *London Times* correspondent Lawley was with Lee's army at the time of the battle and could be expected to give a true story of the Battle of Fredericksburg. See e.g. *Daily Richmond Enquirer*, December 22, 1862; *Memphis Daily Appeal*, December 30, 1862. Lawley's battle account of Fredericksburg appeared in the *London Times* of January 13, 1863.

CHAPTER 8

Editor Forsyth Reports from Kentucky

No PROFESSIONAL newspapermen remained in Beauregard's Army of the Mississippi when it evacuated Corinth at the end of May 1862 and fell back to Tupelo, Mississippi, fifty-two miles south of Corinth. There the army remained for about two months while its commander exchanged angry letters with President Davis about the reasons for Beauregard's retreat. When about the middle of June Beauregard absented himself from camp for a period of rest in Bladon Springs, Alabama, Davis seized on the pretext that he had left his command without permission and on June 20 assigned Bragg to the command of the department in Beauregard's place.[1]

Beauregard had long been a favorite of the Confederate press, and the Western newspapers in particular were not overly enthusiastic about the appointment of the morose Bragg to succeed him. The *Montgomery Advertiser* accused the president of gratifying his spleen at Beauregard's expense, and characterized Bragg as "a General who uniformly sets at defiance the laws of his country for the appointment and promotion of officers and usurps all the powers of judge, jury, and executioner in the treatment of his men."[2] This plain speech of the *Advertiser* editor referred to the stern discipline Bragg had practiced at Corinth, where he shot captured deserters and lined up his soldiers to watch the executions.

In spite of Bragg's unpopularity with the press and with many of his soldiers, his skill as an organizer soon made itself felt. Both the health and the morale of the army improved as it became clear that the Federal commander Halleck had no intention of leading his army into the interior of Mississippi to attack the Confederate encampment at Tupelo.

A vivacious portrait of life in the Western army at this time was provided by a correspondent of the *Mobile Tribune* who somehow

---

[1] S. F. Horn, *The Army of Tennessee* (Norman, Okla., 1952), p. 155.

[2] *Montgomery Daily Advertiser*, July 9, 1862. On July 21, 1862 the Grenada, Mississippi correspondent of the *Atlanta Confederacy* remarked: "Bragg is growing somewhat unpopular, owing to his rigid and almost tyrannical system of discipline." *Atlanta Daily Southern Confederacy*, July 29, 1862.

eluded Bragg's vigilance. Beginning his letter with the query, "Reader, have you ever been at Tupelo?" the *Tribune* reporter went on to say:

If you are a philanthropist and have not been here, come at once! You will have more opportunities to exercise patience and charity and display philanthropy here than at any other place I wot of. . . . Your initiation will commence as you step from the cars, and before you have foothold, by being asked if you brought any watermellons to sell? Although you may reply in the negative, with a look as fierce as that of the chief clerk of a post commissary, you are importuned to "sell one for two dollars!" Probably you will be amused at this attempt to make you a first vender, but your good humor will disappear when, as you are rushing with the crowd to the hotel, some one captures your arm and insists upon your signing a provision return, not appearing to care that he is at the moment keeping you from your own provision returns. . . .

You mingle with the crowd and are asked where *my* regiment is. No, you *don't* know, and turn upon your heel, when a half frantic passenger, who is to leave on the train just starting, asks you to come to the Provost Marshall's office. Of course you consider yourself under arrest and proceed there. When your companion asks you to write him a pass to go to Mobile, you are astonished, and so is he, for the gentleman he was in quest of had stepped out, and he took you for him. His anger increases with his astonishment as the train is leaving, and you are fortunate if he don't knock you down for your failure to be somebody else.

You carry a newspaper in your hand, and are assailed on every side— "any more 'em papers to sell?" "Is that the *Tribune*—is Chattanooga fighting?" "Say, meester, where did you buy that paper?" Hastening on to the telegraph office, you are surprised to find immediately under its sign—"Enquire next door;" and you turn to do so, but find your mistake, when you see the following notice posted conspicuously:

"This is the telegraph office. We have no time or inclination to answer questions; nothing for sale or to eat; can't fill requisitions; don't command the post; don't know where any brigade, regiment, battalion, company, officer or private is. Enquire next door."[3]

On June 10 General Halleck began to break up the large army he had used to capture Corinth. Later in the month the Confederate press began to report the advance of Buell's army on Chattanooga along the line of the Memphis and Charleston Railroad. Reporter Sam Reid was in Chattanooga at the time, having arrived there earlier in the month from the West. Reid had made stops en route in Mobile, Montgomery, and Atlanta. In Mobile he had concluded arrangements with Editor Clark of the *Register* to correspond for that newspaper at $30 a week.

[3] *Mobile Daily Tribune* as reprinted in *Wilmington Daily Journal*, August 20, 1862.

The *Montgomery Advertiser* had agreed to pay him an additional $20. In Atlanta he had conferred with Editor J. Henly Smith of the *Confederacy* but apparently without coming to terms.[4] Reid had not enjoyed his experience in Atlanta. He had detected, he said, a "slight perceptible odor of Yankeedom" in the town, and he was obsessed by the phobia that the "Gate City" was alive with Yankee spies. It was his impression that: "Our passport system is a perfect humbug. On leaving any of our cities for a train of cars, you find, generally, an ignorant, illiterate boy with a musket in hand stationed at the doors of the cars, who asks you if you have a passport; on answering 'yes,' you are at once admitted, without the document being demanded for inspection. In my whole journey from Corinth to this place, I have not once shown my passports, and if I had, I doubt if the ignorant boys and men, detailed for this service, would have been able to read them!"[5]

Reid arrived in Chattanooga just in time to witness a bombardment from across the Tennessee River by a detachment of Federal troops under the command of Brig.Gen. James S. Negley. In his diary Reid recorded "great consternation" among the civilian population, and on June 8 he dashed off a letter to the *Mobile Register* describing the bombardment.[6] Negley made no attempt to cross the river, however, and soon withdrew to middle Tennessee. For reasons other than the threat that had just been dispelled, Reid was convinced there was no more important point in the Southern Confederacy at that time than Chattanooga. He referred to it as "the New Castle of our country," possessing an abundant supply of coal for locomotives and steamers and the saltpeter essential for the manufacture of gunpowder. It ought to be possible, he thought, if the gorges in the mountains were properly defended, to hold Chattanooga against any force "and make a Thermopylae of it."[7]

On July 4 Reid paid a call on Maj.Gen. Edmund Kirby Smith, commander of the Department of East Tennessee.[8] Smith may have discussed with the reporter some of his numerous worries. He was not simply menaced by Buell's advance from the West, but at the opposite end of his department a Federal brigadier general named George W. Morgan had encircled Cumberland Gap and compelled its Confederate

[4] Diary of Samuel C. Reid, Jr., Reid Papers, Santa Cruz, California.
[5] *Mobile Daily Advertiser and Register*, June 10, 1862.
[6] Reid Diary, Reid Papers; *Mobile Daily Advertiser and Register*, June 11, 1862.
[7] *Mobile Daily Advertiser and Register*, June 10, 1862.
[8] Reid Diary, Reid Papers.

garrison to evacuate. Finding the situation too difficult to contend with, Smith called on Bragg for help; on July 20 Bragg began moving the main part of his army east from Tupelo toward Chattanooga.[9]

Misleading reports about Bragg's movements, probably inspired by the Confederate War Department, made their appearance in various Southern newspapers. The *Atlanta Southern Confederacy* reported that the army at Tupelo had been divided, one part of it going into western Tennessee and another to Richmond. Almost two weeks after Bragg reached Chattanooga the Tupelo correspondent of the *Mobile Register* was writing that "rumors of Gen. Bragg's being on the march for Memphis are oft repeated, and the invaders are in constant and uncertain terror."[10]

With an artillery outfit attached to Cheatham's Tennessee division was a correspondent of the *Memphis Appeal* who wrote under the pseudonym of "Leigh." In a long letter to the *Appeal* "Leigh" described the toilsome march of his detachment from Tupelo to Chattanooga that ended on August 16. He reported that he and his fellow marchers had travelled 430 miles in twenty-four days and that the horses had held out better than expected. He told also about the crowds of people, invariably kind and hospitable, who came out to watch them as they marched through.[11]

At Chattanooga, where Bragg had arrived on July 29, the two generals agreed that Bragg should advance into middle Tennessee while Smith, with the help of Cleburne's division of the Army of the Mississippi, would attempt to recapture Cumberland Gap. Once that was done Smith was to cooperate with the invasion of middle Tennessee. Smith returned from Chattanooga to Knoxville to prepare the campaign against Cumberland Gap. Then he considered the alternative of bypassing Cumberland Gap and striking north into central Kentucky.

[9] Horn, *Army of Tennessee*, p. 159. Bragg had already sent McCown's division of 3,000 men to Chattanooga several weeks before. Grady McWhiney, "Controversy in Kentucky: Braxton Bragg's Campaign of 1862," *Civil War History*, VI (March 1960), 9.

[10] *Atlanta Daily Southern Confederacy*, July 26, 1862; *Mobile Daily Advertiser and Register*, August 13, 1862. For critical comment about a statement in the *Richmond Daily Dispatch* relating to the movements of the Western army see the Diary of Thomas Bragg, January 21, 1862, Southern Historical Collection, University of North Carolina.

[11] *Memphis Daily Appeal*, August 26, 1862. Editorial censorship removed from "Leigh's" letter the statistics he included about the number of cannons, the designations of the brigades whose wagons accompanied them, and the length of the train in miles.

By the middle of August he was on his way along the Wilderness Road to Lexington with an army of 12,000.[12]

At the end of August, with an army of 30,000 men, Bragg marched up the Sequatchie Valley to Pikeville and across the mountains to Sparta, passing around Buell's left wing. As Buell fell back to Nashville to protect his communications Bragg continued north, entering Kentucky at Tompkinsville and reaching the Louisville and Nashville Railroad at Glasgow on September 13.[13]

None of the Confederacy's leading war correspondents was with Bragg during his invasion march into Kentucky. When *Register* reporter Reid applied for permission to accompany the army, he discovered that Bragg had issued a general order on August 20 stating that "no person not properly connected with this army will be permitted to accompany it—whenever found within the lines, they will be arrested and confined."[14] Curious to know whether the order applied to him, Reid wrote to Bragg on August 22 asking permission to accompany the Army as the correspondent of the *Mobile Register*. After a couple of days he was informed that there was no "answer" to his note; on August 25 the acting inspector general, Col. E. D. Blake, notified him that General Bragg had ordered him to leave Chattanooga. No cause was given for Bragg's decision, and Reid observed with resentment that another press correspondent had been permitted to remain. In retaliation he prepared an exposé of Bragg's discrimination against him which he submitted to the *Charleston Mercury* for publication.[15]

Reid was mistaken in his supposition that it was he and he alone who had inspired Bragg's wrath against the army newspapermen. It seems likely that an army correspondent of the *Montgomery Advertiser* named Wallace Screws had been equally responsible for provoking Bragg into issuing the order against the army press. Ever since the un-

[12] J. H. Parks, *General Edmund Kirby Smith, C.S.A.* (Baton Rouge, 1954), pp. 205-206.

[13] J. H. Parks, *General Leonidas Polk, C.S.A., The Fighting Bishop* (Baton Rouge, 1962), pp. 255-56.

[14] *Mobile Daily Advertiser and Register*, August 29, 1862.

[15] Sam. C. Reid to General Braxton Bragg, August 22, 1862, Bragg Papers, Western Reserve Historical Society. The exposé appeared in the *Charleston Mercury* of September 26, 1862. Reid provided a veiled explanation of his motives for submitting his attack on Bragg for publication in the *Mercury* rather than the *Mobile Register* in *Mobile Daily Advertiser and Register*, September 25, 1862. It seems probable the real reason was that Editor John Forsyth, a close friend of Bragg, would not have published Reid's slashing attack on Bragg in his columns.

friendly remarks about Bragg that the *Advertiser* had published on July 9, the general had fumed. And when on July 29 the *Advertiser* published a comment by its army correspondent about the movements of the Army of the Mississippi, Bragg promptly placed Screws under arrest. On August 21 Editor Samuel G. Reid of the *Advertiser* addressed a propitiatory letter to Bragg, having already cautioned Screws against mentioning anything relating to army movements in future letters. Five days later Bragg replied through the medium of his inspector general, James E. Slaughter, accusing Screws of a "gross violation of all known rules in armies—not to declare to the enemy the movements of troops." Slaughter went on to say: "It is well ascertained that the enemy receive your papers and others regularly and by that means are kept constantly advised of our operations. As long as you confined yourself to personal abuse and detraction, though false and malignant . . . Gen. Bragg cared nothing for it. But when you assail our cause and expose our plans to the enemy, it becomes his duty to interfere; and you may rest assured he will do it, regardless of the support you have in the Cabinet."[16]

When Editor Reid received this tart communication, any vestiges of the admiration of Bragg's superior discipline which he professed once to have had vanished. On August 11 a reply to Bragg which could hardly have improved the general's peace of mind issued from the *Advertiser* office in Montgomery. In part the reply stated:

Allow me to say the arrest of our correspondent, on the pretense of giving information to the enemy, can only be regarded by all free-thinking men as another exhibition of that petty tyranny and vindictiveness for which you have gained an unenviable notoriety. No one doubts the correctness of the rule of the army not to give information to the enemy, but all will question its application to this case. The necessary inference from your words is that Wallace Screws is a spy, and that the people in the heart of the South, for whose information he was writing, are enemies to the country. . . . The offense of our correspondent, if offense it may be called, in repeating the vague and uncertain reports about the movements of your troops, is not so grave an offense as that previously committed by yourself in authorizing the publication of a dispatch that your army was on the move. Here is a dispatch which appeared in our columns, by order of Gen. Bragg:

"Mobile, July 24.— There has been unusual activity at Tupelo within the

[16] *Montgomery Daily Advertiser* as reprinted in *New York Daily Tribune*, September 1, 1862. See also *Memphis Daily Appeal*, September 5, 1862. Apparently the cabinet member whom Slaughter referred to was Attorney General Thomas H. Watts, an Alabamian. Diary of Thomas Bragg (entry for July 18, 1862), Southern Historical Collection.

last few days. The grand army under command of Gen. Bragg, is on the move, and the loyal people of Memphis may soon have occasion to rejoice. One or more divisions will pass through here in a day or two, *en route* east."

I was not in the office at night when this dispatch came, or we should not have published it. Everybody I met on the street was surprised that such a piece of information should be given an opportunity to go to the enemy. On inquiry, however, I was informed that the telegraph operator of this place had at first refused to receive the dispatch, but was assured from Mobile it was Gen. Bragg's order. Now, no impartial man can read that dispatch and then read the following extract from the letter of our correspondent, published July 26, to which it is understood you take exception, without ascribing more guilt to you than to him, if your movements were made known.

"It is reported that a portion of Bragg's men came in to-day, and that large numbers are on the way."

This report, it should be recollected, is stated in the middle of a long letter, where perhaps not one person in a hundred would ever see it, whereas Gen. Bragg's dispatch was published to the world under the telegraph head of nearly every city paper in the Confederacy, where everybody's attention was attracted to it. We doubt the statement that our papers are received regularly by the enemy, and if they are, they derive no information from them of the movements of our troops. This, thousands of daily readers of this paper can testify to. The enemy has much more direct and certain means of getting information through the so-called deserters from the Yankees, allowed to pass through your lines, than by means of Southern newspapers. . . .

Gen. Bragg knows as well as I do that the article to which he refers in relation to the relief of Gen. Beauregard by himself does him entire justice. It is notorious in the army that his collisions with the War Department had become so frequent previous and subsequent to the retreat from Corinth, that he was ordered to an inferior command at Vicksburg, which order was prevented from going into execution by the interference of Gen. Beauregard, who said Gen. Bragg could not be spared at that time, as he himself would have to ask for sick leave. This is a fact which I should not have adverted to at this time, but for the vulgar terms in which Gen. Bragg has been pleased to deny it.[17]

Apparently Bragg decided that it was inadvisable to provoke the influential editor of the *Montgomery Advertiser* any further. He released Screws after a nominal arrest of ten days; with that the quarrel was patched up with a statement on the editor's part that he wished the General "all success in his movements against the enemy."[18]

[17] *New York Daily Tribune*, September 1, 1862.
[18] Newspaper clipping from the *Montgomery Daily Advertiser* of August 27, 1862 in William Wallace Screws Papers, Alabama State Department of Archives and History.

Bragg's order excluding newspaper correspondents from his army during his march into Kentucky made clear, however, his continued distrust of newspapers and newspapermen.

The fact that several reporters were with Smith during his advance into Kentucky indicated a somewhat more favorable demeanor toward reporters on his part. In letters whose transmission to their newspaper was considerably delayed by communication difficulties, two army correspondents of the *Knoxville Register* with Kirby Smith wrote in rapturous terms about the beauties of the Bluegrass Region and their enthusiastic reception by the Kentuckians, "especially by the ladies." A reporter who signed himself "East Tennessee" invoked God's blessing on the Kentucky women for the water, food, and encouragement that they bestowed from the roadside on the marching Confederates. There was a note of pathos in his comment that "many of our men have marched from Cumberland Gap to this place [Frankfort] barefooted," and that the rocks that punctured the irregular surface of the mountain roads over which they marched were "stained with blood from their feet."[19]

Kirby Smith's barefooted marchers did not enter Kentucky without at least token opposition. Near Richmond, Kentucky, a hastily assembled Federal force of about 6,000 raw recruits under Maj.Gen. William Nelson slowed their progress. On the morning of August 30 the Confederates marched into battle, effectively destroying Nelson's command as a military unit in a stubborn fight. The victors captured over 4,000 of Nelson's men, and the remainder were either killed, wounded, or scattered. The Confederate loss was 78 killed and 372 wounded. A *Knoxville Register* reporter told of seeing Smith ride along the lines after the fight was over, raise his hat in the midst of the shouting and rejoicing, and exclaim: "Hurrah, my brave boys. You have done the best day's work ever done in the Southern Confederacy."[20]

The reporting of the affair at Richmond was not without its humorous aspects. The *Mobile Register* and its readers were puzzled by a Southern Associated Press dispatch which asserted that sixteen "mules" had been used to carry "Bull Nelson," the defeated Federal commander, from the battlefield to a place of safety in the rear. It was well known that Nelson was a large man, but this must have been exaggeration.

[19] *Knoxville Daily Register*, October 15, 1862.

[20] *Ibid.*, September 5, 1862; R. U. Johnson and C. C. Buel, *Battles and Leaders of the Civil War* (New York, 1956), III, 4-5.

Investigation by the *Register* disclosed that a careless telegraph operator had substituted "mules" for "miles" and that the discomfited general had been dropped in a fence corner after being transported the sixteen *miles*.[21]

During the next two weeks the Confederate press regaled its readers with the tidings of Smith's victorious progress through Kentucky. It reported that Smith had entered Lexington unopposed on September 2. When John Hunt Morgan's cavalry raided the vicinity of Louisville and went all the way to Covington, opposite Cincinnati, the *Memphis Appeal* published a very misleading dispatch about the military situation. The dispatch, which received wide circulation through the Southern Associated Press, stated that Smith had won another battle in the vicinity of Covington on September 4 and had demanded the surrender of Cincinnati the next day; both the battle and the surrender demand were completely fictitious. On the strength of such rumors the *Mobile Register* issued an extra on the evening of September 8 with headlines about the capture of Cincinnati by Smith's forces.[22]

Meanwhile Confederate newspaper editors and their readers were bursting with curiosity to know the whereabouts of Bragg's army. On September 9 the *Mobile Register* assured its readers at least a portion of that army was more than a day's march beyond the Kentucky line, advancing north "and devouring the distance which separates them from the Ohio at the rate of twenty miles a day." There were likewise unsubstantiated reports that Buell had evacuated Nashville and was in a race with Bragg to see who could get to the Ohio River first. From Knoxville, to which he had gone after leaving Chattanooga, Reid reported that hundreds of refugees were returning to their homes after learning that Huntsville, Alabama, had been evacuated by the "Abolition vandals." Among the refugees he listed was J. Withers Clay, the former editor of the *Huntsville Democrat*, travelling post haste, carpet bag in hand, to repossess his newspaper property.[23]

With Bragg's army at Glasgow was the *Memphis Appeal* correspondent "Leigh," who had somehow escaped the vigilance of Bragg's provost

---

21 *Mobile Daily Advertiser and Register*, September 12, 1862.

22 The *Memphis Appeal*'s report of the surrender demand was published in its September 8, 1862 issue. See also *Mobile Daily Advertiser and Register*, September 9, 1862.

23 *Mobile Daily Advertiser and Register*, September 9, 14, 17, 1862. In an earlier issue of this newspaper Reid had described a "saltpetre expedition" of Clay's during which he trapped a Yankee major. *Ibid.*, July 12, 1862.

marshals. In a letter to his newspaper written several weeks later, "Leigh" spoke frankly about the unflattering reception given Bragg's army when it first set foot on Kentucky soil. He contrasted the avowed Unionist sentiments of the citizens of Tompkinsville, the first Kentuckians the army encountered, with the enthusiastic reception that was extended to Bragg's soldiers at Glasgow.[24]

From Glasgow Bragg's army continued north along the railroad to Munfordville, where on September 16 he captured a Federal garrison of 4,000 under the command of Col. J. T. Wilder. Now that Bragg had very nearly duplicated Smith's stirring success at Richmond, the whole Confederacy expected him to turn on Buell, who had marched up from Nashville to Bowling Green, and inflict a major defeat on him. But their hopes were unrealized. For whatever reason, Bragg abandoned his advantageous position squarely athwart his enemy's line of communication and turned east to Bardstown, leaving open Buell's line of march to Louisville. Bragg had expected Smith to join him at Bardstown on September 23, but Smith was not there when he arrived. So on the 28th Bragg left his army in Polk's charge and went to Lexington, where he made plans for staging an elaborate inauguration of Richard Hawes as provisional governor of Kentucky at Frankfort.[25]

Bemused by the political implications of his invasion Bragg summoned his warm personal friend, Editor John Forsyth of the *Mobile Register*, to Kentucky to help him engage in "psychological warfare" with the enemy.[26] Since he permitted Forsyth to report the campaign for a quartet of leading Confederate newspapers, it seems likely that Bragg also intended to make use of his friend to enhance his military reputation.

On September 5 Forsyth was in Atlanta on his way north to overtake Bragg. Three days later he left Chattanooga with a dozen officers and commissary and quartermaster's clerks, well equipped with wagons, tents, and provisions. Forsyth was unwell when he left; after a few days he became so ill that it was with difficulty that he could sit upright in the saddle. His party followed the track of the army over Walden's Ridge, up the Sequatchie Valley, and across the Cumberland Mountains to Pikeville. Nothing of special interest occurred until they were within ten miles of Glasgow. There a courier informed them that the evening before, 400 Yankee cavalry had dashed into the town,

[24] *Memphis Daily Appeal*, October 16, 1862.
[25] Horn, *Army of Tennessee*, pp. 168-69, 172.
[26] *Ibid.*, pp. 177-78.

made prisoners of some sick soldiers there, and stolen everything they could lay their hands on. The Forsyth party decided in the light of this information to detour to the right to reach Munfordville, where they expected to make contact with Bragg's army. Starting out at sunrise on September 20 with guides furnished by Southern men along the road, they made good progress until about three o'clock in the afternoon. Then as they were strung out along the road, a company of the Seventh Regiment, Pennsylvania Cavalry dashed up and captured Forsyth along with nine others. Before he was paroled at Cave City and his exchange effected through Bragg's efforts, Forsyth lost, according to his own statement, a valuable servant, a black mare he had bought in Atlanta and one other horse, his side arms, and most of his clothes. Even then he had to put in two days of hard riding before he caught up with Bragg's army.[27]

On his arrival in camp he set to organizing a corps of printers on detail from Bragg's army and to accumulate the necessary facilities to enable him to publish an army newspaper. Also, Bragg utilized his services as a ghost writer to compose a sonorous proclamation addressed "To the People of the Northwest," which Bragg published over his own signature at Bardstown on September 26. This document emphasized the common interests of the northwestern states and the South, and urged on the northwesterners the formation of an alliance with the Southern Confederacy as the only possible escape from the enormous war debt with which they were likely to be saddled. Forsyth also wrote a plea to the people of Kentucky over General Buckner's name for them to ally themselves with the Confederacy.[28]

It was about this time that Forsyth's newspaper employee Sam Reid left Knoxville to go to Kentucky. He was in the company of Maj.Gen. John P. McCown, who apparently had given him permission to report from the army. On October 1 Reid wrote to the *Mobile Register* from the north side of Cumberland Gap (which in the meantime had been evacuated by the Federals) with his back against a tree and his knees serving as a desk. He noted that he was writing the letter by the uncertain light of an inch-long candle. Four days later he was at Newland's Tavern in Madison County, Kentucky, where he described the journey from Cumberland Gap in another newspaper letter. A memora-

[27] *Mobile Daily Advertiser and Register*, October 14, 1862; *Atlanta Daily Southern Confederacy*, November 19, 1862.
[28] *Mobile Daily Advertiser and Register*, October 14, 1862.

ble feature of the trip was a night spent in a cattle shed where the fleas were so aggressive that the campers had to bed down on the rocks outside. Reid also told about a conversation with a lady to whom he ascribed "Yankee Puritan blood." The lady said she "hoped soon to see us returning on the back track from Kentucky." When General McCown informed her that he feared she would be disappointed, she snapped back, "Well, I shall live in hopes, if I die in despair."[29]

About this same time Editor Forsyth was observing with disappointment the timorous behavior of the Kentuckians whom Bragg's army was attempting to "liberate." Writing from Bardstown on September 28 Forsyth expressed the belief that the men were "cowed by Federal military rule." "There is little doubt where their sympathies are," he continued, "but they fear to move when liberty, life and property are involved, until they are assured that the Confederate arms can be maintained in Kentucky." In another letter to the *Register* he recalled his being with General Polk on the march to Harrodsburg after Bragg had left to go on his political mission to Lexington. Forsyth declared bitterly that Polk sat on his horse for an hour in the street, waiting for some citizen of Harrodsburg to pluck up enough courage to offer him the hospitality of his house for the night. And when an invitation was finally extended, it was only under duress.[30]

That same night Forsyth, along with two or three other members of Bragg's staff, was quartered in the home of one of the wealthiest citizens of the state. Their host informed Forsyth that "his politics were neutrality. He didn't want to be forced into the contest. He was willing to give up all his slaves to enjoy peace." Forsyth also noticed that: ". . . in the streets, crowds of able-bodied men gazed upon the army with stolid indifference—not a cheer, not a recruit. Up to this time, the only Kentuckian that had actually taken up arms with us was Col Johnston, a nephew of the late Gen. A. S. Johnston. We had then been in Kentucky over two weeks."[31]

On October 1 General Buell gave further impetus to Kentucky neutralism when he marched out with three army corps from Louisville to attack Polk at Bardstown.[32] On October 8, after a week of maneuver-

---

[29] *Ibid.*, October 15, 1862. Reid's letter reporting the evacuation of Cumberland Gap appeared in *ibid.*, September 25, 1862.

[30] *Ibid.*, October 14, 1862; *Atlanta Daily Southern Confederacy*, November 13, 1862; *Augusta Daily Constitutionalist*, October 9, 1862.

[31] *Atlanta Daily Southern Confederacy*, November 13, 1862.

[32] Horn, *Army of Tennessee*, p. 179.

ing, a general engagement between Buell's army and the two Confederate corps commanded by Polk and Hardee took place at the small village of Perryville, about ten miles southwest of Harrodsburg. Both Reid and Forsyth seem to have been present at the battle, along with correspondents of the *Montgomery Advertiser*, the *Columbus* (Ga.) *Sun*, and one or two other papers. Although the Confederate troops were considerably outnumbered, they vigorously attacked and succeeded in driving McCook's Federal corps and a portion of Gilbert's corps more than a mile from their positions. The casualties on both sides were approximately even, totalling about seven thousand.[33]

In his battle report Forsyth admitted: "All my conceptions of all the hurrah and din and dust of a battle were confounded by the cool, business-like operations going on before me. . . . Those badly clothed, some sholess [shoeless] dirty and ragged-looking men walked into the harvest of death before them with all the composure and much less of the bustle that a merchant would exhibit in walking to his counting-room after breakfast. They had not advanced fifty yards before the enemy artillery—before that firing at random—opened with all their fury. In a few moments the sharp, cutting sound of musketry rolled along the line. . . . For nearly two hours our brave troops stood that ground receiving and delivering the deadliest volleys. Our lines could not be ordered forward for, fifty yards further, they would have been enfiladed by a murderous fire of artillery. Two batteries, planted upon a hill with shelving rocks in front, supported by heavy columns of infantry, were in position to sweep the Confederate lines had they moved forward."[34] Forsyth then went on to relate how Brig.Gen. George Maney and his Tennessee brigade captured these batteries and how after that the long line of Confederate infantry drove the enemy from the field.

Instead of following up his victory Bragg fell back to Harrodsburg and joined Smith's troops there. Buell followed him, and there was a prospect of another large-scale battle near Harrodsburg. Yet neither general ventured to attack; on the night of October 10 Bragg retreated to his supply depot at Bryantsville and on October 13 began his withdrawal from Kentucky via Crab Orchard and Barboursville.[35]

[33] Shelby Foote, *The Civil War, A Narrative, Fort Sumter to Perryville* (New York, 1958), p. 737.
[34] *Atlanta Daily Southern Confederacy*, November 13, 1862.
[35] Horn, *Army of Tennessee*, pp. 188-89.

The first news stories about the Battle of Perryville that appeared in the Confederate press were based on dispatches in Northern newspapers of October 10, which stated that Bragg's army had attacked two divisions of McCook's corps and that there had been "desperate fighting." The first information direct from the battlefield was a special dispatch which Forsyth sent from Harrodsburg on October 10 by way of Knoxville and which was not published until October 18. The dispatch claimed that the Confederate troops had fought "like heroes," that they had driven the enemy three or four miles, that they had captured twenty-one pieces of artillery and 500 to 600 prisoners, and that "our army is in the highest possible spirits." It also contained an inaccurate report that Smith had defeated McCook near Frankfort and captured 700 prisoners.[36]

Even before Forsyth's dispatch was published Richmond was rejoicing over the false report that Bragg had telegraphed the War Department to confirm Southern Associated Press reports of a great victory at Perryville.[37] On October 17 the *Richmond Enquirer* heard from Knoxville that the battle had lasted for three days and that Bragg was successful each day, capturing many guns and over 10,000 prisoners. On the twenty-first the *Enquirer* learned that the report of the capture of large numbers of prisoners at Perryville was untrue; as later reports diminished the scope of Bragg's success, anger followed disillusionment. When it became apparent that Bragg's army was in full retreat from Kentucky, a *Mobile Register* editorial expressed indignation at the exaggerated reporting of the battle: "Most fervently do we wish that Southern letter writers, telegraph operators, army officers etc., 'just from the scene of operations,' would more carefully guard against the besetting sin of exaggeration. The two or three days' fighting in the neighborhood of Perryville was no doubt important in itself and its consequences, but why, in the name of truth and common sense, make such astounding estimates as our own loss at from 2,000 to 5,000, and that of the enemy from 20,000 to 30,000? It is a heinous offense, and a gross insult to the public understanding, to magnify a series of indecisive encounters between divisions of the armies into a world-winning battle, in which the field is piled with the enemy's slain, while

[36] *Mobile Daily Advertiser and Register*, October 18, 1862; *Atlanta Daily Intelligencer*, October 20, 1862. The accounts of the battle published in the *Knoxville Register* and the *Mobile Advertiser and Register* are reprinted in Frank Moore, *The Rebellion Record* (New York, 1863), v, 532-535.

[37] *Richmond Daily Dispatch*, October 16, 1862.

the muster of our own survivors shows a mere corporal's guard of killed, wounded, and missing. If in this case the representations of comparative losses were correct it would speak badly for the valor or condition of our army that it should fall back with such a fearfully cut-to-pieces enemy in pursuit."[38]

In a letter to the *Register* written early in the campaign, Colonel Forsyth had predicted that the outcome of Bragg's invasion of Kentucky would depend in part on a third prong of the Western offensive. Bragg had expected Van Dorn and Price, exercising independent command, to keep Grant and Rosecrans occupied while he advanced into Kentucky. As it turned out, neither Price nor Van Dorn was able to clear western Tennessee of the Federals. Instead, Price with 15,000 men barely escaped entrapment at Iuka, Mississippi on September 19. Two weeks later, on October 3-4, the combined forces of Van Dorn and Price met defeat in a hard fight with Rosecrans at Corinth.[39]

At the Battle of Corinth both sides were approximately equal in numbers. On the first day of the battle the Confederates succeeded in driving Rosecrans back to the northern outskirts of the town. Attacking on the Confederate left on the second day, Price's two divisions were initially successful but were later driven back. On the Confederate right Lovell's division of Van Dorn's command gained no ground at all and suffered heavy losses. After losing 4,233 Confederates in comparison with a Federal loss of 2,520, Van Dorn retreated west to Holly Springs accompanied by Price.[40]

The reporters attached to the Confederate forces were prone to excuse the conduct of the Confederate commanders, but their editors were less partial. Van Dorn had created considerable animosity among Confederate newspaper editors when he issued an order at Vicksburg on July 4 that was restrictive of the press. The order stated that any newspaper article revealing troop movements or attempting to impair

---

[38] *Mobile Daily Advertiser and Register*, October 22, 1862. The *Richmond Dispatch* likewise stated on October 23, 1862, "we have had a great many false messages over the telegraph from the Southwest. . . . Hardly one of the hundred and one stories brought by reliable gentlemen from Memphis, Nashville, Louisville etc. about what they saw in the Louisville *Journal* and other Yankee papers, and about what they heard and saw have turned out true." The *Dispatch* mentioned as an example of these exaggerated tales the repeated reports that were entirely without basis of bagging the Federal force under General Morgan at Cumberland Gap; ". . . yet that Federal force finally got away without the loss of a man!"

[39] Foote, *Civil War*, pp. 716-22.

[40] *Ibid.*, p. 725.

public confidence in a commanding officer would result in the fining and imprisonment of the editor of the paper.[41] When therefore the special correspondent of the *Jackson Mississippian* at Holly Springs addressed a two-column letter to his newspaper in which he asked the editor to do justice to Generals Van Dorn and Lovell, Editor Fleet Cooper credited his reporter with "generous emotions" toward the generals but expressed the opinion that they were "played out." Elsewhere in the press Van Dorn was flayed for leading his men "to a slaughter pen with no other result than to expose the whole Valley of the Mississippi to Federal occupation" and was accused of "pitiable imbecility and incompetency, of wild, reckless and criminal conduct of an army."[42]

Reporter Albert J. Street of the *Mobile Register* revealed the existence of division among the Confederate commanders in Mississippi, and stated that he had learned from both Generals Price and Lovell that they had been utterly opposed to the advance on Corinth. Yet according to Street, Van Dorn "with a determined madness, equal to that of Charles XII" had led his army into the murderous trap planted by Rosecrans. Like most Western newspapermen, Street vastly preferred the civilian-recruited Gen. Sterling Price to the West Point-trained Van Dorn. Referring to Price as "the Washington of the West," Street praised him for the modesty and good naturedness which "have kept the people of the Confederacy, who admire him almost to a man, from knowing the trials he has been put to and the indignities offered him. The disregard shown him by President Davis, when at Richmond, has taught the pets of the President to emulate his example. It is time that the people know these facts, and on our part it is not through a disposition to wrangle and bicker, but with a hope to bring these things before their eyes, and have justice done to a justly favorite officer of the Confederate States army."[43] When therefore in the latter part of

---

[41] General Orders No. 9, July 4, 1862, Earl Van Dorn Papers, Alabama State Department of Archives and History. Critical comment about Van Dorn's order by the *Vicksburg Whig* was reprinted in the *Memphis Daily Appeal*, August 23, 1862.

[42] *Jackson Daily Mississippian* as reprinted in *Knoxville Daily Register*, October 21, 1862; *Jackson Daily Mississippian*, October 14, 1862.

[43] *Mobile Daily Advertiser and Register*, October 2, 19, 1862. The Jackson correspondent of the *Register*, "Clint," discovered a more bizarre explanation for the disaster: "It is said that the Federals were thoroughly posted as to the movements of our army. . . . Prostitutes are used by the Federals as spies, and they

October Gen. John C. Pemberton replaced Van Dorn in command of the Department of Mississippi, there was great rejoicing on the part of the *Jackson Mississippian* and many of the other Western newspapers.

Meanwhile a portion of the Confederate press was launching an attack on Bragg for the failure, in their view, of his expedition into Kentucky. The news that reached Atlanta on October 21, that Bragg had fallen back to Cumberland Gap, created a disagreeable impression there, coming as it did only a matter of hours after the city had received reports of a smashing Confederate victory. The *Richmond Whig* snorted that Bragg's movement into Kentucky "has turned out to be simply a fizzle," and Thompson wrote in a similar vein to the *Memphis Appeal* from Richmond on October 20, commenting that Bragg's retreat was a "sad finale" to a campaign which had been expected to bring about the "redemption" of Kentucky. "That the fight at Perryville was a victory we may believe from the direct accounts of our officers and the admission of the [New York] Tribune," he added, "but of what good result are such victories productive, if straightway we must relinquish the State to the occupancy and possession of the enemy?"[44]

When on October 23 Colonel Forsyth arrived in Atlanta on his way back to Mobile, there was great curiosity about the version of Bragg's campaign he would present to the public. During a visit to the editorial rooms of the *Atlanta Confederacy*, Forsyth imparted a preview of the tack that he would follow. He assured Editor George Adair that Bragg's retreat had been successful, that Bragg had brought all the arms, ammunition, and supplies procured in Kentucky back to Knoxville successfully in the face of a largely superior force, that he could have whipped Buell at any time from Louisville to Cumberland Gap, but that such a victory would have been "a barren and fruitless one." Forsyth stated further that the Battle of Perryville would not have been fought if it had not been necessary to punish Buell sufficiently to enable Bragg's army to leave Kentucky without further interference.[45] After he got back to Mobile Forsyth wrote to Bragg, signify-

---

work with diligence and effectiveness. They fly over the roads and lurk for a day or so about the towns and cities, and then disappear." *Ibid.*, October 14, 1862.

[44] *Richmond Daily Whig*, October 20, 1862; *Memphis Daily Appeal*, October 29, 1862. The *Whig* rated Bragg's campaign from beginning to end as "a brilliant blunder and a magnificent failure."

[45] *Atlanta Daily Southern Confederacy*, October 24, 1862.

ing that he had just finished a "memoir" of the Kentucky campaign that would be published in a few days and promising to send Bragg a copy. Forsyth advised Bragg that "the true policy & history of the campaign" had been greatly misrepresented in the press and that he hoped to be instrumental in correcting these errors.[46]

Between November 11 and November 18 Forsyth published a full report of the Kentucky campaign from his and Bragg's point of view in the four newspapers for which he had acted as telegraphic correspondent during the campaign. The four newspapers were the *Mobile Register*, the *Atlanta Confederacy*, the *Augusta Constitutionalist*, and the *Charleston Courier*. Forsyth's report appeared in three installments in these newspapers under the byline of "Press." Forsyth asserted that Bragg's purpose in marching into Kentucky was to give aid to the Kentuckians in casting off the "Abolition yoke." Neither Bragg nor any other sane man in his army ever believed for a moment, Forsyth insisted, that it was in his power with the army under his command to conquer Kentucky and hold it against the Yankees. Forsyth went on to say: "The plan of the Kentucky campaign was based upon the most positive and, as was believed, reliable promises of a general insurrection in that State upon the appearance of a Confederate army. . . . Gen. Bragg's ordnance trains bore fifteen thousand arms to be put into the hands of the insurgents, and when he reached the Kentucky line and approached the villages and towns of that once war-like people he looked for the first rush of the 50,000 men that had been so solemnly promised him.— He looked in vain. There were no delegations from towns and counties coming out to hail his arrival; there were no crowds of Kentucky's stalwart youth flocking to a standard that promised them liberty. He found on the contrary scowling Unionists and friends that dared not express their joy above a whisper." Then when Bragg endeavored to stimulate a rising among the local citizens, there was still no response. "The 50,000 armed men did not come, and after a march of nearly 300 miles, Gen. Bragg found the keystone of his entire plan of campaign dropped out."[47]

[46] John Forsyth to Braxton Bragg, November 3, 1862, Bragg Papers. Forsyth also communicated to Bragg his fears about the safety of Mobile, where the military commander, General Forney, was, he said, incapacitated both physically and mentally.

[47] *Atlanta Daily Southern Confederacy*, November 13, 1862; *Augusta Daily Constitutionalist*, November 13, 1862. The cavalry leader John H. Morgan had been largely responsible for causing Smith and Bragg to infer that Kentuckians

After the Battle of Perryville Bragg's position, as Forsyth viewed it, was a perilous one. "An unprecedented drought had stopped nearly all the flour mills. To subsist the army in bread [*sic*], it was necessary to scatter it and occupy a wide extent of territory. Yet a force of 70,000 enemies near us required our own concentration."

Forsyth insisted, nevertheless, that the campaign had effected some substantial gains, which he listed as follows:

1. The threat to Chattanooga and even Atlanta created by Buell's invasion of eastern Tennessee had been removed.

2. Northern Alabama had been relieved of Federal occupation.

3. The Confederates had regained possession of Cumberland Gap, the key to Knoxville and the Virginia & Tennessee Railroad.

4. The capture of 18,000 to 20,000 prisoners by the Confederates.

5. The capture of far more arms and ammunition than they carried into Kentucky.

6. The procurement of a sufficient supply of jeans to clothe the Army of the Mississippi.

7. The defeat of the enemy in three large battles (Richmond, Munfordville, and Perryville), along with a score of cavalry encounters.

8. The payment of a debt of honor to Kentucky.

He admitted that there had been mistakes. Among them he included the failure to gather supplies and ship them south when the army first entered Kentucky, also the fact that prominent Unionist hostages were not rounded up and carried away to guarantee good treatment of Kentucky secessionists.

Forsyth's news letters aroused widespread discussion in the Southern press. Having been repeatedly assured in private letters from officers in the army that Bragg left Chattanooga with a force of not less than 75,000 men, the editor of the *Columbus Sun* expressed surprise at Forsyth's statement that it had not contained more than half that number.[48] Critics of Bragg were not slow to refute what they regarded as misleading statements by Forsyth. Among the critics were Bragg's short-lived provisional governor of Kentucky, Richard Hawes, a correspond-

---

would enlist in droves as soon as a Southern army entered the State. McWhiney, "Controversy in Kentucky," pp. 11-12. For a criticism of Bragg's "ill-planned and poorly executed march into Kentucky," by a prominent historian see T. D. Clark, *A History of Kentucky* (New York, 1937), pp. 458-59, 464.

[48] *Columbus Daily Sun*, November 12, 1862.

ent of the *Atlanta Confederacy* who signed himself "Louisiana," the *Atlanta Intelligencer*'s "Vidi," and a Kentucky general, possibly General Breckinridge, who contributed a series of letters to the *Columbus Sun* over the initial, "T."

Governor Hawes admitted in a letter which the *Richmond Enquirer* published on November 28 that Forsyth had written with "singular power and adroitness," but Forsyth's correspondence contained, he said, so many "erroneous statements of assumed facts and distortions of many of the essential features of that movement," that he felt obliged to make a public reply. It was not true, declared Hawes, that Bragg had received positive and reliable promises of an insurrection in Kentucky and the rush of 50,000 Kentuckians to his standard when he appeared in the state. Kentucky would scorn an alliance with the South except on the basis of the fair and unterrified vote of a majority of the people of that state. Moreover, he wanted to know why Bragg's army did not fight and conquer Buell's army before the latter reached Louisville, why Bragg fought the Battle of Perryville with only 15,000 men instead of the 25,000 or 30,000 that a junction with Smith would have made possible, why Bragg retreated after the battle instead of concentrating and following Buell, and why he suddenly retreated from Camp Dick Robinson, thereby exposing his wagon train and most of the army's stores to possible capture. Hawes also argued that Bragg's army remained in Kentucky for too short a time to make possible the enlistment of 50,000 recruits, and he questioned the fairness of blaming Kirby Smith for not purchasing hogs, mules, bacon, and other supplies from the time of his first arrival in the state.[49]

Similar arguments appeared in the letters of other newspaper writers. In a letter to the *Atlanta Confederacy* "Louisiana" denied that Bragg's invasion of Kentucky had been conducted with an insufficient force or in such a manner as to justify the expectation of a general uprising of the people. "The expedition into Kentucky had, from the outset, the appearance of only a raid into the State for the procurement of recruits and supplies. It was so looked upon by the citizens, and nothing was done except the issuing of a number of high sounding proclamations, to dispel the belief and lead them to hope that the Ohio river would be made a line of defense. . . . In the absence of all such evidence, is it strange that the people hung back when they felt assured that in a

[49] Forsyth replied to Hawes in a signed editorial published in the *Mobile Daily Advertiser and Register*, December 5, 1862.

few weeks' time the Yankee authorities would again have control, and then, woe to the man who so much as entertained a Confederate officer in his house?" How, "Louisiana" also wanted to know, could Kentucky, having already furnished 15,000 to 20,000 men to the Confederate army, and a still larger number under duress to the Union army, be expected to provide Bragg with 50,000 more, and when and where were so many as 18,000 or 20,000 prisoners captured within the state?[50]

Another controversial item in connection with the campaign was the 1,500 wagons loaded with "spoils" which Bragg was supposed to have brought back from Kentucky. A correspondent of the *Atlanta Intelligencer* who accompanied the army during the retreat thought the term "plunder" was more applicable to the wagonloads than a term indicating that they had been taken away from the enemy in accordance with the rules of legitimate warfare. In numerous instances, the *Intelligencer* reporter indicated, these "spoils" had been taken from private citizens, being sometimes paid for and sometimes not. That the amount of goods secured was considerably less than the reports from Bragg's army indicated was the conclusion of the reporter Peter Alexander in Richmond. Learning through official channels that Smith's quartermaster had been mailing urgent appeals to the government ever since his return to Tennessee, for stores, blankets, and other supplies, Alexander made it his job to investigate the facts. Having done so, his conclusion was that "the trains, forty miles in length and filled with all kinds of supplies, which, it is said, followed him out of Kentucky, have their existence for the most part only in the imagination."[51]

Not all of the Confederate press joined in the hue and cry against Bragg. Editorial defenses of his campaign performance appeared in newspapers such as the *Knoxville Register*, the *Atlanta Intelligencer*, and the *Mobile Register*, but the quantity of press condemnation far exceeded the amount of editorial praise. Said the editor of the *Columbus Sun*: "All the silly efforts upon the part of a certain class of newspaper correspondents and 'small editors' to manufacture a great man out of General Bragg have failed. His late campaign in Kentucky

---

[50] *Atlanta Daily Southern Confederacy*, December 10, 1862.

[51] *Columbus Daily Sun*, October 30, 1862; *Mobile Daily Advertiser and Register*, November 11, 1862. In the *Atlanta Daily Intelligencer* of October 28, 1862, its correspondent "Vidi" alluded to the "wholesale robbery of which our army was guilty while returning from Harrodsburg to the Gap." The *Chattanooga Daily Rebel* of November 5, 1862 thought the "wholesale robbery" charge was exaggerated, but called for congressional investigation of its validity.

speaks for itself—speaks in language which all cannot fail to understand. . . . After three months tramping, he has returned to East Tennessee, having nothing to show for his campaign but a train of supplies or 'spoils,' most of which were purchased with Confederate Notes, whilst a portion was captured by the superior generalship of a subordinate officer, acting perhaps without instructions from the General-in-Chief."[52] In far off Richmond, Editor John M. Daniel concurred. His verdict on Bragg was quite as absolute as most of his other judgments: "Of genius, military or civil, he has none. Even in judgment and sagacity, for large affairs he is notoriously deficient. As commander-in-chief, he is worse than inexperienced, for he has grown old and hardened in a subaltern position of a regular army. With an iron heart, an iron hand, and a wooden head, his failure in a position where the highest intellectual faculties were demanded was predestined."[53] Yet it seems apparent that Confederate army correspondents glossed over the details of what one of them referred to as "that fearful retreat over the mountains," in which ragged, barefooted soldiers labored over difficult roads under the additional handicap of receiving only half rations.[54]

Press criticism of Bragg and the complaints voiced by Bragg's subordinates inevitably raised questions in Jefferson Davis's mind. So on

[52] *Columbus Daily Sun*, October 31, 1862.

[53] *Richmond Examiner* as paraphrased in *Columbus Daily Sun*, November 22, 1862. Especially critical of Bragg was a letter in the *Columbus Sun* of November 19, 1862 from its correspondent "T.," which contended that Bragg "was not the man to secure the confidence of the people. He is unpopular with the troops under his command . . . his discipline on which his friends rest his claims to being a great General consists simply in a determination to have his own way—in many cases a violation of law, justice, and humanity. . . . A Confederate officer heard a Kentucky Colonel say to a friend upon the streets of Danville: 'I have disbanded my regiment. I raised them to fight under Smith, but Bragg has come up here and taken command. I know him; I was with him in Mexico. He has no heart—no soul. He is a tyrant, and fit for nothing but to be a captain of an artillery company; and I will not put up such as my regiment was composed of under his command.' "

[54] *Ibid.*, November 20, 1862. Reid stated in the *Mobile Daily Advertiser and Register* of November 9, 1862 that he had already sent that paper an account of the retreat of Kirby Smith's army from Bryantsville to Cumberland Gap. Apparently his letter never reached the *Register*, however. Equally mystifying was Reid's failure to submit a substantial report of the Battle of Perryville. Indeed Reid's diary is disappointingly silent about his activities at Perryville. On the other hand the *Chattanooga Rebel* stated with regard to Reid's arrival at Chattanooga that he "looks nothing the worse for his retreat from Kentucky, though it seems he did have a bad time 'bridling that horse' at Perryville."

October 23 the War Department summoned Bragg to Richmond to give an accounting of the campaign. In Richmond, Bragg attempted to shift the blame for the misadventure on Polk, but Polk also stood high in the president's favor; he too was summoned to Richmond. Reporting that Bragg had lost the confidence of his generals, Polk recommended that Joseph E. Johnston supersede Bragg if the latter was going to be removed. Unwilling to believe that Bragg was as incompetent as he was widely reputed to be, Davis took the halfway measure of placing Johnston in command of a new department that included the commands of Bragg, Smith, and Pemberton, and sent Bragg back to the field to establish his headquarters at Murfreesboro.[55]

On December 5 Reporter Reid was on a special train leaving Chattanooga with General Johnston and his staff on board. Johnston was going west to inspect Bragg's army, henceforth to be known as the Army of Tennessee. The weather was miserable, but Reid found some compensation for it when the train stopped at Decherd. There he dined at a tavern kept by the Widow Davis, who in times gone by, "especially before the locomotive whistle took the place of the stage horn, kept the best and cleanest table d'Hote in Christendom." Reid used the opportunity afforded by the train ride to scrutinize Johnston, whose remarkable long upper lip, hazel colored eyes, and Roman nose attracted his attention. Reid also made respectful mention in his letter of Johnston's eleven wounds, nine of which he had received in Florida and Mexico and the other two at the Battle of Seven Pines.[56]

Other reporters besides Reid were assessing the stature of General Johnston. The general's departure from Richmond for Chattanooga and the West had caused Alexander to improvise a profile of him, which was published in the *Mobile Register* and other newspapers. Alexander pictured Johnston as a man about five feet, ten inches tall, weighing about one hundred and sixty pounds, with a florid complexion, short, gray hair, and closely trimmed side whiskers and goatee. His general appearance and self-possessed air reminded Alexander of a gamecock. The reporter rated him intellectually as the equal of any of the five generals in the army and possibly as superior to them.

---

[55] Parks, *Polk*, pp. 277-78. Grady McWhiney denies that Bragg had lost the confidence of his army, and alleges that of the twenty generals directly under his command only Polk and Hardee expressed dissatisfaction at this time. McWhiney, "Controversy in Kentucky," p. 40.

[56] *Mobile Daily Advertiser and Register*, December 13, 1862.

Alexander went on to say that Johnston possessed a very high reputation as a strategist among military men. "In his operations, he regards masses and general results, rather than isolated bodies and mere temporary effects. And hence the opinion prevails with some that he lacks energy and enterprise. This, however, is a great mistake. No man is more watchful of his adversary, or more ready to strike when the right time comes; and when he does strike, he delivers the blow of a giant. He sees but little advantage in picking off a man here and there, or in precipitating small bodies of men against each other. Instead of frittering away his strength, he seeks rather to husband it until the auspicious moment arrives, and then he goes to work with an energy and a resolution that are wonderful."[57]

When a few days later President Davis himself came out from Richmond to obtain a firsthand view of the situation in Bragg's army, a special correspondent of the *Chattanooga Rebel* accompanied the president from Chattanooga to Murfreesboro and composed a description of him similar to that of Johnston. The *Rebel* reporter described Davis as, "a man rather above the middle stature; of slight but well proportioned figure; features decidedly handsome, for a middle-aged gentleman, and wearing a perpetual expression of good humor. . . . His head is slightly sprinkled with grey, and his whiskers are grey; yet he is a younger man in appearance and in feelings than we had conceived him to be; his voice soft and persuasive, yet distinct and full-toned, and he is in the habit of speaking occasionally an exceeding good thing in a most quiet, accidental sort of way."

"His dress was plain and unassuming and his baggage limited to a single leather valise, with the initials 'J.D.' marked upon the side. Attended by one body servant alone, his mode of travel was without ostentation or parade, and I could not help contrasting the President of the young Confederacy traveling securely as a citizen and incognito from one extreme of his native Southern land to the other without even so much as a body guard, with the miserable despot of Abolitiondom carricoling through the streets of Washington with a file of armed dragoons [on] each side of his coach of state, and in constant apprehension of the assasin's dagger in his capital."[58]

During late November and early December the reporters with

[57] *Ibid.*, December 6, 1862.
[58] *Chattanooga Daily Rebel*, December 17, 1862. It is fairly obvious that this picture of Lincoln's security arrangements was based merely on conjecture.

Bragg's army, for the most part, provided reassuring information about the army's health, discipline, and morale. Yet a Tullahoma correspondent of the *Columbus Sun* reported that both civilians and soldiers were "profuse in vituperation of Gen. Bragg" and that a recent number of the *Murfreesboro Rebel Banner* had contained many strictures on his conduct.[59] In a letter from Murfreesboro to the *Mobile Register* on December 11 Reid described a party of Union prisoners that had been brought into town the day before. He concluded that they were "the most motley, heterogeneous commixtion of humanity that I ever saw, being composed of German Hessians of all ages from the decrepit old man to boys of sixteen; there were also a number of Irish, freshly imported, and the few native Abolitionists among them were of the most ignorant classes—a set of ragamuffin jail birds, incomparably inferior to Falstaff's company, and these are the creatures sent to subjugate us. As they marched through the streets to the Court-house, the little boys amused themselves by crying out, 'there go the Yawyaws,' 'Nix come-rouse,' &c. 'What are you fighting for?' asked one of the lads of a brutal looking Hessian. 'Vel den, I ish fighting vor der Union and mine pay!' replied the wretch. 'How long have you been over, Pat?' asked another of a green-looking Patlander. 'Faith and it's myself that wishes I'd niver seen the country for the three months I've been in it,' replied Pat. 'How do you like fighting for the niggers?' asked one of our soldiers of an Illinois officer. 'We are not fighting for niggers, but for our rights under the Union,' replied the fellow. 'Yes,' said another Lincolnite, 'and if the d———d Dutch had not thrown down their arms and run, we could have bagged your party, and then you'd have found out what we were fighting for'!"[60]

Another *Mobile Register* reporter, Albert Street, who returned from a two-week period of captivity in the North in mid-December, was more respectful of the valor of the Union army in the West than Reid was. Describing the enemy's cavalry as one of the best arms of its service, well appointed in every respect, Street characterized the Western army of the United States government as "large and powerful, and commanded by some able officers, and may well be regarded with reasonable fear."[61] His evaluation was soon to be tested under battle conditions.

---

[59] *Columbus Daily Sun*, November 29, 1862.
[60] *Mobile Daily Advertiser and Register*, December 18, 1862.
[61] *Ibid.*, December 16, 27, 1862.

During the last week of December Rosecrans, who had replaced Buell in command of the Union army at Nashville, began to give signs of going on the offensive. Bragg had about 37,000 soldiers at Murfreesboro, compared with Rosecrans' effective strength of 81,729, but detachments for garrison duty and other reasons permitted Rosecrans to bring into action hardly more than 44,000. Had Stevenson's division not been sent from Bragg's army to reinforce Pemberton a fortnight earlier by President Davis's order, Bragg's army would actually have outnumbered Rosecrans' in the coming battle. On December 27 the Union Army of the Cumberland began advancing on Murfreesboro in three parallel columns along the roads between the two cities.[62]

Reid noted in his diary for December 27: "Enemy approaching— our army ordered out in line of battle." In a letter to the *Mobile Register* which he mailed the following day, he referred to the heavy rainstorm of the afternoon of the twenty-seventh which "fell in pitiless torrents on our poor troops as they marched out to the expected battle ground. At night it cleared off, and the young moon, in all her resplendent beauty, illumined the surrounding scene with dazzling silver brilliancy. Our men bivouacked by their camp fires, fully expecting a fight to-day. The morning broke clear and bright. It was as balmy as a spring day. The greatest activity prevailed in all the military departments. Military stores and other property were being removed to the rear, and indeed provision was being made for every emergency. As a portion of Hardee's corps marched through the town to the battlefield with colors flying, and the bands playing inspiring airs, the troops marched with a firm and buoyant step, and displayed the most undaunted and cheering spirit. There was evident alarm felt among many of the inhabitants, who prepared to leave the town in case of disaster, while others moved out to the country. No church bells tolled for morning service, the dread preparation and the hourly expected conflict having wholly engrossed other thoughts. Noon came, however, without any advance of the enemy, and the sun went down without the day having been disturbed by the roar of artillery or the flowing of human gore."[63]

By December 30 the three corps of Rosecrans' army were in position for attack facing east along Stone's River northwest of Murfreesboro.

[62] Shelby Foote, *The Civil War, A Narrative, Fredericksburg to Meridian* (New York, 1963), pp. 81-82.

[63] *Mobile Daily Advertiser and Register*, January 4, 1863.

The Confederate army also was composed of three corps, with Hardee on the left, Polk in the center, and Breckinridge on the right on the opposite side of the river from Crittenden's line. Both commanders had identical battle plans, calling for an advance on the left against the enemy's right.[64] What happened the next morning provided the subject matter for a part of Reid's battle report for the *Richmond Examiner*:

On the morning of the 31st the grand battle was opened by McCown's division, with Cleburn [*sic*] advancing upon the enemy's right wing, under General McCook, just at grey dawn. The enemy was taken completely by surprise, their artillery horses not even being hitched up. Such was the impetuosity of the charge that the enemy fell back in dismay, our troops pouring in a most murderous fire; with such rapidity did our men cross the broken ploughed field, that our artillery could not follow them. . . . The enemy, having gradually recovered, now disputed our further advance, and the battle raged with terrific violence. They continued to fall back, however, under our fire until we had swung round nearly our whole left on their right, as if on a pivot, driving the enemy some six miles towards his centre. . . . The enemy now took a commanding position on an eminence overlooking the plain and which was protected by rocks and a dense cedar wood. Here he massed his batteries, numbering some thirty pieces of artillery, and made a desperate stand.

It was now about noon. We had already captured some five thousand prisoners . . . nearly thirty pieces of cannon [and] some five thousand stand of arms and ammunition wagons. It was now determined to carry the enemy's stronghold at all hazards, and the brigades of Chalmers and Donelson, supported by Manley's and Stewart's brigades, with Cobb's, Byrnes', Charles Smith's, and Slocomb's batteries, were ordered forward to prepare for the charge. It was a forlorn hope, but our men faced the mighty whirlwind of shot and shell with heroic firmness, and did not fall back until they had captured two batteries; the brigades of Generals Adams and Jackson, of Breckenridge's [*sic*] division, who held our right, were now ordered to relieve our broken columns, and advanced toward the enemy's grand battery with a like coolness and heroism, but they were also repulsed and fell back under the enemy's terrible fire. No further effort was made; the enemy, however, was also fearfully punished, and whether fearing that his position might be flanked, or from some cause that it was not secure, he abandoned it that night, only to take up a still stronger one in the bend of the river, towards the Lebanon pike, on a couple of hillocks, which he again crowned with his strongest batteries. That night it was cold to freezing. Upon the battle field lay thousands of the enemy's dead and wounded, who froze stiff, presenting a ghastly scene by moonlight.[65]

[64] Foote, *Civil War, Fredericksburg to Meridian*, pp. 85-87.
[65] *Daily Richmond Examiner*, January 16, 1863.

Although Bragg's losses had been heavy that day, the enemy's had been even heavier; Bragg could not view the battle other than as a Union defeat. Confidently expecting that Rosecrans would be in full retreat toward Nashville the next morning, Bragg wired Richmond that evening: "we have driven the enemy from every position, except on the left. Our troops now occupy the battle-field. We have captured 4,000 prisoners, 30 pieces of artillery, and 200 wagons. Among the prisoners are two Brigadier Generals."[66] The information thus received from Bragg and similar information from the Southern Associated Press of the defeat of the enemy at Murfreesboro was reflected in the happy faces *Memphis Appeal* correspondent Thompson encountered on the streets of Richmond on New Year's Day.[67] Although no further word came over the wires from the battlefield during the next forty-eight hours, newspapers like the *Richmond Examiner* and the *Atlanta Confederacy* concluded that Rosecrans' army had been "hopelessly defeated" and that Bragg had a good chance of "bagging" the entire Federal army.[68]

Rosecrans' army was still in line of battle on New Year's morning, however. Probing attacks by Bragg during the day disclosed that the Federal commander intended to remain. Unable to exploit his success of the previous day, Bragg suddenly became sensitive about press reports concerning the situation. When Reid attempted that evening to send a telegram from Murfreesboro to the *Mobile Register*, he learned that the field commander had refused to permit any press dispatches to be telegraphed and that he (Reid) would not be permitted to visit the battlefield. Indignant at these curbs on his reporting privileges, Reid systematically omitted Bragg's name from the battle account he mailed to the *Register* the next day.[69]

On January 2, the third day of the confrontation of the two armies, Bragg became convinced that the security of his army was endangered by a Federal division that occupied a hill commanding the Confederate

[66] This newspaper version of Bragg's dispatch is a condensation of the text printed in *O.R.* (Army) Ser. I, vol. xx, pt. 1, p. 662.

[67] *Memphis Daily Appeal*, January 10, 1863.

[68] *Daily Richmond Examiner*, January 3, 1863; *Atlanta Daily Southern Confederacy*, January 3, 1863.

[69] *Mobile Daily Advertiser and Register*, January 9, 1863. In *ibid.*, January 8, 1863, the editor of the *Register* made sarcastic reference to the omission of Bragg's name from the account of the battle that Reid contributed to the *Register*, observing that it was "the play of Hamlet, with the part of Hamlet left out."

right, east of Stone's River. Bragg therefore directed Breckinridge to drive the Federals from the hill; under protest Breckinridge attempted to do so. The result was a fiasco. Within a little over an hour's time Breckinridge lost 1,700 men, or better than one-third of his command.[70] The following morning, forty-eight hours after he had clamped down on all wire reporting from Murfreesboro, Bragg relaxed his censorship sufficiently to permit the Associated Press to give a short account of the repulse of Breckinridge, based on Bragg's official dispatch to Adjutant General Cooper in Richmond.[71]

None of the newspaper accounts of Breckinridge's charge was an example of good reporting. Capt. Theodoric Carter, the "Mint Julep" of the *Chattanooga Rebel*, who was an eyewitness of this episode, completely misinterpreted its outcome and confessed his inability to understand "why we retreated." Perhaps the most widely reprinted account of the disaster was the handiwork of the editor of the *Murfreesboro Rebel Banner*, who seasoned his battle report with liberal doses of imagination. Typical of his inflated rhetoric were passages such as: "Preston rushes to the front like a maniac with a brigade of fiends incarnate following close at his heels."[72]

Confronted with evidence that the enemy had been reinforced and that a rise in the river level threatened to isolate the two parts of his army, Bragg decided on the morning of January 3 to retreat to Shelbyville and Tullahoma. At least one reporter thought his retreat was "very badly executed" and that it showed "a remarkable want of foresight, discipline, and management."[73]

The Confederate press was understandably bewildered by the sudden change in the military fortunes of Bragg's army. The *Richmond Examiner* took stock of the situation:

"So far the news has come in what may be called the classical style of the Southwest. When the Southwestern army fights a battle, we first hear that it has gained one of the most stupendous victories on

---

[70] Foote, *The Civil War: Fredericksburg to Meridian*, pp. 99-100; Horn, *op. cit.*, pp. 207-208.

[71] *Mobile Daily Advertiser and Register*, January 10, 1863.

[72] Reprinted in *Chattanooga Daily Rebel*, January 13, 1863; *Knoxville Daily Register*, January 15, 1863. "Mint Juleps'" account appeared in the *Rebel* of January 15, 1863. For unceremonious treatment accorded the editor of this Murfreesboro paper by a Confederate guard see *Atlanta Daily Confederacy*, February 3, 1863.

[73] *Chattanooga Daily Rebel*, January 18, 1863. Apparently, to judge from this reporter's statement, the retreat was characterized by a lot of straggling.

record; that regiments from Mississippi, Texas, Louisiana, Arkansas, &c., have exhibited an irresistible and superhuman valour, unknown in history this side of Sparta and Rome. As for the Generals, they usually get all their clothes shot off, and replace them with a suit of glory. The enemy is, of course, simply annihilated. New day, more dispatches come, still very good, but not quite as good as the first. The telegrams of the third day are invariably such as to make a mist, a muddle and a fog of the whole affair. But we are still assured that our troops are victorious; and only after seven days more does the unpleasant truth leak out that they are not quite victorious, but have, in fact, lost a little ground, after gaining some very brilliant successes."[74]

Probably the best accounts of the Battle of Stone's River from the Southern point of view were Reid's *Richmond Examiner* report and the special correspondence published in the *Memphis Appeal* and the *Chattanooga Rebel*.[75] The *Rebel* claimed that two-thirds of Bragg's army at the time of the battle were Tennesseans, that the battle was an open field fight, and that "our fortifications were merely temporary earth works and rifle pits, if, indeed, we had any at all." Reid attributed the unfortunate outcome of the battle to the detachment from Bragg's army of Stevenson's division, to reinforce the defenders of Vicksburg. In an editorial entitled "Untimely Censure," the *Augusta Constitutionalist* called Reid's opinion "mere conjecture" and defended the decision of the president to assign priority to the safety of Vicksburg over the possibility of recapturing Nashville.[76] Apparently the *Examiner* gave Reid more latitude to express his opinions than Editor Forsyth would allow. Yet fully a month after Bragg's bugles had sounded retreat, the complaint was made that no satisfactory detailed account of the battle had appeared in the Southern press. In the opinion of the editor of the *Columbus Sun*, this lack could best be explained by the "peculiar animosity" of "some of our military leaders" toward an independent press. The *Sun* went on to say:

"Newspaper reporters have been repeatedly banished from within

---

[74] *Daily Richmond Examiner*, January 6, 1863.

[75] *Ibid.*, January 16, 31, 1863; *Chattanooga Daily Rebel* as reprinted in *Wilmington Daily Journal*, January 13, 1863; *Knoxville Daily Register*, January 17, 1863; *Memphis Daily Appeal*, January 22, 1863. Relatively little attention was given in the Confederate press to the important part played by the Confederate cavalry during the Murfreesboro campaign. Wheeler's circuit of Rosecrans' army is described in J. P. Dyer, *"Fightin' Joe" Wheeler* (Baton Rouge, 1941), pp. 80-84.

[76] *Chattanooga Daily Rebel* as reprinted in *Charleston Mercury*, January 6, 1863; *Augusta Daily Constitutionalist*, January 16, 1863.

the 'lines,' either because of their disposition to contribute to impartial history by the simple delineation of facts as they transpire; or because the papers they represent have never condescended to administer to military vanity, in preference to maintaining an independent tone. Hence there is generally a tacit condition which is precedent to the entrance of newspaper correspondents in the lines. The nature of this condition is usually such that but few representatives of the press care to comply with it, and none but the official *minstrels* are enabled to enjoy the scenes behind the curtain. These minstrels, however talented and conscientious, usually have their organs of vision too well filled with the glory of their patron to be cognizant of the deeds of the private soldier or the incidents of the battle field. They are not responsible for this. They merely act as other mortals would act, under similar circumstances. They may be presumed to write by a sort of military square and compass, and adjust their paragraphs with reference to the precedents before them—the vision of arbitrary arrests. Under such circumstances, a partial history of a brilliant engagement is natural. It could not be full and complete owing to the very nature of things. And it is somehow in this manner, perhaps, that officials sometimes get a brilliant newspaper reputation without being able to show much record of their great deeds."[77]

At least one Southern newspaperman gained a new respect for the courage of the enemy fighting man as a result of his experience in the Battle of Stone's River. He remarked: "I have often heard it said that the Yankees will not fight. This is altogether a mistake, or possibly it may be true with reference to *Yankees*, but Rosecran's army, in the opinion of one who was in the battle, certainly contested every inch of ground most gallantly. Nothing but the guidance of an Omnipotent hand, and that indomitable courage which pervades our army, ever enabled us to whip them. . . ."[78]

Bragg's animosity toward the press, which the press reciprocated, had militated against comprehensive newspaper coverage of the campaigns in Kentucky and Tennessee during the latter half of 1862. Yet already the press had sketched the outlines of the image of the Army of Tennessee as an ill-fated command whose victories were barren of result. The disturbing effects of this by no means untruthful image

[77] *Columbus Daily Sun*, January 30, 1863; *Savannah Republican*, January 28, 1863.

[78] *Columbus Daily Sun*, February 3, 1863.

on public morale would become more evident as time went on. It remained to be seen whether future victories would dispel the unfavorable impression of Bragg that this image had helped to create and whether Bragg would provide a freer atmosphere for reporting in his army.

CHAPTER 9

Misleading Dispatches and
Misspent Opportunities

THE FOCUS OF press coverage in the West after the Battle of Stone's River was a river port nestled on a chain of hills that looked down on a hairpin bend in the Mississippi River. Two attempts to capture this "Gibraltar of the West," first by siege and later by assault, had failed. Yet in January 1863 it seemed likely that a joint Federal army and navy expedition under the command of Grant and Sherman would make still a third effort to seize Vicksburg and assist Banks to achieve the same objective at Port Hudson, Louisiana, about 235 miles by river below Vicksburg. So a number of special correspondents of Southern newspapers—the *Mobile Register, Memphis Appeal, Chattanooga Rebel,* and *Columbus* (Ga.) *Sun,* among others—were in Vicksburg at the beginning of 1863 to report military developments in that area.

A lieutenant general from Pennsylvania named Pemberton, whose Yankee origin rendered him suspect in some quarters, was in command of the Confederate Department of Mississippi. This was Pemberton's first field command; to hold that long stretch of river between Vicksburg and Port Hudson and defend the remainder of the state of Mississippi and eastern Louisiana he had at most about 34,000 soldiers. Particularly crippling was the loss of the major portion of his cavalry, which had been sent north into Tennessee to assist Bragg at the end of December.[1]

"Vicksburg never was a prepossessing place," reflected the correspondent of the *Columbus Sun* in a letter to his newspaper during the latter part of January 1863.[2] Even at that time great holes in the sides and roofs of its houses and in churches, ships, and fences, resulting from the bombardment of the previous summer, marred the appearance of the town. It was difficult for a reporter to know whether the local

[1] Bruce Catton, *Never Call Retreat* (New York, 1965), p. 7; John C. Pemberton, *Pemberton, Defender of Vicksburg* (Chapel Hill, 1942), pp. 89-90.
[2] *Columbus Daily Sun,* January 31, 1863. The activities of speculators in Vicksburg were also the theme of a letter which the *Mobile Register* correspondent contributed to that newspaper. *Mobile Daily Advertiser and Register,* March 10, 1863.

smallpox epidemic or the presence of the enemy's fleet at Young's Point to the north of Vicksburg presented the greater danger to its defenders. But such perils evidently were not very important to the ubiquitous speculator, whose profitable transactions provided the newspaperman from Georgia with copy for a racy letter.

See him behind the counter there with a small lot of ready made clothing before him. He bears about him the unmistakable evidences of his descent from the despised and outcast children of Israel. He is endeavoring to sell a pair of common brown jeans pants to a soldier whose honorable calling brings him the lucrative salary of eleven dollars a month. He asks thirty dollars for the pants and swears that they cost him twenty-seven and a half when goods were low. The soldier looks at his seedy overalls, worn and torn in front and rear, says something about fighting for Vicksburg swindlers, pays for the pants and walks off with his pockets lightened of four months and six days wages. Your boots are getting thin. You never were in the habit of wearing mended boots. So you look around for a new pair. Well, this shop is the place to get them. You walk in and inquire the price of a good pair of heavy, winter boots? . . . Sixty dollars. Sixty dollars for a pair of boots! You start and look at your old ones. They are not so bad after all, and you ask the obliging son of St. Crispin if he thinks they are worth mending. Certainly he does. It will never do to throw away as good boots as those in such times as these. They need nothing in the world but a pair of half-soles to make them as good as new. Just take a seat and wait half an hour, and they shall be fixed for you. You draw your boots, the shoemaker hands you the morning Whig, and before you are aware of the time that has passed, your boots are handed to you ready mended. That is a good job, sir—what is to pay? Seven dollars. Seven dollars for pegging half soles on a pair of boots! You wonder what leather is worth here, and are surprised to learn on inquiring at the next store that a pair of half soles are worth one dollar.

But it is dinner time, and stamping around in this Mississippi mud makes one as hungry as a wolf. . . . Those great golden letters above that door— restaurant—tell of good things within that make a soldier think of home. . . . The smiling individual who meets you at the door evidently understands his business. Dinner for one? Yes, sir, what will you have? What have you got? Coffee, real Rio—this is always mentioned first, for everybody likes real Rio— beef, mutton, pork, potatoes, butter and bread. A hungry man eats everything with pleasure, but this coffee certainly has a strong smell of villainous rye; and the beef is poor enough to have fasted ever since it left the verdant plains of Texas; and the butter smells as if it had made a trip from Texas too, or had even run the blockade from some foreign country across the deep blue sea. There is, however, no use in grumbling about what one has eaten, and, after all, this dinner is so much better than camp fare, that you feel good and pull out your pocket book with the air of a man who has been benefitted and wished to compensate his benefactor. What do I owe you,

sir? Two dollars and a half. Two dollars and a half! You are exor- And before you can finish the sentence your accommodating host begins talking in
such an excited manner about paying forty cents a pound for flour, fifty
cents for pork, three dollars for butter, five dollars for coffee, so much for
wood, house rent &c &c that you feel ashamed that you have said anything
and are glad to beat a hasty retreat. . . .[3]

The Vicksburg correspondents of the Confederate press were also
watching closely the movements of Grant's army above Vicksburg and
coming to the conclusion that he was trying to get below the city to
obtain a more favorable approach for an attack.[4] Attempts by Grant's
engineers to construct alternative water routes on the Louisiana side
of the river to avoid the dangerous passage of the Confederate batteries at Vicksburg gave the reporters there plenty to write about. So
too did the efforts of Federal Admiral Porter to run the Vicksburg
batteries by stealth.

The first of Porter's dangerous experiments took place on February
2 when the ram *Queen of the West* scampered past the Vicksburg batteries in broad daylight. The Vicksburg newspapers (*Sun, Whig,* and
Citizen) were furious with the lack of vigilance or poor gunnery that
had made this exploit possible, but the *Memphis Appeal* correspondent
rationalized the apparent failure as "part of a regularly laid scheme
. . . to entice the Yankees into an inextricable trap."[5] Other Yankee war
craft succeeded in running past the batteries at night, but the local
journalists felt somewhat better about it when, below Vicksburg, the
Confederates captured first the *Queen of the West* and then the new
ironclad *Indianola*. A special correspondent of the *Memphis Appeal*
who used the pseudonym "American Rifles" was an eyewitness of the
capture of the *Indianola*. His account of the action, written from on
board the sidewheeler *Dr. Bailey*, vividly reconstructed the ramming
of the *Indianola*, the incessant play of musketry, the yelling of the
Confederate crews, and the capitulation of the Yankee skipper just as

---

[3] *Columbus Daily Sun*, February 17, 1863.

[4] See e.g. *Memphis Daily Appeal*, January 26, March 3, 1863. For optimistic
reports by Confederate war correspondents of widespread disaffection and desertion in the Northern army near Vicksburg, see *Mobile Daily Advertiser and Register*, January 30, February 15, 1863.

[5] *Memphis Daily Appeal*, February 4, 1863; *Vicksburg Daily Whig*, February 3,
1863. For a ridiculous report, credited by the Vicksburg papers, of a Federal gunboat standing on end, see *Memphis Daily Appeal*, March 30, 1863.

the Confederate boarding party was about to descend on the deck of the *Indianola*.[6]

The Confederate reporters noted improvement in the performance of the Vicksburg artillerymen as the weeks went by. Yet they continued to complain about the large number of "idle and incompetent officers" among Vicksburg's defenders. Even the press itself did not escape criticism for publishing reports of the damage inflicted on Yankee gunboats and "turreted monsters."[7] The Confederate journalists were alternately contemptuous and apprehensive of the none-too-successful attempts on the part of Grant's army to dig through the Louisiana bayous to bypass Vicksburg. Probably they became more hopeful, and even slightly envious, when in March the correspondent of the *Memphis Appeal* at Port Hudson wrote a stirring battle report of a naval action in which only two of the seven ships in Admiral Farragut's Yankee squadron managed to squirm past the Port Hudson batteries on their way upstream.[8]

During the early part of April, misled by intelligence reports from Pemberton's headquarters indicating that Grant was sending reinforcements to Rosecrans' army in middle Tennessee, the correspondents at Vicksburg reported that Grant had raised the siege of Vicksburg and that the Yankees were returning to Memphis. They admitted, however, the possibility that the apparent withdrawal might be only a ruse; their suspicions were confirmed when on the night of April 16 Porter ran a fleet of gunboats, empty transports, and barges past the Vicksburg batteries. Although some of them were mystified about the purpose of this new movement, the correspondent of the *Memphis Appeal* made the fairly accurate guess that Porter intended to use these gunboats to support the operation against Port Hudson.[9] A few nights later a reporter for the *Knoxville Register* was on hand to describe a second

[6] *Memphis Daily Appeal*, March 11, 1863.

[7] *Ibid.*, April 11, 1863; *Daily Richmond Examiner*, March 7, 1863.

[8] *Memphis Daily Appeal*, March 20, 1863. Reprints of the *Appeal's* battle report appeared in the *Daily Richmond Enquirer*, March 30, 1863; *Wilmington Daily Journal*, April 1, 1863.

[9] See e.g. *Memphis Daily Appeal*, April 9, 11, 15, 16, 1863; *Mobile Daily Advertiser and Register*, April 12, 18, 19, 1863; *Vicksburg Daily Whig*, April 14, 1863. "Nestor's" estimate of Porter's intentions appeared in *Memphis Daily Appeal*, April 18, 1863. For accusations of "partying" among Vicksburg officers that undermined the efficiency of the Vicksburg defenses, see *ibid.*, April 21, 1863; *Jackson Daily Mississippian*, April 24, 1863.

successful run past Vicksburg by six Federal river steamers with the loss of only a single ship. The *Register* representative told how as the town clock chimed the hour of midnight:

The alarm was sounded, and when the boats had gained the point where they are within range of our uppermost batteries, a ten-inch Columbiad welcomed them with an iron messenger in the shape of a shell. In less time than it takes to relate it, five transports, heavily laden with provisions, and one gunboat were receiving the fire of these death-dealing monsters that grin defiance from the hills overlooking the Mississippi. At this juncture, it was fearfully grand and awfully sublime to see the flaming metal gushing forth from the mouths of our blackthroated defenders, which had been aroused and angered by the insolence and audacity of the foe in venturing within their dominions. Our officers had taken the necessary precaution to have the river lighted by setting fire to several of the houses on the opposite shore, whenever the enemy's boats attempted a passage. The fires burning dimly at the beginning, the first craft went by with but slight damage, compared to what the rest received. In a few minutes, however, the flames burst forth and illumined the river sufficiently to enable our gunners to get accurate range of the whole number. There they were, strung out one after another; our men had only to choose—the red glare from the Louisiana shore diffusing light enough to discern with the naked eye the smallest object on the boats, even the names of some of the steamers could be distinguished.

The dull, deafening roar of the heavy guns mingled with the sharp sound of musketry, making the night hideous and leaving on the mind of the beholder an impression not easily forgotten. The scene in the city proper was not less interesting to one whose feelings permitted him to enjoy it. Whilst men, women, children and negroes were gathered promiscuously, some under shelter of the hills for safety, others on the summits to gratify their curiosity, the different species of animals, mules, goats, cats and oxen might be heard making all kinds of noises as though "chaos was come again." The groans of the wounded on the enemy's boats could be heard distinctly by people near the river bank. On one boat the wounded called out to our men for God's sake to have mercy on them, that they were sinking—of course we ceased firing, but instead of heading for the shore as they appeared to be trying to do at first, the boat (Yankee like) moved down the stream and away they went. Ah! but they paid dearly for their perfidy—instantly perceiving the object of the cunning Yankee, our guns again opened with greater fury and more deadly aim than ever. Anon, it was plain to all that she had received her just deserts, as she was now sinking rapidly.[10]

The *Register* man inaccurately reported that two of the six enemy vessels were sunk and that the others were badly damaged; he interpreted the encounter as a successful feat of arms for the Vicksburg

[10] *Knoxville Daily Register*, May 7, 1863.

cannoneers. The *Memphis Appeal* correspondent more correctly viewed this as the most recent demonstration that Federal transports were able to "run our batteries at pleasure" and admitted that he was puzzled by the lack of success of Vicksburg's defenders. "The men in the batteries are vigilant and skilful, the guns are good, our troops are brave and determined, and nature has provided us with means to blockade the river so that it would be entirely impenetrable. But there is a want somewhere, and in due course of time the proper exposition will be made."[11]

In Vicksburg, to which he had moved his headquarters from Jackson at the end of April, General Pemberton was as confused as any reporter about Grant's plan of campaign, which had undergone an important change. When Grant marched down the Louisiana side of the Mississippi during the last two weeks of April, he intended to support Banks in a movement against Port Hudson. Learning, however, that Banks had changed his mind and was marching in the opposite direction, Grant decided instead to strike at Vicksburg from below. Avoiding the heavily fortified Confederate position at Grand Gulf, he crossed into Mississippi at Bruinsburg, 10 miles below. Simultaneously Sherman's corps made a diversionary attack at Snyder's Bluff, north of Vicksburg, and a Union cavalry raid out of Memphis which stirred up plenty of trouble in eastern Mississippi before the raiders reached Baton Rouge on May 2, added to Pemberton's state of confusion. As a result there were only 8,000 Confederate troops under Brig.Gen. John S. Bowen near Bruinsburg to meet Grant's invasion force. Bowen waged an all-day fight with the Federals against heavy odds on May 1 at Port Gibson, a few miles inland from Bruinsburg. Following the battle, Bowen retreated across the Big Black River toward Vicksburg, leaving Grand Gulf exposed.[12]

Confederate editors and reporters later criticized Pemberton for not marching with his entire army to the support of Bowen. During the first week of May, however, the Confederate press was as much at sea about the situation below Vicksburg as Pemberton was. While Grant was heading east toward the capital of Mississippi, editors whose reporters were strangely silent made what sense they could out of the

[11] *Memphis Daily Appeal*, April 24, 1863.

[12] Shelby Foote, *The Civil War, Fredericksburg to Meridian* (New York, 1963), pp. 346-348. The Confederates evacuated Grand Gulf on the morning of May 2 after destroying its magazine and spiking the guns. *Columbus Daily Sun*, May 12, 1863.

meager and largely inaccurate reports of the Battle of Port Gibson. A special correspondent of the *Mobile Register* who interviewed Governor John J. Pettus in Jackson on May 4 learned that the governor could not make public the military dispatches in his possession without first consulting with General Pemberton. As Pemberton was then in Vicksburg, forty miles away, Pettus was fairly safe in making this stipulation. He assured the reporter, nevertheless, that no serious disaster had yet befallen the Confederates at Grand Gulf and that reinforcements then on their way to Bowen would not only check Grant but "probably" dislodge him from his foothold in Mississippi.[13] Meanwhile the *Vicksburg Whig* had dispatched one of its staff members named John Armstrong in the direction of Port Gibson to gather information about the fate of Bowen's men. But a fire that destroyed the *Whig* newspaper office on May 9 ended the career of that paper.[14]

On May 19, 1863 the *Augusta Constitutionalist* published a letter from its special correspondent "Novissimus" that had been mailed from Vicksburg about a week earlier. The reporter for the *Constitutionalist* alluded to the fight at Port Gibson, which apparently he had not witnessed, and described the retreat during the following night of the survivors of Bowen's command, accompanied by pale women, shivering children, and a few faithful slaves. "Novissimus" confessed he had had little opportunity to observe or speculate about the situation during a week of much labor and little glory, often for twenty-four hours in the saddle without rest or sleep. He stated as a fact, however, that the Confederates had lost the left flank of their position, some guns and stores, a portion of their rear, and a battle. He declared that he still regarded Vicksburg as "invulnerable against all, but starvation." His further statement, that "we had better lose Richmond—but I trust shall not lose either" demonstrated his understanding of the vital importance of the city Pemberton was defending.

By this time Editor Cooper of the *Jackson Mississippian* was fully aware of the acute peril Grant's invasion of Mississippi presented. As a special correspondent of the *Mississippian*, Cooper had accompanied

[13] *Mobile Daily Advertiser and Register*, May 9, 1863. On the following day the governor issued a proclamation calling on the people of Mississippi to rise to the defense of their homes.

[14] Marmaduke Shannon to "Dear Ma," May 2, 1863. Crutcher-Shannon Papers, Mississippi State Department of Archives and History; *Mobile Daily Advertiser and Register*, May 15, 1863.

a cavalry expedition from Jackson in pursuit of Grierson's raiders,[15] and on May 5 he published an editorial in which he called on General Pemberton "in the name of his country and the army . . . to combine his forces and lead them against the foe and crush the foe at any cost." Then without waiting to see whether Pemberton would take his advice, he dispatched a long communication to President Davis, stating that the soldiers and citizens of Pemberton's department lacked confidence in his capacity and loyalty and were asking for his removal.[16]

Pemberton's inability to slow Grant's advance on Jackson seemed to justify Cooper's skittish behavior. At Raymond on May 12, McPherson's Federal corps brushed aside a Confederate brigade under General Gregg, that had just come up from Port Hudson and compelled it to retreat toward Jackson after a fight that lasted several hours. When General Johnston arrived in Jackson from Tullahoma on the second day after the fight at Raymond to take personal charge of the city's defense, he found only two brigades there to resist the onslaught of two Federal army corps. Concluding that the defense of Jackson was hopeless, Johnston fought a delaying action in the entrenchments west of the city on May 14 to cover the retreat of his forces northward.[17]

The refugee *Memphis Appeal*, which had been published in Jackson since its retreat from Grenada in November 1862, made its escape just before Sherman's troops marched in; but the *Jackson Mississippian* was not so fortunate. One of the casualties of the brief Federal occupation was the destruction of the *Mississippian's* printing plant. Later the *Mobile Register* attributed the "capture and sack" of the capital of Mississippi during the next three days to "a rash and needless exposure of its military weakness at the time by a newspaper then published in that city."[18]

Military censorship kept the Confederate Associated Press from publishing the news of the fall of Jackson for several days. Apparently the censors killed the story after it left the Mobile telegraph office, but

[15] *Memphis Daily Appeal* as reprinted in *Atlanta Daily Southern Confederacy*, May 8, 1863.

[16] *O.R.* (Army) Ser. I, vol. lii, pt. 2, pp. 468-69. In reply Davis informed Cooper that "time does not permit the change you propose" and advised him to be more trustful of Pemberton.

[17] G. E. Govan and J. W. Livingood, *A Different Valor, the Story of Gen. Joseph E. Johnston* (Indianapolis and New York, 1956), pp. 198-199.

[18] *Richmond Daily Dispatch*, May 21, 1863; *Mobile Daily Advertiser and Register*, November 17, 1863.

failed to notify the *Chattanooga Rebel* in time to keep it from appearing in the May 15 issue of that newspaper.[19]

A blackout of special correspondence from northern Mississippi afflicted the Confederate press as Pemberton headed east from Vicksburg along the railroad line to Jackson in pursuance of Johnston's orders to strike at Grant. None of the special correspondents who had been at Vicksburg seems to have been with Pemberton's army, and the Federal occupation of Jackson had caused the newspapermen who previously had been there to quit the vicinity. At Senatobia, an important news center in northern Mississippi, Grierson's raiders had "gobbled up" the telegraphic correspondent of the *Memphis Appeal*, M. W. Barr, thereby temporarily silencing one of the more important news transmitters in the area.[20] As a result there was no consistent news coverage by the Confederate newspapers of the crucial military events of the next few days, during which Grant drove Pemberton back to the fortifications of Vicksburg.

How Pemberton tried in vain to sever a supply line which vanished into thin air, how faulty communication prevented the junction of Johnston's and Pemberton's commands at Clinton, and how the rapid advance of the Federals west from Jackson forced Pemberton to assume a defensive posture at Champion's Hill, midway between Jackson and Vicksburg, was essentially an untold news story in the Confederate press. A reporter for the *Mobile Register* who returned to Jackson on May 17 after Sherman left the city heard ugly tales about the misconduct of some Georgia regiments at the Battle of Baker's Creek on May 16.[21] But the details of that Confederate defeat and of the rearguard action the retreating Confederates fought at the railroad crossing of the Big Black River the following day were unreported by the Confederate newspapers. Gradually rumor crystallized into the acknowledged fact that Pemberton had fallen back to the defenses of Vicksburg and that Grant had reestablished his supply line to the North.

The first definite information about these events that reached the Eastern press was a Press Association report from Mobile from the Jackson correspondent of the *Mobile Register*. The dispatch related

[19] *Richmond Daily Whig*, May 19, 1863.

[20] *Chattanooga Daily Rebel*, May 23, 1863.

[21] *Mobile Daily Advertiser and Register*, May 30, 1863. Further investigation caused the *Register* reporter to conclude that he had been misled and had done an injustice to these regiments. *Mobile Daily Advertiser and Register*, July 11, 1863.

that the Confederates had lost thirty pieces of artillery spiked and abandoned in the fighting at Baker's Creek, that heavy losses had been sustained in the retreat across the Big Black River the following day, and that "Vicksburg is closely beseiged [*sic*] and the enemy is closing in on every side."[22] False reports from Yankee sources which reached Richmond on May 27, that Vicksburg had fallen, added to the public's anxiety.[23] Richmond morale improved somewhat, however, when official information was received from General Johnston of the repulse with heavy losses of enemy assaults on the defenses of Vicksburg. Similar information about the repulse was transmitted by the Confederate Press Association, based on reports published in the resuscitated *Jackson Mississippian*. The Jackson reporter of the *Mobile Register*, who was somewhat embarrassed by widespread disapproval of his statement about Vicksburg being "closely besieged," added for good measure the grisly information, "Pemberton is burning tar and using other disinfectants to save his troops from the effect of the stench of the Yankee dead who are rotting in front of our works. The slaughter of the Yankees has been far greater than in any other battle of the war." Commenting on the use the Yankees were making of their own dead "to stink our forces out of that stronghold from which their valor had failed to drive us," the editor of the *Atlanta Confederacy* quipped that this represented "a new kind of strategy—a new *offensive weapon* of warfare not laid down in any of the authorities in military science."[24]

During the next six weeks, with an army that was continuously being reinforced Grant drew an ever tighter ring around Pemberton's 18,500 harassed men. Unable to break out of the trap, Pemberton looked for deliverance to Johnston's slowly increasing army at Jackson and to the largely inchoate forces in the Trans-Mississippi Department. Beginning May 20 Admiral Porter's mortar and gunboat fleet on the west side of the Vicksburg peninsula, and the 248 heavy guns of Grant's field artillery, subjected the Vicksburg defenders to almost daily bombardment.[25]

The fury of the bombardment was pictured by a correspondent of the *Memphis Appeal*, whose report was not published until after the

[22] *Atlanta Daily Southern Confederacy*, May 23, 1863.
[23] *Memphis Daily Appeal*, June 6, 1863.
[24] *Daily Richmond Examiner*, May 29, 1863; *Richmond Daily Dispatch*, May 27, 1863; *Richmond Daily Sentinel*, May 27, 29, 1863; *Atlanta Daily Southern Confederacy*, May 28, 1863.
[25] Pemberton, *Pemberton*, p. 185.

surrender of Vicksburg. The reporter for the *Appeal* told how Vicksburg came under simultaneous fire from Grant's light and heavy artillery in the rear, from the Union mortars on the opposite side of the river, and the gunboats that lay between them. Only the pen of a poet, he conjectured, could do justice to the hideous concatenation of booming cannon, clashing mortars, the banging of small arms, the howling of shells, the whistling of Parrotts, and the popping of minie balls. The Parrott shells, he declared, "were the most dreaded of the enemy's missiles, their flight being so rapid that they would find their target or go whistling by before the report of the gun could be heard. The mortars, on the other hand, were excellent things as signals, because in the night the shells could be seen at a great distance coursing through the air like fiery monsters. Sometimes in dark nights their parabolic evolutions would present a beautiful spectacle, particularly at times when all the mortars were discharged simultaneously, when they could be seen passing overhead with their burning fuses, as if striving for the pirotechnic championship. . . . I never could learn how many mortars were engaged, but the greatest number of shells I saw overhead at one time was five, all going at the rate of about 3 miles in 40 seconds. So accustomed did the people become to this that those living in the lower end of town would sit in front of their doors at night and watch the shells flying overhead at an elevation so great that the spark of the burning fuse was almost invisible. Experience also taught them to know by the manner in which the shell revolved whether it was going to burst or not, and in fact, toward the last it became so familiar that mortar shells were rather regarded as pets than otherwise."[26]

The Confederate press had to depend for information about the situation at Vicksburg almost exclusively on dispatches emanating from the Press Association reporter at Jackson and the Jackson correspondents of the Mobile newspapers. To reduce the cost of telegraphic news reporting, Thrasher, the general manager of the Associated Press, had instructed his news agents to exclude prepositions, conjunctions, and other verbiage from their dispatches. Wagner, the Jackson correspondent of the Press Association, apparently was an apt pupil of Thrasher; as a result his dispatches were often incomprehensible to editors who were used to the old style of telegraphic reporting. Editor Daniel of the *Richmond Examiner* referred to the P.A.'s wire service from Jack-

[26] *Memphis Daily Appeal*, July 27, 1863.

son as "an unintelligible compound of gas, braggadocio, blunder, absurdity, and impossibility" and accused Wagner of wild exaggeration in reporting enemy losses in the neighborhood of Vicksburg and Port Hudson. The *Mobile Register* entered the plea, in defense of the Press Association, that Vicksburg was cut off from regular communication with Jackson by telegraph, rail, or stage and that the reticence of General Johnston successfully inhibited knowledge by reporters of his plans and movements.[27]

Practically the only information about what was happening at Vicksburg that newspapermen at Jackson could obtain was the product of questioning the army couriers who from time to time managed to slip through the enemy's lines. From one of Pemberton's couriers who reached Jackson on June 11, the editor of the *Mississippian* obtained the not altogether reliable statement that " 'our boys' at Vicksburg are in good health, fine spirits, have plenty to eat . . . and are eager to be led against the Vandal hordes of old Abe. . . ."[28]

During the latter part of June David Flannery, the superintendent of the Southwestern Telegraph lines in Jackson, forwarded to the editors of the *Richmond Enquirer* a copy of a somewhat misleading letter written ten days earlier by a telegraph operator in Vicksburg, which he had received that morning. The operator assured Flannery that he was "not scared, nor shelled, nor starved out of existence yet, as you may perceive, nor even driven to live on worse fare than beef and bread, with the customary concoction of corn coffee. Indeed, no one here is starving, nor are there any fears of it entertained. The idea of surrender, for any cause, is never dreamed of here. . . . Compared with the fury of the bombardment since the investment the casualties are very small. In the entrenchments, the danger is very little, unless to the curious, who, duck-like, are given to popping their heads over the

[27] *Daily Richmond Examiner*, June 6, 25, 1863; *Mobile Daily Advertiser and Register*, June 12, 1863; *Augusta Daily Constitutionalist*, June 17, 1863. On April 18, 1863 the *Savannah Daily Morning News* displayed to its readers the following specimen of Press Association telegraphic literature from Jackson: "Jackson, April 17. — Eight boats passed Vicksburg last night; one burnt two disabled five succeeded. Rumor canal Milliken's Bend reach Mississippi near New Carthage believed construction Batteries opposite Vicksburg Jew paid burn bridge Big Black Vicksburg attacked within ten 10 days all officers absent ordered report opposite Vicksburg sixty-four 64 steamers left Memphis for Vicksburg soldiers niggers no papers allowed below Cairo Yankees fortifying Rolla R R north Memphis Bulletin argus suppressed editors arrested."
[28] *Jackson Daily Mississippian*, June 12, 1863.

breastworks, which the Yankee sharpshooters promptly pop at, frequently popping the owner into eternity. But the tedium and monotony of trench duty is its most disagreeable feature."[29]

On the basis of these and similar reports the Confederate press portrayed the situation at Vicksburg as being one in which the defenders had ample food supplies to hold out for several months, in which the position of Grant, located between the armies of Pemberton and Johnston, was precarious and becoming progressively more so, in which help for Pemberton was on its way from the Trans-Mississippi theater and other commands, and as a result of which the enemy was suffering staggering losses. The press reported as solid fact or probable truth rumors that Smith, the commander of the Trans-Mississippi Department, had thrown a column of 10,000 men into Port Hudson, had seized both Helena, Arkansas, and Milliken's Bend on the west bank of the river, had opened communication with Vicksburg, and was ready to supply it with men, munitions, and provisions without limit.[30] When Johnston displayed no signs of activity as the weeks passed by, the Jackson correspondent of the *Mobile Register* expressed the comforting opinion that Johnston "is fighting Grant daily by giving him a 'terrible letting alone,' and after all it may be the safest and surest way of whipping Grant. With the navigation of the Mississippi closed, his supplies cut off, and harassed and menaced at every point, he will have but one alternative, that of raising the siege and giving Johnston battle on his own ground."[31]

To improve the news coverage of the *Jackson Mississippian* in northern Mississippi, the newspaper sent its assistant editor, J. H. Thompson, to Grenada at the beginning of June. Thompson's instructions were to act as a roving correspondent in the region between Panola, Batesville, and Senatobia and forward by telegraph or otherwise information

---

[29] *Daily Richmond Enquirer*, July 1, 1863. According to the *Mobile Daily Advertiser and Register* of May 13, 1863, the agent of the Press Association in Vicksburg was a newspaper editor and "a very intelligent and experienced gentleman."

[30] See e.g. *Daily Richmond Examiner*, July 3, 1863; *Mobile Daily Tribune*, June 28, 1863; *Mobile Daily Advertiser and Register*, June 30, 1863; *Jackson Daily Mississippian*, June 9, 1863; *Memphis Daily Appeal*, June 8, July 6, 1863. On July 19 the Jackson correspondent of the *Mobile Register* informed his newspaper that the approval by the military authorities of Press Association dispatches was a security measure and was no guarantee of the authenticity or correctness of the news contained in the dispatch. *Mobile Daily Advertiser and Register*, June 23, 1863.

[31] *Mobile Daily Advertiser and Register*, July 7, 1863.

gleaned from Northern newspapers smuggled through the lines from Memphis. Thompson's observations led him to conclude that illegal trading activity and the disloyal sentiments of a troublesome minority of the inhabitants were injurious to the effectiveness of Confederate cavalry operations in that area.[32]

At the end of May the *Knoxville Register* had dispatched its able correspondent, L. J. Dupré, to Mississippi to report the Vicksburg campaign. Dupré, who had just returned to Knoxville from a reporting assignment in Richmond, passed through Selma, Alabama, and Macon, Mississippi, on his way west, reaching Meridian on June 2. There was as much news from Vicksburg in Meridian as at Jackson, he decided; furthermore "Vicksburg is inaccessible, and in Jackson there is neither bread nor abiding place for a stranger."[33]

Dupré was convinced from his observations at Meridian that defeatism was rife among the people of Mississippi and that in many instances they counted Vicksburg as already lost. He attributed their lack of nerve to their onetime illusion that the soil of Mississippi would never be invaded, and expressed confidence that they would recover from the shock that had temporarily paralyzed their energies.[34]

The ravages of war were only too evident in Jackson at this time. On June 10 the Bowman House, the largest and finest hotel in the state, burned to the ground. From an officer who had just left Jackson to go to Selma, the *Selma Dispatch* got the impression that "commercially, pecuniarily, socially, Jackson is a wreck beyond the power of repair."[35] To make matters worse, there seemed to be ill feeling between soldiers and civilians because of a silly rumor, circulated some months previously, that the people of Jackson did not want any soldiers to use their sidewalks. According to the Jackson correspondent of the *Mobile Register*, the rumor had spread through the entire army and was believed, although the mayor of Jackson had taken the pains to publish an official denial in the columns of the *Mississippian*. The reporter added: "The

---

[32] *Jackson Daily Mississippian*, June 4, 9, 1863.

[33] *Knoxville Daily Register*, June 13, 1863. In a letter from Selma dated May 24, 1863, Dupré indicated that he had been delayed everywhere along the route by soldiers and ordnance stores that were being rushed to Vicksburg. "The people here [in Selma] are hopeful in the midst of a degree of anxiety which I have never before seen manifested." *Ibid.*, May 29, 1863.

[34] *Ibid.*, June 9, 1863.

[35] *Selma Daily Dispatch* as reprinted in *Memphis Daily Appeal*, June 19, 1863; *Mobile Daily Advertiser and Register*, June 16, 1863.

troops hoot at their comrades to 'come off them sidewalks.' The Yankees have burnt your town, have they? Glad of it—you are mighty glad to see us ain't you? You'll let us walk on your sidewalks won't you?' "[36]

Another newspaper correspondent, Barr of the *Memphis Appeal*, who had been released after a brief period of captivity in the North, made clear in his reporting that other areas of Mississippi besides Jackson were suffering acutely from Yankee depredations. In a letter from Panola to the *Appeal* which he mailed on June 21, Barr made no attempt to suppress the fact that: "The condition of North Mississippi is deplorable. Mention the name of a town in that raid ridden area, and I will tell you it is burned. Ride with me twenty miles south of the Memphis and Charleston railroad, and I will show you charred chimneys and little fields of luxuriant rose bushes; nothing else remains of all that made that section as prosperous and pleasant as any spot in the Confederacy. The Yankees have been there, and it is a wreck. . . . This is no exaggeration. It is true. A live body has ridden from Holly Springs to La Grange in a hearse. Every article which tends to comfort, help production, or betokens civilization the Yankees have stolen or destroyed."[37]

In a letter to the *Knoxville Register* from Suqulah, Mississippi, on June 17, Dupré admitted that he was having transportation problems. "I am incapable of locomotion save when astride some meek Rosinante; and since I am not inclined to invest $1,000 or $1,500 in a quadruped, and pay five dollars per day for forage, I have deemed it advisable until some active demonstration is made by Gen. Johnston to make Meridian my headquarters."[38]

Dupré had other difficulties, too, resulting from the fact that "the only news that reaches us, comes in the shape of vague, unreliable rumors" and that the latest news from Vicksburg generally contradicted all that had preceded it. Yet with little to go in the way of sifted information, Dupré came to the disturbing conclusion that Grant's posi-

[36] *Memphis Daily Appeal*, June 17, 1863; *Mobile Daily Advertiser and Register*, June 9, 1863. A correspondent of the *Selma Dispatch* who visited the new office of the *Jackson Mississippian* during the early part of June described what he called "the foot-prints of the war dragon" in the editor's sanctum. "A large map of the former United States was hanging up in the editor's chamber—the Abolitionists cut out the Confederacy and left the Gorilla's dominions intact." *Selma Daily Dispatch* as reprinted in *Mobile Daily Advertiser and Register*, June 12, 1863.

[37] *Memphis Daily Appeal*, June 27, 1863.

[38] *Knoxville Daily Register*, June 24, 1863.

tion was as strong as that of Pemberton. "He [Grant] is strongly entrenched. — While his communication with the river at Snyder's Bluff
is maintained and his supplies uninterrupted, we cannot see how Grant
is not in a better condition than Pemberton." By June 26 Dupré was
considering the possibility that Vicksburg might fall and that Pemberton might be compelled to surrender.[39]

The surrender of Pemberton's army was indeed imminent. Negotiations conducted under a flag of truce on the third of July resulted in
Vicksburg's capitulation the next day. The publication of an extra
edition of the *Mississippian* on Monday, July 6, featuring a dispatch
from its war correspondent, J. H. Thompson, made the surrender
public knowledge on the streets of Jackson that day. The next morning,
however, the Jackson reporter of the *Mobile Register* cast doubts
on the reliability of the surrender report by maintaining that the adjutant general's office in Jackson had no *official* information of the fall
of Vicksburg, although "I am assured by the agent of the Associated
Press, who arrived from the front yesterday, that the news is true."
Before the day was over, Jackson had official confirmation of the surrender.[40]

Richmond had its first word of the disaster in the form of a press
dispatch from Jackson which was received at the capital at 1:00 P.M.,
Tuesday, July 7. The dispatch stated that an officer who had come
through the enemy's lines reported that Vicksburg had fallen. Doubting
the truth of the report, President William S. Morris of the Southern
Telegraph Company submitted the dispatch to the War Department
without notifying the press. Secretary Seddon and the other officials
at the department were surprised and puzzled, and asked why if the
news were authentic it should have been left to the press reporter to
transmit such an important piece of information. The War Department telegraphed General Johnston at once, seeking clarification. About
half past eight that evening a dispatch from Johnston addressed to
Secretary Seddon was received at the War Department, stating flatly
that "Vicksburg capitulated on the 4th instant" and indicating that
the source of the information was an unnamed officer who left Vicksburg on Sunday, the fifth. The War Department and the general public in Richmond, to whom the news was released at ten o'clock the
next morning, were still skeptical about the news of the capitulation.

[39] *Ibid.*, July 2, 3, 4, 1863.
[40] *Mobile Daily Advertiser and Register*, July 8, 10, 1863.

Who was the officer whom Johnston had mentioned, it was asked, and if he got to Jackson, why could not others of the garrison do the same? Some people wanted to know why the dispatch from Jackson was signed Joseph E. Johnston instead of the general's customary signature of J. E. Johnston, and implied that they thought the message was a Yankee forgery. As the hours passed on Wednesday without bringing to light any further information, the *Memphis Appeal* correspondent in Richmond, J. R. Thompson, admitted that the public was gradually coming around to an acceptance of the belief "that we have lost our stronghold on the Mississippi."[41]

The first reaction of the Confederate press to the stunning realization that Vicksburg had fallen was hot resentment of the deceptive news reports that had been accepted at face value up to that time. The *Savannah Republican* commented bitterly, "there is a heavy weight of responsibility resting on somebody's shoulders for the regular and systematic lying that has been put upon the public regarding the ability of this place to hold out. The western Press in the vicinity of the unfortunate city have been quite as badly imposed on as anybody else. We have forty times read reports, coming from Pemberton himself, that supplies were abundant, and the garrison could 'hold out indefinitely'. . . ."[42] The *Mobile Tribune* also emphasized that the calamity was "totally unexpected. . . . Every piece of information, from numerous persons not in concert, led us to believe that there was at least 60 days of vigorous resistance in the garrison; and before that could be expended, it was believed that much could be done by Johnston to thwart the designs of Grant."[43]

[41] *Daily Richmond Examiner*, July 8, 9, 1863; *Memphis Daily Appeal*, July 13, 1863; *Savannah Republican*, July 10, 1863; *Atlanta Daily Intelligencer*, July 15, 1863; *Knoxville Daily Register*, July 8, 9, 1863; Edward Younger, ed., *Inside the Confederate Government; The Diary of Robert G. H. Kean* (New York, 1957), p. 78; S. A. Putnam, *Richmond during the War* (New York, 1867), p. 229.

[42] *Savannah Republican*, July 10, 1863. On July 13, 1863 the *Memphis Appeal* admitted, "from prudential motives of doubtful propiety [*sic*] the discouraging facts were suppressed, while such as could be tortured into encouragement were magnified." An example of the misleading information about which the *Republican* complained was the statement of the *Knoxville Daily Register* on June 3, 1863 that Grant had lost 40,000 to 50,000 men in killed, wounded, and sick since he landed in Mississippi at the end of April.

[43] *Mobile Daily Tribune*, as reprinted in *Atlanta Daily Intelligencer*, July 14, 1863. On June 16, 1863 the *Jackson Mississippian* had stated on the authority of "officers who have lately left the garrison at Vicksburg" that "there are rations enough to last for two months at least, and upon a pinch, their supplies could be

It was not true, however, that the fall of Vicksburg had been "totally unexpected" either by the press or its readers. At least two months beforehand, a few editors and war correspondents had begun to prepare their readers for the possibility that the "Gibraltar of the West" might fall. After they recovered from their first shock, Southern editors sought to cushion the news for their subscribers by maintaining that Vicksburg was only one point on the Mississippi River, that its surrender gave the enemy possession of neither the river nor the valley, that the enemy had paid dearly in the form of casualties for his success, that Pemberton's army had not been "whipped" but rather starved into "honorable capitulation," and that in any case the loss of Vicksburg was more than compensated for by Lee's (supposed) great victory at Gettysburg. Almost simultaneously with the news of the fall of Vicksburg, the *Memphis Appeal* published reports (which proved to be untrue) of the recapture of New Orleans by Maj.Gen. Richard Taylor's command.[44]

Now for the first time the Confederate press revealed the rigors of the siege and the sufferings of the garrison and of Vicksburg civilians while it was going on. A correspondent of the *Chattanooga Rebel* who was shut up in Vicksburg and unable to communicate with his newspaper during the siege was finally able to tell how "there was no safety anywhere; shells passed through and through our hospitals, killing the sick and wounded. Women and children were struck down in their homes and in the streets. . . . The litter bearers were constantly

---

made to hold out much longer." On July 3, the day before the surrender, the *Mississippian* repeated its assurances that "our people need have no apprehension about Vicksburg's being starved out. . . ." In Vicksburg, on the other hand, according to the *Memphis Appeal* correspondent who was in the city at the time, there were exaggerated expectations of the ability of Johnston's army to come to Pemberton's relief. Apparently these expectations were nourished by the misleading reports of the couriers from Johnston who managed to slip through Grant's lines. *Memphis Daily Appeal*, July 27, 1863.

[44] The editor of the *Columbus Sun* had asked the rhetorical question in an editorial published on May 1, 1863: "What if Vicksburg should fall? Gibraltar was once captured, and so was Quebec. We *may* lose a magnificent army there, and with it, the last stronghold we possess on the Mississippi, but what then? . . . Will trade revive? Will the granaries of the Northwest find an outlet for their accumulated wealth of cereals?" Samples of morale-building editorials published *after* the fall of Vicksburg may be found in *Jackson Daily Mississippian*, July 7, 1863; *Mobile Daily Advertiser and Register*, July 8, 1863; *Knoxville Daily Register*, July 10, 1863; *Columbus Daily Sun*, July 14, 1863; *Augusta Daily Constitutionalist*, July 19, 1863.

passing with bloody, ghastly loads. 'Who is shot?' would be the simple question asked. The name would be given and the sad remark, 'Poor fellow, he was a good soldier' made and the poor fellow's body placed in its last resting place."[45]

In one of the most extensive newspaper accounts of the Vicksburg campaign published after the surrender, a special correspondent of the *Augusta Constitutionalist* gave full credit to the valor of the enemy's troops at the Battle of Baker's Creek and contributed a graphic description of the lethal effects of the bombardment and the physical exhaustion of the garrison as a result of its remaining under fire in the trenches day and night for a protracted period. Writing about the events of the siege a week before the capitulation, he said:

"The soldiers now do not get in a day as much as a man usually eats at a meal. . . ."

"Some of the Louisiana regiments eat anything, and some of them called here yesterday with a large wharf rat, and offered to pay fifty cents each for every rat they could get! . . ."

"The lines of the enemy are in some places within ten feet of our ditches, close enough to make scribbling on ship crackers and tossing them into our ditches a favorite amusement. Consequently, one third of the men have to be always watching for a charge, knowing that the occupation of twenty yards of our entrenchments would be fatal to Vicksburg. . . ."

"Inside of this slaughter pen we have the same solid fact as before. Shells the size of half a bushel filled with powder . . . borne in an instant from that red hell beyond the trees . . . come thicker than did the lost angels from the battlements of heaven."

"Batteries of rifle guns also line the opposite shore, and as my office is in front of the river trenches, and not forty yards from the water, I am sufficiently exposed to satisfy the most ambitious."

"A rifle shell came crashing through the window of my bed room a few mornings since, covering me with glass and splinters and effectively waking me up. It went on out through the timbers of the house and buried itself in the hill without bursting."[46]

On the day before Vicksburg surrendered this same reporter was

---

[45] *Chattanooga Daily Rebel*, July 29, 1863. See also *Charleston Daily Courier*, July 17, 1863 for the strange stories about the privations of the garrison told by paroled prisoners.

[46] *Augusta Daily Constitutionalist*, July 26, 1863.

convinced that the garrison's resources for defense were exhausted. Addressing his letter of that date to Editor James Gardner, he announced that the soldiers' rations were exhausted, and went on to say:

I told you we would stay until starved out. Well, rats are a luxury. Small fishes sell at twenty dollars. Chickens at ten dollars each. Corn meal has sold at one hundred and sixty dollars per bushel. Mule meat has sold readily at two dollars per pound, in market, and I eat it once a week. The soldiers have had only one meal a day for ten days, and then one man does not get what a child should have. . . . There will probably be an attempt to cut our way out, but the men cannot walk, much less fight.

I have lately spent considerable time at the lines, and can speak from experience, both of the horrible heat and terrible fire. All the heavy guns captured from us at Snyder's Bluff, Grand Gulf, Port Gibson and Baker's Creek are now in position besides the siege guns of the enemy. I stay in the tent of Col. Barkaloo at the lines, and the shells which pass through the crest of the earthworks pass over the top of his tent just eight inches. As the rush of the huge Parrott shells, which are twenty-two inches long and seven inches thick, can be distinctly heard at a mile's distance, you can imagine the perfect shriek with which the one hundred and thirty pounds of iron rushes by one's head. I have heard them whistle fully as loud as an ordinary locomotive would at a few feet distant.

As to the huge iron orbs of two hundred pounds weight, which yet come by hundreds from the gunboats, they would make a hurricane ashamed of itself.

Several mines have been exploded under our trenches, and while the earth does not produce such terrible results as falling masonry would, still the list of killed and wounded in this way is frightful. Three regiments were blown into the air at once, two days since, by the mining of a long ditch. We countermine all we can, but lack tools and powder. . . .[47]

Seeking a scapegoat for the loss of their vital strong point, Confederate editors engaged in tumultuous controversy over the respective responsibilities of Pemberton and Johnston for the disaster. At first the *Richmond Sentinel*, which was generally regarded as the organ of the Davis administration, was disposed to blame Pemberton,[48] and there were those among the journalistic profession who not simply criticized his military ability but even raised questions about his loyalty to the Confederate cause. Subsequently the *Sentinel* tried to shift the blame to Johnston, but the Confederate press as a whole was more critical of Pemberton than of Johnston, even after the fall of Port Hudson and Jackson only a few days after the capitulation of Vicksburg.

[47] *Ibid.*
[48] *Memphis Daily Appeal*, July 15, 1863.

The Confederate newspapers received their first information of the fall of Port Hudson through Yankee sources in New Orleans. The *Mobile Register* later published detailed accounts of the siege and surrender that were furnished by members of the garrison. Commenting on the first reports of Port Hudson's surrender, the editor of the *Register* stated that he would not have credited them on such doubtful authority, had he not expected the fort to fall "as a sequence to the abominable farce at Vicksburg. We suppose, however, that it is true and that it has succumbed to the same unpardonable causes—the infantile negligence to provision it for a siege of even decent duration. Nothing has happened in the whole war, in which, God knows, there have been official imbecility and blunders enough . . . that appears to us so profoundly disgraceful, reprehensible and injurious as the fall of two such positions as Vicksburg and Port Hudson for the reasons given."[49]

Echoes of the controversy over the loss of Confederate control of the Mississippi River continued to agitate the press for many months. A. S. Abrams, a member of the *Vicksburg Whig* staff who was present at Vicksburg throughout the siege and reported the outcome for the *Mobile Register*, published a book entitled *The Siege of Vicksburg*. In his book Abrams set forth what he regarded as the errors of Confederate strategy, and pinned the blame for the loss of Vicksburg squarely on the shoulders of the general commanding.[50] Most of the soldiers in Pemberton's army probably agreed with Abrams; the result of all the discussion in the press and elsewhere was a harvest of bitterness and misunderstanding.

WHILE reporters in the West were trying to comprehend the Vicksburg drama, newspapermen in Richmond were watching preparations for another test of strength in Virginia. There was uncertainty among the newspapermen attached to Lee's army about the possibility of winter campaigning after the Battle of Fredericksburg. The failure of Gen-

[49] *Mobile Daily Advertiser and Register*, July 14, 1863. The source of the first report of the fall of Port Hudson was the *New Orleans Era* of July 10, 1863. *Daily Richmond Examiner*, July 14, 1863. See also *Atlanta Daily Southern Confederacy*, July 20, 1863.

[50] A. S. Abrams, *The Siege of Vicksburg* (Atlanta, 1863), p. 3. See also *Mobile Daily Advertiser and Register*, July 18, 1863. War correspondent John H. Linebaugh rated Abrams' description of the siege for the *Mobile Register* as the fullest and most intelligent account that had been published. *Memphis Daily Appeal*, July 24, 1863.

eral Burnside's "mud march"[51] during the latter part of January brought *Charleston Courier* reporter de Fontaine scurrying back to Virginia to report any other military operations that might materialize. Three months had elapsed since de Fontaine's previous connection with Lee's Army of Northern Virginia, and he was impressed with what he regarded as its improved health, discipline, and morale. Not finding any military operations in progress, he devoted an interesting letter to one of the comfortable army homes which provided winter quarters for Lee's soldiers.

First then, you alight from your horse in front of a semi-circular enclosure, formed of pine saplings which in itself shuts out the wind. A small opening answers for the gate. As you near the tent there bursts upon you a vision of shirts, drawers, socks, and other articles *ad infinitum*, dangling from the lines and drying in the sunshine. On one side are the quarters of the servants, the stump whereon the prince of the cooking department pounds his steak or minces his hash, an array of saddles and bridles, and finally the green arbor which shelters the animals of the command. Entering the tent you find yourself in a capacious apartment large enough for a city parlor. The clean swept earth is the carpet; a cozy fire sends out its cheering gleams, and gathered round on camp stools, and other improvised articles of furniture, half a dozen gentlemen are discussing pipes, papers, and politics. Over the fire place is a mantel, yet a genuine shelf, not as handsome as marble, but quite as useful, and you there see bags of tobacco, stumps of candles, pens, ink, letters, books, and a small library, including a bottle or two of doctor's stuff. On one of the poles which supports the tent hangs a looking glass; another holds the towels, and still another sustains a comb and brush. The remainder of the toilet department, which is composed of a tin basin and an economical looking piece of soap, reposes snugly in the corner. In another corner, rolled away for the night's use, is the bed and bedding, and in the third is a camp chest and multifarious articles too numerous for mention. In the centre of the apartment, or rather on one side of it, stands a mess table, now a desert without an oasis, but at the hour of dinner as choice a receptacle of edibles, in its way, as ever blessed the optics of a hungry soldier—not that one has anything like luxuries to provoke his appetite, but of good hard, homely fare, such as can be collected in the neighborhood of the army by an industrious forager, there is plenty and some to spare for the sudden guest. Dinner is of course one of the happiest hours in the day. If a man has any fun or talk in him, then is the time that it must come out, and he is an unlucky wight indeed who cannot add his mite to the flow of conversation that is continued in a steady current.

Such is the tent life and surroundings of an officer. The privates are

[51] An unsuccessful attempt by Burnside on January 20-21, 1863 to cross the upper Rappahannock and turn Lee's left flank.

necessarily not all so comfortably fixed, but wherever there is taste there is also an approximation to the domestic associations of a home.[52]

Both "Personne" and the other reporters in camp found material for letter-writing in the various amusements of the soldiers and the religious revivals which were a common feature of camp life at that time. Reporters' letters told about balls, parties, Negro minstrel shows, snowball fights, and bowling at ten pins, making use of bricks for pins and twelve-pound cannon shot for the balls. Verbal byplay, directed indiscriminately at soldiers and civilians, likewise drew the attention of the army newspapermen. A *Richmond Enquirer* reporter told how whenever a civilian with high-crowned hat passed an encampment, a whole chorus of voices would exclaim, "Come out of that hat," "I see your body," "I know you are there," and then would follow such peals of laughter as only soldiers could give vent to.[53]

"Personne" was particularly interested in the thespian activities of the camp, performed in theaters where for fifty cents one could hear as good singing and see as good dancing and burlesque as in any city theater. At a show staged by Jenkins' South Carolina brigade one evening, de Fontaine noted that the performance was housed in a cloth structure, located on a hillside, capable of accommodating 150. The seats were constructed of pine logs, flattened on one side to keep them from rolling. The stage was elevated two or three feet above the ground with a fireplace at each end, a dozen candles constituting the "foot lights," and a tent cloth serving for a curtain. Both officers and privates were the actors; although no lady performers were present at the rehearsal "Personne" attended, he was assured there would be a display of crinoline at the proper time. "I take it for granted there will be no real angels, for specimens of the sex in the army are scarce as hen's teeth. A good looking washer woman has only to pass within a hundred yards of an encampment to call out the whole brigade, who gaze in unmitigated wonder as long as the aparition remains in sight."[54]

The comments visiting newspapermen made about the town of Fredericksburg were tinged with pity and melancholy. Never did a town present such an anomalous aspect, concluded a correspondent of the *Jackson Mississippian*. The life of Fredericksburg civilians had

[52] *Charleston Daily Courier*, February 5, 1863.
[53] *Daily Richmond Enquirer*, January 26, February 28, 1863; *Daily Richmond Examiner*, February 5, 1863.
[54] *Charleston Daily Courier*, February 5, 1863.

returned to normal, even though they, as well as Lee's soldiers, were within speaking distance of the enemy across the Rappahannock and were under the very muzzles of the enemy's guns. Yet the shattered and deserted houses, the lonely sidewalks, and the filthy streets knee-deep in mire could not help but inspire gloomy emotions in a Mississippi newspaperman who was quite possibly of a romantic turn.[55]

The sufferings of the refugees who had fled from the town at the time of the battle of the previous December claimed the attention of the Fredericksburg correspondent of the *Richmond Examiner*. On a tour of the neighborhood he found within a radius of twelve or fifteen miles many former residents of Fredericksburg living in the houses, Negro cabins, and shanties of the area. In some cases as many as four or five families had taken refuge under the same roof, and practically all the refugees were dependent on public charity.[56]

The inactivity of Lee's army during the winter and early spring provided the correspondents with little other than camp routine to write about, and de Fontaine did not remain in camp for more than a few days. Since Congress was then in session at Richmond, that city rather than Fredericksburg became the focus of press activity in the East. Some of the Confederacy's ablest newspaper correspondents were in Richmond at this time, among them Bagby of the *Charleston Mercury*, Thompson of the *Memphis Appeal*, and William G. Shepardson, who joined the *Mobile Register* staff in February 1863. At the end of January a new face appeared on the newspaper scene in the person of Dupré of the *Knoxville Register*. Dupré's knowledgeable reporting soon created a favorable reputation. A Tennessee editor declared that "we have never known any one who had such complete control of his topics, or who handled his subjects with such consummate ability." A feminine fan from Tennessee who signed herself "Jeannie" wrote to him for his photograph.[57] Dupré obliged, jovially passing off the episode as an illustration of the influence of the press.

Bagby, Dupré, and the other Congressional reporters had to contend with the problem that much of the time Congress was in secret session and that when its sessions were public, the reporters frequently had to sit through "long Buncombe speeches" which provided little useful copy. In one of his first letters from the Confederate capital, Dupré

---

[55] *Jackson Daily Mississippian*, April 12, 1863.

[56] *Daily Richmond Examiner*, March 12, 1863.

[57] *Holston Journal* as reprinted in *Knoxville Daily Register*, March 1, 1863; *ibid.*, April 1, 1863.

stated bluntly: "The Congress of the Confederate States is doing nothing. In fact it has very little to do. Were it not for the sake of appearances, and for the purpose of keeping alive the forms of Republicanism, we might very well have our Parliament prorogued till the close of the War. There are but two single questions to come before this Congress which can excite any great interest. The one affects the currency and revenues of the Government, and the other the amendments of the Conscript Act. Both these subjects are now before the House of Representatives, and occasional speeches are delivered. No exhibition of great learning or research has been made, and but little disposition has been evinced to grapple fairly with this question of taxation. Manifold devices have been proposed to *pay* without *paying*, as if the world could be induced to believe that a nominal or apparent payment was a real one, or that a debt was lessened because its shape may be changed. Congressmen are still politicians of the old school. They think oftener of the propriety of a vote, as this may affect their own popularity, than of the advantageous or unfortunate results of any measure, when it has assumed the shape of a congressional enactment. They are patriots, nevertheless, who care not to sacrifice their popularity while promoting the end of patriotism."[58]

Confederate congressmen were no more prone than generals to relish candor on the part of upstart newspapermen. Such a veteran of the political wars as Congressman Charles M. Conrad of Louisiana, who had held cabinet rank under President Fillmore, was a particularly troublesome critic of the Confederate press. During the latter part of January, in connection with a debate on the Exemption bill, Conrad expressed the opinion that there was no need to exempt newspaper editors from conscription, since a man over forty-five could very well edit a newspaper. In fact, he thought the South could do without newspapers for six months. He added that if called on to make a sworn statement as to whether newspapers had done more harm or good during the war, he would hardly know what to say, although he believed that they had actually done more harm than good.[59] Confederate edi-

---

[58] *Ibid.*, January 23, 1863. For an interesting discussion of the various personalities in the lower house of the Confederate Congress at this time see the reprint of a Richmond letter to the *Fayetteville* (N.C.) *Observer* in *Charleston Daily Courier*, March 3, 1863.

[59] *Vicksburg Daily Whig*, February 4, 1863. No reference to the remarks of Congressman Conrad about the press appears in the Journal of the Confederate Congress during the month of January 1863.

tors reacted with predictable spleen to Conrad's disparaging remarks about their profession. They also quoted with approval the statement of Senator Hill of Georgia, recommending that war correspondents be included among the gentlemen of the press whose exemption from military service was being urged by Senator William L. Yancey of Alabama.[60]

Indicative of the animus of other congressmen toward the press was a clash between Senator Albert G. Brown of Mississippi and Reporter George C. Stedman of the *Richmond Enquirer* in February 1863. Senator Brown, like Conrad, had objected vigorously to exempting newspapermen from conscription. Also, Brown took umbrage at a statement in Stedman's report of one of the Senate debates accusing him of making a bid for popularity. Subsequently, on the floor of the Senate, the senator attacked the press, and especially the Senate reporters, whom he stigmatized as incompetent and unworthy of the name of reporters. Stedman, who had the reputation of being the best shorthand reporter in the South, retaliated by appending to his report of that day's proceedings a piquant and telling reply.[61]

Stedman's spunky action placed Senator Brown on the defensive. Brown denied he had said that the press was no better than a "grocery," and signified that his reflections on the reporters were to be construed in a Pickwickian sense. At this point, however, Senator Wigfall of Texas kept the controversy going by submitting a motion for an inquiry into the privileges extended to congressional reporters. The result of the inquiry was that the committee which conducted it recommended the expulsion of the *Enquirer* reporter from the floor of the Senate, and

[60] *Mobile Daily Advertiser and Register*, March 3, 1863; *Savannah Republican*, March 7, 1863; *Charleston Daily Courier*, March 7, 1863; *Atlanta Daily Southern Confederacy*, March 14, 1863. Dupré held that it was unwise of the Southern press to assail Congressman Conrad because of his attacks on the newspaper industry. "He has the advantage of us—his game is a deep one—see how it will result. He will go before his constituents and tell them that he only wished to send preachers and editors to where their sons and husbands are, in the army. Neither the preacher nor editor can answer him. Then to cap the climax of demagogueism he will tell the soldiers and their kindred that he sought to distribute among them the public lands. Who can meet him on the stump? Who can answer such an appeal to the people? It were well to say nothing of the gentleman from Louisiana. He has the vantage ground and will use it. . . ." *Knoxville Daily Register*, February 22, 1863.

[61] *Memphis Daily Appeal*, March 7, 1863; J. B. Ranck, *Albert Gallatin Brown, Radical Southern Nationalist* (New York, 1937), pp. 224-27.

the committee's recommendation was adopted by a large majority.[62]

When news about Congress and the executive branch of the government became scarce Richmond reporters sought material for special correspondence in the hardships of life in the Confederate capital. Dupré was astonished when he arrived in Richmond in January 1863 not to hear any allusion to the war by people in the streets or at the railroad stations. He noticed that everyone he encountered seemed intent on making money and that the shops of the merchants were filled with goods. "The hotels are filled, and restaurants abound with guests. A single meal at one of these establishments—a beef steak, one dozen oysters, and coffee—costs five dollars. . . . The hotels charge from $5 to $7 per diem. Apples cost 25 cents each, and while I am writing this in the gallery of the House of Representatives, a gentleman is making a speech on government finances."[63]

During this same month of January de Fontaine found Richmond overflowing with people of all kinds: refugees, speculators "thick as locusts," gamblers, courtesans, transient visitors, blushing brides, ecstatic bridegrooms, members of Congress, representatives in the State Legislature, department clerks, "officers of no account," and "officers *in transitu.*" He was amazed by the tight military discipline to which the presence of a provost guard at every street corner attested. Everyone who walked the streets was expected to give an account of himself; "Personne" was amused at the jokes sharp-witted individuals practiced on illiterate soldiers. He told in his correspondence about a gentleman who handed the guard an old sugar receipt in lieu of a pass and was permitted to "pass on"; and about the soldier who exclaimed, "My stars, why that's the pootiest pass I seen yet—Government's comin' out, ain't it?" when he received a printed slip from the local telegraph office.[64]

---

[62] *Memphis Daily Appeal,* March 21, 1863; *Charleston Daily Courier,* March 12, 1863; *Mobile Daily Advertiser and Register,* March 20, 1863; *Journal of the Congress of the Confederate States of America,* III, 100, 154, 156-57. The *Memphis Appeal* correspondent, in defense of Stedman, alleged that if the speeches made on the floor of any legislative body were printed in the newspapers verbatim, many legislators who were reported to be orators would fare very badly in the public eye. "The reporter makes the speech presentable, clothes the speaker in good grammatical apparel, mends the unseemly rents that too often appear in his poetical quotations, and not infrequently gives the outward seeming of sense to the boldest and most disjointed nonsense." *Memphis Daily Appeal,* March 21, 1863.

[63] *Knoxville Daily Register,* January 22, 1863.

[64] *Charleston Daily Courier,* February 5, 1863.

By March Dupré was reporting that government clerks in Richmond were receiving $5 a day or less at a time when the Ballard House was charging its boarders $8 a day. "At such a salary, a man can have only two-thirds of the fare furnished at Ballard House, and must go naked when his present stock of clothing is worn out. Not a few of the government employees are looking seedy. The Spotswood will soon close its doors. Many of the private boarding houses have suspended, and nothing is more common than disconsolate looking Congressmen, ejected from exhausted *tables d'hotes*, prowling through the city seeking a spot where food and sleep may reinvigorate their wearied souls."[65]

In a letter from Richmond written on March 5, the *Memphis Appeal* correspondent Thompson reported the existence of a "somewhat senseless panic" in the city for the past several days. The panic was caused by an order of the secretary of war calling for the seizure of every barrel of flour in Richmond for the use of the commissary department of the army. When a month later Richmond women took part in a bread riot of major proportions, Thompson denied that there was any justification for it, and the War Department imposed censorship on the transmission by wire of any news about the outbreak.[66]

Military censorship also discouraged any discussion by reporters or their editors of the logistic problems of Lee's army during the late winter and early spring of 1863. In February Lee sent Longstreet to Richmond with two divisions to counter a Federal troop movement down the Potomac. Meanwhile lack of forage for the army's horses and the shortage of provisions for the soldiers became such serious problems that Lee made appeal after appeal to Commissary General Lucius C. Northrop. When nothing came of these appeals, Lee sent Longstreet on a commissary campaign into eastern North Carolina, where a large volume of bacon and other provisions was known to be available.[67]

[65] *Knoxville Daily Register*, March 19, 1863.
[66] *Memphis Daily Appeal*, March 12, April 11, 1863; *O.R.* (Army) Ser. I, vol. xviii, p. 958; Jno. Withers A.A.G. to Prest. W. S. Morris, April 2, 1863, Southern Telegraph Co. Papers, Carnegie Library of Pittsburgh. Withers likewise requested the Richmond press to suppress any news about the incident. For a recent version of the Richmond bread riot see W. J. Kimball, "The Bread Riot in Richmond, 1863," *Civil War History*, VII (June 1961), 149-54. To judge from the Columbus *Daily Sun* of April 26, 1863, vandalism, unrelated to any food shortage, of a similar nature to the Richmond outbreak had already taken place in Augusta, Columbus, and Milledgeville, Georgia.
[67] D. S. Freeman, *R. E. Lee, A Biography* (New York, 1935), II, 483, 491-95, 500.

On March 19, 1863 the Richmond newspapers carried wire stories of a spectacular cavalry fight at Kelly's Ford on the upper Rappahannock between Fitzhugh Lee's mounted brigade and 3,000 Federal horsemen. Although the official reports on both sides were at wide variance in their interpretations of the results, the Confederate press generally classed the affair as a Southern victory. The alleged victory was flawed, however, by the death of Maj. John Pelham, one of the most promising artillery officers in the Confederate army. Reporter Thompson used the opportunity to contribute to the *Memphis Appeal* a sentimental but moving description of the "gallant Pelham" lying in state in the hall of the Capitol at Richmond, and Maj. John Esten Cooke later supplied the *Richmond Illustrated News* with a memorial sketch of Pelham's career.[68]

There were increasing signs during April of preparations for another Federal offensive against Richmond. On April 17 the *Enquirer* printed an editorial which made it appear that "Fighting Joe" Hooker, Burnside's successor as commander of the Army of the Potomac, was planning to move his army to the York River to duplicate McClellan's great maneuvre of March 1862. Neither Lee nor the Richmond correspondent of the *Memphis Appeal* believed the story, and indeed, it was without basis. Instead, with a magnificent army of 130,000 men, Hooker was planning to throw a huge flanking column across the Rappahannock and Rapidan Rivers upstream and then march eastward to cut in behind Lee's left wing and sever his connection with Richmond.[69]

At 5:30 on Wednesday morning, April 29, the sound of church bells awakened the Fredericksburg correspondent of the *Richmond Dispatch*, apprising him of an enemy movement. After breakfasting satisfactorily on Potomac shad, the reporter spent an hour checking all his available sources of information in Fredericksburg. Hearing reports that the Yankees had crossed the river two miles below town, the *Dispatch* reporter made a reconnaissance of his own along the Telegraph Road and on the hills back of the town. On Willis's hill near Marye's Heights, he saw his old legislative friend Charley Grattan wheeling artillery into position. At intervals a game rooster perched on a caisson crowed

[68] *Memphis Daily Appeal*, March 31, 1863. For Cooke's emotional description of the death of the "gallant Pelham" see Philip Van Doren Stern, ed., *Wearing of the Gray* (Bloomington, 1959), pp. 116-29; statement of John R. Thompson in *Memphis Daily Appeal*, August 3, 1863.
[69] Catton, *Never Call Retreat*, p. 146.

lustily, and the reporter avowed his conviction that the artillery men were like the rooster—all game.[70]

There were no further signs of military activity near Fredericksburg that day, but about ten o'clock that morning this same reporter heard that the Yankees had crossed the Rappahannock in large numbers above Kelly's Ford, that the crossing below Fredericksburg was only a feint; the main fight would be above. That evening a member of the *Richmond Examiner's* editorial staff inquired at the War Department what news they had about military developments along the Rappahannock. The reply, "they had got nothing," brought the reply: "What a wonderful Government that it never receives any dispatches from its armies!" The next day Thompson informed the *Appeal* that the *London Times* correspondent Francis E. Lawley had left Richmond to go to the front, "being specially favored by the authorities with freedom of locomotion within the lines."[71]

While Richmond anxiously awaited more definite information about what was happening to Lee's army, Maj.Gen. George Stoneman's Federal cavalry raiders cut the telegraph line between Fredericksburg and Richmond and got close enough to Richmond to precipitate a wild panic. The *Memphis Appeal* correspondent heard wild rumors in Richmond on Saturday night and Sunday morning. Excitement was increased by the knowledge that a great battle had begun somewhere near Fredericksburg and that a train filled with wounded soldiers was expected in the city sometime Sunday afternoon. The climax came at six that evening when the crowd of four or five thousand who had assembled at the railroad station to look for the train learned that it had been captured earlier that day at Ashland, seventeen miles north of Richmond. A telegraph operator and an engineer who left the next morning with an engine and tender to repair the telegraph line narrowly escaped capture and returned to the city on foot during the afternoon.[72]

What Richmond did not yet know was that Lee had responded magnificently to the threat of destruction posed by Hooker's well-planned

[70] *Richmond Daily Dispatch*, May 1, 1863.

[71] *Ibid.*, May 2, 1863; *Daily Richmond Examiner*, April 30, 1863; *Memphis Daily Appeal*, May 7, 1863. Lawley's eight long letters from Guiney's Station and three from Richmond, reporting the Chancellorsville campaign ran to eleven full columns in the *London Times*, or almost fifteen thousand words. W. S. Hoole, *Lawley Covers the Confederacy* (Tuscaloosa, 1964), p. 51.

[72] *Memphis Daily Appeal*, May 11, 1863; *Daily Richmond Examiner*, May 4, 5, 1863.

movement. On Thursday night, April 30, Hooker was at Chancellors-ville with a force of 50,000; 22,000 Northern troops were on their way to join him. At Falmouth, across from Fredericksburg, Maj.Gen. John Sedgwick had 47,000 more soldiers to distract Lee's attention. By this time, however, Lee realized that the real threat was from the direction of Chancellorsville. With an army of not more than 60,000 he might have been expected to retreat in haste. Instead he left Maj.Gen. Jubal A. Early with 10,000 men on the line of Marye's Heights to contain Sedgwick, and with the remainder of his army marched toward Chancellorsville to meet Hooker.

Instead of continuing to advance, Hooker took a defensive position and awaited an attack—which was a challenge Lee was willing to accept. At a campfire meeting on Friday evening, May 1, Lee and Stonewall Jackson decided to avoid a costly frontal assault and send Jackson off the next morning with the major part of the army to strike the unprotected right flank of Hooker's army.

No one who knew "Old Stonewall" doubted that the hazardous movement would succeed. Peter Alexander had already made sure of Jackson's place in the pantheon of Confederate heroes. In an article published in the *Southern Literary Messenger* early in 1863, Alexander portrayed Jackson as a figure of rather undistinguished mien and manner, looking in repose like an ordinary farmer or country schoolmaster. "But place him on the battle-field—let the cannon begin to thunder, the small arms to rattle, and the sabres to flash in the sunlight—and the quiet farmer, the awkward, calculating pedagogue, becomes a hero . . . full of fire and energy, quick as lightning and terrible as the thunderbolt. . . ." Alexander went on to say that there was some difference of opinion among military men about Jackson's talents as a strategist but none whatsoever about his ability as a fighter. "In his battles he has been attended with a larger degree of success than any officer in the army. He is the idol of the people, and is the object of greater enthusiasm than any other military chieftain of our day. And this, too, notwithstanding the fact that he marches his troops faster and longer, fights them harder, and takes less care of them than any other officer in the service. Indeed, some go so far as to say that if he had no enemy to encounter, and nothing to do but march his troops about the country, he would yet lose one-third of them in the course of a year. This indifference to the comfort of his men is only apparent, however —not real. No man possesses a kinder heart or larger humanity; but when he has anything to do, he is so earnest, so ardent and energetic that he loses sight of everything but the work before him. If, for example, he were required to move his corps from Fredericksburg to Richmond and had two weeks to do it in, he would be almost sure to perform the march in four days, or one-fifth of the time, because he does not know how to do anything slowly."

Alexander attributed to this bold fighter only one weakness, which related to his feeling about his middle name. His admirers generally supposed that his complete name was Thomas Jefferson Jackson, but this was not so, Alexander made clear. "What, then, do you suppose it is, reader? Why *Jonathan*! the name (Uncle Jonathan) by which the United States are personified. The General does not want it to get out that he bears any such name, and it is hoped, Mr. Editor, that your readers will say nothing about it."[73]

Regardless of Jackson's middle name his flanking movement was spectacularly successful. About five o'clock on Saturday afternoon, with a force of 28,000-30,000 men, he rolled up the Union Eleventh Corps on the right wing of the Army of the Potomac, driving it back into the Chancellorsville clearing. In the confusion of the night fighting, Jackson got in front of a North Carolina regiment that was expecting an attack and was shot by his own men.[74]

The army correspondent of the *Richmond Whig*, Richard J. Yarington, had gone up the river from Chancellorsville that day to observe the fighting in what he correctly guessed to be the main conflict. During the night he started back to Fredericksburg, arriving there about ten Sunday morning. As he was in the process of writing up the events of the previous day, his work was interrupted by the sound of sharp skirmishing between Hazel Run and the town. Going out to investigate, he learned that the Confederate pickets had received orders to fall back from the river to the heights behind Fredericksburg and that the enemy was then in the process of crossing the river in front of the town. Returning about three o'clock in the afternoon to the heights where Early's men were posted, Yarington discovered a Yankee brigade advancing on the Confederate works. After eluding them and reaching the Confederate lines by a circuitous route, he took up a position at the "Stone Wall" on Marye's Hill which had been so important in the

---

[73] P. W. Alexander, "Confederate Chieftains," *Southern Literary Messenger*, xxxv (January 1863), 36-37.

[74] Foote, *Civil War: Fredericksburg to Meridian*, pp. 282-87, 292-98.

Battle of Fredericksburg the preceding December and spent the night there. He described in his report what happened next:

"At the first grey streaks of dawn, the enemy were discovered drawn up in line of battle on this side of the canal, which they had crossed in the darkness, and their skirmishers thrown out and confronting ours. Barksdale's Mississippians occupied the position behind the Stone Wall and some distance to the right and left, but without any support in the rear. Presently the enemy began to advance to the attack and the lines of skirmishers were soon sharply engaged. Finding the minnie balls whistling rather uncomfortably around him, your correspondent withdrew to a position in less dangerous proximity. Presently the main body advanced in beautiful order, and when within proper distance were greeted with a volley from our men behind the Stone Wall which caused them to turn and flee in every direction. About forty or fifty fell at the first fire. They rallied and again advanced to the attack, delivered their fire and again fled before the fire of our men. This was repeated a third time."[75]

About eleven o'clock, according to Yarington, a large enemy column succeeded in flanking the right of the Confederate defense line and forced them to withdraw from the heights to another defense line about a mile away. Yarington's narrow escape from capture was similar to the experience of the other correspondents of the Richmond press who were in Fredericksburg at this time. The *Richmond Dispatch* reporter ascribed his deliverance to the crippled condition of his feet which had prevented him from returning to the town on the Saturday night that the Yankees occupied Fredericksburg.[76]

The movement of Sedgwick's command that Yarington had witnessed had been the result of peremptory orders from Hooker's headquarters to occupy Fredericksburg and advance west along the road to Chancellorsville to join Hooker. A reporter for the *Richmond Enquirer* had been an eyewitness of the heavy fighting around Chancellorsville on Sunday when the two wings of Lee's army stormed Hooker's well-fortified position. They marched across open fields in the face of both direct and enfilading fire from artillery protected by earthworks. In his excitement the *Enquirer* reporter boasted, "I have never during the whole war seen so strong a position carried so quickly and with so

[75] *Richmond Daily Whig*, May 8, 1863.
[76] *Richmond Daily Dispatch*, May 11, 1863.

little loss."[77] Having already driven Hooker's main army back toward the river from the Chancellorsville clearing, Lee took the risk of dividing his army again, sending the major portion east to meet Sedgwick. At Salem Church six miles east of Chancellorsville, the Confederate force defeated Sedgwick on May 3, and the following day forced him to retreat across Banks Ford to the north bank of the Rappahannock. Then reuniting his army, Lee intimidated Hooker into recrossing the river, thereby bringing to an end the Northern invasion attempt.[78]

The first authentic information about the battle that Richmond received was in the form of an official dispatch from General Lee to President Davis which the Richmond newspapers published on Tuesday morning, May 5. Up till then the Richmond office of the Confederate Press Association had been unable to obtain any news from the battlefield, since telegraphic communication between Fredericksburg and Richmond was not restored until sometime later that day.[79] Lee's dispatch stated that Jackson had penetrated to the rear of the enemy and that the enemy had been dislodged from all his positions around Chancellorsville and driven back to the Rappahannock. It also revealed that Jackson had been "severely" wounded. Richmond correspondent Bagby was impressed by the fact that Lee had reported a "great victory" and that he had never used the word "great" in any previous dispatches.[80]

During the next few days the Richmond press gave further information about what they rated as one of the greatest victories of the war. In their news columns were to be found the usual exaggerated claims of enemy losses, coupled with underestimates of Confederate casualties.[81] There were complaints, nevertheless, by editors and other news-

---

[77] *Daily Richmond Enquirer*, May 11, 1863.

[78] Catton, *Never Call Retreat*, pp. 155-56.

[79] *Wilmington Daily Journal*, May 4, 1863; *Richmond Daily Whig*, May 6, 1863.

[80] *Charleston Mercury*, May 9, 1863.

[81] Sener's account of Chancellorsville, published in the *Enquirer* of May 8, 1863, estimated the Confederate loss at 5,000, compared with enemy losses of 25,000. The Richmond *Enquirer* correspondent "A." estimated the enemy's loss in killed and wounded at 15,000 to 20,000 and reported 10,000 prisoners. Official estimates of the losses on both sides are Union, 17,287, Confederate, 10,281. *O.R.* (Army) Ser. I, vol. xxv, pt. 1, pp. 192, 809. But the historian James Ford Rhodes, *History of the U.S. from the Compromise of 1850* (New York, 1910), iv, 264, places the Confederate loss at 12,463. For an accusation of lying on the part of the Confederate press about the number of guns captured from the enemy see J. B. Jones, *A Rebel War Clerk's Diary* (Philadelphia, 1866), i, 323.

papermen about the lack of authentic information concerning the battle;[82] from one of the Lynchburg newspapers the president of the Southern Telegraph Company received a vigorous complaint about inefficient news handling by the Lynchburg office of the company. Editor Glass said in his letter to President Morris: "I am sorry to have to complain to you of the manner in which your office is conducted here. On Friday last an important dispatch about matters at Fredericksburg was sent to the Virginian, & not to us. On Saturday night another came about a cavalry fight at Chancellorsville, & it was not sent to us until Sunday morning, too late for our paper. In the first case they say that they neglected to make a copy & in the next they can give no explanation at all. These grievances occur frequently or I would not complain. The fact is you have not a competent man in this office. There is not one of them who can write half as good as your little son."[83]

The Press Association reports of the Battle of Chancellorsville drew heavily on the news columns of the Richmond papers, especially the *Enquirer*. Much of the news about Chancellorsville published in the Richmond newspapers was reprinted in turn from the Northern press. Objecting to the "ridiculously and pitifully false accounts" of the battle that came to him in this form, the editor of the *Augusta Constitutionalist* refused to authenticate them by permitting them to appear in his newspaper.[84]

Probably the best battle accounts of Chancellorsville that appeared in the Confederate press were those furnished to the *Richmond Enquirer* by its special correspondent James B. Sener and a second reporter (possibly J. W. Albertson) who signed himself "A." Since the correspondents of the various Richmond newspapers were at Fredericksburg before the battle, they tended to report the fighting of Early's command in greater detail than the main action in front of Chancellorsville. Sener offered as an excuse for any deficiencies in his reporting the circumstance that although he had been attached to Lee's army for nearly six months as a newspaper correspondent, he had never

[82] On May 14, 1863 the *Richmond Sentinel* stated editorially: ". . . the details of the information received through our own sources have not been as lucid and accurate as usual. We know but little comparatively with certainty, save the grand results as communicated in Gen Lee's official dispatches." For further evidence on this point see the comments of Reporter Shepardson ("Evelyn") in *Mobile Daily Advertiser and Register*, May 19, 1863.

[83] R. H. Glass to Dr. William S. Morris, May 4, 1863, Southern Telegraph Co. Papers.

[84] *Augusta Daily Constitutionalist*, May 14, 1863.

been invited to any corps headquarters, and had been present only twice at divisional headquarters, "and at only one of these by invitation. Yet the correspondent of the London 'Times,' who is writing for the English people, is specially invited to our general headquarters, where he is able to gather many items that would be doubtless interesting to those who are sustaining this war by the blood of their first born and their patrimonial inheritance."[85]

Stung by insinuations by Confederate reporters that he had been at fault in leaving Marye's Hill inadequately defended, General Early entered the columns of the *Richmond Enquirer* in his own defense. Early objected to "the statements of correspondents ignorant of the real facts or writing in the interests of particular commands," and claimed that he had sent two brigades to Brig.Gen. William Barksdale's support at the time of the successful Yankee assault on May 3.[86] Interpreting Early's remark as a reflection on him, Barksdale in turn wrote a letter to the *Enquirer*, declaring that Early's statement about correspondents writing in the interest of particular commands was unfounded so far as his own brigade was concerned, and vigorously defended the performance of his Mississippi troops.[87] The editor of the *Richmond Enquirer*, perhaps suspecting that his paper was the target of Early's complaints, denied that any errors appearing in the *Enquirer*'s reports of the battle were the product of any cause other than ignorance of the true facts. The correspondent of the *Richmond Dispatch*, on the other hand, accused Early of "poking his head into a hornet's nest" and of concealing the fact that he had posted only one or two regiments to hold the line occupied by an entire brigade at the Battle of Fredericksburg.[88]

Once more sectional jealousy was reflected in editorial criticism of the battle reporting. The *Wilmington* (N.C.) *Journal* accused the

[85] *Daily Richmond Enquirer*, May 18, 1863. The *Montgomery Daily Mail*, May 12, 1863 viewed Sener's account, elsewhere reprinted in the *Mail*, as "the fullest and best description of the battle of Chancellorsville which has reached us from Richmond."

[86] *Daily Richmond Enquirer*, May 12, 1863; Jubal A. Early to Messrs. Editors May 11, 1863, Jubal A. Early to the Editors of the [Richmond] *Enquirer*, May 19, 1863, Jubal A. Early Papers, Library of Congress.

[87] Letters of Barksdale to the Editors of the Richmond *Enquirer* as reprinted in *Richmond Daily Dispatch*, May 21, 1863. See also comments of a *Jackson Mississippian* correspondent in the May 29, 1863 issue of that paper.

[88] *Daily Richmond Enquirer*, May 12, 1863; *Richmond Daily Dispatch*, May 15, 1863.

Richmond Enquirer of not doing justice to the North Carolina troops at Chancellorsville, and the *Savannah Republican* complained that during a period of three weeks after the battle, "we have not seen the casualties of a single Georgia regiment in a Virginia paper."[89]

Because of a general feeling that the performance of the special correspondents at Chancellorsville had not been satisfactory, several newspapers sent their best correspondents to the battlefield after the battle to reconstruct accounts of the fighting from interviews with participants. The four-column account of Chancellorsville, based in part on the *Richmond Enquirer* accounts which Peter Alexander prepared for the *Savannah Republican* and the *Mobile Register*, was not published for nearly a month after the battle. For similar reasons Sam Reid came up from Tennessee to Fredericksburg in late May to put together a connected account of the fighting for the *Atlanta Intelligencer*.[90]

In his battle story of Chancellorsville *Enquirer* reporter Sener described the circumstances of the wounding of Jackson as they were communicated to him by Capt. R. E. Wilbourn of General Jackson's staff. Sener told how the messenger who brought the news of Jackson's wound to General Lee found the general on a bed of straw about four o'clock in the morning and how Lee exclaimed, when informed of what had occurred, "Thank God it is no worse; God be praised that he is still alive."[91] Yet apparently no newspaper reporter was an eyewitness of either the wounding of Jackson or his death on May 10.

The news of Jackson's death caused newspapers throughout the Confederacy to drape their editorial columns in mourning, and prompted the editor of the *Knoxville Register* to write: "Would that the battle of Chancellorsville had never have been fought if the brilliant victory have [*sic*] cost us the life of Stonewall Jackson."[92] The Confederate Associated Press reported the presence of "an immense concourse of people" along Broad Street and on Capitol Square when the special train carrying Jackson's body arrived in Richmond on Monday afternoon, May

[89] *Wilmington Daily Journal*, May 25, 1863; *Savannah Republican*, May 25, 1863.

[90] *Savannah Republican*, June 3, 1863; *Mobile Daily Advertiser and Register*, June 7, 1863; *Atlanta Daily Intelligencer*, May 30, 1863.

[91] *Daily Richmond Enquirer*, May 14, 1863.

[92] *Knoxville Daily Register*, May 12, 1863. For the impressions of one of the editors of the *Richmond Whig* about the impact of Jackson's death on the public see Thomas L. Bondurant to Alexander Bondurant, May 13, 1863, Thomas Bondurant Papers, Alderman Library, University of Virginia.

11.[93] The solemn pageant of Jackson lying in state in the Capitol building in Richmond and the removal by another special train of the body
to Lexington for burial were the theme of many somber news stories.

One of the most interesting specimens of reporting the sequel of the
Chancellorsville fight was the *Mobile Register* correspondent Shepardson's account of the arrival of the first Yankee prisoners in Richmond.
Shepardson observed that whereas before the citizens of Richmond had
been prone to treat prisoners with a great deal of courtesy and consideration, on this occasion there was a tendency to insult and hurt
them as they were marched through the streets of the city. Shepardson thought the death of Jackson contributed to the bitter feeling. In
the midst of the shouts of derision coming from every side, a voice
from the crowd wanted to know: "What has Hooker got now?" From
one of the prisoners: "Jackson's *left* arm!"[94]

The Confederate press's reporting of the Chancellorsville campaign
had not been commensurate with the opportunity such a splendid victory offered. It was journalism's misfortune that neither of the Confederacy's two greatest reporters was present at the battle and that Sener
was not provided with the entree at Lee's headquarters that would have
enabled him to obtain a broader perspective of the whole operation.
Whereas Lee and Jackson made effective use of the advantages which
Hooker's loss of nerve put within their grasp, the reporting of the
Confederacy's major achievement of 1863 was, with the possible exception of the *Enquirer*'s performance, a tale of misspent opportunities.

[93] *Augusta Daily Constitutionalist*, May 12, 1863.
[94] *Mobile Daily Advertiser and Register*, May 17, 1863.

CHAPTER 10

"Is Gettysburg Another Antietam?"

IT WAS MAY 15, 1863. In his hotel room in the Confederate capital, the Richmond correspondent of the *Atlanta Southern Confederacy* was writing a routine letter to his newspaper. He concluded his letter with a prediction: "I incline to the opinion that Gen. Lee contemplates crossing the Potomac and letting the cursed cowardly nation of swindlers and theives know something of a war of invasion. My reason for this opinion I reserve for the present."[1] The newspaperman from Atlanta may have been making a wild guess. It is just possible, however, that he knew Lee was in Richmond to confer with President Davis and his cabinet about problems of overall military strategy.

Official circles in Richmond were well aware that the military situation in the southwest was fraught with danger. Secretary of War Seddon wanted Lee to send troops from Virginia to the relief of Vicksburg, but Lee was convinced that in an effort to save Mississippi, Virginia would be sacrificed, perhaps forever. His counterproposal was a second invasion of the North to be carried out by his victorious Army of Northern Virginia. With the prestige of his spectacular successes at Fredericksburg and Chancellorsville weighing heavily in his favor, Lee's persuasion carried the debate. And so Lee returned to his headquarters on the Rappahannock three days later to prepare for the march into Pennsylvania.[2] Perhaps other Richmond newspapermen had access to the same informed sources as the *Atlanta Confederacy* reporter probably had. At any rate, one of their number, Shepardson of the *Mobile Register*, predicted not long afterward that "in less than thirty days our army will besiege Washington."[3]

Lee reorganized his army establishing three corps, each comprised of three divisions. The three corps commanders were Longstreet, Ewell,

---

[1] *Atlanta Daily Southern Confederacy,* May 21, 1863.

[2] Shelby Foote, *The Civil War, A Narrative: Fredericksburg to Meridian* (New York, 1963), pp. 431-33; R. W. Winston, *High Stakes and Hair Trigger; The Life of Jefferson Davis* (New York, 1930), p. 216.

[3] *Mobile Daily Advertiser and Register,* June 3, 1863. Shepardson's letter was dated May 26. According to the *Wilmington Journal* of May 30, 1863, the Richmond papers had given abundant warning for several days that Lee was about to undertake an important movement.

and A. P. Hill (whom Lee regarded as his best division commander). The effective strength of Lee's army in round numbers was about 75,000 (60,000 infantry, 10,000 cavalry, and 5,000 artillery). On June 3, just four days after the reorganization was announced, Lee started the first contingents of his army along the south bank of the Rappahannock toward Culpeper, the concentration point for his northward advance.[4]

On June 7 Lee joined Longstreet and Ewell at Culpeper; four days later the Richmond press printed front-page stories about a cavalry fight at Brandy Station, only six miles from Culpeper. These accounts fostered the impression that Stuart, the Confederate cavalry leader, had been disgracefully surprised and out-generalled, that his headquarters had been fired on before the enemy's presence was even suspected, and that his troops had narrowly escaped disaster. These reports were not very wide of the mark. Supported by two brigades of infantry, a new Union cavalry commander, Maj.Gen. Alfred Pleasanton, had moved up the Rappahannock from Falmouth on June 8 with a cavalry force equal in strength to Stuart's. The next morning he had crossed the river at Beverly's and Kelly's Fords under cover of a heavy fog and surprised the Confederate pickets, driving them back to Brandy Station. After hard fighting that continued all day, the attacking force withdrew the same way it had come, having suffered greater losses than those inflicted. Stuart's greatest loss was his pride; the experience also made him aware that the spectacular raids behind the enemy's lines on which he prided himself were going to be more difficult in the future.[5]

Army correspondent Alexander was only less irritated than Stuart by the expansive accounts of the "surprise" that appeared in the Richmond newspapers on the second morning after the fight. After wiring from Culpeper the general facts about the engagement, Alexander discovered that the telegraphic censor in Richmond had suppressed that part of his telegram relating to the surprise. He sarcastically suggested that "to be consistent the Government should establish a censorship over the mailbags, over the railway trains, and over the minds and tongues of men; for there was scarcely a letter sent from the army the day after the battle that did not admit the surprise, nor was there an

---

[4] Foote, *Civil War: Fredericksburg to Meridian*, pp. 434-436; D. S. Freeman, *R. E. Lee, A Biography* (New York, 1935), III, 8-15.
[5] Foote, *Civil War: Fredericksburg to Meridian*, pp. 437-38; Burke Davis, *Jeb Stuart, The Last Cavalier* (New York, 1957), pp. 305-10.

individual, white or black, who left here by the railroad, who had not heard of it and who would not speak of it."[6]

Leading Richmond correspondents Bagby, Thompson, and Shepardson did not hesitate to blame Stuart personally for his troops having been "disgracefully surprised," alleging that his head had been turned by the adulation of the ladies and newspaper praise. They also regaled their readers with stories (probably fictitious) of Stuart and his officers having been present at a ball in Culpeper on the night before the battle and of their having been summoned from the festivities to the field of combat.[7]

Stuart thought he detected malice in his treatment by the press. A few days before the battle a correspondent from one of the Richmond papers appeared at Stuart's headquarters. He wanted to accompany the cavalry in the next campaign, "which," wrote the general to his wife, "I politely declined. He returns tomorrow with a flea in his ear. Look to see me abused for it." When after the battle, a cavalry staff officer who styled himself "Veritas" presented Stuart's side of the controversy to the *Richmond Examiner*, there were those who thought that "Veritas" was none other than Stuart himself.[8]

Stuart's humiliation affected the timetable of Lee's invasion movement little if at all. As part of the invasion plan Ewell's Second Corps, preceded by a brigade of cavalry, marched north on the day after the fight at Brandy Station, entering the Shenandoah Valley by way of Chester Gap. Longstreet followed, marching northward east of the Blue Ridge to screen the passes, while Hill waited for Hooker to evacuate the line of the Rappahannock before he left Fredericksburg to follow Ewell up the valley. Stuart's mission was to cover the right flank of Lee's army and keep Hooker from knowing what Lee was doing.[9]

With three reporters attached to Lee's army, the *Savannah Republi-*

---

[6] *Mobile Daily Advertiser and Register*, June 19, 1863. During the Pennsylvania campaign Alexander reported from Lee's army for the *Savannah Republican* and the *Mobile Register*.

[7] *Charleston Mercury*, June 17, 1863; *Memphis Daily Appeal*, June 15, 1863; *Mobile Daily Advertiser and Register*, June 19, 1863. For similar charges against Stuart by a volunteer correspondent of the *Mobile Register* who was attached to Ewell's (infantry) corps see *Mobile Daily Advertiser and Register*, June 30, 1863. For a defense of Stuart against these charges see Charles Brewer to the Editor of the *Charleston Courier*, June 24, 1863, J.E.B. Stuart Papers, Huntington Library.

[8] J. W. Thomason, Jr., *Jeb Stuart* (New York, 1930), pp. 409-10.

[9] Foote, *Civil War: Fredericksburg to Meridian*, pp. 439-41; Thomason, *Jeb Stuart*, p. 418.

can was in the best position of all the Confederate newspapers to report the invasion. Writing from "In the Mountains, Va." on June 16, a *Republican* correspondent, Capt. Parks, who was accompanying Maj.Gen. John B. Hood's division of Longstreet's corps, told about leaving Culpeper the day before and marching twenty miles "under the hottest sun we have ever yet sweltered." He further reported that several soldiers (the number was variously estimated at five to fifteen) had died from the intense heat. As Longstreet's corps continued its march by way of Markham Station and Upperville, Parks rhapsodized in his correspondence about the incomparable beauty of the region through which they were passing, with its "deep shady dells and green hills . . . heightened by the rugged spurs of the Bull Run mountains on the one side, and the towering grandeur of the Blue Ridge on the other." At Upperville he rejoiced at the cordial hospitality accorded the "weary, way-worn soldiers" by the citizens of the town. There were handouts of fresh-baked bread, milk, and butter, and Negro servants stood at every gate with buckets of cool water to satisfy the thirst of hundreds of dusty soldiers.[10]

Alexander, another *Republican* reporter, was devoting his attention to a series of hard-fought engagements at Aldie, Middleburg, and Upperville between June 19 and 22, in which Stuart's cavalry participated. Although Stuart was successful in keeping his adversaries from discovering what was going on beyond the Blue Ridge, Alexander continued to be critical of the performance of the cavalry in his reporting. According to Alexander, Stuart's officers were "discouraged and mortified" and prone to question Stuart's qualifications to exercise such a large command; as for his troopers, they were "bordering on a state of demoralization." Alexander reported that the cavalry service had come to be regarded with contempt by all other departments of Lee's army, and that the appearance of a dragoon almost invariably inspired disparaging remarks by infantrymen and artillerymen: this in spite of the fact that the material of which the cavalry arm was composed "could not be better." From Alexander's viewpoint what the cavalry most needed was proper training and discipline and able leadership.

Lest his frank statements about Lee's cavalry arm be ascribed to improper motives, Alexander insisted, ". . . it gives me no pleasure to indite such a letter as this. There is no braver or gallanter spirit than

[10] *Savannah Republican*, June 25, 1863.

Stewart [*sic*]. As a colonel of cavalry he rendered important service at Mason's and Munson's hills near Washington, and as Brigadier he displayed commendable spirit and energy; but the heavy force now under his command is too large for him. . . . I might add much more, and yet not tell all, but I forbear."[11] In view of the injurious effects of Stuart's prolonged absence from Lee's army during the campaign just under way, Alexander's evaluation of Stuart takes on greater significance than it might otherwise have.

Alexander's newspaper colleague Parks was with Hood's division on the twenty-sixth of June when it crossed the Potomac at Williamsport in the wake of A. P. Hill's Third Corps. Parks told about Hood halting his division for an hour after crossing the river and issuing a ration of whisky. The reporter explained: "While I believe a too free use of the "ardent" is injurious particularly to the soldier, I believe the troops were benefitted this time; for all the previous night and until 3 o'clock that evening they were exposed to a cold, drizzling rain. Furthermore we had to wade the Potomac and were not allowed to strip. In thirty minutes after the whiskey was issued, Hood's division presented the liveliest spectacle I ever saw. Good humor and wit ran high, and it was difficult even to hear one's self talk."[12]

Now that Lee's army was north of the Potomac, moving up the Cumberland Valley into Pennsylvania, it became increasingly difficult for the Confederate press to keep track of its movements. The nearest telegraph station and post office to the army was at Winchester, Virginia. Between Winchester and the receding rear of the army the only communication was by courier. The *Richmond Enquirer* reported on June 24 that all roads north of Winchester were strongly picketed and no one was permitted to travel on them for any reason other than government business. As a result, practically the only information the Richmond newspapers could obtain from Lee's army at this time was from gossip brought to Richmond by train passengers from Staunton and Culpeper, private letters to friends in Richmond from Martinsburg and Winchester, and Northern newspapers which reached Petersburg and Richmond by way of flag-of-truce boat. In faraway Mobile, John Forsyth confessed that he did not know whether General Lee had succeeded in eluding Hooker, "but we do know that he has completely

---

[11] *Ibid.*, July 4, 1863. An answer to Alexander's criticisms of Stuart, written apparently by one of Stuart's cavalrymen, appeared in the *Charleston Mercury*, September 12, 1863.
[12] *Savannah Republican*, July 21, 1863.

befogged and bedusted our optics. We are unable to find the remotest clue to his intentions in any of his movements, and are prepared to be surprised by nothing that happens—whether he alights from a balloon in the park of New York City, sweeps like an eagle upon Grant in the great valley, or sails up the Mississippi river on board of the fleet built for the Emperor of China.[13]

Meanwhile the small number of reporters with Lee's army were taking stock of the mixed reception given them in Maryland and the generally hostile demeanor of the Pennsylvanians. At Greencastle, the first town in Pennsylvania, every door was closed and the people looked sad and downcast. At Chambersburg, eleven miles beyond Greencastle, one of the *Savannah Republican* reporters thought he had never seen such long faces and that the features of the women "would have made vinegar ashamed of itself for sourness." This same reporter heard several citizens tell some of Lee's soldiers that they could expect to receive a good thrashing before they left Pennsylvania, that they would be surrounded and cut off, and that not one of them would get back to Virginia to tell the tale. The soldiers retorted that all this might be true, but when General Lee was surrounded and couldn't get out, there would be more Yankees hurt than ever were hurt before at any one time![14]

To *Republican* reporter Alexander, the people along the line of march appeared to be like "a flock of sheep terrified and bewildered by the howl of the wolf and . . . astonished and slavishly thankful that we do not murder, burn, and ravage as we go." He added contemptuously, "these Dutchmen . . . are good farmers and livers, but otherwise . . . a stupid set, but little superior to their sleek cattle and well-fed horses. They know nothing beyond their immediate neighborhood, and fall far below the people of the Confederacy in spirit and intelligence."[15] A reporter for the *Atlanta Southern Confederacy* formed a different impression of the attitude of the Pennsylvanians. At Greencastle, he recalled, "we . . . in vain looked for some development of that peace

[13] *Mobile Daily Advertiser and Register,* June 20, 1863. On June 29 the *Register*'s Richmond correspondent reported that no positive information had been received from General Lee's army "except that derived from the Northern papers, exaggerated as this is by Northern fears. The rumors of army movements brought from Staunton and Culpeper are as a general thing entitled to little credence, being merely the repetition of rumors current in these places." *Ibid.,* July 7, 1863.

[14] *Savannah Republican,* July 14, 1863.

[15] *Ibid.*

sentiment which we had been told existed here. War! war! to the knife flashed from the bright eyes and pretty lips of the ladies, and the stern, mournful, determined countenances of the men showed that, although captive, the unjust spirit that has waged so cruel a war on us has not yet become broken or submissive. At Chambersburg, "the whole population were at the windows and on the sidewalks to see us, and all breathed alike, in their quiet looks, the most unmitigated scorn and hatred to us. We could afford to be generous. We laughed at their demonstrations, and to the malignant blurt of beauty we had naught but smiles and polite salutations to return. . . . Even amidst their sackcloth and ashes they showed every evidence of their character and we could not help but admire the firm, unshaken manner in which they uphold their accursed cause."[16]

The reporters with Lee's army were more willing than their editors to justify the strict orders against the impressment of private property issued by General Lee. They were also of the opinion that in general these orders were obeyed by the troops. Parks admitted, however, that he had seen and heard about the misconduct of one of the Virginia regiments, which he identified and which while on duty in Chambersburg, he said, entered the stores and helped themselves to what they pleased. He expressed the conviction that General Lee should and would punish such acts of vandalism, "even against our enemies."[17]

On Sunday, June 28, Lee's army was widely dispersed. Ewell's corps, the advance of the army, was at York and Carlisle, threatening Harrisburg. Longstreet's corps was at Chambersburg, and Hill's three divisions were encamped eight miles to the east. Lee still did not know that morning that Hooker's Army of the Potomac had left Falmouth, crossed the Potomac near Edward's Ferry, and moved on to Frederick, Maryland. Lee had been kept in ignorance of Hooker's movements up to this time by the protracted absence of the greater part of his cavalry forces. Stuart had left the main body of Lee's command on June 24 on one of those characteristic raids of his. Not until the night of the twenty-eighth did the Confederate commander receive word that the Army of the Potomac was in his rear on the north side of the Potomac, presenting a serious threat to his line of communications. The receipt of this disturbing intelligence prompted Lee to countermand a general

[16] *Atlanta Daily Southern Confederacy* as reprinted in *Charleston Mercury,* July 15, 1863. See also *Atlanta Weekly Southern Confederacy,* July 14, 1863.
[17] *Savannah Republican,* July 21, 1863.

advance on Harrisburg and give orders for his army to concentrate east of South Mountain in the vicinity of Gettysburg.[18]

In a letter to his newspaper, written at Chambersburg that day, Alexander mentioned a report that a Confederate mail carrier had been captured at Hagerstown the day before with the mail he was bringing from Winchester, by a squad of Federal cavalry. This incident accented the importance of cautious statement in special correspondence until Lee's communications with the rear had been placed beyond danger.[19]

Of the nine Confederate reporters attached to the Army of Northern Virginia at this time, one, Jonathan W. Albertson, was an agent of the Confederate Associated Press and three were affiliated with the Richmond newspapers. Two of the three Richmond newspapermen were accredited to the *Enquirer*; the third was a reporter for the *Richmond Sentinel*. The *Charleston Courier*'s ace reporter, de Fontaine, had been prevented from accompanying Lee's army into Pennsylvania by his wedding in Spartanburg, South Carolina on June 10, 1863.[20]

Apparently none of the correspondents with Lee's army was in the right place to give an account of the fighting north and west of Gettysburg on July 1, 1863. It seems likely that most of them were with Longstreet's corps, which was not involved in the fighting on the opening day of the Battle of Gettysburg. Their failure to be on hand to see Hills' and Ewell's Graybacks fight it out with advance elements of General Meade's Army of the Potomac was the more unfortunate because of the generally successful performance of the Confederates that day. After pursuing the fleeing Federals through the streets of Gettysburg to the high ground south of the town, the Confederates were forced to give battle during the next two days on ground of their opponents' choosing.

Alexander was in the vicinity of Chambersburg on the morning of the first day at Gettysburg. He was sitting on the wet ground propped up against a tree writing war correspondence when he saw General Lee and his staff pass by, riding in the direction of Cashtown and Gettysburg. Alexander watched Anderson's division of Hill's corps march in the same direction, followed by Johnson's division of the same corps. But since Longstreet's corps, to which Alexander was attached, was still

[18] Freeman, *Lee*, iii, 60-62.

[19] *Savannah Republican*, July 14, 1863.

[20] *Ibid.*, June 20, 1863. Besides the three Savannah reporters and the Atlanta *Confederacy* man the *Mobile Tribune* had a correspondent with Lee's army during the Gettysburg campaign.

four miles from the battlefield at midnight, Alexander did not reach the scene of the fighting until the morning of the second day.[21]

With the exception of sporadic artillery fire and some skirmishing near the Peach Orchard, there was no action on the battlefield until the late afternoon of July 2. Extending almost five miles, the Confederate line was crescent-shaped, with Ewell's corps on the left, facing south toward a powerful Union defense position on Culp's Hill, southeast of Gettysburg. Hill's corps in the center was drawn up along the northern extension of Seminary Ridge, a long hill running north and south to the west of the town. At the southern end of Seminary Ridge, on the Confederate right, Longstreet's corps faced east toward the left of the Union line on Cemetery Ridge. About 4:00 P.M. Longstreet threw two divisions against an exposed salient on the Union left and all but captured Little Round Top, the key to the Union position in that part of the field.

Savannah Republican correspondent "Tout-le-Monde," who was with Brig.Gen. Henry L. Benning's brigade of Hood's division, described the attack from the viewpoint of that command. "Tout-le-Monde" reported that Benning's Georgians were dubious about their ability to drive the enemy from his strong position, and that "every man had nerved himself for death." These troops had to make a gradual ascent across a field a mile wide; as they began their march they came under fire from the enemy's artillery on the high ground in the distance. "Our batteries now began to open in the rear, sending the hissing shot over answering to the enemy's guns in front. They hardly attracted the fire of any of his, but all seemed concentrated on the advancing lines. Down the plunging shot came, bursting before and around and everywhere tearing up the ground in a terrific rain of Death. Still the old brigade moved on in its solid and beautiful line, the red star gemmed cross [the Confederate battle flag known as the "Southern Cross"] floating defiantly in the midst. As it approached the guns, the rain of grape and canister began, mingling their sharp cries with the shrill whistle of the mad minnie balls which seemed to come in showers. The ranks began to melt away, but springing forward with a shout the undismayed line steadily rushed on, determined this time to sacrifice every life or carry the cannon-crowned hill before them."[22]

Lee's plan called for Anderson's division of Hill's corps to support

[21] *Savannah Republican*, July 22, 1863.
[22] *Ibid.*

Longstreet by attacking the Union center on Cemetery Ridge. A reporter for the *Augusta Constitutionalist* described the fighting in that part of the field from the vantage point of Wright's brigade of Georgia troops. The correspondent of the *Constitutionalist* had been so ill the day before that he could no longer remain upright in the saddle and had to look for a bed in a farmhouse. Now, however, he was sufficiently recovered to describe the dance of death in which his brigade was participating: "As soon as we emerged from the woods and came into the open fields, the enemy poured a most terrific fire of shells into our ranks. We rushed down the hillside and reaching the valley found it was broken by a series of small ridges and hollows running parallel with the enemy's line on the mountain; and in the first of these depressions or hollows our line paused for breath. Then we rushed over the next ridge into the succeeding hollow, and thus we worked our way across that terrible field for more than a mile, under the most furious fire of artillery I had ever seen. When we reached the base of the range upon which the enemy were posted, they opened upon us with their infantry, and raked our whole line with grape and cannister from more than twenty guns. We were now within a few hundred yards of the enemy's guns and had up to this time suffered but little loss—the small ridges I have spoken of protecting our men from the enemy's fire, except as we would pass over their tops, which we always did in a run, thus exposing ourselves but very little to the enemy's fire. But here we were in a hot place, and looking to the left through the smoke, it was apparent that neither Posey nor Mahone had advanced and that Wright's left was whole [*sic*] unprotected. A courier was dispatched to General Anderson informing him of the fact, that both Posey and Mahone had been ordered in and that he would reiterate the order that our Brigade go on."[23]

Meanwhile "Tout-le-Monde" was watching the fierce struggle of Benning's brigade in the Devil's Den, a "jumble of boulders" interlaced with vines just west of Little Round Top. He told how the courageous Georgia regiments—2d, 15th, 17th, and 20th—clambered over the rocks and broke the enemy's line, forcing it to retreat to higher ground. "The enemy formed his lines and swept down the hill to recapture the guns, but the steady fire of the old brigade swept him away and broke his ranks in every futile effort. Again and again he formed and desperately stormed at the hill which contained his guns, but at each time his

[23] *Augusta Daily Constitutionalist*, July 23, 1863.

ranks were broken and hurled back on the mountain heights. All the while the summits were blazing with cannon. The shell and shrapnel shot descended, exploding in the earth and hurling the rocks to an amazing height, but in spite of all, our men held their places firmly."[24]

By this time the brigade the reporter from Augusta was accompanying had accomplished its mission, only to discover that the brigade on its right (Berry's) had given way, that it was unsupported on the left, and that it was about to be enveloped on both sides by flanking columns of the enemy. The only escape from death or capture was to face about and cut their way out, and this is what they did. But when they finally reformed their line a half-mile to the rear, only 554 men were left of the brigade of 1,600 that had begun the attack.[25]

The fighting these two reporters had described was typical of the action everywhere that afternoon on the second day at Gettysburg. At both ends of the line and in the center, Lee's army had driven the enemy back and inflicted heavy casualties, but as Alexander saw it, the great strength of the enemy's position and the lack of previous knowledge of the character of the terrain had prevented the Confederates from holding the positions they had gained at such cost.[26]

Early Friday morning, July 3, the correspondent of the *Augusta Constitutionalist* watched a large number of cannon being placed in line in front of the right and to the left of his brigade. He also heard that a general attack was about to be made along the whole line, with the focus of the thrust to be directed against the Union center. Some 10,000-15,000 men were to be committed to the attack. Maj.Gen. George Pickett's division of 5,000 Virginians, the only division of Longstreet's command that had not previously taken part in the battle, was to spearhead the attack, supported by two of Hill's divisions.

About 1:00 P.M. the 130 pieces of Confederate artillery along Seminary Ridge began the most tremendous artillery bombardment of the war. Eighty Union big guns took up the challenge. The correspondent of the *Richmond Enquirer,* who may have been the Associated Press correspondent Albertson, concluded: "I have never heard such tremendous artillery firing. . . . The very earth shook beneath our feet and the hills and rocks seemed to reel like a drunken man. For one hour and a half this most terrific fire was continued, during which time the

[24] *Savannah Republican,* July 22, 1863.
[25] *Augusta Daily Constitutionalist,* July 23, 1863.
[26] *Savannah Republican,* July 20, 1863.

shrieking of shells, the crash of falling timber, the fragments of rock flying through the air shattered from the cliffs by solid shot, the heavy muttering from the valley between the opposing armies, the splash of bursting shrapnel, and the fierce neighing of artillery horses, made a picture terribly grand and sublime, but which my pen utterly fails to describe."[27]

About two-thirty the fire from the Union batteries slackened. Almost immediately the Confederate attack force prepared to advance, under the delusion that the Union batteries had been silenced. Viewing what happened from the position of Wright's brigade, which was being held in reserve, the *Augusta Constitutionalist* reporter was certain he had never seen troops start out better than these men. "Pickett pushed firmly and steadily forward, going over the identical ground our Brigade had passed the day before. Pettigrew followed in fine order. Our artillery now ceased firing, and upon inquiry, I learned they had exhausted their ammunition! And at such a time! There is Pickett and Pettigrew half across the valley; the enemy have run up new guns and are pouring a deadly fire into their ranks.—The enemy's infantry have opened upon them—they fall on every side—Generals, Colonels, Captains, Lieutenants, privates as thick as autumn leaves they strew the plain. And our guns, will they not re-open? Is there no succor for those brave spirits who are so nobly and steadily bearing their country's flag in that terrible fight. . . . I ask myself, 'can they stand this fire much longer?' and I see Pickett still vigorously pushing on dealing a deadly fire at every step."[28]

The correspondent of the *Richmond Enquirer* was watching the North Carolina troops on Pickett's left, and this is what he saw:

Now Pettigrew's command emerge from the woods upon Pickett's left, and sweep down the slope of the hill to the valley beneath, and some two or three hundred yards in rear of Pickett. I saw by the wavering of this line as they entered the conflict that they wanted the firmness of nerve and steadiness of tread which so characterized Pickett's men. . . . These were mostly raw troops, which had been recently brought from the South, and who had, perhaps, never been brought under fire—who certainly had never been in

---

[27] *Daily Richmond Enquirer,* July 22, 1863; Frank Moore, *The Rebellion Record* (New York, 1864), VII, 112. The *Richmond Enquirer* correspondent used the initial "A." as his byline. "A." could not have been Peter Alexander, since Alexander was not present at the Battle of Chancellorsville, although Richmond *Enquirer* correspondent "A." evidently was.

[28] *Augusta Daily Constitutionalist,* July 23, 1863.

any very severe fight—and I trembled for their conduct. . . . But on press Pickett's brave Virginians; and now the enemy open upon them, from more than fifty guns, a terrible fire of grape, shell, and canister. On, on they move in unbroken line, delivering a deadly fire as they advance. Now they have reached the Emmetsburgh road, and here they meet a severe fire from the heavy masses of the enemy's infantry, posted behind the stone fence. . . . Now again they advance; they storm the stone fence; the Yankees fly. The enemy's batteries are one by one silenced in quick succession as Pickett's men deliver their fire at the gunners and drive them from their pieces. I see Kemper and Armistead plant their banner in the enemy's works. I hear their glad shout of victory.

Let us look after Pettigrew's division. Where are they now? . . . I turn my eyes to the left, and there, all over the plain, in utmost confusion, is scattered this strong division. Their line is broken; they are flying, apparently panic-stricken, to the rear. The gallant Pettigrew is wounded, but he still retains command and is vainly striving to rally his men. Still the moving mass rush pell-mell to the rear, and Pickett is left alone to contend with the hordes of the enemy now pouring in upon him from every side. Garnett falls, killed by a minie ball, and Kemper, the grave and chivalrous, reels under a mortal wound and is taken to the rear. . . . The order is given to fall back, and our men commence the movement, doggedly contending for every inch of ground. The enemy press heavily our retreating line. . . . Armistead is wounded and left in the enemy's hands.[29]

The battle was now virtually over. On the following day (Saturday) both armies remained on the field, facing each other. That evening Lee's army began its retreat in the rain along the road to Fairfield in the direction of Hagerstown. Among the dead they left behind was army correspondent Parks of the *Savannah Republican*.[30]

A considerable scare, created by the advance of some Union troops up the Peninsula from Fort Monroe, had distracted the attention of the people in Richmond from the gruesome events in Pennsylvania. On the day Hood's Texans were fighting and dying in the Peach Orchard, Richmond reporter George Bagby was responding to a militia summons. The fire bell of the guard house in Capitol Square interrupted the writing of his daily newsletter to the *Charleston Mercury*. From the street below Bagby could hear the brisk command, "Fall in! fall in, men!" With a grimace he left his lodgings to shoulder his eighteen-pound Tower musket and "march, gracious knows how many miles, under this scorching sun."[31]

[29] *Daily Richmond Enquirer*, July 22, 1863; Moore, *Rebellion Record*, VII, 112.
[30] The circumstances of Parks' death are briefly described in the *Savannah Republican*, August 11, 1863.
[31] *Charleston Mercury*, July 8, 1863.

The first information that Richmond received about the battle was from Northern news sources. Richmond editors were understandably skeptical about a Yankee version of the fighting, although the *Examiner* concluded that the enemy accounts were "more favorable to us than any the Northern Government has yet permitted [to] appear immediately after a battle."[32] "Is Gettysburg another Antietam?" John M. Daniel asked in an editorial the *Examiner* published on July 6. In response to his own question the editorial writer expressed confidence that although in many ways the two battles seemed parallel, Lee would remain north of the Potomac, as he had not been able to do in 1862. On the day the editorial appeared, Bagby still believed that not all of Lee's army had been engaged in what he referred to as the "heavy skirmishing" at Gettysburg. Yet if the battle had been as indecisive as an informant who was on the flag-of-truce boat from Baltimore, that brought Northern papers of July 3, had indicated, why, Bagby wondered, had Governor Andrew G. Curtin of Pennsylvania called for reinforcements?[33]

The very next day the population of Richmond was considerably excited by wire messages from the superintendent of the telegraph office in Martinsburg, reporting that General Meade was retreating toward Baltimore pursued by Lee and that in a continuation of the battle on Sunday, July 5, Ewell and Longstreet had captured 40,000 prisoners! After releasing these telegrams to the press, Dr. Morris, the president of the Southern Telegraph Company, called on his friends for the largest Confederate flag in the city to hang from his window.[34]

The first reaction of the press to the 40,000-prisoner story was one of mingled incredulity and consternation. The *Richmond Examiner* sagely remarked that "'Forty thousand' is a phrase in telegraphic language equivalent to x in algebra. It means that the reporter does not know how many."[35] The *Enquirer* editor scented a Yankee trick in the alleged refusal of the prisoners to be paroled, and wondered about the prob-

[32] *Daily Richmond Examiner,* July 6, 1863.

[33] *Charleston Mercury,* July 9, 1863.

[34] *Daily Richmond Enquirer,* July 7, 8, 1863; *Savannah Republican,* July 8, 1863; J. B. Jones, *A Rebel War Clerk's Diary* (Philadelphia, 1866), II, 370-71. It seems likely that the author of this highly misleading information was Maj. J. T. Coldwell, superintendent of the Confederate Military Telegraph, who was credited with constructing fifty-seven miles of telegraph line during the Gettysburg campaign. *Richmond Daily Whig,* April 30, 1864.

[35] *Daily Richmond Examiner,* July 8, 1863.

lem of transporting them to Richmond under guard. Would it not be advisable, he asked, to provide the guards with a large supply of cartridges and at the first sign of insubordination shoot the prisoners without mercy?[36] Bewilderment gave way to disillusionment when it was learned that Lee was back in Hagerstown instead of on the road to Baltimore and that the number of prisoners as reported from Martinsburg had shrunk from 40,000 to 4,000.[37]

Difficulties in communication caused considerable delay in transmitting the battle reports of the various Confederate army correspondents to their newspapers. The letters and telegrams carrying dates of July 4 and 5, which Alexander had addressed to the *Savannah Republican* from the Gettysburg battlefield, were returned to him at Hagerstown on July 7 with the explanation that his courier had been unable to cross the Potomac because of the high water.[38] The delays in transmitting the battle reports of the Richmond newspapers caused the Richmond press to hurry additional reporters to Winchester to gather whatever information they could from wagoners and civilians. Among this second group of reporters were Sener of the *Richmond Enquirer* and Yarington of the *Whig*. By sifting reports from army couriers and wounded soldiers returning from the battlefield, Sener was able to construct a substantial narrative of the Battle of Gettysburg which was published in the *Enquirer* almost a week earlier than the accounts of its reporters who were actually present at the battle.[39]

The most widely reprinted and probably best Southern newspaper account of the battle was the story Alexander furnished to the *Savannah Republican* and the *Mobile Register*. In his reporting, Alexander raised questions about Lee's accepting battle at the time and place that he did and about his decision to attack Meade's army on the second day of the battle without having first made a proper reconnaissance of the

[36] *Daily Richmond Enquirer*, July 8, 1863.

[37] For the "sickening depression" to which these "unfounded and extravagant" telegraph stories gave rise see editorial in *Richmond Daily Dispatch*, July 10, 1863.

[38] *Savannah Republican*, July 21, 1863.

[39] *Daily Richmond Enquirer*, July 13, 1863. Yarington's comparatively brief and not very informative account of the Battle of Gettysburg appeared in the *Richmond Whig* on July 14, 1863. The *Richmond Dispatch* reporter "J.," who apparently was not familiar with military terminology, confessed that the repetition of brigades, divisions, and the regiments of brigades with the names of their various commanders by the reciter who was familiar with them had so greatly confused him that as yet he had been unable to reconstruct an account of the battle. *Richmond Daily Dispatch*, July 13, 1863.

ground. The only reason Alexander could offer was that Lee must have thought his troops were able to carry any position, however formidable. Although Alexander expressed confidence that Lee's army was capable of doing what any other troops in any period of the world's history had done, he was convinced that there were some things that even *they* could not accomplish.[40]

Both Alexander and the *Richmond Enquirer's* correspondent "A." were criticized by some of Lee's officers and soldiers for inaccuracies in their reporting of the second day at Gettysburg. On July 29 Maj.Gen. Richard H. Anderson, one of Hill's division commanders, wrote a letter to the *Richmond Enquirer* taking exception to statements made by both correspondents. The statements had to do with the alleged failure of two of his brigade commanders, William Mahone and Carnot Posey, to cooperate in the movement against the Union center on the afternoon of July 2. Anderson defended his own performance in the battle, and asserted that his corps commander supported him in this. Replying to these strictures, Alexander pointed out that none of his critics had denied that Posey's and Mahone's brigades had failed to take part in the attack. His error, he frankly admitted, was in not realizing that both the division commander and the two brigadiers were acting in accordance with orders received from Hill. That division commander R. H. Anderson was more culpable than he admitted at this time is the conclusion of a recent, informed student of the battle.[41]

Once again, as had happened in connection with earlier battles of the war, disparaging statements about the performance of the North Carolina troops by Virginia newspapers aroused the ire of the press of the "Old North State." North Carolina editors objected in particular to the biased treatment by these same Virginia newspapers of what they called "Pickett's Charge." North Carolinians were quick to point out that Pickett's Virginia division made up less than half the attack force at the time of his charge. The *Raleigh Register* and other North Caro-

---

[40] J. J. Mathews, *Reporting the Wars* (Minneapolis, 1957), p. 96. Alexander's battle account appeared as special correspondence in the *Savannah Republican* on July 20, 1863 and in the *Mobile Daily Advertiser and Register*, July 21, 1863. Reprints of this account appeared in the *Charleston Mercury, Augusta Constitutionalist, Columbia Guardian,* and many other Southern newspapers.

[41] W. W. Hassler, *A. P. Hill: Lee's Forgotten General* (Richmond, 1957), pp. 161-62; *Daily Richmond Enquirer*, July 31, 1863; E. P. Alexander, *Military Memoirs of a Confederate* (New York, 1907), p. 401. General Anderson kept the controversy going with another letter to the editor of the *Enquirer*, which the newspaper published on August 10, 1863.

lina newspapers also objected to the description of the North Carolina troops in Pettigrew's and Trimble's divisions as being "raw troops recently brought from the South."[42] In this they were substantially correct, as Pettigrew's brigade included some of the best-drilled regiments in the Confederate army. North Carolina editors were infuriated by the implication in the *Enquirer's* principal account of the battle that the failure of these two other divisions to support Pickett's charge led to its disastrous outcome. That they were more nearly right than the *Richmond Enquirer* reporter conforms to the opinion of a present-day military historian who contends that Pettigrew's division delivered the main bolt of the attack after Pickett's division had been brought to a halt.[43] Subsequently Governor Zebulon Vance requested permission to send a newspaper correspondent with Lee's army to insure that justice was done the North Carolina troops. When his request was refused, he addressed an indignant letter to the War Department, withdrawing his application and appealing to history for the justice which, he said, would never be done North Carolina troops in Virginia by their associates.[44]

Governor Vance was not the only prominent figure who was irritated by newspaper comment about the Gettysburg campaign. In a letter to President Davis written several weeks after the battle, General Lee expressed regret at the censorious comments about the performance of his army which had appeared in the *Charleston Mercury*. Lee concluded, however, that the object of the writer and his publisher was to cast discredit upon the government and those connected with it and that the sentiments voiced in the article gratified feelings more to be pitied than envied.[45]

On July 17 the Richmond press published the news, in the form of an official dispatch from General Lee to President Davis, that Lee's army had recrossed the Potomac into Virginia. A *Richmond Dispatch*

[42] *Daily Richmond Enquirer*, July 28, August 5, 1863; *Raleigh Register*, July 25, 1863.

[43] Glen Tucker, "Some Aspects of North Carolina's Participation in the Gettysburg Campaign," *North Carolina Historical Review*, xxxv (April 1958), 194-96. Thomason, *Jeb Stuart*, p. 442, states that Pickett's report of the charge of his division at Gettysburg was destroyed by Pickett himself at Lee's request.

[44] Jones, *Rebel War Clerk's Diary*, i, 391 (entry for July 30, 1863).

[45] R. E. Lee to Jefferson Davis, July 31, 1863 in Clifford Dowdey and L. H. Manarin, eds., *The Wartime Papers of R. E. Lee* (Boston, 1961), pp. 564-65. The letter of the Richmond correspondent of the *Mercury* (Bagby) to which Lee objected was published in the July 22, 1863 issue of that newspaper.

reporter who described the details of the crossing was unwilling to speculate about the reasons for the retrograde movement. He sought to put the best face on the situation, however, by arguing that the capture of ten thousand excellent horses in Maryland and Pennsylvania, the benefits received by the Confederate commissariat during the campaign, and the time afforded for harvesting the Virginia crops were sufficient justification for the apparent "failure."[46] Rationalizations such as these were the best solace the Confederate press could offer for the disappointing sequel to magnificent expectations.

WHILE Southern news editors were evaluating the results of the Battle of Gettysburg, Charleston, South Carolina, was once more becoming the center of war news. Ever since the beginning of 1863 there had been rumors that a Federal attack on Charleston was planned. Confederate journalists were not in doubt that Charleston was high on the list of Yankee military objectives. Not simply was it the "Cradle of Secession"; blockade runners entering and leaving the harbor made it one of the biggest loopholes in the Union coastal blockade. Beauregard had been back in Charleston since September 1862 working to strengthen the city's defenses against the expected attack.[47]

From time to time during early 1863 various newspapermen connected with out-of-town newspapers visited the city to report the attack if and when it materialized. Early in February Willis G. Clark, one of the owners of the *Mobile Register*, and *Register* reporter Sam Reid arrived in Charleston to observe Beauregard's defensive preparations. Reid was elated by a surprise attack that Beauregard's two lightly armored rams had made on the blockading squadron just before the pair of newspapermen arrived in town, and jumped to the mistaken conclusion that the rams had succeeded in breaking the blockade. Later Reid paid a visit to Fort Sumter and expressed surprise at the extent to which the fort had been strengthened since April 1861.[48]

The letters of newspaper correspondents from Charleston enlarged on the wide scope of its commercial activity and the efficiency of its police regulations. Another correspondent of the *Mobile Register*, who signed himself "Winyah," described the quays as being full of life and

---

[46] *Richmond Daily Dispatch*, July 21, 1863.

[47] T. H. Williams, *P.G.T. Beauregard, Napoleon in Gray* (Baton Rouge, 1955), p. 166.

[48] *Chattanooga Daily Rebel*, February 13, 1863; *Mobile Daily Advertiser and Register*, February 18, March 1, 1863.

reported that a half-dozen fine steamships could always be seen loading or unloading at the wharves. Every night for the past five nights, he went on to say, there had been a steamer in from Nassau in the Bahamas. One of these, the *Georgianna*, had been sighted by the blockaders and so hotly chased that her commander had found it necessary to beach her at Long Island, just north of the harbor. The most important item in the *Georgianna's* cargo was a half-dozen English rifled cannon of heavy caliber which Beauregard was still hoping to retrieve.[49]

During the first week of March Alexander arrived from Richmond, looking for material for war correspondence. He was disappointed to find no signs of military activity in Charleston other than the familiar sight off the bar of the Federal blockading ships with their black funnels and sharp tapering masts. Yet he was not unobservant of the damaging impact of the war on Charleston. In his correspondence he told about whole blocks of retail establishments being closed for want of clerks because Charleston's young men were away at war.[50]

The long-expected attack on Charleston finally came on Tuesday afternoon, April 7, when Rear Adm. Samuel F. DuPont appeared off the bar with nine Yankee ironclads, armed with guns of the heaviest caliber which had been used only for naval combat up to that time. Both Alexander and "Personne" were in Charleston to describe the exciting contest. To their delight, the Union fleet failed miserably to silence the Confederate shore batteries. Indeed, DuPont's ironclads proved unable to face the terrific fire from Beauregard's guns and had to withdraw after losing one of their ships. To Reporter Alexander the fight was a "magnificent spectacle." "The white puffs of smoke issuing from the port holes of the ironclads with a tongue of fire in the centre, the solemn waltz kept up by these huge monsters as they were led past the forts, the fantastic festoons of smoke that garlanded the heads of the forts and slowly floated off to the north, the bursting of 15 inch shells in mid-air and the deep booming of the titanic guns engaged in the conflict, the appearance of the Confederate rams Chicora and Palmetto State steaming energetically up and down their chosen fighting position, the silent city, and the breathless multitude who crowded the house tops and promenade, made up a spectacle at once grand and imposing."[51]

[49] *Mobile Daily Advertiser and Register*, March 25, 1863.
[50] *Savannah Republican*, March 10, 12, 1863.
[51] *Ibid.*, April 8, 1863; Williams, *Beauregard*, p. 175.

De Fontaine was amused by Alexander's reference to the "solemn waltz" of the gunboats. In token of his amusement "Personne" passed along the quip by a mutual friend, "who is probably much more familiar with Terpsichorean joys than 'P.W.A.,' whose initials indicate that he is Pretty Well Advanced," that Alexander should have used the term "schottische" rather than "waltz" to characterize the stately motion of the gunboats.[52]

In "Personne's" story of the fight, probably the most complete Southern newspaper account of it, he told how at two o'clock that afternoon the enemy attack force steamed down the main ship channel in two lines of battle, each composed of four monitors. The first line slowly advanced in the direction of a buoy fourteen hundred yards distant from Sumter, the *Passaic* in the lead. "Personne" then went on to describe the scene of excitement at the various batteries as men and officers, most of whom had never been under fire, prepared for battle. At Fort Sumter, even the men who were confined under arrest for some infraction of military discipline, besought their commander, Col. Alfred Rhett, "for God's sake, let us come out and go to our guns!"

As the slow-moving fleet came within range about 3:00 P.M. Fort Moultrie opened fire on the leading monitor; Fort Sumter, Battery Bee, Forts Wagner and Beauregard, and the battery on Cumming's Point soon joined in. After engaging these opponents for thirty minutes, the *Passaic* sheered off and moved out as the three other vessels of the first line and the Union flagship *Ironsides* exchanged fire with the shore batteries.

As soon as the frigate [*Ironsides*] turned, the second line of monitors advanced led by the Keokuk—a boat which differed from the others in having two turrets. Taking the track of the first line and passing under the stern of the Ironsides, she came gallantly into action, and took position within nine hundred yards of Fort Sumter. . . . in forty minutes she, too, withdrew from action so badly crippled in both turret and hull, that it was not without difficulty she was prevented from drifting ashore. . . . The projectiles . . . aimed at her from every battery soon finished her short career, and with riddled smoke stack, perforated turret, and ragged sides from which the steam escaped without restraint, the doomed Keokuk made her way out of the fight only to sink on the following morning at her anchorage. . . .

The whole fleet had retired and ceased firing at twenty-five minutes after five o'clock, the battle having lasted two hours and twenty-five minutes. . . .

There is little doubt that every one of the enemy's boats was damaged;

[52] *Charleston Daily Courier*, April 11, 1863.

and where they now lie, four thousand yards from the Fort, the workmen can be seen making repairs. . . . Why all did not come nearer is properly a subject of inquiry, but it is answered by their own fears of submarine monsters[53] over which they could not and never can have control. It is surmised that the reason why the attack was made so late in the day was to take advantage of the flood tide in case either of the vessels should get aground. The channel in which they fought was three quarters of a mile wide and about sixty feet deep.

The enemy fired eleven and fifteen inch shot and shell, but with great deliberation, as it requires from ten to fifteen minutes to load the guns. The turrets revolve slowly—not oftener than once in a quarter of an hour. Probably less than ninety balls were fired by the monitors during the entire engagement and of these only about forty struck Fort Sumter. The effect on the walls is not as bad as many officers had predicted, and the damage has been so quickly repaired that the Fort is now even stronger than before the battle.[54]

Other newspapermen flocked to Charleston during the next few days in the expectation that DuPont would make a second attempt. Among the party of visiting journalists were James Gardner and Patrick Walsh of the *Augusta Constitutionalist*, Sneed of the *Savannah Republican*, and *Wilmington Journal* editor James Fulton. On his way to Charleston Editor Fulton encountered the correspondent of the *London Morning Herald*, M. Butt Hewson, and Stedman of the *Richmond Enquirer* going in the same direction. Hewson assured Fulton that a great interest was felt in England as to the result of the trial of ironclad warships versus forts.[55]

When Fulton arrived in Charleston on the day after the battle, the enemy fleet was still inside the bar, but around the point of Morris Island so as to be invisible from the city. Puzzled by reports of the long range at which the monitors had engaged Fort Sumter, Fulton tried to find out the extent and nature of the damage done to the fort. He was surprised to find that although the wall had been decidedly pitted, no rent, crack, or break could be seen. Indeed, the injury to the parapet had already been repaired, and like de Fontaine, he was persuaded that the whole fortification was at least as strong as it had been at the beginning of the bombardment.[56]

[53] "Personne" presumably meant the mines, generally referred to as "torpedoes" at this time, which Beauregard had placed in the channel between Moultrie and Sumter.

[54] *Charleston Daily Courier*, April 11, 1863.

[55] *Ibid.*, April 10, 13, 1863; *Wilmington Daily Journal*, April 13, 1863.

[56] *Wilmington Daily Journal*, April 13, 1863.

The difficulties of reporting a naval bombardment like this were the subject matter of a letter Alexander sent to *Savannah Republican* after the battle. The *Republican* reporter commented that in a naval action the damage inflicted on the attacking party, especially when his ships are protected by an armored exterior, can only be known when the enemy sees fit to publish it. "It is very different when the combatants meet on land, where the line of battle is frequently several miles in extent, the ground uneven and often admitting of a variety of evolutions, and where the beaten party leaves behind him his dead and wounded to tell the tale of his disaster."[57] The precise amount of damage inflicted on the enemy might be difficult for Alexander and the other Confederate correspondents to determine, but the return of the Yankee fleet to Port Royal after only a little more than two hours' fighting gave some indication that Charleston could never be taken by naval attack alone.

Early in July 1863, one week after the Battle of Gettysburg, wire stories disseminated by the Confederate Associated Press indicated that the 567-day siege of Charleston was about to begin. A.P.A. dispatch carrying a Charleston dateline of July 10 announced that "the attack here has commenced," that a large Yankee fleet was off the harbor, and that there had been heavy firing since five o'clock that morning. This time a Federal army commanded by Maj.Gen. Quincy A. Gillmore was cooperating with the Union navy. During the day Gillmore's soldiers overpowered the weak defenses on the south end of Morris Island and overran about three-fourths of the island. When they attempted, however, to sweep past Battery Wagner to reach the northern end of the island, they found the fort too difficult to take.[58]

Editor Sneed happened to be at Charleston in a position to report the attack. The gloomy tone of his reporting reflected what appears to have been the low morale of the Charleston press and citizenry at the time. In Sneed's opinion the capture of the lower battery on Morris Island was a "disaster" attributable to bad engineering, for which somebody (he did not say who) should be held responsible. But by the next day he had recovered his confidence sufficiently to express doubt that Battery Wagner could be taken either by infantry assault or fleet bombardment.[59] To report this new phase of the fighting around

[57] *Savannah Republican*, April 13, 1863.
[58] Foote, *Civil War: Fredericksburg to Meridian*, pp. 696-97.
[59] *Savannah Republican*, July 14, 15, 1863.

Charleston, the *Courier* hastily summoned de Fontaine from the interior of South Carolina. "Personne" returned to the city in time to report a second major attack on Battery Wagner on July 18.

From early that morning until six o'clock in the evening, approximately seventy U.S. army and navy guns subjected the fortification of palmette logs and sandbags to a pulverizing bombardment. "Personne" was impressed by the peculiar grandeur of the setting for this struggle as viewed from the Charleston battery. "Grey old Sumter lay like a half aroused monster midway of the scene, only occasionally speaking his part in the angry dialogue.— Far in the distance were the blockaders, taking no part in the fray. To the right on Cumming's Point was a little mound of earth, and every now and then we could see a band of artillerists gathered around the guns, a volume of smoke and far to the right exploding in the vicinity of the enemy's batteries. Still to the right of this was Battery Wagner clustered above which, now bursting high in air and letting loose their imprisoned deaths, now striking the sides of the work, and anon plunging into the sand on the beach and throwing up a pillar of earth or dashing into the marsh and ricochetting across the water, could be seen the quickly succeeding shells and round shot of the enemy's guns. . . ."

At dark the firing ceased, and two brigades of Federal infantry advanced to occupy the fort. The Confederate garrison had suffered relatively little from the bombardment, however, and the Federals were beaten back after a desperate fight, among them a Negro regiment commanded by a Boston patrician named Robert Gould Shaw. When "Personne" visited the scene of the fighting the next morning, he concluded that probably no battlefield in the country had ever presented such an array of mangled bodies in such a small space. "The ground in front of the Battery was thickly strewn, but in the ditch around the work the dead and wounded, white and black, were literally piled together. Blood, mud, water, brains and human hair matted together— men lying in every conceivable attitude, with every conceivable expression on their countenances, their limbs bent into unnatural shapes by the fall of twenty or more feet—the fingers rigid and outstretched, as if they had clutched at the earth to save themselves—pale, beseeching faces, looking out from among the ghastly corpses, with moans and cries for help and water, and dying gasps and death struggles— these are some of the details of the horrible picture which the night of Saturday had left to be revealed by the dawn of a peaceful Sabbath.[60]

"Personne" had already revealed his distaste for the use of Negro troops by the enemy. In a letter from James Island written two days before, he described the capture of fourteen Negro soldiers, including a sergeant and a corporal, nine of whom were runaway slaves. One of the prisoners was shot, perhaps accidentally, as he was in the act of surrendering his musket to his captors. According to "Personne," the captured Negroes expected to be hung; they gave as a reason for the valor with which they had fought that they would rather die of a bullet than a rope. In de Fontaine's opinion, it was "a nice question whether they are to be recognized as belligerents or outlaws, and the indignation of our troops is not concealed at the thought that a white man may by virtue of these captures be one day exchanged for a negro."[61]

After the July 18 fight the Federal army commander abandoned frontal assaults and resorted again to siege. During the next fifty days, Battery Wagner was the target of almost continuous bombardment as the Federals edged nearer to the fort. Since more than half the garrison consisted of North Carolina troops, the editor of the *Wilmington Journal* was vociferous about the hardships of the fort's defenders.[62]

Shortly after the middle of August Rear Adm. John A. Dahlgren's Federal warships began a series of large-scale bombardments of Fort Sumter which eventually reduced it to rubble. On August 23 Editor Sneed visited the Confederate harbor defenses to see how well they were standing up under the heavy punishment. A friend provided him with a boat to visit Fort Sumter, but as he drew near it the enemy fire became so intense it seemed foolhardy to approach any nearer. So he headed for Fort Johnson. He reported that the entire Southern face of Sumter was "one vast ruin. A pile of rubbish—brick, mortar, stone, timber and guns—rises from the water and forms an inclined plane to the original parapet, some fifty feet in height." The inability of the Confederate defenders to prevent this destruction and the strengthening of the enemy's position he ascribed to the fact "that the enemy have a *navy*, while we have none. This has been the secret of nearly all their successes in the present war."[63]

[60] *Charleston Daily Courier*, July 20, 21, 1863.

[61] *Ibid.*, July 17, 1863.

[62] *Wilmington Daily Journal*, August 12, 1863. The reality of the hardships was confirmed in an eyewitness account by a member of the Battery Wagner garrison, published in *South Carolina Historical Magazine*, LVII (January 1956), 5-11.

[63] *Savannah Republican*, August 26, 1863.

Meanwhile the newspaper correspondents in Charleston began to experience the rigors of writing under fire within the city itself. Reid, who had returned to Charleston on July 16 to report for the *Atlanta Intelligencer* and the *Mobile Tribune,* mentioned in his correspondence Gillmore's threat to open fire on Charleston if Sumter and Battery Wagner were not immediately surrendered. At half past one in the morning on August 22, Reid witnessed the first bombardment of the city by an eight-inch gun on Morris Island, four miles away. He reported that the "Swamp Angel," as the gun was called, fired thirteen shells weighing 200 pounds each, and that although they caused great consternation and excitement, no one was injured by them.[64]

When the "Swamp Angel" opened fire on Charleston for the second consecutive night, Reid witnessed a general exodus of women and children from the city. He also reported that generally all the stores were closed and the streets were desolate. "The usual crowds that visited the City Battery and the elegant and liveried equipages that were wont to roll along the fashionable drive in front of the battery promenade have all vanished."[65] Sneed had been careful to avoid mention in his correspondence of the localities reached by the enemy's shells lest he provide data for correcting the range of their guns, but when the Charleston papers disregarded this caution, he felt at liberty to reveal that some of the shells had lodged as far up the peninsula as Society Street.[66]

By this time the Confederate press was preparing its readers for the possibility that Fort Sumter might not hold out much longer. An Augusta newspaperman admitted that "brick or granite cannot stand the steady blows of solid bolts," but pointed out that even if Sumter fell, there were still powerful sand batteries on both sides of the harbor.[67] Viewing the situation with anxiety, Editor Rhett of the *Charleston Mercury* told his brother, the commander of Fort Sumter, that he had

[64] *Atlanta Daily Intelligencer,* July 23, 1863; *Mobile Daily Tribune,* August 27, 1863. For a description of the bombardment written by an English correspondent see W. S. Hoole, *Vizetelly Covers the Confederacy* (Tuscaloosa, 1957), pp. 94-95.

[65] *Mobile Daily Tribune,* September 1, 1863.

[66] *Savannah Republican,* August 26, 1863.

[67] *Augusta Daily Constitutionalist,* August 25, 1863. The editor of the *Wilmington Journal* agreed: ". . . Sumter is a thing of the past, and brick walls as opposed to rifled cannon are little better than so many screens of paper, while on the other hand sand forts seem to be virtually invulnerable." *Wilmington Daily Journal,* August 24, 1863.

just had a conversation with General Beauregard and that Beauregard expected Sumter to hold out from one week longer to fifteen days. "Beauregard expects to evacuate Morris Island *after* Sumter is gone one or two days. But not before."[68]

Events proved otherwise. Although Sumter did not have a gun left with which to reply to the enemy, it was still in Confederate hands when the Confederates evacuated Morris Island on the night of September 6-7. The increasing intensity of enemy bombardment preceding the evacuation was the theme of a news story Editor Rhett wrote for the *Charleston Mercury*. Rhett described the bombardment that continued all day Saturday, September 5 and throughout the following night as "beyond all doubt the most fierce and long continued which has taken place against Wagner since the beginning of the siege." He estimated the rate of firing as often more than sixty per minute. He further declared that it was almost impossible to describe the "terrible beauty" of the scene in Charleston Harbor, bathed in a misty autumn moonlight on that memorable Saturday night. "From Moultrie almost to Secessionville, a whole semi-circle of the horizon was lit up by incessant flashes from cannon and shell. As peal on peal of artillery rolled across the waters, one could scarcely resist the belief that not less than a thousand great guns were in action. . . ."[69]

In reporting the evacuation the *Richmond Examiner* broke the news gently by assuring its readers that the necessity for the evacuation "had long been forseen and provided for" and that everything of value on the island had previously been transported to the mainland.[70] By this time the editor of the *Memphis Appeal* was in the city to see for himself the situation at Charleston and to recruit a reporter to provide the *Appeal* with special correspondence from there. The local newspapermen told Editor John B. Dumble that he could do no better than get de Fontaine who was already reporting the siege for several other newspapers, including the *Mobile Register* and the *Savannah Republican*. Dumble was impressed by the fact that a much larger proportion

[68] R. B. Rhett, Jr. to Col. Alfred Rhett, August 20, 1863, Robert Barnwell Rhett Papers, Huntsville, Ala.

[69] *Charleston Mercury*, September 7, 1863. In what was evidently the editor's own file of his newspaper, the initials "R.B.R. Jr." are inscribed in ink in the margin of this news report.

[70] *Daily Richmond Examiner*, September 8, 1863; D. D. Wallace, *South Carolina, A Short History* (Chapel Hill, 1951), p. 539.

of the population (at least three-fourths, he estimated) had left the city than he had at first supposed.[71]

There was a certain amount of friction between the army and the newspaper correspondents at Charleston because of security leaks about military movements and the weight and position of the Confederate guns. On September 2, 1863 the *Augusta Constitutionalist* published a report from one of its correspondents in Charleston describing a huge gun weighing twenty-two tons for which a temporary track had to be laid along King Street to move it from the railroad station to White Point Garden. Yet on the whole, the press relations of Beauregard's command were good, in part because of the affability and good sense of his chief of staff, General Jordan. As the siege progressed, there was increasing satisfaction on the part of the Confederate press with the quantity and quality of the Press Association's reports from Charleston prepared by its Charleston agent, B. R. Riordan.[72]

Although Riordan reported that on October 30 Fort Sumter had been subjected to its heaviest bombardment to date,[73] it was becoming increasingly clear that the Federal assault on Charleston had failed and that the possibilities of its capture were still as remote as they had been six months earlier. Sneed attributed, perhaps mistakenly, the slackening of enemy fire at the end of August to the wearing smooth of the enemy's rifled guns. Also, the very presence of Fort Sumter, still in Confederate possession after the enemy had done his worst, and the fear of harbor obstructions kept Dahlgren's monitors from getting any closer to Charleston from then on until the end of the war.[74]

[71] *Memphis Daily Appeal*, September 5, 8, 1863; *Mobile Daily Advertiser and Register*, September 10, 1863. On September 10, the *Appeal* stated that it had secured the services of de Fontaine as its special correspondent during the siege of Charleston.

[72] *Charleston Daily Courier*, September 10, 1863. Favorable comment in the *Savannah Republican* about the efficient and careful press reports of Riordan were widely reprinted in the Confederate press. See e.g. *Memphis Daily Appeal*, September 25, 1863; *Columbia Daily Southern Guardian*, October 6, 1863. De Fontaine testified likewise to the accuracy of the Press Association dispatches from Charleston. Writing under the pseudonym of "Quel Qu'un" to the *Memphis Appeal*, he assured its readers that "what goes to you from Charleston, by telegraph, may be believed. Much that travels by word of mouth on the cars is doubtful." *Memphis Daily Appeal*, September 18, 1863.

[73] *Richmond Daily Dispatch*, October 31, 1863.

[74] *Savannah Republican*, August 28, 1863; J. E. Florance, Jr., "Morris Island: Victory or Blunder?" *South Carolina Historical Magazine*, LV (July 1954), 151-52. Florance expresses the view that Gillmore, the Federal army commander, made a disastrous blunder in landing on Morris Island in July 1863 instead of attacking

In December 1863, the *Richmond Dispatch* stated editorially that General Beauregard was entitled to the gratitude and admiration of the Confederacy for his magnificent defense of the city, adding that "the defense of Charleston stands without a parallel." Claiming that the *New York Times* now virtually admitted that Charleston could not be taken, the *Dispatch* exulted: "What a lame and impotent conclusion of all the gigantic efforts and prodigious vaperings of the vindictive foe!"[75] But another Confederate newspaperman was more perceptive and candid than the *Dispatch* writer. This journalist, a reporter for the *Augusta Constitutionalist,* conceded that in at least one respect the enemy had been highly successful. The extensive trade that had been carried on between Charleston and the West Indies was now, he said, "effectually broken up, at least for the present." Indeed the possession of Morris Island by the enemy and the large number of blockading vessels in the vicinity had rendered such trade "a very unprofitable business."[76]

THE SUMMER heat of July and August gave Southern army correspondents little to write about in the period of about a month and a half that followed the conclusion of the Gettysburg campaign. The armies of Lee and Meade had been severely punished in the fighting in Pennsylvania; there was need for a breathing spell to bury their dead, obtain fresh supplies of food and ammunition, repair broken-down transportation, and renew the energies of both men and animals. In late July Shepardson of the *Mobile Register* reported that everything was remarkably quiet in Richmond. "The whole community seems to wear a wondering, expectant air, as if asking one another what is to come next. When the evening bulletins are posted, a crowd collects around, and for a time some little bustle and excitement is visible. Then follows the same painful, expectant quiet. Just as the sunset shadows fall upon the suburban hills . . . the President can be seen riding through the shaded and quiet streets, looking quite well, and generally puffing a fragrant Havana. Sometimes, as on yesterday, a lady accompanies him, while on a pony beside them rides his little son. During the day, when the sun

---

James Island, which in Florance's opinion provided a better approach to the city of Charleston.

[75] *Richmond Daily Dispatch*, December 12, 1863.

[76] *Augusta Daily Constitutionalist*, October 18, 1863. See also *Daily Richmond Enquirer*, October 3, 1863 for the editor's admission that "Holding Morris Island. . . . they [the Federals] can shut up the harbor to trade, as they do the mouths of our Virginia rivers. . . ."

shines hotly, the capitol square is the favorite resort. The fountains are kept playing, and the large lindens form a cool protection from the heat. Lying around on the heavy grass are seen hundreds of idle forms, generally emaciated and careworn with some portion of their bodies bound closely in bandages, or with some other evidence of mutilation. It is a favorite place for convalescent wounded, and they break away from the hospitals on every occasion and seek its shades. So go the hours; and one by one old Time checks off the days."[77]

Since the return of the army to Virginia there had been rumors in Richmond of dissension between President Davis and Lee. Shepardson assured the readers of the *Mobile Register* that these stories were untrue. He reported that Lee had recently spent a week in Richmond and that during his stay he was almost constantly with the president, breakfasting and dining at the latter's Clay Street mansion and walking and chatting with Davis in the spirit of friendship. "The President writes familiarly to Lee when in the field; Gen. Lee takes salt with the President when in the city."[78]

Along the Rapidan River, where Lee's army was based in August, apparently there were only four special correspondents to represent the Southern press: Alexander of the *Savannah Republican,* Sener of the *Richmond Enquirer,* and one reporter each for the *Richmond Dispatch* and the *Atlanta Confederacy.* Although Sener complained about uncivil treatment by unidentified officers, he apparently had a good relationship with General Longstreet, who, he said, had promised to provide him with all the necessary facilities to obtain accurate news reports of the operations of that general's command.[79] Unfortunately Longstreet's departure from Virginia shortly before the middle of September to join Bragg's army in Tennessee deprived him of this arrangement.

Cavalry operations offered the principal subject for army reporting during August and September. Stuart, the Confederate cavalry leader, was still suffering from a bad press because of his inept performance

[77] *Mobile Daily Advertiser and Register,* July 31, 1863.
[78] *Ibid.,* September 23, 1863.
[79] *Daily Richmond Enquirer,* August 10, 25, 1863. For an expression of resentment by Sener of the privileged status accorded the *London Times* correspondent Francis E. Lawley during the Gettysburg campaign by the Confederate high command and for Sener's complaints about snubs inflicted upon correspondents of the Richmond press at this same time see *Daily Richmond Enquirer,* July 21, 1863.

in the Gettysburg campaign. During the first week of August Shepard-son published reports current in Richmond that General Hood was slated to replace Stuart as chief of the cavalry arm of Lee's army, and Alexander stated flatly that there was a woeful lack of discipline in the cavalry service, for which he held Stuart responsible.[80] When in a cavalry fight at Liberty Mills on September 22 Stuart narrowly missed losing his artillery, he occasioned further press criticism. The Rich-mond correspondent of the *Memphis Appeal*, Thompson, considered such criticism unjust and contended that Stuart had not been "whipped" at Liberty Mills. "On the contrary, he gave the Yankee cavalry a very heavy check and undoubtedly prevented their advance upon Gordons-ville and Charlotteville [*sic*] . . . where they might have inflicted upon us grievous injury."[81]

A contributor to the *Savannah Republican* who wrote to that news-paper in defense of the cavalry advanced the opinion that one of the chief reasons why it was held in such low esteem was that army cor-respondents had been ignorant of its performances and had failed to report them. He went on to say that during the fall of 1861 the in-teresting letters the *Richmond Dispatch* correspondent "Bohemian" had written from Stuart's headquarters near Centreville had helped to make Stuart famous throughout the Confederacy. Since then, how-ever, no newspaper correspondent had succeeded in keeping up with the cavalry; therefore the public had been deprived of firsthand knowl-edge of their exploits. The regular correspondents of the press, he as-serted, "rarely see the cavalry, and know nothing of what they are doing. They usually live at the headquarters of an infantry General. In the large battles they accompany these Generals, or take a position favorable for seeing the fight. They naturally write about what they see and hear from the Generals, the staff, and from such acquaintances in the line as they happen casually to meet. . . .

"The cavalry meanwhile are upon the flanks, or in the front beyond the army. They never see or are seen by the bulk of the army.— They have no intercourse even with the higher officers of the main army,

---

[80] *Mobile Daily Advertiser and Register*, August 11, 1863; *Savannah Republi-can*, September 11, 1863. These same rumors about Hood replacing Stuart are mentioned by war department clerk Robert Kean, in Edward Younger, ed., *In-side the Confederate Government* (New York, 1957), p. 90. For criticism of Alexander's adverse comment about the performance of Stuart's cavalry by a Confederate dragoon see *Savannah Daily Morning News*, November 1, 1863.

[81] *Memphis Daily Appeal*, October 3, 1863; Thomason, *Jeb Stuart*, p. 463.

except by couriers, who have neither time, nor opportunity, nor permission to converse with any but the officers to whom they are sent. Hence, the unavoidable ignorance and consequent silence of correspondents in reference to the cavalry."[82]

Early in October there were indications in the press that Lee was going on the offensive again. On October 2 the *Richmond Dispatch* published the news, which had reached Bagby's ears several days before, that two army corps had been detached from the Army of the Potomac to reinforce Rosecrans' Federal army in Tennessee. The detachment of 12,000 soldiers from Meade's army reduced the odds against Lee's command from two to one to only a little worse than eight to five. On October 9 Lee's army marched up the south bank of the Rapidan and crossed the river to the west of the Union right wing. Lee hoped to make a turning movement along the Warrenton turnpike to intercept Meade's withdrawal along the Orange and Alexandria Railroad.[83]

The premature publication in one of the Richmond newspapers of the news that Lee's army was in motion and had crossed the Rapidan caused the general to protest to Secretary Seddon. Lee told Seddon that "all such publications are injurious to us. We have difficulties enough to overcome interposed by our enemies without having them augmented by our friends. I wish you could impress upon the editors the importance of rejecting from their papers all mention of military movements until the result has been obtained."[84]

During the next few days the correspondents with Lee's army seem to have acted in the spirit of Lee's letter to Seddon. At any rate, they gave sparse coverage of the forward movement of the Army of Northern Virginia which carried it all the way to the Centreville heights during the following week. By this time Alexander had gone west to report Bragg's Chickamauga campaign, and Sener had ceased to report for the *Richmond Enquirer*. As a result, the repulse of A. P. Hill's corps at Bristoe Station, accompanied by the loss of five guns and 1,300 prisoners, was largely unreported in the Confederate press.[85]

[82] *Savannah Republican* as reprinted in *Daily Richmond Enquirer*, November 7, 1863.

[83] Foote, *Civil War: Fredericksburg to Meridian*, pp. 786-87, 789; *Charleston Mercury*, October 2, 1863.

[84] R. E. Lee to James A. Seddon, October 11, 1863. Dowdey and Manarin, *Wartime Papers of Lee*, pp. 607-608.

[85] Hassler, *Hill*, p. 179, states, however, that "reaction to this costly and humili-

At Centreville Lee might have turned Meade's position and forced him to fall back on the defenses of Washington. Adverse weather conditions and the poor equipment of the Confederate army decreed otherwise, however; thus on October 17 the men in butternut uniforms began falling back along the railroad to Orange Court House, skirmishing with the enemy cavalry as they retreated. Stuart's cavalry operations during the retreat were the topic of a complimentary letter by the correspondent of the *Richmond Dispatch*. The *Dispatch* reporter expressed admiration of Stuart, saying: "It is a matter of surprise to me how Gen. S. has escaped uninjured in this war. He is in every skirmish and battle, and his apparel has been perforated time and again by the enemy's bullets, but one has never made the slightest impression of his skin yet. He is one of the 'Bravest of the brave' and . . . a terror to the enemy."[86]

The difficulties of campaigning in such desolate country were alluded to from time to time by army correspondents. The *Dispatch* reporter described the region now occupied by Meade as "a vast territory of ruin and desolation. . . . There is not a house standing on the railroad from Manassas Junction to Rappahannock river, a distance of more than thirty miles. All enclosures on the farms have been pulled down and destroyed; extensive fields once yielding rich harvests are cut to pieces by military roads. In lieu of valuable crops of corn may be seen bramble and high weeds waving triumphantly over the land."[87] In a similar manner a correspondent of the *Richmond Examiner* described the almost impenetrable forests, bottomless bogs, the "Amazonian character of the women," and the abundance of robbers operating with impunity in Prince William County, where he accompanied a scouting party. As an illustration of the wildness of the country, he told about meeting a gray fox while threading one of these jungles on foot and how the animal stood still and stared for fully a half-minute, "as if astonished to see a human being in such a secluded spot."[88]

After being substantially reinforced in early November, Meade decided to stage a counteroffensive. Advancing to the Rappahannock he

---

ating defeat was quick and sharp throughout the ranks, press, and official circles." It is possible that Hill's Virginia origin influenced the Richmond press to gloss over the defeat.

[86] *Richmond Daily Dispatch*, October 27, 1863.

[87] *Ibid.*, November 5, 1863.

[88] *Daily Richmond Examiner*, November 3, 1863.

wiped out a Confederate bridgehead at Kelly's Ford on the north bank of the stream, killing or capturing all the troops in two Confederate brigades except six hundred men. The Confederate press reacted much more violently to this fiasco than to the affair at Bristoe Station. The *Richmond Enquirer* recommended the dismissal of the brigade commanders involved (Hoke and Harry Hays), and denounced what it called "the mysterious and unaccountable silence" of the Confederate authorities about the disaster at Kelly's Ford. The *Examiner* was more cautious, explaining that the two brigades had been "unexpectedly attacked by the enemy in overwhelming numbers," credited their members with having fought with "desperate courage," and stated that "it is believed [they] would have prevailed against their assailants but for the giving out of their ammunition." On the other hand, Richmond correspondent Thompson declared that such a surprise in the army of General Lee had never been heard of before and that since these brigades were in the division of General Early, it was his responsibility to give a proper explanation of the affair.[89] Noting that Lee was silent, "as he always is when the day goes against him," Bagby pettishly classified this trait as one of the general's weaknesses.[90]

Meanwhile Lee withdrew to the south bank of the Rapidan River. After a two-weeks interval, during which the two armies remained inactive, Meade crossed the Rapidan to strike at the Confederate right flank. By this time Sener was back in Lee's army, acting as a special correspondent of the *Richmond Dispatch*. He addressed letters to the *Dispatch* on November 27 and 28 describing the crossing by the enemy at Ely's and Germanna fords and a fight on the Fredericksburg plank road about sixteen miles east of Orange Court House. Sener expressed doubt that the enemy's loss in the fight had been as great as the Confederate. "They fought, I am told, quite well and fired more accurately than usual." On December 1 he reported that the two armies were still confronting each other along Mine Run, a tributary of the Rapidan, about ten miles west of the old Chancellorsville battleground. Sener expressed fear that the enemy would refuse to offer battle and that

---

[89] *Daily Richmond Enquirer*, November 14, 1863; *Daily Richmond Examiner*, November 10, 1863 as quoted in *Atlanta Daily Intelligencer*, November 18, 1863; *Memphis Daily Appeal*, November 16, 1863. In D. S. Freeman, *Lee's Lieutenants, A Study in Command* (New York, 1944), III, 267, Freeman estimates the loss of the two brigades at 1,674 killed, wounded, and captured.

[90] *Charleston Mercury*, November 16, 1863.

after their supplies gave out, failing an attack by General Lee, they would retreat to winter quarters at Fredericksburg.[91]

Sener's estimate of the situation was only partially correct. Concluding that Lee's position along Mine Run was too strong, Meade fell back across the Rapidan on the night of December 1, and the campaign was at an end. In his concluding letter to the *Dispatch*, Sener angrily exclaimed: "A mountain in labor, and behold at parturition a mouse is brought forth. Meade has marched up the hill and then marched down again . . . . doubtless some of your hot-house critics in Richmond . . . will animadvert upon Gen. Lee for not having fallen upon Meade and crushed him before he could get back across the Rapidan. . . . I believe that Gen. Lee was disposed to have attacked Meade on Tuesday [Dec. 1], but was dissuaded from doing so by the advice of his Lieut. Generals, and it is equally true that he intended to have fought Meade on Wednesday certain, but Meade *had gone*."[92]

By this time the attention of newspapermen in Richmond was shifting to the opening of the next session of Congress on December 7. Looking ahead to this event, *Mobile Register* correspondent Bagby, who had replaced Shepardson as the *Register's* Richmond correspondent,[93] predicted that the rescue of Confederate finances and army appropriations would constitute the chief business of this session. The Richmond correspondent of the *Atlanta Intelligencer* analyzed the composition of the new Congress as a combination of a minority of new members and a majority of old members who had had more or less experience in legislation. In cynical terms he rated more than one half of its members as "useless lumber, composed of inefficient, time serving and moderately informed men, incapable of forming a sound and independent judgment on any subject of public interest . . . [and] thinking more of their per diem and their personal consequence than the good of their country."[94]

[91] *Richmond Daily Dispatch*, November 30, December 3, 1863.

[92] *Ibid.*, December 8, 1863.

[93] During the latter part of November, 1863 Bagby's old friend William M. Semple, who was a member of the *Mobile Register's* editorial staff at this time, wrote to Bagby, informing him that Editor Clark "wants to get you to write, but thinks your terms rather steep. I told him . . . that your letters were more readable than any others that came from Richmond. To this latter proposition he very cheerfully assented." William M. Semple to George W. Bagby, November 21, 1863, Bagby Papers, Virginia Historical Society.

[94] *Mobile Daily Advertiser and Register*, December 10, 1863; *Atlanta Daily Intelligencer*, November 19, 1863.

Recurrent themes of Richmond reporting at this time were the moral decadence of the city's floating population, political corruption, the housing problem, and the runaway inflation in living costs. The reporters for the out-of-town newspapers wrote in terms of obvious disapproval about the gambling halls that abounded on the principal thoroughfares of Richmond, courtesans robed in silks and satins jostling the plainly dressed pure-minded woman who walked these same streets, government officials and army quartermasters losing as much as $40,000 at a single sitting in one of the faro games, and two-story dwellings renting for as much as $1,000 a month. The *Memphis Appeal* correspondent Thompson claimed that not a single row of tenements had been built in Richmond since 1860 and that "nobody can finish what they have already commenced."[95]

If Bagby was right, Richmond was very gay during the closing weeks of 1863, notwithstanding problems such as these and the generally unpromising military situation. The gayety, he admitted, was mainly confined to what he called the "loose classes." These people were given to practices such as marriages of doubtful authenticity, lending their presence to exhibitions of "living statuary," "stunning" manners, and astounding costumes.[96] In another descriptive piece, he reported that French conversation classes were the latest "rage" among the young ladies of the town. He also pictured the bootblacks who were a common sight on the streets of Richmond with a wooden contraption containing their equipment slung around their necks, and the numerous Negroes "squatted on their hams, at the street corners and public places, selling apples."[97] Probably Bagby's description of the mood and manners of Richmond was not greatly overdrawn. Undoubtedly it provided the basis for a better comprehension of the Richmond scene for the wide range of newspaper readers for whom the perusal of "Hermes'" column had become a pleasant habit.

[95] *Memphis Daily Appeal,* October 5, 1863. For some other examples of the reporting of life in Richmond at this time see *ibid.,* October 10, 1863; *Mobile Daily Advertiser and Register,* December 13, 1863. Even the names of the thousand and one drinking and eating saloons in Richmond reflected the influence of the war. They included such appellations as "Bull Run," "Manassas," "Secession Club," "290," "The Chickahominy," "The Ape" (referring to President Lincoln), "Beauregard," and "Stonewall." *Daily Richmond Examiner,* December 5, 1863.

[96] *Mobile Daily Advertiser and Register,* December 10, 1863.

[97] *Charleston Mercury,* November 24, 1863.

CHAPTER 11

Bragg's Final Reckoning
with the Press

On a Wednesday evening in January 1863 the *Mobile Register* correspondent in the Army of Tennessee, Sam Reid, received some disturbing information. A certain O'Hara, whom he did not otherwise identify, informed him that General Bragg intended to arrest him "tomorrow." Reid's previous contacts with Bragg had been sufficiently unpleasant that the prospect of inhabiting the general's prison seemed even more ominous than it otherwise would. Preferring flight to imprisonment, Reid left Tullahoma on horseback about nine o'clock that very night in the company of an orderly. The night was dark and rainy; being unable to follow the road, Reid and his companion decided to camp beside it until daybreak and then ride on to Winchester, fourteen miles southeast of Tullahoma, the next morning. Apparently Bragg made no attempt to give chase, for after remaining in Winchester for more than a week, Reid went on to Chattanooga without interference and did newspaper work there and at several other places in the East during the next several months.[1]

Probably Bragg's difficulties with his generals in the Army of Tennessee loomed larger in his mind than the fleabite of an army reporter. Early in February the *Charleston Courier* broke the news that on his arrival in Tullahoma after the Battle of Murfreesboro, Bragg had addressed a circular letter to his corps and division commanders, asking if there was any foundation for rumors of lack of confidence in him by the army. According to the *Courier*, all the generals with the exception of James M. Withers and B. Franklin Cheatham, replied in the affirmative, adding that it would be in the interest of the service if Bragg would ask to be relieved. The outcome of this controversy was an investigation of Bragg's leadership by the department commander, General Johnston, which, not altogether to Davis's liking, resulted in Bragg's retention.[2]

[1] Diary of Samuel Chester Reid, Jr., Reid Papers, entries for January 21, 22, 1863.

[2] *Charleston Daily Courier* as paraphrased in *Columbus Daily Sun*, February 11, 1863; S. F. Horn, *The Army of Tennessee* (Norman, Okla., 1953), pp. 222-27.

During the first half of 1863 there was a prolonged period of military inactivity in middle Tennessee which provided the army correspondents with few opportunities for interesting letters. While Rosecrans' Army of the Cumberland remained near Murfreesboro, Bragg's army was strung out along the Duck River in the form of a crescent, with its left wing under Polk at Shelbyville, its right under Hardee at Wartrace, and cavalry posted on either flank. Bragg's headquarters were at Tullahoma, thirty-eight miles south of Murfreesboro on the main line of the Nashville and Chattanooga Railroad. In the absence of any real news, the army newspapermen treated their readers to stories about large-scale Union desertions and the supposed intention of Rosecrans to evacuate Murfreesboro and retreat north to Nashville and Bowling Green. There was even an erroneous report in a Shelbyville paper, of the death of Rosecrans from pneumonia. Editor Daniel of the *Richmond Examiner* was impatient with such absurd reporting. Daniel expressed "grave uneasiness" with Rosecrans' threat to the Confederate position in east Tennessee, "unquestionably the first General the United States have in the field, at the head of one of the most powerful armies that ever made the ground tremble with its tramp. . . ."[3]

The letters which a certain "John Burley" contributed to the *Richmond Enquirer* during the spring of 1863 give some idea of the life of a Western army correspondent at this time. "John Burley" may have been the pseudonym of the famous journalist Henry Watterson, who was then connected with the newspaper establishment of the *Chattanooga Rebel*.[4] "John Burley" (or Watterson) held an unflattering opinion of Tullahoma, whose citizens had mostly left town, perhaps to create housing room for the Confederate generals and their staffs.

[3] *Charleston Daily Courier*, March 23, April 2, 1863; *Shelbyville* (Tenn.) *Banner* as reprinted in *ibid.*, February 12, 1863; *Daily Richmond Examiner*, February 12, 19, 1863. In a letter from Shelbyville dated February 22, 1863, T. D. Wright of the *Atlanta Confederacy* informed his newspaper that although there had been reports of thousands deserting the Union standard, "we occupy the extreme front . . . of Gen'l Bragg's army, and the enemy show no signs of deserting to us." *Atlanta Daily Southern Confederacy*, February 28, 1863.

[4] There is no direct evidence to substantiate the guess that "John Burley" was Watterson. In the *Daily Richmond Enquirer* of April 7, 1863, however, "John Burley" states that McMinnville, Tenn., Watterson's birthplace, is "mine own home and roof-tree." Also at this time, Watterson was a member of the editorial staff of the *Chattanooga Rebel* and may have been corresponding for that newspaper in Bragg's army. Third, there are similarities in the style of "John Burley's" army correspondence and Watterson's letters and editorials written at this time. In this connection see J. F. Wall, *Henry Watterson, Reconstructed Rebel* (New York, 1956), pp. 31, 39.

"The idiosyncrasy of this village is—it were hard to say—not mud, truly, for it will be as dusty tomorrow; nor bats, nor owls, either, for the fleas are quite as numerous. . . . I do not believe it has any peculiar features by which it can be distinguished and denominated. Sir, it is nondescript. A hell of a place the soldiers say. . . ."

The *Enquirer* reporter quoted a pretty young married woman as having written of Tullahoma: "The headquarters of an army are situated among a few squalid black jacks, a few trim cottages and a great many empty and rotten casks, indiscriminately scattered over a plateau which has not hill or stream to enliven the monotonous level. . . . Add that there is not a hotel, . . . a saloon, . . . a bath house, . . . not even a cage, and that there is a depot, several commissary and quartermaster's offices, and a lively assortment of camps, and the daguerreotype is complete."[5]

With Tullahoma as drab as it apparently was, it is hardly surprising that the *Enquirer* correspondent was frequently on the move, shuttling back and forth between Tullahoma, Shelbyville, and Chattanooga. Once he told about riding out from McMinnville on the extreme right of the Confederate line the night before with a scouting mission which netted a train of five wagons, twenty-eight mules, and a guard of ten Yankee soldiers. On another occasion he described an outing in Chattanooga at which he danced eleven sets, drank half a bottle of champagne, and came away at four o'clock in the morning "horribly in love!"[6]

In spite of Bragg's well-known hostility toward newspapermen, there were other reporters besides "John Burley" in the Army of Tennessee at this time, among them Albert J. Street of the *Mobile Register* and the *Savannah Republican* and a reporter for J. S. Thrasher's Press Association, who arrived at Tullahoma during the first week of April. Later Thrasher fired his reporter when he discovered that the man had inserted news obtained from Northern sources into a press report that had already been cleared for publication by Bragg's provost marshal general, Col. Alexander McKinstry, and that he had forged McKinstry's signature as a means of getting the material approved for transmission by telegraph.[7]

[5] *Daily Richmond Enquirer*, April 15, 1863.

[6] *Ibid.*, March 26, 30, April 7, 1863.

[7] *Chattanooga Daily Rebel* as paraphrased in *Columbus Daily Sun*, April 7, 1863; *Mobile Daily Advertiser and Register*, November 17, 1863.

To lend interest to their reporting, the correspondents in Bragg's army described the more colorful personalities among the officer corps with whom they came in contact. Since Bragg's cavalry was more active than his infantry at this time, the reporters paid more attention to dashing cavalry leaders Bedford Forrest and John H. Morgan than to the infantry division and corps commanders. "John Burley" described Forrest as "a swarthy, dark-eyed, Spanish-looking Caballero . . . who has a soul after your own heart, a fearless spirit of his own, and a keen, trenchant military perception." Later, during a visit to McMinnville, the same reporter sketched a pen portrait of the cavalry raider Morgan and his wife, who, the reporter said, had passed his window in each other's company only five minutes before.

"Know, then, that John Morgan is not my model for an Adonis, nor his wife altogether a Venus de Medici.[8] In strict observance and good breeding, they are both fair types of the better class of men and women in the twin States from which they [respectively] spring. The one tall, florid and full—an athlete, . . . used to exposure, hard riding and fatigue, clear blonde of hair and beard, and eyes of grayish blue; the other, a comely girl, . . . lissomely graceful as are most young women of health and education. . . . I saw the present Mrs. John Morgan (Miss Mattie Reedy [sic] who was) in the days when she was the most youthful star in quite a hemisphere of beauty. I believe her to be handsomer now, that the teens have ripened into the full-blown twenty; certainly more apropos to the sterling manhood of Morgan. She loves him very ardently, and I doubt not that the affair was entirely one of the affections. They take long strolls every afternoon, and the evidences of attachment . . . are delicate and dignified upon both sides."[9]

The dynamic Forrest provided one of the biggest news stories of 1863 when in April he led the pursuit and capture of a large party of Federal cavalry under Col. Abel D. Streight, which was operating in Bragg's rear. A special correspondent of the *Atlanta Confederacy* who accompanied the pursuit told how Forrest set out after the raiders from Spring Hill, Tennessee with a force of less than 500 horsemen, caught up with them at Decatur, Alabama and after five days and nights of almost incessant fighting and marching captured the whole

[8] Obviously a slip for Venus de Milo.
[9] *Daily Richmond Enquirer*, April 1, 7, 1863. Morgan had married Miss Mattie Ready, a belle of the Murfreesboro section, the previous December in a military wedding at which General (Bishop) Polk officiated.

band of 1,800 fugitives between Gadsden, Alabama and Rome, Georgia. Editor Adair, an old friend of Forrest, made a special train trip from Atlanta to Rome to interview him and obtain from his own lips an account of his thrilling exploit.[10]

In general the reporters in middle Tennessee spoke favorably of the morale and condition of Bragg's army at this time, although there were occasional complaints about monotonous fare and other deficiencies in the army's living arrangements. A correspondent of the *Columbus Sun* writing from near Shelbyville on April 5 acknowledged that "our troops are well clothed now," but "our rations are horrid; corn bread and fat bacon, day after day, is too much for the stomachs of many of our men, and the result is a prevalence of diarrhoea through the whole army." Two months later a soldier correspondent of the *Mobile Register* reported from Wartrace that "we are short of clothes; short of shoes; short of what we want to eat. The paymasters are out of funds and can't pay us, and if we have a bushel of Confederate money we cannot get the Lincolnites around us to take it."[11]

In the early part of June, after reporting the Chancellorsville fight from Virginia, Reid left Chattanooga to try his luck again in the Army of Tennessee. His connection with the *Mobile Register* had ceased at the end of April after a disagreement between him and the editors over military policy. Because of Reid's hostility toward Bragg, Colonel Forsyth had directed that none of his letters or dispatches should go to press until the colonel himself had inspected them. When through somebody's oversight the *Register* published some of Reid's correspondence without Forsyth having seen it, the colonel decreed that "Ora" should go to Charleston instead of returning to Bragg's army. Although Reid did go to Charleston at the beginning of March 1863, he gladly accepted an offer of a new employment from the *Register's* newspaper competitor in Mobile.[12]

---

[10] *Atlanta Daily Southern Confederacy*, May 8, 17, 1863. Adair characterized the capture as "the boldest game of bluff on record" and "one of the most extraordinary and brilliant achievements of the war." In *ibid.*, May 9, 1863 is a card signed by Adair inviting others to join him in presenting a fine war horse to General Forrest.

[11] *Columbus Daily Sun*, April 12, 1863; *Mobile Daily Advertiser and Register*, June 16, 1863. For an army correspondent's charges that the common soldier in Bragg's army was being victimized by army contractors see *Atlanta Daily Intelligencer*, July 3, 1863.

[12] Dr. J. C. Nott to General Braxton Bragg, March 1, 1863, Braxton Bragg Papers, Western Reserve Historical Society; undated newspaper clipping from

On his way back to middle Tennessee in June one of Bragg's officers clapped him under arrest at Shelbyville for going there without a pass, and ordered him to leave town by two o'clock the next afternoon. At that juncture one of Bragg's cavalry commanders, Maj.Gen. Joseph Wheeler, interceded with Bragg for Reid and obtained permission for the correspondent to remain in the army. An entry from Reid's diary for the following Sunday illustrates his feeling of personal triumph: "Shelbyville—Sun Jun 14. Went to hear Dr. Palmer preach—Met Gen. B. Bragg, who bowed to me!—"[13]

Before he left Chattanooga to return to Bragg's army Reid had obtained a glimpse of the "copperhead" Ohio politician, Clement L. Vallandigham, who had been banished from the United States and deposited within the Confederate lines under a flag of truce. Reid viewed Vallandigham rather unsympathetically, styling him "an avowed alien enemy" and declaring, "there is nothing which entitles him to the sympathy of our people in his career." He described the refugee Ohioan as "about fifty years of age, five feet eight inches high, brown short hair, slightly grey, a large twinkling blue eye, aquiline roman nose, full face, ruddy complexion, rather stout, has a very affable, pleasant manner, and smiles most graciously, exhibiting a white set of teeth. . . . He is what may be called a good looking man, with a very prepossessing popular manner, and admirably adapted to electioneering and stump speaking. He remarked that we had published nearly everything that the Northern papers contained, and therefore we must be well posted up."[14]

Toward the end of June the Union army began the offensive movement against Bragg's line that Editor Daniel had dreaded back in February. On June 24, while Maj.Gen. David S. Stanley's Federal cavalry staged a heavy demonstration against Polk at Shelbyville, Rosecrans' main army conducted a flanking operation against the Con-

---

Mobile Daily Tribune c. April 15, 1863, in S. C. Reid Papers. An invitation to Forsyth from Bragg to visit the army during the "hot months" evidenced the continuing close relationship between the general and the editor of the *Mobile Register*. (John Forsyth to Braxton Bragg, June 15, 1863, Bragg Papers.) Apparently Forsyth did not accept the invitation.

[13] Reid Diary, entries for June 8, 9, 14, 1863.

[14] *Atlanta Daily Intelligencer*, May 31, June 5, 1863. For a more sympathetic portrait of Vallandigham by another Southern army correspondent see *Atlanta Daily Southern Confederacy*, June 11, 1863.

federate right wing through Hoover's and Liberty Gaps, which were only lightly fortified.[15]

The army newspapermen were more than slightly confused by what followed. A correspondent of the *Mobile Register* who used the pseudonym "Look-Out" attributed the retirement of Bates' Tennessee brigade from Hoover's Gap to the exhaustion of its supply of ammunition, estimated the enemy's loss in that fight at ten times the Confederate's, and announced the recapture of the gap by reinforcements which Hardee hurried forward. Later the *Register* correspondent admitted he had been wrong about the recapture of the gaps.[16] Although Reid tried to make it appear that Bragg had outwitted Rosecrans by the retreat which followed the flanking operation, he implied by his reference to the "disgraceful" surprise at Hoover's and Liberty Gaps that Bragg's tactics had not been altogether successful.[17] Other reporters were critical of Wheeler's unsuccessful effort to protect the withdrawal of the Confederate wagon train from Shelbyville. Wheeler himself had barely escaped capture, and many of his troopers had not been so fortunate.[18] Baffled by Rosecrans' flanking strategy Bragg evacuated Tullahoma, fell back across the Elk River, and retreated across the Cumberland Mountains to Bridgeport on the Tennessee River.[19]

A general order issued on June 28 imposed censorship on wire reporting of the retreat while it was in progress.[20] To avoid the censorship most of the army reporters had to return to Chattanooga and forward their reports by mail from there. Although in general they put the best

[15] R. S. Henry, *"First with the Most" Forrest* (Indianapolis, 1944), p. 164; Horn, *Army of Tennessee*, p. 235.

[16] *Mobile Daily Advertiser and Register*, July 1, 8, 1863.

[17] *Atlanta Daily Intelligencer*, June 30, July 7, 8, 1863.

[18] *Chattanooga Daily Rebel*, July 2, 1863; *Mobile Daily Advertiser and Register*, July 8, 1863. The army correspondent of the *Augusta Constitutionalist* defended Wheeler's performance in a letter published in the *Constitutionalist* on July 24, 1863.

[19] J. H. Parks, *General Leonidas Polk, C.S.A.* (Baton Rouge, 1962), pp. 316-17; Henry, *"First with the Most,"* pp. 167-68.

[20] *Mobile Daily Advertiser and Register*, November 17, 1863; *Atlanta Daily Intelligencer*, July 3, 1863. For a critical comment about the reporting of Bragg's retreat by the Associated Press agent at Atlanta see *Richmond Daily Whig*, July 7, 1863. The Confederate Press Association had no regular reporter nearer to Bragg's army than Chattanooga at the beginning of July. The Chattanooga correspondent of the *Memphis Appeal* said regarding this: "The superintendent of the Associated Press reporters has withdrawn Mr. Butler at the very moment when he is most needed." *Memphis Daily Appeal*, July 3, 1863.

face possible on Bragg's retreat, they admitted that it had cost the temporary loss of middle Tennessee and northern Alabama; a soldier correspondent of the *Augusta Constitutionalist* alluded to the "singular and baneful antipathy" between the cavalry and the infantry that had been evident during the retreat. "It showed itself conspicuously on the march—generally provoked by the infantry. They call us by many opprobrious names, such as cowards—always spoke of our courage disparagingly. This came with an exceedingly ill grace from the men whose retreat we alone protected, but it shows how deep is the animosity, for which there is no cause."[21]

A reporter for the *Macon Telegraph* was at Bridgeport on July 5 when Bragg's army evacuated the town and crossed to the east side of the river, applying the torch to everything of value in and about the town except an old saw and grist mill. The same correspondent described the burning of the new bridge over the main channel of the Tennessee River, which he wistfully estimated had cost nearly $200,000.[22]

Some members of the Confederate press made the Press Association the scapegoat for the suppressed irritation that the retreat and Bragg's news censorship caused. The *Chattanooga Rebel* cited the provision of the constitution of the association, which required that a regular press reporter be stationed at all important points in the Confederacy, and wanted to know why none had been assigned to Chattanooga. From Augusta came the complaint that the P.A. reporter at Atlanta had neglected to send the press a dispatch about Bragg's recent movements until every paper in Atlanta had reached there with the news. Replying to this latter complaint, Editor Steele of the *Atlanta Intelligencer*, who had been acting as press agent at Atlanta for the past month, pinned the blame for his silence on interference with his press dispatches by the military commander in Atlanta.[23]

During the next six weeks both opposing armies remained stationary with the broad expanse of the Tennessee River and the thinly inhabited Cumberland Mountains region between them. The greater part of

[21] *Augusta Daily Constitutionalist*, July 24, 1863. For an earlier indication of such antipathy see letter of army correspondent "Bayonet" in *Mobile Daily Advertiser and Register*, April 29, 1863. In "Bayonet's" opinion, one infantry soldier was worth five cavalrymen "and costs only one third the money."

[22] *Macon Daily Telegraph*, July 10, 1863.

[23] *Chattanooga Daily Rebel*, July 8, 1863; *Augusta Daily Constitutionalist*, July 2, 1863; *Atlanta Daily Intelligencer*, July 7, 1863.

Bragg's army was massed at Chattanooga and along the Tennessee River upstream of the city. On the left Wheeler's cavalry stood guard over the long stretch of river from Chattanooga into northern Alabama.[24] Dupré of the *Knoxville Register* arrived in Chattanooga during the first week of August to study the military situation. He came to the conclusion, after talking with soldiers, that the morale of the army was higher than he had been led to believe. He also dismissed as untrue the stories of large-scale straggling and desertion by Tennessee soldiers during the recent retreat from Winchester and Shelbyville.[25]

The commanding general of these soldiers drew the attention of a *Macon Telegraph* reporter at Chattanooga, who wrote to his newspaper over the signature, "Achile" [*sic*]. According to "Achile," Bragg's headquarters was in a building atop one of Chattanooga's hills. "Any afternoon you may see the Commanding General, like a gray owl, on the front porch. To do Bragg justice, he is not an Adonis. He is a long, dismal looking man—ungraceful, but as I am told, not ungracious—with painful wrinkles round the eyes and mouth—a man without much knack or tact. What a pity that Bragg ever attempted to deal with the newspapers! For my own part, it is not a matter of any personal feeling . . . and I think some of his adversaries of the pen deserve hanging richly; but in the main, the man has, by indiscriminate folly, ruined himself with the press. . . ."[26]

Editor Watterson of the *Chattanooga Rebel*, on the other hand, did not endear himself to Bragg when he went to tea one afternoon at the Chattanooga residence of a Mrs. Reese Brabson. Watterson had been waging a vigorous editorial campaign for Bragg's replacement by General Johnston. At the tea he expressed his views about military strategy with his usual vivacity to a group that included a military gentleman to whom he had not been introduced. The "military gentleman" seemed to be displeased with Watterson's opinions; becoming aware of constraint among other members of the group, Watterson finally asked the grave listener if he were General Bragg. "I am," was

[24] J. P. Dyer, *"Fightin' Joe" Wheeler* (Baton Rouge, 1941), p. 110; Henry, *"First with the Most,"* p. 169.

[25] *Knoxville Daily Register*, August 6, 1863. Allegations that a considerable number of Tennessee soldiers had deserted from Bragg's army during the retreat appeared in the army correspondence of the *Mobile Register* during the early part of July 1863. *Montgomery Daily Mail*, July 12, 1863.

[26] *Macon Daily Telegraph*, July 23, 1863.

the grim reply which came from the general just before the editor hastily excused himself.[27]

Another newspaperman reporting for the *Mobile Register* wrote about the thin detachments of conscript soldiers who were shuffling into Chattanooga to fill the gaps created by the Tullahoma campaign. Describing a squad he had just met, the reporter told about an old fellow near the upper age limit who greeted him with the words, "Halloa, stranger, this ain't no fun, is it? I had rather be a knot on a dog's tail than to be a conscript." The *Register* man silently reflected that the conscript looked about as useful for army purposes as a "knot on a dog's tail." The reporter noticed another conscript paying ten dollars to an enterprising merchant for a watermelon. "The last of my money, and the last of me, too, maybe, for I'm just gwine into camp." Yet it was just such material, the correspondent remarked, who made very useful members of old regiments when mingled in the ranks with veteran troops.[28]

About mid-August the Confederate press became aware that Rosecrans was beginning a general advance on Chattanooga. On August 21 Crittenden's Federal corps reached the Tennessee River opposite Chattanooga and staged a surprise bombardment of the city as part of a demonstration to convince Bragg of Rosecrans' intention to cross the river above Chattanooga. Linebaugh, the special correspondent of the *Memphis Appeal,* was at the Presbyterian church in Chattanooga attending fast day services when the congregation was startled by the sound of artillery. The members immediately dispersed as the word was passed that the enemy was on the heights, across the river overlooking the town. As Linebaugh was hurrying back to his lodgings an officer turned him about, saying that a shell had exploded nearby, killing one man and wounding another. Confederate artillery was already replying, and the firing was still going on at five o'clock that afternoon when Linebaugh left the city.[29]

Neither Bragg nor any of the reporters at Chattanooga knew that the main part of Rosecrans' army was below Chattanooga, advancing

[27] D. C. Seitz, *Braxton Bragg, General of the Confederacy* (Columbia, S.C., 1924), pp. 331-32.

[28] *Mobile Daily Advertiser and Register*, August 13, 1863.

[29] Henry, "First with the Most," p. 173; *Memphis Daily Appeal*, August 22, 1863. Another reporter at the interrupted Presbyterian church service was Israel Gibbons, an occasional correspondent of the *Mobile Register. Mobile Daily Advertiser and Register*, August 28, 1863.

along the main line of the Nashville and Chattanooga Railroad. Throughout the campaign Bragg had been handicapped in scouting the enemy's movements by the detaching of a large part of his cavalry force to accompany Morgan's raid through Indiana and Ohio. On August 29 two of Rosecrans' three infantry corps crossed the Tennessee River below Bridgeport and marched eastward across the mountains. While Bragg was pondering whether to evacuate Chattanooga, there was a general exodus of citizens and army stores from the city. When Reid arrived from Atlanta on September 5 after a prolonged stay in Charleston, he found Chattanooga almost completely deserted, even more desolate than Charleston. Although Spencer's Hotel near the depot and the *Chattanooga Rebel* were still in business, army headquarters, the telegraph office, and the post office had been moved about two miles out of town at an inconvenient distance from each other.[30]

The next day Bragg notified his corps commanders of his decision to abandon Chattanooga and march on Rome, Georgia, Rosecrans' supposed objective. Watching the situation closely from Richmond, Davis and Lee decided that the time had come to reinforce Bragg substantially to enable him to remove the threat to Atlanta and roll back the tide of Yankee invasion. As a result, on September 8 Longstreet's corps was detached from Lee's army and started southward by train to join Bragg in northwest Georgia. Likewise orders went out to Johnston to send two divisions to Bragg from Mississippi; Buckner's corps, which had been pushed out of Knoxville when Burnside's Army of the Ohio invaded east Tennessee, moved down to unite with Bragg.[31]

Yet Bragg's evacuation of Chattanooga and its occupation the next day by a Yankee force caused consternation in some quarters of the Confederate press. Both the *Memphis* (Atlanta) *Appeal* and the *Atlanta Southern Confederacy* conjured up a gloomy picture in their "situation articles," and the editor of the *Richmond Examiner*, while conceding that the surrender of Chattanooga was essential to a successful defen-

[30] *Mobile Daily Tribune*, September 9, 1863. According to a special correspondent of the *Mobile Register*, the removal of military equipment from Chattanooga began on the day after the first shelling of the town and was completed by the following Monday. The only remaining civilian institution was the *Chattanooga Rebel*, whose editors continued to issue a war gazette until only a few hours before the enemy entered the city. *Mobile Daily Advertiser and Register*, September 8, 1863.

[31] Hal Bridges, *Lee's Maverick General, Daniel Harvey Hill* (New York, 1961), p. 198; D. B. Sanger and T. R. Hay, *James Longstreet* (Baton Rouge, 1952), pp. 198-99.

347

sive policy, hinted at his real feelings by exclaiming, "Let us hope that Bragg is a reproduction of [Nathaniel] Greene; but O! for an hour of Jackson! — O! for a day of our dead Dundee!"[32]

By this time Rosecrans had scattered his three corps so widely that none of them was in a position to support the others in the event of a vigorous counterstroke. Suddenly realizing his opportunity, Bragg tried in vain for a whole week to pick off the isolated units—while the Confederate press was almost completely at sea as to what was happening. The most knowledgeable reporters in the vicinity of Bragg's army were *Memphis Appeal* correspondent Linebaugh and Reid of the *Atlanta Intelligencer* and *Mobile Tribune*. Linebaugh had gone home to northern Alabama at the end of August because of the serious illness of his daughter, and was on his way back to the army when he learned that Federal troops were between him and Chattanooga. To escape capture, he reversed his course, crossing Sand Mountain and passing around the southern tip of Lookout Mountain to Rome. At Rome he boarded a train for Dalton, then headed back to Rome and from there to Kingston on September 14 in a not very successful effort to find out what was going on. Reid was in Atlanta on September 13; five days later he was in Tunnel Hill, north of Dalton, attempting to reach the rear of Bragg's army.[33]

Just about this time Bragg's feud with the press reached the boiling point. The Press Association was the first victim of Bragg's attempt to seal off his army from the press. Thrasher had dispatched P.A. reporter Will O. Woodson from Atlanta to the scene of operations in northern Georgia on September 3. When Woodson reached Kingston he was informed that Bragg's army was moving toward Rome. At Rome, Woodson was unable to obtain any positive information as to Bragg's whereabouts. After being informed by Colonel McKinstry that no press dispatches could be forwarded without his approval, Woodson returned to Kingston, where he learned that Bragg had established army headquarters at Lafayette, west of Dalton, about twenty-five miles south of Chattanooga. At Bragg's headquarters on the morning of September 16 Woodson tried unsuccessfully to obtain permission to report from the army or a pass to enable him to remain until such permission

---

[32] *Mobile Daily Tribune*, September 16, 1863; *Daily Richmond Examiner*, September 14, 1863. For a criticism of Reid's fault-finding about the "croaking" comments of the *Appeal* and the *Atlanta Confederacy* see *Mobile Daily Tribune*, September 17, 1863.

[33] *Memphis Daily Appeal*, September 8, 12, 16, 17, 1863.

could be granted. Unable to secure transportation cross-country to Re-saca, twenty-six miles away, Woodson started out on foot and reached his destination twelve hours later. From Resaca, which was on the rail-road, Woodson explained to Thrasher the reasons for his failure, adding that the reason assigned by the army authorities for their uncoopera-tive attitude was "the indiscretion of special correspondents in regard to army matters."[34]

The second newspaperman to run afoul of Bragg was Linebaugh, who had become increasingly critical of the general since the begin-ning of the Tullahoma campaign. On September 17, two days before the Battle of Chickamauga, Capt. J. P. Baltzell, the post commander at Rome, arrested Linebaugh and jailed him on a charge of treason. Baltzell held Linebaugh in custody until detailed orders for his arrest were received from Bragg. Linebaugh was then sent to Kingston and on September 19 transferred under a strong guard to a military prison in Atlanta. Learning of his reporter's plight, *Appeal* editor Dill hired a lawyer and instituted habeas corpus proceedings. Within a matter of hours after attorney Amos Hammond of Atlanta served Judge O. A. Bull's writ on the commander of the Atlanta military prison, the com-mander whisked Linebaugh out of Atlanta and placed him in the custody of the provost marshal at Ringgold, northwest of Dalton. There the correspondent remained until October 4, when he was released in accordance with legal proceedings conducted by Judge Bull. Bragg's arbitrary action, which neatly prevented Linebaugh from reporting the Battle of Chickamauga, may have been caused by a dispatch in which the *Appeal* correspondent mentioned troop movements, but a more obvious reason for the action was the allegations in Linebaugh's correspondence that Bragg was unwilling to fight the Federals.[35]

On the day Baltzell arrested Linebaugh, Bragg's army was moving north from Lafayette to face Rosecrans across Chickamauga Creek about ten miles below Chattanooga. By Friday, September 18, ele-ments of Bragg's army began crossing to the west side of the creek

[34] *Knoxville Daily Register*, September 21, 1863; Q. C. Wilson, "Confederate Press Association, A Pioneer News Agency," *Journalism Quarterly*, xxvi (June 1949), 165; *Mobile Daily Advertiser and Register*, November 17, 1863.

[35] *Charleston Daily Courier*, September 26, 1863; *Memphis Daily Appeal*, Oc-tober 7, 1863; *Mobile Daily Tribune*, October 13, 1863; George Sisler, "The Ar-rest of a Memphis Daily Appeal War Correspondent on Charges of Treason," *West Tenn. Hist. Soc. Papers*, xi (1957), 76-92; T. H. Baker, "Refugee Newspaper; The Memphis Daily Appeal, 1862-1865," *Journal of Southern History*, xxix (Au-gust 1963), 337.

although only the first contingents of Longstreet's nine brigades from Virginia had reached the battlefield after a long and circuitous journey via Wilmington, Charlotte, Augusta, and Atlanta.[36] On the morning of the nineteenth all but three of Bragg's eleven infantry divisions were across Chickamauga Creek, facing Rosecrans' army. At its maximum strength during the two-day battle, Bragg's army amounted to 66,000, with 198 guns. The field on which the battle was to be fought extended from Chickamauga Creek on the east to Missionary Ridge on the west. Much of the terrain was heavily wooded; the remainder consisted of open fields, pastures, and a few small houses. Bragg's plan of attack was to lead with his right so as to cut Rosecrans off from Chattanooga and force him back into a pocket of Lookout Mountain called McLemore's Cove.[37]

Whether Bragg planned it that way, apparently the only reporter on the field to witness the fighting of either day was "Tout-le-Monde," the army correspondent of the *Savannah Republican*. "Tout-le-Monde" had accompanied Hood's division of Longstreet's corps on the long train ride from Virginia and was with that division near the center of the Confederate line on the first day of the battle. In his battle story "Tout-le-Monde" alluded to the cheerful greetings exchanged between the soldiers of the Eastern and Western armies when Hood's division marched over from Tunnel Hill, and the tonic effect on Bragg's Westerners at seeing the reinforcements in the flesh.[38]

The fighting began early Saturday morning, September 19, when Forrest's cavalry on the Confederate right came in contact with Brannan's Union division as it was reconnoitering toward Chickamauga. When Forrest fell back after a brisk skirmish, a Confederate infantry division moved to its support, forcing back and badly mauling two Union divisions. The fortunes of battle changed when another Union division struck the flank of the Confederate division and drove it back with heavy loss. From that time until the end of the afternoon the battle was a dogfight, with each side sending in divisions, brigades, and even

[36] Horn, *Army of Tennessee*, p. 245. Not all of Longstreet's corps had been sent to Bragg. Pickett's division remained in Richmond, and Anderson's and Wise's brigades were ordered to Charleston. J. P. Dyer, *The Gallant Hood* (Indianapolis, 1950), p. 201.

[37] Bridges, *David Harvey Hill*, p. 204; Horn, *Army of Tennessee*, p. 257; Parks, *Polk*, p. 331.

[38] *Savannah Republican*, September 29, 1863.

regiments piecemeal.[39] Yet at the end of the day, although Rosecrans had lost some ground, his left flank was still intact along the Lafayette road. As the sound of fighting died away, "Tout-le-Monde" caught sight of the harvest moon through the dense smoke that hovered over the battlefield, in a silence which was broken only by the shrieks of the wounded.[40]

Shortly before midnight Longstreet rode into Bragg's headquarters from Ringgold, where his troops were still being unloaded from the cars. Longstreet learned from Bragg that the army was being reorganized into two new grand divisions, with Longstreet commanding the left wing and Polk in command of the right wing. Bragg's plan called for Breckinridge's division on the extreme right to attack at daylight and for the other divisions to go into action successively from right to left. Through a communication mixup, Breckinridge failed to receive Bragg's order until the next morning; as a result the attack was not carried out until about 9:30 A.M. In his report of Sunday's battle, *Savannah Republican* correspondent "Tout-le-Monde" pictured Longstreet riding along the lines with impassive countenance before the fighting began and Hood, smiling as he told his soldiers, "Boys, all went well yesterday on the right."[41]

On the left, the Confederate advance was stalled during the morning by the fierce resistance of the Union corps commander Thomas's troops, fighting behind the heavy breastworks they had thrown up during the night. Yet D. H. Hill's repeated assaults caused Thomas to keep calling for reinforcements. In the process of shifting troops from his right to his left, Rosecrans inadvertently opened a gap in his line which Longstreet's attack column of eight brigades discovered. Longstreet's impetuous charge split the Union line, causing the right and part of the center to crumble and retreat to Chattanooga. Thomas's corps with the remnants of the two others remained on the field, however, and bitter fighting continued until late afternoon when Thomas withdrew in the direction of Rossville. In the opinion of Reporter "Tout-le-Monde," with three more hours of daylight the remainder of Rosecrans' army would have escaped "only in squads."[42]

[39] Horn, *Army of Tennessee*, pp. 257-58.

[40] *Savannah Republican*, September 29, 1863.

[41] Bridges, *David Harvey Hill*, pp. 206-208; Horn, *Army of Tennessee*, pp. 259-60; *Savannah Republican*, September 29, 1863.

[42] Bridges, *David Harvey Hill*, p. 221; *Savannah Republican*, September 29, 1863.

On the morning after the battle "Tout-le-Monde" walked over the battlefield where most of Bragg's army were still encamped. According to him, some of the soldiers were amusing themselves by rifling the pockets of the dead and wounded enemy. From time to time they read to each other with ribald comments extracts from the love letters of Yankee soldiers or compared the pictures of the Yankee's girl friends. "The attitudes for grabbing 'truck' from the capacious pockets, the looks of surprise in drawing forth some unusual thing, the Southern names applied to and Southern remarks upon the various productions in course of exhumation was a scene to see and hear."[43]

Alexander and Reid arrived on the battlefield too late to witness the fighting. Before he left Richmond about the middle of September to join the Western army, Alexander had arranged with the *Richmond Dispatch* to represent the paper in Bragg's army, along with the *Savannah Republican* and the *Mobile Register*. On his way to Chickamauga he stopped in Savannah and did not begin the second leg of his journey until the second day of the battle.[44] Reid was at Tunnel Hill, to the east of Chattanooga, on Saturday morning, September 19, trying to find transportation to Ringgold. Unable to buy a horse for less than $1,000, he was still in Tunnel Hill Sunday, unable to locate transportation or anyone to approve his dispatches. He could hear distinctly the roar of musketry and artillery from the battlefield some fifteen miles away, although the sound had died away by the time (one o'clock in the afternoon) he ended his letter to the *Mobile Tribune*. Reid finally reached Chickamauga the next evening after walking nine miles from the railroad station at Ringgold.[45]

The first news of the battle to pass over the wires was an official dispatch from General Bragg telegraphed from Ringgold Sunday night. The first attempt to send it had failed when the telegraph instrument refused to work. After a Canadian officer from Morgan's cavalry, who had worked with Morgan on wire-tapping, made his instrument available, the dispatch was quickly sent. As Maj. B. J. Semmes of the 154th Tennessee Regiment recalled, the dispatch was written in pencil at a time when General Bragg did not realize the extent of his victory and therefore underplayed it. The message stated that the fighting had been "energetic," that a great number of men and officers had fallen, that

[43] *Ibid.*, October 6, 1863.
[44] *Ibid.*, September 18, 21, 1863.
[45] *Mobile Daily Tribune*, September 23, 25, 29, 1863.

the Confederates had captured twenty pieces of artillery and twenty-five hundred prisoners, that the Army of Tennessee held the field, but that "the enemy still confronts us." In a dispatch dated the following day Bragg revised his estimate, reporting that "the victory is complete" and that his cavalry was pursuing the enemy.[46]

Since the P.A. reporter was still excluded from the army, Thrasher prepared a report of the two-days' fighting at his Atlanta office on the morning of the twenty-first and submitted it to the post commander for transmission to the members of the Press Association. The executive officer refused to approve the report; it was not until Wednesday, the 23rd, that the P.A. account of the fighting, compiled from the statements of the wounded who had been brought to Atlanta, was published. By that time the P.A. reporter had returned to the front. Apparently Thrasher's difficulties with Bragg were still not resolved, however, for on September 29 P.A. reporters were still being kept away from Bragg's lines.[47]

Alexander reached the scene of the recent battle in time to write a two-column account which he mailed to the newspapers he represented. Since he had arrived there too late to see the fighting, he was, he admitted, almost wholly uninformed about the organization of the various units of which the Army of Tennessee was comprised. He, was therefore compelled to rely on the statements of others. It was hardly surprising in view of his lack of familiarity with the Western army that he was tempted to assign particular credit for the victory to the troops he knew best—Longstreet's veterans from Virginia. Alexander told how these reinforcements had "travelled from the Rappahannock in crowded box cars, upon open platforms, and upon the tops of the cars, in the rain, in the dust, and in the sun, and with but little food or sleep. They had passed by their own homes without stopping to embrace the loved ones there—homes which some of them had not seen since the commencement of the war; and had rushed to the scene of action without rest or transportation, halting only long enough to clear their eyes of the dust of travel and replenish their cartridge boxes. The officers were without horses, and the men without wagons to trans-

---

[46] *Confederate Veteran*, III (October 1895), 293; *Daily Richmond Enquirer*, September 23, 1863; *O.R.* (Army) Ser. I, vol. xxx, pt. 2, pp. 22-23.

[47] *Knoxville Daily Register*, September 21, 1863; *Memphis Daily Appeal*, September 23, 1863; *Daily Richmond Examiner*, September 30, 1863; R. F. Tucker, "The Press Association of the Confederate States of America in Georgia," unpub. Master's thesis (University of Georgia, 1950), pp. 63-65.

port their supplies. There was not time to furnish either; the battle was about to be joined. Arrived in front of the foe, these veterans were placed in the van and led in every attack by the left wing where our success was most signal and where the day was really won."[48]

Although Alexander's account was widely reprinted and praised in the Confederate press, Reid's battle report, which he prepared with elaborate care, was probably the most complete and informing Confederate newspaper account. This account, which he worked on for nearly two weeks and which first appeared in print in the *Mobile Tribune*, was published in pamphlet form at Mobile in November 1863.[49]

Reid's battle story ran to about ten thousand words and was both readable and generally accurate. Although in his eyes Chickamauga was a "great and glorious victory," Reid reported the battle with some degree of objectivity. He admitted that Saturday's fighting ended without Bragg having gained any decisive advantage, and that up until Sunday noon the Confederate right had been repulsed by the enemy's "superior numbers." His account also contained effective descriptions of the divisions of Hindman and Bushrod Johnson advancing like "tigers on the foe" and of the forest being ignited by the enemy's artillery fire.

In describing military operations Reid perhaps wrote too exclusively from the Southern point of view. He made no attempt to identify any of the Union corps or division commanders and even implied that Crittenden did not take part in the battle. In addition, it could be argued that his version of what happened was often excessively partisan. Almost invariably he referred to Rosecrans' soldiers as "the Abolitionists" or the "abolition infidel foe"; just as frequently Bragg's troops were "glorious heroes" who "press forward undaunted . . . while the terrified enemy . . . [give] way before them."

Although his account of the events of the battle was substantially correct, there were some notable exceptions. He did not seem to have

[48] *Savannah Republican*, September 28, October 1, 1863; *Richmond Daily Dispatch*, September 29, 1863; *Mobile Daily Advertiser and Register*, September 29, 1863. Only portions (five brigades) of two divisions of Longstreet's corps arrived at Chattanooga in time to participate in the battle. Horn, *Army of Tennessee*, pp. 259-60. For critical comment by the army correspondent of the *Columbus (Ga.) Enquirer* about discrimination against the corps of Buckner, Polk, and Walker in Alexander's reporting see *Augusta Daily Constitutionalist*, October 10, 1863.

[49] *Mobile Daily Tribune*, October 25, 1863; S. C. Reid, *Great Battle of Chickamauga* (Mobile, 1863).

been aware, for example, some fifteen days afterward, that Longstreet and Hood achieved their decisive breakthrough before noon on September 20. He incorrectly gave the time of the breakup of the enemy's right and center as "about 5 o'clock" and presented a rather confused version of what happened after that, although evidently he was aware that Rosecrans provided the opportunity for Longstreet's success by moving a "heavy body of troops" from one wing to the other. But he indicated incorrectly that the direction of the enemy's troop movement was from Rosecrans' left to his right.

The statistics Reid used in reporting the battle were in some instances approximately correct, but in others considerably wide of the mark. The 8,000 prisoners and forty-nine pieces of captured artillery that he cited were almost identical with the figures given in Bragg's report. Yet he underestimated the Confederate loss by at least 6,000, and placed the enemy's loss at almost double the actual figure. He also made the Confederate victory seem even more remarkable by stating, inaccurately, that Rosecrans' available force on the field outnumbered Bragg's by at least 30,000. He claimed with some degree of exaggeration that not since the Battle of Crecy in 1346 had the artillery arm of the service been more effective on both sides.[50] The fact is that the wooded country in which the battle was fought interfered to some extent with the use of artillery, especially by the Confederates.

Much of the exaggeration and most of the more obvious inaccuracies that appeared in print about Chickamauga were a product of the telegraphic reporting of the battle. The Press Association first reported that the battle took place on Peavine Creek rather than the Chickamauga, and Alexander sent a special dispatch from Ringgold to the *Mobile Register* on September 22, asserting that the Confederates had captured forty thousand prisoners![51] On September 23 the *Memphis Appeal* stated "with great certainty of the correctness of our information" that Rosecrans had burned the city of Chattanooga with all his stores on the south side of the river and recrossed the Tennessee on Monday night, destroying his pontoons to escape pursuit; that careful reconnaissance had failed to discover any Federals on the south side of the river on Tuesday; and that an engine had gone in to Chattanooga from Cleveland on Tuesday evening and returned in safety. This story was en-

[50] Reid, *Great Battle of Chicamauga.*
[51] *Mobile Daily Advertiser and Register,* September 23, 1863; *Macon Daily Telegraph,* September 24, 1863.

tirely without basis; within twenty-four hours the *Appeal* had to admit that it was untrue. Telegraph dispatches from Atlanta also reported on September 22 that General Hood had died as the result of a wound received in the battle which had caused his right leg to be amputated. On the day after this story appeared in the *Richmond Examiner* the *Examiner* printed a denial in another dispatch from Atlanta stating that *"General Hood is not dead. . . .* He says he will live to fight the Yankees at least another battle."[52]

Although both Forrest and Longstreet had besought Bragg to vigorously pursue the enemy, Bragg consumed several days moving his army slowly toward Chattanooga. Not until Wednesday, September 23, did he establish his headquarters on Missionary Ridge overlooking the city.[53] In a letter to the *Richmond Dispatch* written from Lookout Mountain five days later, Alexander confirmed earlier reports that "Rosecrans has not evacuated Chattanooga nor is there any reason to believe that he has any such intention. The long lines of infantry, cavalry, and artillery reported by the signal corps some days ago to be crossing the Tennessee to the north side, are now believed to have been forces sent out for the purpose of escorting provisions and forage trains to Stevenson and McMinnville, whence the Federal army obtain their supplies. . . . Possibly the place could have been carried by storm, though not without heavy loss, had we pressed forward from the victorious field of Chicamauga. If any mistake has been committed it was in not making the effort at that time—It is too late now, I fear."[54]

For a matter of hours or days there had been covert hopes on the part of Confederate journalists and their readers that Bragg's victory, won at such heavy cost,[55] would result in the recapture of Chattanooga and the repossession of Tennessee, Kentucky, and even Mississippi. Yet the

[52] *Daily Richmond Examiner*, September 25, 1863.
[53] Bridges, *David Harvey Hill*, p. 226.
[54] *Richmond Daily Dispatch*, October 6, 1863.
[55] Total Confederate casualties of 18,454 exceeded the Union total by more than 2,200. In a number of the Tennessee regiments and in several other Confederate regiments the percentage of loss was 60 percent or more. As usual the first reports by telegraph underestimated the Confederate losses and magnified those of the enemy. In a special dispatch from the battlefield on September 23, Reid estimated the Confederate loss at between eight and ten thousand and the enemy's at twenty-five to thirty thousand. Yet an Associated Press dispatch from Atlanta the day before conceded that the Confederate losses might reach fifteen thousand. Shelby Foote, *The Civil War, A Narrative: Fredericksburg to Meridian* (New York, 1963), p. 758; Horn, *Army of Tennessee*, p. 273; *Mobile Daily Tribune*, September 24, 1863; *Atlanta Daily Intelligencer*, September 24, 1863.

experience of Stone's River, where Bragg's claim of a complete victory had been the prelude to a retreat, made for some degree of skepticism even in Richmond, where the first reports of Chickamauga caused pleasure to "beam" from every eye and where *Mobile Register* correspondent Shepardson heard shouts of "Hurrah for Bragg!" and "Bully for him!"[56] Perhaps many a Richmondite felt as the *Memphis Appeal* correspondent did, that unless the hated Yankees were driven from Kentucky and Tennessee, the Battle of Chickamauga had been fought in vain.[57]

ON A MILD autumn morning during the first week of October John Forsyth took time out from proofreading the daily edition of the *Mobile Register* to compose a letter to his favorite general. Bragg's victory at Chickamauga had put the editor in an exultant mood that was reflected in his letter, along with an undertone of anxiety. Forsyth told Bragg:

"Everything conspires to make your triumph conspicuous—the magnitude of the stake for which you fought, the chosen army of the enemy which you have overthrown, the sneers & gibes & abuse of your enemies which you have silenced. I thank you for our common country & personally I do most inwardly enjoy your triumph. Indeed, I feel as if I had a personal share in it, for that triumph has fulfilled my promises & vindicated my opinions of what you could do if ever you had a chance. . . .

"We are all watching the scene of your operations with interest . . . heightened by the mystery which hangs over the two armies. How Rosecrans feeds his men . . . shut up in Chattanooga & cut off from . . . R. Road communication is a puzzle to us. I pray God you may be able to give him a finishing blow—a *coup de grace* that will end him & all Yankee hopes in the West."[58]

Reid of the *Atlanta Intelligencer* and the *Mobile Tribune*, who was south of and across the river from Chattanooga at this time, was less hopeful than Forsyth that Bragg was about to administer the *coup de grace* for which Forsyth so hungered. Writing to the *Intelligencer* on September 28, Reid stated flatly that there was no probability of an encounter with Rosecrans' army "for some days." He reported that Bragg's army was in a semicircular shaped valley extending from the

---

[56] *Mobile Daily Advertiser and Register*, September 30, 1863.

[57] *Memphis Daily Appeal*, September 28, 1863.

[58] John Forsyth to Braxton Bragg, October 2, 1863, Bragg Papers, Western Reserve Historical Society.

base of Lookout Mountain on the left to Missionary Ridge on the right and that the enemy's position was strong and well fortified, "they taking advantage of the works we had constructed, besides having since erected three lines of entrenchment fronting South."[59]

Three days later, in his correspondence for the *Tribune*, Reid revealed that Bragg was devoting more attention to warring with his generals than to following up his victory. Similar information, to the effect that Bragg had placed Generals Polk and Hindman under arrest "during, or immediately after" the Battle of Chickamauga for failure to carry out his orders, reached the Richmond press on October 4 through the medium of some railroad passengers direct from Atlanta.[60] Yet the press failed to obtain, or refrained from publishing, detailed information about the disharmony between Bragg and his subordinates. It was perhaps just as well from the standpoint of Southern morale that the Confederate press did not reveal the complaints about Bragg that Polk, Longstreet, and Hill were making to the authorities in Richmond. In letters to Secretary Seddon, President Davis, and even General Lee, Bragg's lieutenants made clear that they thought the army's welfare required Bragg's removal. Davis dispatched his aide, Colonel Chesnut, to Bragg's army to ascertain what lay back of these complaints. When Chesnut wired Davis that his immediate presence in the army was "urgently demanded," the President left Richmond, arriving at Bragg's headquarters early on Friday, October 9.[61]

In Atlanta, where he had gone on a shopping expedition, Alexander professed uncertainty as to the object of the President's visit. "Has he come to mingle with his soldiers and encourage them by his presence?" Alexander wanted to know, "or has he come to compose the strifes of officers, and, if need be, to institute a change in the command of the army?"[62] There was little doubt among the army correspondents at Bragg's headquarters that Davis was there to perform the latter function. De Fontaine, who had just arrived in the army from Charleston

[59] *Atlanta Daily Intelligencer*, October 1, 1863. *London Times* correspondent Francis E. Lawley, who visited Bragg's army about a week after the Battle of Chickamauga, was convinced of Bragg's utter incompetency. W. S. Hoole, *Lawley Covers the Confederacy* (Tuscaloosa, 1964), pp. 72-73.

[60] *Daily Richmond Examiner*, October 5, 1863.

[61] Bridges, *David Harvey Hill*, pp. 228-29; Parks, *Polk*, pp. 342-43; Sanger and Hay, *Longstreet*, pp. 212-15.

[62] *Savannah Republican*, October 14, 1863; *Richmond Daily Dispatch*, October 15, 1863. Alexander was with difficulty shopping for winter clothes in Atlanta. "A suit of winter clothes at $500—think of that."

to cover operations for the *Charleston Courier, Richmond Whig,* and *Memphis Appeal,* let it be known in his published correspondence that he thought Davis's visit was very desirable, to dispel "the spirit of complaint which I am free to state prevails throughout the army."[63]

The first news event in connection with Davis's visit was a review he conducted on the day after his arrival. According to the Press Association reporter, who apparently was in good graces again, the President rode along the entire line of the army within range of the enemy's shells, and not a gun was opened upon him. The generals who constituted the President's escort provided copy for a descriptive piece by "Personne," in which he made use of such characterizations as the "dignified" Bragg, the "facetious" D. H. Hill, "stately" Breckinridge, "rough and ready" Buckner, "impetuous" Jenkins, and "dashing" Cheatham. "Personne" explained the lack of enthusiasm among the troops on the Confederate left during the review as being prompted by concern for the President's safety, since the Confederate position was within a thousand yards of the enemy's batteries. "Personne" refrained from saying anything about the near mutiny in the army that General Pemberton's presence in the President's entourage was supposed to have occasioned.[64]

Davis remained with the army five days, during which he sought in vain to bring about a reconciliation between Bragg and his generals. Disregarding positive evidence of lack of confidence in their commander by the generals, Davis kept Bragg in command and acquiesced in the removal of Polk, Hindman, and Hill. Not knowing what was going on at the top military level, the army correspondent had to fall back on misleading platitudes about the visit of the executive having restored harmony where it had not previously existed.[65]

Reporter Reid grasped at the opportunity to ferret out the real story about Davis's visit, however, when he found himself on the same train with Davis bound from Tunnel Hill to Atlanta. Presuming on his previ-

---

[63] *Charleston Daily Courier,* October 20, 1863.

[64] *Memphis Daily Appeal,* October 19, 1863; *Richmond Daily Whig,* October 26, 1863. De Fontaine did allude to the presence of Pemberton in the army and to the surprise among the men. He also correctly guessed that Pemberton had come there to replace Polk as a corps commander. Reluctantly Davis and Pemberton came to the conclusion that no one in the army wanted to serve under the command of the general who had surrendered Vicksburg. D. C. Seitz, *Bragg,* pp. 382-83.

[65] See e.g. *Charleston Daily Courier,* October 27, 1863.

ous acquaintance with the President, Reid employed one stratagem after another to draw him out, but was baffled at every turn. When, for example, Reid spoke slyly about certain plans in relation to Tennessee, Davis blandly agreed that they would be very desirable. When next the reporter mentioned a certain rumor about a movement in middle Tennessee, his travel companion made the noncommittal comment that it would be a fine country to be in. When finally their conversation progressed to another topic whose nature Reid did not specify in his correspondence and about which Davis deftly queried, "What do you think about it, sir?" Reid rallied the President with the rejoinder,

"Well, sir, if I was President Davis I could tell you a great deal more on that point than I am at present supposed to know."

Thereupon the President, "taking an additional puff of his cigar, and with one of his blandest smiles," retorted,

"You may be sure I shall not enlighten you, sir, and so you need not attempt to pump me."

"Not for a moment," replied Reid hastily, somewhat disconcerted at Davis's insinuation. "Having known you, sir, for the last twenty years, I should not attempt at this time of life to apply to you the hydraulic pressure."

President Davis seemed willing to accept this explanation, whereupon the journalist and the President shook hands and parted, without Reid being any the wiser for the experience.[66]

Davis had hardly left the army before he became a party to another controversy involving the press. The difficulty was occasioned by the Confederate Associated Press report of a speech that Davis had made at a serenade following his visit to the Chickamauga battlefield on October 13. The P.A. credited Davis with having made a short speech complimenting General Bragg in the highest terms, adding: "He said that notwithstanding the shafts of malice that had been hurled at him [Bragg], he had bravely borne it all, and the bloody field of Chickamauga plainly stamps him as a military commander of the first order." The *Columbus Sun* reported that when the President stopped at Atlanta on his way back to Richmond, General Polk, who had gone there after his removal from command, called Davis's attention to the telegraphic synopsis of that part of his speech and asked for an explanation. According to the *Sun*, Davis denied he had ever used such lan-

[66] *Mobile Daily Tribune,* October 21, 1863.

guage. The *Chattanooga Rebel* (now published in Atlanta) confirmed the *Sun's* story and quoted Davis as having said in Atlanta that far from eulogizing General Bragg he had not even mentioned his name during his speech and had used extreme caution to avoid any allusion which would offend the large number of gallant officers who were antagonistic to Bragg.

Following a complaint to the superintendent of the Press Association, the agent who had transmitted the inflammatory report was discharged. Thrasher did not deny having discharged him, but in a public statement he issued on October 23 he presented the explanation given to him by his agent, Woodson. Woodson admitted that he had not heard the speech of the President that he reported, since he was en route to the army from Atlanta at the time. He identified as the sources for his version of the speech Bragg's provost marshal general, Colonel McKinstry, Colonel Walters and Captain Read of General Bragg's staff, and "numerous gentlemen who told me the same."

In a letter to the *Atlanta Intelligencer* written after the publication of Thrasher's explanation, Reid, who apparently was not present when the speech was delivered, expressed the opinion, "there is no doubt but that the President was properly reported." He denied, however, the implication in Woodson's statement that the telegraphic synopsis of the speech had been obtained from Bragg's headquarters and was therefore an official statement. Reid concluded that the P.A. reporter had obtained his version of the speech "in the ordinary way," i.e. from officers who were present.[67]

In their reports from Missionary Ridge the army correspondents had already made clear that Bragg's artillery on Lookout Mountain com-

[67] Newspaper clippings from undated issue of *Chattanooga Daily Rebel* and from *Savannah Republican* of October 16, 1863, Leonidas Polk Papers, Southern Historical Collection, University of North Carolina; *Chattanooga Daily Rebel* as reprinted in *Daily Richmond Examiner*, October 22, 1863; *Columbus Daily Sun* as reprinted in *Charleston Daily Courier*, October 23, 1863; *Chattanooga Daily Rebel* as reprinted in *Daily Richmond Enquirer*, October 26, 1863; *Richmond Daily Dispatch*, October 24, 1863; *Charleston Daily Courier*, October 24, 1863; *Columbia Daily Southern Guardian*, October 24, 1863; *Atlanta Daily Intelligencer*, November 1, 1863; Tucker, "Press Association," p. 66. Reid's remarks about the statement of the Press Association may reflect the antagonism against the organization evident in his letter to the *Intelligencer* published on November 19, 1863, in which he objected to the "pilferings and distortions of my special dispatches by Mr. Thrasher." Reid repeated these allegations in the *Atlanta Daily Intelligencer* of December 20, 1863, adding that the *Atlanta Southern Confederacy* was the organ of the Associated Press agent.

manded Rosecrans' supply route between Bridgeport and Chattanooga by rail, road, or river. Bragg hoped to starve Rosecrans' army out of Chattanooga by blockading this supply route; during the early part of October it looked as if the strategy might succeed. On October 16 Alexander briefly described a destructive raid by Wheeler's cavalry in the Sequatchie Valley almost two weeks earlier which had wiped out a Federal train of five hundred wagons bringing supplies to Chattanooga. Yet if food was scarce in Rosecrans' camp, it was scarce in the Confederate camp, too. In a letter to the *Atlanta Intelligencer* Reid described the "trials and tribulations of a correspondent who has a horse to feed and take care of and who especially has to do his own foraging, and no corn to be had at that. . . ."[68]

Alexander expatiated on the discomforts of the Confederate soldiers near Chattanooga, performing guard duty in trenches half filled with water as a result of the heavy rains that set in about the middle of October. Many of the soldiers were without tents and were provided with only one blanket. According to "Personne," fever, ague, and dysentery were prevalent throughout the army, but especially in Longstreet's corps, whose soldiers were not yet adjusted to the Tennessee climate. Although they were better equipped to withstand the weather than the soldiers in Bragg's old army, "Personne" could see that they were not entirely contented. The best indication of their nostalgia for the Old Dominion was the music of their bands. "Carry Me Back to Old Virginia" was by far the most popular air, always giving rise to a pandemonium of cheers, yells and "ki-yis."[69]

One of the best specimens of army reporting of its kind, written in "Personne's" best descriptive style, was a letter he furnished to the *Charleston Courier* describing camp life in Bragg's army under adverse weather conditions:

Autumn is upon us in one of her most savage moods. The picturesque has become puddlesome; the heavens are shedding their floods, the woods their crimson dyes, and the saucy wind, sharp as Shylock's knife, searches to the very crannies of our bones. Such has been the weather which for two days has made us melancholy, misanthropic, and miserable. Rain, rain, rain, that "mournful music of the mind," has drizzled and poured upon us by turns,

[68] *Savannah Republican*, October 21, 1863; *Atlanta Daily Intelligencer*, October 1, 1863.

[69] *Richmond Daily Dispatch*, October 24, 1863; *Charleston Daily Courier*, October 17, 27, 1863; *Mobile Daily Advertiser and Register* as reprinted in *Atlanta Daily Intelligencer*, October 30, 1863.

until camp has become a chaos, and the men dream of Noah's ark and Mount Arrarat as a pastime. Poor fellows! Without shelter, half fed, with no covering at night but a bower of leaves and threadbare blankets, no resting place but the rocky hillsides down which a myriad of muddy rivulets are coursing, with fires inundated, clothing saturated, feet wet, bodies shrivelled, and intermittent agues knocking at the door, it is no wonder that they give vent to a natural mud-puddle infirmity, and grumble at this purgatorial existence.

The soil is soaked and slippery; the mud ankle deep and dotted with "lovely islands in solution;" the streams choked, fords impassible and bridges gone. You attempt to walk, and after reeling like a drunken man attempting to preserve his equilibrium, there are ten chances to one that your locomotive apparatus will fly up, your head down, and a beautiful map of the country done in red clay will be impressed in a most uncomfortable manner in a most inconvenient place. Copyrights of "Life in Tennessee," like these, are dirt cheap all around us.

As an illustration of camp comfort, pardon me for giving you a personal specimen. Towards dusk one evening last week, I called upon a prominent officer. Headquarters, such as they happened to be, were on a declivity of Missionary Ridge, so steep that a stone started at the top would have rolled two hundred yards to the bottom. Fire of logs in the back ground and half a dozen horses tethered to the trees. Fifty yards distant our entrenchments, and a hungry crowd cooking evening rations. Was invited to supper—looked in vain for the accessories—but directly an Ethiopian ganymede produced from a bag that had gone the rounds of a Western campaign, a bone, five biscuits and a pinch of salt. Five minutes more and a tin cup, that served at once for five and table, was set before us, oderiferous [*sic*] with the fumes of smoking hot coffee. Our table was a rock, our spread a blanket, and an appreciative appetite compensated for every other want.

Seated on the ground, around the camp fire, we talked over old times and home affairs until nine o'clock. "Stay with us all night." It was not hard to say—"yes!" I searched fruitlessly for the bed chamber, *alias* tent, but the luxury did not belong to even headquarters. In a few moments, however, an India rubber blanket was spread upon the safest place, leaves gathered to make it still more sylvan, more blankets were laid down, and I was told to "take the middle." With a tolerably stout officer on either side, all three occupying not more than four feet breadthwise, packed like sardines and straight as liberty poles, my friend on the uphill side constantly rolling against me, and I, in turn, pressed against my down hill neighbour, you can imagine the situation, and why it was that before morning the latter unfortunate was obliged to prop himself up with rocks to keep from rolling to the bottom of the hill.

Here with as pretty a picture spread before us, as ever graced the easel of an artist—the clear blue dome of night's dark tent, above—the camps of the enemy in full view, their pickets only six hundred yards distant, thousands of fire lights gleaming like stars transferred from heaven to earth, and the music of the bands of both armies mingling with our "good night"

363

thoughts of home—we slumbered as peacefully as if in the grotto of an houri.

Such is life in camp. You will agree with me that to enjoy it requires tough stomachs and unsusceptible sittings down. Our troops, however, are [as] patient as human nature will permit them to be under the sometimes trying circumstances, and preserve that jolly indomitableness of disposition, which is the ever present characteristic of an American, whether he be climbing an Egyptian Pyramid, bivouacked in a desert, or controverting scripture logic with his Holiness, the Pope.[70]

A considerable portion of the press, including such influential newspapers as the *Richmond Examiner*, the *Atlanta Confederacy*, the *Columbia South Carolinian*, and *Mobile Tribune*, continued to criticize Bragg for not having captured Chattanooga after the Battle of Chickamauga and for retaliating against the generals with whom he had quarreled.[71] Bragg did not improve matters by reopening his old feud with Reid while Reid was in Atlanta on a three-day rest trip from the army. As Reid was preparing to return to the front on October 17, Capt. Charles W. Peden, the provost marshal in Atlanta, refused to permit him to board the train. In an effort to obtain clearance for the *Intelligencer*'s army correspondent, Editor Steele learned that Captain Peden's action was based on an order issued at Shelbyville sometime earlier in the year, and which, not having been revoked, Peden felt obliged to enforce in Atlanta. As soon as he discovered this, Steele telegraphed Bragg to request a pass for Reid, and followed up the telegram with a letter expressing strong indignation. In his letter, written after he had already learned that Reid would be permitted to go back to the army, Steele let Bragg know that the *Intelligencer*, "a journal whose circulation is not surpassed by any in Georgia," had never failed in its editorial support of the general, "simply because its Proprietor and Editor were impressed with your lofty patriotism and military capacity, for neither of us has ever had any personal acquaintance with you." Steele went on to say that the *Intelligencer* had employed Reid as an army correspondent because it wished to obtain the services of an able man whose letters would interest their readers

[70] *Charleston Daily Courier*, October 22, 1863.

[71] The *Daily Richmond Enquirer* of November 23, 1863 classed the *Atlanta Confederacy* as having been "the most earnest and vehement of all Confederate newspapers in entreating for the removal of General Bragg. . . ." R. W. Gibbes, the editor of the *Columbia South Carolinian* and the president of the Confederate Associated Press, was evidently a partisan of Polk. In this connection see his letter to Polk of October 18, 1863, Polk Papers, Southern Historical Collection, in which he enclosed a clipping from his newspaper defending Polk against Bragg.

and because it wished to be "truthfully" advised of occurrences that were suitable for publication. Steele told Bragg that Reid "has not disappointed us in a single particular, and, I am satisfied, has been eminently serviceable in advancing the policy of this journal in all that pertains to your command."[72]

Bragg was not without his defenders, however. Among the newspapers especially friendly to him were Colonel Forsyth's *Mobile Register*, the *Atlanta* (formerly the *Knoxville*) *Register* (which had the reputation of being Bragg's "organ,") the *Richmond Whig, Charleston Courier, Savannah Morning News, Augusta Constitutionalist*, and *Marietta* (Ga.) (formerly the *Huntsville*) *Confederate*. At the end of October Editor John Withers Clay of the *Marietta Confederate* announced that during a visit to the front some ten or fifteen days before he had been authorized to state General Bragg's policy toward the press. According to Clay, Bragg had never excluded press correspondents or telegraph reporters from his lines so long as they were "prudent" and refrained from publishing information inimical to the Confederate cause. Clay also said he had been told that on several occasions newspaper reporters had violated the conditions prescribed by Bragg for remaining within his lines.[73]

On the evening of October 21, after he had received permission to return to Bragg's army, Reid boarded a northbound train on the Western & Atlantic Railroad and arrived at Tunnel Hill the next morning at dawn. A heavy rain set in soon after his arrival; since the railroad bridge between Tunnel Hill and Ringgold was still under construction, Reid decided to accept the offer of a friend to drive him to Lookout Mountain in a buggy. On the way Reid stopped overnight at the home of a Mr. Small near the gap in Taylor's Ridge. There he spent a pleasant evening playing chess with a charming young lady whom he referred to in his diary simply as "Miss Lou." He crossed Chickamauga Creek the next morning (the 25th) at Alexander's bridge, passed over the Chickamauga battlefield where the bleaching bones of the enemy dead were still unburied, and arrived at the camp of Hood's division on Lookout Mountain that evening. From Hood's soldiers he heard that the general was recovering from a leg amputation and that his division

[72] John H. Steele to Gen. Braxton Bragg, October 21, 1863, Bragg Papers.
[73] *Marietta Confederate*, as reprinted in *Mobile Daily Advertiser and Register*, November 5, 1863.

had raised five thousand dollars to procure for him the best cork leg money could buy![74]

Reid's return to the army was just in time to enable him to report the part played by Hood's (now Jenkins') division in the first important clash of arms since Chickamauga. While Reid was in Atlanta there had been a change in command of the Federal army, with Thomas replacing Rosecrans in command of the Army of the Cumberland and Grant being placed in charge of all Federal military operations in the West. While Reid was still at Tunnel Hill on his way back from Atlanta, Grant reached Chattanooga to supervise measures for opening the river supply route. At Bridgeport were the two corps of the Federal Army of the Potomac which Secretary Edwin M. Stanton had rushed to Rosecrans' aid after the Chickamauga defeat. From Northern newspapers and other sources, the Confederate press had become aware as early as the beginning of October that troops from Meade's army were being sent west to reinforce Rosecrans.[75]

Before Rosecrans left Chattanooga on October 19 he had begun to formulate a plan for opening the "Cracker Line," as the Union soldiers called the river supply route. Both Thomas and Grant approved the plan; in accordance with it, a small force of Northern soldiers floated down the river from Chattanooga on the night of October 26-27 to Brown's Ferry, a distance of five miles from Chattanooga by water. From Brown's Ferry, which was safely out of range of the Confederate guns on Lookout Mountain, it would be easy for the Federals to reach Bridgeport either by road or river. Brushing aside the Confederate pickets at Brown's Ferry, the enemy established a bridgehead on the Confederate side of the river and fortified it before Bragg or Longstreet knew what was going on.[76]

In his report of the Brown's Ferry operation war correspondent Alexander charged that the enemy caught the Confederate videttes on the south bank of the river asleep. Apparently Alexander and the other

[74] *Atlanta Daily Intelligencer*, October 25, 31, 1863. See also Dyer, *Gallant Hood*, p. 212.

[75] Bruce Catton, *Never Call Retreat* (New York, 1965), p. 258; Horn, *Army of Tennessee*, p. 292. On press awareness of Northern reinforcements see *Daily Richmond Enquirer*, October 1, 1863. Alexander wrote the *Richmond Dispatch* on October 14 that the Louisville *Journal* of October 3 had reported the arrival at Louisville the day before of General Slocum and two of his brigadiers. *Richmond Daily Dispatch*, October 22, 1863.

[76] Freeman Cleaves, *Rock of Chickamauga* (Norman, Okla., 1948), p. 189; Catton, *Never Call Retreat*, p. 259; Dyer, *"Fightin' Joe" Wheeler*, p. 142.

Confederate army correspondents were also caught napping at some distance from the point of attack, for there is no indication that any of them witnessed the dispersal of Law's Alabama brigade from the vicinity of Brown's Ferry. Yet on the afternoon before the surprise night attack, Reid, Alexander, and de Fontaine had all been together at Breckinridge's headquarters. According to "Personne," Generals Bragg, Longstreet, and Jenkins watched from Lookout Peak on the afternoon of the 28th the arrival at Brown's Ferry of the two corps of the Army of the Potomac from Bridgeport to join their elated comrades.[77]

In a letter to the *Savannah Republican* from Bragg's army that morning, Alexander declared that the important advantages gained by the enemy in the last forty-eight hours would solve the problem of supplying the beleaguered army at Chattanooga permanently unless they were counteracted. Apparently Longstreet was of the same opinion, for that night he attempted to drive the Union troops into the river and close off the river supply line to Chattanooga again. The attack, conducted by a single division and unwisely executed at midnight, failed. In describing what the Confederate reporters referred to as the Battle of Lookout Valley,[78] Reid told how Jenkins' division, seeking to surprise the enemy, was itself surprised by two enemy divisions and Granger's corps and forced to fight its way out of a trap. As a result the Federals secured a workable supply line to Chattanooga.[79]

Both Reid and Alexander showed their awareness of the serious consequences of the Confederate failure. De Fontaine, on the other hand, although admitting that the recent operations had made Federal occupation of Chattanooga a "fixed fact," claimed that Jenkins' division had inflicted heavy casualties on the Federals; in his description of the battle he gave the Confederates the better of the fighting except that for some undisclosed reason they had to retreat at the end. Then, after taking time to consider the matter further, he vigorously took issue with what he styled a misapprehension that Bragg's army had been outgeneraled in Lookout Valley. Unrealistically he argued that Bragg

[77] *Savannah Republican*, November 2, 1863; Reid Diary, entry for October 26, 1863; *Richmond Daily Whig*, November 9, 1863. Horn, *Army of Tennessee*, p. 293, indicates that the meeting of the generals on Lookout Peak occurred on the "morning" of October 28.

[78] Generally referred to as the Battle of Wauhatchie.

[79] Sanger and Hay, p. 218; Horn, p. 293; *Mobile Daily Tribune*, November 5, 1863.

had not been surprised by the Federal advance from Bridgeport, that the retention of Lookout Valley was not worth the risk of a general battle, and that by retaining possession of Lookout Mountain the Confederates had not "lost the advantages of our position."[80]

During the early part of November the war correspondents in Bragg's army watched in vain for the unfolding of the great plan to crush the Yankees which, "Personne" was confident, Bragg had formulated. These newspapermen were well aware that Sherman was on his way from Mississippi with 20,000 soldiers to swell Grant's host at Chattanooga; they must have wondered at Bragg's temerity in sending away two divisions under Longstreet on November 4 to drive General Burnside out of east Tennessee. Seemingly unaware of the crushing attack Grant was planning for him, Bragg kept his army in front of Chattanooga waiting to see what the Yankees would do next. While Bragg's army marked time, Southern reporters kept tab on the eastward progress of Sherman's force, emphasized the need of the Confederate soldiers for blankets and axes to cut firewood, and gleaned indications from prisoner-of-war reports that the Federal army was preparing to storm Lookout Mountain. On November 17 Alexander estimated that by the time Sherman joined him, Grant would have available in the vicinity of Chattanooga 82,000 soldiers exclusive of cavalry.[81]

Alexander was especially worried at this time about the shortage of horses in the Army of Tennessee, which he attributed in part to the "scandalous exhibition of military vanity" on the part of high-ranking officers. In this army, unlike the Army of Northern Virginia, where only General Lee had a small cavalry escort, it was the custom, Alexander said, to allow all general officers above the rank of brigadier to have escorts. He went on to say: "There is one Major General who is reported to have an escort of forty mounted men, and another one an escort of one hundred and twenty-five. A Lieut. General[82] who was lately here is said to have had an escort twice as numerous as the latter. . . . Indeed so universal has this practice become that one seldom meets an officer riding alone. Nearly all of them have one or more

---

[80] *Memphis Daily Appeal*, November 22, 1863.

[81] *Ibid.*, November 6, 1863; *Richmond Daily Dispatch*, November 21, 23, 1863. The figure was slightly exaggerated. James Ford Rhodes, *History of the U.S. from the Compromise of 1850* (New York, 1910), IV, 407n, estimates the effective strength of the Union Army at 60,000, that of the Confederates at 40,000.

[82] Both D. H. Hill and Polk were lieutenant generals who had recently left the Army of Tennessee.

orderlies following after them, including captains and majors of artillery, quartermasters, commissaries, &c."[83] In newspapers other than those by whom he was employed, Alexander's comments about the horse problem were reprinted with obvious agreement, and Bragg hastily issued an order seeking to correct this abuse.[84]

While the storm was gathering around Chattanooga, Bragg once more took action to curb the activities of overly zealous war correspondents. The indiscreet publication by the correspondent of the *Atlanta Register* of the organization of Wheeler's cavalry corps caused Bragg to issue a general order on November 15. The order prohibited all general officers from communicating information of this character to newspaper correspondents and held them responsible for contraband publications.[85]

It seems to have been fairly obvious to the better-informed newspapermen, if not to Bragg, what was about to happen. On November 12 the *Richmond Examiner* stated editorially that "it has become very clear that another huge battle is to be fought in Northern Georgia before the winter begins." Four days later the *Richmond Dispatch* similarly predicted that "the enemy are about to make their supreme effort on that field [Chattanooga]." On November 21, three days before Grant struck, Alexander wrote to the *Savannah Republican*: "the storm has certainly gathered, and the thunderbolt is forged and ready to be launched. . . ." What Alexander could not decide was whether the "thunderbolt" would consist of an attack on Lookout or a flanking movement against the Confederate left in the direction of Rome.[86] Yet the very next day (November 22) Bragg detached another division from his army (Buckner's) to join Longstreet at Knoxville. An army correspondent who obviously was *not* well informed addressed an unrealistic letter to the *Atlanta Confederacy* on November 20. The *Confederacy* special alluded to the harmony "which I believe to be

---

[83] *Savannah Republican*, November 16, 1863; *Richmond Daily Dispatch*, November 17, 1863.

[84] *Savannah Republican*, November 24, 1863. *O.R.* (Army) Ser. I, vol. xxxi, pt. 3, pp. 694-95. For an appreciative comment on Alexander's exposure see *Jackson* (Selma, Ala.) *Mississippian* as reprinted in *Charleston Daily Courier*, December 30, 1863.

[85] The text of General Order No. 206, as it was called, is given in Bragg Papers, Western Reserve Historical Society. The connection between the indiscretion of the *Atlanta Register* correspondent and the issue of the order is stated in *Atlanta Daily Intelligencer*, November 21, 1863.

[86] *Savannah Republican*, November 26, 1863.

returning to our military households" and maintained that he had never felt more hopeful. He added: "I believe we shall winter around Nashville."[87]

On the eve of the Battles of Chattanooga Bragg had an army of less than 40,000 to face Grant, divided into two corps, the one on the right under Hardee, and the one on the left commanded for the time being by Breckinridge. Both corps were located on the crest of Missionary Ridge. Grant's army consisted of three main divisions, with Hooker on the right, Thomas in the center, and Sherman, who had crossed the river at Brown's Ferry and passed behind Chattanooga, on the left. Getting wind somehow of Sherman's movement, which was conducted with elaborate secrecy, Reid wrongly interpreted it as a retreat and telegraphed the *Intelligencer* on the twenty-third that "this move is a virtual abandonment of the taking of Lookout."[88]

The preliminary phase of the fighting took place that afternoon when Thomas's command tested the strength of the center of the Confederate line. Sweeping over two fortified Confederate outposts on the plain between Missionary Ridge and the river, the blue wave fortified the position they had just won and bedded down for the night. At nine o'clock that evening, Alexander began a letter to the *Republican* with the sententious statement, "Gen. Grant has made a move upon the military chess-board to-day . . . that is likely to exert an important influence upon military operations in this quarter." He scouted the idea that the advance had no purpose beyond securing greater maneuvering room and a more abundant supply of firewood. Moreover, he thought that a movement undertaken by the Yankees up the river that afternoon to the right of the Confederates would compel Bragg to weaken his left to meet the threat to his supply depot at Chickamauga Station. He correctly guessed that such a move on Bragg's part would lead to an assault on Lookout "tomorrow."[89]

The morrow in fact brought about an attack on both flanks of Bragg's army. On Tuesday morning, November 24, Hooker attacked the lower slope of Lookout Mountain and pushed back the two Confederate

---

[87] *Atlanta Daily Southern Confederacy* as reprinted in *Mobile Daily Tribune*, November 26, 1863. It is possible that the *Confederacy* reporter's judgments reflected the recent change in the *Confederacy's* editorial position with respect to Bragg noted by the *Daily Richmond Enquirer*, November 23, 1863.

[88] Foote, *Civil War, Fredericksburg to Meridian*, p. 842; Horn, *Army of Tennessee*, p. 296; *Atlanta Daily Intelligencer*, November 25, 1863.

[89] *Savannah Republican*, November 30, 1863.

brigades which opposed him. The Confederate guns on the summit of the mountain were unable to depress their muzzles sufficiently to lend support to the infantry below. At midnight the Confederate division commander ordered the survivors to withdraw to Missionary Ridge to join in its defense the next day. In a letter to the *Republican* written at the same hour, Alexander stated that very few details of the fighting had been received, but that the impression prevailed "in well-informed circles" that the affair had been mismanaged by the Confederate officers in command. He also reported that the fighting had continued until ten o'clock that night; "and even now I can hear an occasional shot while I write." He made no mention of the attack that Sherman had unleashed that afternoon at Tunnel Hill on the Confederate right. Since the telegraph line on Missionary Ridge was not working properly, the *Intelligencer* correspondent Reid had had to ride down to Chickamauga Station in the rain that afternoon to send off a dispatch to his newspaper. Reid reported at five o'clock that no "general engagement" had yet taken place, and expressed doubt that the enemy was in condition to make a general attack.[90]

Whatever may have been Reid's reasons for this statement, Sherman attacked the Confederate right at dawn the next day using six divisions to dislodge Cleburne's single division from the north end of Missionary Ridge; that division of Alabamians, Arkansans, and Tennesseans fought well, however, rolling heavy boulders down the slopes on the attackers and stopping Sherman in his tracks by the middle of the afternoon. But in the Confederate center it was another story.

At about 3:30 P.M. Thomas's four divisions moved forward against the three lines of rifle pits which the Confederates had constructed on Missionary Ridge at an elevation of about three hundred feet. In cold fascination Southern reporters and soldiers watched Thomas's men move out in a line two miles wide on the plain below in what looked to be as futile an effort as Pickett's charge. The Northerners advanced to the base of the ridge, carried the first line of rifle pits, and then found their position untenable because of the murderous fire to which they were subjected. There was no time or opportunity to dig in to escape the fire, and the only practical solution was to retreat or continue the charge. To the surprise of the defenders they chose the latter, crouch-

[90] Horn, *Army of Tennessee*, pp. 297-98; *Savannah Republican*, November 30, 1863. The same letter appeared in the *Richmond Daily Dispatch*, November 30, 1863. See also *Atlanta Daily Intelligencer*, November 26, 1863.

ing low for traction as they surged upward. Because of the contour of the ground, they were shielded as they advanced from the fire of the Confederate guns atop the ridge.

Caught in a crossfire from flank and front, the Confederate Graybacks on top of Missionary Ridge suddenly broke and fled. The charge was all over in an hour. As the Federals reached the top, they saw some of the Confederacy's best soldiers rushing wildly down the hill on the reverse side and into the woods, tossing away knapsacks, muskets, and blankets as they ran. It was such a spectacle as no Confederate newspaperman cared to describe in detail. That night Hardee withdrew from the position he had successfully defended, and Cleburne's division covered the withdrawal to Chickamauga Station on the far side of Chickamauga Creek.[91]

From Chickamauga Station Alexander wired the *Richmond Dispatch* that evening, putting the best face on what had happened. In his dispatch, he stressed that Hardee had repulsed the enemy's assault on the right "with great slaughter," capturing seven flags and some prisoners, then went on to say that the enemy gained a ridge near the center of the Confederate line and enfiladed that line. "The men supposing that the enemy were successful elsewhere gave way on our left, when the Federals occupied that part of the ridge. Our whole army was withdrawn at night, and is now crossing the Chickamauga."[92]

About the same time that Alexander was composing his dispatch, Bragg was sending off an official telegram to Adjutant General Cooper in Richmond admitting that "after several unsuccessful assaults on our lines to-day" the enemy had carried the left center about four o'clock and that the whole left soon gave way "in considerable disorder." Emphasizing that the right had held its ground, Bragg concluded by saying that he was withdrawing his whole army "to this point" (Chickamauga Station).[93] After further consideration the next day, Bragg continued his retreat across country to Dalton on the railroad line to Atlanta.

In the letter Alexander wrote at midnight of November 25-26 to the various newspapers he represented, he was considerably more frank than he had been in his dispatch. Prefacing his letter with the state-

---

[91] Catton, *Never Call Retreat*, pp. 264-65; Foote, *Civil War, Fredericksburg to Meridian*, pp. 852-56; Horn, *Army of Tennessee*, pp. 299-300.

[92] *Richmond Daily Dispatch*, November 27, 1863.

[93] *Ibid.*, November 26, 1863.

ment, "the Confederates have sustained to-day the most ignominious defeat of the whole war—a defeat for which there is little excuse or palliation," Alexander continued: "For the first time during our struggle for national independence, our defeat is chargeable to the troops themselves, and not to the blunders or incompetency of their leaders." The defeat, he maintained, was even less excusable because "the ground was more in our favor than it was at Fredericksburg"; yet having won at Fredericksburg, the Confederates lost at Missionary Ridge.[94]

Racking his brain for other explanations of a disaster that he deemed so indefensible, Alexander placed high on the list the length and weakness of the Confederate line, the odds of over two to one which he claimed the Confederate defenders faced, the error of judgment of sending Longstreet off to Knoxville before the battle, and the intensification of the panic that followed the penetration of the Confederate line that was created by the spectacle of an artillery battery rushing down the hill at the rear to obtain a fresh supply of ammunition. Amplifying his contention that Confederate leadership was not at fault, Alexander insisted that Bragg had done all he could to rally his troops and reconstruct his broken line. "He exposed himself in the most unguarded manner, and at one time it looked as if he would certainly be killed. His staff officers were also conspicuous in their efforts to restore our line. They and their chief were the last to leave the ridge." Alexander concluded his letter with the gloomy words: "It is late and bitter cold, and I must close. We cross the Chickamauga tonight, and then proceed to Dalton. I write under the greatest possible disadvantages."[95]

In Reid's preliminary report of the battle which his newspaper published on November 28 he exaggerated the severity of the fighting, rated the odds against the Confederates much as Alexander did, pinned the blame for the collapse of the Confederate line on Stevenson's division, and minimized the extent of the Confederate loss, alleging inaccurately that it was "not over two per cent of our forces."[96] In a

[94] *Savannah Republican*, December 1, 1863; *Mobile Daily Advertiser and Register*, December 1, 1863; *Richmond Daily Dispatch*, December 4, 1863.

[95] *Savannah Republican*, December 1, 1863. Horn, *Army of Tennessee*, pp. 301-302, indicates that Bragg did not decide to retreat to Dalton until the day after the Battle of Missionary Ridge, but Alexander's statement suggests that the decision had been made the evening before.

[96] *Atlanta Daily Intelligencer*, November 28, 1863. Bragg's army lost 361 killed, 2,180 wounded, and 4,146 captured or missing at the Battle of Missionary Ridge, approximately 18 percent of his army. Horn, *Army of Tennessee*, p. 301.

more detailed account, written five days later, Reid devoted most of his space to eulogizing the heroism of particular commands and moderated his criticism of the troops that had given way. His explanation of the causes of the defeat was terse and perhaps too simple, nothing more or less than the "overwhelming numbers" of the enemy. Also, he came to the surprising conclusion that the collapse of the Confederate center was a blessing in disguise, for if the troops had stood firm they would have been flanked on the left (presumably by Hooker's divisions advancing from the direction of Rossville), and the whole army would have been captured. Thus all was for the best, "and we shall soon be ready for them again."[97]

The other Atlanta newspapers, the *Confederacy, Appeal,* and *Register,* probably had correspondents in Bragg's army during the battle; but if they published accounts of the battle the newspapers in which they appeared have not survived. De Fontaine did not report the Battles of Chattanooga because he had left Bragg's army during the first week of November to accompany Longstreet's command on its march into east Tennessee.

Alexander was with the Army of Tennessee during its retreat on the night after the battle. The road from Chickamauga Station to Ringgold, he said, was as bad as it could possibly be; had it not been for the light of the moon he did not think the army could have made its escape. During the afternoon and evening of November 26 the retreating force with its long wagon train reached the railroad at Ringgold. By that time the enemy had thrown in a pursuit column which was harassing the Confederate rear guard considerably. At one point it seemed the army's supply train would have to be burned to keep it from falling into the hands of the enemy. Once more Alexander's concern for and love of army horses became evident. He wrote: "You will be astonished to hear that the horses in the artillery service, the most important in the whole army, are the most neglected—a fact, however, which quartermasters and even artillerists seem incapable of comprehending. . . . I saw a mule lie down when the harness was removed and go as soundly to sleep in two minutes as an infant, and that while hundreds of wagons and thousands of men were marching by within a few paces of where it rested."[98]

On the night of the twenty-seventh Alexander set out again, on

[97] *Atlanta Daily Intelligencer,* December 8, 1863.
[98] *Savannah Republican,* December 2, 1863.

horseback and with a mouthful of half-cooked beef, for a weary night march to Resaca. In the midst of a downpour of rain he had to seek shelter at the home of a poor woman with ten children whose husband and oldest son were in the army. Reid had a similar experience, arriving at Dalton on Sunday morning, November 29, after riding all night. As there was no hotel or any other place of public accommodation in Dalton, he had to find shelter in a deserted house with the windows out and only his blanket for a bed. "But for the rations I brought with me, I should certainly have starved," he said. At Resaca, Alexander learned of the repulse that Cleburne's division, with the assistance of a small detachment of Wheeler's cavalry, had inflicted on Hooker's pursuit column near Ringgold on the twenty-seventh.[99]

One further obstacle of the kind familiar after defeats, which was placed in the way of the army correspondents, was Bragg's censorship of press telegrams. On the eve of the recent battles, Bragg had requested the Atlanta newspapers through the commander of the district of Georgia, Maj.Gen. Howell Cobb, to abstain "for the present" from giving news of movements at the front, especially in east Tennessee. When Reid arrived in Dalton he found the provost marshal acting as a censor of all telegrams, striking out whatever he thought improper. In its irritation at the news blackout that resulted, the *Savannah Morning News* attributed the scarcity of news to the inefficiency of the Press Association, and asked the accusing question, "Why is there no Associated Press at Dalton? If the Association cannot obtain army news it fails to accomplish the object for which it was formed."[100]

Perhaps the most controversial feature of the reporting of the Battles of Chattanooga was the statements of the reporters about which brigade (or brigades) was the first to give way during the assault on Missionary Ridge. Reid had to retract his strictures against Stevenson's division of exchanged Vicksburg prisoners when it was pointed out that on the afternoon of November 25 that division was with Hardee on the right instead of in the center, where the breakthrough took place. Alexander pinned the blame on Reynolds' brigade of Buckner's

[99] *Mobile Daily Advertiser*, December 3, 1863; *Atlanta Daily Intelligencer*, December 3, 1863. In a letter to the *Mobile Register* from Resaca on November 30, Alexander reported that the main army was encamped around Dalton and that the train and such forces as had reached Resaca had now been ordered back to Dalton. *Mobile Daily Advertiser and Register*, December 6, 1863.

[100] *Memphis Daily Appeal*, November 24, 1863; *Augusta Daily Constitutionalist*, November 27, 1863; *Charleston Daily Courier*, November 30, 1863; Tucker, *Press Association*, p. 67.

division, but apparently changed his mind after Brig.Gen. Patton Anderson admitted that it was his own brigade, commanded during the battle by Col. William F. Tucker, that gave way first.[101]

On the day after the Battle of Missionary Ridge, the *Richmond Examiner* fired the opening gun in a press campaign for Bragg's scalp. Two days later, in a routine telegram to General Cooper, Bragg asked to be relieved of his command. On December 3, forty-eight hours after a rumor to that effect was current in Richmond, the press announced that Bragg had been relieved at his own request and that General Hardee had temporarily replaced him in command of the Army of Tennessee. Immediately editors and reporters began to speculate about who would be the permanent successor, with both Johnston and Longstreet being mentioned as possibilities. Not until two weeks later did the *Mobile Register's* Richmond correspondent George Bagby learn, as other newspapermen soon did, that Davis had mastered his dislike of Johnston sufficiently to name him as Bragg's successor.[102]

When it became known in camp that General Bragg was about to leave the army, Alexander called at the general's headquarters to bid him farewell. Bragg apparently was pleased by this show of attention. At any rate, according to Alexander, he spoke freely and with some feeling about the recent disaster and gave the reporter the impression that he was more concerned about the success of the Confederate cause and the welfare of his troops than about his own military reputation.[103]

Interestingly enough, both of the two leading newspaper correspondents in Bragg's army at the time of his removal (Alexander and Reid) were more ready to defend than criticize him. Alexander admitted that he had come to the army in September with some prejudice against Bragg, produced by the representations of others. Yet an association of nearly three months duration had convinced him that, "in all our army there is not a braver soldier, a more devoted friend to

[101] *Atlanta Daily Intelligencer*, December 1, 1863; *Mobile Daily Advertiser and Register*, December 20, 1863; *Augusta Daily Chronicle and Sentinel*, December 13, 1863; Brig. Gen. A. W. Reynolds to General Hardee, December 6, 1863, Bragg Papers.

[102] *Mobile Daily Advertiser and Register*, December 3, 1863; *Atlanta Daily Intelligencer*, December 3, 1863; *Memphis Daily Appeal*, December 7, 1863. In a letter to his newspaper from Montgomery on December 6, 1863, Bragg's newspaper champion, John Forsyth, stressed that "the universal, popular cry here is for Joseph E. Johnston to assume the late command of Gen. Bragg. . . ." *Mobile Daily Advertiser and Register*, December 9, 1863.

[103] *Savannah Republican*, December 30, 1863.

our cause, a more unsullied patriot, or a man who has lost so heavily at the vandal hands of the enemy." Note that Alexander stopped short of extolling Bragg's generalship. Yet a review of the campaign which he submitted to the *Savannah Republican* for publication concluded with the statement that Bragg had not received justice from either the public or his subordinates. A few days later Alexander ventured to predict that "the country will be amazed when the inside history of the Army of Tennessee comes to be written, the intrigues of some of its officers exposed, and the schemes laid bare by which they have sought to make and pervert public opinion through the instrumentality of an unsuspecting press."[104]

In a generally sympathetic profile of the general, obviously written with some care, which he contributed to the *Republican* at the end of December, Alexander rated Bragg as "simply a soldier" whose heart and soul were devoted to his calling as long as he remained in command of the army. Alexander conceded that Bragg was "destitute of diplomacy, and knows neither friends nor foes in the discharge of his duties." Alexander also admitted that as a disciplinarian Bragg was very rigid, "and has probably had as many [soldiers] executed as any two commanders in the army." Nevertheless, the Georgian reporter credited Bragg with being "the hardest worker I have met with in the Confederate army." While recognizing that Bragg's unsocial habits had made him unpopular with many high-ranking officers, Alexander maintained that Bragg was far more popular with his soldiers and regimental officers than with the other generals.[105]

In trying to be fair to Bragg, Alexander may have been a bit too charitable. Reid attempted, in seeking to clear Bragg of responsibility for "the late defeat before Chattanooga," to shift the blame to the shoulders of President Davis by ascribing to Davis responsibility for dividing Bragg's army in the presence of the enemy and sending Longstreet to Knoxville.[106]

[104] *Mobile Daily Advertiser and Register*, December 8, 1863; *Savannah Republican*, December 19, 24, 1863.

[105] *Savannah Republican*, December 30, 1863. *Memphis Appeal* correspondent J. H. Linebaugh was understandably critical of Alexander's sympathetic appraisal of Bragg. In a letter to General Polk, Linebaugh commented sourly that "Alexander has evidently become a Bragg man, as every correspondent about Headquarters will become out of gratitude for small favors if he has no great amount of self respect." J. H. Linebaugh to General Polk, December 20, 1863, Polk Papers.

[106] *Mobile Daily Tribune*, December 19, 1863.

Ironically, in view of Bragg's stormy relations with the press, the general's stock with some of the newspaper correspondents in his army had never been higher than when he left it to become the military adviser of the president in Richmond. Elsewhere among the press he was regarded much less favorably; it could hardly be denied that under his command the military fortunes of the Confederacy in the West had gone from bad to worse. The concluding disaster on Missionary Ridge had contributed to the permanent loss of east Tennessee, which Reid correctly estimated as "incalculable." But it was de Fontaine rather than Reid who had the opportunity to report the campaign which more than anything else determined the fate of east Tennessee.

THE SUCCESSFUL invasion of east Tennessee by General Burnside's Army of the Ohio and the fall of Knoxville on September 2 had been a stunning disappointment to Southern editors and their readers. The *Richmond Dispatch* described the Federal occupation of what it called the "Switzerland of America" as "the hardest blow that has been struck us since the beginning of the war," rating it the most astounding conquest in history.[107]

The operation plan of Longstreet's counterblow called for McLaws' and Jenkins' divisions to move by rail from Tunnel Hill to Sweetwater, Tennessee and join Wheeler's cavalry there to move against Burnside at Knoxville. De Fontaine, who had agreed to cover the operations for several newspapers, including the *Charleston Courier, Memphis Appeal, Mobile Register*, and *Richmond Whig*, addressed his first east Tennessee war correspondence to the *Whig* from Sweetwater on November 7. Since the whole operation was being conducted with the utmost secrecy de Fontaine was careful not to reveal Longstreet's connection with the expedition, the size of his force, and the military units that it included. He admitted that there were few facts on which it would be prudent to expound, although he let it be known that skirmishing had already taken place within twenty miles of Knoxville.[108]

It was more than a week later before he wrote the second in his series of campaign letters, this time to the *Memphis Appeal*. By then (November 16) Longstreet had left Sweetwater and reached Loudon, where the Virginia and East Tennessee Railroad crossed the Tennessee

---

[107] *Richmond Daily Dispatch*, September 17, 1863; Sanger and Hay, *Longstreet*, pp. 217, 221.
[108] *Richmond Daily Whig*, November 19, 1863.

River on its way to Knoxville and Bristol. De Fontaine exuberantly reported that: "We crossed the Tennessee at Loudon on Friday night, and skirmished severely with the enemy on Sunday night, killing forty to sixty Yankees. . . . Burnside is here in person, with two divisions. We hope to bag him before night. . . . We are now within twenty-two miles of Knoxville, and moving on."[109]

From then on for a period of weeks, de Fontaine's letters failed to reach the newspapers for which he was corresponding, and the Confederate press was unable to obtain much solid information about the progress of the campaign from other sources. On November 21 a correspondent of the *Atlanta Register* mailed a letter to his newspaper from Loudon, in which he described the success of Wheeler's cavalry near Marysville and reported that Knoxville was heavily invested on the opposite side of the river. About a week later the *Register* published the letter; by that time a report of the recapture of Knoxville, attributed to several different newspapers, had been contradicted. Also by November 21 the newspapers had revealed Longstreet's command of the expedition against Knoxville.[110]

During the last week of November the Southern press manifested serious concern for the safety of General Longstreet and his command. On the second day after Bragg's defeat at Missionary Ridge, the *Memphis Appeal* asserted that the enemy's cavalry had cut off all railroad and telegraphic communication with Knoxville, and there was some doubt whether Longstreet's army could remain much longer in east Tennessee unless it received supplies from the outside. The *Appeal* added: "We have literally nothing from Knoxville, except unreliable and conflicting rumors."[111]

On the last day of the month the *Appeal* published a Press Association dispatch personally signed by J. S. Thrasher and dated at Bristol on Saturday, the 28th, stating that persons from the vicinity of Knoxville maintained that the city was completely invested and was being

[109] *Memphis Daily Appeal*, November 21, 1863.

[110] *Atlanta Daily Register* as reprinted in *Richmond Daily Dispatch*, November 30, 1863; *Atlanta Daily Intelligencer*, November 29, 1863. In a letter from Missionary Ridge to the *Republican*, dated November 21, Alexander remarked "it was desired that Gen. Longstreet's connection with the [east Tennessee] expedition should not be made public, but since it has found its way into the newspapers it need not be disguised that he is in command of our forces now operating in East Tennessee." *Savannah Republican*, November 26, 1863.

[111] *Memphis Daily Appeal*, November 27, 1863.

subjected to bombardment by the Confederate forces, also that all the city north of the railroad had been burned by the enemy.

Four days later Richmond correspondent Bagby informed the *Mobile Register* by letter that the night before, Richmond had heard directly from Longstreet for the first time. Longstreet made clear that he had been repulsed, but did not seem inclined to withdraw into Virginia, although he was aware that it was no longer possible for him to rejoin Bragg's army. Richmond correspondent Thompson was still uncertain the next day whether to believe a P.A. dispatch indicating that Longstreet had raised the siege and started to retreat to Virginia, or another press dispatch received later in the day declaring that the siege of Knoxville was still going on.[112] By the ninth of December the press was reasonably sure Longstreet had abandoned the siege and retreated to Bean's Station, forty miles east of Knoxville.

The *Charleston Courier* received its first report from "Personne" since the beginning of the Knoxville campaign on December 12. His letters carrying dates from November 9 to 16, had been approximately a month in transit and had lost virtually all their news value by the time they reached Charleston. De Fontaine had forwarded accounts of the operations during the campaign, sometimes by courier and again through the medium of private parties, but most of them failed to reach their destination.[113]

"Personne's" narrative of Longstreet's unsuccessful attempt to storm the fortifications of Knoxville, which reached the *Courier* office shortly before Christmas, was the best specimen of reporting that the campaign produced. The *Courier* reporter graphically described the strength of the position, with pikes standing at a forty-five-degree angle to impale the attacker and telegraph wires stretched knee high on the edge of ditches to trip him as he clambered upward. Fort Sanders, a large square earthworks on a large hill northwest of the town, was virtually unassailable, but Longstreet knew that reinforcements from Chattanooga were on their way to Burnside's relief and that Federal cavalry was playing havoc with his communications. So he planned a direct assault, making use of four brigades, for the dawn of November 29. As de Fontaine described it:

"Daylight was scarcely breaking, and through the cold thick mist, our troops advanced to the assault. Up, up, up, until within a few yards

---

[112] *Mobile Daily Advertiser and Register*, December 13, 1863; *Memphis Daily Appeal*, December 10, 1863.
[113] *Charleston Daily Courier*, December 23, 1863.

of the great frowning pile the storming party silently advanced, exposed to the irregular and sudden fire of the host behind the parapet; then suddenly dashing forward with the battle cries that have rung on so many desperately contested fields, the Confederates charged to the ditch at the very base of the parapet.

"But now what a scene of confusion! A wire stretched along the edge of the chasm caught the leg of every man who did not suspect its presence, and tripped him headlong into the yawning trap. Others followed, and others and others—those behind rolling like a wave on those before—until the abyss was filled with a seething, boiling, bubbling mass of men and guns, out of which issued the groans, shouts, yells and orders, with the discordance of a pandemonium. There were those in that throng, however, who could not be appalled by any danger, however great . . . officers as well as privates, and remembering the mission in which they were engaged, they still pressed on to its accomplishment. Mounting the shoulders of their comrades, and digging their fingers into the earth, they climbed the opposite side of the ditch as best they could, and then assisting others, a little party was thus quickly gathered who rushed to the top of the parapet and there stood—the heroes of the hour."[114]

De Fontaine had to admit, however, that the attack was a disastrous failure. Most of those who escaped from the ditch retreated back down the hill, along with the remainder of the command; the two hundred or more who still clung to the slopes of the parapet had to surrender. De Fontaine comforted himself with the belief that in five more days the Federals would have been starved into surrender, but Longstreet's dispirited men dared not wait for that. The approach of Sherman and the capture by Federal cavalry of Longstreet's supply base at Loudon compelled the Confederate commander to change his base to the east and discover new means of supply. Early on December 3 the retreat to Rogersville began, sixty-five miles over bad roads.

Apparently the only other account of the campaign by a Southern war correspondent was that of the *Savannah Republican* reporter "Tout-le-Monde." In a letter which required almost two weeks longer to reach Savannah than de Fontaine's letters to the *Charleston Courier*, "Tout-le-Monde" told much the same story as "Personne." In the Savannah man's opinion, Longstreet's soldiers had suffered a "fearful repulse." He expressed ignorance as to whether the Commanding Gen-

[114] *Ibid.*, December 23, 1863. See also D. S. Freeman, *Lee's Lieutenants, A Study in Command* (New York, 1951), III, 293-94.

eral or the subordinates who executed his plan were responsible for the blunder that he was convinced someone on the Confederate side had made. He also conjectured that if the news of Bragg's defeat at Missionary Ridge had reached Longstreet before the disastrous assault at Knoxville the assault would never have been made.[115]

De Fontaine did not mince words in bringing to public attention the miserable plight of Longstreet's men who were faced with the necessity of wintering in the rugged mountains: "There are at this moment [December 11, 1863] from three thousand to thirty-five hundred barefooted men in this army. Some of them are officers high in rank. One whom I know is a Lieutenant Colonel. All of them are fighting men, who, but for this necessity, would be in the front rank in every hour of danger. The weather is so cold that the icicles around the waterfalls are as thick as a man's body. In twenty minutes after sundown liquid freezes solid. The surface of the ground is as hard as a rock, and at every step the frozen edges of earth cut into naked feet, until the path of the army may be almost said to have been tracked in blood. To remedy the evil, I have seen these men, accustomed as they were at home to every luxury, strip their coats and blankets from their backs, and tie the rags around their feet; I have seen them take the fresh hides of cattle, reeking with the warm blood, and fashion therefrom rude moccasins to last them for the day's march; and I have seen them beg in piteous terms of passing horsemen for a brief respite to their painful walk, and where this has failed, offer five, ten, and twenty dollars for the privilege of riding a few miles on their wearisome journey. I mention these as facts that have come under my own observation, and which should appeal to liberal and sympathizing hearts with all the eloquence of suffering, and call for that speedy relief which the emergency demands."[116]

The day before this letter was written, de Fontaine left for Charleston to spend the rest of the winter at home and formulate plans for a newspaper venture in Columbia in conjunction with Henry Timrod.[117] This, his last report from east Tennessee, was perhaps a fitting epitaph for the high hopes that had thus ended in the bitterness of defeat.

[115] *Savannah Republican*, January 5, 1864.

[116] *Charleston Daily Courier*, December 24, 1863.

[117] War Diary of Capt. Joseph Banks Lyle, 5th South Carolina Infantry, "10 (Thurs) [December 1863]," in possession of Elmer O. Parker, The National Archives.

CHAPTER 12

"The War Absorbs All Other Topics"

THE GLOOMY outlook for the Confederate cause at the end of 1863 drew the attention of a portion of the Southern press, especially in North Carolina and Georgia, to the possibilities of a negotiated peace. In the Tar Heel State William W. Holden, the Unionist editor of the *Raleigh Standard,* and J. L. Pennington of the *Raleigh Progress* provided the leadership for the "North Carolina Movement." In Georgia the peace editors took their cue from a group of politicians whose moving spirits were Governor Joseph E. Brown and Vice President Alexander H. Stephens. At the end of March 1864 the well-informed Richmond correspondent, George Bagby, reported that, "with the exception of the regular partisan organ of the Administration there is hardly a press in this city or State which does not sympathize with Mr. Stephens."[1] The Davis administration was unwilling, however, to make peace on any other terms than Confederate independence, which almost certainly meant a continuation of the war.

The winter of 1863-1864 in Richmond and elsewhere in the South had been unusually bitter. One frigid February night froze the ink in Bagby's inkstand, and the last week of March 1864 produced an eight-inch snowfall in Richmond, the heaviest since 1858. At the end of February the capital was thrown into a sudden flurry by the approach of a Union cavalry raiding force. *Memphis Appeal* correspondent Thompson noted in his diary that the "Vandals" pushed to within three miles of Richmond, shelled the home, one and a half miles from the city, of James Lyons, and "committed the most wanton outrages wherever they went."[2] Most of the raiders escaped down the Peninsula, but the press voiced deep indignation over the alleged discovery on the person of their dead leader of plans to release the Union prisoners at Belle Isle, sack and burn Richmond, and assassinate President Davis and his cabinet. Bagby asserted that he had seen the instructions, signed by the leader of the expedition, Col. Ulric Dahlgren; he de-

[1] *Mobile Daily Advertiser and Register,* April 2, 1864.
[2] *Ibid.,* February 25, 1864; J. R. Thompson Diary, entry for March 1, 1864, John R. Thompson Papers, Alderman Library, University of Virginia.

clared that the press was united in urging the immediate execution
of the three hundred captured raiders.[3]

Bagby went over to Capitol Square late in March to see the return
from Northern prison camps of over 1,100 repatriated Confederate
soldiers. While waiting for their arrival he noticed three ladies dressed
in black with two wounded officers, standing guard over several picnic
baskets. The ladies were General Lee's daughters, and they were soon
joined by their brothers Rooney and Custis, the former of whom was
one of the returned prisoners. While Bagby was eyeing the Lee family
with understandable curiosity, he saw a man step slowly in front of
them as if he were about to leave the square. The reporter observed
that the man was entirely alone and that he wore a dingy black wool
hat and a faded blue cloak, which had evidently seen considerable
service. "There goes President Davis," whispered a spectator. Bagby
then recognized the president, and so too apparently did the Lees, who
met and remained in conversation with him until the arrival of the expected party of returned soldiers. Davis was there to greet the returning heroes, along with Governor "Extra Billy" Smith, and to deliver a
welcoming speech. In Bagby's opinion the affair was badly managed,
however. The president had to stand on the same level as his audience,
surrounded by the returned officers. The crowd was the largest Bagby
had seen in Richmond, and the president's remarks were for the most
part inaudible to all but a few of his listeners.[4]

The trees along the avenues of Richmond were just beginning to leaf
in the middle of April as Peter Alexander came up from Georgia to
report the spring campaign for the *Savannah Republican, Mobile Register,* and *Richmond Dispatch.*[5] Lee had not been sure earlier that

[3] *Daily Richmond Enquirer,* March 7, 1864; *Daily Richmond Examiner,* April
1, 1864; *Mobile Daily Advertiser and Register,* March 15, 1864. On March 24 the
editor of the *Richmond Enquirer* replied to a statement of the regular correspondent of the *New York Times* with the Army of the Potomac, E. A. Paul. Paul, who
was the only Northern war correspondent who had accompanied the Dahlgren
raid, accused the Confederate authorities of having deliberately forged the papers
that were said to have been found on the body of Colonel Dahlgren. The *Enquirer*
editor declared that the authenticity of the documents was attested by the sworn
statements of the officers who inspected them and the confessions of the captured
raiders.

[4] *Mobile Daily Advertiser and Register,* March 30, 1864.

[5] Bagby reported Alexander's arrival in Richmond en route to the front on April
18 in *ibid.,* April 27, 1864. For a letter from Alexander to the adjutant general
of Georgia, Henry C. Wayne, written at home in Georgia, February 6, 1864 see
Letters Received, Ga. Adj. Gen., 1861-1865, Record Group 22-11, Georgia De-

there would be a spring campaign in Virginia; it had seemed to him that Tennessee was more likely to be the battleground in 1864. By the end of March, however, the general had come to the conclusion that the Yankees were planning another major campaign against Richmond. To counteract the strategy of Grant whom Lincoln had summoned to Washington to become the overall Union commander, Lee decided to bring Beauregard's army up from South Carolina to protect the southern approaches to Richmond, and recall Longstreet from eastern Tennessee to Virginia.[6]

Within five days after Alexander reached Richmond he notified the *Mobile Register* that the best information available indicated a three-pronged movement against Richmond. "One of these columns, starting from his present lines on the Rappahannock, he [Grant] will lead himself. The second will move under Burnside on the south side of James river, and will seek to cut our communications at Weldon or Petersburg; and the third will move up the Peninsula from Fortress Monroe under Beast Butler."[7] Alexander was correct in his assumption that Lee would have to meet several offensives at once; yet his information was inexact and incomplete. Apparently he did not know about the part Franz Sigel's Union force was supposed to play in the Shenandoah Valley, and he was in error about Burnside's role in Grant's plans, an error which the Fredericksburg correspondent of the *Richmond Examiner* discovered a few days later.

The *Examiner* reporter, quite possibly George H. C. Rowe, was a Virginia gentleman who had been a prominent lawyer in Fredericksburg before the war. Being intimately acquainted with the area north of Fredericksburg, it was his custom when a battle was imminent to mount his horse and reconnoiter behind the enemy's lines. Thus on Wednesday morning, April 27, the *Examiner* correspondent left Fredericksburg to ride up to Dumfries on the Potomac. There he learned that Burnside had arrived at Alexandria from Annapolis with a force estimated at 20,000 to 25,000. Rowe still could not be sure whether Burnside planned to march down Telegraph Road to Fredericksburg or use the Orange & Alexandria Railroad route to join the Army of the

---

partment of Archives and History. In this letter Alexander made his acceptance of an appointment as an aide-de-camp to Governor Brown contingent upon the necessity for him to "leave for the army at an hour's notice."

[6] D. S. Freeman, *R. E. Lee, A Biography* (New York, 1935), iii, 263-65.

[7] *Mobile Daily Advertiser and Register*, May 1, 1864.

Potomac. Discovering that Burnside's Ninth Corps was coming down the railroad route, the *Examiner* man started back to Fredericksburg with this important news. Unfortunately Sheridan's Yankee cavalry had moved in behind him and was in possession of the principal fords and ferries over the Rappahannock. By some means and after some delay, Rowe eluded the enemy and got across the river to Fredericksburg in time to mail his story to Richmond on Saturday. Accompanying his letters were some Northern newspapers he had obtained in Dumfries.[8]

While the *Examiner* reporter was trying to slip through the Union picket line, Newsman Thompson of the *Memphis Appeal* reported a complete halt to railroad travel in and out of Richmond as a result of the troop movements then in progress. Thompson also noted that not even travel by private conveyance was possible, for the government was impressing all the horses not being used for military purposes or bringing supplies to city markets.[9] The truth was, as Alexander had reported in his first letter from Richmond to the *Savannah Republican*, food was abnormally scarce there. Flour was $250 per barrel, meal $50 per bushel, beef $5 per pound, and bacon from $7 to $8.[10]

Longstreet's troops had reached Gordonsville by this time after a march from Bristol. The reporters who accompanied them emphasized their satisfaction at being back in "old Virginny" after their unfruitful campaign in east Tennessee. The prolonged stay in Tennessee seemed like a "hideous nightmare" to a reporter for the *Columbia South Carolinian*; a *Montgomery Mail* correspondent made no bones about saying, "East Tennessee is, in truth, the moral and political Sodom of the South." Apparently what had made Longstreet's soldiers most unhappy was their physical isolation from their old surroundings, the severity of the weather, the shortage of provender and other supplies, and the unfriendly attitude of the civilian population. The reporter from Alabama said he regarded the people along the line of the Virginia and East Tennessee Railway as "the most ignorant, uncouth, illiterate, and degraded race with whom I was ever thrown in contact. . . . I can truly assert that I have not seen a single woman in East Tennessee who did not swear like a trooper; and three-fourths of them chew, smoke and

---

[8] *Ibid.*, May 13, 1864; *Daily Richmond Examiner*, May 2, 1864. The *Examiner* reporter commented on the news in the Northern newspapers he had gathered, making mention of the report in one of them that Burnside's command included five or six Negro regiments.

[9] *Memphis Daily Appeal*, May 3, 1864.

[10] *Savannah Republican*, April 25, 1864.

get drunk. In short the Southern and respectable element have left the country. . . ." The correspondent of the *South Carolinian* thought the experience of Longstreet's soldiers in the West had exerted an injurious and brutalizing influence on them. "There was so much of lawlessness," he recalled, "so many instances of the ruthless robbery of helpless women and children—so many marauding expeditions—so much stealing, and such open disregard for justice and humanity."[11]

As soon as all of Longstreet's men returned, Lee would have about 65,000 with which to contest the advance of 116,000 Federal troops.[12] At nine o'clock on Wednesday morning, May 4, the Confederate signal station on Clark's Mountain flagged the message that Grant's huge army was heading from Culpeper Court House for the Rapidan fords about fifteen miles northwest of Fredericksburg. From Lee's headquarters staff officers carried orders for the two corps of Ewell and Hill to push eastward along parallel roads to intercept the enemy's southward advance and for Longstreet to move up from Gordonsville to take position on the Confederate right. By evening Lee was reasonably sure that Grant was bearing to his left through the Wilderness, as Hooker had done, to crumple the Confederate right flank. Lee's plan was to strike Grant at a right angle to his line of march in the Wilderness, where the Federal advantage in artillery would be largely neutralized.[13]

Correspondent Alexander was on his way to the front that day. Arriving in Gordonsville from Richmond at one o'clock in the afternoon he heard that Grant had crossed the Rapidan at Germanna and Ely's Fords and was attempting to turn Lee's right flank. Mounting his horse, Alexander rode off after Longstreet's troops, in search of the probable point of collision of the two armies.[14]

Earlier that day Press Association reporter Smoot had telegraphed from Orange Court House the somewhat misleading information that

[11] *Montgomery Daily Mail*, April 15, 1864; *Columbia Daily South Carolinian*, April 30, 1864. For further criticism of the behavior of Longstreet's troops in recent weeks, by a correspondent of the *Montgomery Advertiser*, see the May 6, 1864 issue of that paper. According to the *Advertiser* reporter, Vaughan's Tennessee brigade had "made more enemies to the South in North Carolina than the Yankees have since the war began. . . ."

[12] D. B. Sanger and T. R. Hay, *James Longstreet* (Baton Rouge, 1952), p. 261.

[13] Freeman, *Lee's Lieutenants*, III, 269-73.

[14] *Richmond Daily Dispatch*, May 19, 1864. Presumably by this time Alexander had in his possession the camp outfit whose failure to come by express from Georgia had delayed his departure from Richmond to join the army. *Savannah Republican*, April 28, 1864.

Grant's army had "struck their tents and are moving in two columns to flank Lee's army on either wing."[15] The telegraph was silent the following day except for a dispatch from Lee to Secretary Seddon, reporting that the enemy had opened the battle that morning and had been repulsed in all-day fighting. Alexander's first press dispatch, telegraphed from Orange Court House on the sixth, supplied much the same information about the repulse of the enemy as Lee's dispatch had contained, but added, "at daybreak this morning the battle was renewed, and is now raging with great fury."[16]

According to the more detailed letter Alexander wrote later, the battle began about four o'clock on Thursday afternoon, May 5, some four miles west of Chancellorsville. Springing upon Grant's right flank, "like a tiger upon the side of an ox," Stuart's cavalry, in combination with the two corps of Ewell and Hill, had brought Grant's march to a sudden halt. Before turning west to meet the threatened attack, Grant had taken the precaution to throw up strong entrenchments along the Brock Road, his line of march from the Rapidan fords. Then, according to Alexander, Grant attacked repeatedly along his whole line, delivering his hardest blows against the Confederate right. In every case he was repulsed with heavy losses.

Alexander's report made clear that the arrival of Longstreet's corps on the field the next morning, after a night march, narrowly averted disaster on the Confederate right. Alexander was there to behold the consternation of Gregg's Texan Brigade when Lee announced his intention to lead them into battle in person. The Texans remonstrated against their general exposing himself unnecessarily and assured him that they would "whip the fight" if he would go to the rear. This they proceeded to do after they won their point. Alexander also reported the accidental wounding of Longstreet by Confederate bullets as the Georgian was leading a successful flank attack. But the loss of Longstreet did not keep the Confederates from inflicting heavy losses, as they drove Grant's troops back to their entrenchments along the Brock Road.

[15] *Macon Daily Telegraph*, May 4, 1864. "Mr. Smoot" was named as the P.A. correspondent at General Lee's headquarters in the early part of 1864, in Q. C. Wilson, "Confederate Press Association, a Pioneer News Agency," *Journalism Quarterly*, xxvi (June 1949), 165.

[16] *O.R.* (Army) Ser. I, vol. xxxvi, pt. 1, p. 1,028; *Daily Richmond Enquirer*, May 7, 1864; *Daily Richmond Examiner*, May 9, 1864; *Mobile Daily Advertiser and Register*, May 7, 1864; J. B. Jones, *A Rebel War Clerk's Diary* (New York, 1958), p. 367.

In his second telegraphic account of the fighting Alexander correctly guessed that this battle would take its name from the Wilderness in which it was being fought.[17]

At the close of the second day of the battle, Reporter Sener of the *Richmond Dispatch* estimated the Confederate casualties at fully six thousand, "of which a much larger number than usual are officers." He also commented on the "great obstinacy" with which the enemy had fought, and admitted that while in most cases Lee's soldiers had lived up to their past reputation, "some are said to have done badly."[18] Alexander rated the outcome as "another Confederate victory," although not decisive, since the enemy had neither been routed nor driven back across the Rapidan. Apparently Alexander disagreed with Sener as to the performance of the troops on both sides. While contending that Grant's troops had not fought as well during these two days as they had under McClellan, Burnside, or even Hooker, he maintained that the Confederates had never fought better. There was a note of reverence tinged with awe in the closing words of his battle narrative: "Oh, that we may ever have such a leader and such an army!"[19]

Nevertheless, Alexander's reporting of the Battles of the Wilderness was not up to the standard he had set at Gettysburg, Shiloh, and several other places. Apparently he was to some degree aware of this, for he admitted that he had not "gone much into detail" in his reporting. He explained that he had been unable to do so because of "constant changes in the position of the army" and the difficulty of keeping track of the various army units in heavily wooded country. Also, the resentment General Anderson and several other officers had displayed toward his criticism of their performance at the Battle of Gettysburg had, he admitted, made him hesitate to deal specifically with the performance in battle of particular corps and divisions.[20]

[17] *Mobile Daily Advertiser and Register*, May 8, 1864; *Richmond Daily Dispatch*, May 19, 1864.

[18] *Richmond Daily Dispatch*, May 10, 1864. The correspondent of the *Richmond Enquirer* who reported the battle explained that the reason for the heavy losses of Confederate officers was that they "were compelled to go into the fight on horseback and thus became conspicuous marks for the enemy's sharpshooters." *Daily Richmond Enquirer*, May 10, 1864.

[19] *Richmond Daily Dispatch*, May 19, 1864.

[20] See above, p. 317. See also *Savannah Republican*, May 24, 1864. Alexander's report in the *Richmond Dispatch* ran to two columns or about 2/7 of a newspaper page, about one and a half columns less than his account of the Battle of Gettysburg.

Perhaps the most lengthy and highly praised report of the Wilderness campaign that appeared in any Southern newspaper was by an English newspaperman named Butt Hewson, who had lived for some years in Memphis and Helena, Arkansas, as a civil engineer for the railroads. By special arrangement with the *Morning Herald,* "our earliest and strongest friend among the British journals," the *Richmond Enquirer* published Hewson's four-column battle report of the fighting on May 5-6 in advance of its appearance in London. From all sides Southern editors lavished praise on the Hewson report. In the opinion of the *Augusta Constitutionalist* it was the most graphic, clear, and interesting description of the battle that had yet appeared. Surmising that Hewson might have been given access to General Lee's report to assist him in the preparation of his account, the *Montgomery Advertiser* lauded the Englishman because, unlike many army correspondents, he did not view the battle from the standpoint of a single unit, be it brigade, division, or corps. Instead, marvelled the *Advertiser,* "he writes as if he occupied a position where he took in the entire field."[21]

It was a matter of days or even weeks before the newspapers could publish the full-length accounts of the great struggle on May 5-6; there was suspense in Richmond all day Friday, the sixth, as its citizens awaited the outcome of the fighting. Not even the publication of General Lee's dispatch about ten o'clock the next morning, announcing that his army had repulsed the enemy at every point, entirely dispelled this anxiety. The public remained skeptical until nine o'clock that evening when a second dispatch from Lee provided further information about the second day of the battle. Then on Sunday, abruptly changing its mood as reports of victory came in from all directions, Richmond gave itself over to rejoicing. According to the *Richmond Examiner,* there was speculation on the city streets as to the figure that gold would reach in Wall Street the next day, and predictions that "we shall have peace soon—The North is played out."[22]

Then came bad news. Under a new commander, Maj.Gen. Philip H.

[21] *Daily Richmond Enquirer,* May 26, 1864; *Memphis Daily Appeal,* May 6, 1863; *Augusta Daily Constitutionalist,* May 31, 1864; *Montgomery Daily Advertiser,* June 4, 1864; *Charleston Daily Courier,* June 9, 1864. Hewson's strong sympathy with the Southern cause was alluded to in G. C. Brown to Mother and Sister, near Spotsylvania C.H., May 20, 1864, Richard Ewell Papers, Southern Historical Collection, University of North Carolina.

[22] *Richmond Daily Dispatch,* May 7, 1864; *Daily Richmond Examiner,* May 9, 1864.

Sheridan, a force of 15,000 Federal cavalry appeared in Lee's rear on Monday and after destroying the greater part of the army reserve stores at Beaver Dam creek, advanced on Richmond. At Yellow Tavern, seven miles north of the city, Stuart managed to intercept the Federals with a smaller force, but in the fight that followed he was killed. Mournfully the *Memphis Appeal's* Richmond correspondent noted in his diary on May 12: "Genl J.E.B. Stuart died at 8 o'clock P.M. at the house of Dr Brewer on Grace Street in this City."[23]

By this time Richmond was virtually denuded of its male inhabitants and business was at a standstill. The war department battalions and the militia were manning the fortifications, while in what was ordinarily the busiest section along Main Street nobody could be seen but a few gossiping old men. Even the Confederate Congress considered adjournment so that its members could participate in the defense of Richmond. The frantic behavior of the public officials from Governor Smith on down inspired a certain amount of press criticism. The Richmond correspondent of the *Augusta Constitutionalist*, Salem Dutcher, was of the opinion that "in an insane desire to put every man (except themselves) in the ranks" these officials were guilty of acts that were tyrannical to the last degree. He told of how on mere suspicion of harboring a man who was capable of bearing arms they broke down doors and entered houses without any pretense of a legal warrant and how they hustled men into service regardless of age or health. In one instance of which Dutcher said he had personal knowledge, an old man of sixty-five who had thus been inducted collapsed before he could leave the city and was sent back under guard to Castle Thunder (a political prison in Richmond).[24]

In the midst of this atmosphere of gloom and terror Jeb Stuart's funeral was reported in the Richmond press. According to the *Enquirer*

[23] J. R. Thompson Diary, Thompson Papers, University of Virginia. For a description of the efforts of Stuart's cavalry to repel Sheridan's raid against Richmond written by a correspondent who accompanied Stuart see *Daily Richmond Enquirer*, May 14, 1864.

[24] *Daily Richmond Enquirer*, May 9, 1864; *Daily Richmond Examiner*, May 13, 1864; *Memphis Daily Appeal*, May 23, 1864; *Columbus Daily Sun*, May 24, 1864; *Augusta Daily Constitutionalist*, May 22, 29, 31, 1864; *Atlanta Daily Intelligencer*, May 31, 1864. For reports that congressmen were as panic-stricken as other public officials see Edward Younger, ed., *Inside the Confederate Government* (New York, 1957), p. 149; J. Turner to My Dear Suffering Wife [Richmond] May 26, 1864. Josiah Turner Papers, Southern Historical Collection, University of North Carolina.

the scene was "sad and impressive." It told how President Davis sat near the front of the chancel of St. James' Church, "with a look of grief upon his careworn face," flanked by his cabinet and the members of Congress. Although a number of generals and officers of lesser rank were scattered through the congregation, Fitz Lee and the other cavalrymen whom Stuart had so often led were somewhere away from Richmond, continuing the fight in which their leader had fallen. No military escort accompanied the funeral procession, and the dead cavalier was laid to rest on a hillside in Hollywood cemetery while the earth trembled with the roar of artillery and the din of warfare.[25]

The friendship of the newspaperman John R. Thompson with Stuart had been long; at the time of Stuart's death a handsome gift which Thompson had ordered for him from England was on its way to Richmond. A poem Thompson wrote in connection with Stuart's funeral, and which was published in the *Richmond Examiner*, made a strong impression on Stuart's friends and admirers. On the morning the poem appeared in print Attorney General George Davis came to an informal meeting of the cabinet with a copy of the newspaper in his hand.

"Gentlemen, have you seen the *Examiner* this morning?" he asked.

"No," was the reply. "What does it contain? Anything particularly savage against the Administration?"

The attorney general answered by reading the poem, which inspired exclamations of delight from the president's advisers.[26]

In the excitement of the war news no one paid much attention to the proceedings of the Confederate Congress, which had convened a new session just three days before the Battles of the Wilderness began. In Thompson's newspaper story about the opening of the new Congress, he had called attention to the fact that almost half of the lower house was composed of newly elected members, some few of whom were war veterans who had lost a leg or an arm in the service. The attention of the newspaper reporters in the gallery was particularly drawn to the "peace men" among the North Carolina delegation. The reporters noted that one of the North Carolinians, Congressman James M. Leach,

---

[25] *Daily Richmond Enquirer*, May 14, 1864; *Daily Richmond Examiner*, May 14, 1864. For J. R. Thompson's brief description of the funeral see *Memphis Daily Appeal*, May 27, 1864. Thompson predicted Stuart would live "hereafter" in romance and song and the historian's record.

[26] *Memphis Daily Appeal*, June 16, 1864.

created a stir by his admission on the floor of the house that he was for peace "on any terms short of subjugation."[27]

On the Sunday afternoon in early May that Richmond was staging its short-lived victory celebration, *Richmond Dispatch* correspondent Sener was on his way east from Orange Court House, seeking to catch up with Lee's army. A reconnaissance that morning had disclosed that the enemy's fortifications were empty, and Lee had already divined that instead of retreating, Grant was hastily trying to reach Spotsylvania Court House to the southeast. Because of its nearness to Hanover Junction, an important railroad intersection, Spotsylvania was of strategic importance; it was essential that Lee get there first to safeguard his communications with Richmond. By the narrowest of margins the Confederates won the race. According to Sener, the fight that took place at Spotsylvania that Sunday afternoon was one of the first instances of the use of the bayonet in combat during the war.[28]

The next day (Monday, May 9) the newspaper correspondents saw heavy skirmishing. The Confederate line was in the shape of an inverted "V," or horseshoe, with Ewell's corps at the apex. The battlefield was at the edge of the Wilderness. Although the area was wooded, it contained a number of farms and open fields. On the tenth two Yankee divisions struck the left side of the tip, making a considerable dent and taking about 2,000 prisoners. Gordon's division of Ewell's corps counterattacked and after a fierce struggle forced back the attackers.[29]

There was a lull in the fighting the next day, but on Thursday, May 12, the Confederate army correspondents saw what Alexander rated as "one of the fiercest and most obstinate battles of modern times." Launching a mass attack on a very narrow front at 4:30 A.M., the Federals shattered that part of the Confederate line which the soldiers

[27] *Ibid.*, May 8, 10, 1864; *Mobile Daily Advertiser and Register*, May 13, 1864. The fact that no reference to Leach's remark appears in the Confederate House Journal for that date can be explained by the possibility that it took place during an unrecorded secret session of that body. For Bagby's prognostications about the activities of the new Congress and his report of its opening session see *ibid.*, May 7, 11, 1864. Some interesting profiles of the newly elected "peace" congressmen from North Carolina appeared in the Richmond correspondence of the *Augusta Constitutionalist* reporter Salem Dutcher. *Augusta Daily Constitutionalist*, May 11, 1864.

[28] *Richmond Daily Dispatch*, May 19, 1864; Freeman, *Lee's Lieutenants*, III, 298-99, 304, 306.

[29] Col. R. E. Dupuy, *The Compact History of the Civil War* (New York, 1960), p. 297.

called the "Mule Shoe," smashing one of Ewell's divisions and capturing about 4,000 men. Sener reported that the unlucky division commander, Maj.Gen. Edward Johnson, was not with his troops when the
battle opened, and that Johnson rode up to his line and dismounted
just in time to be made a prisoner. Once more Gordon's reserve moved
into the breach and helped to contain the Federal breakthrough. As
Alexander described it: "The battle was soon fully joined, and for nine
hours it roared and hissed and dashed over the bloody angle and along
the bristling entrenchments like an angry sea beating and chafing
against a rock bound coast. The artillery fire was the most sustained
and continuous I have ever heard for so long a time, averaging thirty
shot to the minute, or 1,800 to the hour, for six hours. The rattle of
musketry was not less furious and incessant. At 10 o'clock, when the din
and uproar was at the highest, an angry storm swept over the field,
and thus to the thunders of battle was added 'the dread artillery of the
skies.' "[30]

Sener told how again and again the enemy assaulted the Confederate
lines and in each case wavered and fell back. "Their obstinacy and
courage on this field cannot be gainsaid. They fought with a courage
and devotion worthy of a better cause; whilst our men, safe behind
breastworks, rejoiced in their ability to deal death to the accursed foe
with such slight loss." The *Richmond Enquirer* correspondent "Y." also
attributed the comparatively small Confederate loss in the battle to
the fact that "our army fought for the first time behind breastworks."[31]

It went against the grain for a Confederate war correspondent to
have to admit courage on the part of the "cowardly Yankee." In his
report Alexander supplied an explanation for the unusual behavior of
the enemy which deprived that enemy of most of the credit. There
could be no doubt, he asserted, that Grant's troops had been well supplied with liquor before they went into battle. He found supporting
evidence in the fact that many of the prisoners, including more than

[30] *Ibid.*, p. 298; *Richmond Daily Dispatch*, May 16, 18, 1864; *Savannah Republican*, May 25, 1864; *Mobile Daily Advertiser and Register*, May 27, 1864.
[31] *Richmond Daily Dispatch*, May 16, 1864; *Daily Richmond Enquirer*, May
23, 1864. The Richmond correspondent of the *Augusta Constitutionalist*, who
made the same claim about the use of breastworks as the *Enquirer* correspondent, admitted that at the Battle of Fredericksburg the Confederates had had "some slight protection," but denied that it was equal to the
strength of the Confederate breastworks at Spotsylvania. *Augusta Daily Constitutionalist*, May 27, 1864.

one colonel, were intoxicated when they fell into Confederate hands.[32] Alexander's *Republican* colleague "Tout-le-Monde," who had returned to Virginia with Longstreet's command, supported "P.W.A.'s" allegation that the Union attackers had been "plied with liquor" beforehand. "Tout-le-Monde" stigmatized the practice as "not only disgraceful but brutal . . . [unfitting] men in every way to be effective, and only . . . [giving] them an artificial courage to be murdered like very hogs."[33]

More than one correspondent who reported Thursday's fight, including Alexander, expressed hesitation about describing the battle in detail lest he fail to give satisfaction to some of the officers. Undoubtedly this was what the *Enquirer* correspondent had in mind when he said, "experience has demonstrated that an attempt to enter into details of so extensive an engagement at this early stage must result in unwilling injustice to some portions of our army."[34]

Editor Forsyth of the *Mobile Register* was with one of the Alabama brigades in the battle and was wounded in the hip during the attempt to regain the captured breastworks of the "Bloody Angle." Forsyth was taken to Richmond after the battle to be hospitalized at the Alabama Soldier's Home. When *Mobile Register* correspondent Bagby heard about Forsyth's presence in Richmond, he went to the Soldier's Home to learn about the performance of the Alabama troops from Forsyth.[35]

Another newspaperman who presumably was at Spotsylvania at this time was the same English correspondent whose account of the Battles of the Wilderness had been so greatly extolled by Southern readers. Hewson's story of the Spotsylvania campaign, occupying seven columns of a single issue of the *Richmond Enquirer*, was in the judgment of the editor of the *Augusta Constitutionalist* the most complete and vivid description of the battles that had yet been published. The Richmond correspondent of the *Atlanta Intelligencer*, who was himself a literary figure of some consequence, told of reading Hewson's battle report aloud to a Richmond lady. The result was that: "The vividness of the delineations and the masterly skill with which the accomplished writer grouped together the events which had passed almost with lightning rapidity before the keen eye of the observer—the minuteness and fullness of detail, which left no important point unnoticed, and the elo-

[32] *Richmond Daily Dispatch*, May 18, 1864.
[33] *Savannah Republican*, June 1, 1864.
[34] *Daily Richmond Enquirer*, May 23, 1864.
[35] *Mobile Daily Advertiser and Register*, May 28, June 1, 1864.

quent rush, so to speak, of the diction, which seemed characteristic and significant of the very hurry of the conflict, drew forth from my fair auditor the exclamation, 'what an artist!' "[36]

Because of communication difficulties north of Richmond, the letters and dispatches of the army correspondents were sometimes delayed for more than a week in reaching the home offices of their newspapers. These interruptions resulted from the fact that the army was fighting at some distance from the nearest railroad and telegraph offices and the country between was so infested by the enemy's cavalry that the use of couriers had to be suspended temporarily. Frequent breaks in telegraph communication between Richmond and the Lower South also made it difficult for the newspapers of South Carolina, Georgia, and Alabama to keep informed about the progress of the fighting in Virginia. Within twenty-four hours after the Battles of the Wilderness, Union raiders cut the line of the Southern Telegraph Company at Stony Creek, about twenty miles south of Petersburg, Virginia. About the same time, another raiding party severed the line between Richmond and Danville over the other principal telegraph line between Richmond and the South, thus effectively cutting Atlanta and Montgomery off from Richmond for a whole day. On Sunday morning the Danville line of the Southern Express Company was back in operation, but by that time there was such a backlog of government business the press could not get access to the telegraph.[37]

The failure, for these reasons, of the Confederate Press Association to keep its members supplied with news from Virginia led to repeated complaint and criticism. To get at the root of the difficulty, President Clark of the Press Association telegraphed from Mobile to Superintendent Thrasher in Atlanta on May 16, inquiring what steps, if any, had been taken to obtain news from Virginia by other channels of communication. Thrasher's reply was not entirely reassuring. He explained that he had been trying for four days to send P.A. dispatches, but none had been allowed. "Nobody answers me from Richmond." He claimed, however, that he had sent a special reporter to Petersburg four days

[36] *Augusta Daily Constitutionalist,* June 7, 1864; *Atlanta Daily Intelligencer,* June 8, 1864. For evidence of appreciation by other newspapers of Alexander's "graphic and deeply interesting account of the great battle at Spottsylvania C.H., Va." see *Daily Columbus Enquirer,* May 26, 1864.

[37] *Daily Richmond Enquirer,* May 16, 1864; *Macon Daily Telegraph,* May 16, 1864.

before to see what could be done about reopening news communication by the coastal telegraph route.[38]

The transmission of special correspondence by mail from the army to points below Richmond was hardly more satisfactory than the wire service. At the beginning of the campaign military authorities called the Richmond postal clerks into the field for militia duty; as a result the operation of the Richmond post office was virtually at a standstill during May. The *Mobile Register* did not receive any army correspondence for almost three weeks after the campaign began; on June 7 Bagby was shown an accumulation of nearly 100,000 letters that had been lying in the post office during the previous five days. After waiting ten days to receive its customary newspaper exchanges from Richmond, the *Macon Telegraph* concluded that the Richmond newspapers must have suspended publication because of the invasion threat, and on July 12, for the first time in three weeks, the *Montgomery Advertiser* had the opportunity to excerpt news from a Richmond paper.[39]

Attributing the interruption of communication to censorship by the Richmond authorities, the pro-administration *Charleston Courier* politely asked for a relaxation of the censorship. The *Courier* argued that the public could stand to hear the truth, "even if not up to the most sanguine expectations," and that the suppression of unfavorable news only created a wider field for the dissemination of exaggerated reports. Then, perhaps influenced by the example of Union Secretary Stanton, Editor Yeadon besought the authorities to prepare a daily news bulletin for the Confederate press. Exclaimed the *Courier*: "Must we wait for flags of truce to bring us the earliest reports, true or false, uttered by Yankee journalists? We believe the most prejudiced opponent of General Bragg—who is supposed to be chargeable with the late restrictions on communication—would not have accused him of such revenge. Let him and others in power show in the people a little of the confidence which the people have extended towards our officers and soldiers. . . . Give us the news as to all completed events—we ask not any premature revelations of plans or purposes or numbers, or any information which the most cautious policy should detain."[40]

[38] *Mobile Daily Advertiser and Register*, May 18, 1864; *Atlanta Daily Southern Confederacy*, May 22, 1864; *Charlotte* (N.C.) *Bulletin* as reprinted in Augusta *Daily Chronicle and Sentinel*, June 25, 1864; *Columbus Daily Sun*, June 29, 1864.
[39] *Mobile Daily Advertiser and Register*, May 26, June 21, 1864; *Macon Daily Telegraph*, May 16, 1864; *Montgomery Daily Advertiser*, July 12, 1864.
[40] *Charleston Daily Courier*, May 21, 1864. Bragg's relations with the press

There is no indication in the scanty records of the Confederate government that the *Courier*'s petition was acted on or even considered. Neither Davis nor his chief military adviser Bragg was much interested in currying the favor of the press, and the Confederate Congress was not disposed to go out of its way to facilitate newsgathering. Although in the latter part of May the Confederate Senate passed a bill recommended by its military committee to authorize Press Association reporters to purchase rations and forage from the army quartermaster, a motion to reconsider was agreed to, and the bill was then rejected. In vain, various newspapers pointed out that the proposal applied to only two reporters, one with General Lee's army and the other with Johnston's, that it called for the *purchase* of supplies and not for a government subsidy to the press, and that it made no sense to exempt printers and editors from compulsory military service if the press reporters, operating along lines from ten to fifteen miles long, were denied subsistence for themselves and their horses. Senators like Hill of Georgia and Robert W. Barnwell of South Carolina were convinced that Congress had no constitutional right to permit anyone not enrolled in the military service to purchase rations from the supply department. And there the matter rested.[41]

For almost a week after the Battle of Spotsylvania the two armies continued to face each other without resuming hostilities. Then on May 18 Grant made another attempt to break the Confederate lines below the Bloody Angle. According to Alexander the Union commander first staged a diversionary movement to his left to make Lee think he was shifting to the east, but the stratagem failed and Lee was ready

---

were still touchy. During the last week of May 1864, he wrote a private letter to one of the proprietors of the *Richmond Whig* to express his displeasure with an article the *Whig* had published. It seems likely that the article to which he objected was an editorial entitled "Drunken Officers" in the *Richmond Daily Whig* of May 25, 1864. W. M. Elliott to Gen. Braxton Bragg, May 28, 1864, Bragg Papers.

[41] *Mobile Daily Advertiser and Register*, May 12, 1864; *Daily Richmond Examiner*, May 24, 1864; *Richmond Daily Sentinel* as paraphrased in *Atlanta Daily Southern Confederacy*, June 16, 1864; *Richmond Daily Dispatch*, June 9, 1864; *Richmond Daily Whig*, June 10, 1864; *Augusta Daily Chronicle and Sentinel*, May 26, 1864. Before Thrasher addressed a memorial to Congress requesting this legislation, his application for this privilege had been rejected by Generals Lee and Johnston and Secretary of War Seddon on the ground that they lacked authority to grant it. *Atlanta Daily Southern Confederacy* as reprinted in *Savannah Republican*, May 13, 1864. See also *Journal of the Congress of the Confederate States*, IV, 73, 80.

for the attack. Alexander also reported that although the enemy's artillery fire was very heavy, the infantry assault was feeble, "the enemy at no time coming nearer than seventy-five yards from our entrenchments." From Union prisoners "P.W.A." heard that the assault column consisted of 8,000 troops who had volunteered their services in response to a call from General Grant. The reporter decided that if the Federal army was so demoralized that it was necessary to call for volunteers to attack the Confederate line and if such volunteers showed no more spirit than these, "then the struggle here is approaching its end."[42]

Alexander was honest enough to admit, however, that the morale of some parts of Lee's army was not much higher. Describing a flanking movement attempted by Ewell's corps on the evening of May 19, he conceded that the "unsteadiness" of some parts of the corps limited the success of the movement. He went on to say that "Jones' brigade, of Johnson's division, which did not stand firmly at the Wilderness, and was the first to break in the great battle of the 12th, fled incontinently, and some report that the Stonewall brigade did not do as well as it might have done."[43]

On May 20, Grant marched southeast from Spotsylvania, and Lee kept pace, moving south of the North Anna River to cover Hanover Junction, only twenty-five miles north of Richmond. The weather was hot and dry; Sener noticed that Lee's troops were so exhausted by their marching that whenever their officers called the hourly halt for a ten-minute rest they would fall down where they were and go to sleep instantly.[44] Alexander rated Lee's position along the North Anna as even stronger than his defenses at Spotsylvania. Evidently Grant was of the same opinion, for instead of attacking it, he resumed his crab-like movement to Lee's right on the twenty-seventh and crossed the Pamunkey River into the Peninsula. Lee countered by moving on a line parallel to the enemy's to keep his army between Grant and Richmond. In a letter to the *Mobile Register* from Richmond on May 28, Bagby observed with glee that "Grant is forced into McClellan's old route, and Lincoln is no doubt tearing his hair with mortification."[45]

The next evening Bagby saw Beauregard in Richmond. The dapper

[42] *Richmond Daily Dispatch*, May 23, 1864.

[43] *Mobile Daily Advertiser and Register*, June 1, 1864. According to Alexander the troops in Jones' brigade were from southwestern Virginia, and the "Stonewall" brigade was composed of soldiers from the Shenandoah Valley.

[44] *Richmond Daily Dispatch*, May 24, 1864.

[45] *Mobile Daily Advertiser and Register*, June 1, 5, 1864.

general had been summoned for a conference with Lee from Bermuda Hundred below Richmond, where he had been doing an effective job of stymying Ben Butler's Army of the James. Bagby inferred that the conference was occasioned by reports from Lee's spies that Grant had been ordered to move to the south side of Richmond and "play the Vicksburg game against us." Bagby thought Beauregard was looking well, although the general told the correspondent that his health was not very "firm."[46]

Alexander turned up in town the next day (May 30), and Bagby discussed with him the possibility that Grant's game was to make a sudden attack on Petersburg, which both correspondents considered the key to Richmond. Alexander told Bagby he thought Grant was aiming for Petersburg, but that Grant's losses during the campaign had been exaggerated in both the North and South.[47]

While Alexander pondered the strategy of the two great antagonists he remained on the alert for a good human interest story. Riding along the lines north of the Chickahominy on Sunday, May 29, he saw the soldiers enjoying a much-needed rest after their weary marches and hard battles. "Some were reading their well-thumbed Bibles; some were indicting [*sic*] letters to the loved ones at home, to assure them of their safety; some were sleeping—perchance dreaming of the bloody work still remaining to be done; others were enjoying the music of the brigade bands, as they rehearsed those solemn and touching airs which the grand old masters of the art divine . . . have given to the world; and others again were sitting under the trees, with their arms stacked near at hand, listening to the Word of Life, as preached by those faithful servants of God, the hardy, zealous, self-denying chaplains of the army. As the army thus rested—its great heart quiet, its huge arms unstrung, its fleet feet still—I could but reflect, and wonder as I reflected, that this vast machine, this mighty giant, this great, unmeasured, and immeasurable power, should be so terrible in battle, and yet so calm and gentle and devout in the hour of peace."[48]

[46] *Ibid.*, June 8, 1864. Bagby's guess as to the reason for Beauregard's visit to Richmond was rather wide of the mark. The general had come to explain to Davis and Lee his objections to sending reinforcements from his command to Lee. Freeman, *Lee's Lieutenants*, III, 368-69.

[47] For Alexander's predictions in his special correspondence at this time that Grant would cross the James see *Mobile Daily Advertiser and Register*, June 7-9, 1864.

[48] *Richmond Daily Dispatch*, May 30, 1864.

As Grant advanced on May 31 to Cold Harbor near the 1862 battle-field of Gaines's Mill, Lee extended his lines to the Chickahominy River, about three miles from the outer ring of Richmond's defenses. Grant was running out of space on his left, and so after a successful movement of limited scope the day before, he decided to launch a frontal attack on Lee's lines on June 3. On the evening before, the people in Richmond heard the sound of heavy cannonading from the northeast, and there was great anxiety until the arrival of a dispatch from Sener announcing a successful flank movement by Ewell.

As Bagby came downtown after breakfast the next morning the sound of the guns at Cold Harbor, seven miles away, vibrated in his ears and rose high above the bustle of the city. He went out of his way to climb a hill from which the firing could be heard more distinctly. There he noticed two little Negro urchins lying flat on their stomachs, watching a gang of white boys who were seeing who could jump the farthest, and two old gentlemen seated on a curbstone, protected from the drizzle by their umbrellas as they listened to the hammering of the guns. In the city below, the merchants and tradesmen were attending to their usual duties in spite of the many closed doors along Main Street. As the roar of the cannon showed signs of becoming louder, acquaintances could be heard greeting each other with comments like:

"There seems to be a fuss going on out yonder."

"Yes."

"Somebody will get hurt."

"Yes."

Bagby asked himself the question whether such apparent nonchalance signified insensitiveness or trust in God and in Lee's army. He decided that it was probably both, "but more of the latter I hope."[49]

Grant used detachments from three corps in a futile attempt to crack Lee's strong entrenchments that day. Dutcher of the *Augusta Constitutionalist* told in his Richmond letter how the enemy made as many as

[49] Dupuy, *Compact History,* pp. 302-303; *Mobile Daily Advertiser and Register,* June 21, 1864. Apparently by this time Bagby had replaced Thompson as the Richmond correspondent of the *Memphis Appeal.* The new Richmond correspondent of the *Appeal,* who signed himself "Mercury" (essentially the same pseudonym as the "Hermes" pseudonym Bagby used for his *Charleston Mercury* correspondence) announced that he had been requested by the *Appeal's* correspondent "Dixie" to take his place because of "Dixie"'s "feeble health." *Memphis Daily Appeal,* June 16, 1864. At the end of June Thompson travelled to England, running the blockade from Wilmington, in what proved to be a successful effort to recover from tuberculosis.

fourteen different assaults in heavy columns against Kershaw's division, but each time the assault failed with wholesale slaughter. By eleven o'clock the battle was over. Within less than an hour between 6,000 and 7,000 enemy troops were casualties of the accurate fire of the Confederates. Alexander stated in his report that "the loss of the enemy in front of Kershaw's veteran division is represented on all hands to exceed anything that has occurred during the war." He portrayed the battle as a repetition of Spotsylvania, with the important difference that "our own loss is almost incredibly small. Anderson's loss, including Hoke's, will not reach 500." Sener took the position that the enemy had not fought that day with the vim that they displayed in the holocaust on the twelfth of May. He went on to say that while a Union colonel had been taken prisoner on the Confederate entrenchments and his color bearer shot dead while attempting to plant his colors there, the great majority of the attacking force never came that near.[50]

Following the Battle of Cold Harbor, Alexander announced he would no longer correspond for the *Richmond Dispatch*. The burden of reporting for three different newspapers in such an active campaign was evidently becoming too great for him. Perhaps also his belief that the campaign of 1864 and the war itself were fast drawing to a close helped to motivate his decision. Alexander realized, and had already made clear, that he was in danger of falling into the common error of believing that General Lee was infallible. However much such a feeling might seem justified by the skill and intuitive knowledge of his adversary's plans that Lee had exhibited, Alexander felt duty-bound to sound a note of caution. There was, he reminded himself and his readers, a greater power than Lee upon whom the general relied and to whom Alexander ascribed the good fortune that had been literally showered upon the Army of Northern Virginia during 1864.[51]

On the day after the battle both Alexander and Sener visited Bagby's Richmond office. The two reporters disagreed in their estimate of the results of the battle. Whereas Alexander rated it a "decisive victory," Sener interpreted it as a "temporary check." When Bragg came in from the field at nightfall, he contented himself with observing to Bagby that Cold Harbor was not a "general engagement."[52]

[50] *Augusta Daily Constitutionalist*, June 12, 1864; *Richmond Daily Dispatch*, June 4, 1864; *Mobile Daily Advertiser and Register*, June 11, 1864.

[51] *Savannah Republican*, May 28, 1864.

[52] *Mobile Daily Advertiser and Register*, June 17, 1864.

An exchange of letters between Grant and Lee, in which Grant requested an opportunity to bury his dead, gave the correspondent of the *Richmond Examiner* an idea. Scenting an opportunity to obtain material for his correspondence, the reporter inquired of Lee whether it would be possible to have the correspondence published, presumably in the *Examiner*. The offer was politely declined, and the *Examiner* man had no other alternative than to await the publication of the series of letters in the New York papers via the correspondents at Grant's headquarters![53]

Grant remained in the vicinity of Cold Harbor for more than a week, preparing for his next move. An army correspondent of the *Columbia South Carolinian* indicated that most of Lee's soldiers thought they could guess what that next move would be—a sudden crossing to the south side of the James. Meanwhile they continued to strengthen their breastworks.

An interesting description of everyday life in Lee's army at this time appeared in a letter published by this same correspondent. He reported that about one-third of the men in the army were kept awake during the night to be ready for a surprise attack; this necessary precaution, along with heavy working details, gave the common soldier little sleep. Thanks to the victories won in the Wilderness and at Spotsylvania, the army was now well provided with Yankee fly tents. As a rule the tents were stretched over a pit from two to three feet deep to protect the occupants from chance volleys by night and more or less continuous sharpshooting by day. The *Carolinian* correspondent declared that the soldiers were so habituated to danger that they paid very little attention to sharpshooters; as a result, hardly a day passed without six men or so being killed or wounded in each brigade under fire. Not always, he noted, did recklessness cause death or caution provide insurance against it. At many points, including the front line of this reporter's brigade, the opposing breastworks were so close that conversation across the lines was possible. "The other morning, one of our comic fellows, interrupted while eating by an unexpected volley, shouted angrily, 'why the devil can't you let a fellow eat his dinner in peace.' 'Why the devil,' was the quick reply, 'can't you fellows learn to stop this everlasting shooting during the day. If you will come over this way,' continued the Yank, 'we will give you all furloughs.' 'If you will come

[53] *Daily Richmond Examiner*, June 8, 1864.

this way,' rejoined our spokesman, 'we will give you all, *"Final* Discharges!" . . .' "⁵⁴

By early June, according to the army correspondents, the diet of Lee's
army was more abundant and satisfying than it had been for a long
time. Alexander reported on June 11 that the troops were now receiving full rations of salt meat and bread, coffee and sugar, and a
fair supply of West Indian onions and greens. These latter, he pointed
out, were needed to check incipient cases of scurvy and other dietary
ailments. Reporting that the soldiers also were well clothed and shod,
Alexander asserted that the morale of the army was excellent. He implied that effective work by the supply corps of the army had helped
to bring this about.⁵⁵

On June 12 Grant and Meade began the movement of the Army of
the Potomac to the south side of the James that both Confederate army
correspondents and soldiers had predicted. By the evening of the next
day the Northern army had reached the James; on the fourteenth almost 50,000 Federals crossed over to Bermuda Hundred between the
Appomattox and James Rivers.⁵⁶ The army newspapermen were aware
that the enemy had left Cold Harbor, and had a fairly accurate idea
of Grant's destination, but they did not know how rapidly he was moving. Hardly anyone in Richmond paid any attention to the fact that
Congress had adjourned that day to reconvene in November. In a current newspaper letter Bagby said he could not recall having heard at
any time during the past month and a half, either on the street or in
any of the business houses, discussion of any measure before Congress.
"The war absorbs all other topics. . . ."⁵⁷

Alexander was still in Richmond on June 17, reflecting on the per-
plexities at Lee's headquarters. According to him, it was still not known

⁵⁴ *Columbia Daily South Carolinian,* June 21, 1864.

⁵⁵ *Mobile Daily Advertiser and Register,* June 21, 1864. See also *Montgomery
Daily Mail,* June 21, 1864.

⁵⁶ T. H. Williams, *P.G.T. Beauregard, Napoleon in Gray* (Baton Rouge, 1954),
p. 227.

⁵⁷ *Memphis Daily Appeal,* June 17, 22, 1864; J. R. Thompson Diary, entry for
June 14, 1864. The Richmond correspondent of the *Atlanta Intelligencer* confirmed Bagby's statement about the engrossment of the Richmond population with
war news. "War has again become the all-absorbing theme, to which religion,
literature, politics, law, and legislation succumb." *Atlanta Daily Intelligencer,*
June 25, 1864. Much of the business of Congress had consisted of the discussion
of the habeas corpus issue. For reporting of the congressional debate about it see
the letter of a Richmond correspondent in *Mobile Daily Advertiser and Register,*
May 14, 1864.

at noon that day in Richmond whether Grant had moved the bulk of his army to the south side of the James, although it *was* known that parts of three corps of the Army of the Potomac were across the river. Yet at that very time Grant had over 60,000 troops in front of Petersburg, and more were on the way.[58]

As a result of the confusion in the minds of the Confederate high command as to where Grant was and what he was doing, none of the leading Confederate army correspondents was at Petersburg between the 15th and 18th of June to witness Beauregard's skillful defense of that key point against almost incredible odds. The public had to rely on the wire reports of the Press Association and the daily news summaries in the *Petersburg Express.*

Apparently the first Southern army correspondent to cross the James was the *Richmond Examiner's* "Ivanhoe," who got across on the morning of June 16 and rode to a place called the Half Way House. There he learned about the attack on Petersburg the day before, and how, after losing the first line of entrenchments, ex-Governor Wise had checked any further advance with a strangely mixed force of aged civilians and uniformed soldiers.[59] On the 16th Beauregard still had only 14,000 troops to hold his main defensive line against odds of between 3-1 and 4-1. The ineptitude of Federal corps commanders, Hancock, Burnside, and "Baldy" Smith, contributed as much to Beauregard's success as his own skillful tactics. The story of what happened the next day was essentially a repetition of the happenings of the previous day, and finally on the morning of June 18 the vanguard of Lee's army reached Petersburg. By the time Alexander arrived in town the next day the safety of Petersburg was assured.[60]

REALIZING that it was now too late to capture Petersburg by direct assault Grant shifted to a siege operation, constructing an elaborate line of trenches from north of the James to below Petersburg. He accompanied the operation by a bombardment of the city which frightened the inhabitants but which some reporters insisted did relatively

[58] *Mobile Daily Advertiser and Register,* June 25, 1864; Williams, *Beauregard,* p. 230.

[59] *Daily Richmond Examiner,* June 17, 1864; Hudson Strode, *Jefferson Davis, Tragic Hero, 1864-1889* (New York, 1964), p. 60.

[60] *Savannah Republican,* June 27, 1864; *Mobile Daily Advertiser and Register,* June 29, 1864; Bruce Catton, *Never Call Retreat* (New York, 1965), p. 367; Williams, p. 232.

little damage. Within two weeks after the siege began Alexander reported: "Everybody has left, or is preparing to leave, who is able to get away. The houses, and even the woods and fields, for miles around Petersburg are filled with women and children and old men, who have fled from their homes. Some have provided themselves with tents; others have erected bush arbors, and others are bivouacking under the trees. This is a sad fate for a town so distinguished for hospitality, refinement, and cultivated men and women."[61]

On the 6th of July *Republican* correspondent "Tout-le-Monde" reported that the enemy was continuing to lob shells into the city and that here and there great holes could be seen through the walls, windows were smashed, colonnades crushed, and pavements torn up. Although "Tout-le-Monde" seemed to think the effects of this "infamous vandalism" might be evident for years, a soldier correspondent of the *Mobile Register* believed that all the damage except shattered window glass could be repaired within a few days. According to the *Montgomery Mail* reporter, the loss of life among civilians was comparatively small.[62]

The summer of 1864 in Virginia was extremely hot and dry, and because no rain had fallen since the first week of June the roads in the vicinity of the army lines were ankle deep with dust. In a letter to the *Savannah Republican* from Petersburg on July 7, Alexander soliloquized: "Everything partakes of the color of dust—the woods, the fields, the corn, the grass, the men, the horses, and the wagons. We breathe it; we sleep in it; we eat and move in it. It is thicker than the darkness that overspread Egypt in the days of Pharaoh; so thick, indeed, that Gen. Butler from his lofty lookout will be able to descry but little else except dust. If there is no wind to blow it away, the dust raised by a solitary horseman is so great that it is impossible at the distance of a few paces to tell whether it is produced by a man, a horse, or a vehicle."[63]

Reporting the daily fatalities from sharpshooters and describing the clouds of dust kicked up by the "mortles," as the North Carolina sol-

---

[61] *Mobile Daily Advertiser and Register*, July 14, 1864. For a description of the bombproofs constructed by the citizens of Petersburg who remained in the city see J. H. Claiborne, *Seventy-Five Years in Old Virginia* (New York, 1904), pp. 204-205.

[62] *Savannah Republican*, July 20, 1864; *Mobile Daily Advertiser and Register*, July 23, 1864; *Montgomery Daily Mail*, July 17, 1864.

[63] *Savannah Republican*, July 14, 1864.

diers were wont to call the enemy's mortars, was not very exciting; so on the 10th of July Alexander went to Richmond for a change of pace and some rest.[64] Early's invasion of the North was the talk of the town when Alexander arrived there. Jubal Early was an eccentric character, a former Union man from southwestern Virginia, with stooped shoulders and a piping treble voice that provided a strange medium for the steady stream of profanity that he emitted. Early had been in the Shenandoah Valley, where Union General David Hunter had been making trouble since the middle of June. In a letter to the *Richmond Dispatch* from Lynchburg on June 16 Reporter James P. Bell indicated that the enemy was approaching the vitally important railroad center and that the editors and employees of the Lynchburg papers had suspended publication to man the trenches. Yet Early reached Lynchburg before Hunter did; on the day after Bell's letter was written, Hunter began a precipitate retreat across the mountains, leaving the Valley highway to the North unguarded.[65]

By July 2 Early was at Winchester, ready to make the demonstration against Washington and Baltimore that Lee had ordered. By so doing Lee hoped to prod Grant into attacking the Army of Northern Virginia in its entrenched position or compel him to withdraw troops from Petersburg for the defense of Washington. Secrecy was essential for the success of Early's movement; therefore Lee was annoyed when he learned somebody in the government had leaked information about Early to a correspondent of the *Richmond Enquirer*. Although the *Enquirer* reporter requested his newspaper not to publish what he had discovered, other newspapermen in the capital could be expected to be less close-mouthed. Consequently Lee implored Davis to notify all the newspapers not to allude to any military movement, directly or otherwise. He explained that, "of course it will not do to particularize that [Early's] movement as it may not be known. I think it would be well to charge the Telegraph operators not to forward a dispatch referring in any way to Army movements."[66]

[64] *Ibid.*, July 20, 1864.

[65] J. S. Wise, *The End of an Era* (Boston, 1899), pp. 227-28; *Richmond Daily Dispatch*, June 18, 1864.

[66] R. E. Lee to Jefferson Davis, June 15, 1864 as reprinted in D. S. Freeman, ed., *Lee's Dispatches* (New York, 1915), pp. 240-41. There was a direct hint of Early's invasion plan, written before the press was notified to keep quiet about Early's movement, in Bagby's letter in *Mobile Daily Advertiser and Register*, June 24, 1864. Apparently Lee himself issued such a warning to the press on June 20. *Columbus Daily Sun*, July 13, 1864.

Direct evidence of the War Department's compliance with Lee's request is found in a letter Editor Pleasants of the *Richmond Dispatch* addressed to Secretary Seddon about a month later. Pleasants cautioned Seddon that however well intentioned his warning to the Richmond press had been, its effect would be lost unless its substance was telegraphed "to the whole press south of us." Pleasants went on to say that the press of Raleigh, Charleston, Columbus, Savannah, Mobile, Atlanta, and Montgomery was liberally represented in Richmond and that the correspondents of these newspapers "write letters communicating everything they hear." To guard against any resentment on the part of a Richmond bureaucrat of his offering this unsolicited advice, Pleasants concluded with the observation that he hoped "this hint will be taken in good part."[67]

For the most part the Confederate press had to depend on Northern journalists for information about the progress of Early's invasion, a dependence dictated in part by the Confederate telegraphic censorship. Also, apparently no more than two newspaper correspondents accompanied Early, one of whom was a volunteer correspondent, and neither had any means of communicating with their newspapers before Early's return to Virginia. The Confederate force of about 13,000 infantry and cavalry crossed the Potomac near Shepherdstown on July 6 and marched toward Washington by way of Hagerstown and Frederick. A correspondent of the *Wilmington Journal*, who was a member of a North Carolina regiment, described the consternation and indignation that was plainly written on the faces of the Marylanders they encountered at this, the third, invasion of their state. On July 9 Early brushed aside a force of 6,000 militia and regulars Maj.Gen. Lew Wallace had brought from Baltimore, in what came to be known as the Battle of the Monocacy. The road to Washington was now open.[68]

By that time the reporter from North Carolina had changed his mind about the sentiments of the people of Maryland. Now he was convinced that "they are with us" and that they were eager "to unite their destiny with the Confederate cause." With similar optimism Editor James Southall of the *Charlottesville Chronicle*, who also was with

[67] Hugh R. Pleasants to Hon. Jas. A. Seddon Secy War [n.d., but received at the War Department July 18, 1864], Office of Confederate Secretary of War, Letters Received 1861-1865, 163-P-1864, National Archives.

[68] *Wilmington Daily Journal*, July 27, 1864. The Battle of the Monocacy is described at greater length in F. E. Vandiver, *Jubal's Raid* (New York, 1960), pp. 164-65.

Early, expressed assurance that Washington would fall if Early's army attacked it. The capture of Washington had not been part of Early's mission, but now he was willing to make the attempt. By the 11th of July he was at Silver Spring, ready to probe the city's defenses. That same afternoon, Wright's U.S. Sixth Army Corps came ashore at the Potomac wharves from Petersburg, to take over the defense of the capital from the miscellaneous collection of home guards, government clerks, and invalid soldiers in the fortifications. Withdrawing from this unexpected opposition, Early's men recrossed the Potomac on the 14th and headed back toward the Shenandoah Valley, carrying with them large quantities of loot.[69]

The results of the campaign were controversial in Southern newspapers. Not knowing its purpose, Southern editors naturally were disappointed that Early had returned to Virginia without capturing either Baltimore or Washington. In a letter to the *Mobile Register* from Richmond on July 18 Bagby declared that few persons there were satisfied that Early had accomplished everything he might have with the force at his command. The pro-administration *Richmond Sentinel* even went so far as to hint that the overly free use of whisky by unnamed parties had been a factor in limiting Early's success. In general, however, most of the Confederate newspapers took a favorable view of what the audacious general had accomplished. The *Mobile Register* and the *Augusta Constitutionalist* expressed confidence that Early's invasion would strengthen the peace movement in the North and exert a favorable effect on European public opinion. They also rated as pluses the cash donations Early had levied on some of the Maryland towns, the three thousand fine beef cattle he had brought back, and the removal, temporary or otherwise, of Northern troops from the Shenandoah Valley.[70]

ALEXANDER belonged to the minority of newspapermen who regarded Early's expedition as a failure. Toward the end of July he notified the *Register* that he intended to go back to Petersburg the next day on the assumption that "Grant will not remain quiet long."[71] His assumption

---

[69] *Charleston Daily Courier*, July 28, 1864; Dupuy, *Compact History*, pp. 346-47; Vandiver, *Jubal's Raid*, pp. 164-65.

[70] *Mobile Daily Advertiser and Register*, July 16, August 2, 1864; *Augusta Daily Constitutionalist*, July 26, 1864. For the vigorously expressed point of view that Early's movement was a failure see *Daily Richmond Enquirer*, July 28, 1864.

[71] *Savannah Republican*, July 27, 1864; *Mobile Daily Advertiser and Register*, August 12, 1864.

was correct, although he probably did not anticipate the form Grant's activity would take. For some time there had been rumors in Lee's army, which had attracted the attention of the press, that Grant was constructing a mine under Petersburg with the intention of blowing it up. Sener alluded to these reports in a letter mailed to the *Richmond Dispatch* on July 21, saying that they were of a speculative character but by no means incredible. He did not mention the fact that Confederate engineers had sunk countershafts along the lines in an attempt to verify the reports and had failed to locate any Federal miners. Indeed, expert opinion tended to discount the possibility of a tunnel being run the five hundred feet that separated the opposing lines. Lawley, the highly respected correspondent of the *London Times*, who happened to be at Lee's headquarters when the possibility of an enemy mine was first discussed, was sure four hundred feet was the absolute limit for such a tunnel because of the problem of ventilation.[72]

All doubts about the enemy's tunneling were removed on Saturday morning, July 30, about five o'clock, when eight thousand pounds of gunpowder in a subterranean gallery were exploded near the center of the Confederate lines in front of Bushrod Johnson's division. Sener reported that the explosion caused a loud, deep noise,[73] and fragments of earth began flying in every direction, making a breach in the lines of some thirty to forty yards. At the same time the enemy opened fire with their batteries all along the line. According to Sener: "No sooner had the explosion occurred than Burnside's minions—'black spirits and gray'—bounded forward with a hellish yell, pressing back our astonished and, for a while, discomfited troops, gaining possession of . . . four guns, and a number of prisoners. The enemy now held some two hundred yards of our lines, and could be seen hurrying up troops from the rear. . . ." Other correspondents reported that Burnside's Negro troops charged through the breach as soon as the smoke had cleared away, shouting, "No quarter—Remember Fort Pillow," and that the same fate was visited on these troops when the Confederates regained the upper hand.[74]

[72] *Richmond Daily Dispatch*, July 23, 1864; Freeman, *Lee's Dispatches*, III, 464.

[73] The *Petersburg Express*, on the other hand, reported the incidence of several explosions instead of just one explosion. *Petersburg Daily Express*, August 1, 1864. See also Claiborne, *Seventy-five Years*, p. 223.

[74] *Richmond Daily Dispatch*, August 1, 1864; *Daily Richmond Enquirer*, August 1, 1864; *Charleston Daily Courier*, August 8, 1864.

Unfortunately the newspaper accounts of what happened do not square very well with the official reports. There was a great deal of confusion in both camps that morning, perhaps also in the minds of army newspapermen who had been rudely awakened; and neither side acted promptly or with much resolution at first. It was more than an hour after the explosion before Ferrero's Negro division, minus its commanding officer, moved to the attack, after at least one other white division had bungled it, and after Lee had directed General Mahone to use two brigades to recapture the lost works. According to more than one Southern correspondent, Wright's Georgia brigade was unable to carry out its part of the assignment, and an Alabama brigade had to be brought up to do the job. The fighting dragged on in aimless fashion until about noon when Burnside attempted a withdrawal. By that time a considerable number of his troops, Negro and white, had taken refuge in the crater opened by the explosion and after considerable slaughter were compelled to surrender. The so-called Battle of the Crater was something of a repulse for the Federals, in which they suffered casualties more than three times those of the Confederates.[75]

Late that evening one of the editors of the *Petersburg Express* made a personal inspection of what a *Mobile Register* correspondent called "the most horrible sight I have ever seen." "It [the crater] appeared to be about 40 feet in depth, and some 200 feet in circumference, and resembled more what one would imagine to have been the effects of a terrible earthquake than any thing else to which we can liken it. Immense boulders of earth were piled up rudely one above the other, and great fragments of bombproofs, gun carriages, limbers etc. were lying promiscuously in every direction. . . . The sides and bottom of the chasm were literally lined with Yankee dead, and the bodies lay in every conceivable position. In one spot we noticed a corporal of infantry, a sergeant of artillery, and a big, burly negro, piled one upon top of the other. Some had evidently been killed with the butts of muskets as their crushed skulls and badly mashed faces too plainly indicated, while the greater portion were shot, great pools of blood having flowed from their wounds and stained the ground."[76]

The editor of the *Express* noted that this was the first time the Army

[75] Bruce Catton, *Stillness at Appomattox* (New York, 1954), pp. 244-52; Dupuy, *Compact History*, pp. 379-82.

[76] *Petersburg Daily Express*, August 1, 1864.

of Northern Virginia had encountered the Negro troops of the enemy. On the basis of the disastrous results (for the enemy) of the experiment, he concluded—perhaps prematurely—that "this favorite element of the Yankee army" was no match for Confederate white soldiers.

Alexander's newspaper account of the explosion and its aftermath was, surprisingly enough, not one of his more satisfactory reporting efforts of the campaign. Although apparently he was in Petersburg at the time, he was not an eyewitness of the incident. He obtained the facts and figures for his report from the "industrious telegraphic correspondent of the Associated Press."[77]

One of the soldiers in Wright's Georgia Brigade wrote in protest to the *Augusta Chronicle* and *Sentinel* about the statement in the *Petersburg Express* which indicated that his brigade had failed "to take that portion of the works assigned them." The soldier, who signed himself "One of the Brigade," maintained that the *Express* had been misinformed. He claimed that his brigade "or that portion which was unmasked" had charged and planted their colors on the works that were their objective. He also contended that this brigade had suffered a higher number of casualties than any other in Mahone's division.[78]

Fearing that Grant would continue to plant explosives, Lee encouraged his engineers to drive countershafts. On August 8 Alexander reported the springing of an experimental mine three days earlier, which he regarded as a successful experiment. Apparently there was room for disagreement about this, for a correspondent who also wrote for the *Mobile Register* pronounced it a "miserable failure." According to the correspondent the possibility that the enemy might be pursuing other projects of the same kind as the gigantic explosion of the thirtieth was creating a suspense that "is beginning to tell upon the best of us."[79]

About this time reports that Grant was moving troops down the James caused the correspondent of the *Montgomery Mail* to reach the mistaken conclusion that Grant was withdrawing from the Petersburg line. When Lee decided that these troops were being sent to the Shenandoah Valley to be used against Early, he dispatched an infantry division and the greater part of a cavalry division to Culpeper to reinforce his lieutenant in the Valley. To prevent Lee from detaching

[77] *Savannah Republican*, August 8, 1864. In contrast with the *Express* editor, Alexander reported that "the negroes behaved in the fight quite as well as their white associates. . . ." *Mobile Daily Advertiser and Register*, August 14, 1864.

[78] *Augusta Daily Chronicle and Sentinel*, September 13, 1864.

[79] *Mobile Daily Advertiser and Register*, August 17-18, 21, 1864.

412

any more troops for this purpose, Grant decided to threaten the Richmond defense lines from the east.[80]

When the Union Commander sent two army corps with a cavalry division north of the James, Lee made an equivalent countermove. Ordering Hancock and Birney to continue the demonstration in that sector, Grant prepared to strike below Petersburg at the Weldon Railroad, which had been an important objective of his for some time. The Richmond correspondent of the *Augusta Constitutionalist* had already described in his newspaper the network of railroads radiating from Petersburg, over which Lee's army drew its supplies. Running due south from Petersburg was the Petersburg and Weldon Railroad providing a direct connection with Wilmington and linking up there with the seaboard line to Charleston and Atlanta. Running west from Petersburg was the Southside Railroad, connecting at Burkesville with the Richmond and Danville and continuing on to Lynchburg. At Danville the Richmond and Danville met a newly constructed line, the Piedmont Railroad, which provided an indirect approach to the rich corn belt of northwest Georgia.[81]

On August 18 Warren's corps of U.S. troops bore to the left of the Petersburg line to strike the Weldon Railroad at Globe Tavern. Lee responded by detaching troops from the James River sector to dislodge Warren from the railroad. Alexander, in Richmond at the time, was eager to return to Petersburg to report the fighting, but he was handicapped by the fact that more than ten days ago he had shipped his horse to the Shenandoah Valley in anticipation of important military movements there. Moreover, he was convinced that "such a thing as hiring a horse in Richmond is utterly impossible, though one should offer as much for one as King Richard did."[82] The more fortunate *Dispatch* correspondent Sener was on the spot, however, to write what one correspondent later classed as the best description of the fighting that followed.

Sener began his report with the ominous words: "To-day, for the first time in the history of the campaign of the Army of Northern Virginia, the Confederate arms have suffered a check and repulse." Then,

[80] *Montgomery Daily Mail*, August 23, 1864; Freeman, *Lee's Dispatches*, III, 479-80.

[81] *Augusta Daily Constitutionalist*, July 26, 1864. For a useful sketch map and description of Lee's main railroad supply lines to Petersburg and Richmond see Freeman, *Lee's Dispatches*, III, 451-52.

[82] *Savannah Republican*, August 24, 1864.

after alluding briefly to the fight on the 19th in which A. P. Hill attacked the enemy near Globe Tavern and captured 2,700 prisoners, Sener reported that fighting was not resumed the next day "for reasons which would be injudicious to state." Then he described the climax of the struggle on August 22, when Heth's division attacked in front and Mahone attempted a flanking movement. Heth's effort was only partially successful, and Mahone's advance met a raking and destructive fire from the Federal artillery. "For awhile our brave boys press boldly forward, but in an evil moment, a brigade of ours gives back, and despite the efforts of their gallant commander, refuse to rally. The contagion spreads; other troops give way, and soon the whole mass comes rushing back pell-mell, exposed to as murderous a fire in retreat as that to which they were subjected whilst advancing."[83] After two hours the fight was over. Sener explained the failure by saying that the enemy had two whole corps massed on the railroad, and since they had formed their line in the shape of a crescent with the arc confronting the Confederates, Mahone could find no flank to strike. Confederate newsmen now realized that the Weldon Railroad was securely in Grant's possession.[84]

Back in Petersburg once more, Alexander acknowledged in a letter to the *Mobile Register* that Grant had maneuvered his army with much skill during the operation against the Weldon Railroad. As Alexander saw it: "He [Grant] not only put nearly all our cavalry in motion towards the Rappahannock, and compelled Gen. Lee to detach a considerable force of infantry to the north side of the James, but before we could recall our troops he moved out a heavy column upon the railway at a time when we were too weak to prevent it, and is now so strongly fortified that it would be exceedingly difficult to drive him away."[85]

As summer blended into autumn the letters of army correspondents reflected the boredom of soldiers with trench warfare and other evidences of gradually declining morale. The correspondent of the *Mobile*

[83] *Richmond Daily Dispatch*, August 22, 1864. For the high rating given to Sener's description of the battle by a fellow correspondent see *Montgomery Daily Advertiser*, September 2, 1864.

[84] See e.g. *Montgomery Daily Mail*, September 4, 1864. Editorially the *Richmond Enquirer* rationalized the loss, however, contending that "practically the Weldon road has been of little use to us for several months past." *Daily Richmond Enquirer*, August 25, 1864.

[85] *Mobile Daily Advertiser and Register*, September 1, 1864.

Register who used the signature "Bohemia" described the disenchantment of his fellow soldiers with the confined life in the trenches, eating cold bread and bacon, and listening to the incessant popping of rifles on the picket line and the almost unceasing howling and bursting of shells. Probably the increased amount of illness in the army at this time, mainly "intermittent fever" and dysentery, was a factor in generating soldier discontent. According to Alexander, who was sick himself during the last week of August, there was then as much illness in the Army of Northern Virginia in proportion to its numbers as there had been at any time since the first year of the war.[86]

A soldier correspondent of the *Montgomery Advertiser* affirmed the superiority of Confederate sharpshooting over that of the Yankees, but not because "Johnny Reb" was a better marksman. In his opinion, as well as that of some other Southern correspondents, the English Enfield rifle musket with which the Confederate soldiers were equipped was superior to the Springfield rifle generally used in the Army of the Potomac.[87]

The correspondent of the *Advertiser* also spoke with scorn about the tendency of some soldiers to shirk combat duty and of the encouragement given by officers to such practices. With unusual frankness he said:

"No one outside of the army can form any estimate of the number of men, who never carry a gun, and never see an enemy. A general order from Gen. Cooper positively forbids officers to employ soldiers as servants. 'There must be mudsills in all society,' and it is surprising how many of these 'mudsills' there are in the Confederate army. The general order is repeatedly and openly violated by officers of all grades from subalterns up to Generals. Around headquarters of general officers are always hangers on, professedly privates of some company on extra duty, but in reality 'shirkers from duty,' whose money, whose political influence, or whose relatives in Congress whom it is desirable to pro-

[86] *Ibid.*, September 2, 8, 13, 1864. For the high incidence of intestinal disorders in the Confederate army throughout the war see H. H. Cunningham, *Doctors in Gray* (Baton Rouge, 1958), pp. 184-88. "Intermittent fever" was another name for malaria.

[87] *Montgomery Daily Advertiser*, September 8, 1864. See also *Mobile Daily Advertiser and Register*, September 13, 1864. The *Advertiser* reporter's statement was probably correct. The Springfield was generally realized by this time to be inferior to both the Sharps and Spencer rifles manufactured in the North. R. B. Bruce, *Lincoln and the Tools of War* (Indianapolis, 1956), pp. 284-85, 287.

pitiate, keep out of the ranks and far off from danger. Newspaper correspondents do not usually mention these things. They are often the pets of 'headquarters,' and their business is to please and magnify the names of their employers and protectors."[88]

What the *Advertiser* correspondent did not disclose was the steady attrition of the number of soldiers in Lee's army as a result of the incessant sharpshooting and bombardment. As one of Lee's soldiers later admitted: "Without fighting a battle . . . [Grant] was literally destroying our army."[89] The decline in morale that accompanied this steady drain of army strength *was* admitted, however, by an army correspondent of the *Columbia South Carolinian* in a letter which his newspaper published: "That our army is not now what it was in spirit some months ago, and cannot now be made to charge with the dash and determination that formerly distinguished it, is a mortifying fact." He cited two explanations for a weakness painfully illustrated by the failure of Lee's soldiers to retake Fort Harrison. The first was the practice continued for many months of fighting from behind breastworks; the second was the loss in the many fights of a long campaign of most of the officers who at its commencement were wont to lead the charge. Consequently, "regiments and brigades are now largely commanded by officers who are incompetent from mental weakness, or are so timid as to say 'go on' when they should shout 'come on. . . .' "[90]

During the early part of September Newspaperman Bagby decided to go to Petersburg from Richmond to obtain a firsthand impression of the situation in the army. He found transportation on an ambulance train, and occupied his time during the journey in reading the morning newspapers and conversing with some officers on their way back to the army. Bagby was surprised to learn that the army was very much in need of assistant surgeons, who were for the most part young men, "just graduated," who entered the service in hopes of a comfortable berth in a hospital behind the lines. When they were called on to undergo the hardships of field service instead, they were prone to neglect their duties, take to using whisky or opium, and eventually return home to recover from the effects of their dissipation.

From Dunlop's Farm a few miles outside Petersburg, where the train

[88] *Montgomery Daily Advertiser*, September 8, 1864. During World War II newspaper columnist Drew Pearson exposed the same practices in the U.S. army.
[89] G. C. Eggleston, *A Rebel's Recollections* (New York, 1875), p. 176.
[90] *Columbia Daily South Carolinian*, October 22, 1864.

discharged its passengers to avoid coming within range of enemy shelling, Bagby drove over to Lee's headquarters with a cousin who evidently lived in the vicinity. The reporter found headquarters in a grassy yard shaded by ancient trees. The general was in an unpretentious tent as Bagby and his cousin went by to have a look at him. Bagby observed with deep interest that, "The old fellow was seated in a split-bottom chair, engaged in reading one of the morning papers through a pair of spectacles. The back of his head was turned to us, so that we were hardly paid for the pains of our sly observation. Not far from the great Captain's tent, the inside of which looked very clean and cozy, was his ambulance,[91] and under it a number of chickens were pecking about. One of them, a cock, is said to be a great pet with the General, who has had him with him from the beginning of the war, and carries him wherever he goes. I suspect the secret of this apparent whim is nothing more than a very rational desire for fresh-laid eggs for breakfast, for the rooster is not deprived of his harem."[92] Bagby admitted a strong desire to intrude on the general and find out his views about the military situation and Confederate prospects. Recalling, however, the general's well-known secretiveness and having some qualms about disturbing him, he drove on to town without stopping.

As the two visitors entered the trenches below town, they could hear the popping of the sharpshooters and the bursting of shells in the distance. Presently Bagby overheard his cousin, who was behind him, ask someone, "Digging a grave?" The reply was "Yes," and turning around, the reporter saw the gravedigger lift the first spadeful of earth. The corpse lay beside the trenches, almost touching Bagby's elbow.

"Was he killed by a sharpshooter?"

"No, his head was carried away by a round shot."

"How long ago?"

"This morning some time."

Bagby was struck by the matter-of-fact manner in which the episode was described, a reminder of the cheapness of life in the combat zone. The two men continued on their way to the front lines, where they entered the crater that had been opened by the mine explosion on July 30. There they found some soldiers occupying their time in making

[91] Probably a passenger vehicle used for moving the sick and wounded.

[92] *Mobile Daily Advertiser and Register*, September 25, 1864. For a flattering description of Lee at the beginning of the campaign by another reporter see *Columbia Daily South Carolinian*, May 10, 1864.

pipes out of the blue clay which the powder charge had thrown up from below the surface. Bagby discovered that the crater was greatly changed from what it had been like on the night after the explosion, having been reduced in size by breastworks thrown up in the rear and tramped down so that the original ghastliness was now hardly perceptible.

The soldiers nearby laughed inoffensively at the newspaperman as he ducked whenever a bullet whistled over his head. Made thus aware that the enemy's rifle pits were no more than twenty yards away, Bagby wasted little time in getting back to the rear. He reported that the Confederate trenches were now dry, and not too uncomfortable even in the heat of the day; "but what a life the occupants will lead next winter."

ABOUT A WEEK after Bagby's return from his sightseeing expedition to the army, the Richmond press reported severe fighting in the Shenandoah Valley. The opposing commands of Early and Sheridan there had been maneuvering for about a month, testing each other's strength. On the eighteenth of August a special correspondent of the *Richmond Enquirer* had described a fight near Kernstown the day before in which the enemy had been driven through the town without either side losing many men. The *Enquirer* correspondent also alluded to the pall of smoke—caused by the enemy's burning of barns, hayricks, and pastures—that overhung the Valley from Strasburg to Winchester. He conceded, however, that the enemy's behavior at Winchester had been generally good; his estimate of the size of Sheridan's Army of the Shenandoah, "not less than 45,000 men," was close to the mark.[93]

Another reporter, who wrote for the *Petersburg Express*, was unduly impressed with the "splendid condition" of Early's cavalry, which he rated the most important element of the service—obviously the professional bias of a cavalryman, for he also thought the enemy's cavalry was "infinitely superior to their infantry in point of true metal and discipline."[94]

There were rumors in Richmond on Wednesday morning, September 21, that a fight had taken place near Winchester on Monday in which

[93] *Daily Richmond Enquirer*, August 26, 1864.
[94] *Petersburg Daily Express*, September 23, 1864. Bagby stated, however, in his Richmond letter of September 14, 1864 that "from another source I learn that our infantry have a contempt for Sheridan's infantry, but respect his cavalry." *Charleston Mercury*, September 20, 1864.

the Confederates had been disastrously defeated. Rumor continued to enlarge the scope of the disaster until the War Department later that day released an official dispatch from General Lee that had been sent the day before. Lee's dispatch, based on information supplied by Early, stated that Early's command had resisted the enemy's attack near Winchester all day Monday and had then been "compelled to retire" to Newtown and from there to Fisher's Hill. Early admitted that his loss had been "severe," that a major general (Rodes) and a brigadier general had been killed, and that three pieces of artillery had been captured. He reported on the other hand that the army's train had been safely removed.[95]

The first particulars of the battle received from the Associated Press agent in Lynchburg provided a more guarded statement of what had happened than Lee's. The P.A. telegram placed the scene of the fighting on the Berryville road two miles below Winchester, stressed that the earlier part of the action had been "decidedly in our favor," and explained that it was a flanking maneuver by the enemy's cavalry that had led to the "retrograde movement" (i.e. retreat) of Early's force. Making no mention of Confederate losses, the P.A. reporter added that Early's withdrawal had been effected "in an orderly manner, and without confusion."[96]

On the day after the Richmond papers published what may well have been a censored version of the affair, the *Lynchburg Republican* revealed that the Battle of Winchester had resulted in a "severe reverse." It attributed the defeat to the "shameful and cowardly conduct" of a portion of Early's cavalry which were "stampeded" by the enemy's cavalry and to the numerical superiority of the enemy. Yet the *Republican* denied stories of Early having been "surprised," and derived some satisfaction from the information that Early had retreated to Fisher's Hill in good order. The *Charlottesville Chronicle*, which also reported the defeat at Winchester, defended Early's handling of his troops, but admitted that his army did not behave well in the fight at Fisher's Hill on September 22. In the latter engagement, according to the *Chronicle*, a unit of dismounted cavalry that was on the Confederate left gave way, causing the Confederate line to be flanked and leading to a hasty withdrawal of the infantry.[97]

[95] *Richmond Daily Dispatch*, September 22, 1864.
[96] *Richmond Daily Whig*, September 21, 1864.
[97] *Lynchburg Daily Republican*, September 22-24, 1864; *Charlottesville Chronicle*, as reprinted in *ibid.*, September 30, 1864.

Perhaps the most unflattering account of the behavior of the Confederate cavalry at the Battle of Winchester was forwarded to one of the Raleigh newspapers by its correspondent in Winchester and later reprinted in the *Richmond Whig.* The Raleigh reporter alluded to the "disgraceful stampede" of a brigade of Confederate cavalry who, he said, referred to themselves as "Imboden's men." He went on to tell how as they fled through the streets of Winchester shouting, "The Yankees are coming!" they communicated their fright to the other soldiers, as well as to the various hangers-on in the rear of the army—teamsters, ambulance drivers, stragglers and skulkers, and vagrant Negroes. According to the Raleigh man, "officers who have seen much that is exciting about battlefields tell me they never witnessed anything that will begin to compare with the stampede at Winchester."[98]

The protest expressed in the newspapers against the unrelieved frankness of this report was hardly surprising. A reader of the *Richmond Whig,* who refrained from identifying himself otherwise than by a pseudonym, wrote to the *Whig* to say that he was incredulous about Imboden's men having been involved in the stampede. He also questioned the reliability of the reporter's sources of information. Later the colonel who commanded Imboden's brigade during the battle denied categorically the statements in the Raleigh newspaper about his brigade, claiming it was McCausland's cavalrymen who made up the principal part of the stampeding crowd. He made clear, however, that he did not consider either McCausland or his men at fault for having retreated in the face of "superior numbers." The colonel also claimed that the only fighting at Fisher's Hill was by his own division of cavalry and that there it was the *infantry* who "ran away."[99]

The tendency of the Richmond newspapers to gloss over Early's defeat caused the editor of the *Charleston Courier* to take them to task. Singling out the statement in the *Richmond Dispatch* that "with the exception of the loss of ground, all the advantage of the battle remained on our side," the *Courier* editor chortled. "A slight exception verily—

[98] *Richmond Daily Whig,* October 1, 1864.

[99] *Ibid.,* October 7, 12, 1864. Alexander displayed disillusionment about the cavalry in a letter published in the *Mobile Register* on October 4, 1864. He stated that the Valley cavalry were "utterly worthless" and could not be relied on, either to procure reliable intelligence of the enemy's movements before the battle, or to stand their ground after the fighting had occurred. Contemporary evidence of the validity of Alexander's opinion can be found in James Conner, *Letters of General James Conner, C.S.A.* (Columbia, S.C., 1933), p. 164.

and a kind of advantage that could be claimed very well for Bragg's campaign in and out of Tennessee, and Pemberton's fourth of July celebration at Vicksburg."[100]

Following his twin defeats Early retreated down the Shenandoah Valley past Waynesboro to a point between Port Republic and Brown's Gap, while General Sheridan's army systematically laid waste the valley. Writing to the *Dispatch* from camp near New Market on October 10, its correspondent "Asa Tennet" applied the epithet "Chief of Barnburners" to Sheridan. According to the *Dispatch* correspondent, scarcely a barn was left standing in the valley from Strasburg to Staunton, and in many instances the dwellings as well had been put to the torch. "I passed one plantation on which not a house was left, the cattle lay dead in the field, and even the shocks of corn as they stood in the field were burned."[101] Still another casualty of Sheridan's "scorched earth" policy was the newspaper plant of the *Rockingham Register* in Harrisonburg. The *Richmond Whig* declared that this was the second or third time that the Yankees had destroyed the type and presses of the newspaper, but expressed confidence that its editor, John H. Wartmann would soon be back in business again.[102]

At the end of the third week of October the Richmond agent of the P.A. wired an account from there of another battle between Early and Sheridan on Wednesday, the 19th. The P.A. account, which apparently the Richmond newspapers were not allowed to print, quoted official dispatches as stating that Early had attacked Sheridan's camp at Cedar Creek before dawn that day and had surprised and routed the 18th and 19th corps and driven the 6th corps beyond Middleton, capturing eighteen pieces of artillery and a number of prisoners. Then the enemy made a stand and at some later time attacked Early, causing his line to give way and capturing thirty pieces of Early's artillery. According to the P.A. dispatch, Early's loss in killed and wounded was less than a thousand, while the enemy's loss in the two fights was "very severe."[103]

The background of the clash, which was omitted from this news re-

[100] *Charleston Daily Courier*, September 27, 1864.

[101] *Richmond Daily Dispatch*, October 14, 1864; Dupuy, *Compact History*, p. 250.

[102] *Richmond Daily Whig*, October 15, 1864.

[103] *Savannah Republican*, October 22, 1864; *Mobile Daily Advertiser and Register*, October 23, 1864. No A.P. dispatches appeared in the *Richmond Whig* until October 24, and the language of the dispatch published then was carefully guarded.

port, included an advance by Early up the Shenandoah from New Market to Fisher's Hill on October 12. After passing through Strasburg the following day Early's scouts located the enemy in strong force on the north bank of Cedar Creek, a tributary of the Shenandoah River. Following an indecisive exchange of fire, Early fell back to Fisher's Hill, from which three days later he decided to launch another attack. Not feeling strong enough to make a frontal attack on the entrenched Union position north of Cedar Creek, Early decided on a flanking movement against Sheridan's unprotected left flank and rear. After a night march the well-coordinated attack occurred on schedule, achieving the complete surprise mentioned in the A.P. dispatch.[104]

The *Richmond Dispatch* correspondent reported that the enemy was driven through their camp which was some two or three miles in length. He also stated that they vainly tried to make a stand on three different occasions, once from behind a stone fence, but were finally driven into the woods beyond Middletown. Early's victory was complete by half past ten according to the account of the battle published in the *Charlottesville Chronicle*. Then he ordered the pursuit of the enemy halted so that he could reorganize his lines and collect stragglers. It was the consensus of the army correspondents that Early's men used the pause of three to four hours for plundering.[105]

About an hour before sundown, according to the *Richmond Enquirer* correspondent, the Federals counterattacked with fresh troops. First Gordon's division broke and fell back, then Kershaw's, and then Ramseur's. The *Charlottesville Chronicle* reporter told how: "Five or six guns in the rear were immediately driven back when the line broke, and placed on a high hill, where, with no aid from the infantry, who were flying in every direction, they kept the enemy at bay for an hour or more. Having exhausted their ammunition, they were compelled to withdraw."

"By this time Wharton and Pegram's men had caught the panic, and the field became covered with flying men. The artillery retired, firing slowly, and sustained only by Pegram's old brigade and Evans' brigade. All of our artillery, as well as that captured from the enemy were

---

[104] W. B. Wood and J. E. Edmonds, *The Civil War in the U.S. with Special Reference to the Campaigns of 1864 and 1865* (London, 1937), pp. 220-21; J. A. Early, *Autobiographical Sketch* (Philadelphia, 1912), pp. 437, 442-43; E. J. Stackpole, *Sheridan in the Shenandoah* (Harrisburg, 1961), pp. 283-85.

[105] *Richmond Daily Dispatch*, October 29, 1864; *Charlottesville Chronicle* as reprinted in *ibid.*, October 27, 1864.

gotten safely over Cedar creek. Just then a small body of the enemy's cavalry crossed the creek and charged over the hill, but were driven back by a few scattering muskets. After the creek was crossed, Pegram's and Evans's brigades participated in the demoralization—the road was filled with fugitives. Their cavalry charged again in the rear of our train and not a gun was fired in its defence. Many ordnance and medical stores, and twenty-three pieces of artillery, besides those taken by us in the morning, were captured."[106]

At dusk Early's army of something less than 12,500 was in complete rout and stampeding toward Fisher's Hill. His casualties were only 2,900, compared to nearly double that for Sheridan, but the Confederates had lost heavily in officers, and the Yankees had captured twenty-four Confederate cannon besides retrieving their own captured guns. Whatever the press might think or say, Confederate resistance in the Shenandoah Valley was now virtually at an end.[107]

The Confederate newspapermen who had witnessed the debacle generally blamed Early for halting his pursuit of the enemy prematurely and ascribed much of the responsibility for the defeat to the diversion of plundering by his soldiers. The *Dispatch* reporter alleged that although strict orders were given that no one should stop to plunder, a great many soldiers did, and they did not afterwards rejoin their commands. When, therefore, about four o'clock in the afternoon, Early formed a line of battle to check the enemy's counterattack, about one-third of his army was in the rear.[108]

Another explanation of the defeat received attention in the press when news of Early's defeat became public. At the time of the Battle of Winchester Peter Alexander had mentioned in his Richmond correspondence the stories that had come to his ears about the role of "John Barleycorn" in the defeat at Winchester. September was the sea-

[106] *Daily Richmond Enquirer*, October 29, 1864; *Charlottesville Chronicle* as reprinted in *Richmond Daily Dispatch*, October 27, 1864. General Gordon's version of the concluding phase of the battle is given in J. B. Gordon, *Reminiscences of the Civil War* (New York, 1905), pp. 347-49.

[107] Dupuy, *Compact History*, p. 353.

[108] *Richmond Daily Dispatch*, October 29, 1864; *Selma Daily Reporter*, November 25, 1864. For Early's explanation of the defeat, which added up to emphasis of the fact that he was heavily outnumbered, see Early, *Autobiographical Sketch*, pp. 448-51. According to Early, his force did not consist of more than 1,200 cavalry and 8,500 "muskets," i.e. infantry. Sheridan probably had an "effective" strength of about 40,000 at Cedar Creek. See Table 4 in Appendix B of Stackpole, *Sheridan in Shenandoah*.

son of the apple harvest around Winchester; this, along with the scarcity of grain to keep the distilling industry in business, had caused both
officers and men to patronize freely the distributors of apply brandy.
Alexander had said in a letter published in the *Savannah Republican*
that "officers of high position—yes, of very high position—have, to use
an honest English word, been drunk—too drunk to command themselves, much less an army, a division, a brigade, or a regiment." In the
wake of the Cedar Creek disaster, these stories of drunkenness on the
part of Early and other high-ranking officers in his command were
revived. Alexander made clear that he still believed in the truth of the
accusations, and called for a congressional investigation of their accuracy. While the Richmond press generally defended Early, who, they
could not forget, was a Virginian, the Confederate Senate, after referring the troublesome problem to its military committee, decided against
making further inquiry into the causes of the recent reverses in the
Shenandoah.[109]

Alexander, who to be sure had not been present at either the Winchester or the Cedar Creek defeat, wrote bitterly about the refusal of
the Congress and the Senate military committee to discharge their
duty, as he saw it. "We pass laws against drunkenness in the army," he
stated, "but never enforce them except against privates and officers of
inferior grade. . . . I cannot recall an instance in which an officer has
been tried under the act of Congress 'to punish drunkenness in the
army.'" He recounted numerous instances of this offense by corps and
brigade commanders which he had seen, along with army surgeons
"so stupefied by liquor that they could not distinguish between a man's
arm and the spoke of a wagonwheel, and who would just as soon have
sawed off the one as the other."[110]

In the wake of the disaster there were demands from the press for
Early's removal, although some newspapers, such as the *Richmond*

---

[109] *Savannah Republican*, September 29, November 21, December 4, 1864;
Charleston Daily Courier, December 1, 1864; *Journal of the Congress of the Confederate States*, IV, 431; *Daily Richmond Examiner*, January 10, 1865. For a
spirited defense of Early's officers against charges of intoxication see *Daily Richmond Enquirer*, October 26, 1864.

[110] *Savannah Republican*, December 4, 1864. For earlier remarks by Alexander
in condemnation of intemperance in the Confederate army, this time in the Western army, see *Mobile Daily Advertiser and Register*, December 8, 1863.

Whig, sought to excuse Early and even minimize the seriousness of his defeat.[111] What Southern editors said about this was quite as much designed to influence public opinion in the North on the eve of a Presidential election as to inform its readers about the situation and sustain Southern morale. There was general recognition by the Confederate press, however, that the reverses in the Shenandoah Valley demonstrated the need for a reorganization of the cavalry. As the *Richmond Dispatch* saw it, it was the "cavalry" in the valley that had failed, or rather the mounted infantry that masqueraded under that name, "for cavalry, properly so called, we have none." The *Dispatch* editor sadly acknowledged that during the past year the enemy had evolved genuine charging cavalry, which had now beaten the Confederates on two important occasions. He added plaintively: "We must have *cavalry,* real *cavalry,* to confront the Yankees if we do not wish to be beaten in every battle."[112]

BACK IN Richmond newspapermen were discouraged by what appeared to be a further deterioration of the position of Lee's army. Near the end of September Grant had captured Fort Harrison, a strong point in the outer line of Richmond's defenses. In the emergency, newspapermen were included in Bragg's call upon every able-bodied man in Richmond between sixteen and fifty-five for defense service. On September 30 the *Whig* was the only newspaper in Richmond that was able to go to press as usual. Bagby wrote a panicky letter to the *Mobile Register* in which he stated that Richmond "is certainly in great danger, greater, perhaps, than ever before. . . ." He went on to tell how that evening when the firing within three miles of the city was at its hottest, he could find in the crowds gathered on Shockoe and Richmond Hills only four white men, three of whom were over fifty and the other an invalid. Bagby regained his courage after he had taken some ribbing from the *Richmond Enquirer.* And when at the end of October Lee repelled a massive assault against the Southside Railroad, Bagby

---

[111] *Daily Richmond Enquirer,* October 25, 1864; *Richmond Daily Whig,* October 25, 27, 1864. Although critical of Early's personal habits, Alexander realized that there was danger of the press going too far and denying Early the merits "which he unquestionably possesses." Alexander conceded that Early was a good division commander, but argued that invariably he had failed in the exercise of independent command. *Mobile Daily Advertiser and Register,* November 6, 1864.

[112] *Richmond Daily Dispatch,* October 29, 1864.

gently chided the general for understating the magnitude of his success.[113]

By October Alexander was giving attention in his Richmond correspondence to the question of enlisting black soldiers to fight for the Confederacy. In a letter to the *Mobile Register* from Richmond on October 14 he let it be known that the subject was attracting a great deal of attention at the capital and in the army. He further stated that there were few persons who would not approve of the use of Negro soldiers in the event that Lincoln were reelected and should make another attempt to bring a large army into the field. Three weeks later Alexander hinted that General Lee was in favor of Negro enlistment; on November 23 he stated positively that both the general and the Army of Northern Virginia "generally" were in favor of this. Bragg and Davis were opposed, however; and so too was the Richmond press with one exception. Alexander was certain Negro soldiers never would be placed on an equality with Southern white troops. He expected them, if conscribed, to be organized in separate commands under carefully selected white officers. On the other hand, he believed that the Southern slave, although inferior to the white soldier, would perform better in combat than the Northern free Negro, "and no doubt is entertained that negroes will do to fight negroes."[114]

In another letter to the *Register* on November 8, Bagby made known the general opinion in Richmond that the 1864 campaign in Virginia was virtually over. He said Alexander thought so too and was talking about going home for a short furlough.[115] A familiar name among the Confederate war correspondents arrived at the capital before the month was out, however, to have another try at reporting. The new arrival was de Fontaine, who had been editor of the *Columbia South Carolinian* since January 1864.

In the first of two letters written to the *Carolinian* over his familiar nom de plume "Personne," de Fontaine evinced an optimistic, even jaunty tone. In Richmond, he assured his readers, one looked in vain for signs of doubt or trepidation. Hungry thousands shopped in well-filled markets. Restaurants, "of which there are scores kept in a style

[113] Wood and Edmonds, *Civil War*, pp. 136-37; *Savannah Republican*, October 5, 1864; *Mobile Daily Advertiser and Register*, October 11, 28, November 8, 1864.
[114] *Mobile Daily Advertiser and Register*, October 21, November 19, 20, December 2, 30, 1864.
[115] *Ibid.*, November 22, 1864. A statement by Alexander to this effect appears in his letter of November 2 to the *Register* of November 18, 1864.

of magnificent abundance," featured venison, birds, turtle, and the choicest wines in their *cartes de visite*. And among the crowds that thronged Main Street throughout the day could be seen representatives of the fair sex, "attired with a richness and elegance, and in raiment that you will see nowhere else in the Confederacy."

In contrast to the dress and fashion of what de Fontaine referred to as "metropolitan scenes" was the army camp, where everything spoke of war. The editorial correspondent from Columbia was writing his letter, he indicated, at the headquarters of one of the Confederate generals; yet "headquarters" was only a deserted Negro hut, partitioned off by strips of canvas. The woods had been leveled for miles around to provide material for an abatis to protect the outer line of entrenchments. Although more than thirty or forty men were being killed or wounded by sharpshooters daily, the soldiers were at work constructing log huts with well-thatched roofs for winter quarters. De Fontaine thought the engineering art had rendered these fortifications impregnable. "It is estimated that behind them one man is equal to eight assailants and that allowing Grant to advance by regular siege approaches, it will take him just two years and a half to dig his way to Richmond."

De Fontaine admitted that of all the generals that had confronted Lee during the war none had given him more trouble or occasioned more anxiety than Grant. Although repeatedly beaten, Grant refused to acknowledge it. "And he still clings with a death-like tenacity." The only lack of the Yankees, de Fontaine declared, was the ability to withstand "the superior prowess of Southern men."

"Personne" made an oblique reference to the fact that no less than 60,000 soldiers were absent without leave from the army. The reasons for this large-scale absence—"Personne" carefully avoided the use of the term "desertion"—were the lack of good officers, of suitable discipline, and "those healthful restraints which appeal both to the feeling and judgment of a Southern man." His letter made clear that he did not approve of the system of permitting soldiers to elect their own officers. This system, he declared, tended to make popularity rather than competence the criterion for selection; as a result whole regiments had been demoralized by the inefficiency of their commanding officers.[116]

"Personne's" description of life in Richmond was obviously written

[116] *Columbia Daily South Carolinian*, November 23, 1864.

427

for its propaganda effect. He made no mention of the high prices in the Richmond restaurants which put them beyond the reach of all but a few soldiers and the class of wartime profiteers. There was also no indication in his letters of the low civilian morale in the capital or the forebodings of public officials. Even Lee had come to realize that the fall of Richmond was a possibility to be reckoned with.[117] As for "Personne's" belief in the impregnability of Richmond's fortifications, they remained to be tested under combat conditions when large-scale hostilities resumed the next spring.

On December 9 Alexander mailed the last installment in his series of war correspondence from Virginia before his return home. His letter reflected his preoccupation with the danger that Grant might be on the move again, whether toward Weldon or Goldsboro he could not say.[118] Alexander did not then know that this was his last campaign with the Army of Northern Virginia and that his newspaper in Savannah would within a little more than a fortnight become a refugee, like many other Southern newspapers in the war zone. The newspaper voice of the Confederacy was being silenced.

[117] Freeman, *R. E. Lee, A Biography,* iii, 505-507 mentions the first instance, which occurred about this time, of Lee alluding to the fall of Richmond as a possibility, in a letter to the secretary of war. The potential influence of "Personne's" letters on Confederate public opinion probably was increased by the fact that they were reprinted in other papers. See e.g. *Charleston Daily Courier,* November 26, 1864; *Daily Richmond Enquirer,* December 7, 1864.
[118] *Mobile Daily Advertiser and Register,* December 30, 1864.

CHAPTER 13

"Rover" Reports the Fall of Atlanta

THE SURRENDER of Vicksburg and loss of Chattanooga had alerted Georgia newspaper editors to the fact that their hour of serious danger was at hand. Bragg's costly triumph at Chickamauga had provided a brief respite for the Confederacy's Empire State, but the disaster on Missionary Ridge signified that Georgia was about to undergo the same bitter ordeal of invasion that Tennessee, Mississippi, Alabama, and Virginia had already experienced.

The Atlanta newspapers made no effort to conceal the fact that their city was the primary objective of the Yankee host entrenched at Chattanooga. Located in north central Georgia some 125 miles southeast of that threatening army, Atlanta was a comparatively young city of about twenty thousand in 1864, bustling with industrial enterprise. Hardly more than twenty years before, the site of Atlanta had been a wilderness. The location of the town had been determined by the decision of a Georgia railroad convention to build a line from the Chattahoochee River to the Tennessee to tap the trade of the Northwest. The post office of White Hall became the hub of a railroad network connecting it with Augusta, Savannah, Macon, Montgomery, and Chattanooga. In 1845, after having successively been named Terminus and Marthasville (in honor of Martha Lumpkin, the governor's daughter), it was rechristened Atlanta. When two years later the rapidly growing town became a city, its corporate limits were a circular area about two miles in diameter whose center was the zero milepost of the vastly profitable state-owned and -operated Western & Atlantic Railroad.[1]

Running generally northeast and southwest, Whitehall Street was the heart of the business section. Decatur Street, where Whitehall ended, was the beginning of Peachtree Street, which a *Charleston Courier* reporter regarded as the most beautiful thoroughfare in Atlanta. Along with some of the city's finest residences, its leading hostelry, the Trout House, fronted on Peachtree Street. From the windows of that hotel one could see on a clear day the gray eminence of Stone Mountain with its observatory on top, the female seminary, also on a hill top, and the

[1] E. Merton Coulter, *A Short History of Georgia* (Chapel Hill, 1933), pp. 244-46.

dome of the Atlanta Medical College. Near the center of town was a mineral spring that was the fountainhead of the Ocmulgee River and a favorite destination for the ladies' sunrise promenades.[2]

As the central office of Thrasher's Confederate Press Association, Atlanta was the most important source of news about the Western army of the Confederacy. In the highly competitive newspaper world of Atlanta, whose journalistic enterprise was now rated second only to that of Richmond,[3] refugee newspapers like the *Memphis Appeal* and the *Knoxville Register* compared favorably with the more strongly entrenched establishments of the *Intelligencer* and *Southern Confederacy.*

Newspapermen who visited Atlanta from time to time found it an exciting place, with abundant material for descriptive writing. A correspondent who was there in the summer of 1864 when the proximity of Sherman's army was already depopulating the city still believed it conveyed the atmosphere of a metropolis to a greater degree than any other Southern city. The president of the Confederate Associated Press, Dr. Gibbes, apparently reached the same conclusion when he came from Columbia in 1863 to attend a convention of Southern newspaper editors. Recalling the primitive appearance of Atlanta when he had last visited it eighteen years before, Gibbes noted the quality of "go-aheadativeness" which then as now seemed to be characteristic of Atlantans. All day and far into the night the steam-engine whistles screamed as the trains at the Western & Atlantic railroad station arrived and departed, crammed to the doors with the floating population that the war was bringing to town. Reporter Israel Gibbons, on his way back to Bragg's army from a furlough to Mobile in September 1863, described Atlanta as a great "railroad whirlpool" and auction mart where thousands of people rotated daily, "where the locomotives are eternally shrieking, and the auctioneers incessantly shouting; where big niggers with hotel brands on them, are ceaselessly scrambling around piles of trunks, and little niggers scramble through the streets with red flags and auction bells, as though the devil himself had turned auctioneer, and let the imps loose. . . . where the side walks are paved with goober-shells and apple peelings and the plays at the

[2] *Atlanta Daily Southern Confederacy*, July 13, 1861; *Charleston Daily Courier*, March 20, 1863.

[3] A comment to this effect by the war correspondent F. G. de Fontaine appeared in the *Savannah Republican* of July 15, 1864.

theater nightly joined in by the audience; where the all-pervading spirit of the people is trade, trade, trade, and where the only material thing is the news boys who merely run as fast as they can, and sell their papers in the usual way."[4]

In the opinion of a *Charleston Courier* reporter wartime society in Atlanta was unique but agreeable, constituting a kind of mosaic of various shades of caste and kind. He saw the refugees as providing a pleasant addition and the government officers stationed there as welcome escorts for the society belles. "A few months ago and the pretty Puritans raised their white hands and frowned from their pretty brows at the *mere idea* of dancing; indeed one of the fairest Georgians affirmed that she would not, at such a time, attend a soiree dansante; but the musical parties soon merged into 'hops,' and gay quadrilles replaced the dignified 'sonata,' or monopolizing 'reverie.' "[5]

At Dalton, a hundred miles north of Atlanta, the Army of Tennessee remained in camp throughout the winter of 1863-1864. The Confederate press had generally approved of Davis appointing Johnston to the command of the army in December, although Johnston was hardly more approachable to newspaper correspondents than Bragg had been. Even before the *Atlanta Intelligencer* published the news of Johnston's appointment, it had sent Assistant Editor Alexander S. Abrams to Dalton to check on the morale of the army in the wake of its demoralizing defeat. Perhaps Abrams saw what he wanted to see or what he thought Editor Steele wanted him to publish. At any rate, he reported in the columns of his newspaper that the "morale" of the troops was greatly improved over what it had been represented to be only a short time before. Abrams deduced that a desire for revenge had succeeded the feeling of humiliation that the recent defeat at Missionary Ridge had inspired. He also reported that the troops were quite satisfied with the change of commanders, even though many soldiers told him they would like nothing better than to witness the return of General Beauregard to command. It was several months later before another Confederate army correspondent stated in flat contradiction of Abrams that at the time Johnston took command of the army on December 27 it was a "demoralized wreck," scattered about a valley Johnston regarded as militarily untenable. According to this same reporter, Johnston re-

[4] *Columbia Daily South Carolinian* as reprinted in *Atlanta Daily Southern Confederacy*, May 23, 1863; *Mobile Daily Advertiser and Register*, September 24, 1863.
[5] *Charleston Daily Courier*, March 20, 1863.

luctantly remained at Dalton rather than risk further depressing public morale by surrendering more territory to the enemy.[6]

Perhaps for security reasons the Confederate press had little to say about the reorganizing and refitting of his command that Johnston effectively carried out during the next four months. By the middle of April the *Mobile Register* could boast that for the first time in its history the Army of Tennessee had no "barefooted soldiers" within its ranks.[7]

What few reporters were at Dalton during the first part of 1864 were mostly volunteer correspondents. During the first week of April Capt. Theodoric H. Carter, who had previously reported for the *Chattanooga Rebel* over the signature "Mint Julep," announced his return from a period of four-months' captivity in the North in a letter to the *Atlanta Confederacy*. Carter had been a prisoner on Johnson's Island in Lake Erie for the greater part of the time. He had escaped near Masillon, Ohio while being moved to another prison. Travelling incognito by train to Pittsburgh, he stopped overnight at Pittsburgh's leading hostelry, the Monongahela House, with a Union soldier from a Pennsylvania regiment. The Pennsylvanian snored away quite lustily, unaware that his roommate was an escapee "Rebel" army correspondent.

Carter told of strolling along the streets of Pittsburgh the next morning and stopping in at a beer saloon where three convivial Yankee soldiers were fraternizing with a deserter from Imboden's cavalry. Leaving the deserter in the act of protesting his devotion to the Union cause, Carter boarded a train for Cincinnati, which stopped in Columbus about midnight. There he had a narrow escape from being caught by sentries on the alert for escaped prisoners from Camp Chase. With the help of a barroom acquaintance who was also a Union officer, Carter eluded the sentries and arrived safely in Cincinnati. While on the train from Cincinnati to Memphis he quieted the suspicions of the baggage master by passing himself off as a fugitive from the Confederate conscription officers in Tennessee; after several other hair-raising experiences Carter reappeared in Dalton to rejoin his old regiment.[8]

[6] *Atlanta Daily Intelligencer*, December 18, 1863; *Memphis Daily Appeal*, May 2, 1864.

[7] *Mobile Daily Advertiser and Register* as reprinted in *Montgomery Daily Mail*, April 14, 1864.

[8] *Atlanta Daily Southern Confederacy*, April 8, 1864.

A special correspondent of the *Confederacy* who had no such colorful tale as Carter's to unfold described the disagreeable lot of a reporter in Johnston's army at the time. The *Confederacy* correspondent complained about innumerable vexations and annoyances, among which was the experience of being snubbed at various headquarters by everyone from the assistant adjutant general to the orderly. Along with such distasteful treatment the reporter had to contend with casual acquaintances accosting him with the stale query, "What's the news?" Still another standard approach which he recognized was that of the military mendicant who wanted to know why the reporter never mentioned his particular regiment or brigade. Two-to-one, before the day was over the same epauletted individual who had snubbed the reporter that morning would take him by the arm, lead him around the corner, and ask confidentially why "you never say anything about 'the General' in your letters."[9]

The theme of army life in camp had worn very thin by this time, and reporters had to exercise considerable ingenuity to find anything new about camp life to write about. Stock subjects of special correspondence were descriptions of the rolling country around Dalton, snowball fights between the soldiers, and the popularity of religious revivals in the army.

General Johnston was so adept at keeping his own counsel that none of the army newspapermen seems to have known of the steady pressure from Richmond on him to undertake a late winter or early spring offensive in Tennessee. Realizing he was heavily outnumbered by the Yankee force Sherman was building up at Chattanooga, and that he would encounter serious problems of supplying his army in middle Tennessee, Johnston resisted the pressure and stayed where he was. Reporter Sam Reid noted in his diary on February 26 that there had been skirmishing in front of the army all day. On the 27th he rode out to Tunnel Hill to watch the pursuit of the retreating enemy. During the quiet period that followed these hostilities Reid went back to Atlanta to read proof on an article at the office of the *Atlanta Register*. There he had further difficulties with the city marshal, who first arrested him "for spite" and then released him.[10]

[9] *Ibid.*

[10] Samuel C. Reid Diary, entries for February 27-March 4, 1864. In a letter to his friend General Stuart on January 21, 1864, Johnston acknowledged that he regretted his assignment to the command of the Army of Tennessee and confided,

A new arrival in Dalton was the convalescing General Hood, who had come from Richmond to become a corps commander in the Army of Tennessee. Johnston apparently was well enough satisfied with Hood and his other corps commander, Hardee, unaware that Hood was carrying on a secret correspondence with Davis and other Richmond officials in violation of regulations. Hood, for his part, thought Johnston was too defensive-minded, and too prone to assure his Richmond friends that the army was in better shape than Johnston said it was.[11]

On Saturday, May 7, after Grant and Meade had launched their attack on Lee in the Wilderness, Sherman's army of about 100,000 was ready to march from Tunnel Hill. The next evening special correspondent "Waverly" of the *Memphis* (Atlanta) *Appeal* wired his newspaper from Dalton that "the ball has opened" and that the enemy had advanced up Mill Creek Gap that afternoon. Grossly underestimating the size of the opposing army and carefully refraining from stating the number of Confederate troops, "Waverley" cautioned his readers against expecting his letters to be carefully prepared or elaborate. He explained that the physical ordeal of riding a half-day over rocky hills permitted little time or energy for rhetoric. He promised facts in place of rhetoric, "hints of the goings-on in these parts; stray gleams of suggestive interest," and the avoidance of anything sensational.[12]

As many as eleven army correspondents, representing ten different Southern newspapers, seem to have been in the vicinity of Johnston's army at the beginning of the Atlanta campaign. Among the identifiable reporters were Reid of the *Montgomery Advertiser*, Abrams of the *Atlanta Intelligencer*, John S. Ward ("Shirley") of the *Atlanta Register*, Captain Matthews ("Harvey") of the *Memphis Appeal*, Press Association reporter Forbes, and another correspondent who apparently doubled as the "Shadow" of the *Mobile Register* and "Waverly" of the *Memphis Appeal*.[13] The well-known newspaperman Henry Watterson

---

"I have never believed . . . that we had the means of invading the enemy's country." J.E.B. Stuart Papers, Huntington Library.

[11] J. P. Dyer, *The Gallant Hood* (Indianapolis and New York, 1950), p. 226; G. E. Govan and J. W. Livingood, *A Different Valor, The Story of General Joseph E. Johnston, C.S.A.* (Indianapolis, 1956), pp. 248, 250, 256.

[12] *Memphis Daily Appeal*, May 9, 1864. See also reprint from *ibid.* in *Augusta Daily Constitutionalist*, May 11, 1864.

[13] For evidence that the editor of the Mobile *Register* believed "Waverly" and "Shadow" were different pseudonyms of the same reporter see *Mobile Daily Ad-*

also was at the front the day before Sherman advanced, possibly in the capacity of an editorial correspondent for the *Atlanta Confederacy*.[14]

Watterson was probably with Hardee's corps when Federal Generals Thomas and Schofield made a heavy demonstration in front of Dalton while McPherson streaked south behind the mountains to cut Johnston's railroad link with Atlanta. Reid also was with Johnston's army at Dalton at this time. On Sunday afternoon, May 8, the *Advertiser* reporter rode up Rocky Face Mountain with two friends to watch the heavy skirmishing at Mill Creek Gap.[15] Reid had erred in selecting his observation point, however. He would have been better advised to have been fifteen miles below Dalton at Resaca, where a detachment of Confederate soldiers under Brig.Gen. James Cantey arrived from Mississippi just in time to deflect McPherson's thrust at Johnston's vital railroad connection. Some cavalry commander had blundered by leaving Snake Creek Gap unguarded, through which McPherson had made his flanking approach. But Johnston made amends by directing Polk, whose corps was at Rome, Georgia, on its way to Dalton from Mississippi, to take command at Resaca, where three of Hood's divisions were ordered to meet him. Johnston evacuated Dalton shortly after midnight May 12-13 and headed for Resaca with the rest of his army, guessing correctly that Sherman was on his way to join McPherson.[16]

War correspondent Reid left Dalton, just seven hours before Johnston started for Resaca, on a train for Atlanta, presumably to serve as his own dispatch bearer. The correspondent arrived there the next morning, and after spending the day started back north. Unfortunately

---

vertiser and Register, June 4, 1864. The possibility that this reporter was the *Memphis Appeal* correspondent John H. Linebaugh is unlikely, in view of Linebaugh's letter to Vice President Stephens, April 7, 1864 (Alexander H. Stephens Papers, Library of Congress), in which Linebaugh stated that he had given up his connection with the *Memphis Appeal* and that it was doubtful that he would be associated with the press in the future.

[14] In the Henry Watterson Papers in the Library of Congress is a letter to Watterson from General William Bate, dated May 7, 1864, in which Bate expressed his willingness to furnish Watterson with a horse to accompany his command "whenever consistent with your wishes & convenient to yourself." Watterson tells in his *Marse Henry, An Autobiography* (New York, 1919), i, 80, of accompanying Governor Isham Harris on a morale-building tour of the Army of Tennessee just before the Atlanta campaign opened.

[15] Samuel C. Reid Diary, entry for May 8, 1864.

[16] Bruce Catton, *Never Call Retreat* (New York, 1965), p. 323; Govan and Livingood, *Johnston*, pp. 267-268.

he reached Calhoun too late to watch the battle a few miles west of Resaca on May 14. Several other reporters managed to be there that day, however, to report what some of them called the Battle of the Oostenaula. One of the lucky ones was Abrams of the *Atlanta Intelligencer*; the others were the *Memphis Appeal's* "Waverly" and a *Columbus Enquirer* correspondent who signed his letters "J.T.G." A correspondent of the *Savannah Republican* who had gone to Resaca that morning and procured a pass decided to return to Calhoun when he heard there was not likely to be any fighting. But the train on which he had come up from Calhoun had already left when he arrived at the railroad station, so he made the journey on foot, unaware of the battle in progress while he was tramping in the wrong direction.[17]

In the battle that this newsman failed to report most of the fighting was on the left and right flanks, commanded respectively by Polk and Hood. When Johnston learned that Sherman was massing his forces against Polk he ordered Hood to attack the enemy's left. Hood achieved some success in fighting that lasted until dark, and prepared to renew the fight the next day. Reports, later proven false, that the enemy had crossed the river downstream to strike the rear caused Johnston to countermand Hood's movement. Then, when the crossing was made later that day, Johnston withdrew across the Oostenaula on the night of May 15-16.[18]

The most complete and probably most widely-read Confederate newspaper account of the battle was Abrams' eyewitness report for the *Intelligencer*. In his three-column story, Abrams vividly described the repeated charges of the enemy against the Confederate right. "The minnie balls of the Yankees poured over our line in an increasing stream, and in such numbers that the air seemed black with them. The sharp and musical whiz they emit was no longer heard; it was an angry and discordant imitation of a peal of thunder rolling along the clouds, while the booming of the artillery and the bursting of the shells as they came flying over our line, formed a fire unequalled, perhaps, since nations first made war upon each other." He also revealed what a telegraph censor might have suppressed when he stated that only the fact that the Yankees fired much too high had saved the Confederates from a fearful loss. Even so, they had lost, he estimated, nearly two

[17] *Savannah Republican*, May 20, 1864.
[18] J. H. Parks, *General Leonidas Polk, C.S.A., The Fighting Bishop* (Baton Rouge, 1962), p. 377.

thousand men, compared with about three times that number of the enemy.[19]

Abrams' account was more favorably received by the public than those of some of the other Southern army correspondents. A fanciful paragraph in the battle report of *Appeal* correspondent "Waverly" brought a mixture of praise and ridicule. The paragraph described poetically how when the battle was at its hottest a shell came screaming across the lines from a battery in front of the Confederate left, hovered for a moment above the spot where Generals Johnston and Polk were standing, and before exploding, whistled a half-dozen notes "as clear as a fife to the drum-like rattle of musketry." Then before the sound had died away the attention of the generals allegedly was drawn to the branches of a tall pine tree, where a mockingbird gave a good imitation of the whistle of the shell. Although the Confederate press widely noticed this ingenious product of "Waverly's" imagination, Reid made a slighting reference to the "mocking-bird style" of battle reporting. He jeered the idea of a Yankee shell remaining suspended in the air over a general's head, of the shell whistling like a top, of it emitting a half-dozen notes *before* exploding, and of a mockingbird on a tall pine having the leisure and desire to imitate such unreal sounds. "That beats cock fighting" was the way Reid derisively summed it all up.[20]

Abrams criticized Ward of the *Atlanta Register* for the lavish praise he gave Stewart's division of Hood's corps. Abrams took issue with Ward's statement that the Yankees charged the segment of the line held by Stewart's men *seven* times. Abrams asserted that not simply was the statement erroneous; it was misleading of Ward to argue that Stewart's troops had done the major part of the fighting. There was a strong hint in Abrams' remark that correspondents in the rear should verify the reliability of their information before communicating it to the press and that the *Register* reporter was not an eyewitness of the operations he so extravagantly praised.[21]

Reid was still in Calhoun on May 16 when Johnston's army reached there after crossing the Oostenaula. Unable to find a favorable defense position, Johnston retreated south eight miles to Adairsville. There he

[19] *Atlanta Daily Intelligencer*, May 18, 1864. For a reprint of Abrams' battle report see *Augusta Daily Constitutionalist*, May 19, 1864.

[20] *Memphis Daily Appeal*, May 19, 1864; *Montgomery Daily Advertiser*, May 23, 1864.

[21] *Atlanta Daily Intelligencer*, May 23, 1864.

worked out a plan to trap his opponents, which called for a further withdrawal to Cassville. The plan miscarried as a result of the blundering tactics of Hood and Polk. Thus Johnston had to go on the defensive again after having issued a stirring battle order implying that he had abandoned the policy of retreating. When Hood and Polk insisted that their line was untenable, the army again retreated, this time across the Etowah River to Allatoona during the night of May 19-20.[22]

The army correspondents were hesitant about using the word "retreat" to describe the succession of backward movements. A *Memphis Appeal* reporter said that these movements were "improperly called a retreat by those who do not comprehend them . . . ," and Reid applied the euphemistic "retrograde movement" to the withdrawal from Cassville, which he represented as having been accompanied by less straggling than he had ever seen before on a "retreat." Reporters paid more attention to the stream of refugees from Cassville and other points along the line of retreat than to army stragglers. Reid stressed the understandable fear of Yankee brutality among the ladies of Cassville. It was these same ladies who had waved black veils at Streight's Union cavalrymen when they were led through town as prisoners in April 1863, as an indication of the kind of treatment the ladies thought they deserved. One of the refugees who soon turned up in Atlanta was Editor Melville Dwinell of the *Rome Courier*. Dwinell had so little warning of the Yankee approach that in his sudden flight he had to leave behind most of the equipment of his newspaper office.[23]

By the time the army reached Allatoona Abrams was back with it again after a quick trip to the *Intelligencer* office in Atlanta. In Cartersville on the return trip he ran into difficulty when he failed to locate the officer to whom he had entrusted his horse when he left Adairsville. After discovering that his horse had been taken to Marietta by mistake, he managed to procure a mule to help him get to the front.

Like the other reporters, Abrams had difficulty explaining to his readers why the army kept retreating. The best explanations he could give were the necessity of using this means to counter the enemy's

[22] Govan and Livingood, *Johnston*, pp. 271-72, 273-77.

[23] *Memphis Daily Appeal*, May 23, 1864; *Montgomery Daily Advertiser*, May 23, 1864; *Augusta Daily Constitutionalist*, May 24, 1864. The inaccuracy of Reid's generalization about the amount of army straggling is hinted at in the statement by the army correspondent "Volo" of the *Atlanta Confederacy* published on July 9, 1864, that "there is less straggling from the army now than there was two weeks ago."

438

flanking strategy, and Johnston's apparent unwillingness to risk a general engagement. Abrams was confident, however, that a battle would soon be fought between the Etowah and Chattahoochee Rivers, and that it would halt the Yankee invasion.[24]

There is evidence in Confederate war correspondence that this retreating was getting on the nerves of soldiers as well as civilians. Reid passed on to his readers the comment of a soldier who was supposed to have told General Johnston on the day of the battle near Resaca, "General, don't fall back any farther, we are getting mighty tired." "I am not retreating," the general was said to have replied. "The enemy is on our flank and rear, and we must face the foe." "Bully for you," cried the soldiers as his comrades gave the general three cheers.[25]

To avoid creating more uneasiness of this kind, the military authorities imposed strict censorship on all press dispatches from the army, using as an excuse an Associated Press dispatch alleging that McPherson had cut the Atlantic & Western Railroad at Resaca. They also directed that the control of the censorship should be taken away from the provost marshal and given to the inspector general, who apparently took his duties more seriously than his predecessor had. On the day the army fell back to Adairsville, the general manager of the Press Association went up from Atlanta to see what he could do about restoring daily press service from the front. Evidently Thrasher did not find Johnston receptive to his pleas, for during the succeeding weeks the P.A. had to depend for its news reports about Johnston's operations on letters rather than telegrams from its reporters, visits to Atlanta by the reporters, interviews with wounded soldiers who had been brought back to Atlanta for hospital care, and the rather unreliable reports of railroad passengers. Thrasher also seems to have been having difficulties with his reporters, for on May 27 he dispatched two ("competent") new telegraphic reporters to Allatoona, both of whom were suitably mounted and instructed to operate on either wing of the army.[26]

Meanwhile Confederate newspaper editors were generally trying to

[24] *Atlanta Daily Intelligencer,* May 19, 21, 1864.

[25] *Montgomery Daily Advertiser,* May 20, 1864.

[26] *Daily Columbus Enquirer,* May 19, 1864; *Macon Daily Telegraph,* May 17, 1864; *Savannah Republican,* May 19, 1864; *Charleston Daily Courier,* May 27, 1864; *Atlanta Daily Southern Confederacy* as reprinted in *Augusta Daily Chronicle and Sentinel,* May 28, 1864; R. F. Tucker, "The Press Association of the Confederate States of America in Georgia," unpub. Master's thesis (University of Georgia, 1950), p. 68.

convince their readers that a retreat was not a defeat, that Johnston's retreats were masterly, that he was not retreating anyway, that Sherman's losses were of shocking proportions, while those of the Confed-. erates were comparatively light, and that the Army of Tennessee was as buoyant and cheerful as ever. An editorial allusion in the *Atlanta Intelligencer* on May 18, to those "panic-stricken individuals" who were accustomed to lose their heads over the most absurd rumors, suggests that such morale-building efforts were not effective. "Please quit hooting like owls," the *Intelligencer* begged its readers. "We think the skies are still bright and do not see reverses or danger in prospect." Yet the writer of this article admitted three days later that the military situation was so obscure and clouded with rumor that he was unable to determine what was happening. Johnston still seemed to be falling back; although the *Intelligencer* insisted that this in itself should not be any great cause for alarm, it belied these assurances by advising every able-bodied man to arm for the defense of Atlanta rather than make foolish exertions to remove his property to a safer place. The editorial containing this curious mixture of confidence and fear concluded on a note of desperation: "Atlanta must not fall. Do you hear it? It cannot, must not be."[27]

While Atlantans were pondering this doleful warning Sherman was preparing to leave the railroad and strike directly at the city. When Johnston learned from cavalry reconnaissance what Sherman was about to do, he shifted his army to the left to block the Federal advance. On the morning of May 25 Hooker's Federal corps attacked Hood's corps on the Confederate right. By mid-afternoon sharp skirmishing had flared into heavy fighting, the brunt of which fell on Stewart's division of Hood's corps. Army correspondent "Shadow" of the *Mobile Register* reported, "for a time the result seemed doubtful; but stubborn pluck, a good position and excellent artillery carried the day at last. By 5 o'clock the enemy had retired and we were masters of the field. . . ." Both "Shadow" and the *Memphis Appeal* editor, who also was present at the battle, accurately reported that Hooker's loss exceeded that of Stewart's valiant defenders by a wide margin.[28]

[27] *Augusta Daily Constitutionalist*, May 15, 1864; *Atlanta Daily Intelligencer*, May 18, 21, 1864.

[28] *Mobile Daily Advertiser and Register*, May 31, 1864; *Memphis Daily Appeal*, May 27, 1864. The casualty figures on the Confederate side in the fighting on May 25 were estimated by General Johnston at about 450 killed and wounded. Union losses totalled 1,389 men. *O.R.* (Army) Ser. I, vol. xxviii, pt. 3, p. 616; Walter Hebert, *Fighting Joe Hooker* (Indianapolis, 1944), p. 277.

Reid was in Atlanta that day, having left the army the afternoon before to escape the restrictions of army censorship. In a letter mailed from Atlanta to the *Montgomery Advertiser*, he explained that the difficulty of finding the proper officer to approve dispatches, and the irregularity of the mail service, made regular news reports from the front almost impossible. He complained that the censorship of press dispatches was often a "humbug" and that the prejudice or caprice of the officers who took turns in inspecting dispatches determined the latitude reporters were permitted. Reid was so frustrated by the whimsical behavior of the censors that he urged his editor to advocate the termination of their function. To replace the censorship, he recommended the passage of a law making reporters and editors responsible for censoring their own dispatches and subjecting them to fines and imprisonment for violations of security regulations.[29]

As a result of having missed the repulse of Hooker, Reid made only a casual reference to it in the letter he mailed to Montgomery following his return to Marietta. Later, however, he objected to the way the battle was reported by certain correspondents whom he accused of giving all the credit to Stevenson's division of Hood's corps. Reid maintained that only one of Stevenson's regiments took part in the action and that Stewart's division performed so admirably that Hood complimented it on the field of battle.[30]

Continuing difficulties with censorship caused Reid to miss another severe fight which took place on the Confederate right on May 27. Reid had gone to Marietta, 18 miles east of Dallas, and the nearest telegraph station to the rear of the army. Unable to find a provost marshal to approve his dispatches or any facilities for mailing them, he hopped a freight train bound for Atlanta at midnight May 26-27. Unfortunately the train was held waiting for various northbound trains to pass, and Reid took eight hours to travel a distance of twenty miles.[31]

Shortly after Reid arrived in Atlanta Sherman unleashed a furious late-afternoon attack against Cleburne's division of Hardee's corps which failed. The Confederates then counterattacked at night, which was only partially successful. With some exaggeration *Mobile Register* correspondent "Shadow" described the engagement as "the bloodiest affair of the campaign." Writing for another newspaper he character-

[29] *Montgomery Daily Advertiser*, May 27, 1864.
[30] *Ibid.*, June 13, 1864.
[31] *Ibid.*, May 29, 1864. For the difficulties of another reporter in locating the provost marshal's camp see *Atlanta Daily Intelligencer*, June 18, 1864.

ized the fight as "the most bloody [spectacle] mine eyes ever beheld," and pictured the mangled forms of the enemy dead, most of them "shot through the head" in an area extending for a hundred yards in either direction. "One fellow was . . . found to have received fifty-seven balls. Another received seventeen."[32]

Reid and the other correspondents had relatively little to say about the check their own army sustained when it made a small-scale attack on the 29th. The troops involved—Bate's division of Hardee's corps—lost rather heavily when they went into action against the Union right. The only reporter who described what happened with any degree of frankness was a correspondent of the *Augusta Chronicle,* who signed himself "Kentuckian." The *Chronicle* man, whose pseudonym identified the state from which he came, unhesitatingly denounced the failure as "one of the most wicked and stupid blunders of the war," and assailed the "incompetency or bad management" of the division commander. He admitted that Bate, a Tennessean, was a man of courage and probably a good regimental commander, but declared that the Kentuckians under Bate's command believed him to be unqualified for the responsibilities of directing a division.[33]

The Atlanta press was doing its best during the last week of May to suppress information about the panic that the enemy's advance had caused there. An editorial in the *Appeal* on May 21 tried to make it seem that there was little excitement in Atlanta, but this was not the situation army correspondent "Shadow" beheld when he arrived there on the morning of the battle at New Hope church. "Shadow" had already blurted out in one of his newspaper letters that he regarded the city's defenses as inadequate to withstand a siege, and had predicted that the crossing of the Chattahoochee River by the enemy would mean the loss of Atlanta. The fright of a large number of its citizens which the *Register* reporter witnessed in Atlanta caused him to become panic-stricken himself and to depict the apprehensive mood of the people with uncomfortable precision. "Shadow" declared that the city was "utterly demoralized . . . confused, bewildered; a whole city like one moving household, hurried, up-torn, panic-stricken." He contended that the panic was fed by the speculator class, which had made millions of dollars from exploiting the Confederacy's need, and

---

[32] *Mobile Daily Advertiser and Register,* June 3, 1864; *Memphis Daily Appeal,* May 31, 1864.

[33] *Augusta Daily Chronicle and Sentinel,* June 16, 1864.

by the refugees who were pouring into Atlanta from every quarter. The sufferings of the refugees had already been the theme of a number of letters from Confederate army correspondents, and "Shadow" had obtained glimpses in Marietta of these unfortunate people fleeing in all directions and in every conceivable form of conveyance, leaving behind them their homes, farms, and, in some cases, all their personal belongings.

He said of them: "For the most part they are irresolute and uninformed, the women in tears and the men in fearful perplexity. You may see them on the highways jogging along in a hopeless sort of manner, in search for a hiding place, or at the little stations along the railroad, huddled together in box cars, negroes, dogs and household goods indiscriminate. . . . Doleful, inexpressibly doleful. Let the grim picture pass on."[34]

Every street corner in Atlanta that "Shadow" passed was a gathering place for excited men exchanging the latest reports with all the exaggerations that fancy could devise. Cars were moving out of the railroad depot "with heavy loads of spoils and merchandize"; the provost marshal's office was besieged with petitions for passes to Mobile, Macon, and Augusta; and the Jewish merchants were in a frenzy. "Shadow" depicted the plight of his "little friend," Abednego Levi:

" 'Got for tam ze speculators,' says he, 'I vish dey vas all dead! Dey geet all ze car, ze express, ze wagon, and leef honest peesness man to go to h———l, or any other seaport, shust like five hundred tousand tevyl, by got! I go to Sheneral Wright. He say, "vat you want?" I say, "transportation for a leetle goods." He say, "I got no transportation." Den I poots der goots on one, two, three dray, and I geets to Stone Mountain. Der I meets der cavalry. Dey stop me and say, "ope ze box or I shoot you ded." Den I opes ze box, and takes out ze boots, ze shirts, ze brandy, and tells me I go on. I says "to where?" — And dey says "to hell," and I tinks so, for I coom back to ze Atalanty. Dey calls demselves cavalry, but dey acts more like roppers! Got for dam, ze speculators. I vish dey vas all dead.' "[35]

"Shadow" admitted that occasionally one met along Atlanta's streets a quiet, unconcerned individual who probably was a former soldier.

[34] *Mobile Daily Advertiser and Register*, May 28, 1864.

[35] *Ibid.*, May 29, 1864. For confirmation of the essential accuracy of "Shadow's" description of the turmoil in Atlanta see the comments of the Augusta *Constitutionalist's* new army correspondent, "Grape" (Henry Watterson), in *Augusta Daily Constitutionalist*, May 29, 1864.

The veteran doubtless had lost all he was worth, was accustomed to retreats, and having no local attachment for Atlanta, possessed no personal interest in its fate, although he was not unmoved by the threat to the public welfare. Like the soldier, "Shadow" was not indifferent to the implications of the events that were agitating Atlanta's citizenry. He warned his readers that the Gate City was in imminent danger, that if the events leading up to the loss of Nashville and Chattanooga were a fair guide, "Atlanta will fall." The best chance of averting this calamity, he believed, was a decisive victory by Johnston's army on the banks of the Chattahoochee and the prevention of further flanking operations by Sherman.

"Shadow's" letter, one of the best specimens of realistic reporting that the Confederate press published during the war was widely read and commented on. In the same issue of the *Mobile Register* in which it appeared, the editor explained that "Shadow" was "slightly demoralized" when he wrote the letter and that he had been wrongly influenced by the panic which he described as gripping Atlanta. Although the *Register* refrained from dismissing him for his candid reporting, the *Atlanta Intelligencer* was representative of the press of its city in speaking critically about his "hyperbolical assumptions" and denying that General Johnston, the citizens of Atlanta, or the editor himself believed that the city would fall.[36]

After returning to the army the next day "Shadow" announced that he felt more cheerful about its prospects, but when on the day after "Shadow's" return Reid journeyed to Atlanta, Reid confirmed the reality of a "considerable panic" there among those whom he identified as "weak-kneed and of 'little faith.'" Reid was inclined to pin some of the blame on Mayor James M. Calhoun who had demonstrated his lack of confidence in Johnston's army by sending his family out of the city. Then, a few days later, the mayor had issued a proclamation calling on the citizens to take up arms in defense of the city, and advising all those who were unable or unwilling to bear arms to leave immediately![37]

[36] *Atlanta Daily Intelligencer*, June 1, 1864. Although "Shadow" continued to furnish the *Mobile Register* with special correspondence, there is no evidence of any letter correspondence over "Waverly's" signature in the *Memphis Appeal* after June 1, 1864.

[37] *Mobile Daily Advertiser and Register*, May 31, 1864; *Montgomery Daily Advertiser*, May 29, 1864. Although the *Augusta Chronicle and Sentinel* of June 3,

The consternation "Shadow's" letter produced among Confederate journalists was in proportion to their realization of the damage it might do to their efforts to sustain morale. Most editors and reporters were doing their best to convince their readers that Sherman's troops were on half rations, that they were "much dispirited," that the Yankee invasion was simply a gigantic raid similar to Sherman's Mississippi expedition in February 1864,[38] that Sherman was about to retreat toward East Tennessee, and that his retreat would inevitably effect his ruin. A correspondent of the *Augusta Chronicle* charged that the enemy was making free use of whisky to sustain the courage of its men and that several recently captured prisoners had been partially intoxicated.[39]

With Johnston at this time were Confederate reporters who made a practice of objective reporting rather than special pleading, however. In a letter to the *Mobile Register* from New Hope church on June 2, "Shadow" expressed doubt that the enemy had reached the point of half rations, noting that prisoners coming through the lines seemed to be shouldering full haversacks. Another *Register* correspondent disputed the accuracy of statements claiming declining morale among Northern soldiers. This reporter concluded that the enemy seemed determined and that if Johnston's army conquered them, "as it inevitably will," the Army of Tennessee could pride itself on having repulsed or annihilated "the best army the North has ever had."[40]

Sherman's army began shifting back east at the end of May toward the line of the railroad, with Johnston keeping a parallel movement. On June 5 Abrams reported to the *Intelligencer* that to keep his right flank from being turned Johnston had withdrawn to a new line about ten miles long from Lost Mountain to the railroad north of Kennesaw

---

1864 professed its inability to see any ground for "Shadow's" despondency, it reflected the editor's uneasiness about the safety of Atlanta.

[38] In February 1864 Sherman had marched east from Vicksburg to Meridian, Mississippi to launch an attack on Mobile. Although newspaper editors in Alabama and other parts of the South were panicky, Sherman returned to Vicksburg without penetrating Alabama when his cavalry failed to beat off an attack by Forrest. Catton, *Never Call Retreat*, pp. 302-304; R. S. Henry, *"First with the Most" Forrest* (Indianapolis, 1944), p. 225.

[39] *Augusta Daily Chronicle and Sentinel*, May 29, 1864; L. T. Griffith and J. E. Talmadge, *Georgia Journalism, 1763-1950* (Athens, Ga., 1951), p. 80. An Associated Press dispatch from New Hope church descanting on the supposed low morale of Sherman's army appeared in the *Mobile Daily Advertiser and Register*, June 4, 1864.

[40] *Mobile Daily Advertiser and Register*, June 7, July 10, 1864.

Mountain. Abrams was having trouble with the transmission of both his telegraphic and letter correspondence to his newspaper. Yet at the same time he was impatient with the Confederate Associated Press because of its "glaring misrepresentations." "Shadow" similarly questioned the truth of the stories of special correspondents about skirmishing and the large incidence of night attacks which he deemed essentially fictitious. The almost incessant rainfall in northwest Georgia during early June made campaigning so difficult that relatively few correspondents continued to report from the field.[41]

But Reid was too seasoned a campaigner to withdraw under these circumstances. On June 8 he paid a visit to General Johnston's headquarters, where he found the general bivouacked in the woods under a shade tree. The reporter had expected Johnston to exhibit a careworn and haggard appearance, and was surprised to find that this was not the case. Instead the sparkling eyes and merry laugh of the usually reserved Johnston inspired him with renewed confidence in the army's commander. Reid gave no indication in his correspondence that he talked with the general. Apparently the purpose of his report of the incident was to flatter Johnston and reassure the public.[42]

Reid assessed the next day a prominent visitor to the army, the controversial governor of Georgia, Joseph E. Brown. Brown was there to consult with Johnston about the military defense of the state, and Reid correctly surmised that the governor was one of Johnston's partisans. This was probably the first of a series of visits to the army by Brown which other correspondents mentioned.[43]

About a week after these two Reid reports "Shadow" wired the news of an unusual tragedy to his newspaper in Mobile. On the left side of the Confederate line and slightly in front was Pine Mountain, a low elevation occupied by Bate's Tennessee division. Apprehensive about its exposed position, Johnston asked Polk and Hardee to accompany

[41] *Atlanta Daily Intelligencer*, June 3, 7, 1864; *Mobile Daily Advertiser and Register*, June 7, 14, 1864. An example of the kind of special correspondence to which "Shadow" objected appeared in the *Montgomery Daily Mail* of June 4, 1864. An occasional correspondent of the *Mail* related, perhaps with a double dose of his own imagination, how "thousands of soldiers slumbering in their rough bivouacs are night after night aroused by the earth-shaking cannon and the simultaneous discharge of hundreds of small arms."

[42] *Montgomery Daily Advertiser*, June 11, 1864.

[43] *Ibid.*, June 13, 1864. Biographer Louise Hill says nothing about any visits to Johnston's army by Governor Brown at this time in her *Joseph E. Brown and the Confederacy* (Chapel Hill, 1939), pp. 182-88.

him on a tour of inspection on the morning of June 14. While the three generals were together on the summit of the mountain, a Federal battery opened fire from a half-mile away. The third shell struck Polk in the side and killed him instantly as the other generals were moving to a safer place. In his letter describing the incident more fully, "Shadow" indicated that the tragedy had affected him personally. Identifying the dead commander as "my Bishop, my General and my friend," the *Register* reporter told of having ridden with Polk in battle under fire, and of how "I always fancied somehow that there was safety within the magic circle of his presence. . . ."[44]

While relating the circumstances of the general's death, Watterson, now reporting for the *Augusta Constitutionalist*, recalled an experience earlier in the campaign. About noon on the day before Johnston's army retreated from Resaca, General Polk spread out his lunch of cold ham, hardtack, and a piece of mutton, and noticing Watterson standing nearby, offered to share the lunch with him. When the reporter declined with thanks, the general refused to drop the matter.

"I see from your hungry face," he said, "that you have had no breakfast, and I insist upon it—there's quite enough for both of us."

"Very well, General, but suppose I look us up a safer place."

"Certainly, certainly that will be more agreeable," said the bishop-general as a brace of shells screamed through the air above their heads.

Watterson selected a tree at the bottom of the hill and the two men devoured their lunch under it. Presently a piece of shrapnel ripped the branches from the trunk just above them and showered them with leaden debris as it exploded.

"Humph," exclaimed the general with a shrug of his shoulders. "You're a nice fellow to send out after a safe place. I guess we'd as well move back to the front."[45]

---

[44] *Mobile Daily Advertiser and Register*, June 15, 21, 1864. "Shadow" also commented at this time about the fact that there were "few or no" Negro regiments among the Union troops at the front, stating that they had been left behind to do garrison duty in middle Tennessee and perhaps to be gobbled up by Forrest. "Shadow" referred sarcastically to the "shrewd foresight" of the Yankee in this exposing the Negro to the possibility of becoming a "patriotic sacrifice." *Ibid.*, June 14, 1864.

[45] *Augusta Daily Constitutionalist*, June 21, 1864; J. F. Wall, *Henry Watterson, Reconstructed Rebel* (New York, 1956), p. 46. The death of General Polk was the subject of considerable comment in the Confederate press, which was prone to compare his death with those of Stonewall Jackson and other Confederate war heroes who had fallen in battle.

On June 16 "Shadow" was back in Atlanta for a brief furlough. The difference between the situation at the front and in the rear he described as:

the difference between new corn whisky and champagne. This thing of going where glory waits you is not what it is cracked up to be by poets who have never smelt powder, and pretty women who can very well afford to hurry their heroes off to the wars while they loll on sofas and flirt. Glory, forsooth! D'ye mind what I tell you now, it's not the only thing that welcomes you. The fleas give you greeting, the sand ticks and camp itch, and maybe an ugly bullet with its cursed song that doesn't make any music at all! To lie in the trenches, mud up to the eyes; to sleep in a ditch of bilge water, with a chunk for a pillow and a snake for bed fellow; to cook your own rations and sit down to a bit of bacon and hard tack, and consider coffee of the blackest description, sans sugar, a luxury for a king; to be shot at by every Dutchman that blunders upon a sight of you, and be kept from morning till night dodging the visits of the shells as one dodges a dun around the corner—that's one picture.

To be invited out to dine, where there are a brace of beauties full of music, love and sympathy, and a service of silver; to recline in a saloon with a carpet which melts like wax beneath your tread, rosewood furniture and marble slabs, and mirrors which reflect your satisfaction from every wall; to sit at a table with roasts and fricassees, and wines and sweetmeats, a napkin in your lap and the gentle embraces of an easy chair pressing against you; to drink *cafe au lait* out of china cups; to listen to delicious music! . . . I tore myself away from an enthusiastic party to write you these lines, and to explain the difference between the city and the field. You have it here indifferently written down.[46]

Five days after Polk's death the army fell back to a new line anchored by Kennesaw Mountain, an elevation of about seven hundred feet, four miles northwest of Marietta. Reid described the view of the surrounding country from the top of the mountain as magnificent, but a reporter for one of the Atlanta papers laughed at the idea of trying to watch military operations from that point.[47]

On June 21 Johnston shifted Hood's corps from the right end of his line to the extreme left to check an advance by Hooker. Then Hood counterattacked without preliminary reconnaissance and lost about a thousand men without any equivalent gain. The P.A. reported the affair inaccurately, making it appear that the enemy, rather than Hood,

---

[46] *Mobile Daily Advertiser and Register* as reprinted in *Atlanta Daily Southern Confederacy*, June 25, 1864.

[47] *Montgomery Daily Advertiser*, June 18, 1864; *Memphis Daily Appeal* as reprinted in *Daily Richmond Enquirer*, July 7, 1864.

had initiated the fight and had been repulsed with heavy loss. "Shadow" partially contradicted this report by expressing doubt that the enemy had been repulsed "with great slaughter," but the *Columbus Enquirer* seems to have been the only Southern newspaper that nailed down the falsehood of the P.A. reporter.[48]

At this point Sherman began a new phase of a campaign that to one Confederate reporter seemed to have degenerated into a meaningless succession of indecisive, yet more or less costly, combats. Instead of continuing his flanking tactics, Sherman launched a frontal assault on the Confederate center at Kennesaw Mountain on the morning of June 27. Reid was in Atlanta again that day, partially disabled by camp-contracted illness, but he came back up to Marietta the next day to gather material for a report of the battle. In his letter to the *Montgomery Advertiser* Reid told how, after a general bombardment and some preliminary skirmishing, the enemy "advanced at a charge in front of Gen. Hardee's corps, four columns deep, our men reserving their fire . . . until the foe came up within forty yards, when they opened a murderous fire upon them. Rank after rank went down, but still on they pressed only to meet the same fate, until impeded by the piles of their own dead. With undaunted bravery and madness, they rushed on until they gained our works, and mounting our breastworks, planted their colors upon them. Scores of their officers were shot down in mounting our entrenchments, and a Colonel and Lieutenant were taken prisoners by being pulled into our trenches and others bayoneted. That they fought with intrepid daring none can deny."[49] Reid did not report the fact (probably he did not yet know) that the enemy's attack had failed disastrously.

"Shadow" also missed the fight, but he reported on June 29 that Johnston had won a "complete victory," the chief advantage of which was that "we lost so few men," and that the Associated Press dispatches had actually understated the enemy's loss. "Shadow's" estimate of five thousand Union casualties was probably fairly close to the truth. Also, in several Southern newspaper accounts, the peril of the Union wounded when the woods around them caught fire was described at some length. Reid told about the chivalrous behavior of an Arkansas

[48] Govan and Livingood, *Johnston*, pp. 291-292; *Mobile Daily Advertiser and Register*, June 28, 1864; *Daily Columbus Enquirer*, June 26, 28, 1864.

[49] *Augusta Daily Constitutionalist*, June 28, 1864; *Montgomery Daily Advertiser*, June 30, 1864.

colonel who ordered his men to cease firing to permit the Yankees to transport their wounded to a place of greater safety.[50]

Captain Matthews, the "Harvey" of the *Memphis Appeal*, related an interesting story of how, during the truce after the battle to permit the Yankees to bury their dead, a number of officers and enlisted men from both sides had a friendly meeting. Generals Cheatham and Hindman were two of the Confederate officers present. According to "Harvey," Cheatham was in shirt sleeves; his easy pleasant manner so pleased one of the enemy soldiers that the "Yank" nudged the general in the side and effusively informed him, "I think you are a good reb. Give me a drink, old fel." As the general politely handed him his water canteen, one of the Confederate soldiers asked the friendly Yank if he knew whom he was talking to. The Yankee did not, but when he learned that the "good reb" was General Cheatham, a crowd of Northern soldiers swarmed around the two Confederate generals to present their pocket books for autographs![51]

The bloody defeat in front of Kennesaw Mountain caused Sherman to resume his flanking tactics, and Johnston fell back once more, evacuating Kennesaw Mountain and Marietta. While there were predictions in the *Atlanta Intelligencer* that Johnston would be flanked to the Gulf and then to Richmond, other newspapers wondered why Wheeler's cavalry had not been turned loose to raid Sherman's communications. What apparently the press did not know was that all of Johnston's small cavalry force was needed to protect the flanks of his army and keep him informed about Sherman's movements. Johnston had been pleading with Richmond for weeks to release Forrest's and S. D. Lee's cavalry on Sherman's railroad communications. Both Davis and Bragg had taken the position, however, that the cavalry was more urgently needed in Mississippi than in Georgia.[52]

Press criticism of Wheeler nettled the Alabamian no end. Attributing it to the machinations of certain members of Forrest's staff, Wheeler related to Bragg in a private letter, "I have begged General Johnston to allow me to go to the enemy's rear nearly every day for the last three

---

[50] *Mobile Daily Advertiser and Register*, July 3, 1864. An eyewitness description by a Confederate officer of the colonel's humane act is given in S. G. French, *Two Wars, an Autobiography* (Nashville, 1901), p. 211.

[51] *Memphis Daily Appeal*, July 1, 1864. For an interesting report of fraternizing by rival pickets see *Augusta Daily Constitutionalist*, July 3, 1864.

[52] Govan and Livingood, *Johnston*, pp. 286-87; *Atlanta Daily Intelligencer*, July 5, 1864.

months and he is anxious that it should be done but states that my presence is necessary upon the flanks and here I am with one third rations of corn for horses, with my men building and defending rifle pits and the papers abusing me for not being in Sherman's rear. . . . General Johnston tells me not to mind the papers and I try not to do so, but these things are disagreeable."[53]

General Wheeler also had his defenders among the army correspondents; at least one reporter thought Wheeler's friends were too sensitive about public opinion. Both Reid and the *Intelligencer* correspondent Abrams were partisans of Wheeler, the former for reasons that were perhaps significantly related to Wheeler's championship of him against General Bragg. Reid assured his readers that Wheeler's cavalry had made a name for itself in the campaign of which they might well be proud and that Wheeler himself was in the saddle "night and day," rendering the most distinguished service to the Confederate cause. In the last letter Abrams wrote to the *Intelligencer* before he left the army, he too declared that he had formed a much more favorable opinion of Wheeler during the campaign than he had had before he gained firsthand knowledge of the general's capabilities.[54]

Although Wheeler was not in a position to crack down on unfriendly newspapermen within army lines, General Johnston was and now did so. His punitive order, issued shortly before the Battle of Kennesaw Mountain, was not specifically directed against criticism of the military. Instead it threatened expulsion from the army of any newspaper correspondent who was guilty of "magnifying small skirmishes into great battles, and sending off sensational dispatches and letters which only humbug and delude the people for 24 hours." The Atlanta papers had been accused by some reporters of exaggerations of this kind; the Montgomery correspondent of the *Mobile Register* remarked during the first week of July that Alabamians were beginning to lose faith in the statements of the correspondents with Johnston's army. Since the order also prohibited all subordinate commanders from communicating military information to newspapermen, the army reporters now generally went back to Atlanta. That city was only fourteen miles from the

[53] Jos. Wheeler to Braxton Bragg, July 1, 1864, Braxton Bragg Papers, Western Reserve Historical Society. For examples of press criticism of Wheeler's cavalry emanating from army reporters see *Augusta Daily Constitutionalist*, June 8, 1864; *Mobile Daily Advertiser and Register*, June 14, 1864.

[54] *Mobile Daily Advertiser and Register*, July 5, 7, 1864; *Montgomery Daily Advertiser*, June 13, 27, 1864; *Atlanta Daily Intelligencer*, June 30, 1864.

front after Johnston pulled back from the Kennesaw Mountain line and Marietta. According to one correspondent it was now a better place for gathering and promptly transmitting army news than any place along the railroad to the north.[55]

"Shadow" correctly prophesied in a letter to the *Mobile Register* from Atlanta on July 3, that Johnston would soon fall back again, to the admirable defense line his engineers had constructed along the north bank of the Chattahoochee. Fully one month before, Reid had predicted almost to the letter the very move that Sherman now made. Reid had guessed that the enemy would probably move upstream to cross the river at Roswell, twelve miles northeast of Marietta. It was just below Roswell that, to avoid the casualties a frontal attack would almost certainly cause, Sherman crossed to the south bank of the River on July 8. By the next day the reporters in Atlanta were heating up the wires with dispatches about "Yankees Crossing the Chattahoochee."[56]

Confederate newspapers tried at first to make it appear that Hardee had driven Sherman back across the river. When this story was disproved they substituted statements about the remarkably good order with which Johnston's retirement across the Chattahoochee on the night of July 9-10 had been conducted. Yet they could hardly ignore the excitement that the news of the retirement had generated in Atlanta. According to the eyewitness report of the *Mobile Register* correspondent, the city's streets were crowded with wagons piled high with household effects, and every train of cars, freight or otherwise, was loaded to capacity with refugees struggling to leave the city. "The excitement beats anything I ever saw, and I hope I may never witness such again."[57]

There was hardly less consternation in Richmond, where President Davis had become increasingly apprehensive about the consequences of Johnston's retreats. On the same day that Johnston crossed the Chattahoochee the President ordered his military adviser Bragg to go quickly to Georgia to explore the advisability of changing commanders. The

[55] *Montgomery Daily Mail*, July 6, 1864; *Memphis Daily Appeal*, June 28, July 3, 1864; *Augusta Daily Chronicle and Sentinel*, July 7, 1864; *Mobile Daily Advertiser and Register*, July 6, 1864.

[56] *Montgomery Daily Advertiser*, June 13, 1864; *Augusta Daily Chronicle and Sentinel*, July 12, 1864.

[57] *Augusta Daily Chronicle and Sentinel*, July 12, 1864; *Mobile Daily Advertiser and Register*, July 14, 1864.

few reporters who were still with the army when Bragg arrived there on July 13 were curious about the reason for this unexpected visit, but Bragg did not reveal it even to Johnston. He made it appear that his visit was "unofficial," that he had come to help secure reinforcements for Johnston from the other Western commanders.[58]

Another new arrival in the front lines of the Army of Tennessee was the seasoned war correspondent de Fontaine, who had left the employment of the *Charleston Courier* at the beginning of 1864 to become the owner of the *Columbia South Carolinian*. The critical situation of Johnston's army and of Atlanta had caused de Fontaine to return to the field during the first week of July to report the great battle that seemed imminent, for the *Savannah Republican* and for his own newspaper. De Fontaine met Johnston and his chief of staff on the same day Bragg arrived from Richmond. The reporter was doubtless gratified to learn that Johnston had agreed to issue military press releases similar to the war bulletins of General Lee.[59]

This promise to relax the army censorship came too late to benefit de Fontaine and the other reporters, however. Davis had already decided to remove Johnston; apparently the only uncertainty in his mind had to do with the choice of a successor. Bragg preferred Hood to Hardee, although he admitted that Hood was not a great general. And so, although Lee expressed misgivings about Hood as an army commander, Davis decided to appoint the aggressive Texan. The biggest news story in the Confederate press on July 18, 1864 was the Associated Press report that Johnston had been removed from the command of the Army of Tennessee.[60]

The Southern press was divided in its editorial comments. Both the *Richmond Whig* and *Examiner* criticized the President's action, while the other Richmond newspapers defended it. The Georgia press generally followed the lead of Governor Brown in deploring the change of commanders. Among the leading reporters who championed Johnston

---

[58] Govan and Livingood, *Johnston*, p. 309; Hudson Strode, *Jefferson Davis, Tragic Hero* (New York, 1964), p. 72; *Mobile Daily Advertiser and Register*, July 23, 1863.

[59] *Savannah Republican*, July 16, 1864. A covert sympathy for Johnston, at a time when Bragg's unexpected visit to the army made his tenure as army commander seem more shaky, is disclosed in another of de Fontaine's letters, in *ibid.*, July 20, 1864.

[60] Govan and Livingood, *Johnston*, pp. 313-17; Strode, *Davis, Tragic Hero*, pp. 72-73; R. W. Winston, *High Stakes and Hair Trigger* (New York, 1930), p. 233.

were Richmond correspondent George Bagby and the *Montgomery Advertiser's* Sam Reid, now in Charleston, attempting to recover from an attack of rheumatism. Reid published his defense of Johnston in the *Charleston Mercury*, a leading anti-administration newspaper.[61]

An indication of how Bragg attempted to manipulate the press to quiet the controversy over the change he had recommended appears in a letter Editor A. D. Banks of the *Montgomery Mail* wrote to Johnston several weeks later. Banks told his friend Johnston about a meeting that took place in Montgomery on the morning after Johnston's removal was announced. The participants included Colonel Forsyth of the *Mobile Register* and former Secretary of War Walker, who came up from Mobile after receiving a telegram from Bragg asking them to meet him in Montgomery. While Forsyth and Walker were waiting for Bragg to appear, they took breakfast with Banks and expressed their indignation about the removal of Johnston to him. Immediately after their meeting with Bragg, Banks again talked with Forsyth, who by this time had experienced a change of heart. Forsyth communicated to Banks Bragg's representation of the factors underlying the President's decision, saying that Bragg had told him that "it was important the change should be sustained by the Press and public opinion set right on the causes of the change."[62]

Bragg was evidently effectual in dictating the *Mobile Register's* editorial policy, but it seems unlikely that he directly influenced any other newspapers. Some reporters—de Fontaine for one—sought to minimize the extent of dissatisfaction in the army with the removal of Johnston and to exaggerate the not very great popularity of Hood among the troops.[63]

The reporters of out-of-town newspapers in Atlanta did not miss the significance of the preparations for a hasty departure that the daily newspapers there were making. On the very day (July 6) that an

[61] See e.g. *Richmond Daily Sentinel,* July 21, 1864; *Mobile Daily Advertiser and Register,* August 2, 1864; *Charleston Mercury* as reprinted in *Augusta Daily Chronicle and Sentinel,* July 29, 1864 and *Columbus Daily Sun,* August 3, 1864; Griffith and Talmadge, *Georgia Journalism,* p. 81; Mrs. Burton Harrison, *Recollections Grave and Gay* (New York, 1911), p. 192. According to the Richmond correspondent of the *Augusta Constitutionalist,* Salem Dutcher, "the removal of Johnston has excited a degree of animosity here [in Richmond] toward the President which it is painful to witness." *Augusta Daily Constitutionalist,* July 29, 1864.

[62] A. D. Banks to Gen. Joseph E. Johnston, August 21, 1864, Joseph E. Johnston Papers, Huntington Library.

[63] *Savannah Republican,* July 21, 1864.

Intelligencer editorial was beseeching the citizens of Atlanta to "stand firm," the *Intelligencer*, along with the *Confederacy* and *Register*, was planning a precipitate exit. In reporting their timorous behavior to the *Mobile Register*, "Shadow" pointed out that these were the same newspapers that had dissented so violently a month earlier against his prediction of the fall of Atlanta. "The Confederacy goes to Macon. The Register to Augusta. The Intelligencer to Milledgeville. And the Appeal, which is considered a bird of ill omen, is pluming its wings to descend like a raven upon the unoffending capital of Alabama." Before the end of July the *Intelligencer* had moved to Macon, instead of Milledgeville, and was about to resume publication from the office of one of the Macon papers. The *Confederacy* followed the *Intelligencer* to Macon, and true to "Shadow's" prediction, the *Register* shifted its base of operation to Augusta. Although the *Appeal* shipped its type and presses to Montgomery the day before the Battle of Atlanta opened, both the *Appeal* and the *Confederacy* left small staffs in the beleaguered city to issue handbill-sized extras from proof presses.[64]

HARDLY any reporters were still with the Army of Tennessee on the afternoon of July 20 when Hood opened the Battle of Atlanta near Peachtree Creek. Reid had written his last report from this army and was about to undergo a long siege of illness several hundred miles away. Abrams, the "St. Clair" of the *Atlanta Intelligencer*, presumably had followed his newspaper to Macon, to report no more from the field during the war. One of the *Mobile Register's* correspondents, who evidently was a Mississippian, had gone home from Atlanta to recover his health in the midst of a damaging Federal cavalry raid on the railroad line to Montgomery. At Opelika, railroad service was completely suspended. The *Register* reporter had to walk the remaining fifteen or twenty miles into Montgomery.[65] The departure of the correspondent was an unlucky development for Colonel Forsyth's newspaper, since just about this time its principal army reporter, "Shadow," became mysteriously silent and did not regain his voice for a month. Apparently

---

[64] *Mobile Daily Advertiser and Register*, July 17, 1864; Griffith and Talmadge, *Georgia Journalism*, p. 81; excerpt from S. P. Richards diary in F. M. Garrett, *Atlanta and Its Environs* (New York, 1954), I, 622.

[65] *Mobile Daily Advertiser and Register*, July 26, 1864. Another war correspondent whom a campaign-contracted illness rendered inactive was the special correspondent of the *Augusta Chronicle*, a certain "Aristides." *Augusta Daily Chronicle and Sentinel*, July 9, 1864.

de Fontaine was the only war correspondent of any note in the neighborhood of Atlanta to report the battles that would test Hood's capacity as a general.

The first of the battles of Atlanta began with Hood's attempt to strike Thomas's corps as it was crossing Peachtree Creek, the last water barrier before the city. Thomas's corps constituted the Union right; Hood felt there was no time to lose, as Schofield was approaching the city from due north and McPherson had already cut Hood's railroad connection with Augusta east of Decatur. In a letter to the *Savannah Republican* from "Behind the Chattahoochee" on the day of the battle, "Personne" told about riding along the army lines the previous evening and watching the defenders of Atlanta construct entrenchments. At dawn the next morning he had ridden to headquarters on the edge of the city, fairly near the center of the line. There "Personne" found Hood and his corps commanders holding a grim council of war. About noon, as "Personne" was awaiting the outcome of their deliberations, Hood appeared at the doorway of his headquarters, arrayed in full uniform, leaning on his crutch, his eyes flashing with what the newspaperman described as "a strange indescribable light." Grasping "Personne's" hand, Hood informed him in what must have seemed an unusual display of confidence: "Mr. de Fontaine, at one I attack the enemy. He has pressed our lines until he is within a short distance of Atlanta, and I must fight or evacuate. I am going to fight. The odds are against us, but I leave the issue with the God of Battles." With that the general rode off, accompanied by his staff, toward the front line while de Fontaine remained at headquarters to prepare a letter describing the background of the action that was about to begin.[66]

But the battle did not develop according to Hood's plan. Just as he was about to strike Thomas and roll his corps back into the triangle between river and creek, an emergency flared up on the Confederate right. McPherson with a force of 25,000 was heading straight for Atlanta along the railroad from Decatur, driving Wheeler's cavalry before him. To keep from being outflanked, Hood had to shift Cheatham's corps to the right, thus creating a gap in his line and a three-hour delay in the attack. When the attack came, it was poorly coordinated, and Hood lost several thousand men without achieving his objective. De Fontaine concealed his disappointment by alleging that he was too weary to describe the fighting in detail and that the possibility of his

[66] Dyer, *Gallant Hood*, pp. 253-54; *Savannah Republican*, July 25, 1864.

letter being intercepted between Atlanta and Macon by the enemy made it imprudent to do so.[67]

The second phase of the battle began with a turning movement, not unlike Stonewall Jackson's famous maneuver at Chancellorsville, involving a night march by Hardee through and southeast of the city. Hardee accomplished a tactical surprise, although he was late in reaching his destination; but in the meantime the exposed left flank of the enemy had changed its position and received reinforcements. Consequently Hardee was repulsed in the second of the battles of Atlanta, even though he captured two thousand prisoners and inflicted heavy casualties, including the death of the Union army commander James B. McPherson. Also, the unreported Confederate loss appears to have been considerably greater than that of the enemy.[68]

With greater patriotic fervor than fidelity to the truth, the Associated Press reporter in Atlanta portrayed the result of Hardee's march as a glorious victory. His inaccurate report inspired joy in Richmond when it was posted on the newspaper bulletin boards early the next morning. On the strength of that report four of the five Richmond dailies published extras, and the *Evening Whig* made journalistic history by issuing two editions. Some Richmond citizens doubted the reliability of the news, but an official dispatch from General Hood claiming a "brilliant success" which arrived later that day silenced the skeptics.[69]

The letter de Fontaine wrote to the *Savannah Republican* on the night after the battle was equally misleading. "Personne" interpreted the outcome of Hardee's attack as a splendid success, in which the enemy was forced back a mile and a half. He admitted, however, that the enemy's resistance had broken a Confederate brigade, which he

[67] Dyer, *Gallant Hood*, pp. 255-57; J. B. Hood, *Advance and Retreat* (Bloomington, 1959), pp. 168-71. Hood's silence on the extent of the Confederate loss caused the editor of the *Mobile Register* to infer that "we suffered considerably" and to criticize the policy of refusing to trust the people. *Mobile Daily Advertiser and Register*, July 29, 1864.

[68] Dyer, *Gallant Hood*, pp. 258-62; Hood, *Advance and Retreat*, pp. 194-95. In reporting the death of General McPherson, the *Columbia Tri-Weekly South Carolinian* of July 26, 1864 gave him more credit for ability and skill than it or any other Confederate newspaper had done during his lifetime.

[69] *Augusta Daily Chronicle and Sentinel*, July 24, 1864; *Savannah Republican*, July 25, 1864; *Augusta Daily Constitutionalist*, July 30, 1864; *Daily Richmond Enquirer*, July 25, 1864. For an indication of the dramatic effect of the news of Hood's supposed success on the flickering morale of the citizens of Montgomery, see the report of the Montgomery correspondent of the *Mobile Register* in the July 26, 1864 issue of that newspaper.

refused to name. He also revealed that the night march through Atlanta had created the impression that the city was being evacuated, and that this false conception had led to considerable vandalism. "Personne" himself was a victim of the pillaging, losing all his personal effects except the clothing he was wearing.[70]

It was six days after the repulse of Hardee that the third of the battles of Atlanta was fought west of the city in the vicinity of Ezra church. Once again Hood was the attacker, and as before the result was failure with heavy loss. The only compensation was Wheeler's success in thwarting a Federal cavalry raid, undertaken before the battle began, along the railroad running south from Atlanta to Macon. Neither of these events was adequately reported in the Confederate press. De Fontaine apparently returned to Columbia after his mishap with the looters; if there were any other army correspondents in the vicinity of Ezra church on July 28 they refrained from reporting the third of Hood's defeats. Later the *Savannah Republican* revealed that one of the fatalities in the battle was a Captain Ferris, a soldier correspondent of the *Atlanta Register*.[71]

The Confederate newspapers hardly dared reveal that within a period of about ten days Hood's aggressive tactics had cost him almost one-third of the army of sixty thousand men Johnston had turned over to him on July 17. Another general might at this stage have evacuated Atlanta and retreated southward, but Hood retired into the fortifications ringing the city to await Sherman's next move.[72] The letters of the correspondents who remained in Atlanta during the next few weeks described the shelling that had already begun, and improvised variations on the theme that Hood finally had brought Sherman's invasion to a

[70] *Savannah Republican*, July 27, 1864; *Augusta Daily Constitutionalist,* July 29, 1864. For an eyewitness description of this pillaging by cavalrymen who were allegedly members of the 7th Alabama Regiment see F. J. Taylor, ed., *Reluctant Rebel: The Secret Diary of Robert Patrick, 1861-1865* (Baton Rouge, 1959), p. 200, entry of July 22, 1864. According to the *Columbus Daily Sun* of August 9, 1864, Hood severely punished the perpetrators of this vandalism, shooting five of the ringleaders and placing eighty of their companions under arrest.

[71] Dyer, *Gallant Hood*, pp. 265-66; *Savannah Republican*, August 9, 1864. The significance of Hood's "victory" was clearly understood at Macon according to George Bagby, who was there on a visit to his wife's relatives in Georgia at this time. "Your uncle [presumably Mrs. Bagby's uncle] thinks the victory not one to brag of. We whipped 'em but lost more men than they did, a thing we cant afford to do." George W. Bagby to Dear old 'oman, July 24, 1864, Brock Collection, Huntington Library.

[72] Catton, *Never Call Retreat*, p. 283.

halt. They also told about the refugees who sought to escape south; according to the special correspondent of the *Augusta Chronicle* there were few noncombatants left in the city by the middle of August. The newspapermen who were there gave a contradictory picture of the amount of damage caused by the bombardment. Claims of comparatively slight damage were belied by reports of occasional fatalities among women and children and of extensive fires ignited by bursting shells. The *Atlanta Intelligencer* admitted that almost every house in Atlanta "bears marks of the vengeance of the ruthless enemy."[73]

During the first part of August Hood made the mistake of sending Wheeler's four thousand cavalrymen north of Atlanta in an attempt to sever Sherman's railroad communications; soon reporters were dropping mysterious hints about an expedition that would oblige Sherman to retreat. Glowing reports of Wheeler's success drifted back to Atlanta as he galloped north into Tennessee, but Confederate editors were troubled because Sherman was *not* retreating and because he seemed very little disturbed by the mischief that Wheeler was doing in his rear. A *Columbia Carolinian* reporter in Atlanta expressed doubt that Wheeler was doing as much damage to Federal railroad communications as was being claimed; another was skeptical of Sherman's grip on the city being shaken so long as Wheeler remained in charge of Hood's cavalry force.[74]

Before de Fontaine left Atlanta at the end of July he had reported the gist of an interesting interview with Governor Brown, whom he characterized as one of the most remarkable men he had encountered and as not being the dangerous "element of discord" that many Southerners believed him to be. Brown had since called to Atlanta's defense the Georgia state militia, referred to by the newspapermen as "Joe Brown's pets." The appearance of these "gray beards," none too enthusiastic about their summons to active duty, was the topic of a letter to the *Columbia Carolinian* by its army correspondent "Perryman." "Perry-

---

[73] *Augusta Daily Chronicle and Sentinel*, August 19, 1864; *Columbia Tri-Weekly Carolinian*, August 20, 1864; *Mobile Daily Tribune*, August 23, 1864; *Atlanta Daily Intelligencer*, August 24, 1864. At the end of August "Shadow" reported that the casualties in Atlanta during the bombardment of that month had been 497 killed and 691 wounded. "At least 47 houses were destroyed by fire, involving a loss of five millions of dollars worth of property." *Mobile Daily Advertiser and Register*, September 3, 1864.

[74] J. P. Dyer, *"Fightin' Joe" Wheeler* (Baton Rouge, 1941), p. 187; *Columbia Daily South Carolinian*, August 27, 31, 1864.

man" reported: "It is pitiable and amusing to see old men . . . going to the front, burdened with a huge knapsack on their back, a large bag well stored with provisions on their side, and with a gun in one hand and a walking stick in the other. . . . Like the reserves of our State, they believe in good living and plenty of clothes, and many of them bring large boxes, stored with good things and clothes sufficient for two or three men, as if they never intended to move and expected to remain stationary for the balance of the campaign. But there is no discount upon their bravery. They fight like tigers and by their gallantry have commanded the admiration of the army and the commanding general."[75]

The facilities of the Georgia press for collecting news were curtailed by a second cavalry raid which Sherman directed against the Macon Railroad during the third week of August. Although the raiders were beaten off, their depredations brought complaints from the *Columbus Enquirer* and other newspapers about exchanges that were either late or failed altogether and impaired service by the Southern Express Company, the most reliable communication facility.[76]

Toward the end of August "Shadow" resumed his interrupted correspondence for the *Mobile Register*, and early on Friday morning, August 26, he heard some surprising news. At dawn the picket line of the Army of Tennessee had discovered that the enemy had disappeared from his position of the night before, opposite the Confederate right, east of Atlanta. As the pickets advanced, they found the enemy camp deserted and little signs of activity farther west in the sector north of the city. Hood appears to have jumped to the conclusion that Wheeler's raid had finally compelled Sherman to retreat, but "Shadow" was dubious, although he could explain it in no other way. By the 28th he was fairly confident that the siege of Atlanta had been raised, but indicated a difference of opinion in the army between those who thought Sherman was retreating and another group who suspected that the wily Ohioan had started another flanking operation.[77]

By August 29 "Shadow" correctly inferred that Sherman was swinging around Atlanta to the right with his entire army, to do the job of cutting Hood's vital rail communication with Macon that the Union cavalry had failed to accomplish. The *Augusta Chronicle*'s special correspond-

[75] *Columbia Daily South Carolinian*, July 21, August 31, 1864.
[76] *Daily Columbus Enquirer*, August 6, 1864.
[77] *Mobile Daily Advertiser and Register*, August 30, September 1, 1864.

ent "Rover," who had decided three weeks before that Atlanta would be no longer tenable if Sherman gained a foothold on the Macon Railroad, became more optimistic. He expressed confidence that Hood could thwart Sherman's strategy by extending the Confederate left southward to protect the Macon road while leaving a token force to garrison Atlanta.[78]

Most of the Southern army correspondents remained with Hood in Atlanta while Hardee, with two of Hood's three corps, attacked the Union right at Jonesboro, south of Atlanta, on the afternoon of August 31. Apparently the only newspaper reporter at the Battle of Jonesboro was an occasional correspondent of the *Mobile Register* named Ben Lane Posey, who was the colonel of an Alabama regiment in S. D. Lee's corps. According to Posey the march of his command to Jonesboro on the night of August 30-31 was conducted with such frantic haste that at least one-third of the men dropped out of line. Posey's description of his own difficulties on the afternoon of the battle—his utter ignorance of the operation plan, his state of mental and physical exhaustion, his inability to get the men to advance because of the mixture of units, and his apparent distrust of his West-Point-trained superior officers—helps to explain the failure of Hardee's assault against the Union breastworks that day.[79]

Hood's entire plan fell apart after that. Posey was convinced the commanding general lost his nerve after learning of Hardee's failure at Jonesboro and that he ordered the evacuation of Atlanta prematurely.[80] At any rate, Hood evacuated Atlanta, marching southeast along the McDonogh Wagon Road during the night of September 1-2. The correspondent of the *Augusta Chronicle* appears to have been the only war correspondent who published an eyewitness account of one of the most dramatic events of the war.

Augusta Chronicle reporter "Rover" left Atlanta on Thursday evening, September 1, heading toward Decatur after watching the removal of ammunition and other supplies all day. According to "Rover," large

---

[78] *Ibid.*, September 2, 1864; *Augusta Daily Chronicle and Sentinel*, September 1, 1864.

[79] *Mobile Daily Advertiser and Register*, September 20, 1864. Posey subsequently admitted that the content of this letter was "impolitic," and that he withheld it for five days before deciding, after consultation with a friend, to mail it to the *Register*. Also, he dated it September 14 rather than the 9th to make it appear more current. *Ibid.*, October 6, 1864.

[80] *Ibid.*, September 20, 1864.

quantities of public stores were distributed among the townspeople and the soldiers who filed through the city as they were withdrawn from its defense lines. The reporter could distinguish expressions of sorrow on the weather-beaten faces of the marchers, all of whom, with the exception of the rear guard left behind to prevent straggling, had left the city before nightfall. By that time also, the Atlanta telegraph office had ceased to function.[81]

Years later a former editor of the *Atlanta Confederacy*, Colonel Adair, recalled leaving Atlanta that night in the midst of all the sorrow and confusion accompanied by the sound of exploding powder kegs and artillery shells. "The old rolling-mills were on fire, and four hundred bales of cotton belonging to old man Wells were burning. On going up a big hill below Atlanta the fire was blazing so brightly I could count the hairs in the horse's tail by the light. Gen. Hood had placed me in charge of the headquarters wagons. I had a wagon of my own, an old-fashioned North Carolina tobacco-pedler's. Just as we were pulling out Henry Watterson, the Louisville editor, who had refugeed here and had been conducting his paper from this point, and 'John Happy' of the Nashville paper, came up and climbed into my wagon. Gov. [Isham] Harris, his bodyservant, Ran, myself, and my 'nigger' Wash, Watterson, and 'Happy' made up the party. We drove all night. It was a sick crowd, sick in heart and mind. . . . I had old Wash to make some coffee for us, which he could do better than any human I have ever seen before or since, and this somewhat revived our drooping spirits."[82]

It was some forty-eight hours after the fall of Atlanta before the Confederate Press Association transmitted the news of the disaster from Macon to all parts of the Confederacy. General manager Thrasher departed for Texas three days after Atlanta fell to reorganize his company's system of gathering news from the Trans-Mississippi Region. His impending departure from Macon and the inability of the Macon office of the P.A. to get in touch with its reporter at Atlanta may have partially explained this strange delay. On the same day that the news went out from Macon, the Richmond office of the P.A. issued a wire report confirming it on the basis of an official dispatch from General

[81] *Augusta Daily Chronicle and Sentinel*, September 6, 1864.

[82] "Reminiscences of Col. George W. Adair" in *Confederate Veteran*, v (August 1897), 402-405. For an interesting account by a Confederate army correspondent of the retreat of Hood's army from Atlanta, and a human interest story in connection with it, see *Mobile Daily Tribune*, October 2, 1864.

Hood. In a more detailed message the P.A. distributed on September 5, it gave its customers the questionable assurance, "whilst the fall of Atlanta is regretted, the people are not at all discouraged."[83]

In spite of the efforts of the P.A. and the Confederate government to cushion the shock, the news of the fall of Atlanta cast a pall over the Southern will to fight. The Montgomery correspondent of the *Mobile Register* alluded to the "sudden paralysis which fell upon the public mind" in the capital of Alabama, and Alexander wrote to that same newspaper from the capital of the Confederacy that neither the fall of Vicksburg nor the unfavorable outcome of the Battle of Gettysburg had produced such a "painful impression" in Richmond as the news of the surrender of Atlanta. A reporter for the *Savannah Republican* discussed the concern of Richmond authorities about the effect of the news on the morale of Lee's army. He asserted that the news was communicated by "slow and torturing rumors" to this army until finally the War Department made "a cleanbreasted confession."[84]

The Confederate press conceded that the capture of Atlanta was a disaster, but took the position that the disaster was not irreparable. The *Richmond Enquirer* said editorially that Northern difficulties with recruiting would keep Sherman from advancing beyond Atlanta and predicted that Sherman would soon join Grant to assist him in the capture of Richmond. Coupled with such comments was a grudging admiration of the spectacular achievement of the Yankee commander. The *Enquirer* acknowledged that Sherman's successful march to Atlanta had established him as the ablest general in the Northern army. The *Atlanta Intelligencer* also rated his nearly uninterrupted course over nearly 200 miles of mountainous country against the opposition of a "most formidable" Confederate army as an almost "incredible romance."[85]

[83] *Augusta Daily Chronicle and Sentinel*, September 4, 9, 1864; *Columbus Daily Sun*, September 5, 1864; *Mobile Daily Advertiser and Register*, September 6, 1864; *Atlanta Daily Intelligencer*, September 6, 1864.

[84] *Mobile Daily Advertiser and Register*, September 10, 13, 1864; *Savannah Republican*, September 21, 1864. Richmond correspondent Bagby reported that as soon as the news of the fall of Atlanta reached Richmond, President Davis summoned General Lee and conferred with him and General Bragg from eight o'clock in the evening until nine o'clock the next morning. *Charleston Mercury*, September 9, 1864.

[85] *Daily Richmond Enquirer*, September 15, 16, 1864; *Atlanta Daily Intelligencer*, September 7, 1864; *Montgomery Daily Advertiser*, September 6, 1864; *Augusta Daily Chronicle and Sentinel*, September 8, 1864; *Columbus Daily Sun*, September 13, 1864.

DURING the first half of September the center of Confederate journalistic interest in the West was the two armies, some twenty-five miles apart—one in Atlanta and the other at Lovejoy's Station, south of Atlanta, refitting for a strike against Sherman's communications. From Macon the *Atlanta Intelligencer* reported a big Yankee celebration at the Trout House in Atlanta that got the *Intelligencer* reporter in difficulties. "Cantin," as the reporter signed himself, implied that Mayor Calhoun had been rather too friendly with the enemy on this occasion. This piece of enterprising journalism exasperated the mayor into writing to the *Intelligencer* to discover the author of the "slanderous" remarks, but the editor of the *Intelligencer* proved evasive. He explained that "Cantin" was now a captive in Sherman's hands, "and therefore I withhold his name. When he is liberated, I will promptly furnish his name. . . ."[86]

On September 21 the newspaper correspondents with the Army of Tennessee followed the army from Lovejoy's to Palmetto on the Montgomery Railroad, about twenty-five miles west of Atlanta. To Palmetto four days later came President Davis (who had left Richmond on the 20th) to investigate the condition of the army and try to remove dissension from among Hood's lieutenants. Apparently the President's visit was unexpected, and the reporters claimed that his reception by the soldiers was not enthusiastic. According to the representative of the *Augusta Chronicle*, the army manifested no disrespect; neither did it voice that general expression of admiration for Davis that had accompanied his visit to the army after the Battle of Chickamauga. The change of attitude was so noticeable during the grand review that, according to this same reporter, the President demanded to know the reason when he returned to headquarters. When no one would tell him, he called a meeting of the generals, from which Hood tactfully absented himself. There Davis learned of the army's wish for a change of commanders and of its strong preference for Johnston. There was some sentiment for Beauregard, too; before the meeting broke up, the President promised to consider the possibility of relieving Hood and substituting Beauregard.[87]

Posey, reporting for the *Mobile Register*, gave Davis another chance to assess army opinion in a private interview which Posey requested

[86] *Atlanta Daily Intelligencer*, September 28, 1864. "Cantin's" letter was reprinted in the *Augusta Daily Chronicle and Sentinel*, September 11, 1864.
[87] *Augusta Daily Chronicle and Sentinel*, October 7, 1864.

and Davis granted. Posey later stated in a newspaper letter that he told the President what was on his mind, "in words terribly plain and earnest. I felt that the peril of our cause demanded it. I feared that his bedizened generals could not or would not tell him what it behooved him to know, and as I neither court his favor nor feared his displeasure, I dared to do it. He gave me a patient hearing, and whether it bear fruit or not, I have done my duty."[88] Posey did not reveal what he told the President, but it seems likely that he was critical of the army's leadership and that he advocated a policy of greater official frankness about the army's poor performance and the dimming prospects of Confederate success.

In light of the speech Davis had recently made in Macon, he could hardly object to a reporter's plea for candor. In his Macon speech, Davis had revealed facts about the large number of deserters from the army, which inspired consternation among Confederate editors. There was widespread speculation about the identity of the "scoundrel" whom Davis said had accused him of abandoning Georgia to her fate. While some thought the president was referring to Governor Brown, others suspected that the target of his wrath was Editor John H. Steele of the *Macon* (Atlanta) *Intelligencer*, a friend of the governor.[89]

President Davis had disclosed before he left the army that an invasion of Tennessee was in store for it. On September 28 the Army of Tennessee, with Hood still in command, crossed to the north bank of the Chattahoochee to pierce Sherman's communication line. "Shadow" was now with the army again, this time in the service of the *Montgomery Mail*. As Hood marched parallel to the railroad, picking off garrisons at Ackworth and Big Shanty, the Confederate press reported the news gleefully. By the 10th of October the army correspondent of the *Columbia South Carolinian* was informing his paper that the Army of Tennessee was beyond Kennesaw Mountain, that Beauregard was with Hood, and that reports from Atlanta indicated that Sherman was trailing Hood with the greater part of his army.[90]

[88] *Mobile Daily Advertiser and Register,* October 6, 1864.

[89] *Atlanta Daily Intelligencer,* October 4, 18, 1864. The *Richmond Whig* (September 29, 1864) thought the president's Macon speech had been "clumsily reported," as did several other Confederate newspapers. See also J. J. Mathews, *Reporting the Wars* (Minneapolis, 1957), p. 86.

[90] *Montgomery Daily Mail,* October 4, 1864; *Columbia Tri-Weekly South Carolinian,* October 18, 1864. For a report of the president's fighting speech to the army on the night before his departure see *Mobile Daily Tribune,* October 2, 1864.

On the next day after this letter was written, Posey was detached from his old command and transferred to Jacksonville, Alabama on some other military assignment. Posey had stated bluntly in one of his earlier letters that the fighting qualities of the Army of Tennessee were very poor and that its organization was "most wretched." It seems likely that these and even stronger statements about the desertion of brave men to the enemy and the low state of public morale had been brought to the unfavorable attention of his superiors after their publication in the *Mobile Register*. Posey explained the interruption of his army reporting as the result of a recent order from Richmond. This order prohibited the publication of any facts or statements in regard to a military operation until a month after it had terminated. For a soldier, the order was binding, although Posey did not construe it as limiting the right to report of a civilian correspondent; so he did not feel at liberty to make further comments about Hood's military operations.[91]

Whereas Posey was prevented by his transfer from reporting the truth about the Army of Tennessee as he saw it, there were other army correspondents who found it possible to portray the austere side of that army's life. The *Columbia Carolinian* reporter told about "whole regiments" in Hood's army going barefooted, of blankets being the exception rather than the rule, and of soldiers in some regiments who had not received any pay for more than a year. By this time Wheeler's cavalry had rejoined Hood after a generally ineffective raid through Tennessee and back into Alabama. Cavalry deficiencies were the theme of a letter by a *Montgomery Advertiser* correspondent, who reported that Wheeler's cavalrymen were for the most part armed with nothing better than a musket to contend with adversaries equipped with repeating rifles, pistols, and sabers. The *Advertiser* man acknowledged that the discipline of the Confederate horsemen was lax, that they were scattered all over the territory from the Tennessee River to the Gulf of Mexico, ostensibly for the purpose of gathering up stragglers and deserters, and that for the most part they failed to perform any military function.[92]

The transition from hunting down deserters to plundering the countryside was fairly easy in the light of the destructive practices of the army as a whole. In a letter to the *Mobile Register* written after his

[91] *Mobile Daily Advertiser and Register*, October 6, 20, 1864.
[92] *Columbia Tri-Weekly South Carolinian*, October 26, 1864; *Montgomery Daily Advertiser*, October 20, 1864.

departure from Hood's army, Posey observed bitterly: "The track of an army is an utter desolation. They steal your horses, they kill your hogs and cattle, they burn your fences, they rob you of corn, fodder, potatoes, indeed everything, and leave you to starve or abandon your home, a wandering refugee. Quartermasters, 'forage masters,' as they call themselves, huge, dirty, whiskered men dash down your fences, drive into your fields and take your corn without so much as saying, 'by your leave, sir' or paying you anything for it. Dirty soldiers come rudely into your house, invading the privacy of your home to ask a thousand questions, to beg, to buy, or to steal something to eat. Day and night they swarm around you, insatiable as a horse—each, and rude as a bear. Thus your home is made a desolation and a hell. The picture is not overdrawn, and thousands can attest its truth. I have witnessed these things for the past 15 days until my heart is sick at the contemplation of them. . . . It is a common remark of people along the line of our march, that it matters little whether the Yankee army or ours visits them. The result is the same—they are ruined."[93]

While Posey was writing these accusing words Hood was continuing north along the Western & Atlantic Railroad, with Sherman in pursuit. The P.A. announced from La Grange, Georgia on October 11 the capture of Allatoona with four thousand prisoners, the virtual destruction of Sherman's railroad supply line, and the encirclement of Atlanta by Confederate troops—an amazing story that was completely false. Allatoona had instead been the scene of the first serious check encountered by Hood since he left Palmetto. Three days after this canard had received wide distribution, it was officially repudiated.[94]

Hood turned west on October 17 after penetrating as far north as the Chickamauga battlefield and crossed the state line into Alabama. After marching about seventy miles, he was overtaken by Beauregard, to whom he was now nominally subordinate in the chain of command. At Gadsden, Alabama the two Generals worked out the details of the campaign into Tennessee that Davis had already announced.[95] Sherman

[93] *Mobile Daily Advertiser and Register*, October 20, 1864.

[94] *Augusta Daily Chronicle and Sentinel*, October 12, 1864; *Mobile Daily Advertiser and Register*, October 22, 1864; Dyer, *Gallant Hood*, p. 280; Lloyd Lewis, *Sherman, Fighting Prophet* (New York, 1932), pp. 426-28.

[95] T. H. Williams, *P.G.T. Beauregard, Napoleon in Gray* (Baton Rouge, 1954), pp. 243-44. The arrival at Blue Mountain the day before of the first colored troops captured by the Army of Tennessee was the subject of comment by "Shadow" on October 25. He was struck by the contrast of their "pinched and emaciated

now gave up the chase and started back to Atlanta, leaving part of his army under Thomas and Schofield to watch Hood. From that point on, the reporting of military operations in the West diverged as the one combat area separated into two.

ON A Friday morning in mid-November the acting superintendent of the Press Association, John Graeme, received an astounding news dispatch in Richmond from Senatobia, Mississippi. Senatobia, in the northwest corner of the state, was an important listening post for Northern news that slipped through the lines from Memphis. The Senatobia dispatch, based on a story published in the *Chicago Times* nine days earlier, leaked the plan for another huge Sherman raid. This time, it appeared, Sherman was going to sweep through Georgia and South Carolina, striking at such widely separated objectives as Charleston and Mobile.

Graeme submitted this ominous news to the War Department for clearance before he undertook to disseminate it to the press. Secretary Seddon or one of his clerks promptly evaluated the story as false and refused to permit it to be communicated by telegraph. Within twenty-four hours the Press Association distributed to the press the substance of the dispatch in spite of the censorship; on the next day (November 20) Gen. Howell Cobb of Georgia wired the War Department to confirm its essential truthfulness.[96]

Sherman's unexpected movement had already begun with the burning of Atlanta. Then on the morning of November 16 his army of 60,000 began marching southeast after severing connections with its supply base at Chattanooga. With Hood far away and moving in the opposite direction, the only organized force to oppose Sherman's army was Governor Brown's Georgia militiamen and Wheeler's cavalry force of about three thousand. The reporting of Confederate cavalry operations during the Atlanta campaign had been comparatively sparse; sparse,

---

faces" with the well-fed countenances of the country "darkeys" who trooped into town to "peep at their brethren in disgrace." *Mobile Daily Advertiser and Register*, October 30, 1864.

[96] *Columbus Daily Sun*, December 20, 1864; *Augusta Daily Chronicle and Sentinel*, November 19, 1864. Neither of the published diaries of the War Department clerks makes any allusion to the suppression of this dispatch by the War Department. The *Augusta Daily Chronicle and Sentinel* of November 20, 1864 offered partial confirmation of the *Columbus Sun* story by revealing that on November 17 Secretary Seddon distributed to the press a denial of the truth of the accounts published in the Northern papers about a movement by Sherman.

too, was Confederate news coverage of the resistance by the token forces to Sherman's march toward the seacoast. In part this was the result of the systematic destruction of the telegraph lines in the path of Sherman's mighty host, which caused the Georgia press to be almost as uncertain about Sherman's movements as the Northern newspapers were. Unaware at first of the extensive damage to the communication system that Sherman's march was causing, a newspaper in Montgomery, Alabama incorrectly attributed the silence of the Confederate Associated Press to official censorship.[97] The newspapers of Georgia, Alabama, and South Carolina had to depend for news about Sherman's advance and Wheeler's hit-and-run tactics on newspaper exchanges that were hardly better informed than they.

The news picture of military operations in Georgia in November 1864 reflected both confusion and wishful thinking. Sherman accentuated the confusion by advancing from Atlanta in two widely separated columns. His right wing rolled south toward Macon, then swung to the southeast to bypass it. The left wing headed east toward Augusta, then turned southeast to Milledgeville, occupying it on the sixth day of the march from Atlanta. While the *Savannah Republican* was complaining about the failure of the Macon office of the Associated Press to report what was happening there, the *Augusta Chronicle and Sentinel* had visions, not altogether uncomfortable, of Sherman threatening Columbus or Montgomery. Fearing for their own safety, the refugee *Atlanta Confederacy* and *Intelligencer* packed up and left Macon, while the *Macon Telegraph* promised to keep publishing there as long as the Confederate flag waved over the city.[98]

Newspapers in Georgia and elsewhere in the South hopefully portrayed Sherman's march as a retreat, bound to culminate in starvation or surrender. The *Augusta Constitutionalist* likened it to the *Anabasis* of Xenophon in which, like the Greeks of old, the unhappy general was seeking to escape to a secure spot on the seacoast. The *Columbia*

[97] *Montgomery Daily Mail*, November 22, 1864. According to the *Columbia Daily South Carolinian* of December 18, 1864, an investigation by an agent of Governor Brown of the damage done to Atlanta during the Federal occupation demonstrated that all the business firms except those on Alabama Street had been burned, that only one hotel, the Gate City, had survived the conflagration, and that the enemy had destroyed over 90 percent of the houses in the town.

[98] *Savannah Republican*, November 19, 1864; *Augusta Daily Chronicle and Sentinel*, November 18, 1864; *Montgomery Daily Mail*, November 24, 1864; *Memphis Daily Appeal*, November 23, 1864.

Carolinian avowed the happy conviction that Sherman was "marching on his Moscow," and the *Richmond Enquirer* spoke mysteriously about combinations, supposedly in progress, to foil the enemy's strategy.[99]

At the end of November the *Macon Telegraph* published the first special correspondence from Wheeler's cavalry that had appeared since the march began. The *Telegraph* reporter gave Wheeler the best of various clashes with the enemy near Macon and at Griswoldville and Sandersville. In reporting the Sandersville fight on November 25 he told how the 8th Texas Cavalry used their favorite weapon, the "repeater," to drive back the foe and in a twinkling converted the Yankee pursuers of a small body of Georgia militia into fugitives. Only the proximity of the Twentieth Corps of Federal infantry, in his opinion, saved the enemy cavalrymen from extinction.[100]

Later the same reporter, "Nosduh" (whose surname probably was Hudson) described a fierce cavalry fight near Waynesboro on the 28th in which Wheeler deflected a Yankee cavalry raid on Augusta. "Nosduh" described the burning of Waynesboro by the enemy and the screams of the terrified women and children he and his fellow cavalrymen could hear as they rode toward the town through "the dark shadows of the Southern pine." As the fighting continued into the late evening of the next day, Wheeler succeeded in isolating the enemy cavalry commander, Kilpatrick, and two regiments from the rest of his command. But Kilpatrick escaped in a dense fog, leaving his hat in the road as a trophy. "Nosduh" admitted that in another fight there a week later, Kilpatrick had the better of it, forcing Wheeler's horsemen "to retire through Waynesboro with more *haste* than dignity. . . ."[101]

[99] *Augusta Daily Constitutionalist* as reprinted in *Charleston Daily Courier*, November 21, 1864; *Columbia Daily South Carolinian*, November 20, 22, 1864; *Daily Richmond Enquirer*, November 23, 1864. The *Richmond Enquirer* was troubled, however, by Hood's army being "switched off on a side track" at Tuscumbia, Alabama, while Sherman was proceeding, virtually unopposed, on what seemed to be a successful raid through the heart of the Confederacy. *Daily Richmond Enquirer*, November 29, 1864.

[100] *Macon Daily Telegraph and Confederate*, November 29, 1864. On December 1, 1864 the *Augusta Chronicle and Sentinel* published as special correspondence a letter from the mayor of Greensboro, Ga., R. J. Dawson, telling about the passage of the Union army through his town.

[101] *Macon Daily Telegraph and Confederate*, December 17, 1864; Dyer, *"Fightin' Joe" Wheeler*, pp. 163-64; E. L. Bell and K. C. Crabbe, *The Augusta Chronicle* (Athens, Ga., 1960), p. 62.

470

On November 26 the Confederate Associated Press reported the departure of Sherman's army from Milledgeville and Gordon toward Millen, a railroad junction fifty miles south of Augusta. By this time the Richmond newspapers were aware that the only means the North had of obtaining news from Sherman was through Southern news channels. This awareness caused them to suppress such news, coupling with their silence hints that their editors knew much more about the situation than they could print. Perhaps to confuse their adversaries the Confederate press continued to offer random conjectures about Sherman's destination. They mentioned Beaufort, Augusta, Savannah, Brunswick, and Darien as possibilities, although by December 4 the *Augusta Chronicle* was sure that the general direction of Sherman's movement was toward Savannah.[102]

Sherman's capture of Fort McAllister at the mouth of the Ogechee River below Savannah and the evacuation of the city by the department commander, Hardee, on December 20, demonstrated the prescience of the *Chronicle* editor. With Hardee's dispirited troops as they left Savannah to cross into South Carolina were the refugee editors of the *Savannah Republican* and *Morning News*.[103]

The other Southern newspapers did their best to exhibit a light-hearted attitude about Sherman's triumphant march to Savannah. The *Columbia Carolinian* sniffed that Sherman had done nothing more than reach a point where a fleet of vessels could have dropped him "months ago," and the *Columbus Times* observed that the morasses and rice plantations of the Georgia coast would be cheap in exchange for the broad, fertile fields, majestic rivers, and inexhaustible coal mines of middle and east Tennessee, then supposedly menaced by General Hood's army. After passing through the area traversed by Sherman's "bummers" on his way back from Richmond to Mobile,

[102] *Mobile Daily Advertiser and Register*, November 29, 1864; *Daily Richmond Enquirer*, December 8, 1864; *Mobile Daily Tribune*, December 2, 1864; *Augusta Daily Chronicle and Sentinel*, December 4, 1864. The Confederate Press Association had identified Savannah as Sherman's probable objective in a dispatch sent from Macon on November 26. *Mobile Daily Advertiser and Register*, November 29, 1864. See also P. W. Alexander to Braxton Bragg, December 2, 1864. *O.R.* (Army) Ser. I, vol. xliv, pp. 923-24.

[103] A. A. Lawrence, *A Present for Mr. Lincoln* (Macon, 1961), p. 215; H. P. Miller, "Life and Works of William Tappan Thompson," unpub. Ph.D. diss. (University of Chicago, 1942), p. 34; *Macon* (Atlanta) *Daily Southern Confederacy* as reprinted in *Mobile Daily Advertiser and Register*, January 29, 1865.

Editor Forsyth attempted to convince his readers that the amount of devastation was comparatively slight.[104]

Southern newspapers did not ignore repeated complaints of depredations by Wheeler's cavalry while Sherman's march was still going on. The press tried in general to defend Wheeler, and a correspondent of the *Augusta Chronicle* blamed the reputation for thievery of Wheeler's men on "prowling cavalry . . . riding through the country . . . . [who] pretend to belong to Wheeler's or Young's cavalry, cut off from their commands. . . ." A prominent critic of Wheeler was the *Savannah News*, which asserted that his cavalry were doing an immense amount of harm and declared that Wheeler had "demonstrated to every man in the Confederacy, except the President and Gen. Bragg, that he is not capable of commanding 10,000 cavalrymen in such a war as this."[105]

LONG BEFORE Sherman left Atlanta a curtain of silence seemed to descend on the area in which Hood's Army of Tennessee was operating. On October 26 the *Savannah Republican* announced that no newspaper correspondents were permitted to accompany Hood's army, "and he himself sends little or nothing to the government." Five days later the Montgomery correspondent of the *Mobile Register* declared that the great question which preoccupied everyone was, "Where is Hood? Has he crossed the river?" The Richmond correspondent of the *Augusta Chronicle* heard from Northern sources on November 2 that Hood had continued west from Guntersville to Decatur, Alabama, had been re-

---

[104] *Columbia Daily South Carolinian*, December 18, 1864; *Columbus Daily Times*, December 21, 1864; *Mobile Daily Advertiser and Register*, December 28, 1864. Relatively little specific information about the misbehavior of Sherman's troops during the march appeared in the Confederate press. Indeed, the *Augusta Chronicle and Sentinel* of December 2, 1864 admitted that the enemy was under strict discipline and that Sherman had issued orders for severe disciplining of soldiers who were apprehended in the act of destroying private property. "Of course stragglers committed depredations with impunity." On the other hand, an editorial in the *Atlanta Confederacy* of December 14, 1864 made bitter complaint about the atrocious and barbarous deeds of the Yankee marchers.

[105] *Augusta Daily Chronicle and Sentinel*, December 7, 1864; *Savannah Daily Morning News*, December 1, 1864 as reprinted in Lawrence, *Present for Mr. Lincoln*, p. 164. A defense of Wheeler's cavalry in the *Columbia Daily South Carolinian* of December 29, 1864, probably written by de Fontaine, attested to the general good order, discipline, and gallantry of Wheeler's men. See also William F. Robert to Jefferson Davis, December 25, 1864. Jefferson Davis Papers, Duke University.

pulsed by the Yankee garrison at that point, and had marched on west to look for another place to cross the Tennessee River.[106]

The statement by the *Savannah Republican* that reporters were excluded from Hood's army was not entirely true. The Associated Press had a competent reporter at the front in north Alabama throughout October, but Hood denied him the right to send any telegrams to the press. Then on November 4, probably as the result of pressure from the Richmond papers, Secretary Seddon agreed to relax the censorship and allow dispatches concerning the movements of the Army of Tennessee to be sent over the wires again.[107] John H. Linebaugh had already started from Richmond for Hood's army to represent the four papers of the newly organized Richmond Press Association. A letter to President Davis, written by Linebaugh before he left Richmond, informed him of this mission and requested the pleasure of paying his respects to the president in person. There is no information in Confederate records of whether Davis responded to this request, favorably or otherwise. A fatal accident prevented Linebaugh from carrying out his intention of reporting for the Richmond Associated Press, however. About five days after he left Richmond, an Alabama River steamboat on which he was a passenger travelling upstream ran aground during the night. In an effort to swim ashore with some of the other passengers Linebaugh was drowned in the swift current of the Alabama.[108]

Although from a journalistic standpoint Linebaugh's death was a misfortune, another reporter, Capt. George E. Purvis of the *Atlanta Confederacy*, was able to report the crossing of the Tennessee River by Hood's army on Sunday, October 30. Purvis made clear in his published correspondence that the army crossed without serious opposition from the Yankee cavalry on the opposite bank. He also made it appear that

[106] *Mobile Daily Advertiser and Register*, November 2, 1864; *Augusta Daily Chronicle and Sentinel*, November 9, 1864.

[107] *Memphis Daily Appeal*, October 27, 1864 as reprinted in *Atlanta Daily Intelligencer*, October 30, 1864; *Montgomery Daily Mail*, November 4, 1864. The "great difficulties" of the Associated Press agent at Jacksonville, Alabama in obtaining clearance for his dispatches from the military authorities are touched on in *Montgomery Daily Advertiser*, October 24, 1864.

[108] *Memphis Daily Appeal* as reprinted in *Montgomery Daily Mail*, October 27, 1864 and *Atlanta Daily Intelligencer*, October 28, 1864; *Mobile Daily Advertiser and Register*, October 28, 1864; J. H. Linebaugh to Mr. President, October 17, 1864, Office of Confederate Secretary of War, 1861-1865, Letters Received, 314-L-1864, National Archives; *Montgomery Daily Mail*, November 16, 1864.

the entrance of the Confederate troops into Florence on the north bank was "something to make the heart and eyes fill. The women were almost frantic with joy. Just in the midst of the rejoicing the band of the 1st Tennessee—by-the-by the best in the army—broke forth in one of its finest and most stirring pieces, and I leave your imagination to complete the picture."[109]

Another two weeks passed before Forrest arrived from west Tennessee to provide cavalry support for a northward advance. The *Montgomery Mail* correspondent, Captain Carter, was one of the auditors of a fighting speech Forrest delivered to Hood's soldiers on the night after his arrival in camp:

"Well, soldiers, I came here to jine you. I'm gwine to show you the way into Tennessee. My conscripts are going, and I know Hood's veterans can go."

"I come down here with three hundred and fifty men. I got thirty-five hundred conscripts. Since May I have fought in every county in West Tennessee. I fought in the streets of Memphis, and the women run out in their night clothes to see us, and they will do it again in Nashville. I have fought a battle every twenty-five days. I have seen the Mississippi run with blood for two hundred yards, and I'm gwine to see it again. I've captured seventy-eight pieces of artillery and sixteen thousand Yankees, and buried twenty-five hundred of them!"[110]

On the day after the *Mail* printed Carter's version of Forrest's pep talk to the soldiers, the *Memphis Appeal*, now being published in Montgomery, criticized what Carter had written. The *Appeal* objected to what it regarded as the attribution of braggadocio and misstatement of facts to the popular Confederate cavalry leader. Watterson, who was now the editor of the *Mail*, stoutly defended his reporter and interpreted the speech as an authentic expression of Forrest's "brusque, eccentric eloquence." Subsequently Watterson let it be known that a cavalry officer who was present when the speech was delivered had confirmed the accuracy of Carter's report.[111]

[109] *Atlanta Daily Southern Confederacy* as reprinted in *Montgomery Daily Advertiser*, November 21, 1864.

[110] *Montgomery Daily Mail*, November 26, 1864.

[111] *Memphis Daily Appeal* as reprinted in *Montgomery Daily Mail*, November 28, 1864. The *Appeal* had resumed publication of its daily edition in Montgomery on September 20 after emigrating from Atlanta. T. H. Baker, "Refugee Newspaper: The Memphis *Daily Appeal*, 1862-1865," *Journal of Southern History*, xxiv (August 1963), 342.

Carter was with Hood's army of 30,000 when it finally got underway for Nashville on the morning of November 21. Once it got started, the army moved with almost incredible speed over roads which sleet, snow, and rain made extremely treacherous. Seeking to interpose itself between a Union force under Schofield and Stanley and Thomas's smaller command, the Army of Tennessee failed by a narrow margin to win the race with Schofield to Columbia. After Hood executed a flanking movement which apparently enabled him to cut off Schofield's retreat at Spring Hill, one of the greatest of the lost opportunities of the war occurred. Somehow Schofield managed to slip past Hood in the night and check his pursuers at the Battle of Franklin.[112]

The battle took place about eighteen miles south of Nashville on the last day of November 1864. Four more days elapsed before the P.A. provided a brief summary of the action supplied by a clergyman who had just arrived from the army at Tuscumbia. The P.A. report explained that:

"A fight took place on the 30th ult. between our forces and the enemy at Harpeth Creek, near Franklin, in which the enemy were routed from their breastworks, losing 4,000 killed and wounded and 6,000 prisoners."

"Cheatham's corps was principally engaged."

"The enemy are falling back to Murfreesboro."

"Forrest is represented to be at Brentwood, between the enemy and Nashville. . . ."

"Our loss is represented to be about thirty five hundred."[113]

Naturally the Confederate press concluded from this report that Hood had won an important victory and that the Yankee army was in a critical position. What the P.A. dispatch had failed to disclose was the fearful price Hood had paid for his interruption of Schofield's retreat. Hood's actual loss in killed and wounded was at least 2,500 greater than the dispatch had stated, and his loss in officers (twelve generals and no less than fifty-seven regimental commanders) was especially heavy.[114] One of the members of Cheatham's corps who perished in a suicidal charge against the well-fortified position of the

---

[112] S. F. Horn, *The Army of Tennessee* (Norman, Okla., 1941), pp. 386-93.

[113] *Montgomery Daily Advertiser*, December 6, 1864.

[114] Hood's losses of 6,202 killed and wounded were almost one-third of the 20,000 infantry he took into action. Sims Crownover, "The Battle of Franklin," *Tennessee Historical Quarterly*, xiv (December 1955), 316.

enemy was the *Montgomery Mail* correspondent Carter. In a magazine article written long after the war, a woman who was a schoolgirl in 1864 told of seeing young Carter lying dead in his father's house near Franklin and his heartbroken sister bending over him, begging for just one word of recognition.[115]

Hood would have been well advised to recognize that the Tennessee campaign was a failure and fall back to a secure position behind the Duck or Tennessee River. Instead he asked for reinforcements from Kirby Smith's Trans-Mississippi Department, then without waiting for them to join him pushed on to Nashville. Hood's badly outnumbered army was completely routed there in a two-day battle December 15-16. Only the skillful rear-guard protection provided by Forrest's cavalry enabled the forlorn remnants of the defeated army to get across the Tennessee River and find a haven at the army's old camp in Tupelo, Mississippi.[116]

A correspondent of the *Selma Dispatch* was with the army on the eve of the Battle of Nashville, but if he reported the battle for the *Dispatch*, the issue in which the report was published has apparently not been preserved. Practically all the information about the battle that appeared in Southern newspapers afterward was from Northern news sources, a circumstance which did not cause the magnitude of Hood's defeat to be understated. Confederate editors doubted the accuracy of information obtained from such sources and advised their readers to do likewise. Also, the P.A. tried to counteract the impression that such bad news might produce by conjuring up a tale of a fight that was supposed to have occurred a week later, in which the enemy had been badly whipped. Indicative of the sad state of Southern journalism at this time was that on the last day of December the latest Southern reports from Hood's army that had been received by the *Macon Telegraph* did not contain any news later than December 14![117]

During the previous seven months the campaign had taken a heavy toll of the correspondents who had been with the Army of Tennessee

[115] *Montgomery Daily Mail*, December 20, 1864; "Inside the Lines at Franklin [Tenn.]," *Confederate Veteran*, III (March 1895), 72-73.

[116] Hood's Nashville campaign is summarized in Dyer, *Gallant Hood*, pp. 295-303.

[117] *Columbus Daily Times*, December 24, 1864; *Macon Daily Telegraph and Confederate*, May 31, 1864. According to the *Richmond Daily Dispatch* of January 28, 1865, the first Southern newspaper account of the Battle of Nashville was published in the *Memphis Appeal* nearly two months after the battle.

when it left Dalton in May. Carter, Ferris, and Linebaugh were dead; Reid was confined to bed in Charleston and would not be able to leave there until the first of the year;[118] "Shadow" had dropped out of sight after reporting the beginning of Hood's Tennessee campaign; and de Fontaine had gone back to Columbia in discouragement after the Battle of Atlanta. The Confederate Associated Press and the newspapers of Georgia, Alabama, and South Carolina had done by far the major share of the reporting of the campaign. Of the Georgia newspapers the press of Atlanta and Augusta had contributed some of the best reporting the campaign produced.

Yet the reliability of the reporting of the movements of both Johnston and Hood had gradually diminished in direct proportion to the sagging military prospects of their armies and the need, as editors and reporters saw it, to sustain morale. As 1864 drew to a close the better-informed journalists were aware that the situation in the West was alarming, even desperate. But only an exceptional newspaperman like the *Mobile Register*'s Ben Lane Posey was sufficiently realistic and courageous to make public acknowledgment of the fact.

[118] Samuel C. Reid, Diary, entry for January 13, 1865.

CHAPTER 14

Fewer Journals, Fainter Voices

THE YEAR 1864, as the editor of the *Columbus* (Ga.) *Times* frankly admitted, had ended like its predecessor—with disaster to the Confederate cause. The coincidence of the news of the fall of Savannah and of Hood's defeat at Nashville spread gloom within Confederate editorial offices and generally among the Southern people. It must have been difficult for the editor of the *Richmond Dispatch* to compose a New Years Day editorial depicting the bright side of the Confederacy's future. In so doing, he followed the propaganda line of other Southern newspapers, claiming that this struggling new nation actually possessed a larger amount of territory free of enemy occupation than at the beginning of the previous year. Moreover, he asserted, without supplying any evidence for his statement, that the Confederate armed forces were as numerous and formidable as they had been twelve months before. He also professed a belief that the errors Confederate generals had made during the campaigns of 1864 could never occur again. Yet he stopped short of claiming, as a Mississippi editor did, that far from being hopeless, the Confederate cause was "brighter to-day, in reality, than in any period of our history."[1]

Such optimism by these two newspapermen was the more remarkable in view of the critical condition of the Confederate press at the time. All five Richmond dailies were still publishing, but Sherman's march through the most prosperous section of Georgia in November and December 1864 had scattered newspaper presses in every direction and sadly deranged their communication facilities. Particularly alarming was the plight of the newspapers of war-ravaged Mississippi. Reporter Israel Gibbons of the *Mobile Register* had earlier described a Clinton, Mississippi, newspaper as "a mere telegraph slip, published daily for three weeks in each month, and suspended during the fourth, or Yankee

[1] *Columbus Daily Times*, December 28, 1864; *Richmond Daily Dispatch*, January 2, 1865; *Meridian Daily Clarion*, January 28, 1865. The Richmond correspondent of the *Augusta Chronicle* appraised the situation more realistically when he said, "the attitude of affairs is less hopeful than it has been at any time since the fall of Fort Donelson. Still we are very far from the verge of despair." *Augusta Daily Chronicle and Sentinel*, December 28, 1864.

week."[2] He further reported that some of the Mississippi papers published nothing but telegraphic dispatches.

The newspaper situation would have been more favorable if the Southern telegraph system had been in a healthy condition, which it was not. For some time there had been sporadic complaints in the press about interruptions in the telegraph service resulting from rotten posts, poorly attached wires, and the dependence of the telegraph companies on earthenware insulators that were useless in wet weather. By the time Sherman's army left Atlanta in November 1864, the Southern Telegraph Company had almost exhausted its supply of materials. Nearly all the telegraph wire in the Confederacy was already on poles, and much of that was virtually worthless because of rust. Further destruction of vital telegraph lines took place during Sherman's move from Atlanta to Savannah.[3]

There was no telegraphic link between Richmond and Mobile most of the time from December 1864 to April 1865. On one occasion during January 1865 the *Wilmington Journal* announced that the telegraph line was in working order between Wilmington and Augusta, but was out of order or down between Wilmington and Richmond. On the 10th of January the acting superintendent of the Press Association wrote a pleading letter from Richmond to the president of the Southern Telegraph Company. In his letter the P.A. man requested that in the event telegraph service was interrupted for some time at Branchville, South Carolina, telegraph rates on news matter would be reduced by one-half during the period of interruption. Under such circumstances it was hardly strange that a Charlottesville, Virginia newspaper should print a parody that many other newspapers copied. The *Charlottesville Chronicle* quipped:

> The wires that once through Dixie's land
> The 'notes' of 'press' men spread,
> Now on their posts as mutely stand
> As if the *Press* was dead.[4]

[2] *Mobile Daily Advertiser and Register* as reprinted in *Montgomery Daily Mail*, December 6, 1864.

[3] J. C. Andrews, "The Southern Telegraph Company, 1861-1865: A Chapter in the History of Wartime Communication," *Journal of Southern History*, xxx (August 1964), 336, 341.

[4] *Wilmington Daily Journal*, January 24, 1865; John Graeme, Jr. to Dr. Wm. S. Morris, January 10, 1865, Southern Telegraph Co. Papers, Carnegie Library of

The mail service available to Confederate newspapers at the beginning of 1865 was little, if any, better. The mail agents of Postmaster General John H. Reagan were experiencing some of the same difficulties that vexed the telegraph employees. The impairment of railroad communication, which had become serious by the end of 1864, and the wretched condition of the Southern road system were major causes of poor mail service. To make matters worse for the press, the requirements of military operations obliged the Post Office Department to give military messages priority over private correspondence. Thus it took one of George Bagby's letters, written for publication in Richmond in January 1865, almost a month to reach the newspaper office of the *Mobile Register* through ordinary mail channels. The difficulties Bagby met with in discharging the duties of Richmond correspondence for the *Columbus Sun* prompted him to notify the paper on January 28, 1865, "this is the last time I shall write you. Mr. Reagan's mails are fatal to correspondence; Letters six weeks old 'don't pay.' "[5]

Under these circumstances Richmond and other Southern newspapers came to rely on the Southern Express Company for the handling of business correspondence and the newspaper exchanges that provided their main source of news. In February 1865 the *Richmond Examiner* acknowledged its indebtedness to the enterprise and energy of the company that had enabled it to receive late Georgia and Alabama papers which would not have been otherwise available. To provide such service, the Southern Express Company improvised wagon routes to compensate for the lack of railroad facilities in areas devastated by the opposing armies, and constructed its own telegraph lines to link up with the lines of the major telegraph companies.[6]

Colonel Thrasher's Confederate Press Association labored under much the same handicaps as its member newspapers in gathering and disseminating war news. The Press Association had suffered a heavy blow when, in August 1864, four of the five Richmond dailies—the *Dispatch, Enquirer, Examiner,* and *Sentinel*—informed Thrasher of

---

Pittsburgh; *Richmond Daily Whig,* January 26, 1865; *Atlanta Daily Southern Confederacy,* February 7, 1865.

[5] *Mobile Daily Advertiser and Register,* February 9, 1865; *Columbus Daily Sun,* February 14, 1865. On March 30, 1865 the *Mobile Register* lamented, "we are almost entirely dependent upon the telegraph for our news. The mails are few and far between, and almost suspended by the current of events."

[6] *Daily Richmond Examiner,* February 16, 1865: *Richmond Daily Dispatch,* February 14, 1865.

their intention to withdraw from the association at the end of the month. In a letter to President Morris of the Southern Telegraph Company in early October 1864, James W. Lewellen of the *Richmond Dispatch* explained that the cause for this action was the desire of these newspapers to form a Mutual Press Association, of which he, Lewellen, was now the president. Apparently Lewellen and his associates hoped to reduce newsgathering costs by persuading editors in other cities to report news on a reciprocal basis at rates to be agreed on by contract with the telegraph companies. Lewellen commissioned Allegre of the *Richmond Enquirer* to go south as the agent of the new press association to invite the newspaper editors in the Carolinas, Alabama, and Georgia to participate in the new arrangement. Lewellen authorized Allegre to engage reliable reporters in Charleston, Macon, Mobile, and Petersburg to forward news reports to Richmond. The promoters of the new press service informed Morris that they were eager to obtain wire rates on the same terms as Thrasher's Press Association, and urged him to establish uniform rates as low as justice to his stockholders in the difficult times would permit.[7]

The Press Association was said to consist of thirty-eight daily newspapers at the time the four Richmond dissidents broke away. To what extent their defection weakened it is difficult to say, although the president of the P.A. claimed at the end of October 1864 that his association serviced eight more newspapers than it had two months earlier.[8]

There had been complaints for some time in newspapers published south of Richmond of the unwillingness of the Richmond press to cooperate with Thrasher's organization.[9] Yet there seems to be little evi-

[7] J. W. Lewellen to W. S. Morris, October 5, 1864; John Graeme, Jr. to Dr. W. S. Morris, August 30, 1864; Wm. S. Morris to John Graeme, Jr., August 30, 1864; John Graeme, Jr. to Wm. S. Morris, August 31, 1864; J. B. Tree to W. S. Morris, October 5, 1864; W. S. Morris to John Graeme, Jr., October 26, 1864, Southern Telegraph Co. Papers; *Daily Richmond Enquirer*, September 20, 1864. In his October 5, 1864 message to Morris, Tree, the superintendent of the telegraph company, proposed a rate of $8.80 for the first ten words of press reports sent by wire from Mobile to Richmond and 52 cents for each additional word.

[8] W. G. Clark to John Graeme, Jr., October 25, 1864; John Graeme, Jr. to Dr. W. S. Morris, October 26, 1864, Southern Telegraph Co. Papers. The *Richmond Whig*, which had not withdrawn from the P.A., inserted a card on September 5, 1864 boasting that the reports furnished by the agents of the association at Petersburg, Charleston, Macon, Mobile, Senatobia, Clinton, etc. were now published exclusively in the *Whig*.

[9] See e.g. *Macon Daily Telegraph*, October 23, 1863; *Atlanta Daily Intelligencer*, October 30, 1864. In a letter to Vice President Stephens on April 28, 1864, Georgia

dence of success on the part of the Lewellen group in detaching newspapers outside of Richmond from the parent group.

Whether the withdrawal of the Richmond papers from the P.A. had anything to do with Thrasher's decision to leave Macon on September 5, 1864 to visit the Trans-Mississippi area is unclear. Thrasher did not return from Texas to Georgia until nearly the end of January 1865. In his absence Graeme, the Richmond agent of the P.A., supervised its business affairs.[10] Another important figure in Thrasher's news organization was a former editor of the *Atlanta Register*, John Hatcher. At the end of January the Press Association sent Hatcher west to Senatobia to report news from Memphis and elsewhere in the North from this important listening post.[11]

In spite of the optimism shown by the *Richmond Dispatch* and a few other Southern newspapers, the Confederate press was unable to conceal the low ebb to which public morale in the South had fallen in the first weeks of January 1865. During a month-long trip from Richmond to Augusta, Peter Alexander encountered a "deplorable state of dissatisfaction, despondency and faction" all along the route. In conversations with both friends and opponents of the Davis administration, Alexander was appalled by their outspoken criticism of public mismanagement. In bringing these facts to light Alexander expressed hope that the authorities in Richmond would take into account the popular discontent with their policies that he was reporting and that the press would moderate its criticism of the government.[12]

The Southern press was both heartsick and confused. At the beginning of January the pro-administration *Richmond Enquirer* announced editorially that it was prepared to urge upon its readers the abolition of Negro slavery throughout the Confederacy if the British and French governments would enter into a treaty with the Confederate States and recognize their independence. The *Enquirer's* trial balloon failed to win

---

newspaperman J. Henly Smith declared, "I am astonished at the Richmond Press. They regard themselves as metropolitan, and ignore anything from any other quarter of the Confederacy. They have all the while been an impediment in the proper working [of] the Press Association." Alexander H. Stephens Papers, Library of Congress.

[10] *Houston Tri-Weekly Telegraph*, December 12, 1864; *Mobile Daily Advertiser and Register*, February 1, 1865.

[11] *Montgomery Daily Mail*, January 28, 1865. Hatcher apparently doubled as the Senatobia telegraphic correspondent "Scantling" of the *Mobile Register*.

[12] *Richmond Daily Dispatch*, February 1, 1865; *Mobile Daily Advertiser and Register*, February 8, 1865.

the support of other newspapers, and the *Montgomery Advertiser* ridiculed the Associated Press for distributing such nonsense in the form of news reports.[13] Another wavering editor was the Benjamin F. Dill whose *Memphis Daily Appeal* was still very much alive in Montgomery. In a letter to Vice President Stephens, Dill asked the vice president to tell him what he thought the real situation was. Apparently Dill did not have complete confidence in the judgment of his Richmond correspondent and was seeking guidance from a public figure who was not identified with the Davis clique. In his letter to Stephens, Dill enclosed a clipping from the January 26 issue of the *Appeal*, in which the newspaper had called on President Davis and the Confederate Congress to make every effort to win peace on honorable terms. Dill professed his belief that there were few "submissionists" even now, but he admitted that public opinion, insofar as he could measure it, reflected "an increased desire for the return of peace."[14]

There were now indications of peace sentiment and war weariness in much of the Confederate press. On January 10, 1865 the editor of the *Mobile Register* avowed, "at no time since the commencement of the war has the popular feeling of despondency as to its result been so general and so deep as at the present moment." In Macon a correspondent of the *Register* discerned a spirit of "discontent and reconstruction" among prominent citizens so subversive of law and order that the reporter thought they merited the epithet of "traitors." When Alexander passed through Charleston on his way home to Georgia, he marvelled at the "querulous and despondent" attitude of the men who had been the most fanatical advocates of secession in 1860. He did not think the Charlestonians were ready to surrender—yet—but he described their city as abounding with "croakers," fault-finders, and speculators who were more intent on salvaging the large fortunes they had accumulated during the war than on fighting for Southern independence.[15]

[13] *Daily Richmond Enquirer*, December 29, 1864; *Montgomery Daily Advertiser*, January 3, 1865. The *Wilmington Journal* of January 18, 1865 stated that the *Enquirer*'s proposal, "so far as we have seen," had not received the support of a single paper in the Confederacy.

[14] Benjamin F. Dill to Alexander H. Stephens, January 26, 1865, Stephens Papers. For a similar inquiry addressed to General Johnston by Senator Wigfall, see Louis T. Wigfall to General Joseph E. Johnston, March 4, 1865, Johnston Papers, Huntington Library.

[15] *Mobile Daily Advertiser and Register*, January 13, 24, 1865; *Richmond Daily Dispatch*, January 20, 1865. Confederate General James Conner told a friend in a letter dated February 2, 1865 of having visited Charleston two weeks before

Perhaps Alexander would have been astonished at the extent to which the craving for peace was now evident in Richmond itself. It was well known there that desertions from Lee's army had reached serious proportions; a series of futile attempts by Congress to wrest control of military policy and civil affairs from the president reflected the discontent of the peace agitators. On the floor of Congress, Senator Wigfall of Texas, whom Bagby credited with being the "head and front of the whole movement," denounced Davis without mercy in a number of philippics which most of the Richmond newspapers dared not print.[16]

In an attempt to intimidate the opposition the pro-administration *Richmond Sentinel* published an article accusing certain unnamed congressmen of introducing a resolution in secret session, to "open irregular intercourse through commissioners with Lincoln for peace. . . ." Perhaps the *Sentinel* article also was motivated by the knowledge that the elder statesman Francis P. Blair had just arrived in Richmond from the North to explore peace possibilities on his own initiative. More than one congressman rose in the Confederate House of Representatives to denounce the insulting language of the newspaper accusation. One of them, Congressman W. R. Smith of Alabama, threatened to resign his seat in protest, but reconsidered after the Davis government dispatched a peace commission to Hampton Roads to confer with President Lincoln and Secretary of State Seward.[17]

The Richmond press was suspicious of these negotiations. When the commissioners returned empty-handed on February 5, the Richmond editors unleashed all their fury on the peace movement, calling on their readers to back the president. In an effort to utilize reviving army morale to sustain civilian morale, the Richmond newspapers printed daily under the standing head "Spirit of the Army" the text of resolutions reaffirming loyalty to the cause adopted by various regiments in

---

and of it being "blue, fearfully demoralized, and they had reason for their fears for I perceived very clearly that the city was being evacuated. . . . But something, perhaps the fall of Fort Fisher, changed the policy, and orders were telegraphed to defend Charleston to the last." James Conner, *Letters of General James Conner* (Columbia, S.C., 1933), p. 169.

16 E. A. Pollard, *The Last Year of the War*, as reprinted in W. B. Hesseltine, ed., *The Tragic Conflict: The Civil War and Reconstruction* (New York, 1962), p. 375; *Mobile Daily Advertiser and Register*, February 12, 1865.

17 *Richmond Daily Sentinel*, January 14, 1865; *Richmond Daily Dispatch*, January 18, 1865; *Mobile Daily Advertiser and Register*, February 3, 1865.

Lee's army and submitted to the press.[18] A number of papers also re-printed a series of articles which the returned prisoner, E. A. Pollard, contributed to the *Richmond Examiner*, setting forth his observations of war weariness in the North. Pollard contended that the Yankees were at the end of their string in the recruitment of soldiers, that Grant's army was seventy-five percent Negro, that the North faced bankruptcy within another year because of war expenditures, and that the outcome of the war depended on whether the South possessed the determination to hold out.[19]

In the Lower South, as well as in Richmond, the press seemed to have regained its courage by the beginning of February, and was mak-ing vigorous efforts to restore public confidence. The *Mobile Register* expressed assurance in an editorial entitled "Stand Like an Anvil" that the current despondency of its fellow citizens would pass and be suc-ceeded by a heroic, perhaps even desperate, frame of mind: "We are frequently asked on the street, 'What do you think of the present situa-tion?' Our reply is, 'You will see in the morning paper what we think.' 'But your private opinion?—you write, of course, for public effect and public good.' We never write except what we think, although it would be absurd to say we write all we think."[20]

Not content with reassuring his readers in this fashion, Editor For-syth took to task those newspapers that seemed to be lending covert support to the peace movement. When a correspondent of the *Mont-gomery Mail* reported that four-fifths of the people in his section of Alabama preferred peace to ruination, and requested the *Mail* to sup-port a peace convention, Forsyth denounced the *Mail* for publishing these "dastardly sentiments." They were unworthy, he declared, of the senior editor of that newspaper, who was away serving his country in its armed forces. Forsyth also levelled scorn at the renegade editor of the *Augusta Chronicle and Sentinel*, N. S. Morse, whom he pronounced "an enemy to Confederate independence within its beleaguered

[18] J. C. Andrews, "The Confederate Press and Public Morale," *Journal of South-ern History*, XXXII (November 1966), 461. According to Richmond correspondent Bagby, the Fredericksburg artillery led the way in the parade of resolutions by army commands, followed by the 53d Virginia Infantry. *Mobile Daily Advertiser and Register*, February 18, 1865.

[19] *Daily Richmond Examiner*, January 16, 1865. Pollard's observations were the product of eight months' captivity in the North, during which as a paroled prisoner he had found the opportunity to visit New York, Boston, Brooklyn, Baltimore, and other Northern cities.

[20] *Mobile Daily Advertiser and Register*, February 7, 1865.

walls—a viper in our bosom who should be driven north. . . ." The *Register* editor signified his willingness to fight a duel with Morse if there was no Georgian on her soil to protect her honor from this "audacious Yankee." When one of a series of mass meetings to drum up support for the war was held in Mobile on February 14, 1865, Forsyth presided over the meeting.[21]

From neighboring Mississippi, where he was attached to Forrest's command, former editor G. W. Adair undertook to act as a special correspondent for the *Columbus Sun* to publicize the high spirits of Forrest's cavalrymen. Adair reported that although the rain and mud had been very severe on their horses, all of Forrest's men had been home, obtained new clothes, new boots, and fresh animals, and were now ready for another battle. Yet he admitted that the Mississippi legislature "is a poor concern—made up of old men and lay outs in the main. I have recently spent some days at Columbus [Mississippi]— heard C. K. Marshall make a long patriotic and eloquent speech—Orr, a long croaking gloomy Joe Brown harangue—then Mr. Phelan, an able review of the war and its history—he was, I thought candid and fair, though on some points too much the eulogist of President Davis. . . ."[22] Perhaps Adair's experience in writing editorials for the *Atlanta Confederacy* was nearer to his heart than performing the duties of a war correspondent. At any rate, the remainder of his letter—in which he appealed to his old Georgia friends to "use every nigger, cur dog, alligator, pole cat, catamount, or anything else than can damage or defeat our common enemy"—sounds more like an attempt at a morale-building editorial than a sober attempt to report the war in northeastern Mississippi.

On his way home from Virginia in January Alexander had reported for the *Mobile Register* and the *Richmond Dispatch* the last campaign of his career as a war correspondent. The setting was the mouth of the Cape Fear River in southeastern North Carolina, where Fort Fisher stood guard over the approach to Wilmington from the sea. In a letter to the *Register* on December 19, 1864 Alexander described the excitement in Wilmington which the departure of a joint Union army-navy expedition from Fort Monroe had created. Later he reported the arrival off New Inlet, at the entrance of Wilmington Harbor, of the

---

[21] *Ibid.*, February 17, 18, 1865; Associated Press report in *Augusta Daily Chronicle and Sentinel*, February 20, 1865.

[22] *Columbus Daily Sun*, March 22, 23, 1865.

Yankee fleet under Admiral Porter, and pictured the bombardment of Fort Fisher on the morning of December 24. His estimate of the size of the enemy fleet, at fifty-nine war vessels carrying 583 guns, was probably slightly in excess of the actual number. Still, the bombardment was evidently of considerable magnitude, for Alexander, who was not given to extravagant language, reported that "such a rain of shot and shell never before fell upon any spot of earth since gunpowder was invented." Yet the defenders were heartened by the comparatively small damage the heavy shelling did to the fort. By December 27 Alexander was in a position to notify the *Dispatch* that a landing attempt by Ben Butler's ground forces had failed and that the landing party had returned to their transports. Understandably the reporter concluded that the mammoth sand fort was probably "the strongest earthwork in the world."[23]

Following the withdrawal of the Federal fleet, Editor Fulton of the *Wilmington Journal* accompanied a party of his fellow townsmen on a visit to Fort Fisher which General Bragg had arranged. The *Journal* editor concluded that the enemy's gunfire had inflicted considerable damage on the fort, although the greater part of its structure was "perfectly intact." From the ramparts of Fort Fisher Fulton could see no other signs of the attacking force than a half-dozen blockading units out at sea and the wrecks of a number of blockade-runners and Federal ships that had been sunk by gunfire from the fort. Fulton agreed with Alexander that the naval bombardment of Fisher had been the heaviest of the war, with over twenty thousand shells having been directed at the fort.[24]

It soon became evident to Col. William Lamb, the commander of Fort Fisher, that the Yankee armada had retired from the scene simply to retool and change army commanders. When it renewed the attack within a fortnight, the only Southern newspaperman who seems to have been present was a *Richmond Dispatch* correspondent identified only as "C." Once more there was a terrific naval bombardment and a landing operation, which this time was successful after bitter fighting. The *Dispatch* correspondent told of watching during the late afternoon of

---

[23] *Mobile Daily Advertiser and Register*, January 4, 6, 7, 12, 1865; *Richmond Daily Dispatch*, January 2, 4, 6, 1865. The first bombardment of Fort Fisher is briefly described in J. G. Barrett, *The Civil War in North Carolina* (Chapel Hill, 1963), pp. 265-70.

[24] *Wilmington Daily Journal*, January 6, 1865.

January 15 the opposing sides fighting hand-to-hand. "I see through the glass, four flags waving from the parapet; three are Yankee flags, one Confederate—I see one torn down, two men are grappling the second; it is down; the third is in the dust, and only the Confederate now floats on the ramparts." Later that night, as the situation changed, he had to report that the fort had surrendered. He added sadly, "All is still and silent as death; the never-ceasing roar of the ocean is all that is heard."[25]

However much the press tried to soften the blow, the news of the fall of Fort Fisher spread dismay throughout North Carolina, where it was realized that the Confederacy had lost its only remaining port. There were grumblings that Bragg had mismanaged the defense of the fort; when Wilmington capitulated more than a month later, the Southern press very largely ignored the surrender. The few details that ultimately appeared in the *Richmond Dispatch* were copied from a Raleigh newspaper.[26]

At the beginning of February 1865 the dread news appeared in the newspapers that Sherman was on the march again, moving north from Savannah into South Carolina. The *Columbia Carolinian* warned its readers, "Sherman has resumed his advance. It is plain that he, at least, is not attending more than he ought to the rumors of peace fluttering in the atmosphere."[27] Augusta and Charleston stiffened to meet the onslaught, but Sherman's army passed between heading for the capital of South Carolina. One of the few journalists who had divined Sherman's target ahead of time was the editor of Columbia's leading newspaper. Not quite a month before Sherman's army appeared there, de Fontaine had published an editorial in the *Carolinian* reproving the citizens for their lethargy in the face of the danger confronting them. If Charleston could be designated the "cradle of secession," he argued, then Columbia, where the convention that took South Carolina out of the Union first met, could be regarded as the very couch of secession's birth. If this were so, he continued, this fact in itself made Columbia peculiarly obnoxious to the enemy and placed its citizens under a special obligation to defend their city.[28]

---

[25] *Richmond Daily Dispatch*, January 24, 1865.
[26] *Ibid.*, March 6, 1865.
[27] *Columbia Tri-Weekly Carolinian*, February 2, 1865.
[28] T. H. Williams, *P.G.T. Beauregard, Napoleon in Gray* (Baton Rouge, 1954), p. 250; *Columbia Daily South Carolinian*, January 19, 1865.

Certainly there was little Jefferson Davis could do to honor his pledge to protect South Carolina. Hardee was at Charleston with a garrison which did not exceed fifteen thousand troops. Columbia was defended by a small force of state militia, a few thousand cavalry under Wheeler and Wade Hampton, and Stevenson's infantry division of 2,600. For the time being, no help could be expected from what was left of the Army of Tennessee.[29]

In the meantime the Army of Tennessee had undergone a change of commanders. The dejected Hood had submitted his resignation before Editor Forsyth wrote to Bragg from Mobile on January 17, admonishing him that Hood's army was not "worth the value of a regiment" if the Texan were retained as its commander. Forsyth informed Bragg that the army had lost confidence in Hood and that its voice was unanimous and earnest for the reinstatement of Johnston in command.[30]

One of Forsyth's correspondents was in Tupelo when the resignation of Hood was made public. *Register* reporter "Shadow" described a speech Hood made to a serenading party that night, in which the general complained about his bad press ever since he assumed command of that army in July 1864. "Shadow" denied that the press opposition to the removal of Johnston had been aimed at Hood. He maintained that the newspapers which had aroused Hood's ire had simply expressed the opinions of the army and the "people," and that the numerous missives which Hood thought were directed at him were actually aimed at the authorities in Richmond. "Shadow" made clear, however, that he did not approve of Hood's disparagement of the courage of his soldiers at the Battle of Nashville.[31]

Beauregard, the departmental commander, placed Lt.Gen. Richard Taylor, rather than Johnston, in temporary command of Hood's army, a portion of which headed east at the end of January to assist in the defense of Augusta and Charleston. Meanwhile editors and reporters presented conflicting views of the morale and physical condition of the unfortunate western army. In Columbus, Georgia, on February 11,

[29] M. W. Wellman, *Giant in Gray, a Biography of Wade Hampton of South Carolina* (New York, 1949) p. 167; S. F. Horn, *The Army of Tennessee* (Norman Okla., 1953), p. 423.

[30] J. P. Dyer, *The Gallant Hood* (Indianapolis, 1950), p. 304; *O.R.* (Army) Ser. I, vol. lii, pt. 2, pp. 808-809; John Forsyth to Braxton Bragg, January 17, 1865, Bragg Papers, Western Reserve Historical Society.

[31] *Mobile Daily Advertiser and Register*, January 22, 1865.

a correspondent of the *Mobile Register* told of having mingled freely with the men in the ranks during the previous three weeks and of having plied them with numerous questions about their willingness to keep on fighting. The reporter, who styled himself "Cousin Nourma," declared that while the peace negotiations were going on, the soldiers were very cheerful and hoped for peace, "with an earnestness that became almost painful with anticipation." A reversal of sentiment had taken place, however, after the failure of the Hampton Roads peace conference; the army was now "more firm and determined than ever."[32]

"Cousin Nourma" did not claim that the condition of the army was everything that could be asked for. When he arrived in Augusta nine days later he was shocked at the small numbers and ragged appearance of Cheatham's old division, with whom he had campaigned in 1863 and 1864. Less than a thousand were left out of the thousands who had fought at Shiloh. Many companies contained only one man, and in some none was left. Another *Mobile Register* reporter revealed the large incidence of straggling all along the route of the army through Georgia, in which Alabama and Florida troops had participated with the Georgians. Yet he defended the misbehavior of the stragglers by alleging that they only intended to take a short furlough and then return to their commands.

The reporter declared that many of the gaps in the army could be partially filled if something could be done to alter the diversion of manpower into post duty and supply corps work. He charged that over 150 district offices in the city of Augusta alone were employing several thousand able-bodied men in clerical positions, and that influence of all kinds was being applied to keep these individuals from being transferred to combat assignments.[33]

De Fontaine's prediction that the citizens of Columbia would be aroused from their beds some morning by the whoop and clatter of Kilpatrick's cavalry was fulfilled in mid-February in a manner which perhaps even he did not anticipate. On February 12 Sherman's army reached Orangeburg, about 48 miles from Columbia, and burned most

[32] Williams, *Beauregard*, p. 249; *Mobile Daily Advertiser and Register*, February 16, 1865.

[33] Miscellaneous Scrapbooks, Mississippi State Department of Archives and History; *Mobile Daily Advertiser and Register*, February 21, March 2, 1865. For editorial criticism of the "doleful wail" of newspaper correspondents about the tattered appearance of the Army of Tennessee see *Augusta Daily Constitutionalist*, February 24, 1865.

of it.[34] Columbia, normally a town of about eight thousand, was packed with refugees; hope struggled with fear in the minds of its citizens, a large proportion of whom were women, children, and elderly men. When it became apparent that the horde of Union marchers and "bummers" was *not* going to veer off to the northeast and was heading straight for Columbia, anxious Columbians clutched at the vain hope that Cheatham's corps of the Army of Tennessee would come to their rescue.

By Tuesday the 14th the authorities had decided to move the public stores to Charlotte, North Carolina, a hundred miles north. On Wednesday the sound of Sherman's guns could be heard distinctly in Columbia. Thursday the Northern army began to bombard the city, directing its fire primarily at the new state house and the arsenal. On the same day Beauregard notified Lee of his intention to evacuate Columbia,[35] and Confederate troops began marching out on the road to Charlotte. An accidental explosion of ammunition at the railroad depot provided the backdrop for Mayor T. J. Goodwyn's flag-of-truce mission to surrender the city at about nine o'clock the next morning. The first Union troops entered the city along the Main Street road about eleven o'clock Friday morning, February 14; within two hours Sherman and his staff rode in.

The next morning the *Richmond Dispatch* published the news that Columbia had fallen, in the form of an official dispatch to the War Department from General Beauregard. The dispatch stated simply that Sherman had occupied Columbia. The first Confederate Associated Press news report of the event, which appeared in print four days later, added little to the information supplied by Beauregard. It said that Sherman's army "of 50,000" advancing in the direction of Charlotte had occupied Columbia for a short time. It gave no indication of the fact, which another Press Association dispatch reported twenty-four hours later, that much of Columbia had been destroyed by a disastrous fire after the enemy entered the town. The second P.A. dispatch, evidently prepared in Augusta, accused the enemy of burning both sides of Main Street, "the whole length," along with some other buildings.

On February 27, exactly one week after Sherman's army left Columbia on its way to Fayetteville, the Augusta office of the P.A. issued a third press dispatch. It claimed that Sherman's army was drunk on the day it entered Columbia and while in that condition "sacked and

---

[34] B.H.L. Hart, *Sherman, Soldier, Realist, American* (New York, 1958), p. 364.
[35] Williams, *Beauregard*, p. 251.

pillaged Columbia, burning the entire length of Main Street and Cottontown, only one house remaining." This dispatch admitted that after the damage had been done, Sherman had ordered the pillagers and bummers shot when caught, that he had left behind, along with his sick and wounded, two hundred cattle, and had provided the citizens with arms to protect themselves against Negroes.[36]

A fourth (undated) P.A. report, published in one of the Augusta papers March 1, was probably intended as official propaganda. Prefaced by the designation of having been prepared by "the Agent of the Associated Press" and of having been "officially approved," it declared: "The evidence of the terrible diabolism perpetrated by the Yankees in Columbia continues to accumulate. The cries of ten thousand hungry, starving and houseless women and children appeal to the sympathies and benevolence of our people. The horrors that attended the destruction of Atlanta were ten times repeated at Columbia."[37] This fourth and last P.A. news report set the tone for most of the stories about the disaster that were published in the Confederate press, although some attempts were made, especially at first, to report the event with some measure of objectivity.

No less than six detailed reports of the burning of Columbia, of varying scope, and length, appeared in five different Southern newspapers. The first was printed in the *Augusta Chronicle and Sentinel*, a newspaper that had often been accused of disloyal sentiments, on Tuesday, February 28. This story evidently was written in the editorial office on the basis of information supplied by an eyewitness named Eagan who left Columbia five days after the fire and walked the entire seventy-five miles to Augusta.[38] In addition to a second account in this same newspaper, written from personal observation by a correspondent signed "Observer," Charles D. Kirk, the Augusta correspondent of the *Memphis Appeal*, and de Fontaine contributed stories treating different aspects of the disaster. Kirk's account, published in the *Augusta Constitutionalist*, was based on information from eyewitnesses with whom he talked in Columbia after Sherman's army had left the city. De Fontaine's story of the preliminaries of the occupation, an eyewitness ac-

[36] *Richmond Daily Dispatch*, February 18, 1865; *Mobile Daily Advertiser and Register*, February 23, 24, March 1, 1865. Eighty-four out of 124 city blocks were burned. D. D. Wallace, *South Carolina, A Short History* (Chapel Hill, 1951), pp. 550-54.

[37] *Augusta Daily Chronicle and Sentinel*, March 1, 1865.

[38] *Ibid.*, February 28, 1865.

count published in the *Richmond Whig*, unfortunately did not cover the events after de Fontaine's departure from the city on Friday morning. The *Columbia Carolinian* of March 7, 1865 also published a report of the burning of Columbia, contributed by "a gentleman direct from Columbia."[39] A sixth newspaper account, and the most extensive, appeared in the *Columbia Phoenix*, a newspaper established after the fire by the poet William Gilmore Simms. With the help of a staff member of the *Columbia Carolinian* named Julian Selby, Simms improvised a press from materials which had escaped destruction in the newspaper plant, to enable him to present his own version of the atrocities he claimed to have witnessed.[40]

Eagan's account was the only one of the six that presented a favorable view of the conduct of the Northern troops. Whereas it maintained that few, if any, private residences were entered by enemy soldiers, "Observer" charged that Sherman's troops began to pillage, plunder, and sack private dwellings indiscriminately as soon as they entered town. Simms' impassioned narrative in the *Phoenix* described in detail the stealing of watches and other robberies both of men and women, and of Negro and white by soldiers without interference from their officers. Simms told about interference by these soldiers with the attempts of the local firemen to extinguish fires, which in some cases were set by soldiers. He asserted that in "hundreds of cases" the incendiaries were "sober soldiers," and avowed his conviction that the destruction of the city had been deliberately planned by an army that was under perfect discipline.[41]

Kirk's report of the destruction of Columbia was probably derived in part from Simms, whom he met there during his reporting assignment to the ruined capital. On Kirk's way to Columbia from Augusta, he travelled in part the route followed by Sherman's army, making note

[39] This account was reprinted in the *Daily Richmond Examiner* of March 10, 1865.

[40] Julian Selby, *Memorabilia and Anecdotal Reminiscences of Columbia, South Carolina* (Columbia, 1905), pp. 101-103. A reporter who met Simms in Columbia after the fire stated that this "Nestor of our Southern literature . . . was here during the scenes of conflagration and pillage, and may yet find time to weave into an historical narrative his experience during these days of suffering and honor." *Augusta Daily Constitutionalist*, March 12, 1865.

[41] The first installment of Simms' account of "The Capture, Sack, and Destruction of Columbia" appeared in the first (March 21, 1865) issue of the *Columbia Phoenix*, a tri-weekly, and ran consecutively through the issues of March 23-April 8, 1865. See also W. P. Trent, *William Gilmore Simms* (Boston, 1896), pp. 280-83.

that practically every dwelling along the way had been burned, presumably by the invader. Kirk's newspaper letters conveyed much the same notion of what had happened in Columbia as Simms'. Kirk told stories, evidently related to him by the citizens, of Sherman giving his troops thirty-six hours of license to pillage, and of soldiers invading "the sanctity of ladies' chambers," cutting the hoses of the firemen, and firing the town indiscriminately.[42]

In the second of Kirk's series of three letters to the *Constitutionalist* he reported that several hundred Yankee sympathizers had left Columbia with Sherman's army to accompany it on its northward march. Among the camp followers was a "fast and fascinating" young lady named Mary Boozer, who was supposed to have secreted in her mother's house in Columbia an escaped Yankee prisoner named Captain Sadlee. The captain was married to Miss Boozer after Sherman's arrival, allegedly stole a carriage and took his wife away with him in it for their honeymoon. The *Augusta Constitutionalist* later reported as "common gossip" that Miss Boozer and her mother had returned to Columbia in an oxcart after discovering that her new husband was already married and after Mary had ended a short-lived affair with the Yankee cavalry leader Judson Kilpatrick.[43]

One of the most interesting items in de Fontaine's Columbia story was his revelation of the misconduct of Wheeler's cavalry at the expense of their own countrymen. De Fontaine revealed that on the day before Sherman's army entered the city, a party of Wheeler's cavalry, accompanied by their officers, galloped into town, tied their horses, and systematically broke into the stores along Main Street and robbed them of their contents. There were attempts by the provost marshal, General Hampton, and others, to stop the looting, "but the valiant raiders still swarmed like locusts, and to-day a hundred miles from Columbia you may still see men smoking the cigars and wearing on their saddles the elegant cloths stolen from the merchants of that city."[44]

The *Augusta Chronicle* correspondent "Observer" was very much impressed by the youth and vigor of the Western troops in Sherman's

[42] *Augusta Daily Constitutionalist*, March 9, 13, 1865. Kirk's opinion was that "Columbia was destroyed and pillaged, if not by Sherman's positive order, by his exulting connivance."

[43] *Ibid.*, March 10, April 5, 1865; Barrett, *Civil War in North Carolina*, p. 307n; J. G. Barrett, *Sherman's March through the Carolinas* (Chapel Hill, 1956), pp. 93, 97.

[44] *Richmond Daily Whig*, March 7, 1865.

army. "It will not do," he warned his readers, "to delude ourselves with the hope of his [Sherman's] easy overthrow; his army is like a sharp weapon in his hand, easily handled for offense or defense. They have the most unbounded confidence in their leader and express themselves as certain to go wherever he directs."[45]

It is difficult to determine how truthful the Confederate reporting of the burning of Columbia was. The question of who was responsible is the subject of a historical controversy that has never been satisfactorily resolved. The biographer of Wade Hampton contends that Sherman lied in his official report when he accused Hampton of responsibility for the fire, and attempts to pin the blame on the Federal army. On the other hand, the historian James Ford Rhodes, after a careful investigation of conflicting testimony, cleared Sherman of complicity in the burning and distributed the blame among a mob of convicts, escaped Union prisoners, stragglers and "bummers," drunken soldiers and Negroes, and Union soldiers who were eager to take revenge on South Carolina. According to Rhodes, Union corps commanders O. O. Howard and John A. Logan labored earnestly during the night of February 17-18 to prevent the spread of fire, and by the next morning had it under control. They suppressed a riot in the process, killing two men, wounding 30, and arresting 370.[46]

Hardee evacuated Charleston on the same day Sherman entered Columbia, but so concerned was the Confederacy with the developments relating to Columbia that the loss of Charleston went largely unnoticed in the Southern press. The *Richmond Dispatch* did say that Charleston was little better than a deserted ruin when the enemy took possession,[47] and an Associated Press dispatch published in the *Augusta Chronicle* on February 26 added the spiteful note, "Charleston is garrisoned by negro troops." It was almost a month after the fall of Charleston before the Augusta correspondent of the *Mobile Register* learned from an officer who had been on duty in Fort Moultrie that a large number of Charleston's original secessionists had remained in the city and had

[45] *Augusta Daily Chronicle and Sentinel*, March 8, 1865.

[46] Wellman, *Hampton*, p. 168; J. F. Rhodes, *Historical Essays* (New York, 1909), pp. 310-13. In his *Never Call Retreat* (New York, 1965), p. 434, the historian Bruce Catton states flatly that Sherman did not order Columbia burned, but conjectures that as the capital of the first state to secede, "Columbia was certain to go up in flames" as soon as Sherman's soldiers arrived there.

[47] *Richmond Daily Dispatch*, February 21, 1865.

taken the oath of allegiance to the United States government.[48] One Charlestonian who did not remain was the editor of the *Charleston Mercury*, Robert Barnwell Rhett, Jr. Rhett suspended publication on February 11 and moved his newspaper plant into the interior before Charleston fell. He seems to have given some thought to resuming publication in Augusta, but apparently his press and other equipment were destroyed, along with the rolling stock of the South Carolina railroads, at the railroad junction in Charlotte, and he ultimately took refuge in Alabama. The rival *Courier* remained in Charleston and continued publication under Federal control.[49]

One of the Augusta newspapers published an Associated Press dispatch on February 23, stating that Sherman was advancing on Charlotte with a force of fifty thousand men, destroying the railroads and other property along his route, and leaving a wide trail of destruction. The belief that Sherman was heading for Charlotte may have influenced Johnston to arrive there about this time, at Lee's request, to take charge of the defense of the Carolinas.[50] De Fontaine, having moved to Charlotte to resume publication of his *Columbia Carolinian*, apparently had a better knowledge of Sherman's movements than Augusta had. Acting as the local representative of the Associated Press, de Fontaine wired the Press Association from Charlotte on February 24. He reported that the enemy was moving in the direction of Camden, Cheraw, and Fayetteville, and that it was a raiding party, not the main column of the enemy, that was menacing Charlotte.[51]

From the viewpoint of both Johnston and de Fontaine, Sherman's decision to bypass Charlotte was fortunate. The troops Johnston had with which to check Sherman's advance were widely scattered. Hardee,

[48] *Augusta Daily Chronicle and Sentinel*, February 26, 1865; *Mobile Daily Advertiser and Register*, April 1, 1865.

[49] *Wilmington Daily Journal*, February 13, 1865; *Daily Richmond Examiner*, March 3, 1865; *Columbus Daily Sun*, March 7, April 4, 1865; *Mobile Daily Advertiser and Register*, March 7, 1865; *Augusta Daily Constitutionalist*, April 4, 1865; William Porcher Miles to Col. R. B. Rhett, March 22, 1865, Robert Barnwell Rhett Papers, Huntsville, Ala.

[50] *Augusta Daily Chronicle and Sentinel*, February 23, 1865. Davis had determined that as long as he was president, Johnston should never again hold command of Confederate troops. He did not think it advisable to refuse, however, when Lee, as the newly appointed General-in-Chief, asked specifically that Johnston be recalled to duty. G. E. Govan and J. W. Livingood, *A Different Valor, The Story of Joseph E. Johnston, C.S.A.* (Indianapolis, 1956), pp. 345-48; Hudson Strode, *Jefferson Davis, Tragic Hero* (New York, 1964), pp. 149-50.

[51] Robert E. Lee, Official Telegrams, Misc. MSS., Duke University.

with the remnants of the Charleston garrison, was near Fayetteville; the troops Bragg had extricated from Wilmington were near Goldsboro in eastern North Carolina; and what was left of the Army of Tennessee was strung out along the road in South Carolina marching slowly toward Charlotte.[52]

A correspondent of the *Mobile Register* with Cheatham's corps described the picturesque features and the discomforts of the march. He admitted that there was considerable enmity between the infantry and cavalry branches of the service. "The cavalry in passing the infantry at rest must take [to] the woods and fields, as the latter will not give an inch of the road. The cavalry call the infantry the 'web-feet' and the former invariably get 'chawed' (in army slang) whenever they attempt to pass a column of infantry." The *Register* reporter also praised the excellent marching of his outfit, and described the amusing expedients to keep up the spirits of the men and prevent straggling. Whenever the march had been prolonged too far without rest, the cry of "Rest" would resound along the column until the general acceded. Also, the appearance of women along the roadside or at their front gates would occasion the cry of "Eyes Right" or "Eyes Left." The correspondent was impressed by the night crossing of the Saluda River, which was brilliantly lighted by large fire on both banks of the stream. The sight of the loaded flatboat traversing the dark waters of the Saluda reminded him of the pictures of Washington crossing the Delaware.[53]

On February 25 Cheatham's corps was about halfway between Columbia and Charlotte. By this time the War Department had subjected to censorship all news reports from that area, requesting the press not to publish anything about the movements of Sherman's or Johnston's armies.[54] As a result, for the next three weeks there was almost a complete news blackout from the Carolinas.

[52] Govan and Livingood, *Johnston*, pp. 349-50; Horn, *Army of Tennessee*, p. 424.

[53] *Mobile Daily Advertiser and Register*, March 10, 22, 1865. The only identification of this reporter were the initials "A.D.M." attached to his correspondence.

[54] The *Daily Richmond Examiner* of February 25, 1865 stated: "We have been officially and properly requested to take no notice, for the present, of military affairs in the Carolinas; and to make our compliance good, we omit all allusions to these from our reports. Our readers will readily appreciate the motives of this reticence." See also *Lynchburg Daily Republican*, February 28, 1865 for an indication that it was General Lee who had requested this action. Lee's distrust of

Sherman was with Logan's 15th Army corps when it crossed into North Carolina March 8 and headed east through Fayetteville toward Goldsboro.[55] Everywhere along the route the destruction of newspaper offices was a primary objective of his army. In Fayetteville Sherman's soldiers completely destroyed the offices of the *Telegraph* and *Observer* and were alleged to have offered a reward of $10,000 for the body of E. J. Hale, the senior editor of the *Observer*.[56] Meanwhile Johnston had moved east from Charlotte and concentrated a force of about 15,000 at Smithfield, 15 miles south of Raleigh. John Spelman, who was both the editor of the *Goldsboro Journal* and the Associated Press agent in Goldsboro, was in Kinston on March 8 to report a skirmish between Bragg's troops and the Union army under Schofield, which Sherman was about to join. Spelman was unable to find an officer in Kinston or Goldsboro to approve his dispatch, and therefore could only publish a report of the action in his own newspaper.[57]

The relaxation of Confederate press censorship in mid-March apparently encouraged de Fontaine's newspaper to publish an account of a holding action fought by Hardee at Averasboro on March 16. The *Carolinian* gave a generally accurate account of the fight, but its estimate of Union losses exceeding the Confederate in the proportion of 7-1 was considerably exaggerated.[58]

No Confederate war correspondent seems to have been present three days later when Johnston's army came to grips with Sherman at Bentonville, sixteen miles south of Smithfield. Except for a brief account which the *Danville Register* somehow obtained independent of government sources, the Southern press had to depend on Johnston's official report of the battle to Lee, which the War Department released

---

the press is partially explained in R. E. Lee to W. P. Miles, January 19, 1865, W. P. Miles Papers, University of North Carolina.

[55] Barrett, *Civil War in North Carolina*, p. 301.

[56] *Charlotte* (N.C.) *Bulletin*, April 4, 1865 as reprinted in *Columbus Daily Sun*, April 15, 1865; *Richmond Daily Whig*, March 29, 1865.

[57] Horn, *Army of Tennessee*, p. 425; *Goldsboro Daily Journal* as reprinted in *Richmond Daily Whig*, March 18, 1865. An official dispatch from Lee to the secretary of war announcing a victory near Kinston, North Carolina was published in the *Daily Richmond Examiner*, March 10, 1865.

[58] The *Richmond Examiner* of March 18, 1865 contained extracts from various North Carolina and Georgia newspapers describing Sherman's military operations in the Carolinas. Excerpts from the *Columbia Carolinian*'s account of Averasboro were reprinted in *ibid.*, March 27, 1865. Johnston estimated the Confederate loss at Averasboro at between 400 and 500. The official report of Union casualties was 682 (95 killed, 533 wounded, 54 missing). *O.R.* (Army) Ser. I, vol. xlvii, pt. 1, p. 66; pt. 2, p. 1,407.

to the Associated Press. Unfortunately the telegraph at Augusta broke down just as the P.A. report was coming over the wires from Richmond, and Augusta readers had to wait until the next day to obtain the last seven words of the dispatch. From the limited information about the Battle of Bentonville the Confederate press came to the conclusion that the enemy had been routed and forced to withdraw eastward. The Confederates lost more heavily in the battle than the Federals, however; the result was only a temporary delay of the junction of Sherman and Schofield.[59]

Within another week there were indications in the Richmond and Petersburg papers that fighting in the vicinity of Petersburg was about to recommence. The Confederate Congress met for the last time on March 18 after passing the bill that Lee had been requesting for some time, to recruit Negro soldiers for the defense of the Confederacy. The refusal of Congress to enact other items of the legislative program which President Davis wanted caused the *Lynchburg Republican* to recommend, "we should have no more congresses," and that Lee and Davis assume dictatorial power at once.[60]

On March 25 a correspondent for the *Richmond Dispatch* reported a surprise attack on Grant's line at Fort Stedman near Petersburg which was initially successful. But in a letter to the *Dispatch* mailed later that day, he admitted that "the affair did not prove so favorable as at first augured" and that the Confederates had had to fall back to their original line.[61] Three days later Grant counterattacked with a turning movement against the Confederate right. On March 30 the P.A. agent in Petersburg reported that a heavy fight had been in progress all day near Hatcher's Run, eight miles from Petersburg. He told about several furious Union assaults, the last of which had driven Bushrod Johnson's

[59] *Danville Register* as reprinted in *Richmond Daily Whig*, March 22, 23, 1865; *Augusta Daily Constitutionalist*, March 21, 22, 23, 1865; *Mobile Daily Advertiser and Register*, April 1, 1865; Govan and Livingood, *Johnston*, p. 357.

[60] *Richmond Daily Whig*, March 20, 1865; *Lynchburg Daily Republican*, March 16, 1865. For criticism of the obstructive attitude of Senator Wigfall and other members of the Congress and a realistic appraisal of the military situation in Virginia see *Lynchburg Daily Virginian*, March 18, 1865.

[61] *Richmond Daily Dispatch*, March 27, 1865. For reporting by the *Petersburg Express*, see *ibid.*, March 28, 1865. The purpose of the attack may have been in part to cover Lee's withdrawal from the Petersburg line to join Johnston in North Carolina. J. H. Claiborne, *Seventy-Five Years in Old Virginia* (New York, 1904), p. 253.

division back a mile and a half, and about a counterattack that had regained the lost ground.[62]

Before the Richmond press could report the disastrous defeat of Pickett's division at Five Forks west of Petersburg on April 1, Lee's Petersburg line collapsed. On April 2-3 all but one of the Richmond newspaper offices were consumed by a fire that resulted from the precipitate evacuation of Richmond. A special correspondent of the *Columbia Carolinian*, who was identified simply as "Cyphax," witnessed the fall of Richmond and reported the catastrophe more dramatically than accurately. Dating his story from Danville, Virginia on the second day after the Federals marched in, he assured his readers: "Richmond and Petersburg have fallen; but they have gone down in a blaze of glory, and with a record unstained by one blot of shame. All that the enemy have gained has been purchased at a terrible price in blood, while our own army, although suffering severely, is still strong, intact, and ready for its future work."[63]

His account of the fighting near Petersburg the previous week was largely fanciful and somewhat ridiculous. "Cyphax" described Lee's army as having mowed down its opponents "by hundreds" on the day before Petersburg fell. While he admitted a Confederate loss of between eight and fifteen thousand during the week's fighting, his estimate of enemy loss at somewhere between forty and fifty thousand was even more exaggerated than such estimates usually had been during the preceding six months.

"Cyphax" was of the opinion that no one in Richmond had anticipated disaster until news of the breakthrough at Petersburg reached there early Sunday, April 2. He described the excited populace that thronged the streets that morning, the "swarms" of Confederate government officials who were busy packing and removing the records of their offices, the application of the torch to all forms of public property by order of the Confederate government, and the vandalism of the retail establishments by a mob which another reporter pictured as being "mostly of the foreign element." "Cyphax" was still in Richmond the next morning to behold "one of the most fearful sights I have ever contemplated." By that time a large part of the city was in ashes.

The *Richmond Whig* was the only newspaper office in the city that

---

[62] *Richmond Daily Whig*, April 1, 1865.
[63] *Columbia Daily South Carolinian* as reprinted in *Augusta Daily Constitutionalist*, April 16, 1865.

escaped fire. When after a suspension of twenty-hours it resumed publication, it was under a new management and displayed the character of a "Union" paper. Strictly speaking, therefore, its extensive account of the city's destruction does not fit the label of Confederate reporting. Indicative of the change of editorial and news policy was the attribution of the source of the destruction to the action of the Confederate authorities in "wantonly and recklessly applying the torch to Shockoe warehouse and other buildings [containing] . . . a large quantity of tobacco." The *Whig* also gave a large share of the credit for extinguishing the fire to the Union soldiers who entered the city on Monday morning; it denounced the pillaging of the stores on Sunday by a band of drunken Confederate stragglers. The paper defined the burned-over area as the main business section of the town, together with between six and eight hundred houses, and estimated the property loss in terms of "hundreds of millions of dollars."[64]

It is possible, although not altogether certain, that a correspondent of the *Columbia Carolinian* was with Lee's army on April 3 when it began retreating westward from Petersburg in an effort to join Johnston's army in North Carolina. With a force of about 12,500 infantry, Lee was heading for Amelia Court House on the Richmond & Danville Railroad, where he expected to find much-needed army rations. From there he intended to follow the railroad southwest toward Danville, where President Davis had arrived on Monday from Richmond. Unfortunately Grant's army had a shorter distance to travel than Lee's to intercept his line of retreat at Burkesville; when Lee's army reached Amelia Court House, the general discovered that a communications blunder had deprived him of the rations needed for his hungry men. Learning that Sheridan's cavalry was between him and Danville, he decided to continue marching west toward Lynchburg and the mountain country. On the way, Grant's infantry overwhelmed his rear guard at Saylor's Creek, destroying a large part of the army's wagon train and two army corps. Three days later at Appomattox Station, Sheridan's cavalry and two Federal infantry corps blocked his line of retreat, thus bringing the Army of Northern Virginia to bay. An exchange of letters

[64] *Richmond Daily Whig*, April 4, 1865; *Danville Register* as paraphrased in *Augusta Daily Constitutionalist*, April 14, 1865; Rembert Patrick, *The Fall of Richmond* (Baton Rouge, 1960), p. 43. Although the proprietor of the *Whig*, William Ira Smith, remained in possession of his establishment, the editor and all but one of the editorial staff departed before the new regime took over.

between Grant and Lee resulted in the surrender of Lee's army Sunday morning, April 9.[65]

What was probably the only detailed Southern newspaper account of the surrender was published in the *Columbia Carolinian*. The newspaperman who wrote it evidently was not present at the McLean house where Grant and Lee met; it is not certain that he witnessed any of the events that were recounted in his narrative. After reporting the unsuccessful effort of General Gordon's corps to cut its way through the opposing army, the *Carolinian* correspondent told how:

Subsequently an officer, said to be Gen Custar [*sic*] of the Yankee cavalry entered our lines with a flag of truce. Whether his appearance was in response to a request from General Lee, or he was the bearer of a formal demand for the surrender initiated by Gen'l Grant, we are not informed. At this time, our army was in line of battle on or near the Appomatox [*sic*] road, the skirmishers thrown out, while 250 yards from there, on an eminence, was a large body of Federal cavalry.

Soon after the return of Gen. Custar to his lines, Gen. Grant, accompanied by his staff, rode to the headquarters of Gen. Lee, which were under an apple tree near the road. This interview is described as exceedingly impressive. After the salutatory formalities, which were doubtless brief and businesslike, General Lee tendered his sword to Grant in token of surrender. That officer, however, with a courtesy for which we must accord him due respect, declined to receive it, or receiving it declined to retain it, and accompanied its return with substantially the following remarks:

"General Lee keep that sword. You have won it by your gallantry. You have not been whipped, but overpowered, and I cannot receive it as a token of surrender from so brave a man."

The reply of Gen. Lee we do not know. But Grant and himself are said to have been deeply affected by the occasion and to have shed tears. The scene occurred between ten and eleven o'clock A.M., when the sad event became known to the army, officers and men gave way to their emotions and some among the veterans wept like children. A considerable number swore that they would never surrender and made their way to the woods. Generals Gray of South Carolina and Rosser of Virginia with a few followers cut their way out and escaped. But the bulk of the army . . . together with leaders like Longstreet, Gordon, Kershaw and others . . . were obliged to accept the proffered terms. . . .

During Sunday and Monday a large number of Federal soldiers and officers visited our camps and looked curiously on our commands, but there was nothing like exultation, no shouting for joy, and no word uttered that could add to the mortification already sustained. On the contrary every

[65] D. S. Freeman, *R. E. Lee, A Biography* (New York, 1935), iv, 57-59, 66, 81-93, 114-43.

symptom of respect was manifested, and the southern army was praised for the noble and brave manner in which it had defended our cause.[66]

There were minor inaccuracies in the report as a whole. The writer in the *Carolinian* incorrectedly stated that the army of General George H. Thomas had effected a junction with Grant before the surrender. Mistaken likewise were the statements that the surrender had occurred at "Lee's headquarters" and that Lee had offered his sword to Grant. Also the disparity in the size of the two armies was sufficiently great without crediting Grant with having 200,000 troops under his command, and there is no evidence that either Lee or Grant wept during their interview, although both men may very well have been "deeply affected."[67]

While the war in Virginia was ending Johnston was retreating through Raleigh to Greensboro, where on April 12 he conferred with President Davis and Secretary of War John C. Breckinridge and then decided to surrender. The announcement by the Confederate Associated Press on April 20 of the conclusion of an armistice between Johnston and Sherman was interpreted by the P.A. in Augusta as "tantamount to peace."[68] Nevertheless the reports of the Confederate Press Association continued to appear in the Augusta newspapers as late as May 2,[69] although by that time all organized resistance to Federal authority east of the Mississippi River had ceased.

In an April 18 editorial entitled, "The End Is Not In Sight," the *Augusta Constitutionalist* argued that final victory and the "glorious in-

[66] *Columbia Daily Carolinian* as reprinted in *Augusta Daily Constitutionalist*, April 23, 1865.

[67] Freeman, *Lee*, IV, 134 makes clear that the surrender took place at the residence of Maj. Wilmer McLean, which Lee's aide-de-camp, Colonel Marshall, had procured for the conference of the two generals. Freeman Cleaves, *Meade of Gettysburg* (Norman, Okla., 1960), p. 308, places the combined strength of Meade, Ord, and Sheridan at 124,700 troops at the end of March 1865. The *London Times* correspondent Frances E. Lawley also was with Lee's army at the time of the surrender. W. S. Hoole, *Lawley Covers the Confederacy* (Tuscaloosa, 1964), pp. 118-20.

[68] Govan and Livingood, *Johnston*, pp. 361-62; *Augusta Daily Chronicle and Sentinel*, April 21, 1865.

[69] On April 16, 1865 the *Augusta Constitutionalist* reported that Colonel Thrasher was in Augusta "on a flying visit to our city." The purpose of his visit may have been to attend the annual meeting of the Press Association which had been scheduled to be held there April 15, 1865. There was no indication in the Augusta newspapers that the meeting was ever held. Augusta came under Union military occupation on May 1, 1865. F. F. Corley, *Confederate City, Augusta, Georgia, 1860-1865* (Columbia, S.C., 1960), p. 93.

dependence of the South" were still possible so long as the Trans-Mississippi area remained unconquered. In spite of periodic government courier service between Houston and Richmond almost to the very end of the war, the Trans-Mississippi, in de Fontaine's words, had for two years been like another world.[70] Because of the faulty communication between the two sides of the river, the Confederate Associated Press and the newspapers it served were poorly informed about the military situation in Texas and elsewhere west of the river. Lacking precise information, they were prone to credit Smith with greater strength than he possessed. His surrender on June 2, 1865, therefore, must have been a disagreeable surprise to Editor James R. Randall of the *Constitutionalist* and other Southern editors east of the river.[71]

The reporting of the collapse of the Confederacy could not help but be affected by the silencing of its newspaper voices. On February 12, 1864 the *Mobile Register* had estimated that there were still 35 daily newspapers in the Confederacy, but the attrition rate had been especially heavy during the last two months of the war. One by one the newspaper voices of Wilmington, Charleston, Richmond, Petersburg, Montgomery, Mobile, Columbus, Macon, and Augusta were being transformed or muted by Yankee occupation or compelled to migrate to safer areas. The last war correspondence in the *Mobile Register* was a dispatch from its proprietor W. G. Clark, dated April 8, reporting a Yankee cavalry raid near Tuscaloosa.[72]

The demise of the *Memphis Appeal* was in keeping with its history of sudden changes of base, one jump ahead of the enemy. As Brig.Gen. James H. Wilson's cavalry raiders neared Montgomery in early April, the staff of the *Appeal* scattered. Editor Dumble fled to Augusta as part of the equipment of his paper was being ferried across the Chatta-

[70] Warren Adams, Maj. A. S. Rose, and a certain "Mr. Reddington" were some of the better-known government couriers who travelled between Texas and Richmond in late 1864 and early 1865. After Thrasher's attempt to establish courier service for his news agency failed because of the opposition of Postmaster General Reagan, the *Mobile Register* became the chief source of Trans-Mississippi news for Thrasher's organization. R. F. Tucker, "The Press Association of the Confederate States of America," unpub. Master's thesis (University of Georgia, 1950), p. 71.

[71] For conflicting newspaper estimates of the military situation west of the Mississippi see *Richmond Daily Whig*, January 2, 1865; *Montgomery Daily Mail*, February 7, 1865, *Houston Tri-Weekly Telegraph*, November 26, 1864; *Richmond Daily Dispatch*, March 1, 21, 1865; J. H. Parks, *General Edmund Kirby Smith, C.S.A.* (Baton Rouge, 1954), pp. 441-47.

[72] *Mobile Daily Advertiser and Register*, April 9, 1865.

hoochee River to Columbus and the remainder was being transported to Macon. With the entry of Wilson's troopers into Columbus on April 16, the *Appeal* ceased to exist. In the *Official Records of the Union and Confederate Armies* can be found the report of the Union provost marshal in Columbus describing the seizure and destruction of "this defiant rebel sheet" and the placing under bond of one of its proprietors, Benjamin F. Dill.[73]

One of the last of the Confederacy's newspaper voices to be silenced was that of Felix Gregory de Fontaine. In Charlotte his transplanted *Columbia Carolinian* had reported the closing events of the war more fully and circumstantially than any other Southern newspaper. In addition he had supplied the Confederate Associated Press with news dispatches which in one instance at least found their way to the intelligence service of General Lee.[74] Yet de Fontaine was not the only Confederate war correspondent still active at the war's end. It will be remembered that Kirk, the "Se De Kay" of the *Louisville Courier, Chattanooga Rebel, Memphis Appeal,* and *Augusta Constitutionalist,* had made the burning of Columbia the theme of his last big war story. On a pleasant April evening in Augusta, Georgia, "Se De Kay" made the transition from war to peace by marrying a girl from Virginia named Sallie P. Miller.[75] By that time there were no more battles to report.

[73] *Augusta Daily Constitutionalist,* April 25, 1865; T. H. Baker, "Refugee Newspaper: The Memphis *Daily Appeal,* 1862-1865," *Journal of Southern History,* xxix (August 1963), 342-43; *O.R.* (Army) Ser. I, vol. xlix, pt. 1, p. 494.

[74] Robert E. Lee Official Telegrams, February 24, 25, 1865, Misc. Mss., Duke University.

[75] *Augusta Daily Constitutionalist,* April 12, 1865.

CHAPTER 15

Final Edition

REPORTING A war, as newspaper columnist and onetime war correspondent Walter Lippmann once remarked, is a very different assignment from almost any other kind of newspaper reporting.[1] Under ordinary circumstances the first requirement for the reporter is to see and hear from everyone immediately concerned with the event. Yet this is just what the war correspondent frequently cannot do. Generals refuse to communicate their plans to him or even talk with him; army regulations and military priorities restrict freedom of movement within his own lines; and the risk of being shot as a spy or encountering other dangers in enemy territory hamper his reporting the designs and maneuvers of the enemy.

These basic difficulties in reporting any war were true of Confederate war reporting. There were other considerations, both general and local, which also affected it. The conflicting aims of news and official propaganda made it difficult if not virtually impossible for a Southern correspondent to tell the whole truth about the military situation. In stating and interpreting the facts the editors and reporters were able to gather, they had constantly to keep in mind the possible damage of their work to the cause to which most of them were sincerely loyal. The Southern press also had to take into account in its management of the news the values peculiar to its region to which the press itself subscribed, the preconceptions long held by Southerners about the materialism and lack of valor of their Northern adversaries, the suppression for a generation or more of critical comment about the South's "peculiar institution" of slavery, and the longtime preference of its newspaper clientele for editorials rather than news.[2] The reading habits of its customers had, to be sure, in large measure changed under the impact of war. Like their Northern counterparts, Southern newspaper readers had acquired an insatiable appetite for up-to-the-minute news which caused the reporting function of the Southern press to assume greater importance than ever before. Yet the editorial aspect of jour-

[1] *Pittsburgh Post-Gazette*, December 28, 1966.
[2] Interview with Clifford Dowdey, Richmond, Va., July 23, 1959.

nalism still possessed an honored place in the eyes of the Southern newspaper public. Both soldiers and civilian readers pored over editorials, not simply because of whatever attachment they had to the political views expressed there but also because the editor frequently was better able to interpret what was happening than a reporter with more restricted facilities of information.

In evaluating the South's performance in reporting the Civil War, one must seek answers to a number of related questions: How extensive was its news coverage? With what degree of accuracy and objectivity did the Southern press report the various elements of the Confederate war effort? How effective as a whole and in relationship to each other were the different components of the Confederate news organization —the handful of special correspondents and volunteer (soldier) correspondents, the Confederate Press Association and the other telegraphic news services that preceded and competed with it, the system of newspaper exchanges, and the arrangements for obtaining newspapers from the North? What were the principal strengths and weaknesses of Confederate war reporting? Did the quality of that reporting improve or diminish as the war advanced? And how did the standards of war reporting in the South compare with those of the North?

It seems reasonably clear from what has gone before that so far as military reporting was concerned, the Confederate press gave fullest coverage to the operations of its two principal armies, the Eastern army which eventually came to be known as the Army of Northern Virginia, and the Western army successively commanded by A. S. Johnston, Beauregard, Bragg, Joe Johnston, and Hood. The press was much less successful in giving publicity to military operations in the outlying areas of the Confederacy, notably the Trans-Mississippi region. For example it obtained its first and almost only direct information about the Battle of Pea Ridge, Arkansas of March 7-8, 1862 over a telegraph line that was at least seventy miles from the battlefield. The *Memphis Appeal* correspondent at Fort Smith who forwarded what little information was known about the battle had to depend on the report of a mounted courier who rode to the telegraph office from the battlefield.[3]

[3] *Memphis Daily Appeal*, March 12, 1862; *Wilmington Daily Journal*, March 26, 1862. The *Little Rock Gazette* had to await the arrival at Clarksville of another courier who rode fifty miles from Van Buren (near Fort Smith) to put the news on the telegraph wire to Little Rock. For a contemporary observation about the neglect of the Trans-Mississippi area in the Southern press see *Daily Richmond Examiner*, September 24, 1863.

At a number of fights and in some campaigns, as well, the Southern press was inadequately represented or not represented at all.[4] For news coverage of the Missouri campaign of 1861 it had to rely on telegrams of doubtful reliability from the telegraph offices of Louisville, Nashville, and Memphis, on accounts published in Missouri newspapers whose allegiance was questionable, and on Northern newspapers that were smuggled through the lines. No correspondent of any Southern newspaper was present at the Battle of Wilson Creek in August 1861 or at any of the other military actions that took place in Missouri that year. As the war progressed, the unsolicited contributions of soldier war correspondents compensated in part for the lack of special correspondence from the theaters of lesser importance. But such letters were often delayed in transmission to the newspaper office, and even when they arrived on time, they might not be sufficiently interesting or important to warrant publication.

Since the South was never able to create a navy that could meet the Union fleet on anything like equal terms, Southern navy reporting as a specialized branch of war reporting was essentially nonexistent. It is true that war correspondents' letters were sometimes written from the decks of Confederate gunboats on the Mississippi, and that during the latter part of the war Shepardson relieved the tedium of his life as a naval surgeon by contributing occasional shipboard correspondence to his old newspaper employer, the *Richmond Dispatch*.[5] But there were no Southern newsmen on shipboard to report the Battle of Mobile Bay, the repulse of the first attack on Charleston, or the encounter of the *Merrimack* and the *Monitor* in the same manner as the Northern correspondent B. S. Osbon reported a number of naval actions for the *New York Herald*. No Confederate newspaperman accompanied the Confederate raider *Alabama* during her long career of commerce-destruction. And for the most part the defense of the Southern coast against the attacks of various U.S. naval expeditions was reported locally by the newspapers nearest the point of attack.

Confederate news coverage of aspects of the Confederate war effort other than straight military operations concerned itself with the care of the sick and wounded, the war production of the Tredegar Iron Works in Richmond and other munition factories, the system of supply

[4] J. J. Mathews, *Reporting the Wars* (Minneapolis, 1957), p. 95.
[5] See e.g. *Richmond Daily Dispatch*, September 22, 1864 for "Bohemian's" report of a recent cruise of the C.S.S. *Tallahassee*.

for the Confederate armies, and problems of transportation, communication, and finance. Newspaper editorials dealt with these and related topics as did articles prepared by newspaper staff members and contributed by informed readers. The analysis of subjects like these had an obvious connection with the reporting of the activities of the Confederate government. After the capital of the Confederacy was moved from Montgomery to Richmond in May 1861, the reporting of the activities of the Davis administration became the joint responsibility of the Richmond press and the Richmond correspondents of the leading out-of-town newspapers. The more important subject matter of such reporting included the proceedings of the Confederate Congress, the speeches and messages of President Davis, and the policies of, and the implementation of these policies by, the president and his advisers.

The reporting of the activities of the Confederate Congress was often censorious, deploring the lack of talent and public spirit and the excess of greed that motivated many of these legislators. An editor from Memphis who visited the capital in March 1862 came to the conclusion that "what these grovelling members lack in talent, in patriotism, and all the essentials which go to make men great, noble and trustworthy they more than make up in subserviency, in partisanship, and in all the acts of the demagogue." The editor of the *Chattanooga Rebel* expressed the same viewpoint, somewhat more picturesquely, when he described the Congress as "strong only on the one point, possessed by the ass, of large appetite, and heed to little beyond the great principle of self."[6]

Representative of the minority opinion that the press had not done full justice to the congressmen was a statement in the published correspondence from Richmond in February 1863 of Dupré of the Knoxville *Register*. Deploring the wholesale abuse of Congress by a segment of the Southern press, Dupré expressed the belief that many of the members of that session of Congress would have been rated as statesmen in any period of American history. That they were not so regarded by many journalists he explained as resulting from the overshadowing of their accomplishments by the achievements of military leaders like Stuart and Morgan. He went on to assert that "there are not a dozen

6 *Memphis Daily Avalanche*, April 2, 1862; *Chattanooga Daily Rebel*, February 14, 1863. For an expression of the *London Times* correspondent Lawley's low opinion of the Confederate Congress in 1864 see W. S. Hoole, *Lawley Covers the Confederacy* (Tuscaloosa, 1964), pp. 86-87.

men in East Tennessee who have ever read a set speech delivered by the Confederate Congress. So thoroughly do the conductors of the press understand the wants and tastes of their readers that you rarely find a speech published. The most that is read is a Congressional proceedings. . . ."[7]

As a result of the limited amount and impersonal nature of the Congressional news that reached the public, the names of comparatively few congressmen were known to the readers of the daily press. Perhaps the most newsworthy, if not the most notorious, congressman was the Tennesseean Henry S. Foote, who was one of the most articulate congressional opponents of the Davis administration. Foote's criticisms of administration policy met with the approval of the newspapers of his own state for the most part and aroused interest and some favorable comment elsewhere. In a letter from Richmond to the *Chattanooga Rebel* published in September 1862, a volunteer correspondent of that newspaper referred in a flattering manner to Foote's silvery locks and eloquent appeals, and recalled how in the years before the war great statesmen like Clay and Webster had leaned on his strong arm for support. The knowledgeable Richmond correspondent George Bagby, on the other hand, regarded Foote as both "erratic" and "inflammable." As the Tennessee congressman's opposition to the war and his identification with what the press generally regarded as subversive activities became more evident, the newspapers came more and more to view him as a crackpot and even as a traitor.[8]

Much of the acerbic tone that was manifest in the congressional reporting permeated the comments of Richmond newspapermen about the president and particular members of his cabinet. Only rarely did these newspapermen communicate to their readers the kind of sympathetic portrait of President Davis that a New Orleans lady on a visit to Richmond in the early days of the war contributed to a newspaper recently established in her home city. With the enthusiasm characteristic of a certain class of Southern women, she described Davis as, "a

---

[7] *Knoxville Daily Register*, February 12, 1863. For the comments of another Richmond correspondent who was favorably impressed by the ability and talent of the Confederate House of Representatives see *Atlanta Daily Intelligencer*, June 8, 1864. The congressmen whom the *Intelligencer* correspondent regarded as particularly able were the chairman of the House Ways and Means Committee, Judge Francis S. Lyon of Alabama and Congressman John B. Baldwin of Virginia.

[8] *Chattanooga Daily Rebel*, September 11, 1862; *Mobile Daily Advertiser and Register*, December 18, 1863.

quiet, middle aged gentleman, with a dignified bearing" who was accustomed to go riding every evening after his four o'clock dinner, dressed in a beaver hat and a suit of black or gray. In the opinion of this lady admirer, "he sits and rides well, though one might fancy from his delicate appearance that he would eschew horsemanship as too fatiguing an exercise."[9]

More typical of press comment on Davis was the carefully phrased criticism of his military judgment that war correspondent Peter Alexander submitted to the *Savannah Republican* in December 1863. Alexander explained that although he was not lacking in respect for the president, he could never bring himself to "accept his opinions as infallible" so long as he recalled Davis's persistence in retaining Pemberton in command at Vicksburg, "against the remonstrances of almost every man and woman in the Confederacy." Another example of this same lack of judgment, in Alexander's opinion, was the president's taking of Pemberton to Chattanooga in the fall of 1863 to place him in command of an army corps, which would have been carried out if Pemberton had not declined the position, "acting upon a hint from a distinguished officer." Still another count against Davis, as Alexander saw it, was that at that late stage of the war, he still persisted "in spite of the wishes of the entire Trans-Mississippi department in forcing Gen. Price, one of the best officers in the Confederate army, to serve under Gen. Holmes, one of the poorest."[10]

On the other hand, the Richmond press paid little attention to Vice President Stephens, who was away from the city much of the time at his home in Georgia. Yet in the controversy between Davis and Stephens over the conduct of the war, which became public in 1864, Bagby acknowledged his partiality for Stephens and his unhappiness with the "fatuity" that had excluded the Vice President from the inner circle

[9] *New Orleans Merchants' and Manufacturers' Journal* as reprinted in *Nashville Republican Banner*, November 2, 1861.

[10] *Savannah Republican*, December 24, 1863. For a glimpse into the mind of the Confederate president who, according to Secretary of State Judah P. Benjamin, "would not be pleased that opinions and ideas so adverse to his own on a subject, in which he was so deeply interested," should be submitted to him by former war correspondent Durant Da Ponte, see Da Ponte's report of a conversation with Benjamin in Richmond in March 1864, Durant Da Ponte Papers, Jackson, Miss. As an army captain Da Ponte had just returned from an arms mission to Mexico and was about to return to newspaper work as an associate editor of the *Richmond Whig*.

of Davis's advisers. In a letter from Richmond on March 26, 1864 Bagby made known to the readership of the *Mobile Register* "what is well known here, that early in the war, while Mr. Stephens lived in Richmond, he was so snubbed and neglected by the Executive and Cabinet that he was compelled to seek his information precisely as every private citizen did.—To use the expression of a friend of his, he had 'to skin around the newspaper and telegraph offices, like Tom, Dick, and Harry.' This was shameful treatment. But the good advice he had given at Montgomery, and which had been rejected, could not be forgiven."[11]

The Confederate press had little to say in the way of praise for the various secretaries of war, Secretary of the Navy Stephen R. Mallory, or Secretary of the Treasury Christopher G. Memminger. Particularly critical of these cabinet members were opposition newspapers like the *Richmond Examiner* and *Charleston Mercury.* The following blast from a Richmond correspondent of the *Mobile Tribune* at about midpoint in the war was typical of the sweeping denunciations of Davis and his cabinet that Richmond newspapermen often made:

"Mr. Davis' cabinet is composed of a set of old fogy broken down politicians, who act as mere *clerks* to the President. Mr. Davis himself is troubled with blindness, is very dispeptic and splenetic, and as prejudiced and stubborn as a man can well be, and not be well. Mr. Benjamin, the Secretary of State, holds a mere sinecure, we having no *foreign relations* to correspond with, and our people are thus made to pay an enormous sum for the support of these salaried clerks. . . . The Secretary of the Treasury is by no means a Rothschilds in his financial talents, and . . . from the many blunders he has made, it is only a miracle that we have had any means to carry on the war. Had the Yankees bagged the whole Cabinet on the occasion of Stoneman's raid, leaving the President to make more judicious selections, the Confederacy would have gained by the operation."[12]

The extent of Confederate news coverage could hardly fail to be

[11] *Mobile Daily Advertiser and Register*, April 2, 1864. The former editor of the *Richmond Enquirer*, Nat Tyler, in a letter to Jefferson Davis after the war, acknowledged that "I . . . distinctly remember his [Stephens'] coming to the [*Enquirer*] office and lecturing the editors on their support of the measures for the public defence; but, as his views were visionary and impracticable, his temper excited and his influence under a cloud, we gave to his person all respect and to his advice the least attention that was possible." Nat Tyler to Jefferson Davis, January 15, 1885. Dunbar Rowland, *Jefferson Davis, Constitutionalist* (Jackson, Miss., 1923), IV, 482.

[12] *Mobile Daily Tribune* as reprinted in *Daily Richmond Examiner*, June 9, 1863.

adversely affected by the problem of finding enough space in a two- or four-page newspaper to satisfy the reader's query, "What's the news?" The reduction of practically all the daily newspapers and many of the weeklies to half-sheets before the war was half over and the steady attrition of newspapers, reporters, printers, telegraphers, and the facilities for newspaper production and communication diminished the amount of war news to minimal proportions by the time it did end.

The accuracy and objectivity of the published news in the South was affected by a number of factors, many of which were beyond the control of reporters and newspapers. Both reporters in the field and the Richmond correspondents had to depend on news sources of varying reliability; repeatedly they complained of the difficulties of sifting truth from falsehood. In a letter to the *Richmond Dispatch* written in the early part of 1862, Shepardson explained:

"The duties of a newspaper correspondent are much more difficult than many are inclined to believe. He is obliged to know everything, hear everything, and do everything at the same time—in fact, he is expected to be ubiquitous. If anything escapes his eye, up jumps somebody and accuses [him] of a willful omission of facts to the prejudice of another; if he be led into error by the statements of others, he is accused of falsification; whether he blame severely, makes what he believes a plain statement of events, or praises but feebly, it is all the same. —Somebody is dissatisfied. What wonder the band of young fellows who began with this war and wrote such pleasant, interesting, and gossipy letters for the Southern papers, has dwindled down to one or two? Who can blame them for leaving a labor that met with little true reward—the appreciation of the country? To have accomplished the task expected of them would have required the fabled lamps of Aladdin; and even then I have my doubts, —while the vast public looks to the pen of the correspondent for news, and for the daily record of events, few individuals are willing to assist him in his search after the truth. —On the contrary, there are many who will rather place falsehoods in his way in order to mislead him into error. While endeavoring to do justice to everybody, to state the truth, and nothing but the truth, it is not surprising that he should sometimes be wrong, and should make some erroneous statements, either through haste in writing or on the responsibility of friends."[13]

[13] *Richmond Daily Dispatch*, March 14, 1862. For the difficulties a prominent general experienced in getting at the truth in a later stage of the war see Mrs. R. A. Pryor, *Reminiscences of Peace and War* (New York, 1904), p. 284.

In his daily work the Richmond newsgatherer had to contend with rumormongers whose ingenious inventions created endless excitement among their credulous listeners. The most extraordinary stories emanated both from irresponsible news scavengers and from reputable and even semi-official sources. They included false reports of the crossing of the Potomac by Beauregard's army in 1861, of the capture of Washington, and the defeat of Grant's army before Vicksburg. The *Richmond Examiner* editor, E. A. Pollard, was once called across the street by one of the most industrious news-manufacturers, a druggist, who was fairly quivering with excitement. "Great God, have you heard the news, Mr. Pollard?" exclaimed the informant thickly. "Jeff Davis has just committed suicide!" Although it can safely be assumed that this remarkable fabrication did not appear in the *Examiner*, the report of the Confederate President's tragic end spread through Richmond within an hour's time, found its way to the enemy's lines, and flew over the telegraph from the James River to the Penobscot.[14]

In the course of time the more talented and experienced Confederate war correspondents became proficient in evaluating their news sources and determining the degree of reliability of news obtained from such sources. Generally officers were better informed sources of information than enlisted men, although they were not as a group more truthful. Other news sources of varying reliability that were tapped by army correspondents were train passengers, scouts, enemy deserters, prisoners of war, civilian refugees—but hardly ever Negroes.

A prominent Richmond correspondent like Bagby or Thompson kept himself informed of what was going on in official circles by daily visits to the War Department and other executive offices, by establishing confidential relationships with congressmen, making the rounds of the Richmond newspaper offices, and picking up sundry items of news and gossip at the dining tables of the hotels, at the local telegraph office, the railroad station, and private gatherings of friends. As editor of the influential *Southern Literary Messenger* and associate editor of the *Richmond Whig*, Bagby had unusual opportunities for access to information. Occasionally pro-administration editors such as Richard Yeadon and John Forsyth came to Richmond to see for themselves what was happening there and check reports received from Richmond correspondents.

The curbs on the dissemination of news imposed by official censor-

---

[14] E. A. Pollard, *Life of Jefferson Davis* (Philadelphia, 1869), pp. 319-21.

ship also affected the accuracy and completeness of the news gathered in Richmond and in the army. Some generals, for example, Joseph E. Johnston, Bragg, Beauregard, and Stonewall Jackson, totally excluded reporters from their armies for long periods of time. Censors in the War Department and at telegraph offices, provost marshals and other staff officers who functioned as censors in military areas altered or suppressed altogether the dispatches of news correspondents, and generally discouraged candid reporting. Editors likewise exercised the prerogative of eliminating portions of a dispatch before publishing it or of refraining from publishing it at all. In a letter to his correspondent in Richmond in November 1861, Editor R. B. Rhett, Jr. explained that in the light of the shaky condition of public morale, he had excluded from the columns of the *Charleston Mercury* his correspondent's last three letters because of their "despondent and fault finding tone." Again in 1862 Rhett wrote to the same correspondent:

"You have perceived that I have struck out of your letters many hits against Davis. However true and necessary to a knowledge of his real character, they savor too much of personal dislike, in the opinion of the public, to effect the object. I would never attack him, except upon public matters, and with infallible proofs. People will not tolerate the expression of mere opinions derogatory to this great little head of a great country. Many even now abuse the Mercury violently. All victories strengthen him. As long as Congress sits in secret, and free from the pressure of public opinion, while at the same time under the stress of executive influence, Davis cannot be broken down.

"Be therefore, I suggest, as amiable as consistent with truth, and give the dear weakly public as much as possible of the bright side of things. The *Courier* here flourishes on flattering every thing and everybody out of which any thing is to be made."[15]

The most overt effort to introduce objectivity into Confederate news reporting took place in connection with the establishing of the Confederate Press Association early in 1863. Its general manager, J. S. Thrasher, directed his correspondents to eliminate opinion from their news dispatches, stick to facts, use care to sift reports, and "not send unfounded rumors as news." The best-informed scholar on the his-

[15] R. B. Rhett, Jr. to G. W. Bagby, November 25, 1861, April 9, 1862, Bagby Papers, Virginia Historical Society. For contemporary criticism of the *Mercury's* opposition to the Davis administration see Ellison Capers to his wife, August 2, 1862, Ellison Capers Papers, Duke University.

tory of the Confederate Press Association has described the result as "a 'complete revolution' in the habits of writers for the Southern press."[16] That the P.A. stressed factual reporting may well have represented a break with the past in Southern journalism, but it is doubtful that Thrasher was as successful in eliminating opinion from the news dispatches of his organization as Quintus Wilson and others who have written about the P.A. have claimed. Indeed, there were complaints by newspaper clients of the P.A. of being made to pay for editorials by telegraph and for the mere speculations of telegraphic correspondents.[17]

The news value and accuracy of the reports of the various telegraphic news services also left a good bit to be desired. The *Wilmington* (N.C.) *Journal* lamented that "most generally we can place very little dependence in its [the telegraph's] advices." The *Columbus* (Ga.) *Sun* sneered that the news reports distributed by the Associated Press agent at Richmond were both "unimportant and uninteresting," and the *Columbia* (S.C.) *Guardian* summarized the shortcomings of the telegraphic news it received as "slowness, delay, unintelligible and illiterate dispatches, stale and dull news, comments and opinions instead of facts."[18] The letters of war correspondents contained their share of inaccuracies and trivialities, too; but generally the letter correspondents had more time to exercise care in verifying their information than the telegraphic reporters did.

The differences in purpose between the wire reporting and letter correspondence of individual newspapers to some extent invalidate a comparison of their news value. To the rather limited degree that Con-

[16] Q. C. Wilson, "Confederate Press Association, A Pioneer News Agency," *Journalism Quarterly*, xxvi (June 1949), p. 162; R. F. Tucker, "The Press Association of the Confederate States," unpub. Master's thesis (University of Georgia, 1950), p. 77.

[17] *Savannah Republican*, December 17, 1863; *Petersburg Register* as reprinted in *Daily Richmond Examiner*, December 19, 1864; *Charleston Daily Courier*, January 6, 1864. On September 12, 1863, the editor of the *Atlanta Intelligencer* observed that "we have frequently noted the practice of telegraph reporters giving their own opinions in their dispatches to the Press, and not confining themselves to a statement of facts."

[18] *Wilmington Daily Journal*, July 11, 1863; *Columbus Daily Sun* as reprinted in *ibid.*, August 11, 1863; *Columbia Daily Guardian*, December 29, 1863. The *Daily Richmond Examiner* of April 29, 1864 alluded to the "worthless character" of the dispatches telegraphed from the southwest by the Confederate Press Association, citing as an example the report that Grant had reappeared in Chattanooga to resume command of the Union western army.

federate newspapers were in competition for news scoops, the telegraph was their most potent ally. The earliest reports of battles and other major news events almost invariably reached the newspaper by telegraph, frequently through the medium of the Confederate Associated Press. These would be accompanied, or followed, by regular news dispatches from the P.A. agent nearest the scene of the event, and in the case of the larger newspapers like the *Mobile Register* and *Savannah Republican,* by their own special dispatches. When such channels of news were blocked, as they often were after a great battle, editors were likely to make space for private telegrams from prominent citizens in the vicinity of the battle area that were made available to them at the local telegraph office. Such reports frequently contradicted each other; the newspapers often had to correct erroneous information that had appeared in their telegraph columns in an earlier edition. The letter correspondents exercised a check on the accuracy of P.A. dispatches and special telegrams. Sometimes, as in the case of Alexander, the same individual functioned simultaneously as the telegraphic and letter correspondent of the same newspaper. After sending a brief wire story of a great battle such as Shiloh or the Wilderness, Alexander would follow it up with a series of letters expanding his original account, rectifying earlier mistakes, and narrating in detail the performance of individual corps, divisions, and brigades.

The letters of special correspondents made possible interpretive reporting and the insertion of human interest material into the reporter's work. Some of the best letter reporting of battles and campaigns was done by editors like John Forsyth, Alexander Walker, George W. Adair, and James R. Sneed, who frequently had better opportunities than reporters to associate with high-ranking generals and partake of the sociability in the officers' mess. This did not always create impartial reporting, as Forsyth's experience with Bragg in the Perryville campaign of 1862 demonstrated.[19] Too close an association with the commanding general could hardly fail to indoctrinate the reporter with headquarters' point of view.

As a rule the special correspondence of experienced journalists had greater news value than that of volunteer correspondents. Often the volunteers were more intent on gratifying their own vanity or giving publicity to the military units to which they were attached than in producing superior war correspondence. In the spring of 1863 the editor

[19] Above, pp. 248-251.

of the *Wilmington Journal* announced that the flood of communications from North Carolina soldiers in camp was far in excess of the space available in his newspaper. He insisted on carefully reading all communications of this kind and making every effort to bring to public attention views which in his judgment merited such attention. "But the little jealousies and squabbles of camp—the little fun enjoyable by those who know the parties and can appreciate any point made—the inconveniences, and perhaps, grievances inseparable from our present position, are hardly the material out of which to make up matter for an interesting newspaper."[20]

Yet among the volunteer correspondents who became special correspondents of newspapers which recognized their merit were some gifted writers, who had a large following among both soldier and civilian readers. Some of these soldier correspondents, such as Israel Gibbons, were former newspapermen. Other soldier correspondents who were unusually skillful reporters were the *Savannah Republican's* "Tout-le-Monde," the *Mobile Register* correspondent "Bohemia," and T. D. Wright of the *Atlanta Southern Confederacy*. A fellow officer expressed keen admiration for Wright's reporting: "What an imaginative brain that boy has! He can positively write more about less than G.P.R. James or even Charles Dickens. We appreciate him for his letters. May his 'shadder never be less.' "[21]

Among the better features of Confederate war reporting were the variety of interesting themes the correspondents developed, the exposure of abuses in army and civilian administration and of misconduct by soldiers and public officials, the realism, truthfulness, and fairness characteristic of some of the best reporters like Alexander and soldier correspondent Ben Lane Posey, and the steadiness with which Southern newsmen upheld the right to report and kept on reporting in the face of monumental difficulties. The Southern army correspondents did their share of battle reporting, depicted the experience of armies on the march, and wrote somewhat euphemistically about armies in retreat. They portrayed life in camp during and between campaigns, told of the fluctuating moods of the soldier, and described, often with an eye to propaganda effect, the heroism of soldiers and plain people. They revealed, especially during the early days of the war, the high incidence of infectious diseases in camp, and they described death in its various

[20] *Wilmington Daily Journal*, March 18, 1863.
[21] *Atlanta Daily Southern Confederacy*, December 28, 1861.

forms with a kind of morbid fascination. Other recurrent themes of their correspondence were guerrilla warfare, the religious life of the army, including the services of the army chaplains, military reviews and the visits of important figures to the army, military executions, the personal adventures of the reporters themselves on the way to and from the front, and the various forms of army recreation. When they wrote about civilian life, as they frequently did, they either minimized or made disparaging comments about disloyalty and defeatism, pictured the plight of refugees uprooted from their homes and fleeing from the enemy's advance, discussed the consequences of wartime inflation and chronic shortages, and revealed the social disorganization of which increasing rates of crime and vice in Southern towns were symptomatic.

In the process of reporting the grim experiences and the spectrum of attitudes of the army personnel and civilians whom they met, Southern newspapermen infused into what they wrote a mixture of their own feelings of fear, dread, horror, hope, patriotic sentiment, hatred of the enemy, race prejudice, resentment of unjust treatment by arrogant officers, sympathy for the unfortunate, and a sense of wonder at the natural beauty of the mountains, valleys, and rivers that surrounded them.

On the railroad journey from Brandon, Mississippi to Mobile in 1863 the attention of the *Memphis Appeal* correspondent William D. Barr was drawn to the wounded soldiers who had been pressed into service as train guards. Barr did not think they were fitted for duties of this kind. Yet he felt it was in poor taste to laugh at them, explaining that in making their way through the crowded cars "their feebly held bayonets threaten heads on all sides, producing laughable cries of terror from timid passengers."[22]

In exposing abuses in army and civilian administration Southern journalists could hardly avoid criticizing the Confederacy's military and political leadership. It was mainly editors rather than reporters who second-guessed the military strategy of generals like Bragg and Pemberton or the policies of the Richmond bureaucrats. Prudence dictated that special correspondents direct their admonitions at the lower echelons of army brass and government officials, or refrain from identifying the authors of the abuses.

Much of the disparagement of army administration by newspaper critics was directed at its primitive system of caring for the sick and

[22] *Memphis Daily Appeal*, August 19, 1863.

wounded. Emphasizing that his remarks were not animated by the spirit of fault-finding, but were intended for the purpose of correcting the defects of army malpractice, Alexander sent to the *Mobile Register* the most telling reproof of the mistreatment and neglect of the wounded by incompetent and callous army surgeons that appeared in any Southern newspaper during the war. He was moved to this reproof by observing the suffering of the helpless victims of the Battle of Antietam in the hospitals around Winchester, Virginia. Alexander began by stating that it was customary after a battle to place the wounded in temporary hospitals or send them to the rear.

At Richmond they were placed in the hospitals in that city; after the second battle of Manassas they were sent back to Warrenton and other towns in the vicinity, and at Sharpsburg they were sent across the river to Shepherdstown, and thence to this place and Staunton. The regimental surgeons dress the wound, and set or amputate the limb, as the case may be before the patient passes from their hands to the rear. Some of these operators perform their work skillfully and conscientiously; others do it hurriedly or ignorantly; whilst a few do it in a manner that can only be properly characterized as brutal. I have known of cases of amputation where the lapping part of the flesh was sewed together over the bone so stupidly that the thread would disengage itself and the bone be exposed in less than twenty-four hours. The object of many of the field surgeons seems to be to get through their work, in some sort of fashion, as soon as possible and turn their subjects over to the hospital surgeons. While engaged at the amputation table, many of them feel it to be their solemn duty, every time they administer brandy to the patient, to take a drink themselves. This part of their work is performed with great unction and conscientiousness. In a majority of cases however, I am glad to say, the field surgeons do quite as well as could be expected of young men who have had but little practical experience in the art of surgery. . . .

But it is when the wounded man falls into the hands of the hospital surgeons that his greatest sufferings begin. I do not mean such surgeons as those in the Richmond hospitals, which are located in a large city, and under the eyes of the Government, and are provided with careful matrons and nurses and an ample supply of hospital stores. The circumstances surrounding these officers if nothing else, would constrain them to perform their duties. But I allude to the surgeons in those hospitals which are improvised in the rear of the army, as at this place and Warrenton, and who, being of little value at Richmond and other central points, are sent to the country.

Alexander then pictured two young army surgeons who had been sent from Richmond to Winchester about two weeks after the Battle of Antietam and with whom he had shared a room at the local hotel. The surgeons were dressed in uniforms profusely decorated with gold lace, and sported carefully polished boots. From listening to their conversation and observing their behavior, the reporter was convinced that such "dainty gentry" would be utterly useless in a dirty hospital filled with men suffering from ghastly wounds and crawling with vermin. He went on to say that the buildings selected for hospitals "are almost invariably located in the most noisy, dusty, and dirty part of the town. It was so at Corinth, and it is so in Winchester. In the former place, they were located immediately around the depot, where the cars were running day and night, and where the wagons from the camps were constantly arriving and departing; whilst the houses in the rest of the town, which the owners had been required to vacate, were occupied by generals and their butterfly staff officers.

"There are several hundred sick and wounded men here, and yet, if I am correctly informed, the surgeons did not bring with them a single cot, bedsack, sheet or towel, or a solitary change of clothing for the wounded! Some of the men are now lying on a scant supply of straw, with a foul blanket over them, who are otherwise as naked as when they first came into the world! The little clothing they had was torn off when their wounds were dressed, and it was impossible to recover their knapsacks after they were wounded. But for a few cots in the York hospital (which is very well kept), said to have been left here by the enemy, the condition of such of the wounded, as could not get into private houses is as deplorable as it can be."

After contrasting the efficient work of the Georgia Relief and Hospital Association at Warrenton with the bungling efforts of the government surgeons who arrived there a week after the Georgians, Alexander concluded his letter with the observation, "one thing has impressed me more painfully than all others connected with the army. It is the little concern which the Government, its officers and surgeons show for the preservation of the lives of the troops. A great parade is made over a single piece of artillery captured from the enemy; and yet what is such a trophy compared with the life of an able bodied man, even when considered as to its military value! . . . A planter who would take as little care of the health of his slaves as the Government does of its soldiers, would soon have none to care for, while he would be driven out of the community by his indignant neighbors."[23]

[23] *Mobile Daily Advertiser and Register*, October 24, 1862. For Thompson's more restrained reporting of the deterioration of the military hospitals in Richmond see *Memphis Daily Appeal*, May 14, 1862.

Together with other reporters like Street of the *Mobile Register* and Dupré of its Knoxville counterpart, Alexander laid bare the deplorable conditions in the Quartermaster's and Commissary Departments of the army. Writing from Orange County, Virginia in August 1863 he attributed the responsibility for such conditions to the outgoing chief of the Quartermaster's Department in Richmond, Col. Abraham C. Myers. Alexander declared that no intelligent effort had ever been made by Myers, so far as Alexander was aware, to provide supplies for the army by utilizing and processing the abundant raw material in the vicinity of Lee's army. Alexander went on to say what he had frequently stated before in his correspondence, that the beef cattle slaughtered for army subsistence furnished hides enough to shoe the army, tallow enough to provide it with illumination, and enough oil to keep all the wagon and artillery harness in good working order. Yet at this late date (well past the mid-point of the war), not one pound of tallow or oil out of a hundred was being used. Meanwhile the hides of the cattle slaughtered for meat were left to rot in the butcher pens or were sold to local tanners at thirty cents a pound and converted into leather for resale to the government at profits of several hundred per cent.[24]

Street blamed the Quartermaster's Department in Richmond for the deficiencies of blankets and wearing apparel from which Bragg's western army suffered in November 1862. Street estimated that at least one-third of the troops in the Army of Tennessee were without blankets. He also declared that an entire train filled with army clothing had been immobile at Oxford, Mississippi for an entire month while the troops, only twenty-five miles away, were "shivering and suffering" for lack of its contents.[25]

In the columns of the *Knoxville Register* Dupré made public information gathered by a congressional investigating committee in early 1863 about alleged frauds in the Commissary and Quartermaster's Departments. Dupré reported that Pemberton's army in Vicksburg had been deprived of food and other necessities through the diversion of transportation to enrich private individuals having a corrupt relationship with the army supply corps.[26]

Although Commissary General Northrop was one of the most un-

[24] *Savannah Republican*, August 26, 1863.
[25] *Mobile Daily Advertiser and Register*, November 14, 1862.
[26] *Knoxville Daily Register*, March 1, April 15, 1863.

popular Confederate officials, the newspapermen reporting from Richmond rarely ventured to attack him. The fact that he was known to be a favorite of the president perhaps explained in part their reluctance. But Davis's partiality for him was insufficient protection from slashing attacks by opposition editors Daniel and the *Richmond Whig's* James McDonald.[27]

Army "specials" were more willing to expose vandalism and other forms of misbehavior on the part of Confederate cavalrymen than to reveal the mistreatment of soldiers by their officers. Rather exceptional, therefore, was an angry letter Assistant Editor A. S. Abrams of the *Atlanta Intelligencer* addressed to his newspaper from the Army of Tennessee near the end of 1863. Abrams wrote of acts of cruelty by officers that he had witnessed as punishment for minor infractions of discipline. He said he had observed several soldiers "riding rails" for nothing more than failing to respond to roll call at morning muster. "I also learned that the commander of the battalion was in the habit of inflicting such punishment as 'rail toting,' 'rail riding,' 'post whipping,' 'stump digging,' and 'thumb lifting' for the slightest offence and then without waiting for the order of a court martial, but on his own responsibility. . . . I abstain this time from mentioning the name of the officer referred to above, but should he continue such unauthorized acts after this notice of them comes to his knowledge (which I shall take good care it does) I shall not only call his name, but make it my business to call the attention of Lieutenant General Hardee to this usurpation of power, as I feel certain neither the Lieutenant General nor his subordinates are aware of such acts being committed in the army or approve of them."[28]

Objective reporting and truthfulness by newspaper correspondents were not common practice, although the editors who employed them from time to time endorsed the principle of truthful reporting. An example of such reporting was the advice Shepardson gave to his readers in the *Mobile Register* about the significance of the draft riots in New York City. Shepardson, the *Register's* Richmond correspondent, told them frankly they could expect no "comfort" from these disturbances, "for they will rather act against than for us. No party is engaged, no leaders are recognized, no principles beyond personal

[27] J. P. Felt, "Lucius B. Northrop and the Confederacy's Subsistence Department," *Virginia Magazine of History and Biography*, LXIX (April 1961), 181-93.
[28] *Atlanta Daily Intelligencer*, December 29, 1863.

safety are involved, and there is nothing in it but the wild excitement of a reckless mob.—The leading men of the country, property holders, are against it, as, indeed, are all able to raise $300, the price of exemption. It will be a light task for Lincoln to restore peace once more, after which the draft will be enforced, and the reins of tyranny tightened. There is little doubt now of the final success of conscription, and we must be prepared to meet the large army to be raised thereby."[29]

Illustrative of the same insight was the letter of another *Mobile Register* correspondent, published almost a year later. The reporter, who used the inappropriate pseudonym of "Rip Van Winkle," observed wryly that it had become customary by that time to call every man a "croaker" who refused to toss his hat in the air and swear that Lee was about to "gobble up" Grant and that Johnston was dishing up the same kind of menu for Sherman. "Rip Van Winkle" denied that he was a "croaker" and professed to believe in military victory by the end of 1864. Yet he confessed doubts of the reiterated statements in the press about Grant's army being already "whipped" and of the cocksure predictions of newspapermen who swore that Lee's adversary would never reach the south side of the Chickahominy or the James. It seemed strange to him that a "whipped" army continued to confront its conquerors, fighting more or less every day or two, and he wondered why Grant was incapable of achieving the same result that McClellan had managed to effect on the Peninsula in the summer of 1862.[30]

Loyal as Alexander was to the Confederate cause he did not shrink from portraying in the *Savannah Republican* on August 26, 1863 the grim situation of the Confederacy, "struggling for independence, without manufactures or diversified pursuits, without a navy, its nationality not recognized by other powers, its ports blockaded, and its whole industrial system embarrassed by a wide-spread invasion."[31]

One of the most interesting examples of an objective viewpoint on the part of a Southern editor appeared in the *Charleston Courier* just after the fall of New Orleans in April 1862. Yeadon, or whichever one of his assistant editors composed the editorial, listed four delusions

[29] *Mobile Daily Advertiser and Register,* July 28, 1863.

[30] *Ibid.,* June 21, 1864. These comments were written from Longwood, Miss., where this reporter was then stationed. The editor of the *Register* expressed disagreement with his reporter's opinions in *ibid.,* June 22, 1864.

[31] Quoted in A. A. Lawrence, *A Present for Mr. Lincoln* (Macon, Ga., 1961), p. 102.

which the South had "hugged to its bosom" since the beginning of the war, and which the writer saw as being the cause of infinite harm: (1) the belief that the dissolution of the Union would not lead to war; (2) that if war occurred anyway, one decisive battle would terminate the struggle; (3) the belief in the omnipotence of cotton to bring about the intervention of England and France and the destruction of the Union blockade; and (4) the assumption that the U.S. government would go bankrupt before it could mobilize its resources for the conquest of the South.[32]

The weak points of Confederate war reporting were partly the result of the rapid turnover of the few newspapermen who were available and the resulting lack of reporting experience, the imperfect understanding of military operations by reporters of civilian background, the inability of most reporters to know what was going on outside the particular regiment to which they were attached, communication difficulties and mistakes in the transmission of war correspondence by blundering printers and telegraphers, and the conflicting objectives of government propaganda and the news.

Of all these handicaps, none was more frustrating to the correspondents than the problem of reconciling the objectives of news reporting with propaganda considerations and the requirements of censorship. In making their news stories conform to the objectives of official propaganda, Confederate newspapermen were hampered by lack of guidance from a government unschooled in the art of public relations. Apart from maintaining an official organ in Richmond, President Davis had little understanding or appreciation of the press as a medium of public opinion, nor did he make any obvious attempt to conciliate opposition editors like Rhett and Daniel. Whereas Lincoln frequently confided in reporters such as Noah Brooks and Henry Villard, apparently none of the Richmond correspondents of the Southern press had confidential relations with Davis, and there are but few specimens of correspondence between him and leading Southern editors.[33]

[32] *Charleston Daily Courier,* April 30, 1862.

[33] J. E. Pollard, *The Presidents and the Press* (New York, 1947), pp. 348, 351, 364-65. An overly optimistic view of the propaganda activities of the Davis administration appears in M. A. Triplett, "The Efforts of Jefferson Davis to Influence Public Opinion during the Civil War," unpub. Master's thesis (University of Mississippi, 1938). In March 1862 the perspicacious Richmond correspondent of the *Memphis Appeal* described Davis's personality as "cold, almost austere (your correspondent can speak from hearsay only)," but conceded that he was

A certain amount of official war news, which originated in a variety of ways, appeared in the Southern press. It might take the form of a private message from President Davis to his wife, which, in the case of the First Battle of Manassas, reached the press through the medium of the War Department. The most common forms of official news were the official dispatches of generals, which the War Department released to the press at its own discretion. From time to time the press urged the government to institute a system of regular new releases, which never materialized.[34] As for the official reports of battles which the generals were called upon to submit to the adjutant general, so much delay occurred in their preparation and clearance for publication that they tended to be of greater historic than news interest.[35]

A sample of the attempts by the press to provide its readers with statements of war aims appeared in the *Mobile Register* on August 3, 1861. The *Register* explained to its readers: "We are fighting primarily for the grand object of 'Independence.' But we are fighting, too, that our planters, and our merchants, and our artisans, and our laborers, may prosper. That our cities may flourish and grow great by profits no longer poured into the lap of the seaports of the Eastern North. That our staple products may no longer pay a ruinous percentage on actual trade in them, and no longer ultimately work [to] the enrichment of the North. That we may have the whole loaf, which should be the reward of the industrial energy of the South, and not give a large proportion of it to the North. That the surplus of our exports should come to us, to whom it properly belongs, and no longer go to the North, enabling it to consume large imports. . . . That we may trade direct, and no longer pay a profit into the hands of the North for acting as

---

popular "with the comparatively small number of our people who have the chance of seeing him frequently. . . ." *Memphis Daily Appeal*, March 28, 1862.

[34] Mathews, *Reporting the Wars*, p. 88. Something equivalent to the system of press releases inaugurated by the Federal Secretary of War Stanton in May 1864 was envisioned in a resolution offered in the Confederate House of Representatives in 1862 by Congressman J. B. Heiskell of Tennessee. First Congress, Second Session, Confederate States, *Southern Historical Society Papers*, XLV (1925), 188-89. The failure of the Confederate government to issue casualty lists to relieve suspense after a great battle was an especially inept shortcoming of its public information program.

[35] Usually a period of weeks or even months elapsed before the official report of a battle or campaign by the Commanding General was released to the public. Beauregard's report of the Battle of Shiloh was not published until a month after the battle, and Lee's report of the Gettysburg campaign was not transmitted to the War Department until six months after its termination.

our agent in foreign trade. That we may no longer pay high prices for merchandise that the manufactures of the North may be protected; and no longer pay high freights that its shipping interests may be prospered. That our institutions may be safe."

One of the standard aims of war propaganda is to inspire hatred of the enemy. To this end, the Confederate press made frequent use of atrocity stories, some no doubt manufactured for the purpose. The Richmond *Examiner*, for example, made it appear that cold-blooded Union soldiers, "drunken with wine, blood, and fury" were permitted to enter every house at their pleasure to "plunder the property, ravish the women, burn the house, and proceed to the next." The *Atlanta Intelligencer* claimed that it had received from its army correspondent Samuel C. Reid a Yankee contrivance for poisoning the flesh by gunshot wounds. The *Memphis Avalanche* reported that the story of McDowell's army being provided with thirty thousand handcuffs for application to the Confederate prisoners they expected to capture in the First Manassas campaign was "fully confirmed." J. R. Thompson of the *Memphis Appeal,* who first accused the Yankees of wantonly burning the town of Hampton, Virginia in August 1861, had to admit later that the Confederates had burned the town by order of General Magruder![36] To inspire ridicule of the cowardly and ungentlemanly behavior of enemy soldiers, Southern war correspondents urged on their readers with tales of Union generals plying their soldiers with whisky before sending them into battle, and published indecent passages from letters written by enemy soldiers that had been picked up on the battlefield.

In publishing news of enemy operations, the Confederate press rarely overlooked the propaganda implications of such news. Editors constantly stressed the wisdom of distrusting news from Yankee sources. Yet Confederate reporting was no more reliable than its Northern counterpart in such matters as suppressing information about enemy successes, resorting to name-calling to personalize war hatred, and otherwise taking liberties with the facts for propaganda purposes. When Sherman's army entered Jackson, Mississippi in May 1863, a

---

[36] *Daily Richmond Examiner*, March 7, 1864 as quoted in J. W. Silver, *Confederate Morale and Church Propaganda* (Tuscaloosa, Ala., 1957), p. 89; *Atlanta Daily Intelligencer*, October 16, 1863; *Memphis Daily Avalanche*, August 16, 1861; *Memphis Daily Appeal*, August 14, 15, 1861. For another contradiction of an atrocity story by Confederate war correspondent J. J. Lane see *New Orleans Daily Delta*, October 31, 1861.

letter that had been left behind by Editor Fleet Cooper of the *Mississippian*, in which his use of propaganda techniques was explained, fell into the enemy's hands. The letter, written to a friend in Louisiana named Douglas Hamilton, described articles written by Cooper for enemy consumption. Cooper told Hamilton that from the beginning of the war it had been his intent to use his newspaper to create dissension between the Eastern and Western troops in the Northern army. The technique he employed was to credit the soldiers from the Northwest with all the achievements of Northern arms and depict the Eastern Yankees as "cowardly, malignant, and intolerant."[37]

The Southern press also planted stories in their news columns to deceive and mislead the enemy. The editor of the *Richmond Examiner* was probably exceptional in being unwilling to permit the *Examiner's* columns to be used for such purposes. Editor Daniel maintained that "the reputation of our paper for truthfulness is our own; and we cannot understand either the right or the policy on our part to bring it into discredit by publishing false statements of fact . . . for the purpose of blinding and misleading the enemy."[38]

Although censorship of the press by the government in Richmond might be supposed to offend the powerful sentiment of states' rights, censorship per se was not unknown in the South in April 1861. Long before the war, laws penalizing publications that advocated the abolition of slavery had been supported by public opinion throughout the South. Indeed, a Virginia statute passed in 1832 prescribed the death penalty on the second offense for any publications tending to incite slave insurrections that were written, printed, or circulated by a slave or free Negro.[39] There was little or no public opposition, therefore,

[37] *Chicago Daily Tribune*, June 4, 1863; *Philadelphia Inquirer*, June 9, 1863.

[38] *Daily Richmond Examiner*, June 23, 1862; J. G. Randall, "The Newspaper Problem in Its Bearing upon Military Secrecy during the Civil War," *American Historical Review*, XXIII (January 1918), 314.

[39] Q. C. Wilson, "A Study and Evaluation of the Military Censorship in the Civil War," unpub. Master's thesis (University of Minnesota, 1945), p. 196; *Acts of the General Assembly of Virginia, 1831-1832*, passed March 15, 1832, section 7 (Richmond, 1832), pp. 21-22. The death penalty did not apply to white men who wrote, printed, or circulated publications inciting slaves to rebel. For a reference to a Virginia statute of 1836 adjudging any white person guilty of a felony under penalty of imprisonment who wrote, printed, or circulated such publications, see Clement Eaton, *Freedom of Thought in the Old South* (New York, 1951), p. 127. The text of the 1836 act is given in *Acts of the General Assembly of Virginia, Passed in Session 1835-1836* (Richmond, 1836), pp. 44-45.

when in May 1861 the Provisional Congress of the Confederate States enacted a bill empowering the president to establish telegraphic censorship. The bill authorized Davis to place special agents of the government in the offices of various telegraph companies to supervise communications passing over the lines, prohibited the transmission of code messages, required the employees of the telegraph companies to take an oath of allegiance to the Confederate government, and imposed penalties of fine and imprisonment on persons convicted of sending news detrimental to the Southern cause by telegraph.[40]

On June 1, 1861, within ten days after the Confederate government assumed control of the telegraph lines, it placed restrictions on postal service. Southern postmasters had been censoring mail and newspapers received from the North for many years prior to the war. The practice now became the official policy of the Confederate government.[41] Yet the letter correspondence of Southern newspapermen was censored at the source only on rare occasions.

To some extent the Davis administration relied on the discretion of newspaper editors and their reporters to withhold information that might prove damaging to the Confederate cause. It will be recalled that Secretary Walker issued a general appeal of this nature to newspaper correspondents during the summer of 1861. Generally the press responded favorably to such appeals, and a year later, General Lee told Secretary of War Randolph of the existence of a voluntary censorship agreement between the newspaper editors and the army commanders.[42]

That the guidelines for voluntary censorship were evident to the press is indicated by statements in various newspapers from time to time and by the Confederate Press Association's instructions to its agents.[43] In an editorial published in the early part of 1862 the *Mem-*

[40] J. P. Jones, "The Confederate Press and the Government," *Americana*, XXXVII (January 1943), 10; Senate Doc. No. 234, 58 Cong., 2d Session, *Journal of the Congress of the Confederate States of America* (Washington, D.C., 1904-1905), xxv (May 9, 1861), p. 202. A telegram from V. E. Shepherd to Dr. W. S. Morris, November 14, 1864, Southern Telegraph Co. Papers suggests that Shepherd may have been acting as a war department censor at this time.

[41] Wilson, "Study and Evaluation," p. 201.

[42] *O.R.* (Army) Ser. I, vol. xi, pt. 3, pp. 635-36. Lee's letter to Randolph was dated July 7, 1862.

[43] The text of these instructions, contained in the 7th clause of the code of instructions to Press Association reporters, is given in a letter addressed to the *Atlanta Intelligencer* by J. S. Thrasher in its October 13, 1863 issue.

phis Appeal spelled out the distinction between contraband and publishable news that had been established by military authority. According to the *Appeal*, forbidden news topics were the movements of Confederate troops, munitions of war, gunboats, or batteries, and the descriptions and locations of forts. It was permissible, on the other hand, to publish all movements of the enemy obtained from whatever source, descriptions of enemy fortifications and munitions of war, "and all intelligence of our own movements taken from northern papers, without giving additional authenticity to the same."[44]

In light of the probable inadequacy of these rules to prevent infractions of military security, more than a year later the *Charleston Courier* proposed for adoption by the press a series of regulations that were evidently intended to plug loopholes in the system of voluntary censorship. The *Courier's* prescription was:

1. Never allude to the number or position of our forces.
2. Never describe points likely to be occupied by the enemy, or utter doubts as to their strength.
3. Never refer to the arrival or departure of troops.
4. Never discuss the events of the future, or hint at enterprises to be undertaken.
5. In describing a battle avoid details of our strength, and confine the narration to things done.[45]

Although voluntary censorship imposed a severe strain on the spirit of news enterprise, Southern editors tried to withhold news that appeared to be injurious to their cause. On one occasion in June 1864, as previously noted, General Lee informed President Davis that he had just learned that the correspondent of the *Richmond Enquirer* had full information about Early's movement against Washington but had cautioned his newspaper not to publish it.[46]

The legislative hall of the Confederate Congress, the Richmond telegraph office, and army headquarters were important places for the application of official censorship. Also, the secret sessions of Congress may be regarded as a censorship device. Whenever matters having to

---

[44] *Memphis Daily Appeal*, February 11, 1862.

[45] *Charleston Daily Courier*, July 18, 1863. See also *ibid.*, October 14, 1863 for another list of items that the *Courier* thought should be carefully excluded from press reports.

[46] Jones, "Confederate Press and the Government," p. 10; R. E. Lee to Mr. President, June 15, 1864, D. S. Freeman, *Lee's Dispatches* (New York, 1915), pp. 240, 241.

do with military operations came before it, it would order the galleries cleared and sit behind closed doors. The same procedure was followed when the House of Representatives requested information about the number and movements of Confederate troops.

Army generals used a combination of persuasion and force to prevent Southern war correspondents from publishing news they wished to keep out of the newspapers. In cases of violation of a general's orders, expulsion of the offending correspondent was likely to follow. If the reporter happened to be in military service, he was all the more easily silenced. For criticizing the inactivity of a major general, the *Knoxville Register*'s cavalry correspondent "Bird" received a verbal command from that general to sever his newspaper connection with the *Register*. After the general recovered his temper, "Bird" was permitted to resume his correspondence.[47] The resentment felt by Southern war correspondents at military interference with their reporting is suggested by the complaint of a *Richmond Whig* correspondent: "We know of nothing to one in quest of war news more vexatiously provoking than to approach one of those members of a General's Staff who ranks very much as a tray of spades does when 'Clubs is Trumps' at a game of 'All Fours,' and when asked in a polite way as to the news from a certain point, to have him draw himself up in an erect position as if about to sit for a photograph for 'The Illustrated News' — and pompously reply: 'We have nothing'; (emphasis on the we) when, at the same time, the enquirer for war news has private dispatches in his pocket that fighting has been going on all day at the point specified."[48]

The press naturally objected to regulations designed to broaden the censorship and render it more effective. Editorial protest was widespread when a bill that failed to pass was introduced into Congress in January 1862 subjecting to severe penalties any newspaper that published information vital to Confederate security.[49] The *Rich-*

[47] *Knoxville Daily Register*, August 14, September 13, 1862. For a rebuke from a lieutenant general to the *Meridian Clarion* for spreading false information see *O.R.* (Army) Ser. I, vol. xlv, pt. 2, p. 761. The communication was dated January 3, 1865.

[48] *Richmond Daily Whig*, June 17, 1864; Jones, "Confederate Press and the Government," p. 13.

[49] See e.g. *Daily Richmond Examiner*, January 11, 1862; *Richmond Daily Dispatch*, January 13, 1862; *Richmond Daily Whig*, January 18, February 3, 1862; *Knoxville Daily Register*, January 19, 1862; *New Orleans Daily Delta*, January 21, 1862.

mond Examiner was soon up in arms again over a new rule preventing reporters from coming to the War Department to copy public dispatches received during the day. When in October 1862 a dispatch from the Richmond Associated Press, reporting Stuart's raid into Pennsylvania, was stopped by the censor until it received clearance from the adjutant general, the *Richmond Whig* protested vigorously. The *Whig* contended that the dispatch was based on reports gleaned from the Northern press, and pointed out that up to this time no special permission had been required to telegraph news obtained from Northern sources so long as its accuracy was not confirmed. A censorship regulation that more nearly conformed to previous practice was a general order issued soon after the Battle of Fredericksburg, placing restrictions on the reporting of the positions of Confederate troops.[50]

The Confederate Congress displayed some impatience with military censorship when, in 1862, General Van Dorn issued an order in which he threatened to fine and imprison newspaper editors who spoke or wrote in derogatory terms about any military officer within his department. Senator T. J. Semmes of Louisiana introduced a resolution calling for the judiciary committee of the Senate to examine the possibility of limiting such abuse of power by military officers; his resolution was approved by both houses.[51]

The opposition of the newspapers that formed the Confederate Press Association to military censorship was one of the factors that brought about the establishment of the association in the early part of 1863; General Manager Thrasher labored with some success to impose restraints upon the censorship. He informed the board of directors of the association that on some occasions the censors had prevented the transmission of news reports because in their judgment they had been "sensational"; in other instances, without giving any reasons censors had stopped news reports after they had been partially transmitted to their intended recipients. When Thrasher wanted to

[50] *Daily Richmond Examiner*, March 14, 1862; *Richmond Daily Whig* as reprinted in *Charleston Daily Courier*, October 20, 1862; *O.R.* (Army) Ser. I, vol. xx, pt. 2, p. 459. For the text of a dispatch from Adjutant General Cooper to the editor of the *Rockingham* (Va.) *Register* of July 11, 1864 explaining censorship regulations in effect at that time, see *Philadelphia Inquirer*, October 6, 1864. Cooper's dispatch was found in the Harrisonburg telegraph office when Sheridan's troops occupied the town. The censorship regulations that were in effect at Savannah in the spring of 1862 are specified in Headquarters, State of Georgia in Savannah, Special Order No. 103, April 15, 1862, Southern Telegraph Co. Papers.

[51] Wilson, "Study and Evaluation," pp. 214-15.

know why this was done, he was referred to instructions issued by the postmaster general, which he then was not permitted to see.[52]

It is the opinion of a leading authority on Civil War censorship of the press that Southern press censorship was relatively effective during the first two years of the war, but became progressively less so after that time. The principal factor in bringing about its lessening effectiveness, as this writer sees it, was the opposition to censorship by the P.A.[53] To the extent that the censorship became less effective after 1862, it would seem that its weakening was quite as much a product of the decreasing strength of the Confederate government and its pre-occupation with problems other than those of preventing news leaks. Nevertheless Congress still gave attention to proposals for strengthening the censorship. In September 1864 the War Department issued an order prescribing trial by court martial of officers and soldiers who wrote any article regarding troop movements for publication less than one month after the campaign had ended.[54] The author of one of the leading histories of war reporting, Joseph J. Mathews, credits Confederate censorship with having been generally more effective than censorship in the North. He explains the difference in terms of the weaker position of the Confederate press vis-à-vis the government and the greater unity of purpose of the region which these newspapers served. Mathews' opinion is probably correct, although he admits that damaging disclosures of military information by the Southern press were by no means exceptional.[55]

Along with slips of this nature, which censorship was unable to prevent, Confederate newspapers frequently exaggerated the importance of small-scale military actions. They also published inflated estimates of enemy losses and minimized the losses of their own troops, distorted the facts and gave a slanted interpretation of them to conform to a pattern in line with their hopes and sympathies, disseminated canards which were sometimes concocted by stock market operators,

[52] *Ibid.*, p. 215; Wilson, "Confederate Press Association," p. 163.

[53] Wilson, "Study and Evaluation," p. 239; Edwin Emery and H. L. Smith, *The Press and America* (New York, 1954), p. 298.

[54] Senate Doc. No. 234, 58 Cong. 2d Sess. xxviii (May 19, 1864), 60; *Atlanta Daily Intelligencer*, May 31, 1864; *Mobile Daily Advertiser and Register*, September 30, 1864.

[55] Mathews, *Reporting the Wars*, p. 94. For official warnings against infractions of the censorship addressed to Southern newspaper editors and telegraph managers see *O.R.* (Army) Ser. I, vol. xxxv, pt. 1, p. 522; vol. xlvi, pt. 2, p. 1,047; vol. li, pt. 2, p. 626.

and permitted their reporters to palm off on their readers faked eye-witness accounts of battles and other newsworthy events.

From his ranch in Texas on New Year's Day 1862, the distinguished Mexican War correspondent George W. Kendall addressed a letter to his old newspaper, the *New Orleans Picayune*, castigating the Southern press for indulging in exaggeration and magnifying trifling skirmishes into pitched battles.[56] The Charleston and Savannah newspapers derided the sensationalism of the Richmond and Atlanta newspapers; not even the reporters of the P.A. were proof against accusations of slanting news. A soldier correspondent of a Georgia newspaper noticed how during the Atlanta campaign: ". . . the press reporters of this army are continually sending dispatches to the press that deserters are flocking to us daily, and that the enemy are completely demoralized. These reports no sensible soldier here believes, knowing that they are predicated upon the statements made by worthless, drunken soldiers, who straggle into our lines. Since my connection with the army, I have had ample opportunities to ascertain what class of men are those who desert their colors and comrades in arms from each army. They are emphatically a worthless race of skunks, totally devoid of honor, truth, and character; at home their testimony would be excluded in a court of justice. Therefore I would suggest to your readers not to place implicit confidence in the dispatches forwarded by reporters in this army. The soldiers in the trenches, who receive and return the fire of the enemy are more competent to judge of the demoralization of the enemy than any non-combatant who sits in the rear over a *fowl plate*, speculating upon the propriety of forwarding another budget of 'sensationals.' "[57]

The *Knoxville Register* identified another aspect of sensational reporting in the graphic descriptions of bayonet charges published in the daily press which made it appear that such events were common occurrences. The *Register* cited the "stubborn fact" that up until that time (January 1863) not a single instance of opposing forces of any

---

[56] *New Orleans Daily Picayune*, January 26, 1862.

[57] *Daily Columbus Enquirer*, June 28, 1864. J. W. Silver, "Propaganda in the Confederacy," *Journal of Southern History*, xi (November 1945), 499, claims, however, that Confederate news distortion was slight and as such was the "natural exaggeration of editors who wishfully misinterpreted reports which at best were extremely unreliable."

considerable number meeting at close quarters in a bayonet encounter could be produced.[58]

At various times during the war, the Southern press received reports by telegraph that General Price had captured St. Louis, that General McClellan had been killed at Second Manassas, that General Banks had surrendered his army "unconditionally" to General Dick Taylor, that General Steele's Yankee army had similarly surrendered to Price at Camden, Arkansas, and that the Confederates had captured forty thousand prisoners at the Battle of Gettysburg.[59] One of the cruelest telegraphic hoaxes of the war was the report of a stupendous Confederate victory that originated with the telegraph operator in Selma, Alabama in September 1863. Preying on the anxiety of the people during the week after the Battle of Chickamauga, the Selma operator concocted a fanciful story about Bragg having attacked Rosecrans, capturing 16,000 prisoners and 73 pieces of artillery, about the seizure of the Federal ordnance train by Wheeler's cavalry, and about Bragg being 30 miles beyond Chattanooga in hot pursuit of Rosecrans' fleeing army.[60]

Probably the last such hoax that was perpetrated during the war occurred in Richmond only two days before Petersburg fell. In the midst of the despondency hanging over Richmond at the time, an early morning train raced to the capital from Petersburg with the news that in a night attack General Lee had crushed the enemy's entire line. This report, which was not official but was asserted to be the forerunner of an official announcement, was generally believed in Richmond. It was even carried to the bedside of the dying editor of the *Richmond Examiner*, John M. Daniel, to comfort him in his last hours. And John Mitchel regretted in the *Examiner*'s editorial column the next day that his chief had died almost at the moment that his beloved Southern Confederacy had gained a great victory.[61]

As for the question of whether Southern war correspondence improved or declined during the war, the opinion has been expressed

[58] *Knoxville Daily Register*, January 6, 1863.

[59] *Richmond Daily Dispatch*, February 1, 1862; *Knoxville Daily Register*, September 7, 1862; *Daily Richmond Examiner*, May 19, 1864; *Savannah Republican*, May 10, 1864.

[60] *Memphis Daily Appeal*, October 9, 1863; W. R. Plum, *The Military Telegraph during the Civil War in the United States* (Chicago, 1882), II, 310.

[61] Pollard, *Life of Jefferson Davis*, pp. 485-86.

by one writer that the period from June 1862 until late 1863 saw a decline in the quality of Confederate war news, that in late 1863 it improved only to deteriorate in the following year as the Confederacy neared its end.[62] No explanation is given for the above pattern; it seems doubtful that this or any generalization other than the hypothesis of a gradual decline in the quality of Confederate news can be supported by the record. The Richmond press published comparatively little special correspondence during the last year of the war, and the *Mobile Register* was almost alone among Confederate newspapers at the time in maintaining an able staff of war correspondents. As late as October 1864 the *Charleston Courier* complimented Forsyth on possessing a corps of correspondents "not equalled—certainly not surpassed in quantity and quality of communications—by any other journal on our exchange list." The *Courier* went on to say that "the editors [of the *Register*] very properly select and prefer good competent correspondents, and let them write what they see, and know, and think of, and for themselves, and do not expect or desire them to take the cue from the editors and write up or down to a party or partisan bias or humor."[63]

In a comparison of Northern and Southern war correspondence the South comes off second best quantitatively speaking. Not simply did the South have fewer reporters, fewer daily newspapers, and fewer large newspapers at the beginning of the war; as its major cities one by one fell into enemy hands, its daily newspapers either closed up shop, acquired managements which aligned their editorial policy with that of the Northern press, or fled to other parts of the Confederacy. During the last year of the war, what little news there was in the Southern press was largely of Northern origin or was reprinted from newspapers published in the parts of the South under enemy occupation.

Qualitatively speaking, Southern war reporting at its best was comparable to the top performances of the North's leading reporters, in terms of reliability, readability, descriptive qualities, and the reporter's ability to grasp the larger significance of the events he observed. Peter

[62] Mathews, *Reporting the Wars*, p. 95.

[63] *Charleston Daily Courier*, October 25, 1864. For an editorial rejoicing at the improvement of Southern journalism as a result of the war and recommending the establishment of a professional association of Southern journalists see *Daily Richmond Enquirer*, September 27, 1864.

Alexander's battle reports of Shiloh and Gettysburg, although somewhat briefer, merit comparison in their sweep, their capacity to enable the reader to comprehend the complicated maneuvers on both sides, and their dramatic quality, with the best efforts of leading Northern correspondents like Whitelaw Reid, Henry Villard, and Charles Carleton Coffin. Alexander combined with his skill in achieving panoramic effects an interest in the common soldier (not unlike that of World War II reporter Ernie Pyle), which caused the Georgian to be idolized by Southern soldiers and civilians. His transparent honesty inspired trust among his readers and gave him entree into military circles from which reporters were ordinarily excluded. Although his loyalty and devotion to the Confederate cause were beyond question, his sense of integrity and courage impelled him to be critical of incompetence and injustice when he felt such criticism was called for. An illustration of his willingness to recognize and admit defeat was the remarkably frank letter he sent to the *Richmond Dispatch,* stating the facts about the disaster of Missionary Ridge.[64]

De Fontaine reported the war in the grand manner of the *London Times* correspondent William H. Russell, whose Crimean War dispatches he apparently had read and which had impressed him. Probably his battle report of Antietam was the apex of a reporting career which was neither so continuous nor perhaps quite so distinguished as that of the great Georgia newspaperman with whom he was associated in the minds of his readers. Other outstanding examples of Southern battle reporting during the war included Leonidas Spratt's account of the First Battle of Manassas, Samuel Chester Reid's fascinating stories of Murfreesboro and Chickamauga, and the controversial reporting by A. S. Abrams and "Shadow" of the Atlanta campaign.

"Shadow" was obviously a product of the literary romanticism so characteristic of the South in the mid-nineteenth century. The sentimental apostrophe addressed to the town of Marietta, Georgia, in one of his war letters exemplifies a descriptive talent that must have been very appealing to the distaff side of his readership. Dating his letter from this Southern small town on May 27, 1864, "Shadow" wrote: "Quaint old Marietta! How thy ways have changed, and thy sweet, smiling summer face altered its expression. Once thou wert the liveliest

[64] For the text of a letter from a number of Georgia soldiers to the editor of the *Savannah Republican,* March 19, 1862, offering to contribute a dollar a month each toward the expenses of keeping "P.W.A." in the field see *Savannah Republican,* March 21, 1862.

in thy suit of green, decorated with roses and honeysuckles. No place was fairer than thy little park. The dells, meadows and streams which bordered upon thy pleasant outlines of villa, street and lane were like the undulations of an Arcadia. It was beautiful to climb the fairy Kenesaw and look down upon thee, resting in thy quiet circle; to note the wealth of garden, worth of grove; to pluck out from the array of roof and balcony the separate ornaments of each broad avenue; to dwell upon thy rising spires twinkling in the last rays of the sun; and to return thither by moonlight through the thick lines of blackberry, box and evergreen. But those times have gone. War has thee now in his rough arms, fragile Marietta! Thou art as bare as a throstle, as ragged and unseemly as a beggar girl. The soldiers have left thee little but the past and thy loneliness. The citizen has deserted his pretty home, the maiden no longer tends the flower beds and the vine. The honeysuckles droop; the blossoms are scattered. Warble on poor bird in the desecrated porch. Thine is the [dirge?] of . . . old, sacked and spoiled Marietta. Goodbye to thee old town! . . . Live only in our memory!"[65]

The political reporting at Richmond of G. W. Bagby, with his eye for picturesque street scenes and his intimate knowledge of public affairs; and of John R. Thompson, the well-informed "Dixie" of the *Memphis Appeal* compared favorably with the best efforts of the Capitol press corps in Washington. Perhaps the principal shortcoming of Bagby's reporting was its rather obvious bias against the Confederate president, whom he once characterized as possessing "the absurd ambition of getting all power and never using it."[66]

Confederate war correspondence at its worst was meretricious and prolix, making use of an inflated style of writing and indulging in empty bombast. It was the practice of less gifted reporters to write about "gory battle-fields bathed in brothers' blood," to describe armies in pell mell retreat as "retiring in good order," to commit errors such as reporting a regiment "literally decimated, losing two-thirds of its men," to stigmatize Yankee soldiers as "ferocious Hessians" and "cowardly hirelings," and to allude piously to "that overruling Providence, which up to the present time has watched over and protected the infant Southern Republic."[67] Even the elegant de Fontaine was capable

[65] *Mobile Daily Advertiser and Register*, May 31, 1864.
[66] *Ibid.*, November 19, 1864.
[67] *Knoxville Daily Register*, April 4, 1862; Journal of Sara Jane Sams, February 6, 1865, Misc. MSS., South Caroliniana Library, University of South Carolina;

of clumsily mingling fancy with invective as in the passage, "the long finger of Morris island that juts into the bay only twelve hundred yards from Fort Sumter is a perfect bee hive, and the island farther on is black with their [the enemy's] vile hordes."[68]

Late in 1864 the editor of the *Mobile Register* gave Southern reporters a much-needed lecture on the virtues of brevity. He began by saying that rarely in these days was there a subject which warranted a column's length.

"Let our correspondents think of it. Are they denouncing Boyce, Stephens and Parsons; let them condense their logic, leave out their rhetoric entirely, and in their recapitulations take *some* things for granted. Are they writing from the front; let them bear in mind that all our soldiers are heroes, and not dwell too much on the gallantry of Major This, or Colonel That, or even of Private So and So—that will keep (if it is worth keeping) till the war is over.

"Did any of our correspondents ever take the trouble of reading one of Cicero's orations by a watch? If they will they will find some of the best of them less than half an hour long. . . . The intellectual fault of our age and nation is verbiage; the times admonish us to correct it. . . . If an idea can be stated in four words instead of five, we implore them to strike out the fifth, if it be but a monosyllable; and, as a general rule, to omit their comments and permit the reader to make them instead. We could say much more, but our theme admonishes us to desist."[69]

As a part of the Confederate propaganda mechanism the Southern press dared not admit to its people that they were confronted with defeat, so long as the South's leadership was determined to keep on fighting. Hence it is difficult to determine from either news or editorial content at what point its newspapermen came to realize that the South had lost the war. Among themselves and in letters not intended for publication, some of them appear to have admitted privately what they could not reveal publicly. Thus one finds Editor J. Henly Smith of the *Atlanta Confederacy* confiding to Vice President Stephens in August 1863, "I confess that I can hardly find a word of encourage-

Savannah Republican, August 11, 1862; *New Orleans Daily Picayune*, October 11, 1861; *Memphis Daily Appeal*, December 24, 1861; *Daily Richmond Enquirer*, July 15, 1861.

[68] *Memphis Daily Appeal*, September 15, 1863.
[69] *Mobile Daily Advertiser and Register*, October 23, 1864.

ment to say in the paper. . . ."[70] According to one of John M. Daniel's editorial writers, the editor of the *Richmond Examiner* had lost all hope of a Confederate victory by the summer of 1864.[71] Yet these and the great majority of other Southern newspapers continued to be optimistic about Confederate prospects until almost the very end. The substitution of fantasy for realism was not entirely out of loyalty to the Southern cause. The herd instinct the press exhibited whenever a newspaper like the *Augusta Chronicle* or the *Montgomery Mail* suggested that peace or reconstruction was preferable to a continuation of the war was enough to whip the waverers into line and silence any minority opinion.

In a recent volume a prominent Southern historian has alluded to the myths of Southern exclusiveness, such as the Cavalier Myth and the Plantation Legend, which are in conflict with the reality of Southern history.[72] It may be suggested that the notion of Southern freedom of the press during the Civil War is another myth that must be discarded in the interest of a proper understanding of the Southern past. It may be true, as the eminent historian E. Merton Coulter has intimated, that in comparison with more than a score of newspapers suppressed or destroyed by the Federal government, military commanders, or mobs in the North, "no newspaper was ever suppressed by state or Confederate authority throughout the war. . . ."[73] Yet this statement fails to take into account that William G. Brownlow's *Knoxville Whig* was suppressed six months after the war began and his press and types destroyed.[74] It is also likely other Southern newspapers would have en-

[70] J. Henly Smith to Alexander H. Stephens, August 20, 1863, Stephens Papers, Library of Congress.

[71] R. W. Hughes, *"Editors of the Past"* (Richmond, 1897), pp. 29-30. For a prediction by another Confederate newspaperman, that "the Stars and Stripes will float over the government works in Augusta before a year expires and Mr. Davis be dead or an exile," see Henry Cleveland to Alexander H. Stephens, June 8, 1864, Stephens Papers.

[72] C. V. Woodward, *The Burden of Southern History* (Baton Rouge, 1960) p. 13.

[73] E. M. Coulter, *The Confederate States of America, 1861-1865* (Baton Rouge, 1950), p. 503.

[74] *Dictionary of American Biography*, ii, 177-78; William Rule, ed., *Standard History of Knoxville, Tenn.* (Chicago, 1900), p. 323. In the margin of the issue of June 11, 1864 of the Library of Congress file of the *Knoxville Whig*, Brownlow's son, John B. Brownlow told how: "The rebellion suspended and destroyed the editor's newspaper property, the most valuable in the whole southern confederacy, bringing him an income of about $10,000. . . . This property was sold by order

countered a similar fate had not public pressure induced a change in editorial policy (as in the case of the *New Orleans True Delta*); had not changes in editorial management been brought about (as in the case of the *Richmond Whig*); or if the offenders had not been forced out of business because of lack of public support.[75] The *Wilmington Daily Herald*, a conservative North Carolina paper, and the *Charlottesville Review*, the leading anti-secession paper of Virginia, suspended publication within three months after the war began.[76]

HAVING purged or silenced the dissenters, the Southern press experienced freedom only within the narrowly prescribed limits its editors fairly well understood. It was permissible within these limits to attack particular individuals and to question the competence of Congress or the president, but criticism of the "peculiar institution" and of the independence movement was quite as dangerous as it had been before the war in the closed society the South had evolved during the period of anti-slavery controversy.

Within the framework of these limitations the Southern press did its best to provide full news coverage of the military and political events of the war. In the process it kept before the eyes of its readers the ideal of a perfect social order based on chattel slavery which the South was committed to defend and which in some obscure way was associated with the ideals of human freedom. It portrayed the heroism

---

of the [Tennessee supreme] court just after he went north and the proceeds deposited by the rebel clerk of the chancery court with the rebel officers of the branch bank of Tennessee, who speculated with the money during the war; and the aforesaid clerk tendered to the editor confederate money after Burnside took East Tennessee, when said trash was worthless. The editor was a heavy loser by the war." J. W. Patton, *Unionism and Reconstruction in Tennessee—1860-1869* (Chapel Hill, 1934), p. 69n.

[75] Both the publisher (John Maginnis) and editor (Hugh Kennedy) of the *True Delta* were Unionists who reluctantly supported secession and war. The obituary of Maginnis which appeared in the *True Delta* on March 7, 1863 states that he often exclaimed after the clash of arms at Sumter: "Great God, how can any sane man see in revolution a remedy for our political or social irregularities; or persuade himself that the sword can permanently divide into peaceful and unaggressive communities a nation like this." How Robert Ridgway was forced out of the editorship of the *Richmond Whig* to bring about its alignment with the war party is described above in Chapter 2.

[76] Dwight Dumond, *The Secession Movement, 1860-1861* (New York, 1931), p. 169. The *Wilmington Herald* apparently suspended publication in May 1861, and the last issue of the *Charlottesville* (Weekly) *Review* was July 12, 1861. Winifred Gregory, *American Newspapers, 1821-1936* (New York, 1937), p. 697.

of a small band of patriots battling as their Revolutionary forefathers had done against overwhelming odds and performing knightly deeds of the kind of which Robert E. Lee and Jeb Stuart were authentic symbols. Although it reflected the fluctuating moods of Southern men and women, it flayed incompetent leadership, castigated defeatism and disloyalty, and struggled to survive in the face of staggering difficulties.

Thus the South reported the Civil War, making known the outcome of the great battles and campaigns, the nagging controversies between Jefferson Davis and his war governors, the frustrating mishaps of the Davis administration in the realm of diplomacy, and ultimately the collapse of the Confederacy itself. The successes of the Southern press in reporting the war were the more remarkable in light of the shortage of Southern manpower, the steady attrition of the transportation and communication facilities which were vital to newspaper operation, and the financial problems the press shared with other forms of Southern business enterprise. Its failures were the natural consequence of an environment that had never made possible genuine freedom of the press and in which the South's leading newspapers gradually succumbed to the ordeal of invasion and military defeat.

1. John M. Daniel, *Richmond Examiner*.
COURTESY OF
VIRGINIA HISTORICAL SOCIETY

2. James McDonald, *Richmond Whig*.
COURTESY OF VIRGINIA STATE LIBRARY

3. Robert Barnwell Rhett, Jr.,
Charleston Mercury.
COURTESY OF
CHARLESTON LIBRARY SOCIETY

4. Aaron Willington, *Charleston Courier*.
COURTESY OF
CAROLINA ART ASSOCIATION

5. George W. Adair, *Atlanta Southern Confederacy.*
COURTESY OF JACK ADAIR

6. Durant Da Ponte, *New Orleans Delta.*
COURTESY OF MRS. HARRY DA PONTE

7. Colonel John Forsyth, *Mobile Advertiser and Register.*
Copy of original Brady Negative.
COURTESY OF LIBRARY OF CONGRESS

8. William Tappan Thompson, *Savannah Morning News.*
COURTESY OF
EMORY UNIVERSITY LIBRARY

RICHMOND CORRESPONDENTS

9. George W. Bagby, *Charleston Mercury.*
COURTESY OF
VIRGINIA HISTORICAL SOCIETY

10. John R. Thompson, *Memphis Appeal.*
COURTESY OF HILLMAN LIBRARY OF
UNIVERSITY OF PITTSBURGH

REPORTERS IN THE FIELD

11. William Wallace Screws,
Montgomery Advertiser.
COURTESY OF MRS. WALLACE S. PITTS

12. Samuel Chester Reid, Jr.,
New Orleans Picayune.
COURTESY OF SAMUEL CHESTER REID

13

REPORTERS IN THE FIELD, CONT.

13. Felix Gregory de Fontaine, *Charleston Courier*. COURTESY OF WADE HAMPTON DE FONTAINE

14. Henry Timrod, *Charleston Mercury*. COURTESY OF CHARLESTON LIBRARY SOCIETY

15. Peter W. Alexander, *Savannah Republican*. COURTESY OF MRS. FLORENCE A. BLOMQUIST

16. William A. Courtenay, *Charleston Mercury*. COURTESY OF UNIVERSITY OF SOUTH CAROLINA LIBRARY

17. James Beverley Sener, *Richmond Enquirer, Dispatch*. COURTESY OF WYOMING STATE ARCHIVES AND HISTORICAL DEPARTMENT

14

15

16

17

Richmond, Dec. 12th 1862.

Sir,

I am the regular correspondent of the Savannah Republican and Mobile Advertiser, & have been with the Army ever since the war commenced — not clandestinely but openly. Last night I applied for a passport to go to Fredericksburg, & was refused. Three other gentlemen connected with the Press in this city were more fortunate: they received passports, & left for the Army this morning.

As the hour is past for seeing visitors, I would thank you to make such endorsement upon this note as would enable me to obtain a passport. For character I refer you to the Hon. Mr. Kenan of Georgia, now in Rich'd, & to Col. Gilmer of Engineers.

Very respectfully,
P. W. Alexander

Hon. Jas. A. Seddon, Sec'y of War.

18. Letter of Peter W. Alexander to Secretary of War James A. Seddon, December 12, 1862, protesting his exclusion from Lee's army on the eve of the Battle of Fredericksburg.
COURTESY OF THE NATIONAL ARCHIVES

Southern Guardian

EXTRA.

COLUMBIA, S. C.

Monday Morning, July 23, 10 o'clock.

From the Mercury's Special Dispatch.

MANNASSAS JUNCTION, Saturday night, July 20. During the greater part of yesterday afternoon we were busy in burying the dead near Bull's Run. We, however, have information that the Northern forces are concentrating against us in immense numbers, and they are throwing up earthworks and planting batteries with great energy as if to renew the attack on our troops. We await the onset with the utmost confidence.

Gen. Patterson, with his entire force, has abandoned Martinsburg, and is now hastening to form a junction with McDowell. Troops are being thrown across the river in heavy bodies from Washington, and everything indicates that our position will be attacked speedily by an overwhelming force.

Gen. Beauregard yesterday afternoon issued orders that all civilians, women, and children, should leave Manassas Junction forthwith ; he evidently expects a great battle here to-morrow.

MANASSAS JUNCTION, Sunday night, July 21, 7 o'clock.—At the stone bridge on Bull's Run near this place the Southern troops are again victorious. The slaughter on both sides was terrific.

Gen. Johnston who had been summoned from Winchester to come to the aid of Gen. Beauregard, arrived here with his entire force in time to take part in the battle. Gen. Beauregard had his horse shot from under him while leading Hampton's Legion into position.

Gen. Johnston, during the hottest of the fight, seized the colors of a wavering regiment and rallied them in person to the charge. It is impossible at this moment to estimate the number of the dead and wounded.

It is reported that the Commander-in-Chief of the United States forces, General McDowell, is mortally wounded.

On our side Col. Francis S. Bartow, of Georgia, who was acting as Brigadier General, was mortally wounded, and is since reported dead.

The battle began at 8 a. m., and lasted until 6 p. m.

The enemy is now in full retreat and hotly pursued by our cavalry.

MANASSAS JUNCTION, July 21.—11½ o'clock, p. m.—Amid the bustle and excitement here it is exceedingly difficult to get the correct particulars of the great battle of to-day.

The enemy opened their batteries of heavy artillery and small field pieces at McLean's Ford, about eight o'clock in the morning. The engagement above the Stone Bridge on Bull Run began about ten o'clock. The enemies force, as near as can be ascertained, was at least 50,000, our own force but 20,000.

Gen. N. G. Evans, of South Carolina, led the brigade first into action. Among the Southern forces prominently engaged, were Col. Sloan's 4th regiment, Col. Kershaw's 2d regiment, and Col. Wade Hampton's legion, all of which, are South Carolina volunteers.

Only three men were wounded in Col. Kershaw's Regiment.

In Col. Sloan's Regiment and Hampton's Legion the loss of life was greater. Adjutant Theo. G. Parker and Capt. James Conner, of the Washington Light Infantry, Hampton's Legion, were slightly wounded; Lieut. Col. B. J. Johnson, of the Legion, was killed ; Captains Earle and Echols were slightly wounded.

Men never fought more desperately than did ours to-day. We have captured eighteen pieces of artillery, 400 prisoners. The number killed and wounded cannot be assertained with any accuracy until to-morrow. Our loss is estimated at 200 killed and 300 wounded, while the loss of the enemy could not have been less than several thousand.

These figures, however, may be wide of the mark, for the line of battle was extended and it was almost dark when the enemy gave way.

The Washington Artillery, of New Orleans, was again in the foremost place, and did most effective work. Their fire fell upon the ranks of the foe with murderous effect.

The Oglethorpe Infantry, of Savannah, were cut to pieces.

Col. Bartow's fine regiment of Georgians were nearly a annihilated. Gen. Barnard, E. Bee, of South Carolina, was mortally wounded. Col. Wade Hampton was slightly wounded. Gen. Johnston commanded the left wing, and Gen. Beauregard the right wing.

The reports that reach us here state that our force was not less than 75,000 men, and that the enemy had over 100,000. These statements are probably exaggerated, but it is certain that the leaders on both sides had concentrated their whole available force to take part in the battle.

Among the officers known to have been killed, in addition to those I have named above, is Kerby Smith, of Florida.

At one time during the battle Shermon's celebrated battery of United States flying artillery was on the point of destroying Hampton's legion, when Col. Garland, of the 11th Virginia was ordered to charge the battery at the point of the bayonet. He immediately led the Virginians to the charge under a terrible fire and after a fierce struggle captured the entire battery, and turned its guns upon the enemy.

19. A Confederate Newspaper Extra—*Columbia Southern Guardian*, July 23, 1861.

MANASSAS, Dec. 27th.

To-day our whole army is engaged in building log houses for winter quarters, or in moving to sites already selected. Several brigades will remain where they now are, near the fortifications in Centreville, and the remainder will fall back a mile or two upon Bull Run.—Gen. Kirby Smith's brigade is at "Camp Wigfall," to the right of the Orange and Alexandria road, near the Run. Near by, the whole of Van Dorn's division are making themselves comfortable in their little cottages which rise rapidly day by day, under the dilligent hands of the soldiers. A few brigades are scattered down towards the Occoquon, where wood and water is plenty, the farthest being by Davis's Ford. The artillery, with the exception of Walton's battalion, has already been located between Cub Run and Stone Bridge. The cavalry has fallen back a little and they are now building stables and houses near Centreville. Gen. Stuart will remain in the advance. It is probable that Gen. Johnston will occupy the Lewis House, on the battle field, and Gen. Beauregard Wier's, his old headquarters before the 18th and 21st. Longstreet's division will, if I am correctly informed, occupy the advanced position, and will remain near where it is at present. The artilleryists, detailed to man the guns in the batteries, will also remain by the fortifications. In case of an attack by the Yankees, it will take about two hours to get the main strength of the army across Bull Run. Information of an approach would be given at least two hours before an enemy could come up, and in that time we could be well prepared to resist any force that can be brought up. That is about the situation of affairs for the winter, and it remains to be seen whether our men are to have an opportunity of a brush with the Yankees, or whether they will be allowed to enjoy their new houses in quietness. When I say all are ready for an attack, I express but feebly the feeling which pervades the army.

Yesterday I rode over the battle-field of the 21st for the purpose of making sketches and gathering relics for a fair friend. The day was clear but cold, and the wind blew across the plains as sharp as Shylock's knife. What a scene of desolation was spread out to our view! Autumn and winter have wrought many changes. The trees are bare and leafless; the golden-rods flame no longer by the wayside; the ice-bound streams are slumbering in their beds; the birds sing no more, and even the lazy buzzard has ceased to wheel his circles over the deserted fields. The Henry House still stands, although more than half destroyed; beside it the fatal field—silent, solemn, cold, as befits the tomb of more than two hundred men. How full of recollections was the spot to me! The rose bushes by the door, the corn stubble in the garden, the withered grass, the shattered house, all were aids to my memory, and assisted in busying the mind with retrospection. What trivial things bring back the acts and scenes of former life! A simple flower, noteless to others, brings up vivid recollections of some bygone bale or bliss; a single glance at alien cornfields recalls the form and features of the fair Ruth of our boyhood. Ah! how well do I remember the hour spent upon this same spot upon the evening of that bloody day, when the ground was strewn with dead and dying men who had fallen in the fight; when poor, wounded, suffering beings

moaned in the agonies of death, and called upon God for mercy and pronounced the name of some far-off mother, perhaps even then praying for the safety of her absent son. The gibbous moon rose clean above the horizon, and for an hour shone as if in mockery upon the pale and ghastly features of the dead, then plunged into the black masses of clouds, whose dark battalions chased each other along the sky. Soon after, thick darkness covered the scene and closed the tragedy of the day—a day the pen of history will recall when those who saw it have lain a century dead. How terrible is war! How terrible to think even of the loss of life that war entails! But yet, where is the man who would not prefer death to dishonor, or the manly heart that would not hazard its life-blood to maintain the honor of his country?

The day grew chill and blustering, and as sketching with fingers stiffened and benumbed with cold is a difficult task, that part of the expedition was abandoned, and we turned our horses towards camp. I would like to give a description of the present appearance of the battle-field, but mere words would fail to give the correct idea of it to be gained by accurate maps and drawings. Up to this time none have been issued worthy a glance, or that are not better calculated to mislead than to instruct. I am happy to learn, however, that a book, with maps to fold in it, is now in press, and will be issued at an early day. Messrs. Warder and Catlett, both practical surveyors of this vicinity, are preparing for publication maps of the battle grounds of Bull Run and Manassas Plains. They have both spent many days in taking the bearings and distances of all the roads, the meanders of the streams, the position of every piece or body of woods, and the location of every house. To this is added the position of the troops during the battle, given in conventional signs. A competent draftsman was employed to give an exact delineation of the surface of the grounds in hill and valley. The context is compiled from the reports of officers. If this book and the maps prove correct, it will meet with a ready sale, and I shall take the earliest opportunity after its publication of examining it, and of giving my opinion to those who choose to receive it.

Christmas eve I made a flying trip up the country, and spent a few hours with some friends at Front Royal. Starting late in the evening, we arrived at nine o'clock, and after spending a few happy hours, returned by the train at three. Riding entirely in the night, I was unable to learn much of the country or the town, but fancied it very pleasant. The journey back by moonlight was delightful, and I was reminded of a little German poem which I have translated, and beg to introduce here.

THE MIDNIGHT RIDE.

I ride the cold and dark night through,
　No moon, or stars, to point the way—
The bleak winds whistle wildly, too.
How oft this lonely road I've made
When golden sunshine round me played,
　And sported with the zephyr gay!

I leave the garden far behind;
　O'er dead and fallen leaves I ride,
While through the branches how's the wind.
How oft this spot, when decked with flowers,
And love held court within its bowers,
　Has seen a fair maid by my side?

Gone, now, is Phœbus's golden light;
Low lie the roses on the ground;
And one loved soul has taken flight.
I wander through the land again,
Through winter storm, and dark, and rain,
　With my thick cloak wrapped well around.

Yesterday a Marylander came through our lines, having left Washington the day previous. He brought some noticeable information as to the disposition of the Yankee troops. It is the opinion in Washington that our commissioners will be given up.

As your Norfolk correspondent says, "War news scarce." BOHEMIAN.

20. The news letter of Reporter William G. Shepardson which led to the expulsion by General Joseph E. Johnston of all Southern war correspondents from the Confederate "Army of the Potomac." This letter was published in the *Richmond Dispatch* on December 30, 1861. COURTESY OF THE LIBRARY OF CONGRESS

Confederate States of America,
WAR DEPARTMENT,
Richmond, 5 January 1862

Sir

Your letter of 30th Ulto. and 1st inst.
have been received —

1 — The President to whom I submitted the
latter declines making any change in his
former order relative to Major Whiting —

11 — On the subject of the publication in
the Richmond Despatch of two articles signed
"Bohemian", I share your indignation at
such an outrageous breach of duty of both
the writer and publisher — I have anxiously

I think some of the mischief from this too
frequent offence arises from your own too
lenient tolerance of the presence of newspaper
reporters within your lines — I will do all I
can to help you, but the application of
military regulations within the army will
be much more efficacious than any attempt
at punishment by jury trial — I feel
persuaded that this man Shepardson is a
spy, and would be found guilty as such
by a court-martial, and if he is caught
again within your Camp, I trust you
will bring him to prompt trial as a Spy —
But if I arrest him here, he will at once
be liberated by habeas corpus and I will
be unable to secure his proper punishment — His
offence is a military one and ought to be
summarily repressed by a military trial —

21. Part of letter from Secretary of War Judah P. Benjamin to
General Johnston, January 5, 1862, recommending a military trial of Shepardson.
"I share your indignation at such an outrageous breach of duty
of both the writer and publisher."
COURTESY OF NEW YORK HISTORICAL SOCIETY

22. Letter of Samuel C. Reid, Jr., to General Bragg, August 22, 1862, requesting permission to accompany his army on the march to Kentucky as the correspondent of the *Mobile Register*.

23. The *Atlanta Intelligencer* office in 1860, from an original water color by
Wilbur G. Kurtz in the collection of Franklin M. Garrett, Atlanta, Ga.
COURTESY OF FRANKLIN M. GARRETT

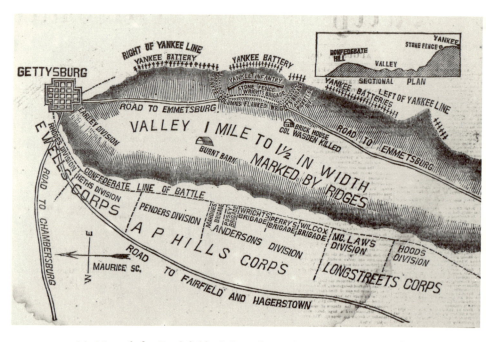

24. Map of the Battlefield of Gettysburg, *Augusta Constitutionalist*,
July 23, 1863. Drawn by an unnamed officer in the field expressly for
the *Constitutionalist*, and engraved by A. Maurice.
COURTESY OF UNIVERSITY OF GEORGIA LIBRARY

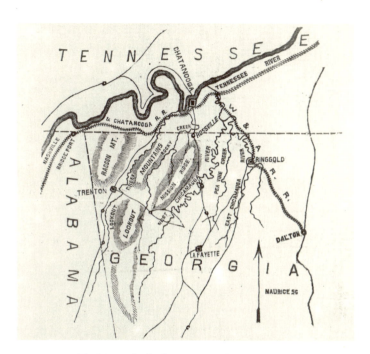

25. Map of Chickamauga and its Vicinity,
Augusta Constitutionalist, October 3, 1863.

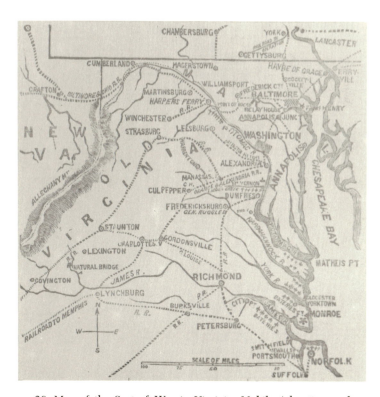

26. Map of the Seat of War in Virginia, *Mobile Advertiser and
Register*, July 14, 1861. Engraved by W. R. Robertson,
Richmond, Va., and stereotyped in New Orleans.

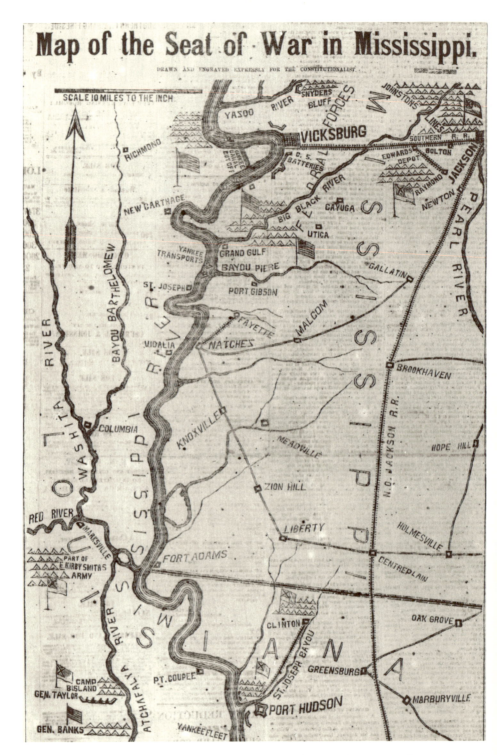

Map of the Seat of War in Mississippi.

DRAWN AND ENGRAVED EXPRESSLY FOR THE CONSTITUTIONALIST.

27. Map of the Seat of War in Mississippi, *Augusta Constitutionalist,*
June 19, 1863. Drawn May 9, 1863 by an unnamed engineer connected with
General Pemberton's Army of the Mississippi.

APPENDIX I

Who Was "Shadow?"

IN MY RESEARCH for this book I have encountered a number of problems of identification of reporters' pseudonyms which have proved more or less baffling. Among the more mysterious are the "J.T.G." who performed competently as a volunteer correspondent of the *Columbus* (Ga.) *Enquirer*, the *Mobile Register*'s "Cousin Nourma," the correspondent "A" who reported Gettysburg for the *Richmond Enquirer* and whom I have only tentatively identified as the North Carolinian Jonathan W. Albertson, and the durable "Tout-le-Monde" of the *Savannah Republican*. In some respects the most interesting of these problems of identification revolves about the question of "Shadow's" identity.

On the 6th of June 1863 the *Memphis Daily Appeal* published the first of a series of able newspaper letters from Chattanooga, written by a reporter whom it identified simply as "Shadow." This reporter continued to furnish war correspondence to the *Appeal* about once or twice a week until the middle of July 1863, after which his byline disappeared from its columns. Almost simultaneously the newspaper began to receive special correspondence from Bragg's Army of Tennessee over the signature of "Ashantee." It is known that "Ashantee" was actually a Kentuckian named John H. Linebaugh (Linebaugh identified himself as "Ashantee" in a letter to Vice President Alexander H. Stephens on April 7, 1864 which is among the Stephens Papers in the Manuscript Division of the Library of Congress). Quite understandably, therefore, in Thomas H. Baker's excellent article on the *Memphis Appeal* in the August 1963 issue of the *Journal of Southern History*, he concluded that "Shadow" and "Ashantee" (Ashante) were different pseudonyms of the same reporter, Linebaugh.

After first assuming, as Baker did, that "Shadow" *was* Linebaugh, I came to rate this assumption as dubious or untenable for the following reasons. During the latter part of May 1864, ten months after the *Memphis Appeal* had stopped publishing any war correspondence from "Shadow," the *Mobile Register* began printing letters from Johnston's army near Dalton, Georgia, that carried the signature of

"Shadow." The "Shadow" series continued to be published in the *Register* about three times a week until shortly after the middle of July. Then after an interruption of about a month and a half, "Shadow's" correspondence for the *Register* was resumed at less frequent intervals, the last letter of the series appearing on January 22, 1865.

There seems to be no evidence that Linebaugh was reporting from Johnston's army, at least for the *Memphis Appeal*, between May and September 1864. Indeed, Linebaugh informed Stephens in the letter of April 7, 1864 referred to above that he had given up his connection with the *Appeal* about two months before and at that time (April) was at home in North Alabama. However, the greatest difficulty about the theory that Linebaugh was "Shadow" is the fact that Linebaugh died on October 26, 1864 in an accident on the Alabama River at a time when apparently "Shadow" was very much alive. Exactly one month and a day after Linebaugh's death the *Mobile Register* published another letter from "Shadow" that was dated at Florence, Alabama on November 23, 1864. If the "Shadow" who reported for the *Register* in 1864 was the same newspaperman who wrote for the *Memphis Appeal* in June-July 1863 over that byline, then Linebaugh and "Shadow" had to be two different persons.

Still another reason for doubting the identity of "Shadow" and Linebaugh was a letter "Shadow" published in the *Mobile Register* on May 28, 1864, in which he described himself as the captain of a company of Confederate pikemen at Nashville after the fall of Fort Donelson in February 1862. Linebaugh, on the other hand, had moved from Kentucky to Alabama before the Civil War and apparently was not in military service at any time during the war.

On the assumption that "Shadow" was possibly a Tennessean, to which his first war reporting assignment with the *Memphis Appeal* lent credence, I constructed two other theories as to his identity. One of these was Albert Roberts, the "John Happy" of the *Chattanooga Rebel*, who was in Chattanooga at the time "Shadow" was writing letters from there in the summer of 1863. When I discovered, however, in the *Mobile Register* of July 16, 1864 a reference by "Shadow" to a statement by "John Happy" supporting one of "Shadow's" opinions about the Atlanta campaign, I reconsidered the idea that "Shadow" could be Roberts.

I then conceived the hypothesis that "Shadow" was Roberts' alter ego on the *Rebel*, subsequently the famous editor of the *Louisville*

Courier-Journal, Henry Watterson. For a number of reasons the Watterson hypothesis seemed to fit the facts rather well. Watterson, a native Tennessean, had been in Nashville writing for the *Banner* of that city at the time (February 1862) "Shadow" claimed to have been there. Also, like Roberts, Watterson was in Chattanooga when "Shadow" was reporting for the *Appeal* from there in the summer of 1863; he had been a member of the editorial staff of the *Atlanta Confederacy* just before "Shadow" began reporting the Atlanta campaign of 1864 from Atlanta and other points in northwest Georgia. Moreover, Watterson had not simply been the army correspondent "Grape" of the *Augusta Constitutionalist* during the Atlanta campaign; he was identified by the *Mobile Register* in October 1864 as "lately army correspondent of this paper."

Then at a given point I uncovered evidence that seemed to prove that "Shadow" was *not* Henry Watterson. The evidence was a letter written from Atlanta on August 19, 1864, and published in the *Mobile Register* nine days later, in which "Shadow" commented that at a time of general exodus of the Atlanta editorial fraternity, "Mr. Watterson is still here, with Messrs. Roberts and Baker." Could it be possible, however, that Watterson, if he were "Shadow," was deliberately referring to himself in the third person to conceal his identity from the military?

Still another piece of evidence that cast doubt on the assumption that Watterson and "Shadow" were one and the same was an indication in a "Shadow" letter in the *Mobile Register* of May 26, 1864 that at some previous time "Shadow" had reported for the *Register* editor, Colonel Forsyth, "in a distant land," penning dramatic criticism and observing the squabblings of opera stars and the scheming of politicians. It seemed likely that the setting of this journalistic activity was in the North and that it must have occurred before the war. Could "Shadow" therefore have been the Washington or New York correspondent of the *Register* sometime before the outbreak of hostilities? Would this mean that he was more likely to have been an Alabamian than a Tennessean? To be sure, Watterson was in Washington just before the war as a correspondent of Colonel John W. Forney's *Philadelphia Press* and as editor of the Southern-sympathizing *Washington States.* While so employed, might he not have augmented his income by addressing a weekly letter to a newspaper in Mobile? It was at least suggestive that the revelation in a "Shadow" letter published in the

Register on July 17, 1864, that "Shadow" had been in Washington on the night after the First Battle of Manassas placed him there at a time when apparently Watterson also was there, before returning in mid-summer of 1861 to Tennessee. Moreover, "Shadow's" companion that night, the novelist and editor Nathaniel P. Willis, is known to have been a friend and correspondent of Watterson.

Having been unable to find any direct evidence in the Watterson Papers in the Library of Congress that Watterson had ever used the pseudonym "Shadow," I wrote to a recent biographer of Watterson, Professor Joseph Wall of Grinnell College. After making a careful comparison of four of "Shadow's" newspaper letters with Watterson's writings, Professor Wall admitted that he was as mystified as I. After reading the first two letters he was convinced that they could not have been written by Watterson. On the other hand, the third and fourth letters were "pure Wattersonian" in style, making use of subject matter with which Watterson often dealt. Could there have been two men writing under the same nom de plume? asked Wall. If not, he rated the odds as being in favor of Watterson's authorship, although he was troubled by the first two letters.

Could "Shadow" have been some other person having a plausible connection with the facts about "Shadow's" life that I had been able to uncover? At one stage of my investigation a member of the library staff of the Carnegie Library of Pittsburgh brought to my attention a certain Stephen Tillinghast Hammond, who had used the pseudonym "Shadow" for books pertaining to hunting and dog training that were published around 1900. According to the Library of Congress catalog cards, Hammond was born in 1831 and was still alive in 1908. Thus he was the right age for a Confederate newspaper correspondent. But I was unable to find any information establishing any connections on his part with Tennessee, Alabama, or the profession of journalism.

If "Shadow" were a Tennessean could he have been the Dr. Fielding Travis Powell who died in Atlanta in 1898 and whose obituary the *Atlanta Constitution* printed on February 19 of that year? Powell had been born in Nashville in 1828 and had remained in Tennessee until 1866, practicing law after attending a Tennessee law school and becoming well known as a war correspondent during the Civil War. Unfortunately the *Constitution* did not reveal the name of the newspaper to which Powell contributed war correspondence that was "widely copied," nor did it refer to any pseudonyms connected with his reporting.

This is where the matter now stands. I have established to my own satisfaction at least that "Shadow" was not Linebaugh and that he could have been one of four different persons—Hammond, Powell, Roberts, or Watterson. Of these four the Watterson hypothesis seems to me the most likely, in spite of "Shadow's" apparent disclaimer. Yet there is no certain proof that "Shadow" *was* Watterson; so I leave the resolution of this fascinating and as yet unsolved problem of identity to any other historians who may be interested.

Southern Reporters

~~~~~~~~~~~~~~~

THIS IS A comprehensive list that includes volunteer soldier correspondents, editorial correspondents, and Richmond correspondents, as
well as professional war correspondents in the field who were attached
to one or more armies.

Abrams, Alexander St. Clair
  ("A.S.A." "St. Clair")
  Atlanta Daily Intelligencer
Adams, Warren
  *Mobile Daily Advertiser and
  Register*
Albertson, Jonathan White
  Confederate Press Association
Alexander Peter Wellington
  Savannah Republican ("P.W.A.")
  *Mobile Daily Advertiser and
  Register* ("A")
  Richmond Daily Dispatch
  ("Sallust")
Bagby, Dr. George William
  Charleston Mercury ("Hermes")
  *Mobile Daily Advertiser and
  Register* ("Gamma")
  New Orleans Daily Crescent
  ("Malou")
  Columbus (Ga.) *Daily Sun*
  ("Pan")
Barr, M. W.
  Memphis Daily Appeal
Barr, William D.
  Memphis Daily Appeal ("B")
Bass, J. N.
  *Atlanta Daily Southern
  Confederacy*
Bell, James Pinkney
  Richmond Daily Dispatch
Britton, E. H.
  Charlotte (N.C.) *Bulletin*

Bruns, Dr. John Dickson
  Charleston Mercury ("J.D.B.")
Bunting, Robert Franklin
  Houston Telegraph
  San Antonio Herald
Carter, Capt. Theodoric
  ("Mint Julep")
  Chattanooga Daily Rebel
  Montgomery Daily Mail
Cooke, John Esten
  Richmond Whig
  *Richmond Southern Illustrated
  News*
Courtenay, William A.
  Charleston Mercury ("Kiawah")
Cox, T. J.
  Columbus Daily Sun
Da Ponte, Durant
  New Orleans Daily Delta ("D.")
Davis, Capt. Richard T.
  Savannah Republican
Dawson, Andrew H.
  *Mobile Daily Advertiser and
  Register* ("Bayard")
de Fontaine, Felix Gregory
  Charleston Daily Courier
  ("Personne")
  Daily Richmond Enquirer
  Columbia Daily South Carolinian
  ("Personne")
  Richmond Whig (F.G. de F.")
  Savannah Republican ("F.G. de
  F.")

Memphis Daily Appeal ("Quel Qu'un")
Mobile Daily Advertiser and Register ("Personne")
De Gournay, Capt. Francis F.
New Orleans Daily Picayune
Dill, Benjamin F.
Memphis Daily Appeal
Duncan, David Grieve
Charleston Mercury
New Orleans Daily Delta
Savannah Morning News
Richmond Daily Dispatch
Dupré, Col. Louis J.
("Sous Lieutenant," "S.L.")
Knoxville Daily Register
Dutcher, Salem
("Tyrone Powers")
Augusta Daily Constitutionalist
Ette, Robert
Memphis Daily Appeal
Farris (Ferris?), Capt.
("Marshall")
Atlanta (Knoxville) Daily Register
Flournoy, J. G.
Memphis Daily Appeal
Foard, N. E.
Charleston Daily Courier
Forbes, ———
Confederate Press Association
Forsyth, John
("Press")
Mobile Daily Advertiser and Register
Atlanta Daily Southern Confederacy
Augusta Daily Constitutionalist
Charleston Daily Courier
Fowler, W. B.
Mobile Daily Tribune
Galbreath, W. B.
("Grapeshot")
Memphis Daily Appeal
Gibbons, Israel
("I.G.")

New Orleans Daily Crescent
Mobile Daily Advertiser and Register
Graeme, John, Jr.
Southern Associated Press
Confederate Press Association
Gray, Alexander
Southern Associated Press
Hatcher, John E.
("Scantling")
Confederate Press Association
Mobile Daily Advertiser and Register
Hotze, Henry
("Cadet")
Mobile Daily Advertiser and Register
Hutchen, Virginius
Columbus Daily Sun
Jenkins, Donelson Caffery
New Orleans Daily Delta
Jeter, Oliver
Mobile Daily Advertiser and Register
Kennedy, Capt. John
Southern Associated Press
Kirk, Charles D.
("Se De Kay")
Louisville Daily Courier
Chattanooga Daily Rebel
Memphis Daily Appeal
Augusta Daily Constitutionalist
Lane, J. J.
("J.J.L.")
New Orleans Daily Delta
Linebaugh, John H.
("Ashantee")
Memphis Daily Appeal
Loomis, ———
Southern Associated Press
Marx, Bonhomme
New Orleans Daily Picayune
Mathews, L. H.
("Nemo")
Pensacola Observer

Matthews, Captain ———
("Harvey")
Memphis Daily Appeal
Meyer, Gustave
Richmond Daily Dispatch
Montgomery, Louis M.
("Louis M. M.")
New Orleans Daily Delta
Parks, Virgil A.S.
("V.A.S.P.")
Savannah Republican
Perry, Maj. Henry H.
("H.P.")
New Orleans Daily Picayune
Memphis Daily Appeal
Pleasants, Hugh
Richmond Daily Dispatch
Posey, Ben Lane
("Ben Lane")
Mobile Daily Advertiser and
Register
Pryor, J. P.
("J.P.P.")
Memphis Daily Appeal
Purvis, Capt. George E.
("Burley")
Atlanta Daily Southern
Confederacy
Reid, Samuel Chester, Jr.
Chattanooga Daily Rebel
("Sparta")
Memphis Daily Appeal
("Sparta")
New Orleans Daily Picayune
("Sparta")
Montgomery Daily Advertiser
("Ora")
Mobile Daily Advertiser and
Register ("Ora")
Mobile Daily Tribune ("Ora")
Atlanta Daily Intelligencer
("290")
Reyburn, W. P.
New Orleans Daily Crescent

Riordan, Bartholomew R.
Charleston Mercury ("Adsum")
Confederate Press Association
Roberts, Albert
("John Happy")
Nashville Republican Banner
Rowe, George Henry Clay
Daily Richmond Examiner
Russell, ———
Daily Richmond Examiner
Ryan, Lipscomb
New Orleans Daily Crescent
Sanderson, ———
Confederate Press Association
Screws, William Wallace
Montgomery Daily Advertiser
Semple, William M.
("Crescent")
Mobile Daily Advertiser and
Register
Sener, James Beverley
("X")
Richmond Daily Dispatch
Daily Richmond Enquirer
Shepardson, Dr. William G.
Mobile Daily Advertiser and
Register ("Evelyn")
Columbus (Ga.) *Times*
Montgomery Daily Advertiser
Richmond Daily Dispatch
("Bohemian")
Sledge, James
Athens Southern Banner
Smith, J. Henly
Confederate Press Association
Smoot, ———
Confederate Press Association
Smyth, Frank
Petersburg Daily Express
Sneed, James Roddy
Savannah Republican
Sossman, ———
Mobile Daily Tribune
Sparnick, Henry
("Sigma")
Charleston Daily Courier

Spratt, Leonidas W.
Charleston Mercury ("L.W.S.")
Stedman, George Clinton
Daily Richmond Enquirer
Stoddard, George W.
New Orleans Daily Crescent
Street, Albert J.
("N'Importe")
*Mobile Daily Advertiser and
Register*
Savannah Republican
Thompson, J. H.
Jackson Daily Mississippian
Thompson, John R.
("Dixie")
Memphis Daily Appeal
Thompson, William Tappan
Savannah Morning News
Timrod, Henry
("Kappa")
Charleston Mercury
Tinsley, H. C.
("T")
Richmond Daily Dispatch
Wagner, A. J.
Confederate Press Association
Walker, Alexander
New Orleans Daily Delta

Ward, John S.
Atlanta Daily Register
Watterson, Henry
*Atlanta Daily Southern
Confederacy*
Augusta Daily Constitutionalist
("Grape")
*Mobile Daily Advertiser and
Register*
West, John M.
New Orleans True Delta
Woodson, Will O.
Confederate Press Association
Wright, Lt. T. D.
("T.D.W.")
*Atlanta Daily Southern
Confederacy*
Wright, ———
New Orleans Bee
Yarington, Richard J.
("R.J.Y.")
Richmond Associated Press
Richmond Daily Whig
Columbus Daily Sun
Youngblood, Capt. J. W.
("Juvenis")
Memphis Daily Appeal

Bibliography

~~~~~~~~~~~~~~~

I. Bibliographical Aids

Cappon, Lester J. *Virginia Newspapers, 1821-1935, A Bibliography with Historical Introduction and Notes.* University of Virginia Institute for Research in the Social Sciences, Monograph No. 22. New York: Appleton-Century, 1936.

Coulter, E. Merton. *Travels in the Confederate States, A Bibliography.* Norman, Okla.: University of Oklahoma Press, 1948.

Crandall, Marjorie Lyle. *Confederate Imprints; A Checklist Based Principally on the Collection of the Boston Athenaeum. With an Introduction by Walter Muir Whitehill.* 2 vols. Boston: Boston Athenaeum, 1955.

Ellison, Rhoda Coleman. *History and Bibliography of Alabama Newspapers in the Nineteenth Century.* University, Ala.: University of Alabama Press, 1954.

Ford, Edwin H. *History of Journalism in the United States; A Bibliography of Books and Annotated Articles.* Minneapolis: Burgess Publishing Co., 1938.

Gregory, Winifred. *American Newspapers. 1921-1936, A Union List of Files Available in the United States and Canada.* New York: H. W. Wilson Co., 1937.

Hamer, Philip M., ed. *A Guide to Depositories of Archives and Manuscripts in the United States.* New Haven: Yale University Press, 1961.

Harwell, Richard B., ed. *More Confederate Imprints.* 2 vols. Richmond: Virginia State Library, 1957.

Jones, H. G. and Julius H. Avant. *Union List of North Carolina Newspapers, 1751-1900.* Raleigh: State Department of Archives, 1963.

New York Daily Tribune Index. 30 vols. New York: Tribune Associates, 1876-1907.

Price, Warren C. *The Literature of Journalism, An Annotated Bibliography.* Minneapolis: University of Minnesota Press, 1959.

Schwegmann, George A., comp. *Newspapers on Microfilm, A Union Check List,* 6th ed. Washington: Library of Congress, 1967.

Swem, Earl G. *Virginia Historical Index.* 2 vols. Roanoke: Stone Printing and Manufacturing Co., 1934.

Bibliography

Westcott, Mary and Allene Ramage. *A Checklist of United States Newspapers (and weeklies) before 1900 in the General Library.* 3 vols. Durham: Duke University Press, 1932.

II. Manuscript Sources

Peter W. Alexander Scrapbook of special correspondence to the *Savannah Republican,* in possession of Mrs. Milton B. Ellis, Savannah, Ga.
George W. Bagby Papers, Virginia Historical Society.
P.G.T. Beauregard Papers, Duke University.
P.G.T. Beauregard Papers, Library of Congress.
Thomas M. Bondurant Papers, University of Virginia.
Braxton Bragg Papers, Western Reserve Historical Society, Cleveland, Ohio.
Diary of Thomas Bragg, 1861-1862, Southern Historical Collection, University of North Carolina.
The Brock Collection, Huntington Library.
Ellison Capers Papers, Duke University.
Durant Da Ponte Papers, in the possession of Mrs. Harry Da Ponte III, Jackson, Mississippi.
Jefferson Davis Papers, Duke University.
Felix Gregory de Fontaine Scrapbook. Microfilmed from the original in the possession of Mr. James B. Coats, 1925 Marion Street, Columbia, South Carolina. Miscellaneous manuscripts, South Carolina Library, University of South Carolina, Columbia, S.C.
Jubal A. Early Papers, Library of Congress.
Richard S. Ewell Papers, Southern Historical Collection, University of North Carolina.
John B. Floyd Papers, Duke University.
Diary of C. R. Hanleiter. Original and typed copy, 1861-1865, Atlanta Historical Society.
William J. Hardee Papers, Alabama State Department of Archives and History.
Isham Harris Papers, Tennessee State Library and Archives.
Albert Sidney Johnston Papers, Tulane University Library.
Joseph E. Johnston Papers, Huntington Library.
Official Telegrams of Robert E. Lee, Army of Northern Virginia, 1862-1865, Duke University.
Robert McKee Papers, Alabama State Department of Archives and History.

W. Porcher Miles Papers, Southern Historical Collection, University of North Carolina.

Diary of Benjamin F. Perry, 1861-1863, Southern Historical Collection, University of North Carolina.

Leonidas Polk Papers, Southern Historical Collection, University of North Carolina.

William Wallace Screws Papers, Alabama State Department of Archives and History.

Samuel Chester Reid, Jr. Papers, in possession of Mr. Samuel Chester Reid, Santa Cruz, California.

Robert Barnwell Rhett Papers, Duke University.

Robert Barnwell Rhett Papers, in possession of Mr. Harry Moore Rhett, Huntsville, Alabama.

Robert Barnwell Rhett Papers, Southern Historical Collection, University of North Carolina.

N. J. Solomon Scrapbook, 1861-1863 (Savannah, Georgia), Duke University.

Southern Telegraph Company Papers, Carnegie Library of Pittsburgh.

Alexander H. Stephens Papers, Library of Congress.

J.E.B. Stuart Papers, Huntington Library.

John Reuben Thompson Papers, University of Virginia.

Josiah Turner Papers, Southern Historical Collection, University of North Carolina.

Earl Van Dorn Papers, Alabama State Department of Archives and History.

T. H. Watts Papers, Alabama State Department of Archives and History.

Henry Watterson Papers, Library of Congress.

Louis T. Wigfall Papers, Library of Congress.

III. Newspapers

No one library comes appreciably near to possessing complete runs for the Civil War period of the major Southern daily newspapers. The most important center for Southern newspaper research for this period is the Library of Congress, containing substantial files of the *Richmond Dispatch, Examiner, Whig*, and *Sentinel*, the *Charleston Mercury* and *Courier, Savannah Republican, Mobile Advertiser and Register*, and *New Orleans Picayune*. Also important for Southern Civil War newspaper research are the Boston Athenaeum, the Western Reserve Historical Society in Cleveland, Duke University, the Confederate Museum, and other libraries in Richmond. One of the more complete files of the *Richmond Enquirer* for the last two years of the war is at the State Historical Society of Wisconsin. The file of the *Memphis Appeal* at the Memphis Public Library is virtually complete through June 1864. The Atlanta Public Library has a nearly complete run of the *Atlanta Southern Confederacy* for the year 1862. Probably the best collection of Montgomery papers is at the Alabama State Department of Archives and History in Montgomery. A file of the *Augusta Constitutionalist* for the entire war period is in the Public Library of Cincinnati. Some other libraries with important runs of Confederate dailies are the University of North Carolina, Emory University, the Charleston Library Society, the American Antiquarian Society, and the Huntington Library. To an increasing extent Southern newspapers for the period from 1861 to 1865 are becoming available on microfilm in many libraries or by purchase from the Micro Photo Division of the Bell & Howell Company.

A. GENERAL

Atlanta Daily Intelligencer
Atlanta Daily Southern Confederacy
Augusta Daily Chronicle and Sentinel
Augusta Daily Constitutionalist
Charleston Daily Courier
Charleston Mercury
Chattanooga Daily Rebel
Columbia Daily South Carolinian
Columbia Daily Southern Guardian
Daily Columbus (Ga.) Enquirer
Columbus (Ga.) Daily Sun
Columbus (Ga.) Times
Houston Daily Telegraph
Jackson Daily Mississippian
Knoxville Daily Register
London Times
Lynchburg Daily Republican
Lynchburg Daily Virginian
Macon Daily Telegraph and Confederate
Memphis Daily Appeal
Memphis Daily Avalanche
Meridian Daily Clarion
Mobile Daily Advertiser and Register
Mobile Daily Tribune
Montgomery Daily Advertiser
Montgomery Daily Mail
Nashville Daily Republican Banner
New Orleans Daily Crescent
New Orleans Daily Delta
New Orleans Daily Picayune
New Orleans Daily True Delta
New York Times

Bibliography

New York Daily Tribune
Norfolk Day Book
Petersburg Daily Express
Richmond Daily Dispatch
Daily Richmond Enquirer
Daily Richmond Examiner
Richmond Daily Sentinel

Richmond Daily Whig
Savannah Daily Morning News
Savannah Republican
Selma Daily Reporter
Vicksburg Daily Whig
Wilmington (N.C.) Daily Journal

B. ANNIVERSARY EDITIONS

The Montgomery Daily Advertiser, Centennial Edition, March 15, 1928.

New Orleans Daily Picayune, Semi-Centennial Number, January 25, 1887.

Charleston News and Courier, 125th Anniversary Edition, May 1, 1928.

Charleston News and Courier, 150th Anniversary Edition, January 11, 1953.

Richmond Times-Dispatch, Centennial Edition, October 22, 1950.

C. NEWSPAPER OBITUARIES

Atlanta Constitution, September 24, 1886 (Peter W. Alexander)

Atlanta Daily Intelligencer, January 12, 1871 (John H. Steele)

Augusta Chronicle, December 24, 1917 (Salem Dutcher)

Augusta Daily Constitutionalist, March 26, 1862 (William H. Pritchard)

Charleston Daily Courier, February 3, 1862 (Aaron S. Willington); January 16, 1864 (Capt. John Kennedy)

Charleston News and Courier, January 13, 1880 (Col. Augustus O. Andrews); May 21, 1883 (John Dickson Bruns); October 5, 1903 (Leonidas W. Spratt); March 18, 1908 (William A. Courtenay)

Hinds County Gazette, August 24, 1881 (Fleet T. Cooper)

Jacksonville Florida Times-Union, June 6, 1931 (Alexander St. Clair Abrams)

Louisville Courier-Journal, March 21, 1907 (Henry W. Cleveland)

Louisville Daily Sun, February 18, 1870 (Charles D. Kirk)

Mobile Daily Advertiser and Register, May 17, 1864 (Albert J. Street)

Mobile Daily Advertiser and Mail, November 13, 1884 (Richard J. Yarington)

Mobile Daily Register, May 11, 1887 (Henry Hotze)

Montgomery Daily Mail, November 16, 1864 (John H. Linebaugh)

Bibliography

New Orleans Daily Crescent, November 2, 1866 (Israel Gibbons); March 21, 1869 (George W. Stoddard)

New Orleans Daily Picayune, February 24, 1862 (Oliver Jeter); March 13, 1870 (Samuel F. Wilson); December 2, 1879 (David G. Duncan); May 20, 1888 (Dr. Hugh Kennedy); August 8, 1894 (Durant Da Ponte)

New Orleans Weekly True Delta, March 7, 1863 (John Maginnis)

New York Daily Tribune, September 1, 1881 (Alexander Mosely); March 22, 1897 (Bartholomew R. Riordan); August 16, 1897 (Samuel Chester Reid, Jr.)

Daily Richmond Enquirer, January 14, 1865 (George C. Stedman)

Daily Richmond Whig, May 12, 1862 (Col. Thomas M. Bondurant)

Richmond Daily Dispatch, November 16, 1893 (James McDonald)

Richmond Times-Dispatch, July 25, 1911 (James P. Bell)

Savannah Republican, July 22, 1863 (Capt. V.A.S. Parks)

Washington Evening Star, November 19, 1903 (James B. Sener)

Wilmington Daily Journal, December 16, 1865 (James Fulton)

IV. GOVERNMENT DOCUMENTS

A. PUBLISHED

War of the Rebellion: A Compilation of the Official Records of the Union and Confederate Armies, 128 vols. Washington, D.C., 1880-1901.

Confederate States of America, War Department
Report of the Secretary of War, Richmond, December 14, 1861
Report of the Secretary of War, Richmond, August 12, 1862
Report of the Secretary of War, Richmond, November 3, 1864

Mathews, James W., ed. *The Statutes at Large of the Provisional Government of the Confederate States of America*. Richmond: R. M. Smith, Printer to Congress, 1864.

Journal of the Congress of the Confederate States of America, 1861-1865. 7 vols. Washington, D.C., 1904-1905. U.S. Congress, Sen. Doc. No. 234, 58 Cong., 2 Sess.

Proceedings of the . . . Confederate Congress. Southern Historical Society Papers 44-52 (1923-1959).

Richardson, James D., ed. *A Compilation of the Messages and Papers of the Confederacy*. 2 vols. Nashville: United States Publishing Company, 1905.

B. UNPUBLISHED

National Archives, Office of Confederate Secretary of War, 1861-1865, Letters Sent, Letters Received, Telegrams Sent, Telegrams Received.

V. BOOKS AND ARTICLES WRITTEN BY CONFEDERATE
WAR CORRESPONDENTS

Abrams, Alexander St. Clair. *A Full and Detailed Account of the Siege of Vicksburg*. Atlanta: Intelligencer Steam Press, 1863.

———. President Davis and His Administration, being a Review of the "Rival Administrations," lately written by E. A. Pollard . . . published in Richmond and Atlanta: Published for the author, 1864.

Alexander, Peter W. "Confederate Chieftains." *Southern Literary Messenger*, 25 (January 1863).

Bagby, George William. *John M. Daniel's Latch-Key, A Memoir of the Late Editor of the Richmond Examiner*. Lynchburg, Va.: J. P. Bell & Co., 1868.

———. *The Old Virginia Gentleman and other Sketches*. Edited and Arranged by his Daughter Ellen M. Bagby [with a] Sketch of Bagby's Life . . . by Douglas S. Freeman. Richmond: Dietz Press, 1948.

———. *Selections from the Miscellaneous Writings of Dr. George W. Bagby* (with a sketch of Bagby's life by Edward S. Gregory). 2 vols. Richmond: Whittet and Shepperson, 1884-1885.

Clarke, H. C. *Diary of the War for Separation, a Daily Chronicle of the Principal Events and History of the Present Revolution, to which is added notes and Descriptions of all the great Battles, including Walker's Narrative of the Battle of Shiloh*. Augusta, Ga.: Steam Press of Chronicle & Sentinel, 1862.

Cooke, John Esten. *A Life of Gen. Robert E. Lee*. New York: D. Appleton and Co., 1871.

———. *The Life of Stonewall Jackson*. New York: C. B. Richardson, 1863.

De Fontaine, Felix Gregory. *Army Letters of 1861-1865*. Issued monthly by "Personne" . . . vol. 1, nos. 1 and 2 [etc.]. Columbia, S.C.: War Record Publishing Co., 1896-1897.

———. *Marginalia; or Gleanings from an Army Note-book*. Columbia, S.C. Steam Power Press of F. G. Fontaine and Co., 1864.

———. "Shoulder to Shoulder, Reminiscences of Confederate Camps and Fields, by 'Personne,'" *The XIX Century* (Charleston, S.C.), vol. 1 (June 1869, July 1869, September 1869, October 1869, November 1869, January 1870).

———. "The First Day of Real War," *Southern Bivouac*, 2 (July 1886).

Dupré, Louis J. *Fagots from the Camp Fire. By "the Newspaper Man."* Washington, D.C.: E. T. Charles & Co., 1881.

Hotze, Henry. *Three Months in the Confederate Army; Printed in Facsimile from the London Index, 1862.* With an introduction and notes by Richard Barksdale Harwell. University, Ala.: University of Alabama Press, 1952.

Hubbell, Jay Broadus, ed. "The War Diary of John Esten Cooke." *Journal of Southern History* (November 1941).

Mathews, Joseph J., ed. *The Capture and Wonderful Escape of General John H. Morgan As Reported by Samuel C. Reid.* Atlanta: Library of Emory University, 1947.

Merrill, James M., ed. "Personne Goes to Georgia: Five Civil War Letters." *Georgia Historical Quarterly*, 43 (June 1959).

———. " 'Nothing to Eat but Raw Bacon'; Letters from a War Correspondent, 1862." *Tennessee Historical Quarterly*, 17 (June 1958).

Reid, Samuel Chester Jr. *Great Battle of Chicamauga! A Concise History of Events from the Evacuation of Chattanooga to the Defeat of the Enemy. Full Details of the Battle, Incidents &c. By S. C. Reid, "Ora," of the Mobile Tribune.* Mobile: F. Titcomb, 1863.

Stern, Philip Van Doren, ed. *Wearing of the Gray*, by John Esten Cooke. Bloomington: Indiana University Press, 1959.

Watterson, Henry. *"Marse Henry," an Autobiography.* 2 vols. New York: George H. Doran Co., 1919.

VI. Books and Articles Dealing With The Press

Allsopp, Frederick W. *History of the Arkansas Press for a Hundred Years or More.* Little Rock: Parke-Harper Co., 1922.

Andrews, J. Cutler. "The Confederate Press and Public Morale." *Journal of Southern History.* 32 (November 1966).

———. "The Press Reports the Battle of Gettysburg." *Pennsylvania History*, 31 (April 1964).

Baker, Thomas H. "Refugee Newspaper: The Memphis *Daily Appeal*, 1862-1865." *Journal of Southern History*, 29 (August 1963).

Bell, Earl L. and Kenneth C. Crabbe. *The Augusta Chronicle: Indomitable Voice of Dixie, 1785-1960.* Athens: University of Georgia Press, 1960.

Bibliography

Brantley, Rabun Lee. *Georgia Journalism of the Civil War Period.* Nashville: George Peabody College for Teachers, 1929.

————. *"History of the Macon Telegraph."* Unpub. Master's thesis, Mercer University, Macon, Ga., 1924.

Dabney, Thomas Ewing. *One Hundred Great Years; the Story of the Times Picayune from Its Founding to 1940.* Baton Rouge: Louisiana State University Press, 1944.

Daniel, John M. *The Richmond Examiner during the War; or, The Writings of John M. Daniel, with a Memoir of His Life, by his Brother, Frederick S. Daniel.* New York: Printed for the author, 1868.

Elliott, Robert Neal Jr. *The Raleigh Register, 1799-1863.* Chapel Hill: University of North Carolina Press, 1955.

Emery, Edwin and Henry Ladd Smith. *The Press and America.* New York: Prentice-Hall, 1954.

Evans, Marvin Davis. "The Richmond Press on the Eve of the Civil War." In *The John P. Branch Historical Papers of Randolph-Macon College.* n.s. (January 1951), vol. 1, ed. W. Alexander Mabry.

Ford, Edwin Hopkins. *Selected Readings in the History of American Journalism.* Minneapolis: University of Minnesota Press, 1939.

Gramling, Oliver. *AP, the Story of News.* New York: Farrar and Rinehart, 1940.

Green, Beulah Gayle. *Confederate Reporter, 1861-1864.* Austin, Tex.: Printed for the Publisher by Burrell Printing Co., 1962.

Green, Fletcher M. "Duff Green, Militant Journalist of the Old School." *American Historical Review,* 52 (January 1947).

Griffith, Louis Turner and John Erwin Talmadge. *Georgia Journalism, 1763-1950.* Athens: University of Georgia Press, 1951.

Halley, R. A. "A Rebel Newspaper's War Story." *American Historical Magazine,* 8 (April 1903).

Harwell, Richard B. "Atlanta Publications of the Civil War Period." *Atlanta Historical Bulletin,* 6 (July 1941).

————. "John Esten Cooke, Civil War Correspondent." *Journal of Southern History,* 19 (November 1953).

Hebert, Mary Alice. "Louisiana Newspapers during the Civil War." Unpub. Master's thesis, Louisiana State University, 1937.

Henry, R. H. *Editors I Have Known Since the Civil War.* Jackson, Miss.: Jackson Clarion-Ledger, 1922.

Hohenberg, John. *Foreign Correspondence: The Great Reporters and Their Times.* New York: Columbia University Press, 1964.

Bibliography

Holden, William Woods. *Address on the History of Journalism in North Carolina, delivered by W. W. Holden at the Ninth Annual Meeting of the Press Association of North Carolina, Held at Winston, June 21, 1881*. 2nd. ed. Raleigh: News and Observer Book and Job Print, n.d.

Houston, Michael. "Edward Alfred Pollard and the Richmond Examiner: A Study of Journalistic Opposition in Wartime." Unpub. Master's thesis, The American University, 1963.

Hudson, Frederick. *Journalism in the United States, from 1690 to 1872*. New York: Harper & Brothers, 1873.

Huff, Lawrence. "Joseph Addison Turner: Southern Editor during the Civil War." *Journal of Southern History*, 29 (November 1963).

Hughes, Judge Robert Williams. *"Editors of the Past." Lecture of Judge Robert W. Hughes Delivered before the Virginia Press Association at their Annual Meeting at Charlottesville, Va. on the 22d of June, 1897*. Richmond, Va.: W. E. Jones, 1897.

Jones, John Paul. "The Confederate Press and the Government." *Americana*, 37 (January 1943).

Jones, Robert William. *Journalism in the United States*. New York: E. P. Dutton, 1947.

Kendall, John S. "The Foreign Language Press of New Orleans." *Louisiana Historical Quarterly*, 12 (July 1929).

King, William L. *The Newspaper Press of Charleston S.C. A Chronological and Biographical History, Embracing a Period of One Hundred and Forty Years*. Charleston, S.C.: Edward Perry (Book Press), 1872.

Kobre, Sidney. *Foundations of American Journalism*. Tallahasseee: Florida State University, 1958.

Lee, James Melvin. *History of American Journalism*. Boston: Houghton Mifflin, 1917.

Livingood, James W. "The Chattanooga *Rebel*." *East Tennessee Historical Society's Publications*, No. 39 (1967).

Lutz, Earl. "Soldier Newspapers of the Civil War" [1861-1865]. Bibliography Society of America, *Papers*, 46 (4th quarter).

McDougall, Clyde D. *Interpretative Reporting*. 4th ed. New York: Macmillan, 1963.

Malone, Henry T. "Atlanta Journalism during the Confederacy." *Georgia Historical Quarterly*, 37 (September 1953).

———. "The Charleston Daily Courier: Standard-Bearer of the Confederacy." *Journalism Quarterly*, 29 (Summer 1952).

Bibliography

————. "The *Weekly Atlanta Intelligencer* as a Secessionist Journal." *Georgia Historical Quarterly*, 37 (December 1953).

Mathews, Joseph J. *Reporting the Wars*. Minneapolis: University of Minnesota Press, 1957.

The Mobile Daily Register. 100th Anniversary, 1814-1914, Alabama State Dept. of Archives and History.

Mott, Frank Luther. *American Journalism; A History of Newspapers in the United States through 260 years: 1690 to 1950*. Rev. ed. New York: Macmillan, 1950.

"The Newspaper Press of America." *Temple Bar Magazine* (January 1863).

Pollard, James E. *The Presidents and the Press*. New York: Macmillan, 1947.

"The Press of the Confederate States." *The* [London] *Index*, vol. 2 (November 27, 1862).

Press Association of the Confederate States of America. *Minutes of the Board of Directors of the Press Association, Embracing the Quarterly Reports of the Superintendent, October and January, Fourth Session—Atlanta, October 14, 1863; Fifth Session—Augusta, January 14, 1864*. Printed by order of the board. Atlanta, Ga.: Franklin Steam Publishing House, J. J. Toon & Co., 1864.

————. *The First Annual Meeting of the Press Association, Augusta, Ga. April 6 1864 with Minutes of the Board of Directors*. Montgomery, Ala., Printed at the Memphis Appeal Job Printing Establishment, 1864.

Randall, James Garfield. "The Newspaper Problem in Its Bearing upon Military Secrecy during the Civil War." *American Historical Review*, 23 (January 1918).

Rosewater, Victor. *History of Cooperative News Gathering in the United States*. New York: D. Appleton, 1930.

Sass, Herbert Ravenel. *Outspoken: 150 Years of the Charleston News and Courier*. Columbia: University of South Carolina Press, 1953.

The Savannah Morning News. Its History and a Description of Its Building, Machinery and Business. Savannah, Ga., 1886.

Sisler, George. "The Arrest of a Memphis Daily Appeal War Correspondent on Charges of Treason." *West Tennessee Historical Society, Papers*, 11 (1957).

Smith, Robert F. "John F. Eakin: Confederate Propagandist." *Arkansas Historical Quarterly*, 12 (Winter 1953).

Stubbs, Thomas McAlpin. "The Fourth Estate of Sumter, South Carolina, *South Carolina Historical Magazine,* 54 (October 1953).

Talley, Robert. *One Hundred Years of the Commercial Appeal, 1840-1940.* Memphis: Printed at the Commercial Appeal, 1940.

Thompson, William Fletcher. *The Image of War: The Pictorial Reporting of the American Civil War.* New York: Thomas Yoseloff, 1960.

Trexler, Harrison A. "The Davis Administration and the Richmond Press, 1861-1865." *Journal of Southern History,* 16 (May 1950).

Tucker, Ruby Florence. "The Press Association of the Confederate States of America in Georgia." Unpub. Master's thesis, University of Georgia, 1950.

Wiley, Bell I. "Camp Newspapers of the Confederacy." *North Carolina Historical Review,* 20 (March 1943).

Wilken, William Herbert. "As the *Telegraph* Saw It: A Study of the Policy of the Macon *Daily Telegraph (And Confederate),* 1860-1865." Unpub. Master's thesis, Emory University, 1964.

Wilson, Quintus Charles. "A Study and Evaluation of the Military Censorship in the Civil War." Unpub. Master's thesis, University of Minnesota, 1945.

———. "Confederate Press Association, A Pioneer News Agency," *Journalism Quarterly,* 26 (June 1949).

———. "Bitter Verbal Battles between Editors during the Civil War Are Recalled." *The Quill,* 25 (January 1943).

———. "Voluntary Press Censorship during the Civil War." *Journalism Quarterly,* 19 (September 1942).

VII. BOOKS AND ARTICLES PERTAINING TO THE CIVIL WAR

Adams, Horace. "Military Operations in and around Jackson, Mississippi during the Civil War." Unpub. Master's thesis, University of Mississippi, 1950.

Andrews, J. Cutler. "The Southern Telegraph Company, 1861-1865: A Chapter in the History of Wartime Communication." *Journal of Southern History,* 30 (August 1964).

Barrett, John G. *The Civil War in North Carolina.* Chapel Hill: University of North Carolina Press, 1963.

———. *Sherman's March through the Carolinas.* Chapel Hill: University of North Carolina Press, 1956.

Bearss, Edwin C. "The Campaign Culminating in the Fall of Vicksburg, March 29-July 4, 1863." *Iowa Journal of History*, 59 (April 1961).

————. "Civil War Operations in and around Pensacola." *Florida Historical Quarterly*, 36 (October 1957).

Bill, Alfred Hoyt. *The Beleaguered City, Richmond, 1861-1865*. New York: Knopf, 1946.

Black, Robert C. *The Railroads of the Confederacy*. Chapel Hill: University of North Carolina Press, 1952.

Brown, Walter Lee. "Pea Ridge: Gettysburg of the West." *Arkansas Historical Quarterly*, 15 (Spring 1956).

Brownlee, Richard S. *Gray Ghosts of the Confederacy, Guerilla Warfare in the West, 1861-1865*. Baton Rouge: Louisiana State University Press, 1958.

Bruce, Robert V. *Lincoln and the Tools of War*. Indianapolis: Bobbs-Merrill, 1956.

Catton, Bruce. *Stillness at Appomattox*. Garden City, N.Y.: Doubleday, 1953.

————. *The Coming Fury*. Garden City, N.Y.: Doubleday, 1961.

————. *Terrible Swift Sword*. Garden City, N.Y.: Doubleday, 1963.

————. *Never Call Retreat*. Garden City, N.Y.: Doubleday, 1965.

Cauthen, Charles E. *South Carolina Goes to War, 1860-1865*. Chapel Hill: University of North Carolina Press, 1950.

Conrad, Bryan. "The Seven Days Campaign, 1862." *William and Mary Quarterly*, 2nd series, 14 (July 1934).

Corley, Florence Fleming. *Confederate City, Augusta, Georgia, 1860-1865*. Columbia: University of South Carolina Press, 1960.

Crawford, Samuel Wylie. *The Genesis of the Civil War, the Story of Sumter, 1860-1861*. New York: C. L. Webster & Co., 1887.

Crownover, Sims. "The Battle of Franklin." *Tennessee Historical Quarterly*, 14 (December 1955).

Cunningham, Horace Herndon. *Doctors in Gray: The Confederate Medical Service*. Baton Rouge: Louisiana State University Press, 1958.

Curry, Roy W. "James A. Seddon, A Southern Prototype." *Virginia Magazine of History and Biography*, 63 (April 1955).

Daly, Robert Welter. *How the Merrimac Won; the Strategic Story of the C.S.S. Virginia*. New York: Crowell, 1957.

Dowdey, Clifford. *Lee's Last Campaign; the Story of Lee and His Men Against Grant—1864*. Boston: Little, Brown, 1960.

Du Bose, John Witherspoon. *General Joseph Wheeler and the Army of Tennessee.* New York: The Neale Publishing Co., 1912.

Dupuy, Col. Richard Ernest. *The Compact History of the Civil War.* New York: Hawthorne Books, 1960.

Evans, Clement A., ed. *Confederate Military History.* 12 vols. Atlanta: Confederate Publishing Co., 1899.

Felt, Jeremy P. "Lucius B. Northrop and the Confederacy's Subsistence Department." *Virginia Magazine of History and Biography,* 69 (April 1961).

Fleming, Walter L. *Civil War and Reconstruction in Alabama.* New York. Columbia University Press, Macmillan, agents, 1905.

Florance, John E. Jr., "Morris Island: Victory or Blunder?" *South Carolina Historical Magazine,* 60 (July 1954).

Foote, Shelby. *The Civil War, A Narrative, Fort Sumter to Perryville.* New York: Random House, 1958.

————. *The Civil War, A Narrative, Fredericksburg to Meridian.* New York: Random House, 1963.

Freeman, Douglas. *Lee's Lieutenants, A Study in Command.* 3 vols. New York: Scribner's, 1942-44.

Gerdes, F. H. "The Surrender of Forts Jackson and St. Philip on the Lower Mississippi." *Continental Magazine,* 3 (May 1863).

Harleston, John. "Battery Wagner on Morris Island, 1863." *South Carolina Magazine,* 52 (January 1956).

Hatcher, Edmund Neuson. *The Last Four Weeks of the War.* Columbus, Ohio: Cooperative Publishing Co., 1891.

Hay, Thomas Robson. "Braxton Bragg and the Southern Confederacy." *Georgia Historical Quarterly,* 9 (December 1925).

————. "The Davis-Hood-Johnston Controversy of 1864." *Mississippi Valley Historical Review,* 11 (June 1924).

————. "Lucius B. Northrop: Commissary of the Confederacy." *Civil War History,* 9 (March 1963).

Henry, Robert S. "Chattanooga and the War." *Tennessee Historical Quarterly,* 19 (September 1960).

Hesseltine, William B., ed. *The Tragic Conflict: The Civil War and Reconstruction.* New York: G. Braziller, 1962.

Heyward, Du Bose and Herbert Ravenel Sass. *Fort Sumter.* New York, Farrar and Rinehart, 1938.

Hoehling, Adolph A. *Last Train from Atlanta.* New York: Thomas Yoseloff, 1958.

Horn, Stanley F. *The Army of Tennessee: A Military History.* Indianapolis: Bobbs-Merrill, 1941.

————. *The Decisive Battle of Nashville.* Baton Rouge: Louisiana State University Press, 1956.

Jervey, Theodore D. "Charleston during the Civil War." In *Annual Report of the American Historical Association,* 1913, ɪ, 167-76.

Johnson, Robert Underwood and Clarence Clough Buel, eds. *Battles and Leaders of the Civil War.* 4 vols. New York: Century Co., 1884-88.

Johnston, Frank. "The Vicksburg Campaign." *Mississippi Historical Society Publications,* 10. Ed. Franklin L. Riley. Oxford, Miss., 1909.

Jones, Allen W. "Military Events in Louisiana during the Civil War, 1861-1865." *Louisiana History,* 2 (Summer 1961).

Jones, Archer. "Some Aspects of George W. Randolph's Service as Confederate Secretary of War." *Journal of Southern History,* 26 (August 1960).

————. *Confederate Strategy from Shiloh to Vicksburg.* Baton Rouge: Louisiana State University Press, 1961.

Jones, James P. and William Warren Rogers. "Montgomery as the Confederate Capital: View of a New Nation." *Alabama Historical Quarterly,* 26 (Spring 1964).

Kimball, William J. "The Bread Riot in Richmond, 1863." *Civil War History,* 7 (June 1961).

Klement, Frank. "General John B. Floyd and the West Virginia Campaigns of 1861." *West Virginia History,* 8 (April 1947).

Lawrence, Alexander A. *A Present for Mr. Lincoln, the Story of Savannah From Secession to Sherman.* Macon: The Ardivan Press, 1961.

La Bree, Benjamin, ed. *The Confederate Soldier in the Civil War, 1861-1865.* Louisville, Ky.: Prentice Press, 1897.

Lee, Stephen D. "The Campaign of Vicksburg in 1863—from April 15 to and including the Battle of Champion Hills, or Baker's Creek, May 16, 1863." *Mississippi Historical Society Publications,* 3.

McMurtry, R. Gerald. "Zollicoffer and the Battle of Mill Spring." *Filson Club Quarterly,* 29 (October 1955).

McWhiney, Grady. "Controversy in Kentucky: Braxton Bragg's Campaign of 1862." *Civil War History,* 6 (March 1960).

————. "The Ordeal of Command, Bragg before Chickamauga." Unpub. Ph.D. Diss., Columbia University, 1960.

Massey, Mary Elizabeth. *Ersatz in the Confederacy.* Columbia: University of South Carolina Press, 1952.

Meredith, Roy. *Storm over Sumter; the Opening Engagement of the Civil War.* New York: Simon and Schuster, 1957.

Merrill, James M. "The Hatteras Expedition, August, 1861." *North Carolina Historical Review,* 29 (April 1952).

Moore, Frank, ed. *The Rebellion Record, Diary of American Events, with Supplement.* 12 vols. New York: G. P. Putnam, 1861-73.

Moore, Ross H. "The Vicksburg Campaign." *Journal of Mississippi History,* 1 (July 1939).

Mosby, John Singleton. *Stuart's Cavalry in the Gettysburg Campaign.* New York: Moffat, Yard & Co., 1908.

A Narrative of the Battles of Bull Run and Manassas Junction, July 18th and 21st, 1861. Accounts of the Advance of Both Armies, the Battles, and the Defeat and Rout of the Enemy, Compiled Chiefly from the Detailed Reports of the Virginia and South Carolina Press. Charleston: Press of Evans & Cogswell, 1861.

Nevins, Allan. *The Improvised War, 1861-1862.* New York: Scribner's, 1959.

Osborn George C. "The Atlanta Campaign, 1864." *Georgia Historical Quarterly,* 34 (December 1950).

Owsley, Frank L. "Defeatism in the Confederacy." *North Carolina Historical Review,* 3 (July 1926).

Patch, Joseph Dorst. *The Battle of Ball's Bluff.* Ed. Fitzhugh Turner with introduction by Virgil Carrington Jones. Lessburg, Va.: Potomac Press, 1958.

Patrick, Rembert W. *The Fall of Richmond.* Baton Rouge: Louisiana State University Press, 1960.

Plum, William R. *The Military Telegraph during the Civil War in the United States.* 2 vols. Chicago: Jansen, McClurg & Co., 1882.

Pollard, Edward A. "The Confederate Congress, A Chapter in the History of the Late War." *Galaxy,* 6 (December 1868).

———. *The Lost Cause; a New Southern History of the War of the Confederates.* New York: E. B. Treat & Co. 1866.

———. *The Second Battle of Manassas, with Sketches of the Recent Campaign in Northern Virginia.* Richmond: West & Johnston, 1862.

——— (putative author). *The Seven Days' Battles in Front of Richmond. An Outline Narrative of the Series of Engagements Which Opened at Mechanicsville, near Richmond, on Thursday, June 26,*

1862, and Resulted in the Defeat and Retreat of the Northern Army under Major General McClellan. Comp. from the Detailed Accounts of the Newspaper Press. Richmond: West & Johnston; Charleston, S.C., Evans & Cogswell, 1862.

Ramsdell, Charles W. *Behind the Lines in the Southern Confederacy.* Baton Rouge: Louisiana State University Press, 1944.

Randall, James G. and David Donald. *The Civil War and Reconstruction.* 2nd ed. Boston: D. C. Heath, 1961.

Reynolds, Cedric Okell. "The Postal System of the Southern Confederacy," *West Virginia History,* 12 (April 1951).

Rhodes, James Ford. *History of the United States from the Compromise of 1850.* 8 vols. New York: Macmillan, 1907. Vols. 3-5.

"Richmond and Washington during the War." *Cornhill Magazine,* 7 (January 1863).

Scharf, John Thomas. *History of the Confederate States Navy.* New York: Rogers & Sherwood, 1887.

Searcher, Victor. "An Arkansas Druggist Defeats a Famous General." *Arkansas Historical Quarterly,* 13 (Autumn 1954).

Silver, James W. *Confederate Morale and Church Propaganda.* Tuscaloosa, Ala.: Confederate Publishing Co., 1957.

———. "Propaganda in the Confederacy." *Journal of Southern History,* 11 (November 1945).

Stackpole, Edward James. *Sheridan in the Shenandoah; Jubal Early's Nemesis.* Harrisburg, Pa.: Stackpole Co., 1961.

Stern, Philip VanDoren. *An End to Valor; the Last Days of the Civil War.* Boston: Houghton Mifflin, 1958.

Swanberg, W. A. *First Blood, the Story of Fort Sumter.* New York: Scribner's, 1957.

Trexler, Harrison A. "The Confederate Navy Department and the Fall of New Orleans." *Southwest Review,* 19 (Autumn 1933).

Triplett, Mary Alice. "The Efforts of Jefferson Davis to Influence Public Opinion during the Civil War." Unpub. Master's thesis, University of Mississippi, 1938.

Tucker, Glenn. "Some Aspects of North Carolina's Participation in the Gettysburg Campaign." *North Carolina Historical Review,* 35 (April 1958).

Vandiver, Frank E. *Jubal's Raid: General Early's Famous Attack on Washington in 1864.* New York: McGraw-Hill, 1960.

Vandiver, Frank E. *Rebel Brass—The Confederate Command System.* Baton Rouge: Louisiana State University Press, 1956.

Walker, Peter F. *Vicksburg: A People at War, 1860-1865.* Chapel Hill: University of North Carolina Press, 1960.

Wiley, Bell I. *The Life of Johnny Reb, the Common Soldier of the Confederacy.* Indianapolis: Bobbs-Merrill, 1943.

Wood, Walter B. and Brig.Gen. J. E. Edmonds. *The Civil War in the United States, with Special Reference to the Campaigns of 1864 and 1865.* London: Methuen, 1937.

Yearns, Wilfred B. *The Confederate Congress.* Athens: University of Georgia Press, 1960.

VIII. Biographies, Autobiographies, Diaries, and Letters

Adkins, William M. "Obadiah Jennings Wise, '50: A Sketch of His Life." *Indiana University Alumni Quarterly,* 24 (Winter 1937).

Alexander, Edward Porter. *Military Memoirs of a Confederate; a Critical Narrative.* New York: Scribner's, 1907.

Anderson, John Q., ed. *Brokenburn: The Journal of Kate Stone, 1861-1868.* Baton Rouge: Louisiana State University Press, 1955.

Andrews, Eliza Frances. *The War-Time Journal of a Georgia Girl, 1864-1865.* New York: D. Appleton, 1908.

Bartlett, Napier. *A Soldier's Story of the War; including the Marches and Battles of the Washington Artillery, and of other Louisiana Troops.* New Orleans: Clark and Hofeline, 1874.

Basso, Hamilton. *Beauregard: The Great Creole.* New York: Scribner's, 1933.

Bean, W. G. *Stonewall's Man, Sandie Pendleton.* Chapel Hill, University of North Carolina Press, 1959.

Beaty, John O. *John Esten Cooke, Virginian.* New York: Columbia University Press, 1922.

Benson, Adolph B., ed. *America of the Fifties: Letters of Frederika Bremer.* New York: The American-Scandinavian Foundation, 1924.

Blackford, Susan Leigh, comp. *Letters from Lee's Army; or Memoirs of Life in and out of the Army of Virginia during the War Between the States.* New York: Scribner's, 1947.

Blackford, William W. *War Years with Jeb Stuart.* New York: Scribner's, 1945.

Bibliography

Borcke, Heros von. *Memoirs of the Confederate War for Independence.*
2 vols. Philadelphia: Lippincott, 1866.

Bottom, Raymond B. "John Mitchel." *Virginia Magazine of History
and Biography,* 60 (April 1952).

Boyd, William K. "William W. Holden." Duke University, Historical
Society of Trinity College, *Historical Papers,* 1895- , Series 3.

Bradford, Gamaliel. *Confederate Portraits.* Boston: Houghton Mifflin,
1914.

Bridges, Hal. *Lee's Maverick General, Daniel Harvey Hill.* New
York: McGraw-Hill, 1961.

Buck, Irving Ashby. *Cleburne and His Command by Irving A. Buck
and Pat Cleburne, Stonewall Jackson of the West, by Thomas Robson Hay.* Foreword by Bell I. Wiley. Jackson, Tenn.: McCowat-
Mercer Press, 1959.

Bunting, Robert Franklin. *Letters of Robert Franklin Bunting, November 9, 1861-April 31 [sic], 1865.* Copied in Cooperation with His Son,
Henry Stanhope. 2 vols. Naples, Fla., 1944.

Canby, Henry Seidel. *Walt Whitman, An American; a Study in Biography.* Boston: Houghton Mifflin, 1943.

Cardozo, Jacob N. *Reminiscences of Charleston.* Charleston, S.C.: Jos.
Walker, 1866.

Chamberlayne, Churchill Gibson. Biographical account of George
William Bagby, in Edwin A. Alderman and Joel Chandler Harris,
eds., *Library of Southern Literature.* 16 vols. New Orleans, Atlanta,
etc.: Martin and Hoyt Co., 1908-13.

Chambers, Lenoir. *Stonewall Jackson.* 2 vols. New York: William Morrow, 1959.

Chesnut, Mary Boykin. *A Diary from Dixie.* . . . Ed. Isabelle D. Martin
and Myrta Lockett Avery. New York: D. Appleton, 1905.

Childs, Arney R., ed. *The Private Journal of Henry William Ravenel,
1859-1887.* Columbia: University of South Carolina Press, 1947.

Claiborne, John H. *Seventy-Five Years in Old Virginia.* New York:
The Neale Publishing Company, 1904.

Clare, Virginia Pettigrew. *Harp of the South.* Ogelthorpe University,
Ga.: Ogelthorpe University Press, 1936.

Clay-Clopton, Virginia. *A Belle of the Fifties; Memoirs of Mrs. Clay,
of Alabama, Covering Social and Political Life in Washington and
the South 1853-1866. Put into Narrative Form by Ada Sterling.* New
York: Heinemann, 1905.

Cleveland, Henry. *Alexander H. Stephens in Public and Private, with Letters and Speeches before, during, and since the War.* Philadelphia, Chicago, etc.: National Publishing Co., 1866.

Conner, James. *Letters of General James Conner, C.S.A.* Columbia, S.C.: The State Co., 1933.

Cotton, John Weaver. *Yours Till Death; Civil War Letters of John W. Cotton, edited by Lucille Griffith.* University, Ala.: University of Alabama Press, 1951.

Crowe, Eyre. *With Thackeray in America.* New York: Scribner's, 1893.

Cullen, Maurice R. Jr. "William Gilmore Simms, Southern Journalist." *Journalism Quarterly,* 38 (Summer 1961).

Cumming, Kate. *Kate: the Journal of a Confederate Nurse.* Ed. Richard Barksdale Harwell. Baton Rouge: Louisiana State University Press, 1959.

Cunningham, Horace H. "Edward Alfred Pollard: Historian and Critic of the Confederacy." Unpub. Master's thesis, University of North Carolina, 1940.

Davidson, James Wood. *The Living Writers of the South.* New York: Carleton, 1869.

Davis, Burke. *Gray Fox, Robert E. Lee and the Civil War.* New York: Rinehart, 1956.

——. *Jeb Stuart, the Last Cavalier.* New York: Rinehart, 1957.

Davis, Jefferson. *The Rise and Fall of the Confederate Government.* 2 vols. New York: D. Appleton, 1881.

Dawson, Sarah. *A Confederate Girl's Diary, with an Introduction by Warrington Dawson.* Boston: Houghton Mifflin, 1913.

Day, Samuel Phillips. *Down South: or, An Englishman's Experience at the Seat of the American War.* London: Hurst and Blackett, 1862.

DeLeon, Thomas Cooper. *Belles, Beaux and Brains of the 60's.* New York: G. W. Dillingham Co., 1909.

——. *Four Years in Rebel Capitals: an Inside View of Life in the Southern Confederacy, from Birth to Death. From Original Notes Collected in the Years 1861 to 1865.* Mobile: Gossip Printing Co., 1890.

Dillon, William. *Life of John Mitchel.* 2 vols. London: Kegan, Paul, Trench & Co., 1888.

Dodd, William E. *Jefferson Davis.* Philadelphia: G. W. Jacobs & Co., 1907.

Douglas, Henry Kyd. *I Rode with Stonewall, Being Chiefly the War*

Bibliography

Experiences of the Youngest Member of Jackson's Staff from the John Brown Raid to the Hanging of Mrs. Surratt. Chapel Hill: University of North Carolina Press, 1940.

Dowd, Jerome. *Sketches of Prominent Living North Carolinians*. Raleigh, N.C.: Edwards & Broughton, 1888.

Dowdey, Clifford and Louis H. Manarin, eds. *The Wartime Papers of R. E. Lee*. Boston: Little, Brown and Virginia Civil War Commission, 1961.

Durkin, Joseph T., S.J., ed. *Confederate Chaplain, A War Journal of Rev. James B. Sheeran . . . 14th Louisiana C.S.A.* Milwaukee: Bruce Publishing Co., 1960.

Dyer, John P. *The Gallant Hood*. Indianapolis: Bobbs-Merrill, 1950.

———. *"Fightin' Joe" Wheeler*. Baton Rouge: Louisiana State University Press, 1941.

Early, Jubal A. *Autobiographical Sketch and Narrative of the War between the States with notes by R. H. Early*. Philadelphia: Lippincott, 1912.

Eckenrode, Hamilton J. *Jefferson Davis, President of the South*. New York: Macmillan, 1923.

Eckenrode, Hamilton J. and Bryan Conrad. *James Longstreet: Lee's War Horse*. Chapel Hill: University of North Carolina Press, 1935.

Eggleston, George Cary. *A Rebel's Recollections*. New York: Hurd and Houghton; Cambridge: Riverside Press, 1875.

"An Englishman in South Carolina, December 1860 and July 1862." *Continental Monthly*, 3 (January 1863).

Fidler, William, ed. "Notes and Documents. Letters [of Henry Timrod] to Rachel Lyons, dated Charleston, Dec. 10, 1861-Sept. 30, 1863 on the author's health, the war, and other matters." *Alabama Review*, 2 (April 1949).

———. "Unpublished Letters of Henry Timrod." *Southern Literary Messenger*, 2 (October, November, December 1940).

Folk, Edgar E. "W. W. Holden, Political Journalist." *George Peabody College for Teachers; Contributions to Education*, Abstract No. 156.

Freeman, Douglas S., ed. *Lee's Dispatches; Unpublished Letters of Gen. Robert E. Lee C.S.A. to Jefferson Davis and the War Department of the Confederate States of America 1862-1865*. New York: G. P. Putnam, 1915.

———. *R. E. Lee, a Biography*. 4 vols. New York: Scribner's, 1934-35.

French, Gen. Samuel G. *Two Wars: an Autobiography*. Nashville: Confederate Veteran, 1901.

Garrett, William. *Reminiscences of Public Men in Alabama for Thirty Years*. Atlanta: Plantation Publishing Company's Press, 1872.

Gilman, Caroline Howard. "Letters of a Confederate Mother, Charleston in the Sixties." *Atlantic Monthly*, 137 (April 1926).

Girard, Charles Frederic. *A Visit to the Confederate States of America in 1863, Memoir Addressed to His Majesty, Napoleon III*. Tr. and ed. with an introduction by William Stanley Hoole. Tuscaloosa, Ala.: Confederate Publishing Co., 1962.

Gordon, John B. *Reminiscences of the Civil War*. New York: Scribner's, 1903.

Govan, Gilbert E. and James W. Livingood. *A Different Valor: The Story of General Joseph E. Johnston C.S.A.* New York: Bobbs-Merrill, 1956.

Gregorie, Ann King, ed. "Diary of Captain Joseph Julius Wescoat, 1863-1865." *South Carolina Historical Magazine*, 59 (January, April 1958).

Hamilton, J. G. de Roulhac. *The Papers of Randolph A. Shotwell*. 2 vols. Raleigh: North Carolina Historical Commission, 1929-31.

Hamlin, Capt. Percy Gatling. *"Old Bald Head"* [Gen. R. S. Ewell]: *The Portrait of a Soldier*. Strasburg, Va.: Shenandoah Publishing House, 1940.

————. *The Making of a Soldier; Letters of General R. S. Ewell*. Richmond: Whittet & Shepperson, 1935.

Harris, Joel Chandler. "Henry Lynden Flash." *The Countryman*, 19 (June 14, 1964).

Harris, William Charles. *Leroy Pope Walker: Confederate Secretary of War*. Tuscaloosa, Ala.: Confederate Publishing Co., 1962.

Harrison, Constance (Cary) (Mrs. Burton Harrison). *Recollections Grave and Gay*. New York: Scribner's 1911.

Hassler, William Woods. *A. P. Hill: Lee's Forgotten General*. Richmond: Garrett and Massie, 1957.

Henderson, George Francis Robert. *Stonewall Jackson and the American Civil War*. 2 vols. London: Longmans Green, 1937.

Henry, Robert S. *"First with the Most" Forrest*. Indianapolis: Bobbs-Merrill, 1944.

Hill, Louise B. *Joseph E. Brown and the Confederacy*. Chapel Hill: University of North Carolina Press, 1939.

Hollis, Daniel W. "Robert W. Barnwell." *South Carolina Historical Magazine,* 56 (July 1955).

Hood, John B. *Advance and Retreat, Personal Experiences in the United States and Confederate Armies.* New Orleans: Published for the Hood Orphan Memorial Fund, 1880.

Hoole, William Stanley. *Lawley Covers the Confederacy.* Tuscaloosa, Ala.: Confederate Publishing Co., 1964.

———. *Vizetelly Covers the Confederacy.* Tuscaloosa, Ala: Confederate Publishing Co., 1957.

Hoyt, James A. "The Confederate Archives and Felix G. DeFontaine." *South Carolina Historical Magazine,* 57 (October 1956).

Hubbell, Jay B., ed. *The Last Years of Henry Timrod, 1864-1867.* Durham, N.C.: Duke University Press, 1941.

Huffman, James. *Ups and Downs of a Confederate Soldier.* New York: William E. Rudge's Sons, 1940.

Hughes, Nathaniel Cheairs, Jr. *General William J. Hardee, Old Reliable.* Baton Rouge: Louisiana State University Press, 1965.

Hunton, Eppa. *Autobiography of Eppa Hunton.* Richmond: William Byrd Press, 1933.

Inman, Arthur C., ed. *Soldier of the South: General Pickett's War Letters to his Wife.* Boston: Houghton Mifflin, 1928.

Jackson, Isaac. *"Some of the Boys . . ." The Civil War Letters of Isaac Jackson, 1862-1865.* Ed. Joseph Orville Jackson with a foreword by Bell I. Wiley. Carbondale: Southern Illinois University Press, 1960.

Johnson, Allen, and Dumas Malone, eds. *Dictionary of American Biography.* 22 vols. New York: Charles Scribner's Sons, 1928-58, I, 492-93 (George William Bagby); III, 486-87 (Jacob N. Cardozo); v, 385-86 (John Esten Cooke); v, 67-68 (John Moncure Daniel); v, 196 (Felix Gregory DeFontaine); VII, 235-36 (Robert Wilson Gibbes); VII, 540-42 (Duff Green); XIII, 35-36 (John Mitchel); xv, 47-48 (Edward A. Pollard); xv, 348 (James Ryder Randall); xvi, 514-15 (William Wallace Screws); xviii, 464 (John Reuben Thompson); xviii, 479-80 (William Tappan Thompson); xviii, 509-10 (John Sidney Thrasher); xviii, 558-60 (Henry Timrod); xix, 337-38 (Alexander Walker); xix, 552-55 (Henry Watterson); xx, 602 (Richard Yeadon).

Johnston, Joseph E. *Narrative of Military Operations, Directed during the Late War between the States.* New York: D. Appleton, 1874.

Johnston, William P. *The Life of Gen. Albert Sidney Johnston.* New York: D. Appleton, 1878.

Jones, John Beauchamp. *A Rebel War Clerk's Diary at the Confederate States Capital.* 2 vols. Philadelphia: Lippincott, 1866.

Jones, Virgil Carrington. *Ranger Mosby.* Chapel Hill: University of North Carolina Press, 1944.

Kibler, Lillian. *Benjamin F. Perry, South Carolina Unionist.* Durham: Duke University Press, 1946.

King, Joseph Leonard. *Dr. William Bagby, a Study of Virginian Literature, 1850-1880.* New York: Columbia University Press, 1927.

Kirwan, A. D., ed. *Johnny Green of the Orphan Brigade; the Journal of a Confederate Soldier.* Lexington: University of Kentucky Press, 1956.

Lawley, Francis E. "The Last Six Days of Secessia." *The Fortnightly Review,* 2 (August 15, 1865).

Lawrence, George Alfred. *Border and Bastile.* New York: W. I. Pooley, 1863; London: Tinsley Brothers, 1863.

Lewis, Lloyd. *Sherman, Fighting Prophet.* New York: Harcourt, Brace, 1932.

Logan, Kate Virginia Cox. *My Confederate Girlhood.* Edited by her Daughter, Lily Logan Morrill. Richmond: Garrett and Massie, 1932.

Longstreet, James. *From Manassas to Appomattox, Memoirs of the Civil War in America.* Philadelphia: Lippincott, 1896.

McCaleb, Walter F., ed. *Memoirs, with Special Reference to Secession and the Civil War, by John H. Reagan.* New York: The Neale Publishing Co., 1906.

McClellan, Henry Brainerd. *The Life and Campaigns of Major-General J.E.B. Stuart, Commander of the Cavalry of the Army of Northern Virginia.* Boston: Houghton Mifflin; Richmond: J. W. Randolph and English, 1885.

Mallory, Stephen R. "Last Days of the Confederate Government." *McClure's Magazine,* 16 (December 1900, January 1901).

Marcosson, Isaac F. *"Marse Henry," A Biography of Henry Watterson.* New York: Dodd, Mead, 1951.

Mason, Edward G. "A Visit to South Carolina in 1860." *Atlantic Monthly,* 53 (February 1884).

Maury, Dabney Herndon. *Recollections of a Virginian in the Mexican, Indian, and Civil Wars; by Gen. Dabney Herndon Maury.* New York: Scribner's, 1894.

Meade, Robert D. *Judah P. Benjamin, Confederate Statesman*. London: Oxford University Press, 1943.

Miller, Henry Prentice. "The Life and Works of William Tappan Thompson." Unpub. Ph.D. Diss., University of Chicago, 1942.

Moncure, John. "John M. Daniel: The Editor of the Examiner." *Sewanee Review*, 15 (July 1907).

Montgomery, Franklin Alexander. *Reminiscences of a Mississippian in Peace and War*. Cincinnati: Robert Clarke Co. Press, 1901.

Mosby, John Singleton: *War Reminiscences and Stuart's Cavalry Campaigns*. New York: Dodd, Mead, 1898.

National Cyclopedia of American Biography. 45 vols. New York: 1893-1962. II, 50 (Patrick Walsh); II, 51 (James A. Cowardin); II, 425 (George W. Adair); VIII, 310 (Leonidas Trousdale); VIII, 471 (John Forsyth); XIII, 279 (Henry Lynden Flash); XVIII, 220 (Henderson M. Somerville); XXV, 210 (James O. Nixon).

Nisbet, James Cooper. *Four Years on the Firing Line and Reconstruction*. Ed. Bell I. Wiley. Jackson, Tennessee: McCowat-Mercer, 1963.

Nuermberger, Ruth Ketring. *The Clays of Alabama, A Planter-Lawyer-Politician Family*. Lexington: University of Kentucky Press, 1958.

O'Conner, Richard. *Hood, Cavalier General*. New York: Prentice-Hall, 1949.

Oliphant, Mary C. Simms et al., eds. *The Letters of William Gilmore Simms*. 5 vols. Columbia: University of South Carolina Press, 1952-56.

Osterweis, Rollin G. *Judah P. Benjamin: Statesman of the Lost Cause*. New York: G. P. Putnam, 1933.

Owen, William Miller. *In Camp and Battle with the Washington Artillery of New Orleans*. Boston: Ticknor, 1885.

Parks, Joseph Howard. *General Edmund Kirby Smith, C.S.A.* Baton Rouge: Louisiana State University Press, 1954.

————. *General Leonidas Polk C.S.A.; the Fighting Bishop*. Baton Rouge: Louisiana State University Press, 1962.

Patrick, Rembert. *Jefferson Davis and His Cabinet*. Baton Rouge: Louisiana State University Press, 1944.

Patrick, Robert. *Reluctant Rebel; the Secret Diary of Robert Patrick, 1861-1865*. Ed. F. Jay Taylor. Baton Rouge: Louisiana State University Press, 1959.

Paxton, Elisha Franklin, Brig.Gen., C.S.A., *Memoir and Memorials*. Printed, not published, 1905.

Pemberton, John C. *Pemberton, Defender of Vicksburg*. Chapel Hill: University of North Carolina Press, 1942.

Poague, William Thomas. *Gunner with Stonewall; Reminiscences of William Thomas Poague, a Memoir, Written for His Children in 1903*. Ed. Monroe F. Cockrell. Jackson, Tenn.: McCowat-Mercer, 1957.

Polk, William M. *Leonidas Polk, Bishop and General*. 2 vols. New York: Longmans Green, 1915.

Pollard, Edward Alfred. *Life of Jefferson Davis, With a Secret History of the Southern Confederacy Gathered behind the Scenes in Richmond*. Philadelphia, Chicago, etc.: National Publishing Co., 1869.
———. *Observations in the North: Eight Months in Prison and on Parole*. Richmond: E. W. Ayres, 1865.

Pollard, Henry Robinson. *Memoirs and Sketches of the Life of, an Autobiography*. Richmond: Lewis Printing Co., 1923.

Putnam, Sallie A. *Richmond during the War; Four Years of Personal Observation. By a Richmond Lady*. New York: G. W. Carleton, 1867.

Pryor, Sarah Agnes (Rice) (Mrs. R. A. Pryor). *Reminiscences of Peace and War*. New York: Macmillan; London: Macmillan, 1904.

Quenzel, Carol H. *Edgar Snowden, Sr.: Virginia Journalist and Civic Leader*. Charlottesville, Va.: Bibliographical Society of the University of Virginia, 1954.

Ranck, James B. *Albert Gallatin Brown, Radical Southern Nationalist*. New York: Appleton-Century, 1937.

Reid, Whitelaw. *After the War: A Southern Tour*. Cincinnati: Moore, Wilstach, and Baldwin, 1866.

Rice, Jessie Pearl. *J.L.M. Curry, Southerner, Statesman, and Educator*. New York: King's Crown Press, 1949.

Roland, Charles P. *Albert Sidney Johnston, Soldier of Three Republics*. Austin: University of Texas Press, 1964.

Ross, Fitzgerald. *Cities and Camps of the Confederate States*. Ed. Richard B. Harwell. Urbana: University of Illinois Press, 1958.

Ross, Ishbel. *Rebel Rose, Life of Rose O'Neal Greenhow, Confederate Spy*. New York: Harper, 1954.

Runge, William H., ed. *Four Years in the Confederate Artillery, the Diary of Private Henry Robinson Berkeley*. Chapel Hill: University of North Carolina Press, 1961.

Russell, William Howard. *My Diary, North and South*. Boston: T.O.H.P. Burnham; New York: O. S. Felt, 1863.

Rowland, Dunbar, ed. *Jefferson Davis, Constitutionalist; His Letters, Papers and Speeches.* Collected and Edited by Dunbar Rowland. 10 vols. Jackson, Miss.: Printed for the Mississippi Dept. of Archives and History, 1923.

Sanger, Donald Bridgman and Thomas Robson Hay. *James Longstreet.* Baton Rouge: Louisiana State University Press, 1952.

Scheibert, Justus. *Seven Months in the Rebel States during the North American War, 1863.* Tr. from the German by Joseph C. Hayes, ed. with an introduction by William Stanley Hoole. Tuscaloosa, Ala.: Confederate Publishing Co., 1958.

Schenk, Martin. *Up Came Hill; the Story of the Light Division and Its Leaders.* Harrisburg, Pa.: Stackpole Co., 1958.

Seitz, Don C. *Braxton Bragg, General of the Confederacy.* Columbia, S.C.: The State Co., 1924.

Selby, Julian A. *Memorabilia and Anecdotal Reminiscences of Columbia, S.C., and Incidents Connected Therewith.* Columbia, S.C., 1905.

Sheppard, Eric W. *Bedford Forrest, the Confederacy's Greatest Cavalryman.* New York: Dial Press; Toronto: Longmans Green, 1930.

Smith, Daniel Elliot Huger. *A Charlestonian's Recollections, 1846-1913.* Introduction by Harold A. Muzon, preface by Alice R. Huger Smith. Charleston, S.C.: Carolina Art Association, 1950.

Smith, Rixey and Norman Beasley. *Carter Glass, A Biography.* New York: Dial Press, 1939.

Sorrel, (Gen.) Gilbert Moxley. *Recollections of a Confederate Staff Officer.* New York: The Neale Publishing Co., 1905.

Stearns, Emiline L. "John M. Daniel and the Confederacy." Unpub. Master's thesis, University of Chicago, 1928.

Stephens, Alexander H. *Recollections.* New York: Doubleday, 1910.

Stevenson, William G. *Thirteen Months in the Rebel Army.* New York: A. S. Barnes & Burr, 1862.

Strode, Hudson. *Jefferson Davis, Confederate President.* New York: Harcourt, Brace, 1959.

————. *Jefferson Davis, Tragic Hero, 1864-1889.* New York: Harcourt, Brace, 1964.

Taylor, Richard. *Destruction and Reconstruction: Personal Experiences of the Late War.* Ed. Richard B. Harwell. New York: Longmans Green, 1955.

Taylor, Walter H. *Four Years with General Lee.* New York: D. Appleton, 1877.

Thomason, John W. Jr. *Jeb Stuart*. New York: Scribner's, 1930.

Thompson, Henry Tazewell. *Henry Timrod, Laureate of the Confederacy*. Columbia, S.C.: The State Company, 1928.

Tinsley, Henry C. *Observations of a Retired Veteran*. Staunton, Va.: Albert Schultz, 1904.

Trent, William P. *William Gilmore Simms*. Boston: Houghton Mifflin, 1896.

Von Abele, Rudolph. *Alexander H. Stephens: a Biography*. New York: Knopf, 1946.

Vandiver, Frank E. ed. *The Civil War Diary of General Josiah Gorgas*. University, Ala.: University of Alabama Press, 1947.

———. *Mighty Stonewall*. New York: McGraw-Hill, 1957.

Wall, Joseph F. *Henry Watterson, Reconstructed Rebel*. London: Oxford University Press, 1956.

Warner, Ezra J. *Generals in Gray: Lives of the Confederate Commanders*. Baton Rouge: Louisiana State University Press, 1959.

Warren Lott. "Henry Timrod." *The Southern Magazine*, 17 (December 1875).

Watson, William (of Skelmorlie, Scotland). *Life in the Confederate Army, being the Observations and Experiences of an Alien in the South During the American Civil War*. New York: Scribner & Welford, 1888.

Wauchope, George Armstrong. *Henry Timrod: Man and Poet, A Critical Study*. Columbia: University of South Carolina Press, 1915.

Wellman, Manly Wade. *Giant in Gray: a Biography of Wade Hampton of South Carolina*. New York: Scribner's, 1949.

White, Laura Amanda. *Robert Barnwell Rhett: Father of Secession*. New York: Century Co., 1931.

Wiley, Bell Irvin., ed. *Letters of Warren Akin, Confederate Congressman*. Athens, Ga.: University of Georgia Press, 1959.

———. *"This Infernal War," The Confederate Letters of Sgt. Edwin H. Fay*. Austin: University of Texas Press, 1958.

Wilkie, Franc B. *Pen and Powder*. Boston: Ticknor and Co., 1888.

Wilkinson, Andrew Newton. "John Moncure Daniel." *Richmond College Historical Papers*, Richmond, Va., 1915. Vol. i, No. 1, pp. 73-95.

Williams, T. Harry. *P.G.T. Beauregard, Napoleon in Gray*. Baton Rouge: Louisiana State University Press, 1955.

Winston, Robert W. *High Stakes and Hair Trigger: The Life of Jefferson Davis*. New York: Henry Holt, 1930.

Winwar, Frances. *American Giant, Walt Whitman and His Times.* New York: Harper, 1941.

Wise, Barton, H. *The Life of Henry A. Wise of Virginia, 1806-1876.* New York: Macmillan, 1899.

Wise, John S. *The End of an Era.* Boston: Houghton Mifflin, 1899.

Younger, Edward, ed. *Inside the Confederate Government: The Diary of Robert Garlick Hill Kean.* London: Oxford University Press, 1957.

IX. The Confederacy: State, Local, and Regional Studies

Armstrong, Zella. *The History of Hamilton County and Chattanooga, Tennessee.* 2 vols. Chattanooga: Lookout Publishing Co., 1931-40.

Arnett, Alex Mathews. *The Story of North Carolina.* Chapel Hill: University of North Carolina Press, 1933.

Ashe, Samuel A., ed. *Biographical History of North Carolina from Colonial Times to the Present.* 8 vols. Greensboro, N.C.: Charles Van Nappen, 1905.

Avery, I. W. *The History of the State of Georgia from 1850-1881.* New York: Brown and Derby, 1881.

Bettersworth, John K. *Confederate Mississippi, The People and Policies of a Cotton State in Wartime.* Baton Rouge: Louisiana State University Press, 1943.

Biographical and Historical Memoirs of Louisiana. 2 vols. Chicago: Goodspeed Publishing Company, 1892.

Boyd, Minnie Clare. *Alabama in the Fifties; A Social Study.* New York: Columbia University Press, 1931.

Bragg, Jefferson Davis. *Louisiana in the Confederacy.* Baton Rouge: Louisiana State University Press, 1941.

Brewer, Willis. *Alabama, Her History, Resources, War Record, and Public Men from 1540 to 1872.* Montgomery: Barrett & Brown, 1872.

Bryan, Thomas Conn. *Confederate Georgia.* Athens: University of Georgia Press, 1953.

Capers, Gerald M. Jr. *The Biography of a River Town: Memphis, its Heroic Age.* Chapel Hill: University of North Carolina Press, 1931.

Chandler, Julian A. C. et al., eds. *The South in the Building of the Nation.* 13 vols. in 7. Richmond: The Southern Historical Publication Society, 1909-13.

Chambers, Henry E. *A History of Louisiana, Wilderness—Colony—Province—Territory—State—People.* 3 vols. Chicago: American Historical Society, 1925.

Chambers, Lenoir. "The South on the Eve of the Civil War." *North Carolina Historical Review*, 39 (Spring 1962).

Christian, William Asbury. *Richmond, Her Past and Present.* Richmond, Va.: Manufactured by L. H. Jenkins, 1912.

Clark, Thomas D. *A History of Kentucky.* New York: Prentice-Hall, 1937.

Cooper, Walter G. *The Story of Georgia.* 4 vols. New York: American Historical Society, 1938.

Coulter, Ellis Merton. *A Short History of Georgia.* Chapel Hill: University of North Carolina Press, 1933.

———. *The Confederate States of America, 1861-1865. A History of the South*, vol. 7. Baton Rouge: Louisiana State University Press, 1950.

Craighead, Erwin. *From Mobile's Past; Sketches of Memorable People and Events.* Mobile: Power Printing Co., 1925.

Craven, Avery. *Growth of Southern Nationalism, 1848-1861.* Baton Rouge: Louisiana State University Press, 1953.

Deland, T. A. and A. Davis Smith. *Northern Alabama, Historical and Biographical.* Birmingham, Ala. 1888.

Delaney, Caldwell. *The Story of Mobile.* Mobile: Gill Printing Co., 1953.

Eaton, Clement. *Freedom of Thought in the Old South.* Durham: Duke University Press, 1940.

———. *A History of the Southern Confederacy.* New York: Macmillan, 1954.

Eckenrode, Hamilton J. *Richmond, Capital of Virginia, Approaches to its History.* Richmond: Whittet & Shepperson, 1938.

Embrey, Alvin T. *History of Fredericksburg, Virginia.* Richmond, Va.: Old Dominion Press, 1937.

Fortier, Alcee. *Louisiana.* 3 vols. Atlanta: Southern Historical Association, 1909.

Garrett, Franklin M. *Atlanta and Environs, A Chronicle of Its People and Events.* 3 vols. New York: Lewis Publishing Co., 1954.

Godwin, Thelma. "Memphis during the Civil War, 1860-1870." Unpub. Master's thesis, University of Alabama, 1947.

Guess, William Francis. *South Carolina: Annals of Pride and Protest.* New York: Harper, 1960.

Halsey, Don P. *Historic and Heroic Lynchburg.* Lynchburg, Va.: J. P. Bell Co., 1935.

Hamer, Philip M., ed. *Tennessee; a History, 1673-1932.* 4 vols. New York: American Historical Society, 1933.

Harden, William. *A History of Savannah and South Georgia.* 2 vols. Chicago: Lewis Publishing Co., 1913.

Harrison, Margaret Hayne. *A Charleston Album.* Rindge, N.H.: Richard R. Smith, 1953.

Hayne, Paul Hamilton. "Ante-Bellum Charleston." *Southern Bivouac,* n.s. 1 (September, October, November 1885).

Hennig, Helen Kohn, ed. *Columbia, Capital City of South Carolina, 1786-1936.* Columbia, S.C.: R. L. Bryan Co., 1936.

Henry, Robert Selph. *The Story of the Confederacy.* Indianapolis: Bobbs-Merrill, 1931.

Hesseltine, William B. *A History of the South, 1607-1936.* New York: Prentice-Hall, 1936.

Hill, Daniel Harvey. *Bethel to Sharpsburg, A History of North Carolina in the War between the States.* 2 vols. Raleigh: Edwards & Broughton, 1926.

Hoole, William Stanley. "Literary and Cultural Background of Charleston, 1830-1860." Unpub. Ph.D. Diss., Duke University, 1934.

Howell, Clark. *History of Georgia.* 4 vols. Chicago: S. J. Clarke Publishing Co., 1926.

Hubbell, Jay Broadus. *The South in American Literature, 1607-1900.* Durham: Duke University Press, 1954.

Johnson, Amanda. *Georgia as Colony and State.* Atlanta: Walter W. Brown Publishing Co., 1938.

Jones, Charles Colcock, Jr. *The History of Georgia.* 2 vols. Boston: Houghton Mifflin, 1883.

Jones, Charles C., O. F. Vedder, and Frank Weldon. *History of Savannah, Ga.* Syracuse, N.Y.: D. Mason & Co., 1890.

Jones, Charles C. and Salem Dutcher. *Memorial History of Augusta, Georgia.* Syracuse: D. Mason & Co., 1890.

Keating, J. M. *History of the City Memphis and Shelby County, Tennessee with Illustrations and Biographical Sketches of Some of Its Prominent Citizens.* 2 vols. Syracuse, N.Y.: D. Mason & Co., 1888.

583

Knight, Lucian Lamar, ed. *Encyclopedia of Georgia Biography*. Atlanta: A. H. Cawston, managing editor and publisher, 1931.

———. *Georgia's Landmarks, Memorials and Legends*. 2 vols. Atlanta: Printed for the Author by the Byrd Printing Company, 1914.

Lefler, Hugh Talmage. *History of North Carolina*. 4 vols. New York: Lewis Publishing Co., 1956.

Leiding, Harriet Kershaw. *Charleston, Historic and Romantic*. Philadelphia: Lippincott, 1931.

Lesesne, Thomas Petigru. *History of Charleston County, South Carolina, Narrative and Biographical*. Charleston, S.C.: A. H. Cawston, 1931.

Little, John P. *History of Richmond; Reprinted from the Southern Literary Messenger*. Richmond: Dietz Printing Co., 1933.

Lynchburg Sesqui-Centennial Association, Inc., *The Saga of a City: Lynchburg, Virginia, 1786-1936*. Lynchburg: The Lynchburg Sesqui-Centennial Association, 1936.

McCain, William D. *The Story of Jackson, A History of the Capital of Mississippi, 1821-1951*. Jackson, Miss.: J. F. Hyer Publishing Co., 1953.

McGinty, Garnie William. *A History of Louisiana* [1528-1948]. New York: Exposition Press, 1949.

McIlwaine, Shields. *Memphis down in Dixie* [1818-1948]. New York: E. P. Dutton, 1948.

Martin, John H. *Columbus, Georgia*. 2 vols. Columbus, Ga.: Thomas Gilbert, 1874.

———. "Montgomery in Secession Time." *The Continental Monthly*, 3 (March 1863).

Moore, Albert Burton. *History of Alabama and Her People*. 3 vols. Chicago: American Historical Society, 1927.

Owen, Thomas M. *History of Alabama and Dictionary of Alabama Biography*. 4 vols. Chicago: S. J. Clarke Publishing Co., 1921.

Patton, James W. *Unionism and Reconstruction in Tennessee, 1860-1869*. Chapel Hill: University of North Carolina Press, 1934.

Powell, Lyman P., ed. *Historic Towns of the Southern States*. New York: G. P. Putnam, 1900.

Ravenel, Beatrice. *Charleston, the Place and the People*. New York: Macmillan, 1906.

Reed, Wallace P., ed. *History of Atlanta, Georgia*. Syracuse, N.Y.: D. Mason & Co., 1889.

Bibliography

Rightor, Henry, ed. *Standard History of New Orleans, Louisiana.* Chicago: Lewis Publishing Co., 1900.

Roland, Charles P. *The Confederacy.* Chicago: University of Chicago Press, 1960.

Rowland, Dunbar. *History of Mississippi, the Heart of the South.* 2 vols. Chicago: S. J. Clarke Publishing Co., 1925.

Rule, William, ed. *Standard History of Knoxville, Tennessee.* Chicago: Lewis Publishing Co., 1900.

Schwab, John G. *The Confederate States of America, 1861-1865; a Financial and Industrial History of the South during the Civil War.* New York: Scribner's, 1901.

Summersell, Charles Grayson. *Mobile: History of a Seaport Town* [1702-1948]. University, Ala.: University of Alabama Press, 1949.

Stephenson, Nathaniel W. *The Day of the Confederacy; a Chronicle of the Embattled South.* New Haven: Yale University Press, 1920.

Sydnor, Charles Sackett. *Development of Southern Sectionalism, 1819-1848.* Baton Rouge: Louisiana State University Press, 1948.

Wallace, David Duncan. *South Carolina, A Short History, 1520-1948.* Chapel Hill: University of North Carolina Press, 1951.

————. *The History of South Carolina.* 4 vols. New York: The American Historical Society, Inc., 1934.

Wiley, Bell Irvin and Hirst D. Milhollen. *Embattled Confederates.* New York: Harper & Row, 1964.

Wilson, Adelaide. *Historic and Picturesque Savannah.* Boston: Boston Photogravure Company, 1889.

Woodward, C. Vann. *The Burden of Southern History.* Baton Rouge: Louisiana State University Press, 1960.

Wooldridge, J., ed. *History of Nashville, Tennessee.* Nashville: Publishing House of the Methodist Episcopal Church South, 1890.

Yates, Richard E. *The Confederacy and Zeb Vance.* Tuscaloosa, Ala.: Confederate Publishing Co., 1958.

X. Miscellaneous

Buchanan, Lamont. *A Pictorial History of the Confederacy.* New York: Crown Publishers, 1951.

Dumond, Dwight L. *The Secession Movement, 1860-1861.* New York: Macmillan, 1931.

Freeman, Douglas. *The South to Posterity; an Introduction to the Writings of Confederate History.* New York: Scribner's, 1939.

Bibliography

Goodrich, Charles A. *The Family Tourist, A Visit to the Principal Cities of the Western Continent.* Philadelphia: J. W. Bradley, 1848.

Harwell, Richard Barksdale. *The Confederate Reader.* New York: Longmans Green, 1957.

Holbrook, Stewart Hall. "Murder at Harvard." *American Mercury,* 66 (February 1948).

McMillan, Malcolm C. *The Alabama Confederate Reader.* University, Ala.: University of Alabama Press, 1963.

Minor, Benjamin Blake. *The Southern Literary Messenger, 1834-1864.* Washington: The Neale Publishing Co., 1905.

Rhodes, James Ford. *Historical Essays.* New York: Macmillan, 1909.

Sideman, Belle Becker and Lilian Friedman, eds. *Europe Looks at the Civil War, an Anthology.* New York: Orion Press, 1960.

Weeks, Lyman H. *A History of Paper Manufacturing in the United States, 1690-1916.* New York: Lockwood Trade Journal Co., 1916.

Index

on the march, 199; reports privations of Lee's army on the march, 199; describes Thoroughfare gap, 200; reports second Battle of Manassas, 200-202; witnesses reception of Lee's army at Leesburg, 204; observes crossing of Potomac by Longstreet's corps, 204-205; describes attitude of Maryland civilians, 205; reports Battle of South Mountain, 208; Antietam battle report as outstanding performance, 213; on results of Maryland campaign, 215; suffers riding accident, 217; returns to South Carolina (October 1862), 217; goes to Virginia (January 1863), 285; describes camp life (January 1863), 285-286; describes Richmond scene (1863), 290; wedding of, 309; reports attack on Charleston (April 1863), 321-322; reports attack on Battery Wagner, 324-325; reports use of Negro troops by enemy at Battery Wagner, 324-325; reports Chattanooga campaign, 358-359, 359n, 362-364, 367-368; on camp life, 362-364; reports Battle of Lookout Valley, 367-368; leaves Bragg's army to accompany Longstreet to east Tennessee, 374; reports Knoxville campaign, 378-382; communication difficulties of, 379-380; reports unsuccessful attempt to storm Knoxville defenses, 380; reports privations of Longstreet's soldiers, 382; returns home from east Tennessee (December 1863), 382; visits Richmond (November 1864), 426-428; reports Richmond scene and camp life, 426-428; reports Atlanta campaign, 453-454, 456-459; on removal of Gen. Johnston, 454; reports Battles of Atlanta, 456-458; victim of pillaging, 458; interviews Gov. Brown, 459; warns Columbia of impending danger, 488; reports preliminaries of Federal occupation of Columbia, 492-494; reports misconduct of Wheeler's cavalry at Columbia, 494;

as agent of P.A., 496; war reporting of, evaluated, 537; mentioned, 505
De Gournay, Capt. Francis F., reports from Pensacola, 62
deserters, 345n
De Witt, Bennett M., as "working editor" of *Richmond Enquirer*, 27; as *Richmond Examiner* editor, 29
Dill, Benjamin F., as *Memphis Appeal* editor, 40; seeks guidance from Vice Pres. Stephens, 483; placed under bond by Union provost marshal, 505
"D." (*Memphis Appeal*), reports New Orleans naval battle, 149
Dumble, John B., recruits de Fontaine as Charleston reporter of *Memphis Appeal*, 327; flees to Augusta, 504
Duncan, David G., reports from Montgomery (1861), 60; meets Gen. Beauregard at Manassas, 72; reports first Battle of Manassas, 83-84, 87n
DuPont, Adm. Samuel F., leads Union attack on Charleston (1863), 320
Dupré, Louis J., as leading Richmond correspondent, 54; on Mississippi defeatism, 277; reports Vicksburg campaign, 277-279; transportation problems of, 278; predicts fall of Vicksburg, 279; arrives at Richmond (January 1863), 287; Richmond reporting of, 287-288, 290-291; quoted, 291; on army morale, 345; deplores abuse of Confederate Congress, 509-510; on abuses in army administration, 522
Dutcher, Salem, as leading Richmond correspondent, 54; on brutality of conscription officers, 391; reports Battle of Cold Harbor, 401-402
Dwinell, Melville, refugee editor, 438

Eagan, news source of *Augusta Chronicle* report of burning of Columbia, 492
Early, Gen. Jubal A., and the press, 299, 424-425; described, 407; Maryland campaign of (July 1864), 407-409; in Shenandoah Valley

quoted, 96; reports arrival of Pres. Davis at Fairfax Court House, 96; reports withdrawal of Johnston's army from the Potomac, 99; criticizes press exaggeration of amount of picket firing, 105; arrives at Memphis, 135; reports Battle of Shiloh, 140-141, 141n, 144; reports conversation between Beauregard and Prentiss, 141, 141n; reports Corinth campaign, 152, 155n; reports Memphis gunboat battle, 157-158

"Perryman" (*Columbia Carolinian*), describes members of Georgia state militia, 459-460; quoted, 460

Perryville, Battle of, reporting of, 244-245

"Personne," *see* de Fontaine, Felix G.

Petersburg, Va., bombardment of, reporting of, 405-406

Petersburg Express, issues extra edition, 173

Petersburg mine explosion, reporting of, 410-412

Peterson, J. S., as Atlanta newspaper publisher, 38

Petigru, James L., 11

Pettus, Gov. John J., and the press, 270

Pickens, Gov. Francis, described, 8-9; erstwhile opponent of secession, 11; questions accuracy of Harvey telegram to Charleston friend, 12n; victory speech of, 21; mentioned, 13

Pillow, Gen. Gideon, in Fort Donelson campaign, 130, 131

planted stories, 185, 530

Pleasanton, Gen. Alfred, at Brandy Station, 303

Pleasants, Hugh R., as *Richmond Dispatch* editor, 33; reports Big Bethel skirmish, 74; on news security problem, 408

Pleasants, John H., as editor of *Richmond Whig*, 28

Polk, Gen. Leonidas, occupies Columbus, Ky., 119; suspended from command after Battle of Chickamauga, 358; in Atlanta campaign, 435-436, 438, 446-447; death of, 447

Pollard, Edward A., as member of *Richmond Examiner* editorial staff, 30-32; early life, 31; characterized, 32; promises cooperation of *Richmond Examiner* in security measures, 193; on war weariness in the North, 485; on rumormongers, 514; mentioned, 88

Pollard, Henry Rives, as news editor of *Richmond Examiner*, 31

Porter, Adm. David D., in Vicksburg campaign, 266, 267

Port Gibson, Battle of, reporting of, 269-270

Port Hudson, La., fall of, reporting of, 284

Posey, Ben L., reports Battle of Jonesboro, 461; interviews Pres. Davis, 464-465; transferred from Army of Tennessee to Alabama, 466; on misbehavior of Confederate troops, 467; quoted, 467; mentioned, 477

Prentiss, Gen. Benjamin M., capture, 141

press, Southern, history and general description, 24-55; wartime problems of, 41-47, 478-480; impatience of with Davis's defensive strategy, 92; general evaluation, 506-542

Press Association of the Confederate States, establishment, 56; copyrights news dispatches, 57; news organization, 57; finances, 57; salaries of reporters, 57; mutual system, 58; business problems, 58, 480-481; in Vicksburg campaign, 272-273, 274-275, 279; in Tennessee campaign of 1863, 343n, 344; in Chickamauga campaign, 348, 353, 355, 356n; in Chattanooga campaign, 360-361; wrongly accused of inefficiency, 375; in Virginia campaign of 1864, 387-388, 396-397, 398, 405; in Atlanta campaign, 439, 448-449, 457, 462-463; reports fall of Atlanta, 462-463; responsible for telegraphic canard, 467; reports plan for Sherman's march, 468; reports Sherman's march to Savannah, 471; in Hood's Nashville campaign, 473, 475; reports burning of Columbia,

Orleans, 150-151; on Richmond morale (March 1862), 170-171; describes Richmond scene (May 1862), 175-176; describes Richmond scene (June 1862), 183; visits Lee's army on the Peninsula, 184-185; reports arrival of prisoners in Richmond from Seven Days battlefield, 188; reports visit to Richmond by Gen. Stuart, 197; on wartime scarcities and high prices in Richmond, 220; on Richmond bread riot, 291; describes death of Maj. Pelham, 292; reports departure of *London Times* correspondent for the front, 293; blames Stuart for Brandy Station "surprise," 304; defends Stuart against press criticism, 331; demands explanation of Kelly's Ford reverse, 334; on housing shortage in Richmond, 336; uncertainty of about Longstreet's situation at Knoxville, 380; on Dahlgren Raid, 383; on situation in Richmond (April 1864), 386; composes poem in Gen. Stuart's honor, 392; replaced as Richmond correspondent of *Memphis Appeal*, 401n; political reporting of evaluated, 538; mentioned, 287

Thompson, William T., reports Sumter bombardment (1861), 18-19

Thrasher, John S., early life, 56; as general manager of Press Association, 56-57; introduces new style of telegraphic news reporting, 274; dismisses untrustworthy P.A. reporter, 339; sends Woodson to Bragg's army, 348; prepares P.A. report of Battle of Chickamauga, 353; dismisses P.A. agent Woodson, 361; and P.A. reporting of Knoxville campaign, 379; attempts to reopen news communication, 396-397; difficulties with press service, 439; goes to Texas after fall of Atlanta, 462; returns from Texas to Georgia (January 1865), 482; directs P.A. correspondents to stick to factual reporting, 515; seeks to restrain military censorship, 532-533

Timrod, Henry, salary as *Charleston Mercury* war correspondent, 48; describes Corinth, 153; quoted, 153, 153n; reports Corinth campaign, 153-155, 157; befriended by J. R. Randall in Mobile, 157

Tinsley, H. C., reports Big Bethel skirmish, 74

"Tout-le-Monde" (*Savannah Republican*), reports Battle of Gettysburg, 310-312; quoted, 310, 311-312; reports Battle of Chickamauga, 350-351; describes Chickamauga battlefield, 352; reports Knoxville campaign, 381-382; on use of liquor by enemy troops, 395; on Petersburg bombardment, 406; mentioned, 518

Trans-Mississippi region, neglected area of news coverage, 507

Trout House (Atlanta, Ga.), 429; enemy celebration at, 464

Tulda, A. E., reports outcome of New Orleans naval battle, 150

Tullahoma, Tenn., Bragg's headquarters during early 1863, 338

Tupelo, Miss., Confederate encampment at, 232

Tyler, Nathaniel, as *Richmond Enquirer* editor, 27

Tyler, Wise, and Allegre, 27

typography, newspaper, 43

Vallandigham, Clement L., described by S. C. Reid, 342

Vance, Gov. Zebulon, objects to bias in Gettysburg reports, 318

Van Dorn, Gen. Earl, issues order restricting press, 246; press criticism of for reverse at Corinth, 246-247; superseded by Pemberton in command of Department of Mississippi, 248

Vicksburg, Miss., as news center, 264; in 1863, 264-266; surrender, reporting of, 279-280; fall, press reaction to, 280-281

Vicksburg campaign, reporting of, 264-283

Vicksburg Whig, newspaper office burned, 270

973.7   An26s   c.2
           Andrews, J. Cutler,
             1908-

           The South reports
           the Civil War

DATE